A Family Living
Under the Sahara Sun

A Family Living Under the Sahara Sun

To God be the glory!

Ruth M. Long

Ruth Long

Library of Congress Control Number:		2011907166
ISBN:	Hardcover	978-1-4628-6833-9
	Softcover	978-1-4628-6832-2
	Ebook	978-1-4628-6834-6

This book was printed in the United States of America.

To order additional copies of this book, contact:
Xlibris Corporation
1-888-795-4274
www.Xlibris.com
Orders@Xlibris.com
94729

Louise King

CONTENTS

PART I

1   Earliest Recollections 1
2   Elementary School Days 4
3   Sunday School and Church 9
4   Grades 7 and 8—1933 and 1934 12
5   First Taste of Camp 15
6   Background—Dad 17
7   Background—Mother 20
8   High School Days 25
9   Working Years 30
10 Wheaton College...32
11 Marriage 36
12 St. Louis, Missouri 38
13 Alaska 40
14 Back to Chicago 43

PART II

1   Candidating...47
2   Paris 49
3   Galmi Hospital...62
4   Onions 66
5   Early Daysat Galmi 69
6   Settling in 87
7   Cameroun Trip 104
8   Anticipating Furlough 115

PART III

1	First Furlough	135
2	Back at Galmi	140
3	New Toys	147
4	Van Lierops	151
5	The Year 1956	155
6	Miango	168
7	This and that 1957	177
8	Tragedy and Triumph 1958	191
9	Pam Plus 1959 Through June, 1960	206
10	Second Furlough—1960-1961	221
11	From Oct. 31, 1961 Through 1962	229
12	Rollie in Wheaton—1961-1965	250
13	1961-1965	263
14	Furlough—June '65—End Of 1966	283
15	Beret—The Summer Of 1998	289
16	Sami, Ibrahim, Lasani, Nikodimu	304
17	1967 and Lance's Illness	325
18	1968	347
19	Leprosy Rounds/A Funeral/Tea Time	365
20	1969	373
21	January-June 1970	390

PART IV

1	Gems From the '50'S	401
2	Furlough – 1970-1972	405
3	1972-1973	410
4	1974-June, 1975	428
5	Sue's Summer Trip to Israel – 1975	452

PART V

1	July 20, 1975	459
2	January Through June, 1976	470
3	Furlough June 1976 Through Summer of 1977	474
4	September, 1977	476
5	1978	482
6	January 29,1979	497
7	1980	508
8	Vacation Trip to Niger	520
9	1982	526
10	1983—1984	531

PART VI

1	E.L.W.A.-Monrovia, Liberia.	539
2	Chad—Republique du Tchad. Jan. - March 1991	550
3	Back to Niger.	560
4	Nigeria, Ho!	589
5	The Last Hurrah!	598

Foreword

October 29, 1995

To my Children,

Why am I writing this autobiography? Mainly, for a pure and selfish reason. I don't want my family to forget me. I want you to pass along to your children and your children's children information about their ancestors. I know little about my ancestors except that they lived in a certain era and died.

This is also a picture of what life was like in the twentieth century. I was not here the first twenty years of it, and as I write this, there are only five years until the end of the century. (1995)

I know it's hard for this generation to believe that there ever was a time when there was no television, no jets, no penicillin or sulpha drugs, no computers, no electronic equipment. In my childhood there were none of these.

The radio was coming into its own. Jack Armstrong, Little Orphan Annie, The Lone Ranger and Tom Mix were our heroes. Saturday afternoon matinees at the movies were a treat. It was usually a cowboy movie and newsreels that gave us news of the world. Someone was at the theater organ playing hits of the day.

As children, it was a few years of innocence. The kids on our block skipped rope together—both boys and girls, played marbles and softball. We rode on our sleds on the prairies of Chicago in the winter, roller skated on the streets in the spring, and on a summer evening played "Kick the Can" on Luna Ave., while our parents sat on the porches watching until the lamp lighter came with his ladder and lit the street lights. Those were days when kids were kids, and I'm glad to have been a part of that era.

We went to Sunday School and church. We celebrated Christmas and Easter in school and nobody objected. We sang songs about our country and pledged allegiance to the flag in school. The worst thing we did in class was chew gum or throw spit-balls. We wore one piece bathing suits, even the boys and men had bathing suits that covered their chests; we didn't know about drugs or alcohol. To be sure, there were a few who snuck a cigarette in the high school bathroom, but they were considered bad girls and the rest of us shied away from them.

My generation saw two World Wars, the Korean War and Vietnam War. My generation saw the advent of miracle drugs, the evolution of the airplane, electronics, nuclear energy, the entrance of illegal drugs and increase in crime. The good and the bad!

We saw the evangelistic explosion with men like Paul Rader, W. R. Newell, Dr. Pettingill, Lance Latham, Jack Wyrtzen, Percy Crawford and Billy Graham to name but a few. Sadly, we passed from a Christian era—a time when most people believed in God and Biblical truth—into a post Christian era. We saw the best of times; the worst of times.

I am glad to have lived in the twentieth century and I want you, my children and grandchildren, to live a part of it through my autobiography.

It is not finished. More will follow as time permits. But it is important that I give what is done to you now lest it never gets to you at all if I wait until I finish it. Obviously it will never be finally finished, because someone else will have to write the last chapter. But even then, it won't be finished, because a part of me will live on in each of you.

Most of the history after we left America comes from letters that I wrote home to Fran and Bill, who saved them and returned them to me. These letters became my journal, so I am grateful to Fran. You will notice that I quote frequently from the letters. This way I am not subject to my memory alone, which could be faulty and perhaps exaggerated. At least the quotes are authentic.

So enjoy, and I hope more will follow.

Love,
Mom

Prologue

Landing in Africa

The airplane circled the runway and came in for a good landing. We stepped out on African soil! We were here—in Africa, the land we had anticipated for so long—Niamey, Niger, French West Africa! All the preparations were behind us! And we were here!

It was July 20, 1950, Burt's 32nd birthday. Early in the morning two days earlier, a van had picked us and our loads up and we headed out to Orley airport in Paris.

With our formal education behind us, we were on our way to Niger Province, French West Africa. Rollie was then 3 1/2 years, Lanny, 15 months. Waiting for us at the airport was a two-engine plane, owned and operated by the Air Transport Company, part of the Transafricaine system. We were the only passengers; the rest of the plane was filled with cargo. About noon we arrived in Algiers, Algeria. We were told that the flight would be interrupted here until about 8 that night, because they didn't fly across the desert during the day—it was too hot. So we had about eight hours to kill with no place to go. Part of the time we spent in the airport, part of the time roaming the streets of Algiers getting our first glimpse of veiled women.

Finally, about 8 that evening, after a meal, we re-boarded the plane and continued our journey. Except for the stars above and an occasional light in the desert, all was black. We slept in reclining seats, Rollie and Burt together and Lanny and I together. At first we started out with Lanny slung in a hammock overhead, but after 15 minutes of silence, I felt him land on me so that was the end of that. About 3 a.m., we landed at Gao, in the middle of the Sahara. We had been sleeping and were asked to leave the plane. We were reluctant to wake up the boys, but they warned us that it was dangerous to be in the plane while it was refueling. So we bundled Rollie and Lanny off the plane with us and walked over to the only building in sight, a mud building about 10' by 10' called a "terminal". A few kerosene lamps were flickering nearby and we noted that everyone was sleeping outside on the sand. We carefully avoided stepping on them as we sought a place to relax. It was hot—even at 3 a.m. Fifty gallon drums were rolled out to the plane and gas was siphoned into its tanks, and in an hour we were ready to go again. No lights on the runway. Miles and miles of darkness. Above, a sliver of moon and myriads of stars. How had he found this strip in the first place? How would he know where to take off? Seat belts fastened, motors revved, a prayer, and we were airborne again.

At the crack of dawn we looked down on the scene below. Vast stretches of sand, of rock, a few scattered huts. The plane offered no food (not even peanuts) and the water was non-potable. Water in France is for bathing, not drinking! Wine is all they need—red,—white or champagne! But they did offer us cokes. When we asked for a coke for Rollie, they exclaimed with their favorite expression, "Mon Dieu! For a child?" They finally brought one, but it was warm! "Ice? For a child?"

Another hour or so and we circled over Niamey. This was it. This was the moment that all our dreams from childhood on up to the present had been focused upon. We didn't know what to expect when we were looking toward it, but now that magic moment was here, and this was it.

The landing! Stepping on African soil!

No one was there to meet us. All alone, four white people surrounded by black Nigeriens in an adobe hut about the size of a mobile home! This housed customs, immigration and police. Burt began negotiating with the customs officials about our personal baggage, the portable U.S. army surplus x-ray machine and his one bag of medical instruments that he had purchased in Paris.

These were the instruments, the only instruments that we had to begin to set up the Galmi Hospital. Finally, after a customs price was settled on, Burt started to pay with travelers' checks, "the money that is recognized the world over." That is, except in Niamey, Niger in July, 1950.

"But, sir, we just landed in your country from Paris. We have no French West African currency. Take these travelers checks. This is money."

"No, we don't know anything about that kind of money. You will have to pay in our money."

"I would be glad to if I had some. Can you tell me where I can change this money?

"No. You will have to leave your things here until you can get some of this country's money."

All this in French!

They wanted cash—not scraps of paper. We were in a quandary. What to do?

Meanwhile, I shepherded the boys over to a few seats at the other end of the room. I had filled four baby bottles with drinking water before we left Paris and had powdered formula and Pablum with us, and by this time most of the water was gone. The boys were tired and hungry, and so were we. I opened up my last miniature can of evaporated milk and in a cup that I had brought along, mixed the milk and the remaining few ounces of water with some Pablum and with one spoon alternated bites with the boys until it was gone. Soon they were crying for water, and we had none to give them.

About 7 a.m., a white man appeared on the scene. Otto Bechtel! An angel! S.I.M. had arranged for him to meet us and get us through the formalities, which even included being finger printed and filling out a lot of forms. He jabbered with the people in the native language, produced the precious French West African currency, and we were able to leave with our baggage and medical supplies.

By this time, it was nine o'clock. We were all still thirsty and hungry, but we piled into Otto's car and soon we were at the Baptist Mission station where Otto's wife, Mary, gave us plenty of water to drink and food to eat. They gave us a lovely room and we relaxed and praised the Lord for our arrival in Niger! This was to be our home for the first few days. How thankful we were for their hospitality.

Tired and dirty, we started a bathing routine that was to last for many years. We called it "dip and pour". Fifty gallon drums of water were filled each day and kept in the bathroom. How good it was to get our first bath, and relax for awhile.

Dinner (lunch) over and rest hour ahead! Rest Hour! The last time I had had rest hour was at summer camp years ago! To be sure, Rollie and Lanny had their naps, but rest hour for us? The Bechtels set off for their rest hour so we made for our bedroom and comfortable beds. This was the beginning of an institution that we came to appreciate and enjoy for our entire missionary career and beyond. Lizards scampered in and out of the room under the doors and through the cracks. All kinds of lizards—little gray ones, silvery, snake like lizards, and the larger orange headed black backed kind. In and out, in and out and to the scampering of the lizard my thoughts went back to the last ten months when we were studying French, then back home to our family and friends whom we loved but had left in order to come to a strange land and minister to a people who were strange to us but included in God's "whosoever".

I dozed off for a bit. What was that horrible noise? Was someone dying? There it was, again and again. Unless you've heard it you wouldn't believe it.

Tea time! Another institution. Well, the nap was nice. We'll try that again. Since when did we ever have tea in the middle of the afternoon? "Tea", we found out, could be anything from a cold drink to hot coffee and didn't necessarily mean tea. It also included a snack. We were beginning to like this relaxed routine, and we found out from the Bechtels that nobody was dying, but donkeys had been braying.

The scene was lovely. Mission house on a hill with the Niger River coursing its way at the foot. Where did our bathing water come from? The river. Where did our wash water come from? The river. Where did our drinking water come from? The river. Our first lesson in boiling water, filtering and cooling it for drinking began that day. The prepared drinking water was placed in large clay pots to keep it cool. We began to learn not to waste water. If we thought water was scarce that day because the river was low, it was because we couldn't foresee the day we would be dipping from puddles left by rain the night before.

A letter to Fran and Bill:

"July 20, 1950 At the Baptist mission in Niamey. Dear Fran and Bill . . . we're drinking Niger River water . . . after it's been boiled and filtered . . . we wash in unboiled river water. The "boys" bring up the water from the river in buckets. Yesterday, one of the "boys" washed the diapers Lanny used on the trip and the other clothes we dirtied. That's a real break, isn't it? Bet you wish you were in Africa. He took them down to the river and washed them.

"This morning Burt and I had to go into town to finish up some business and we left the kids here. When we got home, the houseboy was holding Lanny. He was the only one Lanny would go to—not even Mrs. Bechtel. That pleased the houseboy no end.

"We are gradually being initiated into native customs. This morning . . . market—men, women, children—sitting or walking around, handling food before buying it . . . women vendors with their babies on their backs . . . women who looked like 50 but were probably only 30, carrying water, either two large jugs attached to a pole slung across their shoulders or jugs on their heads.

"Mrs. Bechtel baked a birthday cake for Burt.

"For a long time we had been telling Rollie that we would have to go to Africa and stay there for a long, long time before we'd see Frances and Bill again. Yesterday he said, 'Now can we go and see Frances and Bill?'"

Our instructions were to wait for Mr. Zabriskie and Mr. Osborne to come in our Chevy Carryall and pick us up. Mr. David Osborne was district superintendent of Niger, and Mr. Zabriskie was in charge of the station at Galmi, our destination. The Carryall was ours. That was nice. I had forgotten we had ordered a car before we left home, and here it was, at our doorstep.

A week passed. Mr. Osborne and Zeb arrived in our Chevy Carryall. Before we left Niamey, we did some shopping at the canteen. My previous contact with a canteen was a water bottle that I was introduced to in Girl Scouts. We stopped in front of a small mud brick building, perhaps 10' long by 5' deep. This was a canteen. This was THE canteen. A small shop. No similarity at all to a water bottle. We bought some powdered milk, canned so long before that when we opened the can a week later, the powder wouldn't go into solution. Our other purchases consisted of some tiny cans of tomato paste, some flour and a few cans of peas.

Early the next morning, we said good-bye to Niamey and the Bechtels—to Otto for the last time. During our visit we were impressed with his home made ventilation system, a board hung from the ceiling over the dining room table, attached by pulleys and a rope which he pulled during the meal with one hand while he ate with the other. He explained that formerly certain white officials had used small black boys to pull the ropes during the meals, but that was outlawed now as "slave labor". He and his wife also told about his recent scorpion bite that left him in agony, walking the floor in pain, for several days. Obviously he was more sensitive to insect bites than others. When word came less than four years later that Otto Bechtel had died of a snake bite, we were reminded of his sensitivity.

The road to Galmi was passable, although at one place we had to ford a stream across the road. This was the rainy season, and although the season lasted only three to four months, "when it rained, it poured." It was a common sight to see trucks lined up at the rain barrier, waiting for 12 hours before they could use the road. One could hope that it didn't rain again at the eleventh hour. As we "sped" along the corrugated, bumpy "highway" (Rt. 1—Niger) between 35 and 40 miles per hour, we saw Mr. Osborne and Zeb waving to the Africans in the fields, so we joined in the salutes. They all waved back and seemed very friendly. We detoured a washed out bridge and forded a knee-deep flood over the road. I was surprised and embarrassed to see black women working in the fields with just a cloth on from their waist down. I would get used to it. Most of the men were in their loin cloths. Despite their lack of clothes, they didn't seem as naked as they were. Was it because their skin was black? What if the fields were dotted with white almost-naked people? I think they would have looked very naked indeed. Thus we were introduced to a society in which clothes were not vital.

We stopped for morning "tea" at Dosso, 100 miles along the way, a sister mission station of the Baptist mission in Niamey, where the station was "manned" by two single ladies; then for dinner at Dogon Doutchie, 75 more miles down the road at our S.I.M. station, also "manned" by two single ladies, Edith Durst and Verna Gabrielsen. Where were the men? Why did these missionary women have to stand alone in a society that regarded their women as little more than cattle? Why did our women have to bear the insults of a Moslem male population? Where were the men missionaries?

Darkness was settling as we approached Galmi. Zeb said if we kept looking to our left, we would see the pan roofs of the hospital and house. We remembered the letter Mr. Osborne had written to us while we were in Paris. He said the pan had come for our house. We didn't know what pan he was talking about. Surely we hadn't ordered any pan or pans. So far as we knew, all our pots and pans were still packed in the many boxes and barrels that comprised our "outfit". Now we saw our pan roof glowing in the dusk, and we understood. There were just a few minutes between dusk and dark, and how dark it was! What a welcome sight it was to see a brilliant pressure lamp shining in the west doorway of the hospital. Irene Zabriskie had supper waiting.

Lamps were lit, and we city folk had our first introduction to kerosene lamps, pressure lamps, and Aladdin lamps. This was Galmi. We had arrived. This was the spot in the universe that our Lord had picked out for us to serve Him. This was our destination. This was our home!

Rollie was still confused. At 2 1/2, he had left Chicago after having been born and lived the first half of his life in Alaska. On the DeGrasse, our French liner, he kept asking when we would be home. Then on the boat-train from Le Havre to Paris; then when we arrived at our hotel, he bolted from us back to the taxi. "This is not home. I want to go home." This was not Kedvale Ave. in Chicago. This was not Aunt Fran's and Uncle Bill's home. And here he was now, in Galmi. His latest home. Today he looks back and says "Northwest Africa is my true home. Where else would I rather be?" So the night we pulled into Galmi for the first time, Rollie, then 3 1/2, found his true home.

What was it that brought two young people together to serve the Lord in Africa? It all began when we were children. We lived about six blocks apart on the northwest side of Chicago, but we didn't know each other. As teen agers, we went to the same church, but we didn't associate with each other. Those were the days when the boys had their own clubs, the girls had their own clubs and never the twain shall meet.

In the beginning—THE AUTOBIOGRAPHY OF
RUTH MARGARET HOLLANDER LONG

PART I

Chapter 1

EARLIEST RECOLLECTIONS

When it comes to writing about my earliest years, I realize there is a mixture of actual recollections and hearsay. It is easy to say, "Yes, I remember," but then I ask myself if indeed I did remember that incident or whether I heard it repeated so often that I just think I remember it. I shall try to separate my recollections from hearsay, but if I am wrong, some other member of the family will correct me.

My earliest recollections go back to the time we lived at 1771 Greenleaf Ave. in Rogers Park. I know I was born in Evanston Hospital in Evanston, Ill. at 2:25 P.M. on August 5, 1921. My birth certificate attests to that. Whether we lived on Greenleaf at the time or not, I know not, but it is of little significance. But I do recall living on the second floor on Greenleaf Ave. There were wooden steps leading up the back way. I don't remember a front entrance. I still see the large kitchen (or it seemed large to me then), and I still see myself reading at the kitchen table before I went to kindergarten. (Hearsay says that people were amazed at that feat.) I also recollect a bedroom off the kitchen, and I remember a little red chair that was mine and which I sat on frequently. Why I was sitting on it in the corner in that bedroom, I do not know (but I can imagine), but today I bear in my left little finger the scar that people tell me is the result of the door being closed on the finger and the finger crushed. Fortunately, I do not remember the incident, but I am sure there were screams and tears, a rush to the doctor's, the restoration of the loose digit and

1

remorse on the part of my mother for my being in the corner on the little red chair, for whatever reason.

Another thing I remember about Greenleaf Ave. is Aunt Margaret Jensen. She wasn't a real aunt, but she was the lady who took care of me and lived with us because my mother taught school. Years later, I met her again. She came to Chicago and my Aunt Agnes and I met her in one of the railroad stations downtown. It must have been in my late teens or early twenties because I was not married. She was an old lady then, but still loveable. She remembered me more than I remembered her.

When I was four or five, apparently Aunt Margaret was no longer working for us, because I remember being taken to school with my mother because she had no one to leave me with. She was teaching at Eugene Field School at the time. I was in kindergarten or first grade then, I'm not sure which, but I remember that there was some discussion about where I would fit in since I could already read.

More hearsay is the time when my brother, Bobby, was on the verge of putting our cat through the washing machine wringer, but Mother stopped him before the cat was deprived of one of his lives.

I am told, but I do not remember, that I swallowed a jack, the kind that you play "Jacks" with. I did not swallow it. It wouldn't go down but was lodged in my throat. My mother told Beret to run for help to the doctor's office to ask him to come. Beret ran, but she doesn't remember getting to the office, but someone else, I forget who, told me that she got there and in the midst of all the confusion she was on her knees in the waiting room praying. Beret denies that. Meanwhile, back home, my mother, by some Herculean effort and in answer to the family's prayers, was able to get her finger down my throat and behind the jack and pull it out before I was gone. I'm not sure whether the doctor ever arrived.

Another not so pleasant remembrance of Greenleaf Ave. was the time when a thief ran up the back stairs, pounded on the door and begged for sanctuary. He was being pursued by the police. Father went to the door and talked to him but did not let him in. We were scared. I don't know what happened to him.

There was a cigar store on the first floor on the corner of the building where we lived. I can remember going in there from time to time to buy an ice cream cone. There was a pungent but not unpleasant odor associated with that store that I still recall.

And that is all I remember about Greenleaf Ave. When I was six, the family moved to 5530 N. Luna Ave. on Chicago's northwest side, and that's where I did my growing up.

Chapter 2

ELEMENTARY SCHOOL DAYS

GRADES 1-7—YEARS 1926-1933

5530 N. Luna Ave., Chicago, IL; Palisade 2912

School was the main focus of my life with church running a close second. We enrolled at James Farnsworth School, a half block from our home. Mother taught at the same school so we were in school at the same time. She taught in the older grades—6th, 7th or 8th, so I didn't have her for my teacher. I'm not sure which half grades I skipped, but I know that I graduated in seven years rather than eight, at the age of 12 going on 13 the following August. Some of my teachers were Miss Crokin, Mrs. Bills, Miss Pauley, and Miss Schwatgen. I liked school. I was a good student, both academically and behaviorally. But there was one time that I sewed a few wild oats. When we had a substitute teacher one day, the kids were shooting spit balls and I joined in with them. The teacher said, "Ruth, I am surprised at you." (She also knew my mother.) I melted, was terribly embarrassed and sorry for what I had done.

My brother, Bobby, was a year ahead of me at Farnsworth, albeit two years older than I. I guess we got along as well as any brother and sister, which included our share of fighting. Most of the time, we engaged in the same after-school sports. In season it was baseball, softball or touch football. Then there were rope jumping, roller skating and marbles, either in the ring, or in the pots. Bobby was much better at marbles than I was. He had a lot of marbles. He had a bicycle, too, and because it had a bar on it, I rode it with one leg through and under the bar. You might have guessed it. I was a tomboy!

We enjoyed mutual friends on our block, boys and girls. There were Eleanor and Bessie Buotz, Chester Skiba, Bennie ?, George and Olga Martish (next door), Marty Woods (across the street—I kind of liked him.) Two blocks away the Frankenbergs lived—on Central Ave.—and Florence came over to play with us once in a while, too. To make our playmates complete, I must mention Laddie, our part shepherd and collie dog. We got him as a puppy. Dad brought him home one night from work. He was part of the family, a house dog complete with shedding hair. He raced down the street with us when we were biking or skating, many times pulling me on my skates while I held on tightly to his chain. He played with us both summer and winter in warm weather or snow and cold.

Another favorite sport was racing down the street on our homemade scooters. We took the rubber pads out of our roller skates and nailed the skates to a 2 x 4 about 3 ft. long. Then a wooden fruit box that we acquired from our local grocery store, run by the Novotny family, was nailed to one end of the skate board. A wooden stick across the top provided the handles which completed our home made scooter. We also had a regular scooter but the home made one took precedence for a spell.

The year was 1928. Dad worked nights and when he got home in the mornings, we had already gone to school. He was the chief cook for our noon meals and we would come home for lunch to a prepared meal. One noon I wasn't hungry and complained of a sore throat. I stayed home from school that afternoon and soon our doctor was summoned and he diagnosed diphtheria. The very next day our front door graced a big sign, "DIPHTHERIA", and we were in quarantine. Mother stayed home from school. Bobby stayed home. Fran and Beret moved in with Aunt Sophia and Uncle Fred. Dad slept and lived in the basement, so he could go to work. It wasn't long before Bobby came down with diphtheria, too, so Mother had two sick kids to care for. The month was October. I remember that because in Nov. of that year, Herbert Hoover won the election and became President of the United States while we were recovering. Aunt Agnes brought me a tea set made of china which lasted a good many years, and I think there is still a cup or saucer in the family somewhere. Well, we recovered, and by Christmas time, we were raring to go, but we couldn't go anywhere because we were still in quarantine. That was the Christmas that I got my little 2 wheel sidewalk bike and Bobby got his electric train. I couldn't ride my bike anywhere but I managed to take a few runs around the living and dining room. Mother was a very patient woman. It wasn't until well into January that the quarantine sign came down and we were declared well!

The big crash came in 1929 when I was seven years old. I remember the night. We all went over to Grandma and Grandpa Blix's house on Foster Ave., a few blocks from us. The adults were talking very seriously about the news and wondering what was next for them. We kids didn't quite understand the significance of it. Some changes took place in our family, but it didn't affect my life style. I still went to school every day and Sunday School and church on Sunday. I still played after school. We still ate three meals a day and we still had our house and I still had new shoes and new dress for Christmas. Mother still had her school teaching job and Dad still had his job as an engineer/fireman on the Chicago and Northwestern Railroad—for awhile.

But then things began to change. School teachers were getting paid in script—which was a substitute for money. Not every store honored that "money", but fortunately, our grocery store did, so we could eat. Dad's job gradually eroded and he was cut back from engineer to fireman and finally to substitute fireman. We found out that the mortgage payments that we had paid on our house were not being applied to our credit but went into the pocket of those holding the mortgage and by 1934 we had lost our house and had to move. But that's getting ahead of the story.

Mother enjoyed gardening and summer vacations including working in our flower gardens in the back yard. When we needed black dirt, all we did was go out the back gate, cross the alley and go into the empty lots and dig it. There were two steps up from our yard to the alley, so to make it easier for the wheel barrow, we put a 2 x 8" board from the top to the bottom, making a ramp. One day Bobby was running out and I was chasing him. He got to the top of the steps first and the board came up with his weight, like a teeter totter. I ran right into it and got a square inch butterfly gash in my right leg down to the shin bone. Blood everywhere! Mother called the doctor. Instead of stitching it, which might have been more prudent, he dressed it, and over the course of time, it filled in. I don't fault the doctor for not stitching it because I vaguely remember remonstrating vigorously when the subject was brought up. The scar will be buried with me.

The Zentels lived on Central Ave. Their back yard faced our back yard several houses down. They had a teeter totter. One day Adeline and I were on the teeter totter, and somehow, I forget how, I fell off and landed on my coccyx. The breath was knocked out of me. I struggled to breathe and it seemed like minutes before I could get short breaths, and finally normal breaths. I ran home screaming.

Another time I ran home screaming was when I was hit by a baseball on my right temple. The boys and I were playing baseball, NOT softball, in the empty lot across Central Avenue. It was my turn to bat and I was going to bat left-handed for the fun of it. The pitch came over and I wasn't as good at ducking left handed as I was right handed, and the ball got me in my right temple. As I said, I ran home screaming!

Many times the boys and I played softball on our street, using the manhole covers for bases. An occasional car came down the street causing us to suspend the game long enough for it to pass. For a lark, some of the boys threw their gloves under the cars as they went by. Going over the gloves would startle the drivers, which was the object of the exercise. Not to be outdone, I tried it once, too. But my glove was lighter than theirs, and the wind swept it up onto the hood of the passing car. The driver stopped and gave me back my glove with a lecture. I was frightened to death and my bladder relaxed and I got this warm feeling running down my legs. I ran home that time, too, not screaming, but totally embarrassed.

One Saturday afternoon, several of us kids went to the forest preserve which was only about six blocks away from us and played and played. I had been instructed to be home at a certain time but I delayed intentionally. When I finally showed up in late afternoon, I found my Mother lying in bed with a headache. She reprimanded me for being away so long and sent me to the store to get some aspirin. I was full of remorse. I ran as fast as I could, praying that she wouldn't die before I got home.

7

I was fortunate enough to be able to take piano lessons although I didn't realize it then. I was lax at times in my practice, and one week I was not prepared at all and didn't want to face my teacher, Mrs. Weder. So after school, I asked Mother if I could go to the park, knowing that it was my piano lesson day, and Mother agreed, also forgetting that it was my piano lesson day. Mrs. Weder's husband dropped her off and when Mother opened the door, he went on his way. Mother was embarrassed and apologetic and spent the next half hour visiting with Mrs. Weder until Mr. Weder returned for her. She paid my regular fee of 75 cents. She was an unhappy camper when I got home. I forget what my punishment was but I did get something. I never did that again.

Chapter 3

SUNDAY SCHOOL AND CHURCH

As I mentioned earlier, Sunday School and church played an important part in my life. As soon as we moved over to Luna Ave., Aunt Agnes made it a point to get us to Sunday School. She was going over to a little mission church about 3 blocks from where we lived. Aunt Agnes was not yet married, so she must have been living with her folks on Foster Ave. The building was a converted garage on Catalpa Ave. off of Lynch Ave. It couldn't have held more than 50 people, but it had an upstairs as well as the main room downstairs.

Four maiden ladies had started this mission church, Miss Goldie Hassel, Miss Clara Christopherson, Miss Esther Draeger and Miss Agnes Peterson. It was known as the Grace Gospel Mission, which in later years came to be known as the Grace Gospel Church. Miss Ruth Forsberg also played an important role in the Mission. Our Sunday School classes were spots in the main room with screens partitioning off each class. The girls in my class were my cousin, Lillian Blix, Margaret Truelsen, Bea Boland, Lillian Lockwood, Mary Yuskow and Shirley Roberg. Audrey Roberg, Ruth Freeman, Anna, Irene and Mildred Kralik, twins, Eleanor and Elaine Bauer, June and Marian Jacobson were in another class but we were all close friends and stayed that way through high school. There were others, too, but these were my closest friends. The boys we grew up with were John Ruppaner, Gordon Boland, who died in World War II, Clifford Jacobson, Warren

Bauer, cousin Fred Blix, another cousin, Victor Blix. The Werner boys and Swetman boys came along later.

Each Sunday Mother sent Bob and me off to Sunday School. She didn't go herself except on special occasions and Dad never went. For the most part, "Aunt Esther" Draeger was my teacher, and she had a real interest in "her girls" and to this very day, 1995, some 65 plus years later, she keeps in touch with us. Of the four, she and Agnes Peterson who married Cliff Jacobson are the only ones still living. John Ruppaner married Anna Kralik and Bea Boland married Warren Bauer.

We usually stayed for church, too, but sometimes, Bobby and I would skip church and wander toward home and watch the baseball game in progress on the school playgrounds and manage to get back home about the right "after-church" time. Also, there were times when we "forgot" to put our nickel in the collection plate. In all fairness, I must say that these were rare occurrences. Miss Draeger and the little mission church had a good influence on me and I will always be grateful for the love and instruction that I found there. On Friday nights Aunt Esther had "her girls" over to her apartment for fun and Bible study. I remember the cold, crispy nights, in the winter when we girls would walk to her house on the crunchy snow. We all lived within a few blocks of each other, and we didn't have to worry about being out at night. In those days, we wore warm snow suits, with elastic down at our ankles, not leotards or slacks. We believed in staying warm.

Each summer the ladies held Daily Vacation Bible School. When I was 10 or 11, Miss Jessie Blanchard who was a missionary in Africa told some vivid missionary stories and described African villages with a lot of people who came to the know the Lord through her ministry. This was my first exposure to missionary life and it left a lasting impression. Mr. Simon Forsberg, who was studying at Moody Bible Institute, along with his sister, Ruth, my some times Sunday School teacher, was also helping out in DVBS and spoke about missions. When he gave the invitation for those who would want to be missionaries some day, I raised my hand. Later, "Aunt Esther" told me, "Ruth, you must have really meant it; you raised your hand so high." Simon was the cousin of Malcolm Forsberg who was with SIM. Years later we met Simon and his wife Anne in Alaska when he was a special speaker at Victory Bible Camp which we attended. I reminded him of our early association when I was but a child. When we returned to the "Lower 48" a year or so later, we spent a night with them in Oregon.

On one of those Friday evenings at "Aunt Esther's" house (also "Aunt Clara's" house), we were discussing what we wanted to be when we grew up. I said I wanted to be a missionary, anywhere but Alaska. Little did I know that I would follow my husband to Alaska, not as a missionary, but because of the military.

My early days were happy days. Even though some of those years were depression years, we didn't know we were poor because everyone was poor. We didn't have television, but we did have radio and we would be glued to it in the early evenings listening to "Little Orphan Annie", "Jack Armstrong, the All-American Boy", "Amos and Andy" and "Lum and Abner." Then, of course, in the afternoons when we weren't outside playing, we would listen to the Cubs or White Sox games, and I would make my own score card and record every out and run. Brother-in-law, Bill Bueneman, reminded me often that all I wanted for Christmas was a bat and ball, and that when he came to court my sister, Fran, brother Bob's and my favorite game was traveling from one end of the living room to the other without stepping on the floor, just furniture. Bob and I played marbles on the living room floor in the winter time and we read a lot, too. Salty pumpkin seeds and a book were often my evening activity. We actually had baths twice a week, too, on Wed. and Sat. nights. A far cry from showers every day in this day and age!

Chapter 4

GRADES 7 AND 8—1933 AND 1934

One day in the spring of 1933 I grew up all of a sudden. I was in seventh grade. My mother had been suffering for some time with gallbladder trouble although I wasn't aware of it. The decision was made to have it out. So Sunday afternoon, March 27, we hugged Mother good-bye and she assured us that we would be seeing her again in a week. The operation was on Monday. The doctor was one Dr. Schaeffer in the Norwegian Lutheran Hospital in Chicago. Apparently there was an infection, and since this was before the advent of antibiotics, she did not respond to whatever treatment was available, and a week later, she died. It was April 2. It was early in the morning when the phone rang calling my dad to the hospital. Then Aunt Sophia called and said she was coming right over, which she did. Mother was already gone by that time. We were all stunned. "Aunt Esther" and "Aunt Clara" came over and prayed with us. We couldn't believe it. I was 11, Bob was 13, Fran was 19 and Beret was 21. We couldn't imagine life without Mother. She was the focus of our lives. Hers was the lap I sat on. She took me with her when she went down to the Chicago Historical Society for classes and enrolled me in some art classes, she took me with her when she taught some classes at Wright Jr. High some evenings and enrolled me in other classes. We went downtown in Chicago together with Bob before school started and shopped for school clothes and shoes and again before Christmas. Our favorite store was The Boston Store, perhaps it was because they accepted Script in lieu of cash. She was only 48 years old! And now, my life, our lives, were turned upside down! She was buried on April 5 in the Mount of Olives Cemetery on Narraganset Ave. between Irving Park and Addison Aves. in Chicago. In November, 1993, we kids, all of us old ourselves, finally had a grave stone put in the ground over her burial spot, which read "Amelia Blix Hollander, 1885-1933 Alive in Christ". Dad had never had it done, doubtless there was no money for it.

Miss Schwatgen was my 7th grade teacher. Our class was putting on an assembly for the school, and I had been chosen for the main part, a fairy that waved the magic wand and turned pages introducing story book characters that came out of a big book. The play was to be put on that Spring. Miss Schwatgen asked if I would rather not be in the play because of my mother's death. I said I would rather be in the play, and I was. Some mother in the school made my fairy costume, and the play was a success. Aunt Sophia was there. She was our mainstay after Mother died.

Fran, at 19, became our surrogate mother even though she was younger than Beret by two years. Bill had a roadster car, and he would pick up Fran for church Sunday afternoons, and they piled Bob and me into the rumble seat and off we went to the North Side Gospel Center. The Center was an offshoot of the Chicago Gospel Tabernacle which was founded by Paul Rader. Lance Latham struck out on his own and founded the Center, which consisted mostly of young people. For years the services were held on Sunday afternoons—Sunday School first followed by the service, then a short break followed by the evening service. In that way, those who worshipped in the traditional Sunday morning services could keep up that commitment. And that's what I did.

On March 17, 1934, Fran married Bill Bueneman. The wedding was at Aunt Sophia and Uncle Fred's house. I cried and cried. Mother was gone and now Fran was gone. Beret and Bob and Dad were left, but they didn't take the place of either Fran or Mother.

When I was in 8th grade, we had to move. We moved over on Ardmore Ave., one block north of Elston Ave. and one half block east of Central Ave. That meant I was about 6 blocks away from school, and it was quite a hassle to run home for lunch, find something to eat and run back in an hour. Graduation came in the Spring of 1934 and

Fran and Aunt Sophia were there. I got a new dress for graduation and new shoes which I wore with ankle socks. Most girls my age didn't know the sophistication of silk hose—nylons hadn't been invented yet.

Chapter 5

FIRST TASTE OF CAMP

The summer after Mother died, 1933, I went to Camp for the first time. It was called Camp Mi-chi-dune and was affiliated with the North Side Gospel Center and Mr. and Mrs. Lance Latham were in charge of the camp. The reason I went was because Fran was going to be a leader for a month and she had to drag me along. I was eleven, almost twelve. That was the first of many years as a camper. I loved it. The camp was located at Lake Harbor, Muskegon, Michigan on Paul Rader's Conference Grounds. We were housed in long low dormitories. There was a tennis court just outside the dorm and beyond that, the "moonbeam". There was one cold shower hooked up at the end of our washing troughs outside at the end of one of the dormitories. For my first year, we had to walk a narrow path over the dunes through the woods to get to the dining room dormitory, but after that first year, the dining room was housed at the end of the long dorm. Lake Michigan beckoned down the long dune and up and over a smaller dune. Besides swimming in the cold water every day, this became our giant bathtub at least once a week. It was a long hard trek back up the dunes to the dorms. Besides the Bible hours, the games and activities, one of my favorite times was after swimming, when we gathered on the beds in one of the rooms and listened to our leaders read a story by Grace Livingston Hill or some other like-minded author.

Camp fires on the beach were humongous. We would gather wood from the woods, and Bill Bueneman and Rich Hansen, who were "boy workers" built the fires which were ten to twelve feet high on the beach, and many were the nights that we gathered on the beach around the camp fire, under the stars, enjoying the fires, the singing, the testimonies and the messages. Mrs. Virginia Latham was the catalyst; other leaders were "Frannie Pete" (now Abbey), Grace Gouzoulous, Eleanor Larsen, Ruth Brown, Olga Hodel and Helen Johnson. Others, too, but I have forgotten. Around these camp fires, many commitments to the Lord were made, and I renewed my decision to become a missionary. Some nights we dragged our mattresses down to the beach and slept there. What a job it was to carry them back up the dunes the next morning! In 1934, I was All Around Camp Girl for the Jr. Guards and in 1938, I was All Around Camp Girl for the Sr. Guards. In those days the winners were not determined by points, but on general qualities, friendship, Bible participation, general sports abilities and what not. I'm not sure what all because I was the recipient, not a judge. When time came to go home, we gathered in the Rest—a—While room in the club house on the conference grounds and had a general bawl—room session. Nobody wanted to leave—least of all, I. We traveled those days either by ship across Lake Michigan or by train. It was only years later that the church rented buses to take the campers to and fro.

Chapter 6

BACKGROUND—DAD—Bert Hollander

As I mentioned before, my mother was the mainstay in our family. Dad was there, but he was not a warm person. He was a provider. I recall that he scrubbed the kitchen floor every Saturday. He worked nights most of the time, so we had to walk carefully during the day when he slept. He was an engineer/fireman for the Chicago and Northwestern Railroad. We stayed out of his way most of the time.

We didn't know much about his family. I remember once that his brother visited us. I also met his sister, Sarah Obermaier in Santa Barbara, CA when I was 13 years old. I'll get to that later.

It wasn't until I was in my teens that I learned that Dad was Jewish and born in Budapest, Hungary, and came over as a babe in arms. His father was reported to have been a rabbi in Budapest and in New York when they immigrated. He was born in June of 1883. Somewhere along the line his family moved to Chicago, and it was while he was an engineer or fireman (I know not which) on the Chicago and Northwestern Railroad and my mother rode the train to a teaching job from Winnetka to someplace, I don't know where, that they struck up an acquaintance. This led to their marriage. Grandpa Blix was not pleased with the match but was satisfied after Dad walked down the aisle to profess to accept Christ as his Savior. A year after Mother died, Dad married Ethel Walk and lived with her until he died of a stroke in March of 1960. In Chapter Eight you will sense that I was not too happy that Dad had married. I resented the fact that anyone could possibly take Mother's place. I was twelve, and I didn't understand. I never called her "Mother", always "Ethel". I can see now that Dad needed someone to love and care for and be cared for. After all, he was only 50 years old. To me, that was ancient. She did her best and tried to be a good mother to me.

After I grew up, physically, emotionally and mentally, I came to a greater appreciation of her and the gap she filled in Dad's life.

So the life of my father and his ancestors is very sketchy.

Since writing the above I came across two letters written to us by Ethel after Dad died, and I will excerpt them.

"March 4, 1961, Sedalia, MO—Yes, Ruth, if I hadn't put my faith in God I could never have gone through so much. You'll never know how much Bert meant to me and how I miss him, and I feel he is at peace with God. We had many talks here alone and in my small way I helped him to feel differently about many things as time went on and together we discussed them. Bert was a victim of circumstances and being such a sensitive person, it was hard for him to change his ideas, but I could see a big change in him as time went on . . . I'm waiting on the Lord to take care and when He sees fit, things will shape up. . . . It's just a year ago this very time Bert was so awfully sick and on the 9th of this month, he passed away. I'm still living it over and it's sad. . . . Give my best wishes to all the children and family . . . .

"December 26, 1962 Sedalia, MO— . . . in fact, I think of 'you all' so often. One nice thing in my life is remembering all four of you children and how nice you were to me when I married your father. I'm not complaining, but I always knew we could have been closer, but poor Bert he always wanted to be alone with me, just so contented with nobody around. I think I can understand why though, as he often talked of his past life. I felt so sorry for him, he was a victim of circumstances and his own worst enemy, had what you might call an inferiority complex. I worked on him constantly, and I am happy to know that he did override a lot of it and I loved him VERY much as he had so many good qualities and was so devoted to me. That's why it's so hard for me to lose him. You'll never know—I keep thinking how fortunate I was to have him those 25 years, and I must be grateful. Frances writes and tells me what a nice boy Rollie is . . . . J.C. is so good to me. I am thinking of going to Santa Barbara, Calif. and spend a month with your dad's sister, Sara."

—

Some years after Dad died, on one of our furloughs, Burt and I and some of our children visited Ethel in Santa Barbara. She was living with her son, J.C. and his wife, Betty. She was happy and getting on in years and we had a nice visit with her. She talked about Dad. In her letters she always said, "he was a victim of circumstances" and "he often talked of his past life." I wish I had been more curious at that time and had asked her about those things, because to this day, I don't know what the "circumstances" of his past life were.

Another time later on, we visited with J.C. and Betty. At that time Ethel was in the hospital dying. When we visited her, she was sleeping. It wasn't long after that that she died. It was either in the late 70's or early 80's.

Chapter 7

BACKGROUND—MOTHER—
Amelia Henrietta Blix Hollander

For a more detailed report, I would refer you to the "Norwegian Connection" compiled by cousin Jane Blix (Kenrick) who visited Norway and traced many of the Blix relatives—my mother's family.

Mother's ancestors are covered in the Norwegian Connection, so I will just write my recollections of my mother and what was told me. Mother was born in 1885 to Andrew and Hannah Christophersen Blix in Vega, Norway. Her father came to the States first and a few years later was able to send for his wife and children. Mother was about five when her mother made the trip to the States with her two daughters. They ended up in Winnetka, IL where Grandpa Blix was a carpenter and cabinet maker. Mother's older sister and younger sister died early in their lives, the older one dying in Norway, I believe. The rest of the children were born in the States: Victor, Mabel, Fred, Agnes, Harry and Ruth. Victor died during the flu epidemic in 1918 during the First World War while he was serving in the Army in Texas. I didn't know him. My other aunts and uncles and their spouses were important in my life. Fred married Sophia Ziemer and they had Freddie Jr., Joseph, and Lillian. Joseph died at birth. Lillian was 6 months older than I. Freddie was 3 yrs. older than Lillian. They lived only a few blocks from us, we went to the same school, and I was in the same grade as Lillian. We were very close.

Victor had married Sophia's sister and a son, Victor, Jr. was born to them. We called him Junior. He was just a babe in arms when his father died and his mother died when he was a young boy, so for the better part of his life, he was brought up by the Ziemer family, who lived in Deerfield, IL. I don't know why, but when I was about 10 or so, Victor came to live with Aunt Sophia and Uncle Fred for about a year, and since he was in between Freddie and my brother, Bob, in age, we got to know him quite well during that year.

Another cousin in our age group was Jane, daughter of Harry and Louise Hyler Blix. They lived in Brookfield, IL and we saw them occasionally. Jane was six months younger than I. Some summers, Jane would spend a week with us or at Lillian's house, but more often, we would spend time with the Harry Blixes at their summer cottage at Flint Lake, near Valparaiso, IN. One summer when I was about seven or eight, I went up to the cottage with them to stay for a week, but I was so homesick without Mother, that I cried and cried until they called Mother, and she had to come on the train and get me and take me home after only a day or two. Up to that time, I had always been there with her.

Aunt Mabel married George Perdue and they had two sons and a daughter, George Jr., James (Jimmy) and Carol. These were a little younger than we and lived on the north side of Chicago. Uncle George worked for the elevated company, and he got free passes, so they came to visit us often. Jimmy died in the aftermath of World War II. He was in the navy, on a mine sweeper clearing a mine field in the Pacific Ocean near Japan after the war when his ship hit a mine and went down. I don't know how many survivors there were, but he was not one of them.

Cousin Marjorie Ruth was born to Aunt Ruth Margaret and Charles Roy Hennix around 1930. They lived in Mt. Prospect most of the time that I knew them, so we didn't see them too often as children.

Aunt Agnes was the last to marry and she married Selmar (Sam) Olson, and they had Billy, Johnny and Bonnie in that order. I remember their wedding. They were married at the Grace Gospel Mission where I attended as a child, about which I wrote earlier. They lived on the South Side of Chicago for awhile, and it was during that time, when Johnny was about 5 years old, that he got pneumonia.

I don't know why, but Johnny was treated at the Hennix' house in Mt. Prospect. That was about in 1935 because I remember that Dad, Ethel, Bob and I were living in Mt. Prospect that year, and I recall how Aunt Ruth put mustard plasters on his chest. Johnny recovered. It was after that that their family moved to North Dakota and later to Leonard, near Bemidji, MN and raised their children on the farm. We didn't see them too often. During the year that we lived in Mt. Prospect, the Hennix home was our haven and escape. I will get to that later.

Grandma and Grandpa Blix were the only grand parents that I knew, and Grandma was not my real grand mother. She was grandpa's second wife. Hannah died before I was born, and Grandpa married Anna.

Mother was the oldest living member of the family and she married Bert Hollander. To their union were born Beret Harriet, Frances Virginia, Robert Eugene and myself, Ruth Margaret. I was named after my aunt Ruth. A miscarriage on the part of my mother accounts for the six years between Frances and Bob. In a way it was like two separate families.

Beret was born Jan. 14, 1912, Fran almost two years later on Dec. 19, 1913. There was a time when they were very young that they lived in North Dakota. But most of their childhood was spent either in Winnetka or on the north side of Chicago. Bob was born on Aug. 28, 1919 and I came along two years later on Aug. 5, 1921.

In my recollection, Fran and Beret were never children. My first recollection of them was when they were teenagers, for Beret was almost 10 years older than I. They attended the Chicago Gospel Tabernacle, where Paul Rader was pastor. Paul Rader had earlier been pastor of Moody Memorial Church, which was then located on the corner of Chicago Ave. and either Clark St. or LaSalle, I'm not sure. After he left Moody Church, one summer, he and his committee erected a large temporary, summer structure at Barry Ave. and Clark St., where they held "tent" meetings every night of the week. When the summer was over, the structure was somehow winterized, but not very well. When I was old enough to attend, I recall wooden benches, sawdust floor and pot bellied stoves scattered throughout the building. That temporary structure lasted perhaps 15 years or more. Only eternity will reveal the impact that Paul Rader and the Tabernacle had on the lives of the people, many of whom went into Christian service. The tabernacle held about 2000 people, and you had to come early for a seat. Sunday School and service were held in the afternoon, followed in the evening by another service. Services were usually about two hours long, and Paul Rader preached about an hour and it seemed like 20 minutes. The afternoon, instead of morning services, became the pattern for the North Side Gospel Center, which I have already mentioned.

Most notable among the musical leaders in the church were Lance Latham, Richard Oliver, Sr. and Richard Oliver, Jr., Merrill Dunlap, Clarence and Howard Jones. Lance, Richard and Merrill were geniuses at the piano, Clarence on the trombone and Howard on the trumpet. Richard, Jr. was killed in an automobile accident out East. Lance went on to establish his own church, Clarence was a co-founder of radio station HCJB in Ecuador in the Andes.

The Awana program had its roots in the Tabernacle. It was there that boys and girls clubs were established. The clubs were patterned after the Boy Scouts of America with emphasis on leading young people to Christ. Among the women leaders of the girls' clubs that I remember were Virginia Latham, Naomi Gunderson, Myrtle Bergdahl, Gertie Nelson, and Julia Hennix Spong. Julia was Charles' Hennix sister. She was one of the leaders in the girls' club, ages 9-12, which was called Phi Kappas, and they held their club meetings on Saturday afternoons. Julia made a point of picking me and my cousin Lillian up on Saturdays to go to club. I was about 10 years old. I remember one Halloween meeting when we were escorted through the House of Horrors behind the platform. That was scary. During the meetings, the way of salvation was always presented. From the time I could remember, I had gone to Sunday School and church where the Gospel was preached, but as I listened to those messages from faithful leaders, I could not pinpoint a time in my life that I had ever invited Christ to come into my life. So when the invitations were given, I was very uncomfortable, but not quick to respond, because "everybody knew I was already a Christian". It was probably the next Spring that the group went on a picnic in Lincoln Park, and in conclusion, as we sat under a tree, the gospel was presented again, and this time, I raised my hand to receive Christ, when all eyes were closed. But alas, when it was over, the speaker asked those who had raised their hands to come forward. THAT was meddling! After a pause, I did, and we sat under a tree and I, along with others, prayed a prayer inviting Christ into my life. I count that, at age 11, as my point of conversion because it was a definite act on my part. Whether I had accepted Christ earlier or not, I am not sure, but from that point on, I knew I was a Christian, even though in later years, I sometimes doubted and went through the act again.

Back to Beret and Fran. They both attended the Tabernacle and went to summer camp at Eagle River. As teenagers, they had their boy friends and girl friends. Fran went steady with Bill Bueneman, and they were married on March 17, 1934. Beret never married. Fran and Bill attended the Tabernacle and followed Mr. and Mrs. Latham when they left the Tabernacle to establish the North Side Gospel Center in 1933. Beret did not go to the Center, and she more or less chose her friends from her art and neighborhood associations.

Chapter 8

HIGH SCHOOL DAYS

After I graduated from Farnsworth Grammar School, we moved again. This time it was to 5420 Foster Ave., where Grandma and Grandpa Blix lived. Years before, Grandpa had built this big house—basement, first story and second story, and it was in 1934, in the height of the depression, and he hadn't been able to rent out his apartments. He arranged for Dad and the three of us to move into the first floor apartment and Fran and Bill to rent out the second floor. I don't remember what we paid for rent, but it was probably about $35.00 a month. Grandma and Grandpa lived in one half of the basement which they had made into living quarters.

I was happy with the arrangement because sister Fran was right upstairs. And Bill was so very kind to me. In 1935, Dad surprised us all by marrying again—Ethel Walk. We were shocked because it came as such a surprise. We didn't even know he was seeing anyone, and one morning we woke up to find Ethel in our house, married to our Dad. She had a 19 year old son as well, J.C., and although he was there for a few days, he was on his own and didn't live with us. From 5420 Foster, I went to Carl Schurz High School for my Freshman year. Most of my friends were my cousin, Lillian Blix and those who were also church friends—from Grace Gospel Mission.

I just realized I have left out an important member of our family who lived with us throughout our grammar school days. When we first moved to our home on Luna Ave., when I was about 6 or 7, one day Dad surprised us by bringing home a little puppy dog. We named him Laddie. He was a collie-shepherd with beautiful tan hair. He was a constant companion as Bob and I were growing up. He was an inside/outside dog. He grew to be a little less tall than the average collie. When we mentioned the word "chain", he ran over to where the chain hung in the kitchen and whined. He was ready for a romp. He often pulled us on our roller skates. We loved him very much. Laddie and Mother often walked a few blocks to Central and Milwaukee Aves. to meet Fran or Beret when they came home from church or elsewhere at night and called from the corner drug store. We always felt safe with Mother and Laddie. And Mother was at ease when Laddie was with us kids.

A highlight of my Freshman year in high school was a trip to California. It came about in this manner. The year was 1934. My Sunday School teacher, Miss Esther Draeger, who later became Mrs. Esther Loucks, was taking a trip to California. Knowing that my father worked on the railroad and could get a pass for me, she invited me to go with her. Dad got the pass, and Miss Draeger and I set off for California on the train. The trip itself took several days. We slept in the Pullman car. Each night the porter would come through the car and make up the beds. When the beds were made up and the dark curtains drawn alongside each upper and lower compartment, you had to be careful not to find yourself in someone else's cubbyhole if you went for a walk during the night. We ate in the Pullman dining room—white table cloths, beautiful china and glassware and silverware, with porters to wait on us. We also ate at the Fred Harvey stops along the way. In San Bernardino, we stayed with friends of Miss Draeger. A highlight of our trip was a visit to my aunt and uncle, Sarah Oberrnaier and her husband, Carl, who managed (or owned, I'm not sure) a hotel in Santa Barbara. Sarah was Dad's older sister. We visited them at their hotel. They were most gracious, gave us a hearty lunch in their quarters. Being a sister of my father, she was also born in Hungary. The address I have for them, whether or not it was the hotel address or another, was 227 W. Arrollaga, Santa Barbara. Carl died sometime after that. In the winter of 1966, Burt and I and part of the family were in Santa Barbara on a furlough, and went over to see her. Now her address had changed. She was in a nursing home, Santa Barbara Sanatorium, 2031 De La Vina. She was 83 years old then. When we talked about what we were doing with our lives and tried to witness to her, she adamantly told us that we need not waste our time trying to convert her. She died on April 3, 1972.

The summer after my Freshman year, we moved to Mt. Prospect—304 S. WaPella Ave. That meant being separated from Fran and Bill again, and it seemed as if Mt. Prospect were 100 miles away, not just about 20. That year Bob and I rode the school bus to Arlington Heights High School. It was my Sophomore year and Bob's Junior year. I never did make many friends that year—I was shy, young, a newcomer, a Christian. I did have one friend—Betty Jean Thomas—but I lost track of her when I left that school. The thing that saved me and Bob was that Aunt Ruth and Uncle Charlie and Marjorie lived about 6 blocks from us in Mt. Prospect. We spent a lot of time at their house. The ping pong table in their basement occupied some of our time. We went to the country club with them and played ping pong there, too. On Sundays, they would pick me up and take me to church with them. They were charter members of the Niles Center Bible Church in Niles Center (now Skokie). Two friends that I made there were Grace Clavey (McConnell) and Mary Heiniger with whom I correspond to this day. After Sunday School and church, we always went over to Mabel and Everett Smith's home for dinner and the afternoon, and after the evening service, we came home. I remember riding in the back seat of their car with Marjorie, and Uncle Charlie drove so very fast—50 miles an hour. That was 1935-'36.

I was not happy that year. I missed Fran and Bill and all my church friends. Dad and Fran and Bill talked it over and before my Junior year, I went to live with Fran and Bill—back to 5420 Foster Ave., this time in the upstairs apartment. It had to be a real sacrifice on their part—they had only been married a year, yet they opened their hearts and home to me. Their house wasn't all that big—I slept in the parlor on their hide-a-bed in the winter and on the front enclosed, but unheated porch in the summer time. My dresser was on the porch, both winter and summer. But those were happy years. I was back at Carl Schurz High School and back at church with my friends, and most of all, I was back with my sister and brother—in—law whom I loved dearly.

———

After two years, I graduated from high school in the spring of 1938, just two months before I turned 17. In my Senior year, Patricia Ann was born to Fran and Bill, and we moved over to 5516 Marmora Ave. Now what? There was no money for college. The alternative was to get a job. That summer I also met Burt Long.

We went to the same church, the North Side Gospel Center. He was in Wheaton College but came back to Chicago each week-end to teach his Sunday School class. We didn't notice each other until that summer, although we had been attending the same church for a number of years. First notice on my part—the young people went on a picnic to, I believe, Gages Lake. We rode the church bus. I had brought my tennis racket but didn't get a chance to play. Burt asked if he could borrow my racket.

Second notice. We lived in the same general neighborhood, on the northwest side of Chicago, and rode 3 street cars to get to the Center—Milwaukee Ave. street car to Crawford Ave. (Pulaski), Crawford Ave. car to Fullerton Ave., Fullerton Ave. to Central Park Ave., where the converted furniture store stood with its welcome! Forty five minute trip—seven cents! You wonder what the attraction was! It was the highlight of our lives—from Sunday school classes and church services held in the afternoons and evenings on Sundays, to clubs and Bible studies and choir practices during the week, to special weeks of meetings with giants of the faith such as Paul Rader, William Pettingill, William R. Newell, John Cararra, and others whose names have slipped me. Fran and Bill and I rode the street cars, and so did Burt. Most of the time they were different cars, but one time, we were on the same cars—whether by accident or by design—but he asked if he could walk home with me. Of course! Fran and Bill were there, too. This happened several times.

That summer, some of our crowd were having a roller skating party. By that, I mean roller skating on the streets and going back to Carl and Emily Grothkob's house in Berwyn. Paul, my "supposed boy friend", but not in my mind, was away at camp, and since I was invited and asked to bring a date, I called on my friend, Eleanor Bauer, who lived on the same street as Burt, to ask him for me to go with me. He accepted, thinking at first he was going with Eleanor, but she made it plain it was with Ruth Hollander and not with her. He still accepted. I forget how we got to the party, but I remember that we skated together, and the closest we got to holding hands was his holding on to one end of a short stick and I, on to the other. After that, Paul was no longer in the picture. And that was the beginning of our friendship. Some of Burt's peers (the crowd that was 3 years older than my crowd) didn't like the idea of his dipping down into the next level—"he was robbing the cradle" and I heard about it.

Chapter 9

WORKING YEARS

After high school, I was expected to get a job. In 1938, jobs were scarce. We were still recovering from the depression. There was no way I could afford to go to college although I wanted to. Jerry Thomas worked at Spiegel's on the south side of Chicago, and he was able to get me a job there. It meant leaving the house at 6:30 a.m., riding the street cars for 1½ hours in order to punch the time clock by 8 o'clock. At 4:30 p.m., the ride was reversed. For 8 hours I opened returned goods and recorded what was returned. My pay was $12.00 a week. Five dollars a week went to Fran and Bill for room and board; $1.20 for offering; 70 cents for carfare to and from work; more carfare for rides to and from the Center. The rest, less than $5.00, went for clothes, glasses, and dental bills. There was never anything left over.

I left that job after some months and got a job with Royal Trucking Company. I kept that job until a better one opened up—with Wilson Co. This was a job in a small office which was okay, but Mr. Wilson smoked cigars, and we were in the same room, and my clothes became saturated with the smoke, and it was embarrassing, especially when I went to a church function right from work. It was during the next summer, that Victor Cory, who with his wife, Bernice, had founded Scripture Press, and who went to the Center, offered me a job at Scripture Press. I jumped at the chance. For two years, I worked at Scripture Press, first as Mr. Cory's secretary, then for Marian Siegfried in catalog sales, then for Gladys Siegfried in general correspondence and switchboard. By this time, I was making $15.00 a week. It was during this time that I had an appendectomy, done by Dr. Titus Johnson at the Swedish Covenant Hospital. By this time, Fran and Bill and I, with Pat, moved to Niles Center, now Skokie, and Burt and I were "going steady".

My mode of transportation to and from work was the North Shore line from Harms Woods or walk a mile to Dempster St., and take the north side el. Burt's mode of transportation was sometimes the train, sometimes the el, or sometimes hitch hiking, the latter usually late at night.

It was during these three years out of school that Burt encouraged me to go to Wheaton College. He had already graduated. I had no money but he insisted that I could work and go to school at the same time. I applied. I was accepted and started Wheaton College in Sept. of 1941 with $25.00 in my pocket and the promise of a job.

Chapter 10

WHEATON COLLEGE

Three years after graduating from high school, and with 3 years of work behind me, I entered Wheaton College. I lived in a Co-op house called Lincoln House. There were about 8 of us girls and we had a house parent, Mrs. Wright, and we cooked our own meals and did our own cleaning and contributed a certain sum of money each week toward food. I was working about 20 hrs. a week in the Placement Office for Mrs. MacDonald and going in to Chicago each Saturday to work at Scripture Press. I rode in with Mr. and Mrs. Cory who had moved to Wheaton by that time. They were very kind to me. I didn't mind the trip into Chicago each Sat. because I knew I would see Burt the next day at church. Each Sunday night, he would see that I got on the Aurora & Elgin (Roaring Elgin) at the Central Ave. stop in Chicago and I went back to Wheaton for another week. These two jobs kept me in enough money to pay for my room and board and tuition. I paid the latter in monthly installments. My yearly college bill amounted to about $1200.00. In between work, I went to classes—Bible, English, Anthropology, History, Spanish.

At the end of my Freshman year, Mrs. Smith, dean of women, called me into her office. I hadn't a clue what she wanted with me. I didn't think I had misbehaved! Mrs. Smith told me that there was a woman who paid the tuition of one girl and the one she had been helping out was graduating and she was looking for a new girl. I had been recommended to her as a deserving and needy student and would I like to be helped with my tuition for the next three years? WOULD I? After that, I had only to come up with my room and board money. I worked for Scripture Press during the summers and during the school years, I worked for the Wheaton Bible Church as a youth worker for 20 hours a week and Scripture Press on Saturdays and sometimes during the week when Mr. Cory brought work home for me to do at his house.

In between working, I studied. I decided on Anthropology as my major because it was thought to be best suitable for the mission field. Our head of department was Dr. Grigolia, who had escaped from Georgia, Russia during the Russian Revolution in the 'teens or twenties. He spoke with an accent, and one of his favorite sayings was "plus to dat . . ." Our class was held on the 4th floor of Blanchard—401. It was a full class, with about 50 students in it, and it was thrilling each morning to hear us all sing a cappela such favorites as "Amazing Grace" and "Man of Sorrows" and others. Other courses that stand out throughout my four years were American Literature with Miss Effie Jean Wheeler, Miss Torry in Bible, Dr. Edman for History, Dr. Mixter in Zoology, Dr. Mack in Physiology—which I barely passed, Dr. Thiessen in Ethics and Theism, Dr. Eugenia Price in a Christian Ed Course. In the latter course I got a 95, the highest possible mark, on my final, but because I wasn't a Christian Education major, she gave me only a 90 for the course. I met her one day in a downtown Wheaton beauty shop. She asked me what my major was and I told her. She said, "You should have been a Christian Ed major." Years later, I wish that I had been—either that or an Education major who took some courses in Anthropology because I spent most of my missionary career either teaching or doing Christian Ed work.

During my Freshman year, Pearl Harbor was attacked. It was Dec. 7, 1941, a Sunday. The next day the Tower Bell tolled and as we gathered for Chapel, Prexy Edman, filled with emotion told us that President Roosevelt had declared war on Japan. As we sat in Chapel that Monday morning, Dr. Edman, choked with emotion, reflected on his own experiences in World War I. He warned us of what lay ahead. Death, destruction, separation, loneliness and hardship! Classes were suspended and the day was given over to prayer. One by one, many young men dropped out of school. One day the seat beside me in

Bible 101 was empty. The boy who had sat there never came back. Love for God and country!

Also during my first year, I joined the Ladies Literary Society. Literary societies were the biggest social events of the college, and Friday nights were given over to fine dining by candlelight, soft music, and dispersion to the 8 different societies on campus. During my Junior and Senior years, I was Treasurer and Parliamentarian and Recording Secretary. Lit societies were given over to culture—an appreciation of the finer things in life, but always highlighted with creativity and enjoyment. In my Senior year, a fifth women's society was added. It is too bad that the era of Literary Societies has passed.

During my second year, revival hit the college. I don't remember how it started—whether it was during special services with Dr. Filken—or after. What I remember is that one young man came to the platform and confessed to something. That started a series of confessions that lasted for a few days. Broken relationships were mended and a fresh spirit prevailed on campus.

It was also during my second year that I signed up for the tennis team rather than take gym classes. I made the team and for three years played on the women's team. Mostly I was #3 or 4. Others on the team were Darlene Holstead Gillette, Ruth Jensen Hart, Jane Levering Stam, Jane Wilkens and Marie Fetzer. Of the six of us, three of us became missionaries—Darlene to India and Ruth to South Africa—I to Niger. We have kept in touch all these years. There were two concrete tennis courts. Grass grew between the cracks. We wore shorts under white skirts that came to our knees. Ruth Peterson, later Leedy, was our coach, and we played matches with North Central, DeKalb and Normal Teachers College in Chicago. They were not as hard-hitting, well-organized matches that our teams play now.

With many of the boys dropping out of school to go to war during my four years at Wheaton, the girls outnumbered the boys by 2-1. So if you were asked out for a date, you were pretty special. By the time I entered college, I was pretty much committed to Burt, and after turning down two dates, and after seeing me on campus with Burt from time to time, I wasn't asked out again. And especially when I got my engagement ring in my Jr. year.

I was a cheerleader for my first two years. It was nothing like cheer leading today where the boys throw the girls around. The boys did their thing, including their pyraminds, and we, in our skirts and Wheaton sweaters did our thing and led the crowd in the college cheers and songs.

Intramurals played a part in my life, too, especially basketball, both class competition and Literary society competition. We had a good time.

Graduation finally came in 1945, and I graduated with no special honors with just an 87 average, which is probably equivalent to a B or B—average. I graduated as Ruth Hollander Long because it was during my Spring vacation that Spring that Burt and I were married. But that's the next chapter.

Chapter 11

MARRIAGE

Our wedding took place on Saturday, March 31, 1945 at the North Side Gospel Center on Fullerton Avenue in Chicago. Our pastor, Lance B. Latham, officiated and my bridesmaids were my cousin Jane Blix and friend Gladys Siegfried, and my maid of honor was my sister, Beret. Burt's groomsmen were Pastor and friend Bob Swanson, Carroll Hammer, and Walter Warfield. Pastor Joe McCauley, pastor of the Wheaton Bible Church and his wife were there, and he prayed during the ceremony. Brother-in-law Bill gave me away, and sister Fran was "mother of the bride". The reception was held upstairs at the Center, and the reception was the wedding gift of my aunts and uncles—Olsons, Perdues, Hennixes, Blixes.

For all practical purposes, I was an orphan—for sure I was half a one—but I was surrounded by supportive family and relatives. My Dad was living in Missouri with his wife and did not come to the wedding, but they did send a gift. I had lived with Fran and Bill from the time I turned 15 until my wedding, 8 years later, although for most of the last four years, I was away at college. Since I had no money for a wedding dress, I wore a borrowed one. It was a lovely satin gown with long sleeves, train, and waist length veil.

We were married during spring vacation of my senior year. We were given special permission from the college since that was the time Burt was able to get a week's vacation from his internship at Missouri Baptist Hospital in St. Louis.

Burt was in the second nine months in the hospital as a Jr. Resident. He had made the acquaintance of a woman who worked at the hospital, Mrs. Hansen, and it was her daughter whose dress I borrowed. The Hansen family became good friends of ours, and to this day, we correspond with one daughter.

Chapter 12

ST. LOUIS, MISSOURI

Our honeymoon started at the Sheridan hotel in Chicago and Sunday evening, we boarded the train for St. Louis. We had reservations at the Coronado Hotel in St. Louis and we arrived about 10 p.m. to be told that reservations were cancelled after 9 p.m. It was war time, and hotel rooms were at a premium. It is hard to believe that after the hotel management called all around town on our behalf there were no rooms available. So the Hansens came to the rescue! Burt called Mrs. Hansen, and she offered us her living room hide-a-bed. That's where we spent the second night of our honeymoon. The next day we were able to get our room in the hotel, and we finished the week there. Then I went back to school, and it wasn't until after I graduated in May that we really began to live together. Burt arranged with another woman at the hospital to let us rent her apartment for 9 months to a year until her husband returned from the service since she was living with her mother for the time being. Then when he returned and we had to move, we moved into some condemned, vacated nurses' quarters at the hospital. We lived there the last few months of his third 9 months as a Sr. resident. It was there that I got my first bouts of morning sickness, and Rollie was on the way. During our year in St Louis, I worked for the Huffman Advertising Company and made a very good salary of $135.00 a month.

In St. Louis, we attended the Bible Presbyterian Church where Francis Schaeffer was pastor. We visited in his and Edith's home. I reminded her that when I was a camper at Mich-i-dune, she was a leader and they were on their honeymoon. Also, I reminded her that when we were swimming in Lake Michigan, she and I helped my cousin, Lillian, who was out too far, get back in to shore safely. References are made to their time at camp in her book TAPESTRY. We also made some good friends in St. Louis, some of them being couples from the church and also in the medical profession.

Most important, though, was the friendship of Will and Edna Brunk and their family who were instrumental in starting a church in one of the suburbs. We helped them on Sunday afternoons, spent a lot of time at their house, got to know them and their children—about 9 of them. Will was also in charge of Young Life in that area, and Burt often spoke at their meetings. Hazel Knowlton (before she was Knowlton) was one of the young people who attended. We have kept in touch with Will and Edna and also their daughter, Gwen. Edna died a few years back, and Will is alone but near Gwen. Gwen's husband died also, and she has remarried, and we saw them a few years ago. Gwen formerly worked with New Tribes, so they still have close ties with them.

We attended Youth for Christ meetings on Saturday nights held in Kiel auditorium. Every Saturday the auditorium was filled with young people. What a great time that was. That was the winter of 1945-46. A man by the name of Richard Harvey was in charge, and I have always wondered why Torrey Johnson is claimed to be the founder of Youth for Christ in 1946.

Chapter 13

ALASKA

We returned to the Chicago area and Burt was inducted into the army as a First Lieutenant. He went to Camp Grant for his basic training and was then sent to San Antonio, TX. It was early summer in Texas. I followed Burt there, and by this time, morning sickness really plagued me, and I was sick on the plane all the way. By the time I arrived in San Antonio, I was bleeding, so spent the next few weeks in bed in a hot, sweltering second floor room while Burt spent his days at the barracks. Finally his orders came to go to Ft. Richardson, Alaska, so we headed back home, and I stayed with Fran and Bill again while he went to Alaska. It wasn't until October that I was able to follow him there. The snow was just coming down the mountains—the Chugach Range.

At first, we lived in the basement of Burt's colonel's home. His wife used her influence a few weeks later to get an apartment for us on the base, a nice two bedroom apartment with living room and dining room combined and kitchen and bath, and most important, it was warm in a country notorious for cold weather. We were in the apartment in time to get it set up for Rollie's birth on Dec. 5.

December 3 was one of those 40 degree below zero Fahrenheit days. I'm not talking wind chill. Pains began during the early morning hours. We called the hospital driver's pool and they came for us after awhile. On those bitterly cold nights, some army vehicles were left running all night for the purpose of pulling the rest in the morning to get them started. It turned out that we made it to the hospital in plenty of time, because it wasn't until 36 hours later that Rollie was born!

Our two years in Alaska brought new friends, especially from the Church of the Open Door in Anchorage. John and Nadine Gillespie, were pastor and wife. Roger and Irene Laube were good friends who also lived on the base. Roger was in the law office. They lived only two blocks from us. Then there were the Lahtis, Parmenters, Ericksons, Nelsons, Daisy Graham and others that we have kept in touch with over the years. Life in Alaska included a trip over the Alcan Highway to the Arctic Circle with Agnes John. Although it was summer, it was cold at night, and we slept out in the open in sleeping bags, cooked outside, washed dishes upstream and diapers downstream. At Bethel, we stood on the edge of the Yukon. The highway was not paved, and there were long stretches of wilderness. At least once we stayed all night at a wayside lodge. One night we slept on the ground in grizzly country—we heard about that the next morning. Rollie slept in the car in his sleeper. The scenery was breath-taking—mountains, flowers, rivers, sometimes calm, sometimes raging, water falls! It was awesome.

Another time we spent a week at Victory Bible Camp. It was just new, and we were among the first campers. John and Nadine Gillespie, under the auspices of Arctic Missions, Inc. were the spearheads of the camp. We slept in tents on cots in sleeping bags. Food was prepared on an old wood burning stove out in the open. Rev. Simon Forsberg was the speaker, president of Multnomah School of the Bible. One night we went down to the meeting and left Rollie sleeping in his sleeping bag. During the service I came back to check on him and found him crying and completely engulfed in his bag. I immediately opened up the bag and rescued him. After that, we tied a rope around the middle of his bag so he wouldn't slip down into it. Needless to say, I was quite shaken up. Victory Bible Camp continues to this day and has had almost 50 years of improvements put into it. Simon Forsberg invited us to stay with him and his wife when we returned from Alaska, which we did. Simon was the one who influenced me concerning missions when I was a child. Strange that I should meet him as an adult in Alaska! Later on, we met his cousin, Malcolm, who was also with S.I.M.

—

After almost two years in Alaska, Burt was discharged as a captain. He took his discharge in Alaska, and before returning to the States, we spent a week in Palmer, AK, where Burt did a locum tenums for a doctor for a week. Palmer was 50 miles out of Anchorage, and we had visited there often because Lazy Mt. Children's Home was there, started by Arctic Missions missionaries. Victory Bible Camp was down the highway another 50 miles or so, and a mission station at GlenAllen was not far way. This was started by missionaries Vince Joy and his wife Becky. Today GlenAllen mission station has a radio station and hospital that ministers to the people in that area and along the pipe line. The Joys' mission, I believe it was Alaskan Mission, has merged with SEND. Penny Pinneo's brother was for a long time the doctor at the hospital there. Delta Bond also spent a few years there as a nurse.

Now it was time to head for the States. The year was 1948. Alaska was not yet a state, it was still a province. We took the train from Anchorage to Valdez where we would pick up the boat down to Washington. It was springtime, but Valdez was still inundated with snow piled high on both sides of the streets and sidewalks. The trip down the inside passage was awesome. We saw the little fishing towns along the way, the glaciers that jutted out into the water. As we passed by, the captain sounded the ship's horn and more ice fell from the glacier into the water. It was about a 5 day trip. And finally we reached Washington. John and Inez Nelson had moved to Seattle and we stayed with them, while Burt negotiated with a dealer to buy a new Hudson. The dealer had promised one to us while we were in AK so Burt was going to hold him to his promise, even though post-war cars were scarce. After a few days' wait, we got the car, a long, low beautiful forest green 1947 (1948?) Hudson and our trip across the West to Chicago began.

Chapter 14

BACK TO CHICAGO

It was at this time that we visited Simon Forsberg and his wife in Portland, Oregon. They gave us a tour of Multnomah School of the Bible and treated us royally for a few days. On to Santa Barbara where we visited Ed and Charlotte McDaniel. Ed was Burt's roommate at Wheaton and classmate at Illinois Medical School. Charlotte was a year ahead of Ed and Burt at Wheaton. They eventually went to Thailand, then Siam, as missionaries, working in the hospital at Cheng Mai. Ed's parents had been medical missionaries there before them, and Ed was born in Siam. Charlotte died in her sixties, I believe, and Ed has married again, Katherine, and they are still serving in Thailand. Katherine was a missionary there before their marriage, and is a bit younger than Ed.

Also in Santa Barbara we visited Dad and Ethel. We hadn't seen them for at least five years, and as it turned out this was the last time we saw him because he died in March of 1960. We visited his sister and brother-in-law, Sarah and Carl Obermaier, whom I had visited for the first time when I was a child and once again before she died. I mentioned this in Chapter Eight.

The rest of the way home, we took in the tourist sights. What stands out in my mind is the Grand Canyon. What do you say about something that is so awesome?

Home was at Fran and Bill's on Kedvale Ave. Mrs. Isacksen lived upstairs—she owned the home. She had a room for us upstairs and we ate with Fran and Bill and Pat. Mrs. Isacksen worked for a Salvation Army resale store in Chicago and she brought home many clothes for Rollie and us which was a great help to us. Mrs. Isacksen lived to a great old age, and on one furlough we visited her in a nursing home, Bethany, I believe. She was blind and feeble, and we were not surprised to hear that she had gone home to heaven not long afterward.

After a couple of months we went to Summer Institute of Linguistics in Norman, Oklahoma for the summer. We traveled in our Hudson, and the trip took several days. We piled our bags behind the front seat in such a way that gave Rollie the run of the entire back seat, surrounded by his toys. He was a year and a half at this time. It was his play pen. A far cry from the restraints of today when every child has to be harnessed into a car seat! At SIL besides studying linguistics, we met many who became friends, especially Frank and Sophie Jenista. Frank we had known earlier—he was from Chicago. Rollie played with their son, Frankie, who today is an attaché in the service of the U.S. in Manilla, Philippines, and since Frank's death, Sophie continues in her missionary endeavors, making the embassy her headquarters overseas. We met Dave and Betty Pittman who later served with SIM in Ethiopia. Dave has been hit hard with a stroke. Their son, another playmate of Rollie's at SIL, is now S1M director in Ghana.

After Oklahoma, we returned to Kedvale Ave., and shortly thereafter, we took a locum tenems near Kansas City, MO, working for a Dr. Ellett. This lasted a couple of months. We were able to get back home for Christmas.

After Christmas, we set our faces toward New York—169 W. 71st St.—Sudan Interior Mission headquarters. While in Alaska, we had written to several mission boards, but SIM was the only one to answer and they invited us to come and candidate. Burt was 29 and I was 26, and everything that we had done up to that time had been preparation for what was to come. We were about to embark on a venture that would set the course for our entire future and that of our children. We were not sure what lay ahead—but we knew that what we were doing was right, for each of us since childhood had given our lives to the Lord for missions if that were His desire for us. And now we were at the jumping off place—childhood, schooling, medical training, army—all behind us. This was the beginning of our future!

PART II

Chapter 1

CANDIDATING

It was January, 1949. Two year old Rollie was having his afternoon nap. I lay on the bed, eyes turned upward, following the wire that encircled the room close to the ceiling, wondering what the wire was all about. Burt and I had discussed the possibility that here at 164 W. 74th St., New York City, home of SIM, the wire meant that the room was bugged. We'd better be on our best behavior, even in the privacy of our room. They must really scrutinize their candidates. This afternoon, Burt was having a talk with Jack Percy, Home Director, down in his office.

We thought we had flunked the test the moment we walked into the former hotel, now home of SIM. A week earlier we had arrived just at lunch time, having driven all night and the day before, dirty, unkempt, and of all things, I was wearing slacks. We introduced ourselves to the receptionist. She went into the dining room where lunch was in progress and soon returned with the hostess, prim, sedate, proper Mrs. Trout. I sensed her disapproval, but she looked past us, or through us, and invited us to the lunch table, just as we were. We noticed that the men were in suit coats and ties, the ladies, properly attired in dresses. What a beginning!

A week passed. We were the only candidates. In fact, it was not a real candidate class but just a special time set aside for us to come and have them look us over. We got into the act quickly—dresses for me and suit coats and ties for Burt! We were always seated down at

47

the end of the table with a high chair for Rollie at the corner. A very unrelaxed atmosphere which didn't help much when Rollie burped once! When we said, "Rollie, what do you say?" He said, "I burped". So much for that!

Burt did some odd jobs around the place; I did practically nothing because I was obviously five months pregnant with Lanny and Mrs. Trout apparently felt that I was incapacitated. Or maybe she preferred for me to keep a strict eye on Rollie.

After a week, we came before the Board. I have no idea who was on the Board but there were these ominous looking stately, dignified, older men—about 10 of them—seated in a circle, and they began asking us questions about our background and doctrinal position. It seemed as if it was over in less than 10 minutes (I may have forgotten). Someone said, "We are glad to welcome you to the SIM family." I thought to myself, "What family? This is too easy. We haven't done a thing all week; they interview us for about 10 minutes and tell us we're in the family." It was almost as if they couldn't wait to get their hands on a doctor but didn't want to be too obvious. They told us we could go home and start raising our support, $1200.00 per adult per year plus a small amount for each child.

As I pondered the "bugging of the room", Burt walked in. Jack Percy and he had talked about our assignment. Burt had said he wanted to go to a hard place, somewhere that nobody else would go. Jack said, "We have just the place for you! A town called 'Galmi' in French West Africa." At that announcement, I wasn't so sure I was cut out to be a missionary.

Just before we left, Burt asked Jack about the wired room. Jack laughed and said it was a fire alarm system. It alerted the fire department if there were smoke. Maybe the SIM wasn't too bad after all!

Chapter 2

PARIS

Between the time of our return to Chicago after being accepted by SIM in January of 1949 and our departure in August of the same year, Burt visited many churches with Carl Tanis. By far the most important event during those months was the birth of Lance Vaughn Long called "Lanny", on April 16, named after our Pastor Lance Latham. During those months, we lived with Fran and Bill on Kedvale. We slept upstairs in Mrs. Isacksen's apartment again but took our meals with the Buenemans. Almost everyday Mrs. Isacksen brought home clothes for the boys. We appreciated that and her interest in us.

It was during this time that we visited Bob and Cora in Glenview. For some reason, Rollie (age 2 1/2) called Bob "stupid". Cora reprimanded Rollie and told him to tell Uncle Bob that he was sorry. So Rollie responded with, "I'm sorry you're stupid, Uncle Bob!" I had completely forgotten the incident until our 50th wedding anniversary at Sebring when Bob and Cora were there (and Victor and Fran) and Bob was called upon to say "something nice" about us.

So during that interval, Rollie (and we) got our first introduction to television. We visited Aunt Ruth and Uncle Charlie who were the proud owners of a black and white TV. Rollie walked behind the TV to find the people who were on the screen.

Now it was time to go to New York whence we would sail to Paris to study French for ten months. Excerpts from letters will tell the story from here. All of them are addressed to Fran and Bill. The parentheses are my current additions.

"August 18, 1949 Arrived safely this a.m. at 8 o'clock. Rollie enjoyed the ride. After the novelty wore off, he found a playmate twice his age down the aisle and played 'cars' with him. After supper, all three of us piled into the lower: Rollie next to the window at one end; Lanny, at the other on his 'air nurse', and I on the outside. We were all asleep at 8:00 p.m., we were so tired. When we got up all we had to do was get dressed and get off the train. Took a cab and got here (SIM) in time for breakfast. Burt and the folks got in at 11:30 a.m. Flew all the way. (In our Hudson).

"August 19, 1949 We're not making the Ile de France. There's a chance we'll get a boat Wed . . . (Otherwise) the Marine Flasher on Friday.

"Aug. 22 We sail Wed. at noon on the French liner DeGrasse. We have a cabin with 3 bunks and they said they'd put a crib in extra. I'm so glad we're going on this boat, because on the Marine Flasher, Burt would have been alone with 40 or 50 men, and I and the kids with 10-20 women. Burt cut Lanny's locks off the top of his head. Rollie's getting cabin fever being cooped up inside all the time. He's used to being out."

Burt and I with 2 1/2 year old Rollie and 4 month old Lanny stood at the railing of the DeGrasse waving at the crowd that engulfed Mom and Dad Long. In vain we searched for them. Just minutes before, they were with us on board saying their good-byes, trying to be cheerful, knowing that it would be five years before we saw each other again. Our feelings were a mixture of sadness and anticipation together with apprehension. It wasn't until many years later when I said good-bye to our own children that I realized the price the folks had paid in letting us go with their blessing. We had said good-bye to my family in Chicago. Burt's folks made the trip to New York to see us off. My family was mostly Fran and Bill, who had become surrogate parents to me—caring for me in their own home from the time I was 15 until my marriage eight years later. I owe them a debt I can never repay.

Jack Percy was somewhere in the crowd, too. He had boarded with us also to put us at ease and to make sure that we knew that the word "brassieres" on this French liner meant "life jackets". As we waved, the liner slipped away from the pier, then moved slowly past the Statue of Liberty. The crowd faded and disappeared. Burt thought, "I wonder what crazy thing I am doing—to take my family on such an escapade." My thoughts were on family. We were anything but the dedicated missionaries who were ready to sacrifice life and limb for the sake of the Gospel. How come we didn't measure up to those missionaries who rejoiced to leave family and friends and "go to the regions beyond?" It was too late. We couldn't pull the cord and stop the boat. We saw the statue of Liberty slip away and next it was the shoreline that we lost and we were in open water. Each moment found us farther away from America and closer to France. Burt said, "Let's get something to eat. Remember that Jack Percy warned us to keep our stomachs full, and we wouldn't get seasick." We made our way to the dining room and ordered. Half way through the meal, I said, "I'm not hungry. I'm not feeling very good."

The French liner, DeGrasse, was a hold over from World War I. It had a round bottom that rocked with every wave. It took ten days to cross the Atlantic to LeHavre as compared with five or six days that the newer liners took.

We went down to our cabin, and I mean down, down. It seemed as if we were right next to the engine room. To our surprise, we found a basket of fruit waiting for us in our cabin. From Aunt Ruth and Uncle Charlie! How thoughtful!

"Aug. 30, 1949 aboard le DeGrasse. I had a bout with seasickness from Wed. p.m. to Sat. a.m. Most miserable of all feelings! Couldn't keep a thing down—not even dramamine."

Rollie and Burt kept their stomachs full. As the seas got rougher, the guests in the dining room dropped off, and at one time, Burt and Rollie were the only diners with a dozen waiters to serve them. Tables, chairs, plates, everything was bolted down. First we could see the watery depths as the portholes were covered with water; next we saw the sky as the boat rocked from side to side. I was sure we would never see our families again.

"But all is well now. Burt had a siege one night. The kids are regular sailors . . . With the crib we had standing room only, so we had it removed and are sleeping Lanny and Rollie at either end of a lower bunk. So far yesterday morning was the only time I picked Lanny up off the floor. How long he had been there, I don't know. I woke up to his whimperings. Will post this in LeHavre." On the tenth day, behold, there was land! Did Columbus feel as excited as I? France! Good old terra firma. Debarking. Goodbye, DeGrasse. I hope I never see you again.

Now for a train ride to Paris. It was midnight! What do we do when we get there? Behold, there was an angel named Earl Playfair there to meet us. His French was limited but ours was non-existent. He summoned a taxi which took us to the Hotel Victoria on 14 Rue Gay-Lussae. As we got out of the taxi, Rollie said, "Where are we going?" We said, "We're home!" At the hotel entrance, he turned and made a bee-line back toward the taxi and said, "This isn't home. I want to go home!" We finally convinced him that this was to be our home for the next months.

"September 4, 1949 Hotel Victoria is not as snappy as its name implies . . . a large, old fashioned double bed and a cot, a closet . . . small table and a couple of chairs. The double bed sags in the middle, and we find ourselves meeting each other there or hanging on the sides of the bed for dear life. There is a wash basin in the room and a strange looking basin . . . it's made just like a toilet but without any covers, but it's got a plug and two faucets. The toilet is down a dark hall . . . plus a nail and squares of French newspaper which we assume followed in the evolution from the corncob and catalog. Rollie used the last piece this afternoon . . . we might have to buy a French newspaper even though we can't read it . . . no bathtub, no hot water. There are radiators in the rooms but no heat.

"Yesterday afternoon we attended a meeting which is held every other Sun. in the home of a Christian French middle age couple who also speak English. We had tea and cookies . . . met other missionaries: U.S., French, Swedish, Norwegian, American, Canadian and English." Among the Americans at these Sunday afternoon meetings with Bob and Jeanette Evans, former Wheaton school mates of Burt's. These meetings became the jumping off place for the beginning of Greater European Mission with the Evans as the founders.

"We have a line on a Pension, which is a rooming and boarding house. The price for the family would be 1750 F per day. Francs are 326 to our dollar. We'll know tomorrow. Forgot to ask if they have heat and a bath room!!! I'm looking forward to Africa! More each day."

We did get the pension and we moved in the next Sunday. Price, 1800 francs per day (that includes meals). Our two room "suite" was on the sixth floor. No elevator. Poor Rollie—he had a hard time climbing the stairs. About the fourth floor, he says, "This is right, Mommy." "No," I say, "Two more to go." The next floor. "This is right, Mommy." "No, one more to go." "Carry me, Mommy." "I can't, Rollie. Let's rest a minute." "Mize all rested, Mommy." The next floor. "Here we are, Rollie." Rollie: "That's a long walk!" The bath room (where you take a bath) was on the fourth floor. We were used to a bath or shower a day. Next day we went down to the fourth floor for our baths. The door was locked. We asked the proprietor for the key. No way! You set a time; the servant fills the tub for you. I mean, fills it to the brim. You pay your money and he ushers you in. We all used the same water. That was our first and last bath in that pension. For the next five months we used the sink in our room and that "strange looking basin . . . that looks like a toilet" (bidet—bee day) which we learned was meant for douches but which we also used for sponge baths and basin in which to wash diapers.

"Sept. 13, 1949 We're about two blocks from the school and just across the street from the park . . . the proper name is the Garden of Luxembourg . . . Beautiful with green grass and flowers and lots of playground . . . in the center is a large pond with fountain. The boys delight in sailing their boats in it. The other day we rented a large sailboat and stick for Rollie. You put the boat in the water, give it a push with the stick and wait for it to reach the other side. A couple of kids claimed Rollie's boat at one time, so they and I had a hot argument—they in French and I in English. I won because I kept holding onto the boat. They went off and apparently got their right boat. An impressive building within the park area is the French Senate.

"Your airmail letter came . . . . we showed Rollie the pictures and he was thrilled. He said, 'That's Christie, that's Debbie's home, that's Frances, that's Patsy, there's the mail-box, that's Christie's car, that's Lanny holding Frrr—that's Frances holding Lanny.' His eyes just shone and his whole face lit up with excitement. When we were all through looking at them, he wanted to see them again. He turned each one carefully, and we watched him without his knowing it. He put them up close to his face and every few minutes there'd be a brief smile. He's really a little homesick. The other day he said again, 'I want to go home.'

"He remembers home vividly and he often asks me to tell him the make-believe stories about (make believe) Johnnie and Rollie and the rope, and the ice cream, and the bath. The rope story: Johnnie gets on the table on the back porch and swings on the rope, and the rope breaks, Johnnie gets hurt and doesn't do it again. The ice cream story: Johnnie and Rollie get on their bikes, cross the streets and go up to the corner and get popsicles and when they get home they get spankings because they crossed the streets. The bath story: Johnnie and Rollie have their baths, splash the bathroom all up, go up the stairs—'My stairs, no my stairs, etc.' they say to each other. Then, 'I bet you can't climb into bed.' 'Yes, I can'. Both get into bed, pray, get their night-nights and go right to sleep. Rollie sits ga-ga eyed and listens to them although he's heard each one a hundred times."

We registered at the Alliance Francaise. Burt had classes both morning and afternoon. I had classes for two hours in the afternoon, at the sleepy-time hours. The boys were napping at that time, Burt was home with them studying, and I was trying to stay awake in class. With the care of two small children, learning French did not have top priority for me. But from the first day of class, when Burt walked in to Mme. Vasvari's class and was met with a barrage of French, to which he replied, "I don't know what you said," and to which she answered in English, "You're in the right class!" he set his mind to the class and diligently pursued the subject. In ten months time, he went from Beginners class to "Class Superieur" and received a certificate. Several times a day, we made the descent and ascent from the sixth floor. I was usually carrying a baby and prodding a 2 1/2 yr. old along. We were in Paris with two single nurses whom we met in New York and who sailed shortly before us, Adrianna Raidt and Irene Archer. They remained close friends all through our years in Africa and later.

"September 21, 1949 Yes, Lanny is five months old. We put his Teeterbabe together the other day, and he enjoys sitting up in it. Rollie enjoys bouncing him in it, but we have to hold R. down, or Lanny will fly too high. He still has the sweetest smile and disposition and is the best baby ever. Rollie mentions frequently that he'd like to see Fran and Bill and Patsy and Bramma and Brampa. He comes out with 'I'm going to Akkrika and play in the sand. with my pail and shovel.' "September 29, 1949 Lanny is still the sweetest sweetheart imaginable. He's getting cuter ever day, and his smile is very attractive. His brown eyes seem to be browner all the time. What a boy!

"October 6, 1949 Tomorrow is Friday and we have no electricity on Fridays after 7 a.m. until 12 noon. Then it's off again at 1:00 until 6 p.m. That's one way of conserving electricity. Another way is to use 25 watt bulbs. We complained . . . that we couldn't see to study at night, so he gave us one 40 watt bulb . . . .

"October 14, 1949 Some days I feel as if I'm getting the language, and other days I despair. Dawson Trotman has been here this week holding meetings in the afternoon and evening. We're still in our hotel. No word yet on an apartment. Last Saturday we went to Versailles while one of our nurses took care of the boys . . . 50 min. train ride out of Paris. We saw Louis XIV's palace, now a museum with portraits, pictures, mirrors, furniture, tapestries . . . beautiful gardens.

"Rollie . . . noticed the dust particles in a ray of sunlight coming in the window. He stopped his playing, then said, 'What are those, mommy?' . . . The other afternoon after he was put to bed for his nap, he called me and said, 'Those are my pants that I go swimming in in Patsy' bathtub outside.' He was referring to the pants Debbie's mother gave him when he was playing in Mrs. I's tub. We got our first change of bedding last week after we had been here for 3 1/2 weeks.

"October 28, 1949 Brrr, it's cold. We've been promised heat tomorrow, so here's hoping. One thing about winter, I think the meat will stay fresh longer. All meat markets are open air affairs. At night, when they bar up all the windows on shop fronts . . . they just fence in the meat markets and you go by and see great sides of meat hanging from the ceiling.

"One day a few weeks ago, we were walking down the street, and he (Rollie) said, looking at a car, 'What is that, Mommy?' I said, 'That's a car'. He said, 'No, it's a Renault.' He was right. He just spotted a Mercury. He said, 'That's Bob's car!' Now a television set. 'Mommy, that's Uncle Charlie's picture!' There's a green Ford, Ruth.' He's right—color and make.

"November 5, 1949 When he (Rollie) looked at the pictures the folks sent he said, 'Grandmasss are nice at me. Grandpaaas are nice at me too.' The one with him on the bike, 'That's Rollie in Africa with his big bicycle.' That confirmed my suspicions that he thinks Africa is Chicago and why he's looking forward to it so much.

"November 12, 1949 Sometime ago I noticed an ad in the paper by "The American Diaper Service . . . now I'm getting my diapers washed, ironed, picked up and delivered for 9 frs. each diaper (2 1/2 cents).

"Burt's comment: 'Incidentally, $13000.00 is in for our hospital from one will and $5000.00 for the rest of the station from another one.'

Christmas was on the way—our first Christmas away from home. As I browsed through a department store, I came across a little nativity scene. Mary, Joseph, the baby, the angels, shepherd, wise men and cattle were made of ceramic; the manger, of cardboard. I bought it and set it up on our mantel. We took it to Africa and for the next 35 years, it was part of our Christmas. When we retired, we bequeathed it to daughter Sue and Terry, who were now full-fledged SIM missionaries. Imagine our delight when in 1989 they brought it with them from Kano for Christmas with us at Galmi when we were out for a three-month tour.

"December 22, 1949 Three days before Christmas . . . seven packages have arrived. You should see our mantel. In the center of the mirror is a star, and on the mantel is the little nativity set. We have our Christmas cards strung around the top and two sides and some on the mirror and below. Packages are flanked on and around the mantel . . . adds a festive tone to our room . . . makes us feel that Christmas is coming to us even though we are far from home and loved ones. For a few days he played with the manger set as if it were a toy . . . then I told him about the star and put it up . . . read him the Christmas story from the Bible story book he had received that day.

"The other day I was having difficulty making Rollie understand, and finally in exasperation I said, 'Are you stupid?' He answered, 'I said stupid to Bob.' Do you remember the incident?

"Today he was sailing his ducks and boat in the wash basin in the other room and called to me asking to use the soap. I warned him not to, and he called back, 'Don't talk, Mom.' Yesterday he was sailing his ducks again; Lanny was in his chair watching him. I was in the other room. I heard a squeal out of Lanny and called to Rollie, 'Is Lanny all right, Rollie?' He said, 'He's all right. He's not bothering me.'

"Two nights ago Rollie was having a hard time getting to sleep. After about the fifth trip into the room I told him the next time he'd get a spanking. The next time came. I got him out of bed, ushered him into the other room so Lanny wouldn't wake up and ordered him to take down his pants and lean over. He did say, 'I won't cry, Ruth. Give me a soft one.' I gave him four swats on his bare behind. Burt was watching his face screw up and if I had given him another slap he would have burst out in tears. A look of relief came over his face. He said, 'I didn't cry', pulled up his p.j.'s and marched back to bed and not another peep was heard out of him.

"Last night he pulled the same stunt. I told him I'd spank him again and this time he wanted me to. He said again, 'I won't cry', pulled down his pants and leaned over. This time I spanked him seven times . . . half way through he started to cry. Then when it was all over he sobbed, 'You shouldn't spank me so hard.' His sob was in a voice not of pain but of betrayal. I asked him if he had thought I was teasing him—if it was a joke. All this while I was holding him and comforting him, and he said yes. Then I said it wasn't a joke, and that he should go to sleep like a good boy. After a few more minutes he was ready to go back to bed and he stayed there. Tonight he went to sleep right off the bat. He sure is one sweet fellow.

"We received $40.00 from the Hennixes in four different envelopes . . . . We have received other money from folks too all hoping that their contributions might make our Christmas a little happier we do hope to be able to make a few days trip into Switzerland . . . rent a car . . . Switzerland is only 300 miles from here.

"Last Sunday we went to the usual missionary gathering. After the tea, we had the meeting which included singing Christmas carols in French and English. The Norwegians and Swedes sang in their own tongue their favorite carols."

After Christmas an apartment opened up on the Street of the Pretty Leaves—5 Rue des Belles Feuilles. Other missionaries were living there and told us about it. We were tired of hiking up and down six floors, of sharing the bathroom at the end of the hall with others, with taking sponge baths. We looked at it. There was a living room, small kitchen and a beautiful bathroom all our own. "We'll take it," we said. There was even an elevator now that we were on the second floor.

—

"January 21, 1950 Fran, there's SO much difference in this place than the other . . . . this place has rugs on the floor—the other had none. This place has easy chairs and upholstered straight chairs—the other had two straight backed chairs; this place has heat so one is warm with a sweater—the other had heat so one was still cold with a sweater; this place has HOT water all day—the other had warm water morning and sometimes evenings; here the management is friendly—there they were nasty and suspicious; this place is cheerful and clean, with pretty red drapes and lace curtains—the other was dirty with dark, dirty drab drapes; here we get enough to eat with seconds on everything but meat—there we were hungry when we left the table; here we have a kitchen and I can cook what we want; there, if we munched on anything between meals we did it quietly and with the doors locked; here we have a double bed—there we had singles. The pitch on eating is that we have to take dinner and supper with them in the dining room from Mon. through Sat. Breakfasts and Sunday meals we can prepare ourselves . . . .

"I just got back from grocery shopping . . . . This is how the French shop. They take their net bags or shopping straw baskets . . . first I went to the meat market—picked out a nice looking rolled veal roast . . . then to the fruit market—got some bananas, tangerines and grapefruit. He put in his scale a rotten tangerine which I took out and handed back to him. Then he tried to over-charge me which is very common to foreigners, but I called him on it. Then to the vegetable store—got some onions, tomatoes and lettuce. These they poured right into the bag without even wrapping . . . then I bought some butter and canned peas at another store. Then to the bread store for some rolls and a 'stick' of bread. Finally to a milk store for some milk. My purchases came to 1406 francs or $4.00.

"January 31, 1950 The other day I told Rollie not to do something. He said, 'Yes I will'. I said, 'No you won't'. 'Yes I will'. 'If you do, you'll get a spanking'. He hesitated a minute and said, 'All right, I won't do it.' Then he added, 'Now we are all both happy again, aren't we?' You should see Lanny stand all by himself. He edges around the davenport.

"February 6, 1950 This week Burt and I and Paul and Jane Pendell are going to Switzerland sans kids. Aidie and Irene are going to stay at our place and take care of them. "February 12, 1950 from

Geneva, Switzerland. Switzerland is a clean country . . . Switzerland is mountains and valleys. Geneva is in a valley situated on a large, picturesque, mountain-bordered lake.

"February 22, 1950 Glad to hear of Uncle Fred's spiritual decision. (I understand it was Uncle Charlie who led him to the decision.) I put Lanny in hard sole shoes for the first time. Boy, does he ever crawl! We gave him his first boy's haircut . . . he's really cute . . . he didn't make half the fuss Rollie made. Tuesday was Mardi Gras, the day before Lent. Mardi means Tuesday and Gras means fat—fat Tuesday. Last chance to gorge! We are two blocks from the Eiffel Tower, park and concert hall.

"March 2, 1950 Things are gradually getting back to normal after 5 days of worry, prayer, sleepless nights and days, penicillin shots and aspirin. It all began Sat. noon when he (Rollie) complained of an earache. At 2 P.M., we gave him his first shot, and since then he's had eleven—all in the seat. His temperature . . . Mon. 106 1/2; this noon, 100. We couldn't figure out what was wrong since his ears had apparently cleared up. But last night when Burt looked at them again, he noticed the drums were puffed which meant there was either pus or edema causing the swelling. This noon the swelling was gone . . . Consequently, Rollie is hard of hearing—he doesn't hear anything we say in a normal voice.

"Now it's Lanny's turn. Just noticed this noon that pus was running from the right eye and after his nap his eye was stuck shut. Washed it to open it. Speaking of Lanny, he took eight short steps without falling . . . . He has also found the toilet and if I don't keep it covered or the door closed, he'll get into it. "Speaking of Rollie again. This afternoon when he was lying on the bed, still sick, he said, 'I'd like to see Fran.' I said, 'So would I.' So he hasn't forgotten you or his grandparents.

These were anxious days. We thought we might lose them, especially the night that Rollie's fever went so high. When I touched him, he felt like a furnace. After his fever broke, he broke out in a rash. We decided it must have been measles. Then it was Lanny's turn. Started with pus running from his eyes. After five days, his fever topped at 102. His breathing was very hard. We never were quite sure what Lanny had because he never broke out in a rash, but whatever it was, it was followed by bronchial pneumonia. "March 8, 1950 We see improvements in both the kids. You have never seen Rollie in such sad shape before. He is weak, skinny, lacks his usual punch . . . . he has changed in character, too. He is quieter, shyer and even sweeter. I suppose that will change with the return of his strength. Lanny is still coughing a little. He gets coughing spells and can't stop . . . When Rollie was so sick and he called for water, we noticed that he always said, 'Kank you'.

In late March an Englishman came to Paris for a month's vacation. Ted Emmett. Eighteen months previously, he had lost his wife of five years from cancer. He was staying at the same place that Adriana Raidt was and they began to see a lot of each other. About the same time, a young man from Switzerland came on the scene, Oswald Zobrist. He and Ted became friends, and it wasn't long before he and Irene Archer were double dating with Ted and Aidie. About the same time, Martha Wall arrived to study French. She had already been in Niger and was assigned to work at Galmi with us. She turned 40 while she was in Paris and thought that was the end of the world. Oh, to be 40 again!

"April 14, 1950 . . . it was quite amusing to have Aidie's Englishman here and hear him talk and use different idioms than we use. He's a very nice fellow. (A number of times Burt and I took some long walks in the evening so Ted and Aidie could "sit" with our sleeping kids and have time alone together.) He left yesterday for England and won't see Aidie until the first of July, but it looks like it's all sewed up. Both men applied to S.I.M., were accepted, and both couples married in Africa a year or so later. As I write this, in 1995, I will add that just about a year ago, Aidie went home to be with the Lord, after more than 40 years of marriage and service in S.I.M. Right now, Irene has a recurrence of cancer of the breast which was discovered five years ago. They also have served with S.I.M. all these years.

Uncle Fred died that Spring and Aunt Ruth and Uncle Charlie contributed on our behalf toward flowers. They were always so good to us.

"July 4, 1950 We are packing in earnest now and are scheduled to leave by Air Transport July 14 . . . . We have started our atabrine pills . . . the kids won't swallow them as we do, and they taste bitter. But they'll have to take them every day; I'll figure out some way. "July 13, 1950 . . . we're scheduled now to fly on the 18th, Tuesday. This seems to be final since we have our tickets and seats on the plane. Burt bought scads of instruments which he feels must go on the plane for safety's sake. Also a must is our typewriter and our latest purchase—a second hand accordion for me! Other things will go unaccompanied baggage.

"Tomorrow is Bastille Day, France's Independence Day, so there are big doings and all the stores are closed. (Probably the reason we aren't flying tomorrow.) There will be lavish parades and fireworks. Two blocks from us there is an orchestra stand set up in the street in preparation for dancing, beginning tonight and lasting for three days."

Memories! Space does not allow me to include everything, but we have 44 letters that I wrote to Fran and Bill and which, along with my memory, have been my source of information.

Memories! The number of times our S.I.M.'ers gathered in our small apartment for fellowship and food! Our missionary gatherings at Bob and Jeanette Evans' house that included all evangelical missions which were the forerunner of GEM! The walks to the Eiffel Tower, the Arc de Triomphe, on the Champs Elyses, the outside cafes, the metro rides, the visit by our director and his wife, Mr. and Mrs. Beacham, as they passed through on their way to Africa, picnics in the woods, visits to the zoo, street singers and instrumentalists, our trip to Nice and Marseilles and Cannes, and Menton and Monte-Carlo while Irene took care of our kids, my trip to London with Joan Jackson, the delights we experienced with Rollie and Lanny in their precious early years, and last but not least, the study of French. Burt passed his exams with honor and made the best marks of all the missionaries here. What a guy! What a year! (11 months).

Chapter 3

GALMI HOSPITAL

A hospital in Niger, French West Africa, was born in the hearts and minds of mission leaders in the mid 1930's as a more effective way of reaching through to the hearts of the Moslem people with the Gospel. A request was made to the French Colonial Government and denied. Nevertheless Mr. Osborne and other leaders claimed by faith a site for a hospital some day!

In the meantime, the young man that was God's choice as the doctor of the hospital was finishing high school in Chicago. Early in Burt Long's life, he had come under the sound of the Gospel through the ministry of Paul Rader, founder and pastor of the Chicago Gospel Tabernacle. More closely connected with Burt was the young people's director, Mr. Lance Latham, musician extraordinaire as well. In 1933, when Mr. Rader left the Tabernacle, Lance Latham, along with his wife, Virginia, and a handful of young people from the Tabernacle, started a church of his own, the North Side Gospel Center. Burt was one of the high school boys. Despite a five mile ride one way on Chicago's street cars, Burt was in all the Sunday services, weekly boys' meetings, and as often as he could find the necessary 14 cents round trip street car fare, extra meetings during the week. Under the Bible teaching of Lance Latham and other visiting teachers such as William R. Newell and Dr. Pettingill, Burt grew in the Lord and knowledge of the Word. Special evangelistic services and visiting missionaries, summer camp programs, and an active young people's program all contributed to a desire on Burt's part to give himself to the Lord's service, specifically as a missionary. As a young child, he desired to become a doctor. With these challenges before him, he became focused on becoming a medical missionary. After high school, he worked a year and saved enough for his freshman year at Wheaton College. He graduated from Wheaton in 1940 and was accepted into Illinois Medical School in Chicago from which he graduated in December of 1943.

I was also active at the North Side Gospel and it was there we met. Both of us had a heart for missions and were married March 31, 1945. Courtship, wedding, honeymoon and events that followed are covered in Part I.

While we were studying French in Paris in 1949/1950, things were happening in Niger. After many requests over a period of 15 years, the French Government, albeit reluctantly, granted a site, at Dogaraoua in 1949. The local chief rose up in protest, so the site was moved five miles down the road, out in the bush, just outside the tiny village of Galmi. It was a wide place in the road, covered with rock, far from everywhere—120 miles from Maradi and 300 miles from Niamey. Directly across the dirt road (Rt. 1, Niger) was a lava hill, which we later named Rollie Mountain. This hill retained and radiated heat above and beyond the norm of 120 degrees F. in the hot season. The property looked like a moonscape. Apparently at one time it was covered with water, for we found many fossils later on the hill. The French secretly believed that a hospital wouldn't survive, and I believe they hoped that it wouldn't. They were surprised!

From Mr. Charles Zabriskie's (Zeb's) diary, I quote the following:

". . . in late 1949, Dec. 22, I stopped at the new site near Galmi. There's not much for encouragement as far as the site is concerned. It faces a high hill; it is barren except for two or three trees about three feet high, and a few spots of grassy ground. Several gullies made by water erosion run through the plot. The ground is stony and hard . . . . down at the back several hundred yards away it is low, fertile ground, suitable for dry season gardens. The water level appears to be twelve to eighteen feet deep. The people seem friendly.

63

The chief of the nearest district came over, implying friendliness. Money was on hand to begin to build, made possible by a gift from a Jewish-Christian family who lost their son in World War II."

Jim and Alice Lucas arrived in Africa in the early forties. Jim was a builder and in late 1949 he was ready to build the hospital More from Zeb's diary: "I was helping Jim as he was preparing to go to the Galmi site. Tuesday, Dec. 27, saw the truck and Jeep finally all loaded as we left for Galmi around 9:30. We took some pictures, talked over plans for the buildings, put up a tent for Jim, measured out a three-room house for African help . . . . We then climbed to the top of the hill, from which we noted eight villages easily seen; we did this while having lunch, followed by a time of prayer together . . . . Zeb returned to Madaoua . . . Jim returned late Saturday, saying that approximately three cubic meters of stone had been gathered for building, and he had a well dug in the low land at the rear of the concession . . . He left for Maradi to return in early 1950 with the crew to build the hospital, a residence for the doctor and family and a two-apartment building for the two nurses completing the staff for this new Gospel-light-bearing facility.

Jim Lucas writes:

> "One day while I was living in the tent we had an all day windstorm. I wondered if the tent would be blown away. The sand blowing against the truck seemed to generate static electricity so that if we would touch the truck we would get a shock. We had never experienced wind like that in any other place. When the storm was over, there were little specks on the windshield where the sand had pitted the windshield."

When the first building was finished, a three room boys' house, Alice came with their small son, Steve, and they moved into it while the doctor's house was being built. From there they moved into the doctor's house while the hospital was being built. Jim continues, "We laid out the area for the foundation and began digging the trenches for the center wing first, starting from the north end. When we came to the south end, some of the fellows told us that their grandfathers were buried there. I wondered if we would have to stop digging and move the site, but we kept digging and they didn't make too much fuss so we were able to go ahead and build where we had laid out plans for the foundation.

"When we had some of the walls of the hospital up as high as the top of the windows, one morning the Commandant from Tahoua came with some office workers and said that he had come to approve or give permission to build there. Here we had the walls up higher than a man. He wanted to know who gave us permission. I told him that the plan had been approved and signed by a man in an office in Niamey. He wanted to see the plan which I showed him, and he was satisfied.

"The only water supply was down in the valley. We dug our own well there and hired workers to bring water for mixing mud. They carried it by headload. That was an expensive way to get water so after a time we hauled the rest of the water in a barrel on a home-made cart. We hired men to dig a well on the compound. When it was about 40 feet deep, Kwalkwali, who was at the top of the well to pull up the buckets of dirt, fell into the well. Fortunately he didn't hit the other man down in the well. "We were relieved to find that he was not hurt seriously. Water was found in the well, but it was so hard, it could not be used."

Finally, the hospital was finished. It was T-shaped, the center wing being the stem of the T, which was to be used for outpatients, surgery, pharmacy, storage, X-ray. The top of the T was to be used for patients, men in the west, and women in the east. For the time being, Zeb and Irene made a portion of the west wing their home and the two nurses did the same in another portion of the same wing while they waited for their home to be built.

The Lucases moved on to Madaoua where they lived for the next few years. A building stood there at Galmi waiting. A hospital without a doctor; patient wards without beds; operating room without equipment; x-ray room without an x-ray; pharmacy without drugs; waiting room without patients.

And in God's timing, the Long family boarded the plane in Paris, heading south across the Sahara, not knowing what the future held, but trusting the One who held the future in His hands.

—

Chapter 4

ONIONS

"Do you like onions, Ruth?" asked Zeb on our trip from Niamey to Galmi.

"Yes, I like onions."

I was used to have a sprinkling of onions in my food now and then. I don't remember what Zeb said then, but I soon found out what he meant when he asked the question.

Irene was most kind to us, and she fed us three meals a day until we were settled in. We had onions every day. Sometimes they were fried, sometimes boiled, sometimes covered with batter and deep fried, sometimes scalloped. It didn't take me long to figure out that onions was one of the mainstays of the land. Another staple was rice. Now I don't have anything against rice. But rice everyday along with onions everyday was a bit much. Then there was goat meat, the only meat available in the market. Goats were small, and there wasn't much meat on the bones, but there we were—every noon meal it was onions, rice and goat meat. After I started cooking on my own, guess what we had every noon! Yes, onions, rice, and goat meat.

Breakfast was different, but it was also routine—boiled kunu—wheat ground fine by our cook. A little salt and milk and it tasted quite good—every morning. Supper was sometimes different—maybe a little left over from lunch and perhaps some soup or eggs or a rare tomato. Eggs were something else. We were able to buy some guinea fowl eggs at certain seasons of the year. Peddlers would come to the door with anywhere from a few to a hundred eggs, and we would buy them up. First we tested them. If they floated to the top, they had chickens in them. Rejected! Those who came with a large quantity had kept them for a week or two in their hot huts. Many floated to the top just because they were old. Guinea fowl eggs are smaller than hen eggs and have a tougher shell. They also keep better. If a recipe called for two eggs, we would usually add three. For most of the time, we usually had a supply of eggs on hand, but at a certain season of the year, they were scarce. One day a trader came to the door with an ostrich egg! We bought it, and we had enough scrambled eggs for a dozen mouths.

Milk!

The powdered milk that we had bought in Niamey was so old that it never did go into solution. Therefore, we were fortunate to get milk locally. Every morning Fulani women came to the door with their calabashes on their heads filled with milk. Nana and her clan were the most faithful. But Nana was full of "wayo"—(tricks, cleverness, sometimes to the point of deceit). She had a habit of adding water to the milk so she could charge us for a greater amount. Sometimes the milk was blue, it was so diluted. So we began to test the milk each morning with a hydrometer. If it measured to a certain level, we would buy it; if it didn't, we rejected it. In a sense, we were punishing ourselves in the hopes that tomorrow she would bring pure milk. She brought from 2 to 4 litres a morning, and with our growing family, we were glad to get as much as we could. We called it "Fulani milk", but it was really cows' milk brought to us by Fulanis who were cattle people, herding their wealth. They were nomadic and sometimes when they had to move to greener pasture in the dry season, we had to resort to powdered milk, a new supply. Other times we were able to buy a litre or two from cattle keepers in town. One day when I stepped into the pantry for a minute leaving Nana measuring out the milk, I returned to find my hydrometer broken. Oh ho? Well, we had another one.

Onions, rice, goat meat, ground wheat, eggs and milk. That would be our diet for four years. We didn't know it when Zeb asked me if I liked onions. I recall saying to Burt the first week we were there, "I'll never last four years." But we did! A total of 25 years at Galmi!

Bread! I had never made a loaf of bread in my life. Zeb's wife, Irene, showed me how to do it. I don't remember where I got the yeast and flour. Together we tackled my first batch. First, we had to sift the flour. Sift flour? No problem. I had been sifting flour for years when mixing up batter for cakes and so forth. Irene produced an extremely fine sifter, purchased in the market. Why so fine? To sift out the bugs! I was dumbfounded to see all the bugs being sifted out. This was French flour and very old and was loaded with bugs, so much so, that most of the nutrition was gone. We proceeded. We did everything right. Then put it in our wood burning oven! Three loaves came out flat, hard and heavy. It wasn't until I was able to get fresh English flour from Nigeria that I was able to make delicious, home baked bread.

It was during our first year at Galmi that I became pregnant with Cherry. I recall during those early months of pregnancy dreaming one night of mashed potatoes with a big glob of melted butter in the middle. I knew that people craved watermelon and pickles and other exotic delicacies during their pregnancies, but I had never heard of anyone dreaming of mashed potatoes. Alas, it was only a dream, and I awoke the next morning and the menu for the day was, you guessed it, rice, onions and goat meat.

Chapter 5

EARLY DAYS AT GALMI

"I'll go where you want me to go, dear Lord, O'er mountain, or plain or sea; I'll say what you want me to say, dear Lord, I'll be what you want me to be." That was the response that this eleven year old heart made to the Lord after hearing a missionary message during a summer Bible Vacation School missionary appeal at Grace Gospel Mission. Visions of missionaries living in grass roofed huts, surrounded by jungle, Bible in one hand, other hand raised to emphasize the Message, ill-clad "natives" with spears in their hands listening intently to the Word, danced in my head. Through my growing up years, if anyone asked me what I was going to be when I grew up, the answer was always, "A missionary." So it was with some surprise that I surveyed the house that was to be our home.

I don't know exactly what I expected. I was programmed into a native style house, so I was amazed at what I saw. Instead of a grass roofed house in the middle of a jungle, I saw a corrugated tin roof covering a nice little bungalow with living room, dining room, kitchen, pantry, two bedrooms and a study on the southern edge of the Sahara desert. Instead of "natives with spears in their hands", I saw men and women with hoes on their backs. Instead of a dirt floor, there was a cement floor. The inside walls were mud bricks, but the outside walls were made of rock pointed with cement. In the kitchen was a wood burning stove which any antique buff in the States would like to get his hands on. Two mission beds were set up for the adults. It didn't take long to set up our Port-0-Crib for Lanny and get a Vono cot for Rollie. The dining room boasted a borrowed table and chairs. Crates became dressers and book shelves and desks. Jibbo, our "cook" and Isa, our "houseboy" came with the house—or so I thought. Actually, Zeb had engaged them to work for us subject to our approval. Of course we approved. Either that or chop wood, make the fire for the cook stove, sweep out the dust and sand every day, wash the dishes and take out the garbage, fry the onions, take the stones out of the rice, cook the rice and roast the goat meat, boil the drinking water, cool and store it, measure, strain and boil the milk that the Fulanies sold us. There wasn't too much dialogue between me and the boys with my fragmented French and no Hausa, but we got along by signs and gestures. In addition, the French that these two workers were speaking sounded different from the French spoken in Paris. One day I spilled a little uncooked rice on the floor. I was about to sweep it up and throw it out, but Isa stopped me. He picked it up grain by grain and put it in his pocket. I was beginning to see the poverty that prevailed.

After a few days, Mr. Osborne left to return to Maradi when he was stationed. His final remark to Burt was, "Don't let anyone die! It will get you off to a bad start!" What an impossible charge, since to begin with, only those who had tried everything else and every one else were willing to come to us as a last resort.

Zeb showed Burt how to clean the wick and operate our kerosene Servel refrigerator. While I was getting organized in the home, Burt was ordering furniture made for us and the hospital. Vono cots were ordered from Maradi for the hospital. Eventually, we got dressers and a dining room set made by Fidelis, our carpenter extraordinaire. These lasted us our whole missionary career and are still in use today in Nigeria, where we left them. Sue and Terry have one dresser.

Water was a major problem from day one. Our water supply came from shallow wells down in the valley. Issou, our teen-age water boy, brought water in tulus (large clay pots) slung over the back of a donkey, two at a time. He poured the water into 50 gallon drums—two in the kitchen and one in the bathroom—each day. Then he went on to the hospital and filled up as many drums as he could for them the rest of the day. Issou later became our houseboy and then cook. He came from a family of blacksmiths in Galmi town.

This routine worked well enough until the rains came and washed in the wells. We put our drums under the eaves troughs and caught as much rain water as possible, but often we were forced to dip water from nearby puddles. At times, Zeb loaded up his truck with drums and drove to the large water hole in town and filled the drums for all of us. This was the same water hole that the townspeople and cattle shared. It was tan colored but after it was boiled and filtered, we were able to drink it. Unfortunately, the Africans did not boil or filter the water, and many got diarrhea and parasites because of it

The good news that came with the rains was the greening of the desert. I was reminded of the phrase in Isaiah 35:1 ". . . the desert shall rejoice and blossom as a rose." I commented about this in a letter written on Sept. 21, 1950, our first rainy season in Africa. "Right now everything is green. The grain is up and the trees are in bloom and the grass is growing and a few flowers are blooming. Last week I took a walk up the mountain across the road and found 5 different wild flowers—little tiny things: yellow, pink, two shades of blue and white. It's hard to believe that in a month things will start to dry up and in two months, all will be bleak and barren."

The weather was a symphony of extremes—extreme heat, extreme cold, extreme sand storms, extreme winds, all in their own seasons! "Nov. 17, 1950" . . . The weather is changing fast. Mornings require a sweater until after breakfast. I dress the kids in long pants in the mornings and switch them to short pants in the afternoons when it really gets very hot. It's nice enough in the evening and at 9 o'clock when we go to bed we don't need a covering, but in just a few hours it gets cold enough and windy enough to warrant blankets. And I do mean windy! I've never seen quite so much wind . . . . and we're told it's just beginning. It really does howl!

"Last week Rollie said, 'Let's go for a ride in the car.' We said, 'Where shall we go?' He said, 'We'll ride the car to the bus, take the bus to the airport and take the airplane to Fran and Bill's house." "Yesterday late afternoon he and Lanny were out in front with some torn up bits of toilet paper on the porch. I asked him where he got it, and he said, in his man-like tone, 'Well, Ruth, you see that man up there in the moon? He frowed them down!'

". . . Lanny's actions are very cute. He squints his eyes, or makes faces, and if he's surprised at something or delighted with it, he pulls his mouth together to form an '0' and draws in his breath. One of the things he says is 'Oh, my' if he's wet himself or is reprimanded for something . . . he's turning out to be a beautiful child."

With a limited supply of medicine and equipment, Burt began to see some patients. At first they were afraid to come to see the white doctor, but in desperation a teen age girl came with pus dripping from her head. This had been going on for months, perhaps years, and of course her hair was matted and the odor was not pleasing. Burt saw that the problem was osteomylitis, a piece of bone had fractured and was trying to work its way out but could not. Burt shaved the area, made the cut, removed the piece of bone, put in a drain, and in a few weeks she was well. The ice was broken. Patients began to come.

After finishing building the hospital, the Lucases moved to Madaoua, 23 miles east of us. That was our post–office, and they collected our mail for us and every other Saturday, they came to visit us and brought our mail, and the other Saturdays, we went in to their house for a Saturday afternoon visit and returned with our mail. Their Stevie was four and they had a new born girl, Susie, so Rollie had a white playmate.

"Monday we visited a local chief, about 25 miles away, and he gave us, in parting, a turkey, 2 squash and about 20 limes. Tuesday we received by truck some potatoes and oranges from the Lucases who brought them back from down country. We are also getting field corn now which is a little tough but tastes good instead of rice and onions. And we've also been getting some beef at the market, so our food situation is looking up. "I had to prepare the turkey and roast it this afternoon because we're taking it to Madaoua with us. Also made two squash pies . . . . This week-end is a big one in Moslem land. Saturday is their big feast day. Once a year the chief Moslem malam in the village sacrifices a ram, sheds the blood in commemoration of Abraham's offering of ISHMAEL on the altar. After the religious service, there is a great day of feasting and drinking and dancing. (This is called Sallah!)

Adie Raidt arrived at Galmi about the same time we did. She was as green as we. Martha Wall came three months later. She was a third termer and knew Hausa. They shared living quarters in one wing of the hospital with the Zebs, and a temporary middle wall of partition was erected to divide the living quarters.

It was becoming obvious that we needed to go to Kano, Nigeria, 300 miles from us, to buy some food supplies. This was in October, so Burt wrote to the field chairman asking permission to go. We were given the go-ahead sign and were asked to order supplies for building a duplex for the nurses and a second family house. So we gladly left Galmi after our first three months of breaking in, and set our faces toward Kano, where SIM had a Guest House and an active ministry going on.

Nigeria at that time was a British Colony and it was governed by Britishers. As is always the case, some were very pleasant and some were obstinate and made it difficult for travelers from other countries to enter by making them wait for their visas or travel papers. The Nigerians learned well, and compared to what was to follow in later years, the inconvenience that we suffered at the hands of British Immigration and Customs was mild.

Kano station was lovely with its trees and grass and flowers and hospital and nice houses and electricity and running water. An oasis in the desert. What a contrast to the country we had just left! The food was tremendous and a welcome relief from rice, onions and goat meat. There was food on the store shelves and in the markets, the roads and flower gardens were well kept, and there was a semblance of order and wealth and plenty. This all changed when the British turned over control to the Nigerians and left them to their independence in 1960.

From Kano: "Oct. 19, 1950" . . . we are getting a pretty good line up of food—praise the Lord . . . . We're enjoying carrots, beans, tomatoes, peas—all fresh. Do they taste good! We will be taking back 75 lbs. of potatoes, 100 lbs. of flour and sugar each, lots of canned vegetables and fruits and dried fruits. I also bought a good supply of material, for curtains and other odds and ends. So with the material I had to have a sewing machine. Was going to get a portable but Mr. Osborne . . . and Mike Glerum, who is in charge of buying here said that even if I had to pay 7 or 8 pounds more, I should get a treadle. So I did . . . . It will constitute a nice piece of furniture in our furnitureless home, so I'm not sorry they talked me into it.

"Today Rollie noticed a hole in the ceiling which is meant for getting into the ceiling and storing goods. He asked me what it was and I told him. Then he said that Cora and Bob had one in their house and he would like to go and see them. What a memory! He talks about God a lot and says he wants to go up and see God and when will we go up and see Him. Then he says, 'God loves us.' And when I ask if he loves God, he says he does. Everything he compares as 'longer than the street' or 'higher to the sky' or 'higher up to God'.... 'Remember when I was a little baby and grandpa took me on his knee and said, 'Trit trot to market?'"

We spent 3 weeks in Kano. We had a nice room and three meals a day supplied at the guest house. We ordered lumber and building supplies besides food and material. I also canned 35 quarts of tomatoes and juice and 27 quarts of pineapple, having found canning jars and lids in the stores. Now it was time to go. Back to reality! Back to Galmi! "The other day Rollie asked where the 'Standing Mission' was. I said, 'What?' He said, 'Remember when we came here in our car, you asked the lady where the 'Standing Mission' was!" (Sudan Interior Mission.)

Harvest time was on us, and the villagers were cutting, bundling and bringing in their grain. Mostly it was sorghum (dawa) and for a time Zeb and Burt helped bring in the grain in the truck for a tenth of the harvest. This was a help to us as we paid our workers partly in grain. If Rollie went out on the truck with Burt, he would say, "Don't worry, Mommy, Daddy will take care of me and Lanny will take care of you." Lanny was growing fast and whenever he wanted something he tugged on my skirt and pulled me over to it, especially if he wanted me to play the phonograph.

December 12, 1950 "After supper on his (Rollie's) (fourth) birthday, the Zebs and girls (Adie and Martha) came over for his birthday cake. Then he opened up his presents which also included a sand pail with shovel and rake and molds for him (and an identical set for Lanny) and a hoop from the Zebs made out of raw material on the compound and ... crayons. All day long he asked where his birthday was. We knew he was referring to his cake. He saw me make it but didn't see me put the frosting and candles on it. We brought it in all lit up ... he became awfully shy immediately with all the attention focused on him and buried his head in my skirt.

"Lanny is talking more every day—half in Hausa and half in English. He says 'car' and runs to the door when he hears one going by. He says 'door' and pulls me over to open it for him when he wants to go out; 'co-co' any time he wants a drink, whether it be milk, water, or cocoa. And in Hausa he comes out with 'to' (pronounced 'toe' and meaning 'o.k.'), 'ba bu' (pronounced 'ba boo' meaning 'no') and 'habba' (pronounced hubba and meaning an exclamatory expression). Rollie is doing quite well in Hausa . . . he orders our houseboy around as if he were a little king."

The weather was getting cold as Christmas approached. We were using two blankets at night. With the cold came the winds with harmattan, dust from off the desert. The whole house had to be swept twice a day. At Christmas time, we cut down a little thorn tree and brought it in the house and put a few decorations on it. Packages from home made Christmas special. Dec. 12, 1950 "We received two more packages this week from the Longs. They were all full of games and some food and puffed wheat. Rollie is really crazy about puffed wheat. We opened them when the kids were in bed and will wrap the Christmas presents for Christmas. The other day I took out the 'salt nuts' (pistachio nuts) that I had stored away and handed one to Rollie. Wide eyed he said, 'Did Fran and Bill send us some more salt nuts?' Then when he was sucking the salt off (brave boy) he looked up at me and said, 'I REALLY love salt nuts.' A few days ago he said to me, 'I have diarrhea.' I asked him where he had it and he pointed to his head and said, 'Right here.' This afternoon I'm going to get out our manger scene and tell Rollie and Lanny the story of Christmas again and wrap some packages, so maybe the Christmas spirit will come upon us. Well, the salt nuts are gone, and Rollie said to please ask you to send some more . . . . sob, sob."

"Dec. 19, 1950 The Delahays arrived yesterday from Kano, will be leaving this morning for Madaoua and Tsibiri. They have two girls, one 3 and the other 10 months, and Rollie is having a fine time with Annette. They certainly clicked. The Delahays brought oranges, potatoes and bacon from Kano. We're getting tomatoes locally now, so with our canned goods and your supplements we're eating royally. For Christmas we're having ducks, potatoes, squash, canned vegetables, mince and apple pies and jello salad. We're having dinner at the Zebs with the Lucases and Martha and Adie, and the crowd is coming here for supper."

Conference time rolled around early in 1951. All the Niger missionaries came to Galmi for a few days of spiritual refreshment and encouragement. I don't recall who came, who the speaker was, but I remember a second remark made by Mr. Osborne as he stood looking out over this barren land. He said, "Some day this will be the garden spot of Niger!". I thought he was hallucinating. When we visited Galmi 40 years later, trees were everywhere, flowers surrounded the houses, bushes and shrubs lined the paths, water was abundant, coming from a deep artesian well, and the compound was indeed a garden spot in Niger. Mr. Osborne didn't live to see it.

Being on the southern edge of the Sahara desert with only one road running east and west across Niger might imply that we were alone. On the contrary! National Route #1 was the only "road". There was no Rt. #2 or #3 and so forth and so on. It was a dirt road, corrugated like an old fashioned wash board, but passable. In the rainy season, the road could be barricaded for up to twelve hours, and if you were caught on the road after a storm, you might be subject to a long wait. In the dry season, we ate the dust coming off the road. Fortunately, in the early days, there was very little traffic—maybe two or three trucks a week and a few passenger cars. Years later, the road was paved which was a blessing, dust-wise, and traffic increased.

Burt had to make a trip to Kano for supplies and the boys and I were planning to go with him.

"March 4, 1951 . . . we received a wire from Mr. Osborne, our District Supt., saying that I should stay home because Kano was overcrowded. I'm somewhat disappointed but when Burt pulls out without the kids tomorrow morning, there is going to be weeping and wailing from both, but especially Rollie, who always looks forward to going away. Lanny is getting to be quite a daddy's boy and calls Burt, 'my Daddy'. So what a time I'll have tomorrow morning.

"April 3, 1951—You probably don't think of Rollie and Lanny as they really are. Rollie is a big boy—all boy—with freckles on his straight nose; Lanny is Rollie's age when we left home, so he's doing the cute things that Rollie did. Friday night we had an untimely terrific wind, sand and rain storm. I didn't see it coming, but Burt said the dust came like a black wall. When it hit the house, closing the windows was very difficult. The dust was blowing in and we could hardly breathe as we closed them. When they were all closed, the house was gray with haze and loaded with dirt. It was supper time, but Burt had to go out with the black boys and move bags of cement into the garage so they wouldn't be ruined. The kids and I went ahead with supper and about an hour later when Burt came in drenched, he brought with him a French couple who had been stranded in their open jeep, and they too were drenched. So after they cleaned up and were ready to sit down to supper, along comes another light and it was Jim Lucas coming from Dogan Doutchie going back to Madaoua. So they all had supper here and the French couple stayed all night and took off early in the morning. Sat. we went to the Lucases in Madaoua—our 6th anniversary. Burt gave me a very pretty silver dish with intricate designing which he got in Kano when he was there. I made him a dressing gown out of some native material.

"Last night we resumed our sleeping out again. I had 3 small baby blankets at the foot of Rollie's bed to throw on the kids during the night. At midnight I pulled up Rollie's blanket and covered Lanny. At 1:40 I woke up and noticed Rollie uncovered, and on further examination found there were no covers at all on him and the three small blankets were missing, too. Thieves had lifted them right off of Rollie while he was sleeping, and also took Rollie's slippers and Burt's slippers and socks. What do you think of that?

"April 17, 1951 Lanny is two years old now . . . . we had the girls over for supper Sunday night and brought out his cake with his two candles on it. He was wide-eyed and blew them out with the help of the wind. We ate outside. We didn't have any gifts to give him, but it really didn't matter. This morning Rollie and I cleaned out their toy boxes (plural), put away some and pulled out others, and today they're playing with their cars—old as they are—as though they were new ones. "Lanny has had several boils lately. The worst Burt opened yesterday and the others seem to be taking care of themselves. I have written down some of his vocabulary. So far I have recorded 116 but I just started last night and can't think of them all, so he's not too far behind Rollie's 180 words at his 2nd birthday. It's interesting to note the difference in vocabulary. Lanny's includes scorpion, bite, horse, donkey, sand, stone, bug and fly—none of which were included in Rollie's. He uses 'yah' consistently now in answer to everything. He used to just repeat the word we used if he consented and said 'a-a' if he dissented. But now it's 'yah'. He also repeats 'I love you' real cute. 'I loff you' with rising tone on the second word. He says 'gank you' for thank you and 'peeze' for please. Lanny also has about 10 Hausa words

—

77

under his belt which he uses correctly. Rollie still uses his nite-nite and Lanny realizes that baby stuff isn't for him and sometimes hands Rollie his nite-nite when he goes to bed. I tried several times to give it to Lanny when he went to bed and he said,

'A-a—(No)—It's Rollie's.'

"We are going to Madaoua today for more tomatoes to can. We are expecting an S.I.M. family of four Thursday night through Sunday and perhaps Tuesday." April 23, 1951 Santa Claus arrived Sat. with boxes from you and the folks, so we had Christmas all over again. Now Rollie insists that his birthday is just around the corner, because he keeps asking when it will be, and we tell him not until Christmas time. He holds up 4 fingers and says that's how old he is, and his next birthday, he will be a whole handful and when he's a whole handful and two fingers, then 'we'll go to Fran and Bill's house.' "I just told him I was writing to you . . . he said to write this, 'We love you because you sent salt nuts to us. Now write another letter and say when we see you we will say 'thank you for giving us the salt nuts.' I guess he really appreciates them and so do I.

The kids are especially crazy about the steel trucks and trailers Irene and Norman sent and "Billy" (doll), Johnny's (doll) younger brother. You know the folks had sent Johnny to Rollie for Christmas in Paris, and Billy is for Lanny's 2nd birthday. Well, Johnny has been going around naked for awhile and gotten pretty dirty so immediately Rollie latched on to Billy and said Lanny could have Johnny, he didn't want him any more. Last night there was quite a scene. Rollie wanted to take Billy to bed, but Burt intervened . . . and after many, many tears Rollie went to sleep with Johnny after explaining that the reason he didn't like Johnny anymore was because he didn't have any clothes. So after he was asleep, I scouted around in his old toy box and uncovered Johnny's shoes and hat but that was all. So I spent the next hour making Johnny a shirt and pair of pants while Burt scrubbed him up. Then we dressed him and put him in bed alongside of him, and this morning Rollie was quite pleased and embarrassed and just smiled and didn't say a word. So today they're both happy, playing with both of them and tying them around their backs, native fashion.

"Do you remember the Bechtels with whom we stayed for a week in Niamey on our arrival in Africa? Their boy, Elwin, was quite the idol of Rollie—about 10 years old—and Rollie was especially fascinated by his sling shot. During our stay there he has consistently talked about 'when he gets as big as Elwin'. Burt finally made Rollie a sling shot and last week he has been sleeping with it. Elwin had had several attacks of rheumatic fever and we heard a month ago that he had had another attack but that he was up again. Sat., we heard that he died last week. When Burt told Rollie, Rollie's face fell a mile and then he asked Burt if Elwin took his sling shot to Jesus with him."

We were stunned a year or so later. We heard that Mr. and Mrs. Bechtel had been driving on Niger Rt. #1 and spotted an animal. True to his nature, Otto stopped the car, reached for his gun and followed the animal into the "bush". He had flip flops on. He felt a sting on his heel, knew immediately that it was a snake bite, did all the right things while they drove to the nearest doctor, but he died shortly thereafter. What a blow it was to Mrs. Bechtel, losing a son and husband within two years. They had a daughter, and Mrs. Bechtel and their daughter stayed on for many years and continued to run the guest house for their Evangelical Baptist Mission in Niamey.

Cold season turned into hot season with temperatures in the 100's plus every day.

"May 9, 1951 Eight o'clock and we've been up and at 'em for 2 1/2 hours. Breakfast dishes are done, the milk is here and being strained and boiled, Issu is out washing clothes with the kids' 'help' . . . . The weather has been . . . . hot the last few weeks. At least 100 in the house. Two afternoons ago it was 101 and in the evening a terrific wind and dust storm blew up with a few drops of rain and the temperature took a 28 degree drop down to 73. What refreshment! Our beds were outside all made up for the night, and as Burt was shutting the door he noticed something white flying by but didn't pay any attention to it. I went out the other door to see our blankets flapping in the breeze and one pillow missing. Then Burt realized what the white object had been so set out to find it. At the rate it was going it could have been half way to Dogourawa had it not been stopped by a pile of rocks about 50 yards from the house . . . the wind persisted . . . we moved our beds into the house and enjoyed a cool night's rest. Yesterday the temp was only 90 and we were comfortable once again for a change."

Zeb was spending an hour a day with us trying to teach us Hausa. It was not enough. The medical work was increasing and as there were successes, others heard and came. Martha was designated as interpreter for Burt in the hospital. She would listen to a long list of complaints and in a few words pass the information on to Burt. This became very frustrating to him. He wanted to do his own talking with the patients. He wrote to Mr. Osborne requesting that we go to Hausa language school in Minna, Nigeria. Mr. Osborne balked. So Burt went over his head and wrote to Mr. Beacham, our field superintendent, who okayed it for three months. So exactly a year from the time we landed in Niamey, we packed our Chevy Carryall and headed South. Adie rode with us to Kano where she was to be joined by her Englishman and be married. From Kano we traveled to Jos and from Jos to Minna where our language school was located.

The town of Minna was located in the forest belt. A sharp contrast to the desert we had left. We were part of a group of about a dozen new missionaries whom we met for the first time, and who spent as many years in Africa as we did and are now retired. They were Bill Neef, the Learneds, George Beacham, Evie Smith, Mae Gould, Vince Lohnes, Inez Penny, Harold Fuller, Eric Bowley, Doretta Dail, Ernie Maxwell and Freeda Jones. There were others, too. Helen Lucks helped in the kitchen. Eleanor Forshey was our teacher and the Blunts were station managers. George ended up marrying Mae, Vince married Evie and Ernie married Freeda. Ernie and Freeda were killed in an accident in Canada about 10 years ago, leaving their three young adult children. Mae died a few years ago, and George has married again and lives in Sebring town. Lohneses are here in our village and so are the Neefs and Helen Lucks of our language school days. The others are retired elsewhere.

Our Hausa studies were interrupted for a week due to a visit from Mr. Maxwell, President of Prairie Bible Institute, who was on a tour of our mission areas encouraging our missionaries. I didn't know it then, but this was an annual affair. Each year some speaker from the States would tour the different areas and hold conferences. We had several at Galmi during our years there. Three meetings a day, speaking 1 1/2 hrs. each time. The boys did remarkably well when we took them to the evening meetings which lasted two hours. "Rollie always bows his head and Lanny sometimes bows his head but more often looks around him but he's quiet, and when the amen is said, he says 'all frough?'" We had Jibbo, our cook from Galmi, with us, and he took care of the boys during the day while we were in classes.

Rollie and Lanny had two playmates, Rosalyn and Sharon, daughters of Vernon and Bonnie Smith. They played together well. "All four kids are running around like wild-cats and Lanny is right in with them. He is SO cute. His big brown eyes—still almost black—sparkle with mischief, and he can run surprisingly fast in spite of the way he throws his arms around as if he were loose in the joints. He just stopped by me—I'm sitting on the porch—and gave me some pretty yellow flowers. Then he called out to the kids, 'Wait a minute'. Now he's back and said, 'I fall down, Mommy.' But this time he didn't even have time to let me blow it. He's off again."

"It's seven o'clock now and getting quite dark . . . time to go in and light a lantern. My, the flowers down here smell good. So brilliant in color, too. Those that Lanny brought me are bright yellow and very fragrant. Rollie often brings me flowers, too, for me to wear to supper either on my dress or in my hair. We sure have a couple of nice kids—I guess we're prejudiced. Lanny's boils are all gone now, but Rollie got a few more on his back. There is only one still coming up, and about 7 that have passed the crisis and receding.

"Right now all of the kids are sitting on the porch with books in their hands. Rollie is out in front leading the singing. He just told them to stand up, and now they are all singing—nonsense words and everyone a different tune. Rollie just said, 'Get your Bibles out.' Now he is 'reading' out of his book. Now he's through. Now they are marching with their books. Rollie in front, and they're singing with the books in their hands. Lanny is bringing up the rear, and they have just disappeared around the corner of the house. They're happy and well and haven't had such a good time in a long time as they're having here with Roselyn and Sharon."

One Sunday night on the way home from the church, a bull that was being taken to market for slaughter the next day, was frightened by our lanterns and started to charge our group that was walking together. Two men were holding on to the bull, but he dragged them. Vernon Smith and Burt just left their lanterns in the middle of the road, and we all went for bush. Burt was with Rollie behind one tree and Lanny was with me behind another. Vernon Smith ended up on the other side of a fence with his two daughters. I'm not sure how he got there. Everyone was screaming and yelling and the kids were crying. The men finally got the bull under control after it had passed the lantern. It took several days for Lanny to be assured that the bull was dead and that we had probably eaten his liver Monday noon. After language school the Smiths were stationed at Kent Academy as house parents. It wasn't but a few years later that we heard that Roselyn took sick and died, and I believe she is buried at Miango.

Our three months at Minna were coming to an end, and our third child was due to be born on Oct. 15. On the first of Oct., our S.I.M. plane, piloted by Betty Green, came to take me to Jos. Burt and the boys followed that same day by car and arrived the next day. We had rooms in the guest house. The morning of Oct. 3, I woke up with labor pains. "I entered the hospital at 8:30 and all during the next eleven hours, the pains came anywhere from 5-15 minutes apart . . . at 5:40 they started to come one on top of the other, harder and harder, and I was really sweating it out! By 7:10, the spinal took effect . . . . It's the funniest feeling not to have any feeling, but oh, what a relief!: Twenty minutes later, our little girl was born—Cheryl Michelle. She arrived at 7:30 p.m., Oct. 3, 1951, "the tiniest specimen of humanity that I've ever seen or handled. She weighed in at 5 lb. 9 oz.! "She is real cute and so tiny . . . we praise the Lord for her, for a whole child. A post script to Fran by Burt, "Well, your sis did it again! Ruth fine. Burt." We spent two weeks in Jos—I, in the hospital and Burt taking care of Rollie and Lanny and living and eating at the guest house. Those were the days when mothers were hospitalized for two weeks after their babies were born. It's a practice long since past much to the detriment of the new mother. Even if the birth is normal, a mom can surely use the rest and pampering we got back in those days before she is thrust into her role either as new mother or mother with new baby.

"Oct. 9, 1951 . . . she's very pretty. Eyes are blue with a grayish tint; nose, straighter than Lanny's but not as straight as Rollie's. Mouth resembles Lanny's. I can hold her in one hand without difficulty. Her weight dropped to 5# 4 oz, and today she weights 5# 6 1/2 oz. Her tiny toe nail is about the size of the head of a pin.

"Lanny has taken my departure harder than Rollie, but they have both been very good and Burt has done very well in being mother, father and doctor here at the hospital while Dr. Troup is visiting out-stations this week. Yesterday I went out on the porch for a while to visit with

Lanny. He was tickled pink to be with me since heretofore he could only peek through the window and see me. He was delightful. I held him for a while and we talked and talked and talked and he played and we had a good time together. After a while I said, 'Give Mommy a kiss'. And he started to raise his head and then said, 'Well, I did.' So I asked him if he couldn't give me another one and he said 'No'. So I didn't get my second kiss until the time of his departure. "Now Rollie is another case! A fellow just a bit older than he has alienated his affections from me. It started on Sun. and this is Tues, and I haven't seen him since. Burt says that 'Butch' and Rollie go around arm and arm and insist on sharing their toys with each other. They practically beg the other one to ride his bike. And they can hardly be separated to take time out for tea or meals! Wonder when I'll see Rollie again!" (I believe that was the McElheran boy.)"

Millie Learned delivered five days ahead of me with a 9 lb. 6 oz. boy for her first child. That was almost two of Cherry. S.I.M, Jos was a bit of America in Africa. Meals were delicious. Had potatoes and vegetables again. The weather comfortable at an altitude of 4000 feet!

Two weeks in the hospital were followed by two weeks in Miango. Miango was to become a big part of our lives. Little did we realize how big during this our first visit. Miango was located about 20 miles from Jos and was our S.I.M. rest and recreation spot. More than that, it was the location of Kent Academy where all six of our children spent their elementary school days. More of that later. The grounds at Miango Rest Home were dotted with small cottages of varying sizes to accommodate either singles or families. The central point was the living room/dining room. Meals were delicious and the story was that anyone who gained at least 20 lbs. during their month's stay didn't have to pay. I don't know of anyone who did that, but I do know that many a tired and underweight missionary who spent eleven months out of the year out in the bush, gained weight and refreshment and rest at M.R.H. (Miango Rest Home.) What a wonderful respite was our rest home, but when we went there after Cherry was born, I didn't realize how big a part it would play in our lives.

"Oct. 21, 1951 I am feeling quite well. Lanny and Rollie are having a good time here. Rollie often comes up and tells me he loves me very, very much—'oh, so much!' The other day he said, 'I love you to death.' So I said, 'Not to death, do you?' He said, 'well, that means I love you very, very much'. He's quite taken with Cherry, and if she is crying he tries to comfort her, and last night when he was in bed and Cherry was crying for her supper, he said, 'Don't you love Cherry? Why don't you take care of her, Mother?' Lanny likes to pat Cherry, too, and is very careful of her. They both delight in holding her. We had a very relaxing two and a half weeks at Miango Rest Home. The Worling girls were students at K.A. and they had a doll buggy and let us use it for Cherry, who was so tiny she fit neatly into it. We played a bit of tennis and croquet with other missionaries who were holidaying there. But the time came for us to head back to Galmi, now five instead of four, so we loaded up the Carry-all. Jerry and Paul Craig, who were in charge of K.A., came up with a little box that they had painted white and had a little mattress in it, and they gave it to us for Cherry.

The road between Jos and Kano these days (1996) takes four hours. Listen to what our trip was like back in 1951. "Drove 260 miles on Mon. Started at 7:15 a.m. and went to 5:00 p.m., non-stop except for changing one flat tire and eating our lunch. Ten hours for 260 miles, averaging 26 m.p.h. shows you what kinds of roads they were. Cherry slept most of the way although she bounced around quite a bit and hit her head against the sides of the box. We stayed at one of our stations Mon. night 100 miles out of Kano and arrived in Kano at noon on Tues."

In Kano, we ordered furniture—a davenport and two chairs and four end tables, seat cushions, paint, linoleum. The furniture was what we used all of our 36 years in Africa. Stan Myers was in charge of the furniture shop and he advised us. I bought some material to cover the cushions, a dull yellow with some gray and brown stripes running throughout. Paint was for kitchen cabinets, walls, ceilings and floors. Kitchen cabinets were to be white with red trim. Floors were to be green, walls buff and some green. Linoleum was for kitchen counter tops.

Cherry continued to gain weight and at five weeks she weighed 8 lbs. We received many compliments about her saying what a beautiful baby she is. I remember praying that her personality and character would be as beautiful in the future as it was then, and they are!

Loaded to the gills in our Chevy Carryall with Cherry in her little box and the boys alternating between the front seat with me and on top of the loads in the back, we left Kano and headed back to Galmi. The temperature in Kano and Galmi was just about as hot, but S.I.M. Kano was loaded with trees and bushes and flowers which provided shade which had a cooling effect. Even the city of Kano itself was beautiful in those days of British rule. The canteens (shops) were loaded with supplies of all kinds and the markets were full also, so Kano became our source of supply twice a year. We had at least twenty missionaries stationed there in those days. There was the Eye Hospital founded by Dr. Doug Hursh and his wife, Laura. The clinic was managed by Nyletta Myers, wife of Stan. The guest house was a haven of rest for weary travelers. Even Simair was based there. Friday nights were special, because the whole compound got together at the guest house for supper followed by a sing-song and fellowship. Those were the colonial days in Kano. Things have changed drastically now, but I won't discuss that here.

It wasn't long before the climate of Minna and Jos were forgotten, for the farther north we went, the drier my skin became and my nostrils started itching and drying out. Our usual trip from Kano was to stop at our mission stations at Tsanyawa, about 50 miles out of Kano, then Katsina, about another 50 miles and then on to the border, another 50 miles. The border crossing was always a hassle. First, we stopped on the Nigerian side to check out and then we drove on to the next barrier which housed the Nigerien customs and immigration. This could take quite a while. Our passports and visas were usually in order, but oftentimes the men "on seat" were not "on seat", so many times we had to wait for an hour or two to get through customs. In those early days, the customs officer was usually a Frenchman, and would often be in town drinking and have to be sought by a subordinate. Sometimes, they would ask us to unload all the stuff, most of which was for the hospital. More than likely they let us go through, but they enjoyed giving us a hard time. We usually pulled into Maradi, tired and dirty from road dust, had a meal and slept there, and proceeded in the morning to Galmi, another 125 miles. Back in Niger, we had to remember to drive on the right side of the road again, since in Nigeria the previous four months, we had switched to driving on the left side of the road. We were glad to be back in Galmi, five of us now instead of four. It was almost like starting all over again, but this time, we had some basic Hausa under our belts. This made all the difference in the world so with enthusiasm, we plunged into our second year at Galmi.

Chapter 6

SETTLING IN

Life at Galmi began to take on a routine, but no two days were alike. November 1951 brought about some changes. Ted and Addie Emmett had married and returned to Galmi. With our return, they were free to move to Djougou, Dahomey where they spent many years. Zeb and Irene told us they were being moved to Tahaoua to open up a new station as an outreach to Tuaregs. We were scared to death to have them leave, they were wonderful crutches, and we felt as if we were thrown into the water and left to swim on our own. But, our protests were of no avail, and Zeb and Irene moved to Tahaoua. About the same time, our new house was finished. Francis, the contractor and builder from Nigeria was in charge. We had him make a fireplace in our living room and build in some kitchen cabinets and closets, and we felt very fortunate to have such a nice new house to move into.

Zeb told me an interesting tidbit today, April 4, 1996. Zeb is living in the lodge here at Sebring. He said that early on he had felt called to the Tuaregs but Irene didn't feel the same way. She told Zeb she would go, but her heart wasn't in it. During the war, when they were traveling in a convoy going back (or coming from, I'm not sure) to Africa, the boat they were on was rammed by another boat in the convoy and went down. They were adrift in a lifeboat until they were picked up by another boat and deposited in one of the Caribbean Islands. From there they were flown back to New York and made their way back to the mission home with just the clothes on their backs. Zeb told me that it was this experience that convicted her and she was willing in her heart to go to the Tuaregs.

So now the time had come, and after opening up Galmi and initiating us for a year, they went to Tahaoua and opened up a station there. Tahaoua is located about 80 miles northwest and during the rainy season the road might be washed out for several days by flash floods or heavy rains. Well, we felt somewhat abandoned. We had started out with the Zebs, Martha Wall and Adie. Now we were just three. Elaine Berdan came soon and joined with Martha as our second nurse. In December, Dan and Mary Truax with their 9 month old Sharon were stationed with us as maintenance man and wife, but sadly, Dan didn't know much about maintenance. He was an excellent p.r. man and made friends readily in the village. Besides maintenance, Dan was supposed to be doing trekking, and he was good at it. Unfortunately, Dan knew very little about mechanics and his Jeep seemed always to break down somewhere out in the bush. About sundown, Mary would come over and ask Burt to go and look for Dan. Burt had only a general knowledge of where Dan might have gone, but somehow or other Burt found him and either helped Dan fix the Jeep or drove him home. Life was never dull when the Truaxes were at Galmi. On several market days, Dan would go out on the road in front of his house and offer the passers by "a cup of water in the name of the Lord." Quite innovative! After a couple of market days (Wednesdays), he abandoned the idea. After one term at Galmi, the Truaxes were moved to Nigeria where they were engaged in promoting and selling the African Challenge magazine, a job right up his alley.

During our first year, Martha Wall had led DauDuka to the Lord. He was a Gidan Doutchi young man, perhaps in his late teens, and he quickly caught on to the principle of reading, and in no time at all, was reading the Bible in Hausa and anything he could get his hands on. A conference for Africans was coming up, and Dau Duka and Isu and Mai Daji went to Maradi to attend. Dau Duka came back all fired up and determined to go to Bible School. What a thrill that was for all of us. Our first convert at Galmi! Destined to go to Bible School, wanting to become a preacher! Isu and Mai Daji did not seem to benefit from the conference. Isu and Mai Daji were working for me, Mai Daji as cook and Isu as houseboy. So with their departure, I had no household help for that week. Wouldn't you know we had a lot of visitors that week, too!

"Dec. 12, 1951 The day after the Emmetts left, Mr. Osborne and a Frenchman who is charge of 'Protestantism' in Dakar, and Alberta Simms arrived in time for dinner. They left next day after dinner. Zeb was supposed to have met them here and they were to go to Tahaoua together, but a wire from Zeb said his Jeep had broken down. He managed to get as far as 20 miles out of Galmi during the next day, and Sat. morning, he arrived on a truck in time for breakfast. After breakfast, Burt drove out and pulled him in in his Jeep, and Zeb spent the morning fixing the Jeep and took off for home after dinner. All these guests came during the week the boys were gone, so there were dishes to do, cooking and cleaning. And talk about dirt! We had some terrific winds—about 50 miles an hour at least.

"December 30, 1951 We had a nice Christmas. Even though your pkgs. hadn't arrived, the kids had more gifts than they knew what to do with. The Lucases came from Madaoua and the Zebs from Tahoua . . . . We got a card from Cora and Bob, and Cora said that Bob was only just recently recovering from the shock of Cheryl's name. She's very fat . . . looks to me like Lanny. Lanny's vocabulary is increasing rapidly. But he makes up a lot, too. A pitcher is 'a pouring water'; a scissor is 'a cutting paper'; a hanky is 'a blowing nose'. I'm getting used to cooking for crowds. Tuesday the Darlings with their two girls will be passing through on the way to Tahoua, so we'll have 13 for at least one meal, and we'll probably put them up for the night. Feb. 1-3 is conference here again. and there will be 55 this year!!!!

"Just read in some mission news that Mr. Beacham has gone to Liberia to consult with someone about the radio station work there, so it looks like S.I.M. will have a finger in that radio work . . ." This became the beginning of S.I.M's radio station, E.L.W.A. After W.W. II, a number of former G.I.'s who were studying at Wheaton College began praying, along with Prexy Dr. Edman, about a radio station in Liberia. Some young men with their families pioneered in this field, cleared the jungle, and eventually set up a small station. I believe that Abe Thiessen and Bill Thompson were among them. About 1951/52 S.I.M. got into the act and absorbed the original work and E.L.W.A. began broadcasting and continued to do so with an ever expanding audience and program until 1990 when Civil War broke out. The studio was destroyed with many of the homes, and the station was silent for a few years. It is gradually being put back together again, and today (1996) a new/used 50,000 watt transmitter is being put into service and soon Eternal Love Winning Africa will be beaming across Africa again. When we were there in 1994, E.L.W.A. was broadcasting only locally, and the most popular radio program was "Unshackled". Next most popular was the "man on the street" who interviewed people in downtown Monrovia who wanted to send messages to their loved ones who were refugees in other parts of Liberia or neighboring countries.

(April 13, 1996—Fighting has broken out again this week in Monrovia between rebel Kran and government troops. Fighting seems to be intense, and the U.S. is evacuating its citizens, including our missionaries. There seems to be seven factions that are vying for power. Left on the ELWA compound is Steve Kejr, Randy Wildman and Steve Befus.)

Back to Galmi and our second year. It was hard for us to realize that winter in the desert could be so cold until we experienced it. Strong winds blew, compounding the cold, and we used two blankets at night to keep us warm in bed. Well, I know that cold is relative, but to us who had struggled with the extreme heat, 40 degrees was cold. Needless to say, we enjoyed our fireplace in the mornings. We got to the place later on that we moved our dining room table into the living room each morning so that we could enjoy breakfast in front of the fire. Usually, the weather warmed up during the day. In the morning, the boys were dressed in long pants and sweaters, but by afternoon, they were in shorts and light tops.

Our station custom was to have prayer meeting for the missionaries at 6:30, and since we had small children, most of the time the folks met in our house, and they always enjoyed being greeted by a fire in the fireplace on those cold mornings. Later on, when there were other families with small children, we took turns meeting at different houses.

Conference came and went, and it wasn't as difficult as I thought it would be. It was a time of spiritual refreshment and blessing. Adults numbered 24 and the children, 11. The Truaxes fed the children and we fed the adults. "Feb. 6, 1952 The folks from Maradi and Tsibiri brought lots of fresh fruits and vegetables, so we had oranges, grapefruit, tomatoes, kolorabi, cabbage, cauliflower, celery, green pepper and potatoes. And all the ladies pitched in and helped, and I didn't do much except direct traffic . . . ."

"Many thanks for the packages. We have been enjoying the 'salt nuts' and Rollie especially said that I must write and thank Fran and Bill for sending them . . . . I am sorry to report that Lanny likes them, too, and isn't satisfied now with only the shell. (I can't believe that we ate the nuts and fed him the shells!!!!) We have played 'Puff and Toot' and the circus records to death. I sat down and read 'I'm a Lucky Guy' . . . it was sure funny. I laughed so hard in some places that I almost cried. It was a good tonic."

In February, Paul and Jane Pendell, seven year old "Biz" and their dog, Skipper, arrived from French Camerouns for a nine day visit. It was so good to see them. They were working with the Presbyterian Mission in Batouri, he as a doctor and she as wife and nurse. We had been in Paris with them studying French and became good friends, visited together on holidays especially, and traveled to Switzerland together for a week-end once. I first met Paul at Wheaton. He was a year ahead of me and I didn't know him too well then. They very kindly brought our furniture that had been built in Kano. Jane was quite a seamstress, so the two of us worked together making cushion covers for our davenport and two chairs. We had bought the material in Kano. They also brought with them the news that King George VI had died and Princess Elizabeth was now Queen Elizabeth and her husband would be Prince Consort and sit on his throne a foot lower than the queen. A little over a year later we returned the visit to the Pendells. We set out from Galmi with four children and Isu. More about this trip later. Today (1996) the Pendells have retired and are living in Missouri. (2011—He has since died; she has remarried.)

As I mentioned above, the Darlings passed through just after Christmas to go up to Tahaoua to help Zabriskie build their new station. Don and his family came from Perry, Michigan. He was a builder by trade, and his family had a good business going in Perry, plus owning a hardware store and mill. He and Dorothy and Linda and Beth had arrived in Minna toward the end of our stay there to learn Hausa. So Rollie and Lanny had two more girl friends to play with. They were quite a bunch. They were all about the same age—pre-schoolers. "March 9, 1952 Linda Darling, 5 year old daughter of Don and Dorothy Darling, died Friday morning at 4:30 . . . . A week ago Linda took sick and the French doctor there was called in. He is an excellent doctor. At first they suspected spinal meningitis because of severe headache and rigidity of neck and back. But after a few days she seemed better, her headache was gone as was the rigidity. Well, she was treated for that disease and at the same time treated for malaria for they found a lot of parasites in her blood test. Sulpha, penicillin, increase in anti malaria drugs, fluids internally and externally were given . . . . The first we knew she was sick was when the Fr. doctor passed through Galmi enroute to Maradi. He stopped here about 9:30 that night. Thursday night we all went up to Tahaoua and Burt agreed with the French doctor in diagnosis and treatment, but we could see Linda was a very sick girl. She was resting quietly when we left at 8:30 that night. We left Martha Wall to nurse her. At 4:30 the next morning she died. That news was brought by the French doctor on his way back to Tahaoua who had received an official wire in Maradi. So Burt and Dan Truax set out again Friday about 6 p.m. They had buried Linda the same day she died, about 1 1/2 hours before Burt and Dan got there. The carpenters built a box and the commandant sent over prisoners to dig the grave. She was buried beside the chapel that has just been constructed . . ."

So there you have it. It's one thing for a missionary volunteer to be. willing "to die for Christ". It's another to lay a child to rest on foreign soil for Christ. In a sense it's even harder to do the latter than it is to do the former. Just about a year after the Darlings arrived in Niger, they paid the ultimate price. That wasn't the end of it either as you will see later. "March 20, 1952 About 8:30 the Darlings pulled in from Tahaoua enroute to Maradi. They prefer traveling at night and I don't blame them. Their building work is completed at Tahaoua. They had supper here and went on about 1 1/2 hours later. Beth was with them of course and Rollie was tickled pink to see her. Just before they left, he gave Beth two coloring books—slightly used—and in the presence of us all said, 'This one's for you and this one's for Linda. When you go up to heaven you can give it to her.' The Darlings have certainly taken Linda's death well. Dorothy said last night that the morning Linda died, they hardly knew how to break the news to Beth. When they told her, she cried and cried, not because Linda was gone but because Jesus had taken Linda and left her. But they explained to her that they needed Beth and after a while she felt better."

About this time, John Ockers brought two evangelists from Nigeria to Galmi to hold meetings in the surrounding villages. There was opposition from the Moslem malams in each of the villages who told their people that if they attended the meetings they would perish. The next night the chief of the whole area (Wandara ?) came to the meeting, had a front seat and thanked them for coming. Then he invited the evangelists to come to his own village 5 miles away. The boys who worked for us on the compound were threatened because they were working for us. Our cook was struck on the arm in several places. Our houseboy had a quarrel over the issue. Although only two or three out of the dozen boys who worked for us were Christians, they continued to stand up for us and continued to work for us. The townspeople were trying to get to us, too. We heard that someone had blinded our boys' little donkey's eye.

"Apr. 18, 1952 We're glad you liked the pictures. Cherry is about 2 1/2 months. She is certainly a sweetheart. For about a month she has been running a slight fever every day but hasn't felt bad otherwise. This morning was the first time she was normal . . . sleeping all night again. Happy, too. Sleeps in the morning from about 8:30 to 11 at which time I wake her because I want her to sleep in the afternoon, too, so I can rest. She is in bed for the night about 7:30. She enjoys her Teeterbabe, a gift from one of our churches. She's drinking from a cup now and does very, very well. I started her early because all the nipples I had were wearing out fast. It's a struggle to get her solids down. I think it's probably the heat. It was 105 in the house the other day . . . . We hadn't heard about the plane crash in Gao. We're really isolated. Burt returned from his 700 mile trip a week ago, and the car finally collapsed . . . . He is going to Maradi to see if he can get some repairs done on the car."

We learned later that the plane that crashed in Gao was from the Transafricaine Air Line which was the line that we took from Paris to Niamey two years earlier. It could have been the very same plane.

Entertaining road weary missionaries was becoming a way of life for us at Galmi. We were 300 miles east of Niamey. In the early days, we did not have any missionaries living in Niamey. The Evangelical Baptist Mission (Mid-Missions) was active there, and if we had any business in Niamey, they kindly took care of it for us. That's why Mr. Bechtel met us at the airport when we first arrived and why we stayed with them for about a week before we went to Galmi. We did have missionaries at Dogon Doutchi, Ben and Gwen VanLierop. Their three children were a bit older than ours. There was Bernard, Muriel and John. Ben was American, born of American missionaries to Belgium, so he spent much of his young life in Belgium and of course, knew French well. Gwen was British, with a lovely British accent, a bundle of energy and will be celebrating her 85th birthday next year (1997).

Just outside of Dogon Doutchie was a girls' school where Verna Gabrielson and Edith Durst lived with young school age girls who attended the local school. Guesheme, some miles south of Dogon Doutchie, was opened by Ray and Doris Pollen later on. With Zebs now at Tahaoua, they were located 80 miles north and west of us.

Twenty three miles to our west was Madaoua where Jim and Alice Lucas were located and where the post office was. We had a good relationship with them, and each Saturday they either came our way or we went their way delivering or picking up our mail. We always had supper together and our boys played with their Stevie, who was Rollie's age. They also had Susie who was close to Cherry's age. Later on, Carol was born. Maradi was located 125 miles east of us and was our Niger business hub. Tsibiri was just outside of Maradi. Zinder was another 150 miles east. These were the stations where missionaries were located in our third year.

In later years, we opened works at Maza Tsaye, a farm school outside of Maradi and Dan Ja, the leprosarium, also outside of Maradi on the road to Kano. Way out east, Goure and Maine Soroa were opened, but that was years later. When we arrived at Galmi, Mr. David Osborne was our acting field superintendent until Newton and Doris Kapp returned from furlough. Different couples lived in Maradi through the year, but the one person who was more permanent than anyone was Marcia Mowatt who was in charge of the business department. In the seventies, she had bowel cancer and was operated on. She returned to Maradi and retired in 1985. Several years ago, Marcia moved down to Sebring. Last fall, her cancer recurred, and she chose not to have chemotherapy. Today we buried her. She died Sunday, April 14, 1996.

Some of the people mentioned above have impacted our lives through the years, and in our retirement, a number of them are here with us. Zeb lost Irene about 10 years ago, and he is here. Strange to see him walking with a cane—the one who used to ride a camel. Alice and Jim Lucas are here. The Pollens are in Baltimore, Maryland and we had fellowship with them as we passed through. Pam and Dave are living in Maryland now, so we should see more of the Pollens. As we look over the roster of residents here at Sebring, many of the 135 plus folks have had some impact on our lives the past forty plus years.

Back to Galmi in 1952. We found out early in our missionary experience that letter writing was our life line. Our churches and other supporters needed to be kept current and we needed them to continue to support us and the work in prayer as well as financially. Sometimes it was a chore to write to those we didn't know, but writing to family was like having a one way chat with our loved ones. Fran and Bill and Mom and Dad Long were the ones who received most of our letters. Thanks to Fran's keeping these letters for me, I can be pretty accurate concerning the events that happened and their timing. Memory sometimes plays tricks, as I have found out already when I thought something happened at such and such a time, only to read one of my letters and find it happened at another time or a little differently. So here goes again from letters to Fran and Bill.

"May 4, 1952 We have dug three wells on our compound, going down about 85 ft. to find water, and each time the water has been bad. Two days ago they struck water in the third well, and we thought it would be good, but after boiling and drinking some this morning, it was bitter . . . we must go on. We have been carrying water for over 1/2 mile for two years . . . .

"July 1, 1952 . . . Lanny is still licking out the pan that I stirred up a cake in . . . Rollie just came in with a raw onion and said, 'See? I'm eating an onion, Ruth. I'm eating an onion. It is good.' Cherry is on the pot and quiet. Burt is at the hospital. Dinner is cooking . . . Better take a look at Cherry. Last time she was so quiet on the pot, she had pulled it out from under her and started to eat it and bathe in it. Well, she did what she was supposed to. It's been over a month since she's had messy pants. She does all of her drinking from a cup except for

—

95

her nap time and bed time bottles. Rollie never went to bed with a bottle—I had high falutin' ideas about him. But I found with Lanny and Cherry it saves a lot of tears and is very satisfying to them. Rollie had his 'nite-nite'

"The last three operations Burt has done I've scrubbed with him. I find it very interesting, and enjoy it immensely. Elaine has been circulating. Two hernia repairs, and the third, another leg amputation. The first one I passed out practically in the middle of it and lost my breakfast, so Burt had to carry on alone.

"July 21, 1952 Cherry had a cold a week ago and nose is still running . . . Today Cherry took her first step alone. She stood for a moment by herself, then put one foot forward and kept standing, so I called that a step. She fell immediately afterward, however . . . Lanny and Rollie are enjoying their stay here (in Kano) with all the other children.

"July 31, 1952 We've been back from Kano for a week now . . . . We are still having 'boy' trouble—have only one—and I'm still doing most of the cooking myself, although I don't chop wood for the wood stove yet. Our family has increased this week with Jim Lucas and Stevie. Jim is doing some work for us, so I'm cooking for 8 three times a day. Alice has gone down to Jos for her baby (Carol) who is due the 8th of Aug. She has 2 year old Susie with her." We had a good hard rainfall last night and got about 100 gallons of water off our roof. That lasts us about 2 days. "Cherry's eyes are getting browner all the time. She's 25" tall and 19" around the chest . . . She sleeps from 6 p.m. till 6 a.m . . . . And of course very pretty! After dinner today Burt was playing a record and she held on to the record cabinet and jiggled up and down. She's got rhythm."

Getting water was always a problem. We had been using local wells down in the fadama but when the rains came, they all fell in. A few times Zeb and the boys loaded up the truck and went into the water hole in town and filled our barrels with rain water. Trouble was, the cows and goats were drinking and contaminating the water, the local kids were swimming in it, and the townspeople were competing with us for it, too. When Zeb brought the water home for the three households and the hospital, we had to let it settle, then boil it and filter it. I was still apprehensive about drinking it, but you do anything if you have to. It was a psychological thing more than anything because

I knew the boiling had killed any germs and the filtering had cleared the water. So it was a big event when it rained and we were able to get our water from off our roof.

"Aug. 8, 1952 It's 8 p.m . . . . the kids are in bed, I'm all ready for bed, and Burt is reading. Except for a strong wind which may bring rain, it is quiet. Not even any drums beating in the distance. Last Sat. we had our worst (or should I say best) rainfall of the season. It poured for hours, and we collected 8 barrels of rain water—all the barrels we had and could have collected any number of them. After it had rained for about two hours, we put our cooking pots out on the porch, free from the roof, and collected fresh, cold, heaven-sent drinking water—a day's supply. We have only a barrel and a half left, so we're hoping for another big rain.

"Jim and Stevie went back to Madaoua for a few days, so for two days, I've had lighter work . . . yesterday I had a headache all day long and needed a rest so took advantage of my opportunity. Today I baked myself a birthday cake—Rollie has been wondering where the 'birthday' is for the past 3 days, but until today I had no time to spare. Today when Rollie saw me making the cake, he asked me what I was doing. Told him I was making a cake, and he said, 'Oh, I know, it's your birthday cake. Good!' New missionaries, the Pollens, who have just had two months at Minna Language School, are taking over Madaoua while the Lucases are on furlough. We expect the Pollens for supper tomorrow night. Do you know Eddie Dubisz? He's from the Center, just finished up at Northern Baptist, and the S.I.M. has accepted him for work in French W. Africa.

The other day Lanny wanted to push Cherry in her stroller . . . . I told him to push her outside. So Lanny ordered Rollie to open the front door. Rollie refused. The next thing I heard was loud screaming, with Rollie chasing and teasing Lanny and Lanny pushing Cherry in the house, and then the CRASH came. And then Cherry's screams. Lanny had run into the table (folding) on which was our tape recorder, and the microphone and all our reels were on the floor, and the tape recorder was half on Cherry and half on the stroller. Cherry got a few scratches and a big scare . . . .

". . . we had a lovely evening last night of news reports and music—mostly BBC and we heard the news today. But that's all for awhile, because the car battery is now dead again. We get about 1 1/2 hrs.' play on the recorder on a fully charged battery and about 4 times as much on the radio.

"Believe it or not we've had a regular toilet put into our bathroom, and Jim is digging us a cesspool. Now all we lack is running water. But the fixture looks good even though we're still using the bucket . . . once the cesspool is finished, maybe we can operate the toilet by flushing it down with buckets of water.

"Remember Saidi—our very sick patient whom we thought would die. Well, he went home last week. Certainly it is only an answer to prayer. He accepted the Lord in the hospital, and was a real testimony while he was there convalescing. The dispensary has been running low—today there were 36—because nobody will come during the farming season unless they're really sick." ". . . now my pressure lamp has just run out of kerosene, so I'll have to stop until morning. It gradually died away, and now the study is dark."

"Sept. 10, 1952 wish you could enjoy Cherry with us. She's walking all over now and the last few days has preferred it to crawling . . . . She cut her fourth tooth last week . . . . A little girl is certainly a treasure and after two boys we find in her many things different from Rollie and Lanny. "Both Rollie and Lanny have had little sores on various parts of their bodies . . . tiny blisters, then break, fester, and as the juice spreads, the sores multiply (blister bugs).

"Sept. 23, 1952 Speaking of modern conveniences, we have one now and are quite happy about it. I'm speaking of our flush toilet. We've been using it for a week, and although we functioned quite properly without it, I didn't know how much I'd appreciate having it again. We have a barrel, 50 gal., rigged up outside through which the water flows to fill the cabinet, and the water boy fills the barrel every day. The 'seat warming' day came with Burt giving Rollie and Lanny a lecture, all of us gathering in the bathroom, about the proper use of the toilet. You should have seen the look of pride all over their faces, and the happy expressions. Rollie remarked shortly after the opening day that when we go home to America he'd like to take the toilet with him."

"Burt has been down about 4 days with conjunctivitis. His left eye is about twice the normal size, and it has been one of his most painful experiences. He no doubt contracted it from the patients. He has been in bed with the room darkened, hasn't been able to eat or sleep much. I have been nursing him, washing out the eye, etc. He says it feels better this morning; the pain is less, but he still can see nothing and he is still in bed.

"Rollie and Lanny just came in. Rollie found a pretty yellow flower and gave it to me, saying it was for my hair. Lanny followed him and said he had a cut on his leg. I looked at it and said, 'Let's wash it off.' He said, 'Let's not. It will get bedder with no washing and no medicine.' Then later, 'Kai, dat's a big cut. I cried. But just a liddle.' Lanny hates medicine and I guess he has reason to. He's covered from head to foot with about 30 sores that start as blisters, which when opened, spread to the rest of him. He has only about 3 or four open sores now, the rest have healed to the scabbing point. But he's had a rough time. He head is shaved in spots. We've been putting gentian violet on them, and that seems to dry them up best.

"Rollie had a fever several days this week which probably precipitated the 3 nightmares he had. One afternoon during his nap, he sat up in bed crying. He wasn't awake. He was seeing big objects and trying to chase them away and quite hysterical. It took a couple of minutes before he woke up. That night about 8:30 he woke up again—this time it took him at least 5 minutes to snap out of it. One more the next day to a lesser degree and none since then, so he's getting back to normal.

"I guess it's time to let you know the Longs are 'in the family way' again. Well, four kids aren't too many, I guess. I was somewhat surprised at first, but I've gotten used to it. Burt is going to deliver me here at Galmi. The next month he is going to deliver Mrs. Pollen of her first, and in Jan., Mary Truax of her second. Ours is due the end of Nov. or first of Dec. We're looking for a playmate for Cherry. In Feb. we hope to have our holiday. I'm tired and think I'll lie down for a few minutes before I start to get dinner on the way."

Days and weeks passed. All three kids continued to have sores. Cherry had a fever that lasted five days, I had a tooth ache in my left upper incisor which lasted for a week. Burt got an infection in his thumb and took a course of penicillin which cleared it up. I had a touch of gastroenteritis or something which resulted in false labor so was in bed for three days. The rains had stopped. The people were bringing in their harvest and were happy. The cold season was on the way, which was windy and dusty but more comfortable. The big drawback was the dryness which accompanied it and clogged our noses to the point of getting scabs in them and chapped my skin. My hands were always sore and red with cuts in spite of going through jars of hand cream.

John Richard put in his appearance on Nov. 13, 1952. He weighed 6 lbs. even. Water broke Tues. night, had slight pains for two days. Thurs. at 3 p.m. I started getting regular pains about 10 minutes apart, went over to the hospital about 7:30 and he was born at 8:50 p.m. Greenwich Mean Time. "Burt had just started to scrub when the nurse told him to get over and get ready to catch the baby. So he just put on rubber gloves and after 4 terrific pains, (for the last two I had ether) there was Johnny on the spot. Burt had been sick that day with nausea and diarrhea and as soon as he delivered the baby and sewed me up, he dashed home with a 'terrific urge' leaving the baby in the nurse's care and me on the table and said he'd be back in a few minutes. He didn't show up until 4 o'clock the next afternoon. The nurse, Gen Kooy, tied the cord and they got me off the table and into bed. Burt was sicker than a dog and didn't begin to feel well until Sat. morning. He brought me home Fri. afternoon and I'm feeling fine but spending most of my time in bed."

Johnny was a good baby. Slept most of the time between feedings. His bed was the same little box that we had Cherry in. Cherry is mystified. Rollie and Lanny are very proud of their brother. Conference was on at Maradi and fortunately, we didn't go. The folks from the West passed through enroute and Sat., they returned. Irene and Zeb stayed over the week-end to help out. Johnny was the first white baby to be born at Galmi. "Rollie and Lanny feel very sad if he cries and I don't pick him up. I fed him last night at 8:30; he slept until 1:30 when I fed him again, and he slept until 8:30 this morning."

About this time the Darlings came through again. Don and his brother, Tom, who was visiting, were helping Burt and Dan Truax get started on digging a well. We had given up hope of finding good water on the compound so had to go down to the fadama, the low lying area, about a quarter of a mile from us. First they make a wooden form, put it over the hole, and pour concrete into it. After the concrete hardens, they dig under it and let it fall into the ground. Then they put the form on top of it, pour concrete, and the next day they dig under it and two rings fall down. And so on until they have all the rings they need down. The Darlings then went on to Tahaoua to fix up Linda's grave. Dorothy is pregnant again. Ben Van Lierop came from Dogon Doutchie for a few days. The native doctor had been giving him some anti malaria drugs by shot and he got a terrific abscess in his seat. Burt opened it and got out about 2 cups of pus. Under anesthesia, Ben cried out, "Mon Dieu, Mon Dieu!" He stayed with us for a few days before returning to Dogon Doutchie.

When Don and Tom Darling returned from Tahaoua, I was still in pain with my tooth, so we decided I should go to Maradi or Zinder, wherever the dentist was, with them. So I carried Johnny on my lap, and Cherry sat on Tom's lap, and we traveled some 275 miles to Zinder in Don's Land Rover, where Lena and Gordon Bishop were stationed. The French dentist pulled a molar that was abscessed and filled two others. What a relief from pain! But I was sorry to lose a tooth!

Zinder was the location of the novel, BEAU GESTE, which I enjoyed reading so much so I was quite fascinated by it. Zinder is much sandier than Galmi. I saw the army barracks and the soldiers drilling, not the French Foreign Legion, but the Nigerien boys. "Our former houseboy, Jadi, had been inducted and sent to Zinder, so I decided to look for him in the ranks of marchers. There were about 6 platoons going through their paces, and in the second group I spotted him. I was surprised that I picked him out at all—all black faces look alike—but there he was. I stood for awhile and watched and stared him into looking up. When he did and I smiled at him, his face came alive with recognition, and he smiled broadly. At the same moment, however, the company was ordered to reverse, but since he was looking at me, he kept right on marching and walked right into the fellow in front of him. He quickly recovered however without being reprimanded. I watched for about 10 minutes, then left, not having been able to talk to him." The babies and I flew back to Maradi and the Osteins drove us back to Galmi the next day.

"Dec. 21, 1952 Another young missionary couple has lost their six year old daughter. Barbara Swanson was at Kent Academy, and had recovered from the 3 day measles several weeks before, and Sat. morning felt sick, went to bed, and by Sat. aft. was removed to the Jos hospital. Her father is one of our pilots. Joe was just taking off from Jos to Kano when Barbara was brought into Jos, so he and his wife knew nothing about it. But by the time they reached Kano, the telephone message had beaten them, so he and his wife (they are stationed at Kano) flew back to Jos immediately just before dark. At midnight, Barbara died. Nobody knew what she had. (It turned out to be black water fever.) She was a pretty, dark haired, brown eyed girl, very well mannered. In fact when we visited with the Swansons in Kano both Burt and I remarked how hard it was to keep from looking at her, she was so striking."

"Dec. 23, 1952 Doris Pollen had her baby this a.m. at 5:50. A girl, Judith Ann. 7 lbs. 5 oz."

Christmas came on schedule. We got together at the nurses' house where the Pollens and the new baby were staying. I fixed the ducks, dressing and gravy. The Kapps sent vegetables from Kano/Maradi. We had mashed potatoes, carrots, pineapple and cabbage salad and fruit salad for dessert. Packages came from home. The tree consisted of 3 thorn tree branches tied together. Rollie and Lanny and I made paper chains, and put cotton balls and two red Santa Clauses and some tinsel on the tree and it was quite nice. "We had nothing to give Rollie for his birthday, so we took from those small packages a little red wallet and gave it to him. He was so very pleased with that one small item that it was almost pathetic. The boys (all three) immediately donned their new shirts. The 18 month dresses fit Cherry just fine. Johnny weighed 8 lbs., 12 oz. at 7 weeks. He certainly looks like the Hollander side. His hair is not only red; it's bright red. His eyes are very blue and skin is very fair. He's really very nice looking. Lanny is very cute and very nice looking. When Burt asked him the other day what he'd like to sing in our morning devotions, he said, 'Let's sing, Busher no!' (This Little Light of Mine—Hide it Under a Bushel, No!) Another one of his favorites is the 'House' song (The Wise Man Built His House . . .) Rollie is a freckled face 6 yr. old boy, entering the awkward stage. Wait until he starts losing some teeth!

So the year 1952 passed into history, and half of our first term of five years was over. We had settled into our work pretty much. Burt was occupied at the hospital every day. About 100 out patients were coming daily and he was operating every day. Most of my time was spent with the four little ones, but I was able to help out in the hospital a little bit at times. Nineteen fifty three lay ahead with its adventures, not the least of which was our trip to the Camerouns. I was the ripe old age of 31 and Burt was 34. Looking back I wonder how we had the temerity to be doing what we were doing at that age. Ah, youth!

Chapter 7

CAMEROUN TRIP

The new year started with anticipation of leaving Galmi for two months. We planned to spend a month in Kano at the Eye Hospital while Burt learned some eye surgery and then take our holiday for the second month. When I was growing up, I always thought of a holiday as one special day, like Memorial Day, but when we got to Europe and out here in Africa, a holiday became a vacation. We get a month's holiday (vacation) each of three years. Not bad.

Before leaving, I was able to preserve a number of jars of tomatoes and tomato juice because this was the tomato season. It was also the cold season, and we bundled up with sweaters in the morning and enjoyed our fireplace.

The kids were still delightful. Rollie was always asking for stories, and Burt was a master story teller. Sometimes Rollie would bargain with Burt for a story, "If you tell me one, I'll tell you one." And he made up some corkers, too. Sometimes he asks for "a story I have never heard before." He especially liked the one about Deborah and Barak and Jael and Sisera! Burt tells the boys about Tarzan and makes up stories about him. Rollie especially loves them. Lanny listens for awhile and then walks away. In a letter that Burt wrote, he says, "Lanny is funny just to watch, especially when he is perfectly serious. Prettiest eyes in the family, but partly because of his face, because Cherry has identical ones. Cherry often loses her diaper and walks around with it around her ankles like a hobble."

104

We arrived in Kano the first week in Feb., and Burt was busy at the eye hospital with Dr. Hursh. Delta Bond was one of the nurses working alongside Dr. Hursh. She did surgery too. Burt learned how to do cataracts and lids and more. He attended a two day doctors' conference in Jos. I tended the kids. We stayed in what was called the Dancy house (I guess that's either because at one time the Dancys' lived in it or he built it, or maybe both), and ate our meals at the guest house. In those days, Kano was a delightful place to be. It was like an oasis in the desert. There were about 20 missionaries there, a good camaraderie. The station was beautifully kept with flowers, bushes and trees. A far cry from Galmi, and I felt a little bit sorry for myself stuck way out in the Galmi desert. There were electricity and running water. There was a piano in the guest house which I enjoyed. Every afternoon there was a prayer meeting for the compound followed by tea and fellowship at the guest house. Friday suppers were a station get-together followed by a sing-song. There were two Sunday morning services—one in Hausa and one in English. Even the city itself had traffic circles filled with flowers and it was a pleasure to travel through town and enjoy the scenery. The British were quite proper and careful about their gardens. The shops and market were full. We enjoyed Kano very much.

On the way down to Kano, in Maradi, we both took our second Hausa exams. Burt averaged 86 and I averaged 77. That made us junior missionaries with voting privileges. Somewhere along the line we all got weighed. Burt was 128 lbs., and I was 106 lbs. Really the good old days! Johnny weighed about 12 lbs. then, almost 3 months old.

During our month in Kano, we heard from Fran that the Williams, members of our church at home, were killed in an automobile accident. That left their two children Edith and Don (I believe) orphans in their late teens. Cherry pushed the buggy off the porch with Johnny in it and he suffered a bruised upper lip and nose. Cherry fell out of bed and badly bruised her face. Had a large bump on her forehead, her right eye was 2/3rds closed shut and black and blue, her mouth was cut and her nose was bruised. It's a good thing it wasn't 1996, or we might have been accused of child abuse! It's a wonder kids survive. We had a Wheaton Washington Banquet at the elegant, little bit of England, airport hotel. About a dozen Wheatonites were in the area. We had hors d'oeuvres, cream of chicken soup, fish with sauce, steak, bacon, french fries, boiled potatoes, carrots, cauliflower, tomatoes, cherry pie ala mode, coffee, cheese and crackers. Cost about $1.50 a plate. Then we went to Charlie and Betty Frame's house for impromptus, solos, trios and quartettes and devotions. Dr. Hursh MC'd it. A delightful time. Got home about midnight. I don't remember who stayed with the kids, but I know that someone did, because we didn't have them with us.

Our time in Kano was running out, and on Sat., March 7 we all piled into our Chevy Carryall, along with Issou and a big 50 gal. drum of gasoline and headed for the Camerouns. Rollie had just turned 6; Lanny was almost 4, Cherry was 16 months and Johnny was almost 4 months. Our destination was Batouri, French Cameroun to visit Paul and Jane Pendell. Paul was in Wheaton with me and we met him and Jane and little Biz again in Paris where we had some good adventures with them including a trip to Switzerland. They had visited us the year before in Galmi. The best way to describe our trip to the Pendells is to excerpt a letter to Fran and Bill written from their place. I just re-read it and it exhausted me. "What fools these mortals be!" At one point on our trip, we were actually told we were crazy, albeit not in so many words. Now I tend to agree, but then, we were young and daring.

"Batouri, French Camerouns, March 19, 1953—We pulled in here Sun. night about 11, tired, hungry and dirty. After getting Pendells out of bed, washing off the dirt, feeding the inner man, we hit the hay at 2 a.m. and didn't get off it until 7:30. We're having a good time just relaxing, gabbing, and settling the affairs of the world. As for our health, the last day on the road I developed a diarrhea which I am now just getting control of. Issou, our 'boy', got chicken pox 3 days before we left Kano and yesterday Rollie carne down with it. He spent most of the day in bed, but he is up today, his fever is down but he's got about 50 spots all over his chest, back and face. This morning Lanny and Cherry had about 3 each, so we are waiting for further developments. Cherry was a little hard to handle on the road, forever restless, but Johnny slept most of the time he wasn't eating, and Rollie and Lanny were as good as could be expected considering their long daily confinement in the car. Cherry didn't come down with chicken pox until we got back to Galmi, and Johnny never did get them in that time frame.

"Now to backtrack. We left Kano on Sat. morning, the 7th. We had an elderly lady with us who is a missionary with S.U.M., but who has been in Kano for some time. She had to go to Jos, and we invited her to go with us. Kano to Jos was our first day plan. Left at 10:45 a.m. Had a blowout about 7:30—the only tire trouble on the whole trip—about 80 miles out of Jos. About 40 miles out of Jos we noticed our headlights were beginning to dim and noticed that the battery was discharging. Burt tried tinkering with the wiring but with little success. We managed in about the next 4 hours, after stopping, pushing, starting, to get within 15 miles of Jos before we had no lights and no ignition. Then we quit, took out our camp cots and rolled up in a thin blanket apiece. After about an hour's freezing, we could stand the cold no longer. It was then 3 a.m., so we all piled back into the car and slept sitting up until daylight. At daylight we pushed the car until it started and made our way into Jos on the remainder of the battery, this time not needing the additional juice for lights. At the mission, the Chevy coughed and died. We spent Sunday sleeping. Monday, Burt took the car to the garage, found out the trouble was a burned out generator, got a new part, and on Tues., we managed to shove off, a day behind schedule.

"On Tuesday, we traveled abut 260 miles, 60 of which was getting off the route and retracing our steps. We arrived at McCurdy at dusk, stayed at the D.R.C.M. (Dutch Reformed Mission of South Africa) station, had a good bath, fish dinner and sleep. Left Wed. morning for Ikom. About 10 a.m. we ran into some rain, so Burt got out to fix the windshield wipers. Stopped by a little village and found that most of them were Christians, at least in name, and one young man in particular was in Bible School in a nearby town. Southern Nigeria has been pretty well Christianized.

"About 11 a.m. we ran over a snake about 8' long and about 4" in diameter. He tried to cross the road before we got there but didn't quite make it. We got him right in the middle. We backed up, watched him thrash and writhe, and after 10 minutes of waiting we decided to go on without the skin because he still had some life in him, although he was mortally wounded. (I recall Issou remonstrating with Burt when Burt was considering getting out of the car to cut its head off. This teen age boy had more 'wayo' than Burt at that moment.) Burt was disappointed that he couldn't get his skin and it irked him to have to leave such a prize behind. About noon we stopped at an inviting spot on the road, and in about 30 seconds about 50 boys descended upon us. We found out we had stopped in front of another DRCM mission and these kids were in the school. So we drove about 100 yards to the compound, introduced ourselves, and they invited us to eat our lunch on their veranda and even served us coffee and fruit to boot.

"After that bit of relaxation, we proceeded on to Ikom, arriving about 4 p.m. We had written for a room at the government rest house, and we got it. It was just a room with no fixings whatever. We set up our cots, got out our food box, made supper, had baths all around and turned in. (Reflection: I think it was at this spot that Johnny fussed and fussed and nothing seemed to appease him. He refused his (milk) bottle. Finally, in desperation, I gave him a bottle of water, and he guzzled it down until he was satisfied. After that, he quieted down. I hadn't given it a thought that he might have been thirsty. From that experience, I learned to offer water early on in a dry and dusty land.) That night there was a terrific thunder and lightening storm, but we were high and dry. Next day we could only go as far as Mamfe, 60 miles, because from Mamfe to Bamenda, 90 miles, is a one way road, going one way on Mon., Wed., and Fri., and the other way the other 4 days of the week. Our original plan was to make that stretch on Wed., but having been held up in Jos for car repairs on Mon., we were behind schedule one day already so had to put ourselves behind a second day. Consequently we had no reservations at the rest house—this time it was a catering one—deluxe, and they were all booked so it didn't look good. After serving us an excellent dinner, the district officer came over and by juggling a single guest in with another single guest, they managed a room for us. This one was a room, plus small sitting room and bathroom. With 3 meals, and tea before breakfast and in the afternoon, it cost us about a total of $7.50 for the night. But it was worth it. By this time, all our reservations were null and void because we were two days behind schedule.

"At the rest house in Mamfe we met the Michaelsons, missionaries with the Cameroun Baptist Society, who were going to Bamenda the next day and planning to stay in the same place we were. We wondered how their coming along at the same time we were would affect our housing plans since they were members of the mission. Forgot to mention that between Ikom and Mamfe, we ferried our first river. We all got out, Burt drove the car onto the ferry, we all got on, and the natives started to row. It took about 10 min. to cross, but we landed safely and were on our way.

"Friday morning we got a good start on our narrow, winding, one way road. We were going through dense jungle, climbing, descending, twisting, turning, not able to see 10 ft. into the dense jungle. It was ruggedly beautiful. We had had another thunder storm the previous night. After about 2 hours on the road, we came to an abrupt halt. A giant tree with about a yard diameter was lying across the road. Two cars that preceded us were lined up waiting and another half dozen drove up behind us while we waited for the Africans to chop away on both sides of the road with their little hatchets. When the two pieces were chopped through, they succeeded in pushing it off the road with the help of small trees as a lever. We were on our way in about an hour. We all piled in hopefully, not knowing that 25 yards ahead of us, around a couple more hairpin turns and bends, another tree was down. The Africans were almost through with this one so we had only about a 20 minute wait. No more fallen trees that day.

"Arrived at Bamenda at 3 p.m., an altitude of between 5 and 6000 ft, presented ourselves to the missionaries. The man said they had been prepared for us on Wed. night, that the Michaelsons were due in—we told them they weren't far behind us—but that he would manage somehow to take care of us if the government rest house were full, and wouldn't we please go and see. We did. It was situated on the highest spot in town, another 500 to 1000 ft. climb, in second gear most of the time and in first part of the time. A black boy flunky said they had a place and gave us a room. We unloaded the car and after about a half hour the black proprietor came in and said that his boy had made a mistake, that he was booked up solid and there was no room for us. There was nothing for us to do but pack up again but we decided to come back and have supper there. We returned to the mission. The Michaelsons had arrived by this time and were unpacking, and in the meantime, arrangements had been made for a room for us, so we parked there. We fed the kids in the room, put them to bed, had someone keep an eye on them and retuned to the hill for our supper, then visited with the missionaries for awhile. The hostess was in bed with jaundice so we didn't see her. We had breakfast with them the next morning. It was Saturday.

"We continued climbing until we were in an altitude of about 7000', paralleling the clouds. Our destination was Bafia, which we made about 7:30 that night. This was the first Presbyterian Mission stop. Sun. morning we got a good start for a long ride to Batouri, our destination. We ferried two rivers. These ferries were run by motors. We had lost some bolts on our springs and shock absorbers so now couldn't do over 15 or 20 miles an hour. At that rate it would take us about 15 hours for our 300 mile trip. All along the road were little villages, and we inquired of one man who told us there was a mechanic in a town about 10 miles down the road. We limped in—remember, it was Sun.—and the Frenchman consented to do the job for us. He had to make some parts and it was a good hour before we were on the road again. By that time it was noon. We had made 50 miles.

"About 10 p.m., about 10 miles out of Batouri, we came around a curve and right in front of us was a tree sprawled across the way. We hit it at about 10 mph and were thrown into the ditch. Soon some Africans came along, chopped away the tree and tried in vain to push the car out. In a little while a truck came by and pulled us out, and we went merrily on our way again. And soon we reached the place where the beginning of this letter finds us. "We could see the Lord working things out for us along the way. In respect to lodging, car repair, sending the lone truck on the road along at the right moment. If we had had generator trouble anywhere but near Jos, we'd have been stuck in the middle of nowhere where we could not get parts. And there probably wasn't another garage within 100 miles on Sunday when we needed it. So we have much to thank Him for. Our journey is only half over. We plan to leave here, go on to French Equatorial Africa (Central African Republic today), spend a few days with Florence Almen and go north from there. All of this, D.V."

Well, we made it to the Pendells and Batouri and had a relaxing time with them. Burt and Paul spent time in the operating room and dispensary. Jane was Paul's nurse and scrubbed right along with him. The Pendells' boys did my washing (by hand of course) and ironing. I first met a charcoal burning flat iron at the Pendells. You open up the top, put the hot coals in and your iron is ready to go. (I bought one later in Kano and used it for a while, but charcoal was hard to buy at Galmi, wood being scarce in the desert, so resorted to flat irons for the most part.) It was there that we saw papaya trees

—

loaded so full and heavily that ripe papayas fell to the ground and split open and nobody bothered to eat them. Supply and demand! Wouldn't we like some papaya trees at Galmi! Batouri was right in the grassland area, and it was hot and humid, but there was an abundance of fruit and vegetables. The only meat they had was chicken or game shot in the woods. Burt and Paul and another missionary went out hunting one day, all day. This other missionary was long legged and an inveterate hunter, who could walk and walk and walk. They walked all day until Burt thought his legs would separate from the rest of his body. They walked through tall grass, ever on the lookout for wild game that might approach from behind. They carried their rifles which got heavier by the hour and never fired a shot. They came back exhausted and empty handed. Unfortunately, we had lost two days on our way, so only had two days to spend with Paul and Jane and Biz. On Wednesday morning, we were off again about 10 o'clock.

"We had to go east to cross over into French Equatorial Africa—about 1 1/2 hours drive. We arrived at the first town across the border (as I recall, it was Berberati) about 1 p.m. and hoped to get through customs in a hurry to reach Carnou that afternoon. We knew the siesta customs of the French—everything shuts down from noon to 3, but we were hoping anyway. We were a little chagrined therefore when we had to wait a little while before the French official would see us.

"But our waiting just began. Our passports and visas were in order, but he asked us for a visa for the car. We knew the French were always involved in red tape, but this was a new one on us. Well, we had no visa for the car, so as far as they were concerned we were importing the car for any subversive purpose we might think up as Americans. They directed us to the Swedish mission where they suggested the missionary there might be willing to stand bond for us if we failed to export the car. The wife was home, but the husband had just left and wouldn't be back until the next night or the following morning. So she and Burt went back and she was going to sign for us, but the French, like all Europeans, consider a woman's signature as valid as a child's, so her signature couldn't help us. There was nothing to do but stay with the missionaries until the man got home. "We took over a guest room of theirs and relaxed, enjoying the hospitality of the Swedish missionaries as well as their delicious meals with their fancy fish dishes and Swedish bread. Our conversation was carried on in French, since they knew no English and we, no Swedish. Had a lovely visit, and although we wanted to be on our way, we enjoyed our time with them. The mister came home late Thurs. night so Fri. a.m., he and Burt went down to the office, he signed the paper and we could have gone then except for another delay which held us up until 3 p.m. Fri. In that particular town the police stopped Burt and asked for his driver's license—the only time on the trip—and he didn't have it. He had left it on the desk in our study. So he had to pay a 600 franc fine to boot. We finally got on our way and decided to drive all night and make Bangui by morning. We did—even crossing a ferry at mid-night, getting the ferry man up to do it.

"Arrived in Bangui tired, dirty and hungry Sat. morning and were received by the first Mid Missions station we were to meet. They had been looking for us since Thursday. Stayed there only until after dinner, because we were anxious to spend the week end with Florence Almen, and we were only 100 miles from her, so we pressed on. Arrived about 5 o'clock and completely surprised her. Our letter hadn't reached her, and she had given us up about a month before when we hadn't shown up. We had a nice reunion and stayed there until Tuesday. She is with the Rosenaus who know you and the Marxes well, and I remember them since 1936 when I lived in Mt. Prospect and came into Niles Center to attend the church with the Hennixes. They had been furloughing in Morton Grove." We got a glimpse of Florence's work with the children. On Sunday we were impressed with their large church service. The building had no walls, but a roof and seats. Of course, the climate and setting were tropical

And now we were we were pushing to get back to Kano. The roads were so bad that broken springs were the order of the day. At Ft. Crampel there was a school for missionaries' children. I knew the teacher from Wheaton but forget who it was now. Burt and a young missionary spent the morning fixing a broken spring. From there we crossed the border from French Equatorial Africa into British Camerouns, fearful that our papers might not be in order, but they were. Spent Saturday night with Dr. and Mrs. Chandler of Sudan United Mission—British Board. Somewhere in there we met a missionary and his wife who were working with the Fulani. I forget their names. Had Easter Sunday morning with them, and then left, hoping to get to our (S.I.M.) first station in Nigeria.

"At Maidugari we broke a spring again. It was noon, on Easter Sunday, and we didn't know what to do about it. We stopped to enquire of a police officer, and an auto with two Englishmen drove up and asked us our trouble. They said, 'follow us'. Went to an Arab's garage—big thing with modern equipment. He got the Arab out of bed—at noon—and said, 'Listen, this man needs help—he doesn't need it tomorrow or the next day—he needs it right now. Fix him up!' So with many groanings and excuses about not having any help that day, he started to look for a spring. After a while his wife invited us into their mansion, beautiful and spacious with air conditioning in every room. Gave us drinks, etc. Were very friendly. About 3 p.m. we left, made our mission station, Potiskum, about 8 p.m. (I believe the Rhines were stationed there.) Next day arrived Kano."

Of course, our trip wasn't over. We still had to get to Galmi, but at least we were in home territory. After a day in Kano, we headed north early in the morning, got to the border, checked in and reached Maradi by noon. Left again by 3 p.m. and got home three and a half hours later. It was good to get home after two months away. We dug ourselves out of the dirt, tried to get used to the hot, dry weather again, while our noses crusted and our skin dried out and chapped.

For the most part, during our missionary career at Galmi, our "boys" and "cooks" were Yahaya, Issou, Garba and Uma at different times. They were very good, helpful, and we counted on them. Besides them, there were Mai Daji and Roro, and Hadi, and Sha'aybu, none of them as faithful as the above mentioned four.

During the hot season which was upon us when we returned from the Camerouns, the house would heat up during the day and would get to about 105 degrees with almost zero humidity. The thick walls held the heat of the day, so the house didn't really cool off that much during the night. So move out to sleep we did. The "boy" moved our beds out on the porch at night—six beds—and tied up the mosquito netting. It was beautiful to sleep out with no lights to dim the stars which filled the sky. It had its hazards, too. Sometimes a sudden dust storm would come up and we would awaken to see our pillows flying away. Then we had to chase the pillows, scurry to take down the nets, get our beds back in the house, this time without the help of our "boy". There we sweated out the storm with the windows and doors shut tight to keep out most of the dust. We literally dripped with sweat. Usually rain followed and cleared the air. We got little sleep those nights. And the next morning, our "boy" had the task of sweeping up the dust, washing the floors, shaking out the bedding, and what have you.

Drinking water was a favorite past time for all of us and a necessary one. All of our water was boiled and filtered. We had two filters going at all times and 5 cooling crocks which held almost 3 quarts each. From the cooling crocks we poured the water into pitchers and put them in the fridge. Later on, we set up a large thermos container, put ice in it in the morning and cooled water, and we used that for drinking so we wouldn't have to open our kerosene fridge so often. The kerosene fridge had to be filled each week and the wick carefully cleaned. Our Servel fridge did yeoman service for at least 20 years until we got 24 hr. electricity. Then we got an electric one in Niamey. The Servel was still in good working order, and we sold it to the chief, (Kadiri?) but it didn't last him too long because he or his men didn't bother cleaning the wick very often or weren't very careful about it.

June, 1953 was just around the corner and that marked just 12 months to go before our furlough. But new and different experiences, some good and some not so good, awaited us that last year of our first term.

Chapter 8

ANTICIPATING FURLOUGH

Back in the "good old days", terms were four years long, and if you went to France to study French, that year didn't count. So it was that in the summer of 1953, we had already been separated from home (the U.S.) and family (folks, relatives, friends) for four years, and you couldn't blame us for getting excited about the idea of going home at the end of only one more year.

I'd like to dispel a myth that has grown up about missionaries and where their "home" is. There were times on furlough that people suggested to me that I couldn't wait to get back to Africa and "home". They were sure that I preferred living there in the heat and discomfort of a desert climate without air conditioning, in a culture which was different from what I had been raised in, with people who neither spoke my language nor were knowledgeable about what was going on in the world. (The Africans thought we were kidding when we told them there was someone walking on the moon the day after the first moon landing.) They were sure that I would rather read under a pressure lamp, sweep out after a dust storm, crawl under a mosquito net, boil my drinking water and milk, dip and pour for my shower. "I'm sure your heart is in Africa and you can't wait to get back," they would say. Well, I have news for them! It was hard for me to go back each time. My heart was here with family, not in Galmi. Yes, I liked the people there, and we did have African friends, but they weren't family. It wasn't so much the lack of conveniences in Galmi that made it hard to go back; it was the separation once more from family. It never got easier! The thing that sustained me (us) was believing that this was where God wanted us to be and that settled it. When people suggested that I could hardly wait to go back, I must have given them a puzzled look. For sure, I didn't want to burst their little bubble, but at the same time, I couldn't honestly say I wanted to go back. It was always a struggle. So I made some non-committal remark and let them go on thinking as they wished. I should have asked them to come back with me and get it on the fun.

So, in preparation for furlough, I wrote home and asked Fran to buy me a dress that I could travel in, remembering that "the dress will be holding a child most of the time." My stats at that time were 34/27/35. I was 32 years old. Now in 1996 I am more than double that age, (not size), but I must admit that inches have been added to those stats. And then I reason that if I as a mature person have grown emotionally and spiritually, why not physically? Surely they go hand in hand!

I also asked Fran to buy me a "small, back of the head hat . . . that will go nicely with the dress. Fifteen dollars should cover both the dress and hat!" Just for the record, Bobby Hollander was born, I believe, on April 5 of this year, 1953. Billy Olson was born on that same day years before, and Mother was buried on that day twenty years prior to that.

"May 17, 1953 After six months Johnny is as good looking as the rest of our gang. He resembles Rollie now, has lovely blue eyes and his hair is still predominately red although it is also blondish. He is as good a baby as Lanny. In temperament he is like Lanny. In temperament Rollie and Cherry are alike. Lanny and Cherry are the dark haired, dark eyed ones in our family. Each is entirely different: Rollie, blond, blue eyes, sunburned, rough skin, some freckles, hyper-thyroid, never walking if he can run; Lanny, blond, brownish, slow thinking, slow reacting, loveable little boy; Cherry, dark blond, brown eyes, white skin, shy, coy, self-centered as all 1 1/2 yr. olds are; John, who looks like Rollie and up to now acts like Lanny—what will he be like?"

Well, now that all our kids (even the two who were yet unborn) are older than I was when I wrote those philosophical sentiments, what do you think? My mature wisdom checks me from making character judgments anymore. All our kids are great in their own way and we are thankful that God gave each of them to us. What a great God He is!

Burt's comments about our kids. "Johnny Jack is pretty nice. At first, with his hair and nose combination he looked a lot like Bob (Hollander), but that is passing as he changes. We love his red hair though! Cherry is a pretty girl, looks very much like Pat—real white skin and great big cheeks. Otherwise she looks like Mom (Lasca)—fat and sharp nosed! And the darkest chocolate eyes ever! But very girl-ish-naughty!"

"June 4, 1953 Two main reasons for wanting to get home are one, to see you and two, to show the kids the wonders of America. When Rollie and Lanny feel bad about our refusing them to go into the puddles and swim like their black friends, we have to tell them that when we get home, they can swim in the 'clean' waters of America. Then they want to go right way. Rollie says he remembers television but I wonder. Nevertheless he does remember much of our Paris days and is often referring to the Eiffel Tower or the Arc de Triomphe or the many cars. Time out to feed Johnny."

"June 22, 1953 I took the pad out of the playpen and set it in the center of the parlor with Johnny sitting up on it. Rollie and Lanny and Cherry are marching around it and him while Johnny sits and gurgles. What a gang! Rollie has consistently run a fever every day and is 'always tired'. We don't know what ails him, but he must have some kind of a bug. Now all three kids have left Johnny, and he's sitting there trying to catch the sun's rays.

"With Genny (Kooy) gone (holiday) I've had to help with surgery this past week. Sat. morning it was a large hernia, and this morning it was one cataract and a 'needling'. I'm surprised how comparatively simple the removal of a cataract is—doesn't take more than a half hour. We've been getting excellent results and our fame is spreading abroad and more and more patients are corning in for eye surgery."

Life was pretty routine that year. People passed through enroute elsewhere going east or west, and those that came from Maradi or Nigeria always brought us some fresh fruit and vegetables which was a delightful relief from onions, boiled, fried, scalloped, baked. We planted a small garden and hoped for the best. The rains came, we collected water in our drums. Beef was now available in the market, a nice alternative to goat meat. Beef was very lean, therefore, tough, but succumbed to pressure cooker pressure. The well was finished and the pump was on order. We are building a cistern next to the house on the west side to hold 10,000 gallons of water. Work in the dispensary and hospital was increasing with 200 in the dispensary in the mornings and 40 in-patients (Aug. '53). Church attendance was increasing—57 in church. Some of the patients were coming to know Christ, and the Lord seemed to be working in our midst.

"Aug. 1, 1953 Johnny is 16 lbs. now. Honestly, he is so cute and good. He is the slowest of all our kids in achievement. He sits up well and crawls backwards but has shown no inclination to stand. Cherry, at 8 months, was standing, and at 11 months was walking well. She was our champion. Johnny is very shy. If we smile at him, he smiles back and bends his head down. Cherry and he had their second typhoid shots and Johnny his second DPT shot two mornings ago and were both sick and cried all day . . . it is very difficult to hold two crying babies at a time."

Dau Duka was a bright spot in our church. Martha Wall had led him to the Lord and taught him to read. He went to Bible School at Tsibiri for a year or two and was a natural born preacher. He preached each Sunday in our little church on the compound. Most of the congregation Sunday mornings were hospital patients who were encouraged to attend the service. Very few local people came to church except for those who were working for the missionaries, and it was sort of a given that they would go to church. They were also required to attend morning devotions.

When Zebs were still at Galmi, he gave Rollie and Lanny rides on his camel, and even I had a ride once. You get on the camel when he is in a sitting position, then he rises with a rocking motion, and you slide forward and backward with him, holding on for dear life. When he finally unfolds his legs and is standing, you look down and marvel at how high you are. The ground looks a long way away, and you hope you can stay on this ship of the desert. I think that was my only ride in all my years in the desert. However, some of our nurses were very brave and did some trekking on camels.

On my birthday we went to Tahaoua to visit the Zebs and Davidsons. Both Zebs and Davidsons owned camels and rode them. Tahaoua was Tuareg country, so the missionaries focused on reaching those people with the Gospel, and in preparation, were learning

Tamajaq. On the way back we stopped at two villages and Dau Duka preached. At first when we stopped, the people ran away but when they saw four black boys they came back. This was their first exposure to the Gospel and they were interested.

Two girls in Gidan Doutchie wanted to go to our girls' school at Sura, 100 miles from us. Their fathers refused to let them go. "Aug. 19, 1953 They decided to run away so Dan Truax gave them truck fare to Sura to help them get away. This infuriated their fathers who went after them, saw them, but the girls refused to return home. Then the men went to Konni, our commandant's place, 30 miles west of us. He charged us with kidnapping the girls, and the commandant came to see us when both Burt and Dan were away. I talked with him, and he was very upset and said he would be back the next day. In the meantime he went on. He didn't stop the next day but a few days later the girls came back on a truck. Apparently it was at the doings of the commandant who has us in the dog house. He feels that by Dan helping the girls with money he was an accomplice. A few days afterward, the girls ran away again, this time on their own. But two days ago they were back in their village again, one having been picked up on the road to Sura and the other in a village a little ways from us. The Christians on the compound say they will run away until they get to Sura. They are about 14 years of age—the marriageable age, and their prospective husbands have already begun to pay on the bride price, which amounts to about $40.00." The upshot of this episode was that the girls did not get back to Sura, and their families were very much opposed to us for many years. Kanduwa was one of the girls. Kanduwa married Dau Duka.

The rest of the story of Dau Duka and Kanduwa is not what we had hoped and prayed for. They got along for a number of years, had a family, but Dau Duka got away from the Lord and eventually said he was going to be a Moslem. He took a second wife, and Kanduwa went back to her father's house. His second wife didn't last long—she left him. Eventually, he married Mai Dubu, a quiet spoken girl who was blind in one eye. One night she had a vision of a strong light shining in her face and a voice told her to follow the Christian way. The vision was repeated several times. It scared her, and she went to one of the nurses who led her to the Lord. So here was Mai Dubu, who on her own came to know the Lord, married to Dau Duka, our first convert, now a practicing Moslem. Through the years, Mai Dubu has remained faithful to the Lord, and we applaud Dau Duka for his tolerance in letting Mai Dubu come to church and Bible studies and associate with the Christian women. Eventually they were divorced. Mai Dubu works as household help in the homes of the missionaries, and Dau Duka is a faithful, honest hospital worker, who is a lukewarm Moslem, but deep in his heart he knows that Christ is the only way.

"We gave Johnny his third and final DPT and typhoid shots so he had a rough time yesterday but is better today. It's so unusual to have to baby Johnny, he's usually so good. He's the best behaved one of them all, including Lanny who was exceptional."

When we left home in 1949 Rollie was just 2 1/2 and Lanny, 4 months. Now, four years later, Rollie was 6 1/2 and supposed to be in school. During those four years, I put out of my mind the idea that Rollie might have to go away to school some day. I didn't want even to think about it! But time has a way of passing, and reality set in. Fortunately, we had spent two weeks at Miango when Cherry was born, so we had at least seen Kent Academy and were pleased with what we saw. It was a great school for all those OTHER kids! I sent home for name tags. They didn't come, so I had to embroider his initials on every item of his clothing, even to the last handkerchief. "We hate to see Rollie leave us. About a month from today he goes to school. His foot locker is almost packed and we should be sending that in about a week so that it gets there in time."

"Sept. 3, 1953 Rollie's footlocker has gone and it looks like he's really getting ready to leave us. Three more weeks and we'll take him to Maradi where he'll fly with about six or seven other children from French country. Our mission will be sending all three of our planes . . . Don't forget to be praying for him . . . I don't think he'll be homesick . . . My only concern is that when he gets sick, he gets a fever and gets a semi-delirious spell, imagining he is seeing something, and it takes about 5 minutes to talk him out of it and wake him up thoroughly. I wonder if it sterns back to his serious illness in Paris."

Well, the dreaded day finally came. Zeb had come from Tahaoua on a truck and was going to Maradi with us. Verna Gabrielson and Muriel and Bernard Van Lierop came from Dogon Doutchi. Verna was going to Sura to replace someone going to Jos for a holiday, and the Van Lierop children were going to K.A. along with Rollie. We left on Sat. afternoon, picked up Lolita Harbottle who was going to Jos to have a baby. We were 6 adults and 6 kids in our car, all headed for Maradi, 125 miles east of us. Ordinarily this was a 3-4 hour trip. This one took nine! "About 15 miles out of Madaoua we had our picnic supper and noticed rain clouds approaching. We never got more than a sprinkle but a few hours before our arrival on the road between Madaoua and Maradi, there had been a downpour which made the roads impassable. We were stopped about 10 times with road barriers and had to talk our way through. We thought at one place we would have to wait a few hours until the man saw we were loaded with kids and a pregnant woman. Then he let us go by. Nevertheless, all those stops and having to travel at almost a snail's pace through mud and ruts brought us to Maradi at half past midnight.

"The plane was to pick up the school kids on Monday, but plans were changed and the kids had to go to Katsina in Nigeria to pick up the plane. There is a lot of red tape to crossing the border by air. So they all piled into Mr. Kapp's Jeep Mon. morning at 7 a.m. and took the 80 mile trip to Katsina. Stayed there until Tues. when the plane picked them up and took them to Miango. Rollie climbed into the Jeep like a condemned prisoner, but without a thought of turning back. He was going because he was supposed to go and that was all there was to it, whether he liked it or not. He hardly said goodbye and didn't smile. Zeb sat next to him in the back of the Jeep so I was glad he could sort of keep an eye on him. He and Beth Darling were the two youngest, going to school for the first time. Zeb came through last night on the way back to Tahaoua and said that Rollie was quite sober for a while but by the time they reached Katsina he was singing and laughing with the rest of them so that made us feel good . . . we surely miss him.

"We left Maradi Monday afternoon. It took 2 1/2 hours to go the first 60 miles through mud and muck. Got stuck once and backed out finally after about 15 minutes of trying. This, mind you, was right in the middle of the road. We had our supper and got back in the car about 6 p.m. Forty more miles to Madaoua and 6 more hours. About that time, our motor stopped. We'd wait a bit and then it would start so we figured water was getting in somehow to short the circuit. We found our water line connection to the radiator broken off so the water in the radiator was being splashed back into the engine and killing the motor. When all the water leaked out of the radiator by this means and through our perpetual leaks in the radiator, we were able to start the car. But then we couldn't go more than a mile until the car heated up. We went mile by mile like this for several hours, sleeping in between times, until we came to a puddle of water. We filled up the radiator, then Burt sat on the fender, held the connection up to the radiator, and with hood up, I drove the car the last 15 miles into Madaoua between 5 and 7 miles an hour. We arrived at midnight, told Elvin Harbottle to move over, we were spending the rest of the night there and finally got some sleep. Next morning, Burt got the part soldered by a native blacksmith and after dinner on Tues., we made the rest of the way home. We were tired and glad to get there."

As I look back, I marvel how the kids rolled with the punches. I realize that what we were involved in also involved them. For years, this also meant bottles and diapers (disposable diapers had not been invented yet). Naturally, Lanny, Cherry and Johnny made the trip to Maradi with us—a nine hour trip, and Lanny, Cherry and Johnny were with us on the return ten hour trip. They were good sports! There was no other option. With Rollie gone, Lanny became the big brother, the responsible one. He was all of four years old at this time!

Rollie made a good adjustment at K.A. Paul and Jerry Craig were in charge, and they were wonderful surrogate parents. Jerry reminded me years later of the note we sent along to them with Rollie. It said, "We hope you enjoy Rollie as much as we do." They added, "And we did!" His first letter home consisted of just his name, printed on a sheet of paper. A note from the Craigs said, "Rollie's fine. He's one of our best boys—cleans his room, makes his bed, net, clothes, teeth, bath, etc." Burness Kampen (now Goertz) reminded us years later that the first night when the first grade boys were supposed to be getting their showers, she found Rollie sitting on his bed in his room. When asked why he wasn't showering with the rest, he said, "I don't want to shower with all those naked boys!"

The hospital work was increasing. "About 70 patients in the hospital and doing at least one operation a day. After surgery, there are over 200 out patients for Burt to see and he has to leave his dressings until the afternoon. So outside of the hospital work he has little time for anything else." That became the pattern for the next twenty plus years. Surgery to begin with—usually 4-5 cases a morning and a long waiting list; then seeing patients that the nurses saved for the doctor, rounds in the afternoon. In between times, there were the emergencies.

The Darlings were with us at Galmi for about two weeks doing some more building. He cemented our cistern, built us a storehouse and one for the hospital. They stayed with us. Beth was at school with Rollie. Don and Dorothy had another baby—Don Phillip—and he was 5 1/2 months old at the time.

Conference time was rolling around again and Johnny would celebrate his first birthday during that time. It was at Maradi, and we were excited about going, not only because of the conference but also because we were leaving from Maradi to go to Jos for our holiday, and we would see Rollie again! In the midst of our preparations for conference and holiday, the folks from the West passed through and stayed the night with us. There were the Pollens, the Van Lierops, the Davidsons and Zebs. So we were busy playing hosts as well as getting ready ourselves. Conference would last three days, and we "expect to be in Kano Monday afternoon, get an early start for Jos Tuesday morning—that's a 10 hour drive. So D.V., we'll see Rollie Wednesday a.m. And we'll see you in about 7 months!!"

Well, the best laid plans of men and women often go awry, and we didn't get to Miango by Wed. a.m. Forty five miles out of Kano, our radiator frame broke, so we had to return to Kano to get it fixed and didn't leave Kano until Thursday morning at 4:15 a.m. Got to Miango Thursday afternoon. "How glad we were to see Rollie and he, us. He is doing well in school, and everybody speaks well of him."

The Hurshes were on holiday at the same time, and he checked all the students' eyes and Rollie had 50% vision in one eye and 45% in the other so he was fitted with glasses. Glasses on a six year old kid don't last very long, and I don't know how many pairs of glasses we bought for him during his K.A. days. Fortunately, the eye hospital was in Kano, only a day's journey away. "Rollie says he's the 3rd smartest in his class of 28. Steve Lucas is #1." We were housed in Mountain View. It was the largest cottage on the compound. It had a large sitting room/bedroom combination, a second bedroom with bunk beds and baby beds, and a third little ante room with one bed in it. Rollie stayed with us in our cottage, ate with us in the big house, and went to school during the day. What fun that was! There was an outhouse under the cashew tree, and we got our hot water from the big house in buckets. Our house boy was with us, and his duties consisted mostly of washing and ironing clothes and watching the kids. There was a small "tuck shop" where we could buy snacks. The Rest Home was adjacent to K.A. We relished every day at Miango. There were morning Bible studies, Sunday services, Sunday evening "sing-songs". Even a stunt night was thrown in at times. Tennis and croquet courts were available. "Tea time" was an institution each afternoon. In later years, the outhouse was replaced by inside toilets and running water. Fruit trees were in abundance, so our noon dessert was always cut up fruit—citrus, mango, papaya, cashew. Meals were delicious. This was a perfect holiday place for tired missionaries.

It was during our holiday this year that Ernie Hodges died. He was a young missionary, age 32, married 5 years, father of 3 children and a fourth on the way. They were stationed about 200 miles out of Jos. He was on trek when he became ill. "A fellow missionary traveled all Friday night to Jos to get the plane to come to their station, but the plane had left 20 min. before. So Dr. Jeanette Troup and others drove out Sat., brought him into Jos, doing artificial respiration all the way, got him in an iron lung by 6 a.m. Sun. Burt and Dr. Hursh went in Sunday morning to relieve the other docs and were with him when he died." It was polio. Ernie was buried in the little cemetery behind the chapel where a number of our missionaries and missionary children are buried. Wife Jean was left with a family to raise—her oldest was four years. Two boys and a girl (Ruthie) and the yet unborn child, named Ernie after his father when he was born! Jean and her children moved to Miango where Jean became one of the K.A. teachers.

One day the Darlings arrived at Miango. We were surprised to see them. Then we learned of their most recent sorrow. Little Don Philip was not with them. He was with the Lord. His 7-month old body was buried in Maradi. He had taken ill suddenly. He was sick four days. ". . . don't know what the disease was—meningitis, polio, gastro-intestinal, typhoid? (Later some said that it was a reaction to a prophylactic shot that he had had.) Philip was such a fine healthy baby. He was treated by the French doctor . . . and received as good care as he could have gotten anywhere. Now they have only Beth again, a grave at Tahaoua and a grave at Maradi."

124

Every year at K. A., the students put on Christmas and Spring programs. Rollie's first grade class put on "The Three Little Pigs." Rollie was the "straw man", and he said his one line well, "Very well, little pig, you may have some of my straw." Jerry Craig was the inspiration behind the programs which usually consisted of plays, songs and instrumentalists. These were always done to perfection, and during the course of our kids' stay there, they all figured in some of the plays. Cherry in first grade led the rhythm band. Later she was Pinocchio. Lanny was Rumplestiltskin once and figured later in "A Midsummer Night's Dream". John was an elf; Sue was a story book character that introduced other characters. We saw some of these programs but not all of them. Being so far away and in another country and living in the 50's and 60's, we just didn't travel back and forth when we felt like it. It was contrary to mission policy as well as being a difficult road trip.

We put Cherry's hair in French braids and it looked cute but it was hard for her to be patient. "Johnny is beginning to protest now when she takes something from him, and his protests are enough to make her think twice."

Well, all good things come to an end and so did our holiday. School was out for Christmas holidays, and we all piled into our Chevy Carry-all and with 3 adults and 10 kids made our way to Kano enroute to Galmi. We stayed there for 3 days, left off some of the kids, then waited for the Darlings to arrive by plane and took them back to Maradi. Then on to Galmi and home. What a good feeling it was to be all together again as a family. We cherished every day that we had with Rollie back home for we knew that it wouldn't be long before he had to leave us again. And we wouldn't see him for six months!

The clean-up began. Being away for a month allowed the cobwebs, dust and rat droppings to multiply. In the study one stink mouse got into our bottle of glue and couldn't get his head out and died that way. All the dishes had to be washed, the floors and furniture washed and polished, the curtains which I had taken down before leaving put up again . . . by Christmas eve the place was fairly presentable." We decorated a scrubby thorn tree. Rollie and Lanny made paper chains. All the missionaries had Christmas dinner and supper here. Had guinea fowl, dressing, potatoes, peas, banana salad and radish and carrot jello salad and lemon cream pie. Just like back home!! Then on Sunday we all went in to the Harbottles for another Christmas dinner. She prepared 9 chickens, one to be divided among the kids and one each for the adults, which was a little bit too much.

"We received your Christmas gifts and . . . Hershey bars, plastic nesting blocks and snap on blocks. Burt's folks sent Rollie and Lanny cowboy suits; Cherry, a dress and Johnny a suit and sweater. From us, Rollie and Lanny received 12" cars, Cherry, a set of tin dishes, and Johnny, a musical top, all of which we bought in Jos. Together with a lot of small gifts from Wayne Kletzing's church, the kids had a lot to open up. "It surely is nice having Rollie home with us. He is the only one still up and is making conversation with us. Every night in bed he wants me to talk to him for a while about this and that. He has changed quite a bit and all for the better. We hope the next six months will do him as much good as the last three, although in our opinion he was pretty fine before he left. Mr. Smith, who is house papa says that Rollie is one of the best adjusted and nicest first graders and it shows that he has had some good home training. Rollie informed us yesterday that he likes school better than being home, and instead of making us feel bad we are very happy about it. Knowing he is happy there and enjoying school is a real relief to us. We told him that next year we would be able to let him go to school and live with us, and he thought that was pretty swell. We hope we are able to get Lanny into a kindergarten because he feels the difference between himself and Rollie and it pricks him a bit."

In the meantime, Fran and Bill were looking for a place for us to live in Wheaton while Burt's folks were looking for a place in Chicago. I smile when I read that I wrote, "We don't expect to get anything less than $100.00 a month." Burt had applied for a residency at Hines Hospital and at first was accepted but later was turned down because he wouldn't commit himself for more than a year.

"Glad to hear that Carolyn was saved. How does Richard stand? Received some snaps from Bob and Cora of the baby. Johnny still takes two naps a day, an hour or two each and goes to bed right after supper. In between times he is bubbling over with fun and life. Cherry gets cuter every day. Today Rollie was naughty, so I took him to his room, not knowing exactly what to do about it. Cherry came and said, 'Det it?' I didn't know what she wanted to get but I told her to go ahead. She brought in the window stick that we use to spank with. So I let her spank Rollie, and we all had a good laugh."

Rollie went back to school and life went on. Lanny became big brother again. "It is amazing to see the change in Lanny when Rollie is away. He blossoms out into a big boy. When Rollie is around he is submerged. Cherry has a terrific case of 'mine itis'. Saturday Johnny stood up and walked across the room, and has been doing it ever since. He was the slowest of our gang to venture out on foot. He is 22 lbs., also the lightest of our gang at 14 1/2 months. But he is not a whit behind them in intelligence. "Received a letter from Beret. She says I should write a book about our adventures in Africa." That's what I'm doing now!

I think most of our adventures center around car trouble on our trips. Burt went to Kano for a medical conference.

"He had some car trouble 3/4 the way there, had to stop at Katsina for the night. Coming home, he left Kano Sat. p.m., spent the night and Sunday at Maradi, left Tsibiri at 10:30 a.m. on Monday and arrived home Wed. a.m. at 2 o'clock. Sixty miles from home, as he was sailing along, thinking about getting home in a few hours, getting cleaned up and enjoying a family reunion at the supper table, something went clang, bang, bang and Burt went flying off the road into the sand, the car completely out of control, and finally came to a stop in the sand. The tie rod had broken, leaving the steering gear helpless. That was 12:30 in the hot sun. One truck passed going back to Maradi that afternoon, so he sent word asking them to look for a spare part there. Another truck passed that night going to Madaoua so he sent a note to the Harbottles asking for food and water since he had to stay with the stuff. About 4 a.m. the same truck retuned with food and water, and Elvin Harbottle got a truck to Galmi early Tues. morning. He and Dan Truax pulled out about an hour later in Dan's Jeep and got to Burt about 12:30, just 24 hours after the accident. They took the rod off, returned with it to Madaoua with all of Burt's baggage. Don Darling came from Maradi with word that there was no new part in Maradi. They sent to Kano for it. So finally about midnight, they abandoned the car, leaving two African boys to look after it, and they rolled in here about 2 a.m. An hour later, they were all bedded down. So until the new part comes from Kano, the car is out in the 'daji' (bush)."

Hospital work increased with each passing year. Burt was operating every morning and some afternoons. I helped in the mornings, either scrubbing or circulating. We had over 100 in-patients in a 50-bed hospital into which we squeezed 70 beds. The overflow slept on the floor. Out-patients numbered 200 to 300 daily. We begged for more non-medical workers who could act as chaplains or evangelists in the hospital, doing personal work in the wards and preaching in the dispensary services. But there were none. Our hopes were in Dau Duka who still had 2 years of Bible School. Who would answer the call?

Our houseboy, Issou, (see page 63) made a profession of faith at the annual all-African conference at Tsibiri, and many of the 18 other boys who went from Galmi made professions of one sort or another. Issou (Isu) started working for us about a year after we got here. He worked as houseboy first. He was a nice boy and we all liked him, but he came from a strong Moslem family. And when we made it a rule that all the boys who worked for us had to go to school, he refused, so we had to let him go. Right after Johnny was born, we had some trouble with boys stealing, so we let them both go and Isu asked if he couldn't come back, saying he would go to school. His father had died in the meantime, so the greatest opposition was removed. He had been warming up right along, he went on our Cameroun trip with us, and at this conference (mentioned above), he went forward for salvation. Two evangelists, Malams Gin and Paulo from Nigeria were the speakers.

Speaking of Isu and our trip to the Camerouns, I may not have mentioned that somewhere along the way, Isu came down with a mild case of chicken pox, and wouldn't you know, Rollie, Lanny, and Cherry all came down with it sometime on the trip. Johnny escaped, perhaps because he still may have had some immunity from me, since he was only 4 months old. This was probably one of the reasons that Mrs. Rosenau, with whom Florence Almen worked, told us we were crazy to have undertaken such a trip with four small children. Looking back now, I guess we were! But we were young then and could do anything!

In early April, Mr. Jake Eitzen from Nigeria appeared at our door with Dr. Talbot, Chancellor of Biola and Bruce Linton, his photographer. We had heard that Dr. Talbot was in Nigeria but that he was not going to come to French Country, so we put it out of our minds. So we were surprised when they showed up. We were doubly surprised to see Bruce Linton, who graduated from Wheaton College with Burt. In fact, sat next to him in Chapel for four years! Dr. Talbot was touring and photographing the fields. "He is a nice old man and takes complete charge of the situation whether he is a guest or not. He shot seven pigeons and ordered pigeon stew for dinner the day he ate with the Truaxes. He does things that only a venerable old man can do and get away with in someone else's house, such as going around in suspenders (and pants) without shirt and grabbing the first towel he sees although he has a towel all laid out for him, etc."

Of course, April is one of the hottest months of the year—up to 120 in the sun, and the heat did bother him, but he didn't complain. Instead, he walked into our shower with his clothes on and came out dripping wet until he cooled off and dried out. He repeated this several times during the day. Mr. Eitzen's son, Jim, is also in first grade, and the Eitzens had just returned from K.A. and Miango and had seen Rollie. As they were walking together, Jim said, "I can beat 25 kids in first grade." Rollie, three steps behind, said, "I can beat 26." No grass grows under his feet!

"We received a letter from Rollie saying he had 5 teeth out. One was a molar which Dr. Kraay, our dentist, pulled. Dorothy Darling, who has not been well since her baby died, is at Miango resting. She wrote us and said that some of the French Country kids went on a picnic with some of their parents and she took Rollie with her Beth. At first Rollie was a bit shy about entering into the games, but she encouraged him and soon he was playing hard with the rest of them. During the songs and testimony time he sang loudly and clear and Mr. Thamer called on him for a solo which he rendered in a clear strong voice, 'his missing teeth adding to the attraction'. After that he sang for them in Hausa. The people down there call him 'sarkin Hausa', which means 'chief of the Hausas' because he knows the language so well. Very often he is found in the kitchen talking with the Hausa help who enjoy him a lot.

"Lanny is just as good and cute in his own way. The folks sent him a t-shirt and overalls for his birthday along with some candy. That day we had visitors and he very unselfishly passed out his candy without anyone asking him to and it left him only two pieces. He didn't seem to mind or even notice that he would have very little left if he shared the candy, even though he is fond of it. During rest hour yesterday while Burt and I were reading in the parlor and he was supposed to be resting, he put on his new clothes all by himself, then presented himself to us with a hesitating, questioning, 'If you would like to see me . . .' We took a picture of him in the new clothes today and have put them away for best, which will probably be for the trip home.

"We leave Maradi on the 20th of June. We will meet Rollie there. School is out on the 16th. We plan to spend a day or two in Paris, then continue our flight. Probably be in N.Y., the 25th or 26th. After medical check-ups, home by train from N.Y.

Our last letter home before furlough was May 5, 1954. We were anticipating furlough so much, I could hardly wait. But no matter what I did or thought, each day had 24 hours in it—I couldn't change that. In a way, the days went by slowly, but in another way, they sped by rapidly. There was never a dull moment. Our new Field Director, Ray and Evelyn Davis paid us a visit. They were touring the fields by mission plane in Nigeria and French West Africa. The pilot was Joe Swanson.

"We've had a lot of trouble lately with our 'boys'. Ten days ago the Kapps were here for the week-end, and they are stationed in Maradi, a large town, where wages are high and competition from government officials is keen for services of boys. Kapps' boy got our boys all keyed up with the idea that they should be making more money than they are out here in the bush. So Monday morning 5 of them walked off the job on strike. The strike on their part was a failure since all didn't go. Our cook went, but houseboy and small boy stayed. The main hospital boy left but there was the flunky that remained. The Truaxes were left with one boy and so were the girls. So we weren't stranded. All of the boys were professing Christians and all have returned one by one during the week except our cook and asked for their jobs back. The Truaxes took their cook back and let the other two go since they had too many boys anyway, and the hospital boy is back. Our cook has sent word that he will come back for a 75 franc increase in wages, but we have sent word that it's all right if he doesn't come back, we will manage without him these last few weeks. All our water carriers didn't show up either, so we've had to find new ones which has been inconvenient but not too difficult. Won't it be nice to be back home again where we don't have to worry about boys and water carriers and the likes of them! I wish we could take our 'small boy' home with us. His name is Sha'aybu—about 12 years old—and he takes care of Johnny and Cherry quite well, waters the flowers, sweeps the house, folds washed clothes and does other odd jobs. He's a real nice boy—a professing Christian, and a relative of Dau Duka's. Bible School is out and Dau Duka is back with us and preaching on Sundays and witnessing in the hospital and villages.

"Johnny had a dizzy spell about 10 days ago—a little too much sun. He is very fair with light blue eyes—even fairer than Rollie. Lanny and Cherry are very dark. They tan easily. Although their hair is light, their eyes are dark brown like Burt's. Johnny reminds us of Rollie in many ways, although he is more of a comic than Rollie. He runs everywhere instead of walking. He turns round and round in the middle of the room until he is so dizzy he falls over. Then he gets up and does it over again. He is quite the boy."

And on this note, the saga of our first term has come to an end. That is to say, our letters home stopped. Because who writes letters when you are face to face with the recipients? So from now on starting with our trip home and ending with our return trip a year later, I must rely on my memory, and that may not be exact. I have seen in going through all these early letters that some things that I had thought were accurate were not exactly so, but since I had the letters in front of me, I couldn't deny the truth. So, as I recall—

We made our way to Maradi in our own car, which we left there to be sold. (It sold!) We met Rollie there as planned. (What joy!) On June 20, we flew from Maradi to Niamey. We were booked on Air France all the way home to N.Y. Burt had asked that we be allowed to switch to an American line in Paris, but the French would have none of it. That same night we flew out of Niamey enroute to Paris. The flight originated elsewhere so there were not six seats together, even though we had booked five together. (Johnny rode free.) There we were—7 yr. old Rollie by himself, 5 yr. old Lanny next to a Frenchman, Cherry next to Burt, and Johnny on my lap. Burt asked the steward to please ask others to move so the family could be together, but he said it was impossible. Lanny was not a good traveler, even in cars. On our ascent, he vomited, not only over himself but over the Frenchman sitting next to him, who stood up and yelled at the steward, "Mon

Dieu, get this family seats together!" Suddenly, the steward found that it WAS possible, and we were together

We had several hours lay-over in Paris, which allowed us to clean up and visit with our English friends that we had met during our 10 months in Paris, Dave and Pat Cole. They came to the airport to see us. They were English, doing Christian work in Paris. It was a joy to see them again. During the interlude, Burt went over to the TWA office and arranged to have our flight changed to TWA. Served Air France right!

Our flight from Paris to N.Y. was a long 18 hours. We landed first in Shannon, Ireland for refueling. One reason that we wanted to fly on an American plane was because we knew it would be less crowded than a French flight from Paris to N.Y. TWA had come over full but would not be full going back. And we were right. We each had a bank of 5 seats so we could stretch out and sleep. Our next stop was Boston for refueling and finally we landed in N.Y. It is hard to describe the feelings associated with standing on American soil after five years away. I wanted to stoop down and kiss it but had too much baggage and too many kids to look after.

Medicals taken care of, we made our way to the train station and arrived in Chicago on schedule. What a happy reunion that was! The Longs, the Buenemans, Aunt Agnes, the Hennixes and I don't remember who else, were there to meet us. Even now as I recall and write this, I get a lump in my throat and tears in my eyes. It was so wonderful! We learned later that Aunt Agnes cried when she saw us because we were so skinny. We didn't think we looked so bad, because we were used to ourselves, but apparently Burt being 125 lbs. and I, being 100 lbs., was hard to handle. Well, that didn't last long. Two weeks later, we had both gained more than ten pounds! Our first days were spent with Fran and Bill at 216 Gary Ave. in Wheaton until the house we were to occupy at Seminary and College was available. One chapter in our lives was closed, and we began a new chapter.

PART III

Chapter 1

FIRST FURLOUGH

Once upon a time there was a young lad who, with his parents, was attending a missionary conference in their church. The lad was so impressed with the "real live missionaries", the curios, the stories, the decorations, the music, the challenges, he said to his parents, "When I grow up I'm going to be a missionary on furlough!"

Yes, furloughs were exciting, and our first one was even more so, because this furlough business was new to us! We did not anticipate all the good things that came our way by all the nice people who loved us and were interested in us and our ministry. We moved into our house in Wheaton, and spent the rest of the summer adjusting to the American culture and getting ready for the Fall season. Of course, we went to Camp Awana for a few weeks and we went in to the Center each Sunday for services, because the Center was our church and had been supporting us faithfully from the very beginning of our missionary career, starting with our time in Paris. And of course, we spent time with our loved ones, which was the best of all.

I was so hungry for real Christian fellowship with people who were a part of our culture and enjoyed the same things we enjoyed that I remember fighting to hold back the tears as we sat in the Sunday services at the Center. We heard the choir sing and Doc preach, and not just on my first furlough but on all the others, tears of happiness would run down my cheeks. Words cannot express the feelings that welled up in my chest and throat. I devoured every service to begin with, and then, you know, I got used to it, and sort of took all these good things for granted again until the time got close to leaving it again. Furloughs were not all fun and games.

Speaking was not my forte, but I had to learn how. In most churches I didn't have too much to say because Burt was the speaker and I was given about 5 minutes to "tell all that I did in Africa for the last four years." That in itself was a challenge. What do you say in five minutes that is meaningful and paints a picture of life in Galmi? It would have been easier to have 30 minutes. I did get my 30 minutes in women's meetings and Sunday School classes. But people did not know me for who I was. I was always the "wife of Dr. Long." I can remember times when we visited churches that supported us when after the meeting, people would surround Burt with questions and admiration while I stood alone in the back of the church waiting for him. Sometimes, there was not even an acknowledgement that "his wife" was with him.

But that was not the case in our home churches, the Center and Elmwood Park Bible Church. The latter was an offshoot of the Center, and Bob Swanson, who had so faithfully worked along with Lance Latham at the Center, became the first pastor. Bob was a special friend and he was best man at our wedding. So the Elmwood Park Bible Church was like a second home church to us and they had some of our support for many years, too. They had the best missionary conferences. They lasted two weeks, and were filled with testimonies, messages, prayer, suppers, dinners, slides, movies, women's luncheons, panel discussions and wonderful music. Pastor Bob was a master of detail and had the programs worked out to the minute. Then there was always the "faith promise" offering. It was there that we met missionary colleagues—the Larry and Jean Johnsons, the Dyes, the Periks, with New Tribes Mission, and many others, some of whom we are in touch with yet. The women of the Church had a morning every month given over to sewing for missionaries, and I attended when possible and received many beautiful things for me and the children. Mrs. Alma Johnson was the Bible teacher, and at noon a lovely lunch was served by the women. There was never a more loving, caring group of people than we found at the Elmwood Park Bible Church.

Friends of ours whom we met in St. Louis, Mark and Jane Andrews, gave us their Studebaker for our use on furlough. Mark and

Jane are both in heaven, but their son and daughter still live on earth. Adrianne married Bill Leslie who was long time pastor of Elm St. Church near Moody Bible Institute in Chicago. He died several years ago, and she has since married Bernie Cozette, a college classmate of mine.

School started around Labor Day for Rollie and Lanny. Rollie was going into 2nd grade and Lanny, into kindergarten on our first furlough. Holmes school was on the other side of Wheaton College, on Howard St., so it was about a 20 minute walk for the boys. Burt took the boys to school the first day. Lanny panicked when he realized that Burt had left him and cried and was an unhappy boy that first day.

Now that school was in session, Burt went on a number of trips alone or with Mr. Tanis, our SIM rep in the area. For the most part, I stayed at home with the children, but sometimes we would pile all the kids in the car and go. On one of these occasions, we all traveled to Port Huron, MI where we ministered in the Wadhams Baptist Church. We stayed in the home of Roger and Carol Wilson and their three children who were close in age to ours. Their home was in the process of being built and they were living in the basement at the time. We became close friends of the Wilsons and Ralph and Wanda Conlan. Carol has since died and Roger married Zola, and Ralph has died and Wanda remains a widow and lives in Florida. We still keep in touch with the Wilsons and Wanda.

Once when we were traveling as a family we stopped at a restaurant for a meal. During the meal, a woman who was leaving the restaurant came up to us and complimented us on how well behaved our children were and gave each of them a large candy cane. It was around Christmas time.

Christmases were always exciting. People lavished gifts on the children and the kids loved it. Relatives and church people! They felt sorry for the kids and showered them with gifts to make up for Christmases past and future. The children never felt sorry for themselves before and wondered why people should feel sorry for them, but they loved every minute of it. Special friends were Olga and Henry Staalsen who brought gifts the first Christmas. They remained friends until their deaths.

March came along and so did Suzanne Jeanne. She arrived on March 15, 1955, just nine months after our furlough began. She was born in Elmhurst Hospital and Dr. Brumme was my obstetrician. I believe it was a Wednesday night or early Thursday morning, because Burt left me for a few hours while I was in labor to go to prayer meeting at the Center and got back before the actual delivery. She weighed 7 lbs. 15 oz. Burt's Mom came out to Wheaton to care for him and the children while I was in the hospital.

The last months of furlough were hectic. We purchased clothes, cans of dried fruit and vegetables, medicines, shoes. Will Brunk, who worked for a shoe company in St. Louis, helped us get shoes for five kids for four years at a discount. We figured on a dozen pair for each child in graduated sizes. That meant 60 pairs of shoes, not including shoes for Burt and me. We bought or were given clothes from sizes one to twelve. These were packed into drums in the basement and stacked over at the Tanis' house in preparation for shipping to the docks. We had to return borrowed furniture and supplies. We packed our accompanying baggage suitcases—14 (2 each per ticket). Included in them were dozens of cloth diapers. These would have to be washed enroute. It was before the day of disposable diapers. Getting to the airport on time was always a hassle. It took several cars—the Buenemans', the Hennixes and friends', but we made it. On Sept. 14, 1955, we flew to New York and were met and taken to the mission headquarters at 164 W. 74th St. It was there that we caught our breath.

S.I.M., New York—"This morning as I was dressing the baby after her bath and Burt and the other kids were out, I realized that I was relaxed and not rushed for the first time in weeks. What a good feeling!"

We sailed the next day aboard the French liner, S.S. Flandre.

"The fifth day on board. It is still rough. We have had three stormy days after two very calm days. Waves are like mountains, and the ship rocks up and down, back and forth ceaselessly. Everything is secured fast—furniture and equipment. Dishes are fastened down. Ropes are tied throughout the boat to assist in walking. The waves must break at a height of about 25 feet. No rain. Just wind and rough seas. As we look out the portholes the boat bends to meet the rising waves. Then to the other side. And back once more. All of us are well. Mrs. Saulnier told me that she would make it a special matter of prayer that I wouldn't get seasick. Her prayers have been answered, but I didn't refuse the Bonadoxin either."

"We have nice accommodations. Three double bunk beds, closet space, shower, two sinks, two chairs, writing table and adequate floor space. It is really deluxe for tourist class. We are sleeping until 10:00 each morning, eating two meals a day plus afternoon tea. The usual French cuisine—consisting of umpteen courses—but good! It takes an hour to eat.

"Sue is behaving beautifully. The kids are getting along fine. Rollie and Lanny have found playmates and the corridors are excellent places to play cowboys, etc. Cherry and Johnny are familiar with the surroundings, so they come and go freely. Four days in London. Then to Kano, Nigeria."

We were surprised to find that we were docking in the English Channel outside of Plymouth. It was 1:30 p.m. We were met there by a British scow and were lifted on to it. A ten minute ride brought us into the Plymouth harbor. It took until 5 p.m. to go claim our baggage and go through customs and immigration. Then we boarded the "boat train" to London. It was a four hour ride to London—225 miles. We had supper on the train, and it was after that that Lanny got his finger crushed in a door on the train. I don't remember how it happened, but I think there was a man involved some way and he was very sympathetic. You'll have to ask Lance. He probably remembers. He was a brave boy although there were tears. He lost his nail. We were met at the train station in London and spent four days at our mission home in London. One thing I remember about London was riding the double decker buses.

Our flight to Kano was on B.O.A.C. It took almost 14 hours from London to Kano. The same flight today takes 6 hours. I guess we stopped some place along the way—probably Marseilles—for a few hours, but I don't remember.

So our first furlough was over. We left behind our loved ones who cleaned up the mess we left and finished returning borrowed things, but we carried with us precious memories and did our best to choke back our tears as we said good bye once again to those we loved. Partings were never easy; in fact they became harder as the years passed when we left our own children, one by one as well as extended family.

—

Chapter 2

BACK AT GALMI

Separation came too soon. We arrived in Kano and had one evening together before the boys were flown off to Jos. Rollie knew what he was getting in to, but it was new to Lanny and he was bewildered and we all had a hard time saying good-bye. But word came soon from Jerry Craig that the boys were doing fine and happy.

The rest of us spent a couple of weeks in Nigeria. On our furlough, John Jess of Chapel of the Air called and said if we wanted to go to the port of New Orleans, collect and drive it back home, we could have a 1954 Chevy station wagon that had been designated for a missionary (Miss Flowers?) in South America but that country had denied its entrance. The car had been sitting on the docks deteriorating for several months. It had been purchased by the listeners of Jess's program for this particular missionary lady, but with her permission, he was able to deflect it to us. What an answer to prayer! So while Cherry, Johnny, Sue and I stayed in Kano, Burt flew down to Lagos to pick up the car and drive it back to Kano. We spent our time in Kano buying supplies, and the day after Burt got back, we headed back to Galmi via Maradi. We arrived "home" exactly one month to the day that we left Wheaton. It was good to be back again. Fortunately, the weather was not bad; it was the beginning of the cold season—cold and dirty with harmattan. Everybody was glad to see us, and Burt started work at the hospital almost immediately.

Letters from the boys came regularly. They were in and out of the hospital with minor illnesses, but on the whole they were doing well. We could hardly wait until Christmas vacation. Meanwhile, the three little ones were having their bouts with tonsillitis and colds. Cherry and Johnny played well together, and Sue at eight months was pulling herself up in the play pen. We were all looking forward to Christmas.

But alas, our loads had not come so there were no Christmas presents for the children. Our best Christmas present was to have the boys home with us for two weeks. We loved every minute of it. The first three months at K.A. had done them a world of good.

"New Year's Eve, 1955 They were a bit more subdued and considerate . . . For presents, we dug into our old toys and came up with some gifts. We managed to find some puzzles that had only a few pieces missing. We wrapped them up. Also some Pick Up Sticks, Dominos and Snakes and Ladders. Some caps (for guns) padlocks, tablets of plain paper, books . . . and Rollie and Lanny were quite happy with their gifts. For Cherry we found a coloring book that hadn't been used, and I made her dolly a new dress, diaper and blanket, a colored bag for all her trinkets and she was quite pleased. Johnny took the prize. When he opened up the same mouth organ (harmonica) we gave him for his birthday, his eyes popped open wide, he held it up and proceeded to exclaim about its wonderful qualities. He at once started to walk around the house and blow it. He was also just as pleased to get an animal book which he and Cherry had been reading since our return. He is a real card, that boy. Sue enjoyed playing with all the strings that came off the packages.

"Christmas eve afternoon we had a party for the black people with games and races. It was intended mostly for the Christians and those who work for us, but by the time it was over, there were about 70 people here. We served them peanut brittle, limes, donuts and peanuts. When we women raced, I was out in front and my shoe came off and I went flying onto the cinder road and banged up two hands, two knees, one elbow and leg.

"Sunday evening as Lanny was undressing, I heard him singing the tune of 'God Has Blotted Them Out'. When I got closer, his version turned out to be 'God has blood in the mouth.' When I corrected him, he insisted that 'that's how they sing it at K.A.'.

141

"On Wed. afternoon, we went up to Tahaoua to visit the Zebs and stayed until Thurs. afternoon. The Lees were there building, taking the place of the Darlings, who were still at home in the States."

Speaking of the Darlings, they had another baby, Carolyn. We heard that she had been ill and hospitalized. At five months she was diagnosed with a tumor on her throat. Surgery was done and she recovered. About this same time, Paul Clapp, who was with us studying in Paris as a single man, died of a brain tumor. He had since married and left his wife and two small children. Earl Playfair, son of Guy Playfair, died of a stroke at age 37. He left his wife, Jean, and their three small children.

The two weeks of Christmas sped by too fast and we all left early one morning to get to Maradi with the boys so they could join the others going to Kano with Mr. Kapp.

"Rollie was glad to go but Lanny's last words were, 'I wish I didn't have to go back.' His main complaint was that mommy and daddy weren't there.

"Sue has two teeth now. Johnny is so comical in everything he does and says. He pronounces his 'or's' as 'oy's' ('more' becomes 'moy'). When Burt went out on the motorcycle one afternoon, he said, 'Now not me have a daddy any moy.' Then if he doesn't have a fork at his place, he'll say, 'Me get my foyk, can I'?"

Hospital work continued with no let up. Besides the routine, one man came in with elephantiasis of the scrotum. It hung down and touched the ground. The only way he could walk was to gather it up in his riga and carry it. We operated on it and he recovered but he was impotent after that. Not that he wasn't impotent before that! It weighed 28 lbs.

Another case was a not yet two year old child who had burned her foot two months earlier. By the time she came to the hospital, her foot was just a dangling mess of dead flesh, tendons and bone. We amputated at the ankle, but because of the neglect of her parents, she was minus a foot.

January 1956 signaled conference time again, so we made our way to Maradi for a few days. Conferences were always enjoyable. They were times of fellowship with other Niger missionaries that we didn't see from year to year, and there was usually a special speaker from overseas who came to speak and encourage the missionaries. It was also a time to air our mission business and strategies for reaching the people of Niger, mostly Muslims. It was at this conference that the shocking news came of the murder of the 5 missionaries by the Aucas. Two of the men were Wheaton grads, Nate Saint and Ed McCully, about the class of '49. I did not know them, but I knew their brothers, who were there in my time. They were Dale McCulley and Phil Saint. Phil was a chalk talk artist and later became a missionary to Japan. Two of the other martyrs were Fleming and Roger Youdarian. I can't remember who the fifth one was, and I'm not sure about Fleming. Here at Wheaton, the football field is named McCulley field and there is a dorm called Saint Hall. Nate's widow, Marge, later married Abe VanderPuy. I am reminded that before these men were martyred in Ecuador, five other men were martyred in Bolivia from New Tribes Mission. They did not get the publicity that the later five did. The wife of one of the martyrs, Jean Dye Johnson has written a book about their ordeal. Her first husband was Bob Dye. Along with him was Cecil Dye and three others. Cecil's son, Paul, is a missionary with New Tribes today, and he has an exciting story to tell about his and his airplane's capture and escape from guerillas in Colombia. There is also a video about it.

After that little parenthesis of history, I'll get back to Galmi after the conference. Our loads had come. Included were my pump organ and cans and cans of dried food and preserves. "We shall have to tear down our barns and build bigger ones." Well, we did have our store room behind the house and soon the shelves were filled with all our goodies. We didn't lack for food this term. Also, Christmas presents came, not only for the Christmas that had just passed, but also for Christmases to come. Most of these were stored in drums in the storeroom along with clothes that the children would grow into. Each member of the family had a drum, and as Christmases and school openings rolled around, we went "shopping"—out to the storeroom and into the drums. Boxes and boxes of new shoes were stacked on the shelves, and one by one, they were used.

A big item for the kids came. It was the gym set including swing, teeter totter, glider and horizontal bar. Each of the kids had his turn on them, and when we finally left Galmi, the set went to the Husbands.

Feb. 5, 1956 Cherry has her buggy and a variety of dolls, but we still haven't come across her 'white baby'. Sue is surely cute these days.

She is crawling all over the floor and getting filthy but is very happy about it so we just let her crawl. Soap and water work wonders. Her hair is growing and clings to her head and is very pretty. We shall have to stop long enough one of these days to take some pix of her.

"In January we did 80 operations. With a 5 day operating week, that is 4 operations a morning besides almost a week off for conference. While I am in the hospital mornings Hawa (Eve) takes care of Suzanne and Cherry and Johnny either play at home or sit in one corner of the operating room.

"Wed. afternoon the French Colonel in charge of all medical things in Niger, plus a general and adjutant and captain, all doctors, visited and inspected the hospital. We had 2 hours advance notice of their intended visit. They were well pleased with what they saw. They were surprised to see a woman patient who came from Niamey for her cataracts to be removed, especially since the colonel with his big hospital and staff of doctors is from Niamey."

Since I mentioned Hawa above, I'll mention her husband, Jadi, who was working as my houseboy at that time. He was a pretty good worker, but he got into some trouble, I don't remember what it was, and we had to let him go. Sometime later, we heard that he had been killed. He was trying to hitch a ride on a road grader and somehow in getting on the moving vehicle, his foot slipped and he fell under the gigantic wheel and was crushed. I don't know what became of Hawa.

In March, the Africans had their conference at Tsibiri, so our whole family went. While Burt stayed at the conference with the three kids, the next morning our SIM plane came to Maradi to take me and Ruth Hunt to Jos, Ruth to go on holiday and I to go to Miango for dental work. The bad news was that I got a tooth pulled. The good news was that I was able to see Rollie and Lanny from 3:30 in the afternoon until 11:00 the next morning. I brought some belated Christmas gifts for them—each a tank, Sugar Creek Gang Book, Rollie a game, and Lanny some pencils. I had them excused from classes. They slept overnight in the rest home with me and ate with me at the big house. Next morning they rode with me in the Miango car to Jos where we said goodbye. They returned to K.A. with the car, and that afternoon I took the plane back to Kano, where I spent the night. Visited with the Hurshes. Next morning, I took a truck to Maradi. Then a Jeep ride to Tsibiri when Burt and the three little ones were waiting for me. Bad thing about seeing the boys was saying goodbye again, and I can understand Ruth (Frame) Van Reken's thoughts in her book when she almost didn't want to see her parents again because she knew it was just temporary—she would have to say goodbye again. Nevertheless, we took every opportunity we could to see the kids even though partings were hard.

"March 2, 1956 Rollie and Lanny saw the Queen and Duke when they went through Jos. They certainly have a good time at school and aren't missing a thing that the states offer and get many other things. Lanny still said, however, that he would rather have his mom and daddy there. Have you written to them?

"March 24 We celebrated Sue's birthday today with a cake. Last night a package with a doll came for Sue from the folks.

"April 8 Kent Academy had its field day against Hillcrest School in Jos. The boy that was in competition in the 12 and 13 year olds was sick so he couldn't run, so Rollie had to take his place. Out of six, he came in fourth, and everybody was really proud of him even though he didn't get a ribbon. Little Lanny slow-boy came through in his age group in a running race and got a ribbon. K.A. lost the meet though.

"Less than a week ago Sue started off on her own and has been going since. It surely is interesting to watch her throw her legs in front of her. She is doing very well, and it is a great relief to me to have her off the floor.

"Comments on the boys' report cards: 'Rollie continues to do good work. He is cooperative and pleasant in the classroom.' 'Lanny is a DEAR little boy. He is doing good work and is always conscientious and co-operative.' We got a big kick out of the 'dear'. We hope that Lanny's smile and big brown eyes don't do him more harm than good in later years. Cherry is standing here and says to tell you she is not biting her finger nails anymore. Johnny still sucks his thumb though."

About this time, Carey and Shirley Lees with their three children, Judy, 4 1/2, Jerry, 3, and Joanie—8 months, were stationed at Galmi. He was to take the Truaxes' place. Carey was a real maintenance man, and it wasn't long before he and his crew had laid the 900' of plastic pipe that we had brought out with our loads. He attached it to the lead pipe that we had already and all together, we had about 2500 foot of pipe. He fixed the pump and painted the cracks in the concrete tank, and we finally got running water in the house. The laborers pumped water from our well in the fadama into the 1400 gallon tank behind the chapel. Then he set up the wind mill that we had also brought out in our loads! Burt had gotten it from a farmer in Michigan. "You can't appreciate running water unless you've been without it." Some years later, during a rainy season, we heard a loud noise and a crumble. Upon investigating, we saw the tank a heap of rocks and clay. Back to square one!

"April 8, 1956 Zabriskies are going through on their way to Miango for holiday. About two years ago they were given a little half-caste baby—father a Frenchman in Tahoua—mother a Fulani—and they have been taking care of him ever since. They can't take him with them, so Yakubu is going to live with us for a month. There's always room for one more.

Yakubu (Hausa for Jacques) was a good boy. I recall one Sunday morning after the service, we were all standing outside the church for a bit, and a Frenchman came on the scene. On seeing Yakubu with us and our kids, he raised his eyebrows and had a smirk on his face, giving the impression that here was a missionary who had been indiscreet and has a little mulatto as a result. I don't know whether he was ever set straight or whether we ever saw him again. Yakubu grew to be an outstanding Christian and church leader both in the Maradi and Niamey area, and the Zebs who did not have any children of their own, certainly knew how to raise them. Another of their adoptees was Summai, who went into business for himself in Malbaza, has made a mark both in the business and Christian world. He has been a big help in settling hospital disputes, and although he has been offered the job of hospital administrator has refused to get that involved.

Chapter 3

NEW TOYS

Washing clothes my first term was never a problem for me. My houseboy took our clothes outside each morning and rubbed them on the washboard, rinsed them in the tubs, hung them up to dry, took them down and folded them. Pretty soft for me! But as the days and weeks and months went by, the clothes gradually took on the color of the desert, and I almost forgot what white clothes were supposed to look like. After four years of this, we decided it was time to get a washing machine. So we ordered a gasoline engine Maytag wringer washer and tubs on stands shipped out with our loads. When they came, we installed them in the storeroom with all our drums. I was elated. Strangely enough, having the washing machine meant more work for me. I wouldn't let the houseboy run it. Well, he still heated the water on three rocks outside, filled the machine and tubs, hung, took down and folded the clothes, but to put the clothes through the wringer? No way! I didn't want my precious machine to break right away. One whole morning out of my week was given over to washing clothes, but the whites did stay white.

We had to fill the gas tank with gasoline before each wash, and one day Cherry decided to help me, and before I got out to the storeroom she had taken a can of oil and poured some oil into the gas tank. I don't remember how I discovered it nor my reaction to it, but she got the message that she was never to do that again. We siphoned the oil out of the tank and cleaned it out with gasoline and siphoned it out again and the machine ran fine. The motor made a horrible noise though, especially since it was confined to the storeroom.

It was some years later when we had electricity at night that I got an electric machine. Then we kept it on the side porch—there was no electricity in the storeroom—and I washed clothes at night. I left them in the big white pans overnight for the houseboy to hang the next morning. Even later in our missionary career at Galmi we had electricity some mornings, so I was able to wash clothes in the morning. That's the saga of the evolution of washing clothes at Galmi. I often wondered if I should have just left the washing to the boy and let him scrub away every morning. It would have lightened my load. So what if the clothes turned gray!

The above paragraph alludes to the evolution of light at Galmi. Besides the blazing sun by day and the moon and star-studded sky at night, we were initiated into the world of lanterns, pressure lamps and Aladdin lamps. Except for the necessity of keeping the lamps filled and trimmed and the globes washed, it wasn't too bad. We hung one pressure lamp between the pantry and dining room, and we had lanterns in the kitchen and bathroom and when we went into the bedrooms we carried either a pressure lamp or Aladdin lamp. We had to watch the Aladdin lamps very carefully, because they had a tendency to smoke but they gave off a bright light. Most useful of course were the pressure lamps. They too gave a bright light but had to be handled with care lest the mantle tear. One drawback of these lamps in the hot season was the heat they generated.

Then came Wilf and Esther Husband to Galmi. Wilf was an answer to our prayers for a maintenance man, and he divided his time between maintaining the compound and trekking. One major accomplishment was installing our first generator. It was a diesel Lister from England and I can still see Wilf and the Africans rolling it on logs into the house built for it. This gave us light for 3 hours in the evening. Then we got a second generator and were able to increase our hours of electricity to mornings and evenings. Later we got new and bigger generators and had electricity for most of the day and night before we left Galmi in 1975. This sparked the purchase of ceiling fans for our homes, and some swamp coolers, and electric fridges and other appliances. We even tried air conditioners, but there were too many leaks in the windows to make them practical. If you were to

—

visit Galmi today you would see not one but several large generators at work providing electricity 24 hours a day. The maintenance of the generators requires a missionary and Africans full time just to keep them going.

Of course electricity enhanced the work in the hospital. In the early days, we used daylight for surgery, and any emergency surgeries at night meant the use of pressure lamps for general lighting, a miner's lamp for Burt's head and flashlights to get down into the "hole". During the period of time that we had regular evening hours of electricity, if there was an emergency during the night, Wilf got up and turned on the generators. That was real progress. And when we had it all night long, it was a boon to the patients and nurses and Africans who were on call at night.

Having electricity meant that we could use some electrical equipment, and year by year new machines were installed. There was a new x-ray machine, and when we couldn't get it to work because of a missing part or something, we had to rely on "Old Faithful", the used army surplus machine that we picked up in Paris and brought with us on our first trip. Today, there are modern overhead lights in the operating room and it is air conditioned. The use of modern equipment is routine. Strangely enough, some of the doctors and nurses are not happy with existing conditions. I wish they could have been with us from the beginning when we and the Zebs and Martha Wall and Aidie Raidt (Emmett), Gen Kooy and Ruth Hunt and Liz Chisholm and Jeanne Marie Berney and Joan Jackson and others were a part of the team.

For years we used our Servel kerosene operated refrigerator. It was there waiting for us when we arrived the first time. Each week Burt had to clean the wick and fill the tank with kerosene. The fridge worked like a charm. It provided us with cold water, ice, the ability to keep things in our freezer, and the ability to keep food from spoiling. Some folks who had Servels said they didn't like them, but ours worked perfectly and we used it until our final term at Galmi when we got an electric fridge, not because our Servel wasn't still doing yeoman service, but because it was a lot easier to operate and by that time, we had 24 hour electricity. It still worked well, and we sold it to the chief, Kadari. Burt showed him how to care for it, how to trim the wick every week, how to line it up properly and fill the tank, but he and his men didn't care for it properly and it died some months later.

Wood stoves were our chief and only means of cooking our first term. Along with our other appliances, we brought back a 3 burner kerosene stove with detached oven. Of course, the "boys" still used the wood stove, and I didn't want to part with it because along with cooking meals, it heated 3 big tea kettles of water and it boiled our milk. Routine for the boys was to let the milk boil over. It didn't matter too much on the wood stove, but it was not good for the kerosene stove. Mainly, I used the kerosene stove on Sundays when the "boys" didn't work or for special things I personally wanted to cook. I recall one incident with the kerosene stove. We were always in a battle with cockroaches and I will say that I did a pretty good job of keeping them down. One morning as I went to the kitchen to prepare breakfast (it must have been Sunday), I noticed a cockroach running around on top of the oven. So I lit the burners and watched while the oven started to heat. As it got hotter and hotter, the cockroach ran faster and faster. Unfortunately for him, he couldn't escape. Gradually he slowed down and eventually stopped and fell over. I loved every minute of watching its demise. The kids thought I was sadistic!

Then came the gas stove. That was great. Propane gas. We bought it in small tanks. Now I had three options. I still didn't want to part with my wood burning stove! In Jos later, I even cooked with my electric stove! But believe it or not, I kept my kerosene stove, took it to Jos with me and used it when the electricity was off, which was often.

Chapter 4

VAN LIEROPS

During our first term at Galmi, from 1950 to 1954, we met the Van Lierop family. Conferences and medical needs brought us together. They lived at Dogon Doutchi, about 125 miles west of us.

"April 28, 1956 Two weeks ago we got a wire from Dogon Doutchie. It was sent from the French Commandant in Dogon Doutchie to the Commandant in Madaoua who passed it on to Elvin Harbottle, who was stationed with his family in Madaoua. Elvin brought it out to us. It said that the doctor in Galmi should come urgently to Dogon Doutchie, because the pastor (Ben Van Lierop) had a stroke. So Burt and Gen Kooy and Carey Lees went immediately the 125 miles west, arrived about 8 p.m. Ben met them at the door. He has suffered from violent migraine headaches in the past, and this was one of his worst. When the African doctor and Commandant had come to visit him in the morning, he was somewhat irrational, and the African doctor said he didn't know what to do for him—better call the doctor from Galmi, so the Commandant sent this urgent wire. By the time Burt got there, his headache had subsided."

"This is the month of azumi–which means the Moslem fast. Nothing to eat or drink from sun–up to sun–set–not even to swallow saliva. Because of azumi, the 'fasters' don't swallow medicine, so we expected a drop in dispensary. However, it has kept right up over the 259 mark, and Wed., it was 290. The majority of the people don't keep the fast, as you can observe, although we did expect somewhat

---

151

of a drop. The surgery schedule is still right up there, and we have patients waiting in the hospital all the time for their turn to come.

"This morning Burt and Gen removed a tumor on a man's neck. It was very difficult since it was right on the carotid artery and other important blood vessels. It also went down deep toward the clavicle. It took two hours and Burt said it was one of the most difficult operations he has done. After that we only had time to do one hernia. Yesterday, Burt and I removed an eye from a little girl, did a hernia repair, and removed another neck tumor which wasn't so involved because it was in a little different place. Wed. A.M. Burt and Ruth Hunt removed 9 cataracts. As you can see, the three of us take turns scrubbing with Burt, circulating and dispensary.

"The Lees will be going on furlough in a year. Here's hoping we get the mechanical side of this station operating in that time. In the month they've been here, he has laid the entire pipe from the well to the houses and hospital and assembled the windmill. This past week, they carried the windmill frame down to the well—1/4 mile—and set the legs in concrete. He has two of the legs on hinges at the bottom. This morning, the boys—about 10 of them—carried the head of the windmill down on their heads. The plan is to let the frame down again, attach the head and then with the help of the car pull it back up again. With about 10 fellows, several guy lines, and the car, the windmill has been pulled up and it's a whirling now!"

The Van Lierop saga was just beginning. As it turned out, the situation was more serious than first thought. About a month later, May 15, 1956 two Frenchmen brought Ben and his wife Gwen and son John (4 yrs.). Ben was down again, and he rode in the back of the jeep on a mattress for about 6 hours. They arrived at 1:30 A.M. Next day Gwen and Johnny went back with the Frenchmen and Burt took a spinal pressure reading on Ben and found it to be twice normal which indicated pressure on the brain. That evening he took Ben on to Kano where he conferred with Dr. Whitmoyer (eye doctor) since Ben was seeing double. They called Dr. Troup in Jos and the three of them confirmed the diagnosis and booked him to London on tonight's plane. His wife is English, so if there is to be any brain surgery, it will be done in England."

The diagnosis was a brain tumor and yes, surgery was done in England, with deep x-ray therapy. Ben recovered sufficiently to return to Dogon Doutchie for several more years. But as tumors have a habit of doing, his returned, and this time the whole family picked up and went to the States and settled in Holland, MI, where Ben received further treatment. We were home on furlough in Chicago from July 1960 to Sept. 1961, and it was during that year that Ben had at least one more operation but went home to be with the Lord on Nov 5, 1960. After the funeral, Gwen came to visit for several days and we were able to be of some comfort to her. That was the beginning of a special relationship between us.

In due course, we all went back to Niger, we to Galmi and Gwen back to Dogon Doutchi and Maradi for many years and we became dear friends. When she needed a lift, she came to visit us, either at Galmi or in Jos or back in the States. She carried on the work that she and Ben had started, that of caring for boys who were given to them to raise. They fed and clothed them, sent them to school, taught them about the Lord, helped them to go on to higher education. There with the help of her African "boys," Gwen continued in her role. Her "boys" were her ministry. Most of these boys became Christian leaders. Most notable was Abdou who has grown up and carried on the work at Dogon Doutchie that the Van Lierops began back in the forties. One special boy that was given to them as a baby was a child they named Timothy. Timothy was a cripple and had to be carried about until the Van Lierops went to England with him and had him fitted with braces. He was the only one that they legally adopted, but all the boys were "their boys". As Timothy grew, he was fitted again and again with new braces. He went to Kent Academy for at least one year and African schools for the rest. He is fluent in English and French as well as Hausa. He is married, has children, and works at Galmi hospital.

Abdou, mentioned above, is a grandfather now. His daughter married Istafanus, (Isti), Gen Kooy's "son", whom she helped his mother raise. Isti was the son of Cisu, who died of an aneurism at Galmi. Gen financed all of Isti's education, from early days at Tsibiri and on through post high school work. Isti has a responsible job in Niamey.

We never knew when Gwen would show up at Galmi, usually with a medical need, and she was always welcome. During her many visits we got to know Gwen and her children well. She had many irons in the fire. She was not afraid to go to the officials in Niamey for special help for her "boys." When she left Dogon Doutchi in the capable hands of Abdou, she went to Maradi and established the leather factory there as therapy for and occupation for recovering leprosy patients. She took in girls in her home and was an inspiration to many young ladies. She funded school fees for many needy ones. When she was old enough to retire, she stayed on. There was no stopping Gwen.

She has retired in Toronto, but didn't slow down. She travels to many parts of the States including our homes in Wheaton and Sebring, visits England every year where her son John and his big brother Bernard, both married and with children, live. Muriel, married with children, lives in Toronto. In her eighties, Gwen came to Sebring and was the chief care giver of one of her fellow missionaries and co-worker, Marcia Mowatt, during her last weeks and final bout with cancer. She has touched many lives, and we have all become richer because of knowing her. She has traveled alone on Amtrak, bus and plane and done things that most of us would be afraid to do. Even now as she reaches her 90th birthday, she is still active. The Lord has been her stronghold. We congratulate her on this milestone and praise the Lord with her for His grace to her over the years.

"It certainly is wonderful to have the windmill up and going. We have all the water we want and hot showers any time of the day, and we can flush the toilet twenty four times a day instead of four. The water comes through the pipes almost boiling (in the hot season—cold in the cold season). We have to go down to the well to open and shut the windmill at least twice a day. It's a quarter of a mile down. Last night after supper and in the dark I went down on the motorcycle to put the brake on. I almost reached the well and ran out of gas, and also when the motor stops the light goes off. So remembering what Burt did when he ran out of gas one time, I laid the cycle down and let the gas from one chamber accumulate in the other. It started (to my surprise) and I got down to the well and almost back. Had to push the cycle the last 50 yards. Burt insisted that he could have gotten all the way home on it, and much to my chagrin, he started it this morning, and rode it around the compound to show me before he filled the tank. Well, we do enjoy the motorcycle. Better stop now. It's supper time."

Chapter 5

THE YEAR 1956

You will recall that in Chapter 2 the Zebs left Yakubu with us for a month while they went on holiday. Well, the Zebs returned at night after Yakubu was in bed and asleep.

"June 4, 1956 . . . it was very funny to watch his reaction to them. It took him awhile to warm up to them, altho he knew them, but he was awfully shy and hung on to my skirts for awhile. However, after breakfast was over, he warmed up to them. When they packed up to go in the afternoon, he wasn't sure whether he was supposed to go with them or stay with us. He hung on to me, torn between the desire to get into the Jeep and have me hold him. Then when we gave him to Irene and she put him in the Jeep, he was very happy.

"Just before dark last week, there was a big noise across the street from the hospital and people came from every which way. Soon a boy on a bike came racing and said a car with a white man and the black customs man and his wife had gone over the bridge into the gully, a drop of about 6 ft. The car turned around and the occupants were quite shaken up . . . . The driver was drunk. The three of them were on the way to say good-bye to Gen who left last Tues. We treated them in the hospital for their bruises, the douanne and his wife went to their house and the Frenchman came home with us, had a little supper with us and Burt took him up to Tahaoua where his home and business are. He was very sick, partly because of his being drunk and partly because of his accident. The douanne was in church Sunday

---

155

a.m. the first time in several months. This morning I saw his wife and asked if she and their four little girls would come next week, and she said they would. Perhaps this accident will have some good from it."

With Gen gone for her first furlough we were short handed and her replacement wasn't due for a couple of months. But with the rainy season approaching, we were hoping that the patient load would be lighter. Also with the rainy season approaching, we were preparing to go to Sokoto to pick up Rollie and Lanny. SIMair was to fly them there. We hoped we could get through because just two miles out of Sokoto we had to cross the Sokoto river. If the rains had started we wouldn't get across. So close and yet so far. Most of the year it was a dry gulch, but during the rainy season it was impassable. It wasn't until years later that a bridge was built. We were to combine the trip with a visit to the Leprosarium where Burt held a clinic every three months. "If there were only some way of knowing before we rode the first 78 miles, over bad roads, a trip of 5 hours!"

In the meantime, problems with our Christians! Tanko had made a profession of faith, had studied a little and was taking his turn at preaching in the hospital waiting room. He didn't know much, but at least he was able to give his testimony and share the basic way of salvation. Well, Tanko was accused of having impregnated a village girl, but he emphatically denied it. However, when the girl's father came he finally confessed that he did sleep with her three times but that was about 3 months ago. It turns out that she was 3 months pregnant, so he didn't have a leg to stand on. "The thing was brought to the chief for judgment, and he is supposed to pay a fine of 1250 francs if he doesn't want to marry her, or if he wants to marry her, pay the full price (about 5000 francs). The church has disciplined him for 6 months—i.e., he is not supposed to preach or pray in public . . . that puts a greater load on Dau Duka."

"This morning two more of our believers had a free-for-all. Mamman, the girls' houseboy and his wife, Salama! As is the custom in this culture, they are living with his people. She has a well-known temper and his people, all of them unbelievers, goad her on, even beat her if they feel inclined to do so . . . . Salama and her mother-in-law and sister-in-law had a good fight, then Mamman ran home from the girls' house and beat her up. Now he wants to divorce her. That should make his family happy. We have urged Mamman to move away with his wife from the village and live somewhere else many times, but he can't stand to leave his family (It's a cultural thing} . . . . Salama is all ready to go home, but this evening we urged her to wait a few days at least. Her home is about 30 miles away. All of these palavers have a way of getting us down. Satan is working overtime to destroy the Christian testimony in the village."

"June 30, 1956 We were quite excited about meeting Rollie and Lanny. They came into Sokoto on Tuesday morning by commercial air instead of our mission plane . . . . We left Sue in the car sitting in the car seat. Lanny asked, 'Who is that other little girl in the car?' Sue is quite grown up and plays with the other kids, and as she gets older, her care becomes less. Rollie and Lanny have changed. We sing the praises of Kent Academy very high. They are both avid readers. We are amazed at Lanny's ability to pick up any book and read it. In two weeks time they have each read a half dozen books. Lanny says he is 'tie with the smartest one in first grade.'

"We have had some terrible wind and dust storms . . . . One picked up some kids at the well and carried them a mile to another village. Altho the house is shut up as quickly as possible, the dust seeps under doors, through cracks and broken windows. It takes a day to dig out and it is very discouraging. But they will be less and less as the rains increase . . . . the people have begun to plant.

"This past week Rollie has been suffering with an ear ache. He has had penicillin for about 4 days without much relief and yesterday we gave him pen and streptomycin. He seems some better this morning. Rollie and Lanny have planted peanuts, and with their harvest will have (spending) money to take back to K.A. They are also doing many things around the house which bring them spending money. There is nothing to buy here so they will have it to take back to school.

"We have a motorcycle—125 BSA. Last time Burt was in Kano, he ordered me a motor bike, and it has arrived. (A Lambretta if I remember correctly.) It is lighter than the cycle and easier to handle. Lanny and Rollie have inherited my conventional bike. I have been riding the motorcycle and like it a lot, too, but am just as glad to have the motor bike.

"July 17, 1956 I HAD a motor bike. Burt taught Rollie how to ride it, and now I don't have it anymore. I HAD a bicycle. Lanny has taken that over. I still have two legs, praise the Lord. In order to ride my motor bike I have to sign up hours in advance. We emptied our first tank of gas. The tank holds 3 liters, and we got 80 miles on less than a gallon.

"About 10 days ago Sue began to break out with sores around her mouth. They spread all over her face, arms, legs, body. We painted her with gentian violet, and shot her with pen for 3 days. (That was before the days of oral pen, and the kids really hated those shots. I can't say that I blamed them. They were awful. It broke my heart to hear them cry with the miserable shot with the big needle.) The g.v. has done well by drying up the existing ones, but new ones crop up every day. The pen didn't seem to be doing anything for her, so we discontinued it. 'Did you ever see a purple cow? I never hope to see one. but I can tell you anyhow, I'd rather see than be one.' Sue is a spotted purple cow."

Water was always a problem at Galmi. We tried everything we could to find good water on our compound but to no avail, So we had to go down to the fadama (lowlands) and build a well. The well was solid, made with concrete rings, The workers made rings about 6 ft. in diameter and about a ft. deep. They then laid it in the hole, then added ring after ring which sank the ones underneath until the well was lined all the way down with concrete rings. In the fadama the water was only about 20' down. Then we covered it and put a hand pump on it. When the boys pumped the water for the first time, the elders from Guzarawa who were watching exclaimed, "Ikon Allah." (Power of God!)

Another innovation of ours was to build cisterns to catch the rain water. We built one for our house and the Truaxes' house and the hospital. Ours was just west of the house outside the kitchen and pantry. It was about 8' deep and about 10 x 8 ft. square. An empty drum with both ends cut out provided the entrance into the cistern and we built a wooden cover with a lock on it. The entrance of the cistern was just the diameter of the drum, so it was dark down there. Our eaves troughs directed the water into a down spout that went into our cistern. They worked for awhile. One day we opened up the cover to the hospital one and found that three walls had caved in. That was the end of that one. Our cistern lasted longer than the rest, but eventually, they all died. Our boys liked to go down into the cistern and swim during summer holidays. We used both rope and ladder for the descent and ascent. One time Rollie was going down and just as he touched the water he spied a snake in the far end. He shot up out of the cistern faster than a jack rabbit. "A snake, a snake!" Apparently the snake had fallen into the cistern and had been swimming for a long time so was very tired. Burt got the rake and tied a rope to it and let it down. Immediately the snake grabbed for it and he pulled it up and disposed of it properly. What the snake thought was his salvation became his demise. Is there a moral to that story? I think that was probably the last time the boys swam in the cistern. The one at the Truax house caved in and eventually we quit using ours because the water was slowly leaking out and when we needed the water in the dry season, it was all gone. Nothing ventured nothing gained.

Another effort that didn't get off the ground was the tower that we built behind the chapel. That was the highest ground on the compound, so we built a tower that was at least as high as the church. The idea was to put a tank on top of it in which to store water. Then water would flow down to the houses and hospital by gravity. On our furlough the tower cracked.

"For the past month our mason repaired the tower and added 3 more feet to it to increase the pressure flow. It was all set to have the tank raised—the tank holds 350 gallons. One night last week we had a terrific storm; the next morning after breakfast, there was a terrific thud, and in 10 seconds the tower was completely down. Nothing but rubble . . . . Fortunately, the tank was never raised. More fortunately, no one was near it when it came down. We have abandoned the tower project."

While all these water projects were going on, we were still relying on tulus, clay water pots, that hung in rope saddles slung across the backs of donkeys to bring us water and keep our drums filled. Back to basics. Little by little pipe was laid from the well to the houses and hospital and the day came when we just had to turn on a tap to get water. We built a platform just off the dining room porch and put a drum on it and filled it each day for water for the bathroom and kitchen. In the kitchen, we also made sure that we had two drums filled each day for general use, and there were two or three drums outside the storeroom in the yard which we used for watering our garden. We struggled with a garden, and although it never paid for itself, it was good to get an occasional crop of corn, tomatoes, green beans, melons and papayas—not all at once and not all in the same year. Fresh garden produce did provide occasional spice to our monotonous diet of rice, onions and goat meat. Speaking of meat, a little beef was showing up in the market occasionally. When a cow was on its last legs, it made the ultimate sacrifice, and with the help of the pressure cooker and spices, we enjoyed beef, especially thin slice filets. In later years, beef was always available and we bought it by the chunks. We cut it up the way we wanted it, in roasts, steaks, stew or hamburger. Our trusty meat grinder served us well, but without Issou or Yahaya or whoever, the grinder wouldn't have had a chance to prove its worth.

Speaking of grinders, we had a grist mill set up in the storeroom and the "boy" ground our wheat for us. He put it through several times, so we had fine wheat cereal (kunu) for breakfast every morning. In rare cases, we had cold cereal on Sunday mornings. We bought a box or two in Nigeria when we visited down there. The price of the cold cereal was exorbitant so we didn't indulge too often.

But I am digressing. Back to July 17, 1956.

It is 9 A.M., the temp. is 78, and it is black as night. I'm going to have to light the pressure lamp soon. The sky is black and cloudy, the wind is blowing, and it won't be long before the storm breaks on us. I'll let you know how much water we have in the cistern before I close. From where I sit I can see people running home from their farms, their hoes slung on their backs. We didn't do any surgery yesterday and nothing was scheduled for today, and there probably won't be many dispensary patients either. Here comes the rain! It's 9:15, the storm is over; the threat was worse than the rain. It is getting light again."

It was about this time that the government became very interested in the wages that the Africans were making. On the whole, most of the population did not have jobs. Most jobs available to them, outside of farming for themselves or becoming merchants on their own, were jobs with French or missionary employers who used them for houseboys, cooks, gardeners and laborers. True, we didn't pay much compared to our home country wages, but what they received each week was 100% more than the average person. Those who worked for us or the hospital were considered well-to-do and were envied. But the syndicate (Communist inspired union) influenced the government to double the wages of all workers, get one full day off per week, be paid over-time and severance pay.

"We can't fire the boys without 8 days' notice, plus severance pay which amounts to a month's wages for each year they have worked for us. In some instances, some of the workers have goaded our missionaries into firing them by refusing to do their work properly, just to collect severance pay which is retroactive in some cases for several years.

"The rain has stopped, but it is still dark and thundering so it looks like we'll have more rain. It surely is nice to have R. and L. home. They are at an interesting age in which they can enter into family life and enjoy the things we do instead of having to be taken care of. Judy Lees' birthday is Fri., the 20th, the same as Burt's, so they are having a party for her. She will be five.

"Our expenses have increased. Just getting the boys home from school cost about $50.00—four times a year amounts to $200.00, etc. Read about Dawson Troutman in Time."

More on the cistern:

"Aug. 6, 1956 Rollie and Lanny have been swimming in the cistern . . . . Last week the water was up to their thighs. Burt let them down and pulled them up by rope. They had great fun. Last night's terrific rain storm added enough to make it 33 inches high—up to their waists. But they haven't been able to go in. Last week they each got burns from the exhaust on the auto-bike, the blisters broke and they have had a bit of trouble with them.

". . . Sue also got a small burn on her leg when she touched the exhaust after one of our family rides. I wish you could hear her jabber. She is the only one who has carried on a real conversation that way. She says a whole paragraph, then stops and waits for an answer, then carries on again. She is very serious about it all.

"Johnny said to Burt last night, 'God cemented me up and made me white and gave me to you to take care of.' He is really a cute fellow. He is fast as lightening. He is taking his turn at praying at the table and is also praying at night. Cherry is like the little girl with the curl on her forehead. Sue grabs me by the skirt, leads me to the fridge and points to her bottle. It's time to break her of the habit but she does love it! (the bottle) Gen's replacement was Elizabeth Chisholm from Boston, complete with her accent that continues to this day, 40 plus

---

years later. Ruth Hunt and the Lees completed our missionary roster. Liz was stranded in Madaoua for two days because of rain and truck breakdown. Fortunately we had missionaries at Madaoua who took her in (either the Lucases or Harbottles).

The summer holidays were almost over, and we weren't looking forward to the boys' returning to K.A.

"Aug. 24, 1956, . . . we sure have enjoyed them. No discipline problems or anything like we have when they are home all the time. Everybody's sort of on good behavior and appreciating everybody else because we know the separation is coming."

I was down to my pre-furlough weight and Burt was down, too, but he still had some furlough insulation. I wish I could have kept some of mine, but that wouldn't happen until years later, and now I wish I hadn't kept so much. Ho-hum!

"Sue's impetigo is all gone, no scars. Yesterday she came in holding her vulva and crying. Took off her panties and there was a big black ant with his pincers clamped into her right labium . . ."

The schedule for the Fall included a trip to Kano in Oct. for Doctor's meeting, the annual conference at Maradi in November and a trip to Sokoto for leprosarium visit and pick up the kids for Christmas vacation. I went with Burt on all these trips. Also in December we were scheduled to take our third Hausa exam. We passed. I don't think they would have sent us home if we hadn't passed.

The harvest was good and it was a joy to see the Hausas bringing in their sheaves, mostly slung on donkeys' backs. We were teaching the Christians to give of their first fruits, so the front of the chapel was filling up with grain. The hospital work was increasing with patients coming now that the growing season and harvest were over. Hernias and hydroceles were routine. "We did a bladder stone on a four year old boy. I am down to 105 lbs. All the dresses I brought out hang like flower sacks."

It was time for our Kano trip: "Oct. 17, 1956 We arrived yesterday after an all day trip from Galmi—285 miles . . . . We will be here for doctors' conference today and then a week of leprosy conference. I'm going to write about 50 letters."

You know about best laid plans, don't you? About all those fifty letters I was going to write?

"Oct. 28, 1956 We have been through the wringer this week along with about thirty others, and a couple are still on the way through. Sun. night we had a delicious meal of potato salad, cold sliced beef, carrot jello, topped off by coconut cream pie. Some of the folks started vomiting and having diarrhea about midnight, others didn't go out of commission until Tues. morning. Burt was hit after breakfast Mon. morning, Cherry and I after dinner. Johnny was spared, but Sue had a diarrhea. Cherry and I had fevers. Cherry vomited and 'ran'; I 'ran' without vomiting. Burt did both but had no fever. Everything was shut down; conference collapsed for a day, language school was closed, and the two nurses available spent all their time ministering to the needs of the sick saints. Two were flown down to Jos, and one we hear was still on intravenous fluids two days ago. The doctor's wife here is still not up but is beginning to eat again. I wasn't hit too badly, but Burt and Cherry were in bed until Fri. morning. It apparently was the pie because Johnny didn't eat any pie and wasn't sick. One of the kitchen boys cleaned up a plate of left-over pie and was sick. The lab report came back, 'para typhoid' . . . Burt missed the last half of the conference . . . . He lost another 3 lbs. after having lost 5 lbs. at Galmi two weeks ago with malaria. He now weighs 122 lbs, less than when we went back home. The only ones who weren't sick were those who lived on the compound and had eaten supper in their own homes.

"Kano is wonderful. You can buy anything here. We bought Rollie and Lanny a two wheel bike for Christmas—24"—will they be thrilled! Fourteen British pounds! Red, thin tires, hand brakes, tire pump, tool case. Bought other Christmas presents of lesser value, too."

Our annual conference was a good time of fellowship, food and meetings with about 35 of our fellow missionaries.

"Nov. 16, 1956 Sue is really growing. Smart as a whip. Jabbers like an old woman and really thinks she's saying something when she looks into your eye and keeps up a steady stream of jabber. Johnny had his 4th birthday at the conference. He is so shy it is painful. When they sang, 'Happy Birthday' in the morning, he buried his face in my lap and wouldn't come up to finish his breakfast. At night when they brought his cake he behaved better because we warned him. He still sucks his thumb. We are shooting 100' of movie film (16 mm) of us and the kids at the conference. We bought the film and borrowed the camera from Gordon Bishop . . . . We all recovered from our food poisoning and are gaining back the weight we lost. I'm about 106 lbs. now and Burt has gained some back already."

Back at Galmi again and the hospital work continued to pick up steam.

"Nov. 28, 1956 I scrubbed with Burt this morning on 6 operations—3 hernias, 1 hydrocele, 1 lipoma and 1 fistulotomy. That took exactly 3 hours, an average of 30 minutes an operation, including all the transferring of patients and complete new set-up for each operation. In three days already this week we have done 15 operations. We can't keep up with them."

We spent afternoons painting our living and dining room walls. First term they were all white-washed; now we were getting the real thing done. We were painting the walls a pale blue. The last wall in the dining room was even paler blue because we had to keep adding water to the paint to stretch it. If nobody inquired, they figured it was the 'in' thing to have 3 walls one color and the fourth one another color. Next big job was to put down the tile in our rooms. What a difference it made.

Our Sokoto trip was coming up in December and we combined it with meeting our boys for Christmas holidays. Burt was to examine 600 leprosy patients, and we expected the boys to fly in (to Sokoto) on Thursday. A lot would depend on the harmattan.

"Dec. 12, 1956 Yesterday we did not see the sun and saw only about 200 yards in front of us. We are praying that the weather will clear so the planes will not be grounded and the kids will get home for their Christmas holidays . . . . We have the boys' reports for the first quarter. 'Lanny is making favorable progress in all subjects. I enjoy having him in my class.' 'Rollie does excellent work and is no problem in school. His bright sense of humor and innocent mischievousness make him a very likeable individual. He is the kind of pupil that makes a teacher want to stay in the profession.' R. has a man teacher; L., a woman.

"You should see Cherry. Johnny and Sue are still having their afternoon naps; Cherry doesn't sleep anymore, she just rests a little. She is playing with her white doll (to distinguish from her black doll). She has it on her back, and she just finished 'nursing' it. Took her dress off the shoulder and really gave it to her. Now she's buttoned up again. That sort of thing is so common here that Cherry thinks it is most natural to do. (Well, isn't it?)

"Rollie's letters are a scream and very interesting. He gets 100 in his spelling tests, but his spelling in his letters is abominable.

"I received the two dresses from Jeannette in our last mail . . . . Since our Kano spell of sickness, we have been in good health and gained back some weight. Burt is back to 128 and I to 105.

"We have done 50 operations in two weeks . . . everything from head to feet and in between. Have also been having some good meetings in the afternoon in the various compounds in the villages. Yesterday as I was in one compound, the women from the next compound over asked me to come over to their house. They are locked in their compounds since their husbands are strict Moslems. So today I visited them. Always there is the next compound over, and the same request, so I have been getting into them even though they cannot go out. Usually their husbands aren't there, but sometimes they walk in, and sometimes there is a bit of tension, but most of the times, the men are very friendly despite their religion and invite me back. They are glad to have their women hear. Such is not the case in big cities, and in Tahaoua, for example, where the Zebs are, when Irene has visited one compound one day, the door is shut to her the next because the husbands refuse her entrance.

"Our houseboy's day off was Mon., and he went to the next town (Dogoraoua.) This morning (Wed.) he turned up with the tale that his brother had died, and he had gone home and just got back. His home is 30 miles from here. We were disinclined to believe him since he has been caught in adultery. He is Jadi, the husband of Hawa, who takes care of Sue. We asked him to bring just one witness—just anyone, but he couldn't. Then we asked the boy he went with and who returned the same day, and he said that Jadi was lying and that he had been with harlots. So we dismissed him, for we had given him warning when Burt caught him in the very act sometime ago. Hawa refuses to go with him, so she is still here. He is a professing Christian but has never acted like one. Pray for our Christians."

A sequel to that story is that during our next furlough we got word that Jadi had tried to get on a moving earth mover and slipped and fell under the wheel and was crushed to death.

Well, the boys made it to Sokoto and we delighted in having them home again. We had the usual Christmas programs with the Africans and the church was packed not only on Sunday but also on Christmas morning for the pageant. DauDuka read the Christmas story from the Bible and the Africans pantomimed it out. We counted 120 in the church and another 20 outside. The customs officer and his family were there, and he invited us over to the barracks to repeat the program in the afternoon.

Christmas Eve we gathered at the Lees' house with the nurses and had a carol sing and grab bag. Christmas noon, we all ate together at our house and we included the customs officer. When you talk to an educated African and have him sitting at your table, you don't even think about his being black. Even our kids who play with the Africans don't think about their color or nakedness. When we are with our Christians, we think of them as brothers and sisters in Christ and that's all.

"Dec. 30, 1956 Yesterday we had play day with races, tug-of-war, relays, dodge ball, and afterwards, we invited the Christians into our parlor and gave them pop-corn, doughnuts and Kool-Aid. There were about 30 of them."

This year we got a lot of things from home. Ray Bayne's church had sent us money for a bike for the boys, so that is what we bought for them in Kano.

"Helen and Wayne's church sent us a lot of useful things—dresses for me and the girls, shirts and pajamas for the boys, most of them home made and well done. Candy, toys, favors, were included. We bought a new buggy for Cherry just like the one she got two years ago, but bigger, from some missionaries who were not returning to the field. It was brand new. We cleaned up Cherry's old buggy for Sue. Cherry is just crazy about the doll the folks sent with all the clothes and even a straw hat and glasses! Johnny likes his nail and hammer set very much. We gave Sue the same doll that the folks sent for her birthday. She didn't appreciate it very much then after the first excitement, so I put it away. Now she is happy with it, calls it her 'baby doll' and takes it to bed with her. Fran and Bill's package came on the 27th, and everybody is delighted with what they got, although Sue doesn't know what to do with her diaper bag, so I am putting it away for awhile. Cherry is crazy about her baby bottles. Johnny likes his cars and the boys the erector set. Thursday we went into Madaoua to pick up the mail and have dinner and supper with the Harbottles. Had a nice visit with games and races for us all in the afternoon.

"Dec. 31, 1956 Friday night when Burt was fixing the car spring, he banged his finger and had to take two stitches in it. Consequently we couldn't do any surgery Sat. or Mon . . . Tomorrow is also a day of prayer throughout our mission. We'll be taking the boys to Sokoto on Sun. night, as they are scheduled to fly at 7 a.m. Mon. morning . . . . Rollie made me a darling bud vase with a tin can cover, test tube, clay and paint. It was the fourth grade project. I put one of your tulips in it and used it for a center piece for Christmas dinner along with tinsel and ornaments. Lanny's present was a calendar. A Christmas calendar with a lovely star, and for each month a sheet with a picture that he colored and the days of the month. In three hours, it will be 1957, but we expect to be sleeping it in. We played again the tape you made at Christmas 3 years ago, and enjoyed it and also the music by the Chapel Choir with Marge's emceeing. Remember? Received a letter from Beret—the first in a year. Also heard from Bob about a month ago. A pleasant shock. Good-bye for now, and God's best for 1957."

And so we put 1956 to sleep and entered into 1957. Now forty years later it is Feb. 1, 1997. Years have come and gone. Our kids are adults, they are all middle aged. (over 40) "Train up a child in the way he should go, and when he is old, he will not depart from it." Pro. 22:6.

Chapter 6

MIANGO

I first mentioned Miango in Part 2 Chapter 6. Our first trip to Miango was after Cherry was born. After two weeks in Jos, we were told that we could/should go to Miango. We had never seen it before, so we didn't know what to expect. Miango was about 20 miles out of Jos. It took about an hour to get there over rough and winding roads. Winding roads because we went around and over hills! Some landmarks we came to know along the way over the years were Camel rock, piano bend, the volcanoes, occasional monkeys and later, the airstrip. The reason Camel rock got its name is quite obvious.

Piano bend has a history. It seems that both K.A. and the rest home had ordered pianos, and they were being delivered to Miango by Trevor Ardill. When he arrived at Miango and opened up the back of the truck, lo and behold, there was only one piano there. Then Trevor remembered a thump along the way but had paid no heed to it. So they turned around and went back looking for it and found it lying along the side of the road at a curve in the road about half way back to Jos. From that time on, that curve was known as "piano bend".

The volcanoes were close enough to Miango so that the K.A. kids could take their Sunday afternoon walks to them. On these famous Sunday afternoon walks, the kids often climbed the many rocks and jumped from one rock to another. There were always some daredevils, and then of course, there were those who challenged the more timid to the task. Our own kids had their share of rock climbing, and it's only the grace of God that prevented any great disaster. It was a number of years later that the airstrip was put in just Jos-side of the volcanoes. This was a big aid to getting our kids to and from K.A. About the same time, at the Galmi end, our planes were allowed to land at an airstrip first in Konni, then in Madaoua and Malbaza and finally at Galmi. While we're on the subject of airstrips, I'll digress a bit and mention that on one trip into Madaoua with the Harbottle kids and ours and perhaps more, that the plane came in for the landing dragging a long wire. On examination, we found it to be a telephone wire that the pilot had snagged. Both the pilot and the passengers felt the jolt but the plane came in okay. Humanly speaking, the plane should have somersaulted, but thanks to God, He kept that from happening. It was a very sobering moment. I don't know what reparations SIM made to the town. But we were all very thankful that our kids were home safe and sound.

Back to Miango. Jos and Miango were located on a plateau of about 4000 feet altitude which made it quite comfortable while Galmi suffered in over 100 degree heat. We always tried to book our holidays during our hot season. When we talked about Miango, it meant going to our rest and recreation area to visit our kids. But in fact, Miango was a town about a mile further down the road. Actually, we never went to Miango unless we made a special trip into town. To us, Miango was Kent Academy and the Rest Home. Straight ahead as we entered the compound was the main building which contained the dining room, living room, kitchen, pantry, children's dining room, tuck shop, office and mail boxes. Upstairs was a large recreation room with a ping pong table. It was also a place to dry clothes on wet days. The living room was ringed with upholstered chairs, all made by Mr. Will Craig. In one corner was a radio, and in the other was a piano. I spent a lot of time at the piano. There was always a fresh vase of flowers on the tea table, lovingly picked and arranged by Mrs. Craig. When we went back to visit in 1994, everything looked the same.

Surrounding the main building were cottages consisting of one, two or three bedrooms. When we first went in 1951 there were also little houses like the one under the cashew tree just off of the path between K.A. and the big house. This was called "latrine". Early on we carried water from the big house to the cottages and got our drinking water from the kitchen in liter bottles. Not too many years afterward, each cottage had its own plumbing, and with the advent of the dam and water purification system, we could even drink tap water. What a treat it was to come from Galmi to Miango!

Citrus fruit trees lined the paths, and every noon we had cut up fruit for dessert. Mangos were plentiful as well, and papayas and bananas were purchased at the door each day. What a delightful diet for those of us who came from a dry country.

Behind the big house were the workers' houses and the tennis courts. Our happy hour time was after tea time on the tennis courts. Tea time was an institution at Miango. I can still hear the bell and the announcement at 3:30 each afternoon: "Tea time, time for tea!"

The most important aspect of Miango was the other side of the compound—Kent Academy. First one, then two, then three, four, five and six of our children left our nest for 9 months of the year to be trained by others academically, socially and spiritually. Rollie paved the way. Twelve years later. our youngest, Pam, made her debut. K.A.'s quadrangle consisted of school, dining room, boys' dorm and girls' dorm, housing for dorm staff and the large mango tree. Swings and monkey bars and teeter totters dotted the playground. Just off the quad was the Kirk Chapel, named for one of our earlier missionaries, and down the road were the homes of the teaching staff. Beyond that was the large track field and play ground. Towering behind the compound was Mt. Sanderson. Behind the school was the work shop, the school tennis courts and the road to the dam and purification plant and the pig pens and rabbit hutches.

Hillcrest was the bitter "enemy" of K.A. in sports, and so each year they had their competition. Hillcrest School was located in Jos and was an M.K. school for a consortium of missions. Early on, SIM was not a part of the system, but when SIM began sending our kids to Hillcrest for high school, we became an integral part of Hillcrest. Today, 1997, most of our kids go to Hillcrest for both elementary and high school since K.A. has been devoted for the most part to Nigerian students. If you can't beat them, join them! So we anticipated leaving for Miango in March of 1957, but there were a few items to care for before we left.

March 4, 1957 In Hausa, it's 'huta'; in French, it's 'en vacances'; in American English, it's 'vacation'; and in British English, it's 'holiday'.

Call it what you may, we are packing our suitcases, and in a few days, we will be on our way! And we are ready for a rest! We're anxious to see Rollie and Lanny again. They will be living with us in our cabin and attending Kent Academy as day school students for a month. It will be great fun to be together again."

So it was, year after year. Work, work, sweat, sweat, and it seemed that each year we looked forward to our holiday at Miango. To get away from the heat and the pressures of the work, and most importantly, to be with the children. The only bad thing about it was leaving them again at the end of the month.

"Dr. Culbertson and Mr. Cook from Moody Bible Institute will be at Miango while we are there, as they are touring mission fields in Africa. Also, Rev. and Mrs. Howard Jones, well-know negro evangelist in the States, is in Africa and making a good impression on the Africans and will be in Miango while we are there. His weekly radio broadcast is heard over ELWA in Liberia and has a good reception.

"Our annual African conference was held last week, and all our "boys" have been away. We've been trying to keep up the usual schedule in the hospital and at home, but it's been a drain with all the boys gone. They should be back tonight, and we'll appreciate them all the more for having been without them. We trust that the Lord has done a work in their hearts. About 12 from this area went.

"We have also been having a good time these past few days with Ed Dubisz, who is more than a fellow-missionary and co-worker. He is a friend from way back. Burt was his Sunday School teacher at the Center and had some influence in Ed's choosing SIM. He has been out 4 years and will be going back home in another year, and we are enjoying our visit with him this week. Ed even scrubbed with Burt on an operation this morning—his first experience. He has some good stories about baboons and lions and climbing the nearest tree, too, something we don't see here in the desert but which he sees quite a bit of in the grasslands of Haute Volta."

Just before we left Galmi for Miango, our hospital boy came over with the news that a woman was just brought in who had been in labor four days. She was brought on a cornstalk bed, and fifteen minutes later, we would have been gone. The baby's two arms were hanging outside the mother. The baby was dead and the woman was almost dead. It took Burt an hour to extract the baby. Then we left and never did know whether the mother survived. Her chances were slim. It was cases like this that affected us emotionally. Do you wonder why we were glad to have a reprieve for awhile? But then, the question arises. What would have happened if we had already left? And what will happen during the month that we are gone? Burt was the only doctor. Always there was the cry for more doctors and nurses!

"March 29, 1957. We're here, at Miango. Last Fri. was field day. Hillcrest beat K.A., but it was a thrilling sight to see all the kids do their best. Rollie won 1st in broad jump (boys 9 and 10); 1st in 220 yd. relay race with 3 other boys; tied for 3rd in 100 yard dash. Lanny won second with Johnny Driesbach in 7 yr. old boys' 3—legged race. But Hillcrest got the cup—230-212. The kids got ribbons.

"We're having a swell time here, not accomplishing too much but having a good time doing it. Been playing tennis almost every afternoon. After supper each night and prayers, the parlor comes alive with Scrabble, dart baseball, dominoes, general conversation and tea and coffee. A good crowd is here—about 75. Rollie and Lanny eat and sleep with us, and it's great to be with them again.

"We're getting bananas and paw paws (papaya) and grape fruit or orange juice each day. We even had pork one day last week. They butchered a pig. First pork we've had since we left home."

Miango also boasted a dental clinic so each year when we went on holiday we had our teeth checked and worked on. Also, each K.A. student had yearly check-ups. Dentists came and went, but the one that was there for most of our time was Dr. Wes Kraay. His wife, Charlotte, was K.A. nurse. Their three children were the ages of ours, Ken, Robert and Jan. Char is today retired here at Sebring with us.

Behind the chapel was the cemetery. Occasionally we took walks though it and observed and commented on the graves. Some were of little tiny babies, others of children, still others of missionaries in their prime. There were the Ian Hay children, the Harbottle baby, Ernie Hodges, Art Goosen and his son, Mel, and many others. It was while we were on holiday during our second term that Ernie died. He was stricken with polio. He and his family were in the "bush" on their station. Word came to Jos via radio that Ernie was sick, but it was dark and the plane could not go and get him until morning. So Dr. Jeanette Troup, I believe, and others, drove out to get Ernie, turned around and drove back to Jos. They arrived early in the morning. In

—

172

the meantime, others in Jos were instrumental in tracking down and obtaining an iron lung. Ernie was placed in the lung. Word came to Miango for the doctors there to go into Jos and help. So Burt went in with, I think, Dr. Hursh. But it was all to no avail. Ernie died, and he was buried at Miango the next day. That left Mrs. Hodges with three children and an unborn child who, when he was born, was named Ernie after his late father. Shortly after that, Mrs. Hodges was re-stationed to Miango as a K.A. teacher and it was there that she raised her four children surrounded by loving friends.

It was April, 1958. We sat at tea in the big house. Rollie, then 11 years old, came up to us and asked permission to go to the swinging bridge with the Goosens. Knowing he would be in good company we gave our blessing and consent. The swinging bridge was literally a swinging bridge, made with ropes and wood and wire by one of our early, early missionaries with, of course, the help of the Africans. It spanned a narrow canyon over little rocks, big boulders and troubled waters. It was not unusual for the K.A. kids and visiting missionaries to go down to the sandy beach and wade in the water. At one point, the water hit a boulder which caused it to change course, and in the process, developed a swirl which over the years dug a deep hole in the river bed, unbeknownst to anyone. The Goosens and a few friends had been gone about 2 hours when a car came tearing into the compound, horn ablazing! They were calling for help—for swimmers and doctors to come. "The Goosens have drowned!!!" Apparently, Goosens' boy, Mel, who was also Rollie's age, had gone in wading with a couple of other boys and suddenly he disappeared. As Mrs. Goosen watched her son disappear and saw her husband start to go after him, she cried out to Art, "Don't go! You can't swim." But swimmer or not, Art couldn't see his son disappear and not do anything about it. He was a tall man, at least 6 ft., and he thought he could wade out and reach him. No one was aware of the sudden drop off, and he too disappeared into the hole. Others who went in the water were Johnny Bishop, one of the Wickstrom boys and a Langdon boy, I believe. They were swimmers and made it to safety. Rollie said he didn't go in.

Burt and others went to the scene. They saw some Nigerians diving in search of the men. Our men, including Paul Craig, joined them. The hole was extremely deep and the divers had to struggle against the whirlpool. After about 30 minutes one of the bodies was retrieved, and some minutes later, the other one was. The men gave artificial respiration to both father and son for at least an hour hoping against hope that they would be revived, but the life had gone out of them. Miango radio sent word to Jos to send Dr. Roger Troup with resuscitation equipment. To no avail. It was a sober evening and a night of shock for Jeannette Goosen and her other two children. That night, while some of the men made two boxes, Burt with others prepared the bodies. After a memorial service the next morning, they joined others behind Kirk Chapel in the little Miango graveyard.

A little aside here! Just a few months earlier, SIM had asked all our missionaries to go on Social Security. Art was one who took advantage of this (not everyone did at that time). He had only been on it for about two months when the accident happened. As a result, Jeanette received child support for her two small children until they were of age. A provision ordained by God!

Others buried at Miango included nurse Char Shaw, Dr. Jeanette Troup and pilot Len Dyck. Lassa fever was plaguing Nigeria at this time. A nurse from a bush station from another mission, Laura Wine, came in to Bingham Hospital with a high fever. She had Lassa fever. Since our doctors and nurses had had no prior association with the disease extreme isolation measures were not taken. Our SIM nurse, Char Shaw cared for Laura. Laura died. Then Char came down with it and died. Some of the Africans associated with the hospital got sick. At least one died, others got well. Our nurse, Lily (Penny) came down with it and was sent home where she recovered after a long illness. One of the doctors that worked in the lab at home died. Another recovered after a transfusion of Penny's antibodies was given. Penny's story is told in the book, *Lassa Fever*. Then, sometime later, Dr. Jeanette Troup was doing an autopsy on an African who had died in the hospital. Somehow her glove was punctured. She immediately washed her hands, but she knew that the damage was already done. She felt sure that she would get Lassa and die. Calls for antibodies went out to the U.S. and Liberia, but they did not arrive in time. She died. She is buried at Miango.

Len Dyck was one of our pilots. One of the planes had been worked on and he went up for a test flight. He disappeared. Calls went out to help search for the plane. Other planes arrived and searched. The plane was found by Africans in Sherrie Hills, not too far from Jos.

I was in Jos for having surgery when Chad died

Then the search party went into the hills on foot, because there was no access by any other means. Several days later and after many hours of trekking, they reached the plane and Len's body. They carried out his body which now lies beyond Kirk Chapel with the others awaiting Resurrection Day.

Then there was little Barbara Swanson. She was six years old and in first grade at K.A. She got sick, was taken into Jos. Her parents, Joe and his wife, were working in Kano, and they were sent for. Barbara died of Black Water Fever and was buried at Miango. These are not the only ones who are buried there, but I cannot recall them or the stories behind them now.

K. A. was well known for its Christmas and Spring plays. Over the years our children had parts in them. Interspersed between the acts of the plays were instrumental numbers and choir numbers. When Rollie was in first grade, he was one of the little pigs in the Three Little Pigs drama. Her first year, Cherry led the first grade rhythm band. She was dressed in a really cute red and white outfit. Later she was Pinocchio. Lance was in Shakespeare's "A Midsummer Night's Dream." Lance was Rumplestiltskin. John was an elf. Sue was a narrator. All of them were in the choir from time to time. Jerry Craig was the instrument behind all the special programs. She was the director of the plays and was in charge of the whole program. We weren't able to be there for all of the special events, but we managed to see a few of them. Paul and Jerry Craig were in charge of KA. and what a pair they were! They loved all the kids, and when a youngster had a bad dream and knocked on their door down the hall at night, they took them into their bed and comforted them just as the child's own parents might have done.

Birthdays were special events for the kids at KA. For Lanny's eighth birthday (in 1957) we were invited to KA. for Sunday afternoon tea. Rollie brought in his cake with the candles and Lanny was king for about an hour of the afternoon.

We always had tea and sing song after church on Sunday nights at the big house. Those were always good times, and the older children at K.A. were always invited to join us. Other times we had fun nights. "Friday night we had Fun Night and we laughed 'til we were sore . . . the jokes and stunts were clever and corny and we howled until we hurt."

The next day our holiday was over, and we had to say good-bye to the boys. Good-byes were always hard. Sadness reigned. The only good thing about this parting was that in about six weeks the boys would be back home for the summer. It took the ride from Miango into Jos before I was able to control my tears. It was not just this time; it was always.

"April 18, 1957 Left Jos at 7 a.m. Tuesday . . . heading for Moriki, about 260 miles to check the leprosy patients there. Arrived about 7:00 p.m. (12 hrs. on the road) Found the folks (Dave and Sue John) had gone to Sokoto. Their African boy had access to the house. We raided the ice box, bathed and slept in their beds, went out to the village, checked 250 patients, had dinner, left a note and left at 2:30 for Gummi. Arrived there about 9 p.m. Had supper with the Stades and this morning Burt and Mrs. Stade are checking 150 patients. We will leave after dinner for Sokoto. It's only 100 miles, so barring accident, we should be in Sokoto in time for supper. Hope to reach Galmi on Friday (Good Friday!)."

More will be written about Miango as our letters reveal things that happened on our holidays there over the years. But just so you know, Miango has a big place in our hearts, not only for the beauty of the place, but especially for the part it played in our children's lives and vicariously in ours. There, too, we met many of our missionary colleagues that were stationed far away from us whom we might never have known otherwise. It was a place of rest, spiritual refreshment, friendships made and renewed, and a haven from the heat and pressures of Galmi. We loved it. We know that K.A. and Miango are different today, but in many ways, they are still the same, and they will always be the way we remember them in our hearts.

Chapter 7

THIS AND THAT 1957

"April 27, 1957 . . . back home again. 1400 miles on dusty, washboard, bumpy roads. Broke two springs on the way home, but that is not unusual. The car ran perfectly, and we didn't have a flat the whole trip. Burt is sold on the tubeless tires.

"Biggest news this week is that we cut Cherry's long hair. We braided it, then snipped off the pigtails for posterity, then trimmed it around. It looks very chic. She wanted it cut badly, and then she cried when it was done, because she felt quite shorn. But she likes it now, and it is wonderful for the hot season and very easy to comb. She is very keen on going to school in the Fall.

"We received the spark plug and the box of nuts from Beret . . . We celebrated our 12th (anniversary). How is Aunt Ruth? We got a letter from Beret and Bob. It sounds so different for Bob to be talking about the things of the Lord in a natural way. How come the Kotts left the Bible Church? Who is Bev marrying? In the Wheaton Alumni news we noticed that the Arnold boy was married in a double wedding ceremony at the Center. What was the connecting link to the Center? Who is living in the old house? We saw the Helsers on holiday. Hope you like your job with Mr. Tanis, Pat. He's a nice guy to work for."

Well, it didn't take us long to get back into the swing of things. It was now in the hot season and it was over 100 each day. We were sleeping outside again, under the stars and it was delightful. No lights

177

to hinder a whole sea of stars overhead. I have never seen anything like it before or after. We could see the Southern Cross but not the dippers, so it was a new experience. During this season we had hot water, boiling hot, for showering. In the cold season we had cold water, and then it was we used the dip and pour method for showering. Believe it or not, we tried a little gardening. We had a muskmelon that weighed 5 1/2 lbs. and another one that weighed 5 3/4 lbs., and we had some tomatoes and lettuce. These were the only things that we planted that produced. Our "boys" did the watering, of course, a bucket at a time. We just stood by and watched things grow. We were thankful for whatever we got. It was like a cool drop of water in a barren land.

"May 21, 1958 Last Monday afternoon we had a down pour for about an hour—our first real rain. About 5 a.m. it started to rain today, and it's still raining (9 a.m.) . . . it's about a month early. We went to bed last night outside in a terrific calm. The wind sent us into the house about 2 hours later, and this morning we had our covers on. It's a pleasant 80 degrees in the house now."

I can assure you, the cooler weather did not last.

"These past two weeks we have laid the tile in our parlor and dining room. What a difference it makes. It's gray with black and white and pink lines in it. The contrast from a cement floor is great. The house looks very comfortable and very nice.

"The Zebs were down to pick up Mamman and Mantai, the Christian couple who take care of the little boys that the Zebs have started taking in. They have 5 boys in all. Mantai came down to be delivered of her baby. She got eclampsia and almost died. She was unconscious for two days. Her baby died after two days. Her convulsions started while she was in labor, she had five before the baby came and two, after. But she recovered, and we believe the Lord answered prayer, and they have returned to Tahaoua."

Speaking of the Zeb's boys, the two that stayed with them the longest were Jacques and Summai. Jacques was actually adopted by the Zebs. Both boys grew up to be fine Christian young men. They are both married. Today, 40 years later, Jacques is involved in the Salama church in Niamey, and Summai, as far as I know, is in Malbaza, and considered an upstanding business man. He was also involved in the peace making conferences in connection with the strike that Galmi hospital had a few years ago. It's hard to picture them in their late 40's or early 50's with families of their own.

Another young man that became "family" was Isti, (Istiphanus—Stephen), who was Gen's boy, the son of Cisu and Hassana. Cisu died suddenly of a ruptured aneurysm when Isti was a baby. Gen helped Hassana raise him and she sent him to school, paid all his expenses, and he has turned out to be a fine, young man, married to the daughter of Abdou of Dogan Doutchi, the Van Lierops' protege. Isti has a responsible job in Niamey. Gen also raised Aminatu whose mother came to the hospital, bringing her with her when she was about 4 years old. Her mother died at the hospital and left the little girl. Gen took her in, and after awhile, was given permission to adopt her by the relatives. Gen sent her to school as well. Aminatu married a Nigerien young man and had several children. He was a police man in Niamey and was killed in a traffic accident. Later, Aminatu married another fine Christian man and is living in Nigeria.

But to get back to 1957

"Sue just got out of the barrel (of water) where she and Johnny were having a good time until she hit Johnny over the head with a can. John is still in, but Sue has had enough for today. She is too small to reach the bottom—the barrel is full to the top, but she holds on at the top and just floats. Then when she gets tired of holding on she turns around and 'sits' on the water with her feet holding her up by pushing against the opposite sides of the barrel. Cherry chose not to go in today, but when three are in the barrel, it's quite cramped. These are the same barrels that you helped pack in Wheaton. Cherry and Sue are drinking 'kool-aid' through macaroni straws.

"Monday Burt leaves for Sokoto, will do the rounds of the leprosy segregation villages and pick up Rollie and Lanny on the 20th.

"We have started putting name tags on Cherry's clothes, and she is very excited about going to school. We are glad for that. I wonder what John and Sue will do without her.

"We had three good rains, and the Africans planted, but there hasn't been a rain for two weeks". It's been threatening several days since, and we've had some good dust storms, which in five minutes covers the house with a 1/4" layer of dirt and sand, gets in your eyes

179

even when you're in the house and you start chewing it in a matter of minutes.

"We are looking forward to a good time when the boys come home. Now that they are older, it raises the general level of the discussion around the table. They range farther and get into the villages and get a lot of older boys hanging around the place. The little kids sort of take a back seat, but they are all proud of each other so they learn a lot from the older ones and the older ones like to teach the things they know and be boss on the projects. When we first came back, Rollie built a mud and stone ramp to the porch for the trikes and wagons, and Johnny and Cherry have kept it up, and we use it for bike and motorcycle, too. Of course they get into a lot of things they can't finish and then we have to take time off and complete it for them. They make up for it in the work they do and the help they give in many ways. They want an allowance but don't get one, so we pay them for jobs they do. There is nothing to spend the money on though except rogo (cassava root) in the market, which is so cheap they get all they want for 5 or 10 francs. So they see who can save the most. So it all ends up back in our safe as a savings account. We gave Ruth Hunt some money to get the boys cokes while she was on holiday and they thought that was pretty nice. At school each parent who permits his child to have candy supplies a box of candy and they are allowed a piece or two after lunch two days a week. Certainly doesn't seem to be much, but they are all in the same boat and don't seem to mind. But when we do get them a coke, it is something very special. It is nice to have kids who consider every little thing as very special; makes them delightfully appreciative."

"July 6, 1957 The rainy season is on, the hospital work has slowed down, Burt has gone to Sokoto to do leprosy rounds and pick up the boys from school. The plane brought them in from Jos about 2 p.m. They left Sokoto immediately. Unfortunately we had a terrific rainstorm here that Friday morning which extended all the way to Sokoto. But they decided to try it anyway. As a result, they spent the night in the bush in a mud hole. They were only 35 miles from home, had just come within sight of the douane's place in French country, saw that the road was bad, and detoured around into the bush for about a mile. Lanny was given the job to direct them over an especially bad place and he didn't do such a good job of it. As a result, they got stuck. Burt thinks that four feet away they could have made it and been home for supper. As usual, the Nigerian roads were passable; the French roads were the bad ones. After many unsuccessful attempts on the part of about 20 Africans to lift the car out, they gave up, and slept the night there in the car—Lanny on the front seat, and Burt and Rollie stretched out in the back of the station wagon. In the morning Burt walked the mile into the douane's place, left the boys with the car, got some drinking water and a truck from the traveaux publique which got stuck going out to get them, but finally managed to get himself out and pull Burt out. They had a can of beans for breakfast. Arrived home for dinner covered with mud and dirt and with a good appetite and plenty of mosquito bites. So they've been home for two weeks now and it's good to be all together again. Rollie got all A+'s on his report card except one which was an A. Lanny doesn't get marks yet, just checks, until third grade but he also passed."

Zebs went through again on their way to Maradi to pick up a little black baby for their hostel. "She is very cute; her name is Rabi. She is 9 months old. Her mother died at her birth, and one of the single missionaries, Edith Durst, has been taking care of her since, but now Edith is going home on furlough." The little baby had a great future. Her father was a school teacher in Maradi who went on to be a Minister in the Niger government in Niamey. He allowed Edith to adopt her, and when Rabi was eleven or twelve, Edith went home to stay and took Rabi with her. Rabi had every advantage that an American girl had plus music lessons. She became an accomplished vocalist and pianist, eventually competing in Russia with world performers. We saw her again when she was in her thirties. When Howard Duncan and Lena Bishop got married, she was invited to be the soloist. What a voice she has! She lives in California and sings and plays for a living.

Along with Zeb's visit, he administered our third and final Hausa exam: 10 sentences from Hausa to English, 10 from English to Hausa, 5 questions on Islam, a 20 minute sermon which the examiner chooses from 5 which we have prepared, write an essay on one of three subjects we have prepared and which the examiner chooses, recite 4-6 memory verses, 7 proverbs, give a free translation from a newspaper, reading on sight, interpret a Hausa sermon which the examiner gives. Besides that, we had to have read the Hausa New Testament through, read 10

Bible Study books and three good sized books. Well, we passed but I don't remember by what mark. 70 was passing. That made us "Sr. missionaries". How about that!

We took a trip to Tahaoua with the family. "August 4, 1957 Went up Wednesday afternoon, arrived in time for supper. Then Thursday we went out about 15 miles for a hunt and a picnic. Zeb got a guinea fowl on the road, and Burt got a duck in the swamp. Had a real nice time with them—we certainly enjoy them. Came back Thursday night. We noticed our battery was discharging all the way home, couldn't figure out why until yesterday when Burt examined carefully and found that the fan belt was worn out, wasn't turning the fan which didn't reach the generator with the proper stimulus or what have you. We (i.e., Burt) put on the new fan belt which arrived in a recent mail."

I mentioned Jadi in a former chapter. Now, comes the letter that tells about it. He fell off the road grader while reaching for his falling shoe. The wheel ran over his head. This happened about 125 miles west of us. I wonder if he knew the Lord. He talked a good talk but did not walk a good walk. Hawa went back to her village with Burt when he went to Sokoto and we never saw her again. Hawa had been Sue's primary baby sitter.

Remember Lucia Spicer? She was with us for awhile. She came to the field in 1956 with her trousseau and was scheduled to be married in Kano on July 4. She called off the wedding two or three days before the date. So we had her with us for awhile.

"School starts Sept. 12, so I must begin in earnest to get the kids' clothes ready. We will miss Cherry very much this year, but we know it will do her a world of good. She is somewhat lost around here without Judy Lees, and she doesn't enjoy playing cops and robbers with the boys. She is excited about going . . . it makes it easier for us to let her go. Kent Academy has done so much for the boys, we anticipate it doing the same for her. We have noticed, too, that as each one goes, the next one in line assumes a greater responsibility as he comes out from being the underdog and advances into a new role of the biggest one in the family. We hope it will help Johnny in that respect.

"The boys are into "Tarzan" books and borrowed *Tarzan* and *The Return of Tarzan* and have devoured them this week. Lanny is starting in all over again. Burt picked up *Tarzan* and now all three of them are pressing me to read them, so I guess I'll have to keep abreast of the family. Incidentally, Fran, Rollie has a memory like an elephant. He said you said that on his tenth birthday you would send him a camera that works, and 'here, my tenth birthday is passed and I still don't have a camera.' I think that problem was solved because I have opened the next letter which sheds more light on the subject.

"Sept. 8, 1957 The electronics fair sounds out of this world. (That was in 1957—what's going on today [1997] wasn't even dreamed of then.) When the Africans see me washing clothes in my Maytag and hear the motor roaring like an outboard motor on a boat (there in the desert they didn't know anything about the latter either), they think it is positively wonderful.

"I read *Tarzan* and *Tarzan Returns*. You'd better read them, Fran. They're terrific.

"A couple weeks ago a truck going to Sokoto from this direction went over a bridge and crashed through the side. Forty nine people drowned or died by other ways. They said the driver had a 10 ton load on including 70 passengers, and the bridge had a 6 ton load limit.

"Rollie was pleased to get your letter. He is quite happy about the prospects of getting a camera. About their Christmas presents, Rollie asked me to write the letter instead of him. He has a streak of laziness in him. I can't understand how he got that! He says he would like a "Walkie Talkie with the longest cord possible"; Lanny says, "I want a camera, too." Cherry says, "I would like a stove—a real one that cooks when I put in a plug." I explained to her that that was impossible out here. "Well, then, if they can't send that, I would like a cleaning set like she got back home—oil mop, broom, etc." I said that might be hard to send. So she doesn't know what she wants, but she always likes dolls, coloring books, and paper cut-outs. The boys always like books. As for Johnny, dear boy, he says, "Anything they want to send me is all right." Sue doesn't care—at least she doesn't say—but I think she would like a doll.

"Cherry, Rollie, and Lanny are down in the cistern—their last chance. The water is up to their knees. They get let down by a rope into 10 feet of darkness. Then they get used to the dark and have a splashing good time."

Well, the day came and Cherry joined her two big brothers and off to K.A. they went. Cherry was looking forward to going, and we were glad that she had her brothers with her. Cherry rode in the back seat and we could just barely see the top of her curly head (I had given her a perm) as they prepared for take off. We left them in Kano, and as usual, a part of us went with them. And then there were two! Johnny and Sue! We did our business in Kano, then headed back to the desert, and while we waited for mail from K.A. we became involved once again in the work of the hospital and other things.

The next is from Burt's letter home of Sept. 23

"One day at the market, I saw a butcher preparing the entrails and odd pieces of meat, including the vagina cut out and separated from the uterus. I asked if he were going to throw it away, and he said of course not, and reached out, bit off a piece of it raw and dirty, and put it in his mouth, chewed and swallowed it. I guess he was watching me for my reaction, which of course I took in a completely blasé manner, even though I couldn't have followed his example.

"One woman came in with a ten or fifteen year 'pregnancy' which we laughed at, then we took it out and found a calcified ovarian pregnancy of that many years. When they saw it, they said, 'See, it WAS a pregnancy!' So they had us that time.

"Jack took a whack out of Sue's hair the other day so Ruth started to even it out yesterday; then she decided I should shingle the back, which I did, then she cut the sides real short to match, and now except for a little side hair in front of the ears she looks like a boy. It gets the hair off her neck, however, and she is comfortable. Sue and Johnny (Jack) are finding it necessary to play with each other now."

Lolita Harbottle arrived unannounced about 5:00 o'clock one afternoon with her three kids and a black baby. She was with us for five days—just had to get away from it all. I don't blame her. There were many times I would like to have gotten away from it all, but where to go? Like the Eskimos who walked out into the frozen tundra, I could have walked out into the desert, but there was no future in that. So I thought I'd just better stick it out. Her husband Elvin was usually out trekking most of the week so most of the care of the children fell on Lolita. And now she was straddled with a baby whose mother had died. They stayed in the empty Lees' house and ate with us. They baby was five months old and malnourished. The Harbottle children at that time were Kathy, 4, Linda, 2, and Joyce, six months. When the baby was well enough, they gave it to the black evangelist and his wife who were living on their compound.

"Sept. 24 We had quite a time with my pump organ a few days ago. White ants got into it. I hadn't played it for two weeks, so they had plenty of time to make inroads. It was literally packed with the ants—I couldn't press the keys down. I was devastated. After dinner we started to take it apart—layer after layer, not sure what we were doing. From 1 p.m. until 10:30 I worked on that, taking every key off several times and every reed out and cleaning them several times. What a job! But to my utter amazement, when we put it together again, it played! (Not by itself of course. It needed some hand and foot manipulation.) The termites ate some of the felt linings and a little of the wood, but didn't do too much real damage. I never expected it to play again."

"Oct. 21, 1957 We are loaded with stink bugs tonight. Haven't seen a blister bug yet tonight (whoops, I spoke too soon.) If they land on you they may emit a fluid that brings out a blister. If the blister is broken the fluid spreads and more blisters result. Johnny had a tiny one on his wrist this morning—some get as big as a quarter. Very painful if they break. The reason for the influx of bugs is that harvest is in full swing. The bugs are in the grain, and when they are robbed of their home, they seek another one. Despite our screens, they manage to get in. In another month the winds will start to blow very hard and for three months or so, we'll be blown off our feet (or almost) when we step out of the house. Then the bugs will be gone. Gone with the winds! It's impossible to ride a bike in that season unless you go with the wind. But you do have to come back sometime. Even on our motor bikes, if we start to coast, we slow down to a stop. We like the season for its cool weather. That's when we pull out the flannel and woolen blankets and make a fire in the fire place every morning. And that's when the Africans freeze".

That last paragraph brought to mind Pam's ordeal with blister bugs. This will be covered in a future chapter. At this point in our story, Pam isn't here yet. Apparently one morning she couldn't wait for breakfast. So she decided to sample a dead one. Stink bugs were little green backed bugs that liked to congregate in a group on the walls. We used to take the dust pan and brush and sweep them down off the walls and put them into our wooden cook stove and enjoy the snap, crackle and pop

"I mentioned the harvest. The boys are bringing in their grain. They tie them in bundles weighing about 25 lbs. Then they load them on their donkeys or on their heads and carry them in. Yahaya, our cook, has harvested 200 bundles and expects to get another fifty. He has brought in 20 bundles to the church so far—his tithe. He is the only one who has brought his tithe so far and if they all bring in their tithes, the church will be full. It is with great difficulty that they are able to give a tenth, to say nothing of the offerings above and beyond. But Yahaya said that this year he was going to bring his full tenth (last year he only brought in six bundles) and be an example to others. We send this grain to the native evangelists and their wives—one at Tahaoua and one at Madaoua."

Speaking of Yahaya, it is a good time to speak of him. Yahaya was an older man when we first knew him. He worked for us on and off through the years. He made a profession of faith early on. He had two wives at the time and was convicted about it, so he built a hut for his second wife, a younger wife, and cared for her but said he would be faithful to his first wife, an older woman. Whether his faithfulness was toward his first or second wife, is a question. You just had to take his word for it. At any rate, he cared for them. Eventually, Aishatu, (I think that was her name), his older wife, died. So he still had his second wife. Yahaya ran hot and cold spiritually. At this time, he was a gung-ho Christian. When we left Galmi in 1975, he was not an outstanding Christian, rarely coming to church. But when we were in Jos, word began to trickle in that he had really come back to the Lord and was witnessing and boldly speaking out for Christ. About a year or two later, he died, but his life was a testimony in his twilight years.

"First word from the kids from school was that Cherry was homesick—she broke down usually at meals—according to Mrs. Craig. Next letter, Mrs. Craig said that Cherry was happy all the time and seemed to love life at K.A. Rollie and Lanny are having a great time. We go up to Jos for doctors' meeting this year. About the time you get this, we'll see Rollie, Lanny and Cherry for a few days. They don't know we're coming and we're going to surprise them. We leave here Nov. 8".

186

Here is an excerpt from a letter Burt wrote to his folks with a carbon copy to Fran and Bill.

"Last Tuesday, Ruth and I both went to Madaoua for mail, one on Ruth Hunt's new motorcycle, a 150 cc (ours is 125), each of us with a child aboard. Ruth was always afraid to make the trip alone in case something mechanical went wrong, but she enjoyed it. All of us were good and tired when we got home and slept well. These are little two cycle one cylinder motors, with the oil in the gasoline . . . the big Harley 74 back home is equivalent to 1200 cc so you see how small these really are. Ruth Hunt learned easily and goes all over now, albeit slowly. Lolita Harbottle (Madaoua) went all the way in first gear for a couple weeks before she dared to shift to second, then likewise for several weeks until she would try third. 'So it wouldn't go too fast for me.' Couldn't convince her she could go as slow as she wanted to even in third. But now she comes all the way out here with a baby aboard. Being out in the bush, or even being a missionary does something to one. I could never be a normal US citizen again. (Maybe you think I never was—ha! I beat you to it.) I never would have tried to overhaul a cycle at home. Here I have to. It's just work, but not complicated, just dirty."

Ruth again.

"Sunday, Oct. 27, 1957 I made a cake yesterday with a nice white fluffy frosting, and at dinner when I went out to the kitchen to get it, Johnny followed me and asked if that were his birthday cake. Right there I decided that it was, so we put on 5 candles and we brought it into the dining room. He was thrilled. Could he have smiled wider, he would have broken his face. His eyes sparkled. He has been asking when he was to have his birthday for the past two months. And since we will be in Jos on his birthday, I intended to have a cake for him before we left anyway. Now he is 'five', and if you tell him he is 'not quite five', he thinks we are teasing and contradicts us strongly. He is a real character."

"December 15,1957 Burt leaves tomorrow a.m. for 3 days at Sokoto, then on to Kano where he will pick up the kids and he hopes to be home on Thursday night. The two cameras came . . . Burt's Dad was in the hospital for 3 blood transfusions for his leukemia. We have all our Christmas decorations up, and the house is cleaned up, and it's still 10 days till Christmas . . . Presents are all wrapped and on the table. Johnny is very anxious, but the kids don't touch them. The stockings are hung and filled. But the kids know they're not supposed to peek, so they don't.

"We are beginning our busiest season of surgery now. In the first week back from Jos, we did 23 operations in a 4 day operating schedule. We are averaging 4 to 5 a day. It keeps us very busy, for we have only two nurses besides myself. We have one African dispenser, one ulcer dresser and clean up boy, and one operating room boy. The latter folds linens for sterilizing, washes and boils instruments, buries limbs and cleans up in the operating room. He earns his money. He is a Christian, but not long ago married an unbeliever and she refuses to come to church or to believe, so he is beginning to repent in leisure. His name is Tanko. So if you think of him, you can pray for him and his wife as well."

Friday noon, the 20th, Burt arrived with the children. Oh, how good it was to have them home again even though it was to be for only two weeks. The gifts were wrapped and out on the table, the big red flannel stockings were hung and filled. Four days of suspense, and on Tues., we opened the gifts along with Ruth Hunt and Gen Kooy. The cameras had arrived. The folks sent billfolds for the boys, dishes for Suzanne, a beautiful purse for Cherry, and a plastic cowboy on a plastic horse for Johnny. They were very happy with them.

"When we were in Kano and Jos last time, we bought the boys some all metal Dinky gas tank trailers, Cherry, a bead threading set and some cut outs, Sue, some cut-outs. And we also had some things stored away from Christmas back home, and all together the kids had an enjoyable time. We had Christmas dinner with the nurses—duck and all the trimmings, including olives, pickles and cranberry sauce.

"Isu, our boy, had a baby the week before and his naming ceremony fell on Christmas morning—the 8th day. We were glad he chose to have a Christian naming ceremony. He is the only one besides Dau Duka that has had the nerve to resist a Moslem ceremony. So we all went down to the village, gathered around, and instead of Moslem malams conferring the name, Burt announced the name—Ibrahim. Then he cut the ram's neck for the feast to follow. We didn't stay for the feast, but later in the morning, they sent us a leg and the girls a leg and a leg for all the Christians.

"In the evening, we had a party for the Christians here. About a dozen came, each with a grab bag gift. We did the latter in order to teach them that the business of giving at Christmas time was not something that the whites were to give to the blacks, but the custom was that friends exchanged gifts as a reminder that the Wise Men brought gifts to Jesus. We had a great time, and we laughed and laughed. They were stupefied at the 'Black Magic' game of putting 9 books out and having someone go out and guess the book that was chosen, by 'this' and 'that' method. You should have seen their eyes pop out. We pinned the tail on the donkey and then had the grab bag. Kanduwa had brought the leg of lamb for the Christians in a pan, raw. We had roasted the two legs we got for a surprise for the Africans, so I picked up the raw leg, did some hocus pocus over it and said it would change into roasted meat. A quick switch and I brought out the meat we had roasted and presented it to them. You should have seen Tanko's and Idi's eyes pop out. And all the rest were surprised, too. Did we ever laugh!

"Thursday morning we had the Christmas program with the Christmas pageant. Thursday noon we had dinner with the Harbottles in Madaoua—each of us had a stuffed roasted chicken apiece! Were they delicious! And your remaining packages were there! The truck for Johnny! And is he ever thrilled. It arrived in perfect condition, and he's been towing it ever since. The two dolls came and are delights to the girls. The boys have exposed a roll of film each. Lanny, on picture 8, wanted to show Burt something, so he took off the top, thus exposing the last picture before Burt could stop him. Live and learn. Ed Rei's gifts came. Cherry got a washing machine, Rollie a target and revolver set, Lanny, a walkie talkie, Johnny, a game (which is beyond him), and Suzanne, an educational toy, one with balls that go around and around and come out here. It was very nice of them to send those gifts. The Lucas's sent us a box including food, etc., two dresses for me and two for Sue. We were surely surprised.

"Ben Van Lierop and family came from Dogon Doutchi Thurs. night, left this a.m. He's the one who had the tumor removed from his brain. He has seasons of depression as a result of x-ray therapy and comes every couple months for psychotherapy, which consists of about an hour's talk with Burt. He came very depressed but left buoyed up considerably, 'feeling 100% better'.

"We're terribly busy in surgery these days. Hysterectomies, ovarian cysts (one weighed 25 lbs.), thyroidectomies, bowel resection, and the usual amount of hernias, hydroceles, tumors, etc. We do about 5 operations a morning, and it really keeps us hopping."

Nineteen fifty seven ended and with it came an end to the kids' vacation. Back to school for them, and we began counting the weeks until we would see them again on our holiday in April. Work was so heavy, though, it didn't give us time to grieve. But why grieve? They were in the best situation possible, in those days the only situation possible for them to have a good education and a social climate and make friends with those who would be some of their best friends forever. We shall always remember K.A. and the staff with great fondness and appreciation.

Chapter 8

TRAGEDY AND TRIUMPH 1958

In Jan. of 1958 we enjoyed a visit from Dr. and Mrs. Wes and Charlotte Kraay who were on their holiday. He is the mission dentist and she is the K.A. nurse. We had planned this visit with them over 2 years ago. They brought a little bit of Miango with them, and telling us about our kids brought them a little bit closer home. We surely enjoyed their visit.

"Jan. 31, 1958 Monday we had a bit of a scare. Sunday I had spanked Sue for striking a match. So Monday she hid behind the couch in a corner and sat down and struck a match. It fell on her dress. I was in the kitchen when I heard a scream. Sha'aybu heard it too, and he ran first. It was an unusual scream, one that I had never heard before. I thought perhaps something had fallen on her, and I followed Sha'aybu immediately. He couldn't see her for she was well hidden. Then he saw flames shooting up out of the corner and ran to her and started beating out the fire with his hands. In just a few seconds I was there too and fell on her and beat out the fire too. Scared? She was terrified! Her dress was burned away in front. Her undershirt and underpants were scorched but not burned through. She suffered only a little redness on her body, face, and a tiny blister on her lip. How we praise the Lord for His protection. Also, that we were in the house and not in the garden or elsewhere when it happened. She has learned her lesson and so have we. No more leaving matches within her reach.

—

"My, we are busy. We did 190 operations in January. Tuesday morning the doctor came from Madaoua with a woman in labor, the baby half out. We put her out with ether then Burt delivered a monstrosity with two heads, four arms and four legs and one body. Of course the thing was dead by this time. In order to deliver it, Burt had to cut off one head, deliver the rest, then the second head. We had never seen anything like that . . . The woman is doing fine now."

More on that monstrosity—"four arms, four legs, 2 heads and one body". The (French) doctor in Madaoua brought her after she had been in labor for 3 hours and he saw that she had delivered 3 legs already. They don't have a good set up in Madaoua and that doctor was just new (right out of Paris). They are building a new hospital—6 or 7 beds."

"Did I tell you that one of our recent hysterectomies was a 17 lb. uterus? It was as large as a basketball. She is almost well now.

"I have a regular Thursday afternoon Bible class in the village. Also spent part of two other afternoons in the villages this week, so time just leaps. Am in the hospital all morning 5 days a week. We have a 3rd nurse in sight. She is due from Paris soon and is to come here for three months and help us in our rush season, then go to Kano for Hausa language study. We are getting pretty tired, but we are keeping our health and getting enough sleep at night—usually a minimum of 8 hrs. We are looking forward to April and holiday. Our regional conference is Feb. 13-16, so that will be a bit of relaxation. It is in Maradi. Dr. and Mrs. Helser and Mr. Ritchie Rice from England are to be the speakers. Bye for now."

Conference came and went and Burt went on a two week trip to Sokoto Province to make his leprosy rounds. While he was gone I tackled a heaped up basket of mending. I also got things ready for holiday which was coming up in April.

"Feb. 11, 1958 The French doctor came today to take the woman back home. She happens to be the first of four wives of the son of the chief of Madaoua. And she is very young. Has been married since she was a little girl. And locked up. About half the women cannot go out of their compounds in Moslem society here. Sometimes she says her husband takes her and his other wives for a ride in the car to see some friends, but then they are heavily veiled. What a life!

—

192

"I know the boys will like the books and Cherry her cut-outs. We will take them to them when we go on holiday. You really went to a lot of trouble to make this Christmas a happy one for the kids. The cameras, incidentally, take very good pictures. We got some back recently. The only trouble with most of the shots was that the kids took some of them facing the sun. Then there was the blank negative which must have been when Lanny opened it up to show us that there were 8 pictures on the roll!

"Tonight Suzanne was sitting in the same corner where she hid to strike her match. When I noticed that it was very quiet. I said. 'Where's Sue?' She piped up from behind the davenport. "Here I am. I'm having prayers". We have 'morning prayers' here on the station every day, and she is accustomed to it. Also, when I pray in the morning, she gets down on her knees by the side of the bed with me (John does too) and after about 30 seconds she whispers 'I'm finished' and gets up. When the kids were home for Christmas, we had a regular line up around the bed, each one getting up off his knees at different times when he was finished. Cherry was up in about a minute, and the boys usually took two minutes. Johnny's an awfully good kid!"

Holiday time came and we arrived at Miango and it was so good to see Rollie, Lanny and Cherry! We were having a good time when tragedy struck about half way through our time there.

I first mentioned the Goosens' drownings in Chapter 6, Miango. I wrote it from memory. Now I have come to the letter that I wrote to Fran and Bill about the accident and I can say that my long term memory is not bad. Short term memory is a different story. Here are my exact quotes.

"April 17, 1958 A tragedy occurred last Saturday. A missionary and his son were drowned in the river at the 'Swinging Bridge'. Mr. Art Goosen and his 12 yr. old son, Mel, a K.A. boy! They took a group of boys, including Rollie, to the bridge. There was no thought of going in swimming, but the big boys teased until they were allowed to wade. Then, according to Rollie, they just 'accidentally on purpose' got a little wetter and deeper. Rollie and Gordon Helser were the only ones who didn't go in. I asked Rollie why later, and his first answer was that he didn't have his swimming trunks, then immediately after, he answered 'and I didn't think you'd like me to'. The current began to carry the boys over a sudden drop, and Mel started to sink. Dave Langdon tried to help him, but Mel was so panicky that he pulled Dave down with him and Dave had to push Mel away to escape himself. Then he noticed John Wickstrom and John Bishop struggling. He pushed John Wickstrom over to a rock and John Bishop grabbed Dave's leg as he went by and those two boys were saved but exhausted. By this time Mel was out of sight. Mr. Goosen, against the pleas of his wife, who knew he couldn't swim, started to run after him. Apparently he didn't know of the sudden 14 foot drop and figured he was taller than Mel and could just wade out and help Mel. He was over 6 feet tall. And it was no more than 10 or 15 feet from shore. So he went in, shoes, clothes and all, and disappeared. The boys say he came up twice and then went down for good. Mrs. Goosen was there with her 5 year old girl and 1 year old boy. When she realized what had happened she started for help, running up a steep hill with her baby in her arms. She intended driving the car back to Miango—at least a 10 min. drive—but just as she reached the top of the hill, the Emmett's drove up. The Swinging Bridge is a favorite picnic spot. Adie took Mrs. Goosen back in their car, while Ted went down to the water. He took a rope from their car, went into the water with it tied on his body and the other end to Dave Langdon who dived for the bodies while Ted hung on to the rope. Those of us who were at Miango heard a horn tooting from a long way. I and others, too, thought someone's kid was sitting on the horn. But we soon learned differently, and in a minute, the volley ball court and tennis courts were deserted, and the cars were pouring out of here. By the time the first ones arrived, the accident was already 20 minutes past. By the time I arrived in our car (Burt had gone on before) the whole area was filled with white men and black men, about 30 of them, all diving for the bodies. Mel's was found first—25 min. in the water. But it was 10 more minutes before Art's body was recovered. The drop was estimated at 14 feet. An African prodded with a stick and finally discovered the body. Paul Craig made the dive and brought him up. Gordon Bishop found Mel's body. Artificial respiration was started immediately, but after 3 hours without a let-up, they were pronounced dead at 8:00 P.M. Oxygen came from Jos but that was of no avail. They were dead when they were brought out of the water—but naturally every effort was made. Jeannette Goosen in the meantime was back at Miango and everyone was praying and clinging to the slightest ray of hope. Sunday she had a very hard time and was under Burt's care, but Monday she seemed to have found victory and real peace. The funeral was Sunday morning. It was a beautiful sunshiny day in contrast to the rainy weather we've been having. Saturday night after the men and bodies were brought back, the men worked at making caskets until 3:30 A.M., and Burt and others washed and prepared the bodies. It was a beautiful service, and Mr. Davis, our field director, gave a message that brought hope. The whole thing, from the time of the accident to the funeral, took only 19 hrs. Things happen fast in Africa. Jeannette is planning to return to her station and carry on along with the single worker there, Helen Vetter. It's been a terrific shock to all, and a time of stock taking. Several of the kids from K.A. have been saved through it and others have made their salvation sure. We asked Rollie and Lanny if they would have been ready, and they were sure of their salvation."

Everyone, young and old, was moved by the tragedy and our hearts went out to Mrs. Goosen and her children. It made those of us who had our loved ones appreciate each other all the more. Our family became more precious to us than ever.

(Here is an aside. Today is July 1, 1997. Last week I was at Camp Awana and I mentioned to John Bishop that I had just been writing about the accident. Then he spontaneously added, "Yes, and Rollie didn't go in. He said his parents told him not to." That made me feel pretty good.)

"April 29, 1958 Our holiday is almost over. We have enjoyed great fellowship with about 60 fellow missionaries. The school program was held last week, and it was wonderful. The kids from all grades put on an operetta on Rumplestiltskin. It was terrific. Lanny was Rump. and he was wonderful the way he bounced around. And his curtain call brought down the house—a quick hop and jump. He was dressed in a brown suit with elf style hat, elf shoes and a beard. Cherry led the rhythm band and was stunning in her white and red outfit. She did an excellent job. I hope they leave her out of a few things for a while—she thinks she's pretty cute. She was in the wedding, (Berdan/Carpenter—flower girl), then took 4 ribbons on Field Day, and now this, and everybody makes over her. Of course, we are proud, but it doesn't do her much good. You might say Rollie is the best actor of them all, for not many fellows can stand in the choir and move his mouth and say the words and not sing. He was one of those few

195

whose voices are changing and he can sing neither high nor low well. The choir not only sang some beautiful songs, they also did choral reading—about Peter walking on the sea. Besides that, there were piano recitals, a marimba solo, and a piece on bells. One of the girls plays them beautifully.

"Saturday night was fun night, and we old folks had a take off on Rumplestiltskin which also brought down the house. Instead of changing straw to gold, we changed gold into straw, and it was a riot. Believe it or not, this time I was Rumplestinklestein."

Back at Galmi and it was hot. So what else is new? In the 100's but dry. In between our daily routine, we were getting ready to welcome our three oldest kids home from school. Ken Kraay, the 13 yr. old son of Dr. Wes and Char Kraay was coming back with our kids for ten days. Since he was always stationed with his parents at Miango, he knew little about bush missionary work. This would be a good experience for him. Then he would meet his parents in Kano as they were on their way home for furlough.

"May 20 The other day we were looking for the key to the windmill in order to turn it on. We looked high and low, asked the kids and everything. The black boy had returned it to Burt at the supper table the night before, and we all remembered seeing it last on the table, but this particular morning it wasn't there. After searching for about an hour, including outside where it might possibly have been shaken out with the table cloth, Johnny wanted to know what he could do, so in exasperation, I said, 'Help look for the key, or we won't have any water.' Then the light went on (in his head) and he said, 'If you give me something like a nail file, I will find it for you.' Immediately we produced a nail file, and he proceeded to pry it out from under the leaves of the table. So we had water." To this day, I don't know whether he put it there or whether he was just table height and saw it there.

"We went to Madaoua yesterday, met the French doctor in the post office, so went over to his house for drinks. Saw his dispensary and maternity and hospital. He has a wife and 2 year old son. Very nice, but lonesome. How anyone could come out here except for the Lord's work, I don't know."

"Sue is a most unusual girl—an extrovert. Makes friends with everybody and anybody, while John stands behind the couch embarrassed to tears. And she's sharp as a tack, too. Sings beautifully. Since she was 17 months, she's carried a tune, sits for devotions with her legs crossed and hands folded like a prim old lady. John is coming out of his shyness a little lately and I think when he gets to K.A. it will help him a lot. We sent for the Calvert course—he's not eligible for K.A. this year since his birthday is in Nov.

"June 16 Your letter with all the news of weddings, babies and engagements and graduations came last week . . . We are looking for the kids with the Van Lierops Friday night. Then we will have our house full of our arrows. We're expecting another arrow in January. Now let the tongues start wagging and the telephone wires start humming. We had a Christian wedding here a week ago and in the evening had a celebration with the Christians. There were about 20 believers. We had a treasure hunt, did some 'black magic', played musical chairs, had devotions and Kool Aid and cake. We've had 3 rains and the people have started to plant. We planted peanuts. We are eating muskmelons out of the garden."

"July 6 This past month has been one of nausea, vomiting and discouragement. A good part of each day I have spent in bed because I have felt so rotten, but I have tried to keep going because getting one's mind off the situation helps too. Today I feel better. I have had 3 good days in a row. It's good to have the kids home again. Cherry has learned to ride the girl's bike—she rides it the way I used to ride Beret's. Lanny has read about a dozen books already . . . we have limited him to one a day. 'Those Bobbsey Twin books are terrifically good!' Rollie is out with the boys from morning to evening except when he is doing his work—drying dishes, cleaning the bathroom, watering the garden, setting table, cleaning their room. Rollie, Lanny and Cherry rotate with the work—except Cherry doesn't do the watering. We had more than 30 melons last month. Unfortunately they didn't agree with me, so I had to give them up. Now they are gone. We are having sweet corn from our garden tonight."

It was about this time that Kaltungo Hospital in Nigeria was ready to open. Every time the British medical officer came for a final inspection, he always added some more obligations. We heard that the mission had to supply mattresses and flush toilets for the patients. Then they said that the patients had to have pillows, a chrome operating table and a nurse for every 5 patients! "It's all so silly, because these are bush people, many of whom have never slept on a bed, much less with a mattress and pillow. One thing about the French, they leave us pretty much alone after they get our money. The British should see our hospital. When the beds get filled up we put the patients on the floor! We have 3 nurses for 100 patients.

I found a letter that Cherry wrote to Fran and Bill at this time, so here it is:

"July 10, 1958 Dear Fran and Bill, How are you. I hope you are fine. I remember you. How do you know that Daddy's birthday is in July 20. First I thought he was in the 60 or 70, but he is going to be 40 years old this year. We have fun in rainy days. We go in the puddles. Thank you for the Bobbsey Twin books. Goodbye for now. Love, Cherry."

August 5, 1958—my 37th birthday! A few days earlier we had received the box from Fran and Bill. Burt was unpacking it in the garage. Out came the roller skates for Lanny. When Burt got to the bottom of the box, Johnny came in sobbing, "I didn't get any skates". Minutes later, Sue came in sobbing, "I didn't get any skates." I wasn't surprised when Cherry followed Sue, "I didn't get any skates." John insisted that he knew how to skate, that he had skated back in America. So we put them on him. John was so surprised that he couldn't stand up on them and we all had a good laugh. He was chagrined and took them off. But you know Johnny, within a few days he was skating.

Another crisis

"August 5, 1958 A week ago Wednesday the Zebs came down for a visit. Zeb had a headache at the time. They went back on Thursday and Thursday night Zeb had a fever and he's been in bed ever since. They wired for Burt to come up on Monday so we all went. His fever was 103 and we brought him down on Wednesday morning along with Irene and Yakubu. We have been having heavy rains and the road was bad. We went through water up to the running board for 100 yards in one valley. Burt drove Zeb's Jeep back, and I drove our station wagon with Zeb lying on a heavy mattress in the back. The roads on the hills were all washed away, leaving big holes and just the rocky road bed. The hills were especially bad where the water had run down them. Going up this particular hill, I had the car in second and near the top shifted into first, but the motor died. And our battery was shot. Couldn't start it. Decided to roll downhill and see if I could start it in reverse, but got stopped by a big stone and couldn't go forward or backward. Pulled on the emergency brake and waited for Burt. We removed the rock and Burt started it up by rolling down in reverse. Then he took it up the hill

"This is Tues. Zeb's fever fluctuates between 101 and 103 and refuses to break. Burt has diagnosed it as cerebral malaria and he is very, very sick. Yesterday he quit fighting and said to Gen to say 'good bye' to Irene. But he rallied and is back to his previous situation but is very depressed and discouraged. Irene herself is on the verge of breaking down. He is dangerously ill and needs prayer. We can't understand why the fever won't break. He's completed two courses of malarial treatment and is on the third. Yesterday I drove the car to Madaoua to send a wire to Maradi (the Bishops) since Burt didn't feel that he could leave Zeb."

"Aug. 18, 1958 Zeb is making progress. His fever is gone and he is able to sit up for about 5 minutes at a time a couple of times a day. Well, Zeb did improve to the point where we were able to send him to Jos to recuperate. In October the Zebs drove through on their way back to their station. He spent five weeks in Jos at the mission hospital and Miango recuperating. This whole episode lasted three months. Zeb and Irene served for many more years. About 10 years ago, Irene died. Zeb lives in Sebring in our SIM village, is in his 80's, and he still takes his daily walks around the little lake and in front of our house.

Time for school again and we took our family to Kano to put the three older ones on the plane. Also with us was Johnny Van Lierop, their youngest. Ben and Gwen had brought Johnny as far as our place and we took him to Kano with our three. The older two, Bernard and Muriel were in England in school. They are British—Gwen is British; John is American—Ben was American. The immigration officials gave us the usual hard time because John V. L.'s passport had not arrived before he left home (it was sent later), and our three children were on my passport and they said that because I was not staying in Nigeria with the children, each had to have his own passport. Well, finally they relented and let them all through. It was Thursday, school had started that morning. The kids finally got on the mission plane at 3 p.m. just in time to get to Jos before it got too dark to land. We had been detained since Monday. We went about getting individual passports for them.

When the Van Lierops dropped off their John, they went to Sokoto to do some shopping. On the way they managed to get through the place where Burt got stuck the year before with our boys. Their return trip was another story. "They encountered new rivers that had just developed from underground springs this rainy season. They found themselves in water up to their windshield and spent the whole day with the help of the men from the village getting them out. Just as the sun began to set, they got out and started the last 100 miles to their home. What a nightmare! They wired us from Dogan Doutchie not to plan to return from Kano via Sokoto."

Johnny was excited about having his own school at home; the Calvert course had come, so we settled into a routine. It worked okay at first, but Jerry Lees next door didn't have to go to school—he was a bit younger—and Johnny got tired of school after awhile and wanted to play with Jerry, so it was a struggle. The whole procedure didn't work out too well and when it was time for him to go to school next year, there was some question about whether he should go into second grade, but he did. We found that all through his K.A. years, he didn't do too well. (I mean he only got C's and D's instead of A's and B's). Whether it was lack of motivation or lack of a first grade foundation or refusal to be measured by his brothers and sister, we don't know. At any rate, in consultation with his teachers they and we felt it would be to his advantage to repeat 9th grade, since he was young for his class. In retrospect, we wonder if it harmed him emotionally or psychologically. Hind sight is usually 20/20. We found out later that when he was motivated, as in college, he did very well.

It was about this time that we had another set back in our fledgling church. Dau Duka, upon whom we had such high hopes that he would be the pastor of our church, and who had had some Bible School, had some family problems. He and Kanduwa were squabbling and she taunted him by saying that since they were Christians, he couldn't divorce her. Dau Duka was the best preacher in all of Niger at that time—excellent in content and presentation.

He finally had enough and gave her a paper of divorcement. He left town and engaged another woman. Against our pleadings and those of the national Christians, he went ahead and married her. Kanduwa did not leave his compound so he had two wives. Now starts the church discipline.

Also at this time, Ibrahim, who was a Galmi boy who worked for the Lucases, stole a large sum of money, 12,000 francs ($60.00). Eventually, Ibrahim repented and returned to Galmi, and as far as we know, he never repaid the Lucases. But over the years he became a "pillar of the Galmi church". He and Lydia had a fine compound in Gidan Doutchie and we held our Awana clubs there for a while. They had a number of children, one of whom drowned one rainy season in the fadama in back of our compound. He was about 12 and a fine boy who professed to know the Lord and was a good Awana boy. Ibrahim died a few years ago while attending a conference in Maradi. A heart attack! Lydia continues to work at the hospital.

I was gaining weight about this time. Gained 12 lbs. in six months and was up to 120 lbs!

"Sept. 26, 1958 Mon. night the Van Lierops came from Dogon Doutchie and are visiting this week. Ben is the one who had the brain tumor operation. Every once in awhile, the going gets a bit rough and Ben has to get away from it all, and this is their 'city of refuge'.

Ben lived another two years. Finally in 1959 or '60 they returned to the States for further medical treatment. They were living in Holland, MI, where Ben's relatives were. We were in the States on furlough at that time, living on Circle Ave. in Chicago. In the Fall of 1960, we got the call from Gwen that Ben had gone to be with the Lord. Shortly after the funeral she came to visit us and stayed for some days. Gwen has always been a special friend and in her widowhood has found in us the refuge that she needs from time to time. Gwen returned to Dogon Doutchie and spent many years there and in Maradi and retired about ten years ago. She is now 85 plus, so she retired somewhere in her 70's. When Marcia Mowatt was on her death bed in Sebring, two years ago (1995) Gwen came from Canada and stayed with her for about 3 weeks until just before Marcia's home going. Gwen is a real trooper

The next remarks are from a letter Burt wrote to his folks and to Fran and Bill.

"Oct. 5, 1958 . . . I did two radical breast excisions the last two weeks, my first two by myself although I have scrubbed on many. These were the first 2 that came early enough. Usually they are too far gone. I had one a month ago that was open and gangrenous and I only did a simple mastectomy thinking it too far gone. Of course I cannot get lab confirmation or diagnosis so I don't know for sure that they are cancerous. But I did it and found no nodes in the axilla, so it may have been a gangrenous ulcer. Anyway, I did a skin graft to cover up the part I couldn't close and she recovered with no sign of anything. May live longer than I will.

"Jack and Sue play well together. Jack comes down to Sue's level except when he can't be boss or when they are fighting. Then Sue gets the worst of it. Sue has had a lot of bad infections on her skin; we had to give her a course of penicillin in Kano and they cleared up. Then another after we got home. Today I started another. She had some blister bug blisters and they get all infected too.

"Another operation we did Friday was a mass on right jaw of a woman. Size of a small cantaloupe. Jaw bone cystic tumor. Broke through the jaw at the upper end, but had to saw through it at the chin. Of course this leaves no lining on the mouth on the right and no teeth from the chin but she is eating all right and swallows down the left side. Is nursing her baby too. Had a lot of post operative swelling the first day but is doing all right now."

Rollie wrote that he had been given a New Testament from the Pocket Testament League which had come to Nigeria for two years. He promised to read it every day. He said, "That's easy, but it's kind of 'akward' to carry it around all the time. But I'm doing it, except when I go to bed at night."

"Nov 14, 1958 We just got back from conference. Boy, is it ever hot! Well, it's only 93 with 15% humidity. It's been hotter. Practically windless. We're having trouble getting water because one of the leathers is worn out and more than half of the water per stroke goes back into the well with just a little wind pumping it. This morning, we took some boys down to pump by hand, got one drum for the hospital, 2 drums for our house and 3 for the nurses' house when the pump handle broke. Are sending the handle to Maradi for welding. If Carey Lees would get here in a hurry, he could fix the pump since we now have the proper size leather. The Lees finally arrived two weeks before we went to conference, and now the Maradi crowd is holding him up for 2 weeks for work there. You can't win.

"Burt went to Doctor's conference, was able to spend 3 days at K.A. with the kids. Lanny, a week previously had tried to play Tarzan and was jumping onto a tree limb, fell and landed on a rock, got a big bump on his head. They took him to Jos for x-rays and found everything intact. Just before Burt got to Jos, Cherry had been in the hospital getting 9 stitches in her leg. She was jumping from her wardrobe to bed and missed. What next? Johnny's birthday was spent on the road yesterday, so he had his present and cake today. Rollie is taking trumpet and piano lessons. Prefers the trumpet.

"We are expecting the Van Lierops tonight on their return from conference. They will spend the night. Zabriskies will be coming through tomorrow noon. Folks by the name of Halls will be coming from the other direction tomorrow night, spend Sunday here. The Pollens will be going through on their way to Guesheme on Monday or Tuesday. Hope we have drinking water and bath water for them." Guess who fed and prepared beds for all the people who came through!

"Dec. 8, 1958 Burt leaves in a few days to pick up the kids for Christmas holidays. Saturday the doctor from Madaoua brought two patients just as we were about to begin our own surgery schedule. One man had fallen off a truck and was badly cut in many places and the worst was on his knee which had most of the flesh torn back. The other man had been in a fight—he with a stick and his opponent with a sword. They were fighting over this man's wife. (Cherchez la femme!) This man got 9 sword wounds—his left ear was cut in half and just hanging. His right arm was fractured where the sword cut through; his left elbow was separated at the joint and the bone broken. Other sword wounds on his head, legs, arms and back! What a mess! His wounds were dressed and the fractures set.

"Two weeks ago we had the French doctor from Madaoua and his wife and 2 year old son over for Sunday dinner. They returned the invitation, and we spent yesterday with them. Had a delicious French style dinner. Started with hors d'oeuvres—radishes, sliced salami and sliced ham; sliced tomatoes, sliced hard boiled eggs, liver sausage, French bread. Main course consisted of rabbit and little potatoes french fried. Then lettuce with salad oil on it. The next course was

3 different kinds of cheeses with more bread. Then a French pastry, soggy with some kind of brandy with whip cream on top of it. Finally, a dish of fruit for us and tangerines for the kids. Then followed the usual cup of strong coffee. We drank water but they had their bottle of wine on the table. The doctor had made a trip to Maradi on Thursday and bought all of these cold cuts, cheeses and fresh fruit. They are flown in from France by air. Expensive. Most of the French doctors in the overseas service are army men. He is just a young fellow and a lieutenant. Their term of service is 2 1/2 years; he says he will not choose to return to this area. (I wonder why!) All the conversation was in French, so I didn't say much. Burt does very well."

Christmas came and went. Burt and the children got home on Sat. the 20th. It was such a good feeling to all be together again! I hated the idea of being separated from them but knew it was for the best. The children were thrilled with their gifts from Fran and Bill. The boys loved their watches, Cherry and Sue their dresses. For some reason or other, Johnny's gift hadn't arrived but he had other gifts from us to make up for it. And the prospect of Fran and Bill's gift to come.

"Dec. 28, 1958 If we say it's 4:30 o'clock, meaning in general, one of the boys will say, 'no, it's 28 after,' or 'check your watch, Rollie (or Lanny).' So we have to be very accurate. Christmas eve we were at the Lees for a get-together; Christmas day we all had dinner here, each contributing a part of the meal. We had one duck and 4 chickens, mashed potatoes, canned corn, cole slaw and lettuce, cranberry sauce, dressing, squash and mince pie with ice-cream and coffee. Not bad for the desert. The Harbottles have invited us to dinner on Jan. 1. Christmas morning the believers had their pageant on the birth of Christ. Fri. night we had a party here for them, which they all enjoyed.

"A new couple, the Husbands, have been asked to come to Galmi. They won't be finished with language study until April, and should come after that. Another doctor has been accepted for Galmi. (The VerLees) We don't know when they will be arriving in Africa, but they will have language study for six months in Kano before they get here. We will need at least one new house, and right now funds for building are about nil.

"Next big item will be the arrival of our little one. The kids are all very excited about it, and each has his own choice of name—Stephen and Mike running first and second for a boy. The kids can't quite make up their minds on a name for a girl. Due date is 3 weeks from today. Good-bye for now."

And that brings 1958 to a close and leaves you hanging until next year to find out if it was Stephen or Mike or someone else!

Chapter 9

PAM PLUS 1959 THROUGH JUNE, 1960

Our quiver is full! It wasn't Stephen and it wasn't Mike. It was Pamela Marjorie born at 9:05 a.m. on Jan. 16, 1959. She weighed 7lbs. 10 oz., same as Sue. Very fair.

"Water broke at 10:45 Thurs. night We went over to the hospital about midnight, and pains were irregular and not too bad until 6 a.m. After that I went to work. I was hoping she would be born on Beret's birthday, but the day came and went. Cherry's the one who got her wish as to the baby's sex. Solves a bedroom problem. We'll only need two bedrooms for the kids—a girls' dormitory and a boys' dormitory.

"The hospital work has been very heavy. Burt is not getting home for lunch until 3 or 4 p.m.

Pam's arrival ushered in the cold, windy, harmattan season. It was also the busiest season of the year and we were hard put to finish the day's schedule. And there were always emergencies. We were scheduling non-emergency surgery four months down the road. Below is an excerpt from Burt's letter home.

"Jan. 30, 1959 Yesterday we had a more interesting day than usual in which we removed one cataract, repaired one hernia, removed a large lymphoma as big as a man's hand from the back of his thigh, removed half the lower jaw (from chin to temporal mandibular joint at upper ear level) for a meloblastoma, did a skin graft and opened a hand infection."

Our Maradi boys' school was an agricultural school as well and they were beginning to reap the harvest. We, too, benefited because every two weeks they shipped us a basket of fresh vegetables. We were able to get cabbage, egg plant, carrots, beans, tomatoes, radishes, lettuce, kohlrabi, turnips and paw paw. In fact, our own paw paw tree was beginning to produce. So things were looking up, food wise, not like it was almost ten years earlier.

Pam gained weight, she slept well, she nursed well. You might say she was a perfect baby. After one month she was sleeping from 10 p.m. until 5 or 6 a.m. "Her hair is as red as Johnny's and her complexion is like his, too, so it looks like we'll have two red heads in the family. Her eyes are gray blue."

"Feb. 13, 1959 Johnny is coming along all right with his school, but he doesn't like to have it interfere with his play. If he's in a dark mood, he can pout and refuse to give the answer even though he knows it. Then we come to a road-block; I fume and he pouts. So he sits until he says the answer—which he knows and stubbornly refuses to say."

About this time, we received word that another doctor was in the pipe line—Jim and Mary Ver Lee. He was a Wheaton grad of '49. It would be a year before they appeared on the scene because they were still raising support and then they would have six months of language study when they arrived in Africa.

"Dau Duka made a public confession in church Sun. of his sin, but his repentance has not produced any restoration. That is, he still has his second wife. His first wife is in Konni, and rumors are that she has remarried. So the whole thing is quite a mess, and we don't know what the answer is or can be."

I was still helping out at the hospital on a limited basis. I would leave the house after Pam was down for her morning nap, and Sha'aybu would come to the hospital and get me when she woke up. We saw some extraordinary cases. In one day, we operated on a 14 year old Buzu girl who had no vagina and had never menstruated but the blood had piled up in her uterus and tubes for several years. Since she could never have children, we removed the uterus to prevent further menstruation and build up of blood.

We saw pseudo hermaphrodites—maybe a half dozen that term. We operated on a girl who had no peritoneum and removed an eye which had a tumor about the size of an orange protruding from it which had pushed out the eye. Burt removed a bladder stone and repaired a bowel which had been perforated some time back by the Tahoua doctor when he tried to repair a hernia. Then Burt looked at the patients that the nurses had saved for him. No wonder he wasn't getting home for dinner until 3 or 4 o'clock.

At school, the kids were excited about Pam. In devotions one night John Herr asked for prayer requests and Rollie asked prayer for his mother who was going to have a baby. John Herr asked if I was in Jos, and Rollie replied, "Oh no, we get them on our station."

"Cherry has been writing notes to the new baby for weeks. Rollie wrote, 'We have got the news about the baby and I thank God that it's alive and I hope it doesn't get sick and die till the Lord's purpose for it on earth is over. Pamela isn't a bad name. There are better ones I suppose. But I couldn't think of any. Your son, Rollie.' Lanny wrote to Pam. 'Dear Pam. How are you? I'm fine. I hope you are. I'm your big brother. Love, Lanny.' Cherry sent Pam a home made valentine."

From Burt's letter in March, 1959:

"Kids all like the baby immensely; Pam is doing well; her eyes are getting muddier gray and are going to turn brown, I think. So we will have a red head with blue, and a red head with brown eyes. This, her second month birthday, finds her at 11 lbs 8 oz., 4 lbs over birth weight, a nice steady normal gain. She is still breast feeding but is too hungry for that only now and is on cereal, fruit when available, and supplemental feedings at times. Sleeps through the nights now most of the time. Sue is plenty wise and can find her way around situations when she wants to, but she is getting cuter as her light blondness increases, and in fluffy pink dresses, like Fran sent for Christmas, she is a beauty. The Madaoua (French) doc has only a little boy, and he is crazy about Sue, but she won't give him a tumble. Partly because she doesn't understand his French and figures it as a good thing to avoid. Even Jack finds it hard to extend his hand for a handshake which is very French and even for the kids, all shake around when we meet."

The Hausas have given Pam two names—one, "sarauniya" which means "queen" because she is queen of the household; the other, "mai hankori" which means "patience" because John and Sue always want to hold her or touch her or play with her.

Our holiday was in April, and we had the usual good time. Some of my time was taken up with Pam's needs and John's home schooling. There was the usual fellowship with the missionaries, the Bible classes during the week, dental appointments, shopping in Jos, teas and tennis. Meals for pre-schoolers were one half hour before others, and they ate in the "children's dining room", under the supervision of their parents. I think we probably had Issu or Yahaya with us and he looked after the children while we ate and he did our washing and folding and sweeping daily.

"We've met lots of new missionaries, including the parents of Rollie's girl friend! He and Sherilyn Kliensasser have been 'friends' for 3 years now, and they both have taken a lot of razzing this holiday from both sets of parents. We asked Rollie how he shows his affection! Sometimes they exchange candies on candy day and sometimes go for a walk or sometimes they hold hands. He blushes crimson when she is mentioned!

"Cherry has been a little mother to Pam this holiday and Lanny was delighted to hold her, but Rollie, the oldest and most reliable, was afraid to hold her or pick her up. For him, she was too fragile.

In June, 1959, we looked for the return of the children from school. They were to fly to Kano, come by car with the Maradi bunch to Maradi and then with the Van Lierops the rest of the way. In the meantime, Sue and John were enjoying the plastic pool on the back porch that Grandma Kletzing and Neva had given them. Pam was watching them from her Teeter-babe (the same one we used for the other kids). Our melons had ripened and we were enjoying them. There was a slight let-up in the hospital work since the first rains had come and also because of the big Muslim feast. They kill a ram in celebration of Abraham's sacrifice of "Ishmael". I was able to get over to the village together with some of our Christian young women. We now had three nurses and the new doctor and his family were on the way. A new sect of Islam was taking Gidan Doutchi by storm. We heard their chants until the wee hours of the morning.

"For 3 days and 3 nights the people waited on the road for 'a great prophet' to pass by and touch them on his way to Mecca. He passed by all right but overhead. He flew to Mecca. A few days later, a lesser disciple came along and blessed the crowd, and when the crowd pressed him, he got into his modern car and took off again."

Contrast that with Jesus' patience with the crowds who were always pressing Him! I learned a lot of patience, too, because with the whole family home and a never ending arrival of guests, preparing food and beds seemed to take a lot of my time. Pam was in her seventh month and crawling all over the place and was not content to be in her play pen or Teeter-babe sine she had found greater freedom. The Lees were back and with their five and our six, we had quite a compound full. We had visitors from other missions passing through, some going to Miango for their holidays. They could only book Miango in the rainy season since SIM had it all booked up for the other months of the year. Rains were late and the people had planted three times and most of the first two plantings had died. It didn't look good.

"July 31, 1959 Do you remember Francis and Edith Schaeffer who were at Camp Mi-ch-dune for a summer while we still had camp there? They were in St. Louis when we were there, too, as pastor of Bible Presbyterian Church which we attended more frequently than any other. We lost track of them through the years, although we knew they had gone to Switzerland for Children for Christ shortly after we left St. Louis. Then a year or so later through friends in the mission who receive their prayer letters, we got in contact with them again, and have been receiving their prayer letters ever since. They are terrific! They work with young people now and have a peculiar ministry in which they open their home to students or other young people and just talk over their spiritual problems with them. Their days are full of appointments and meetings with visitors who may stay for an hour or for days. They make special trips to England and other countries for weeks at a time, and each hour is taken with special personal or group meetings in a home. It is thrilling to read how these young people—many of them intellectuals—come with their doubts and questions and find Christ as a result."

This was the beginning of L'Abri (the Shelter), the great work that grew out of their initial ministry in Switzerland. We continued to receive their letters and follow them as they expanded and became well known. We met with them again several times in later years, and a few years ago when we were returning from a short trip to Africa, we visited L'Abri together with the Emmetts. The Schaeffers weren't there, but one of their daughters was, and she gave us a tour of the place. Dr. Schaeffer died in Rochester, MN and Edith still lives there and continues her ministry from there. L'Abri continues in Switzerland and England and other places. It is good to look back and remember that we knew them as little people like us, before they became famous.

From Burt's letter to his folks Aug. 14, 1959

"I think one reason for our babies being so good lately is that Ruth is an expert mother. She sure gets organized rapidly when one comes along. One reason we didn't bother having her go to Jos; she had it one day and even though resting had things nicely organized and controlled from then on. (Ruth speaking now—I couldn't have done anything without the help of our house boys and cook and help from the children and other ladies on the compound.)

"We are all okay, but it is the wettest part of the rainy season, and it is either wet or raining all the time, so it is pretty messy in the house with all the tracking in and out, and the kids don't have much way to let off steam. Rollie and Lanny go hunting with Carey Lees a bit and really enjoy it. Mostly ducks and turkeys and owl.

"A snake medicine man put on quite a show in the market yesterday. Had six 8 ft. hooded cobras and six large vipers like rattlers but no rattles. He played with them, stroked them, provoked them to strike, but they always struck short of him. Claims he has "magani" (preventive medicine) and can't be bitten. Sells the magani (a red colored string) for 10 francs each. People here, except the young ones, know better though, because a year or so ago one of them died after being struck. But it is quite a show to see a cobra all reared up with his neck piece all flared out swaying back and forth with the man, looking him in the eye, gyrating around as the man does, just like hypnotized. Then the guy waves these colored threads over them, and they turn over upside down and lie there for half an hour, till he snaps them out of it. (Proves the strong nature of the medicine!) A month ago a fellow was sold some medicine (2000 francs) to make him invulnerable to knives. He then plunged a knife into his belly to prove it and came in here to have his abdomen wall and stomach sewed up. Every day I asked him if his medicine had caught on yet and pricked him lightly with a knife. By the time he got out, he claimed he was going hunting for the one who sold it to him and get it out of him. He wouldn't pay me the same for sewing him up though."

School time was fast approaching and I was busy sewing name tags on the kids' clothes—this time for four of them. Three K.A. ladies visited us about that time and they pitched in and helped with the sewing. They said they "see Rollie all over again in Johnny Jack." They saw him running one day and thought of it.

Our summer with the kids was good. A few weeks before the summer ended, Johnny said, "I'm not going to get on that airplane!" Then several days later he said, "I'm going to take second grade with Mommy too, and go to school next year for third grade. I'll be a big boy then." This came as quite a shock to us. This was the first time in a long time that he did not claim to be a big boy already. But at this point, there was no turning back. We didn't have any second grade books and since he had resisted first grade at home so much, and had always said, "Me a big boy, me go to K. A." we were dumbfounded. Neighbor Jerry Lees was going to first grade and was enthusiastic. No backing out for him. We felt that we should go with the plan of sending him, knowing that he had 2 older brothers and an older sister there.

Cherry learned to use the pedal Singer sewing machine that summer and did a little on the accordion, too. Rollie had taken trumpet lessons for a year. The Pollens and Van Lierops arrived with their children, picked up ours and the Lees, went on to Maradi where they loaded into the Powers' truck for Kano. Spent the night there and flew to Jos the next day.

Meanwhile Pam was beginning to stand up and was a good baby. She enjoyed her thumb. Her eyes were getting very dark. It was strange to see such dark eyes with her red hair and fair skin. She was a good sleeper too which I appreciated very much.

When the four oldest were gone, part of my heart went with them. The place was quiet, and Sue was the big girl and Pam, the baby. As Issu said, "The house is too big now," meaning there weren't enough kids around.

During the afternoon of Oct. 2, the whole village disappeared. Fear gripped the people. They huddled in their huts. They thought the world was coming to an end. The sky darkened and the sun

212

disappeared. The people didn't reappear until the almost total eclipse was over and the sun shone again. As for us, we watched it with darkened glass, but for me the glass wasn't dark enough and for about two weeks my eyes pained me, and I had to wear my dark glasses around the house. Fortunately, there was no permanent damage—I think.

The next day the Drapers from Dahomey (now Benin) arrived with six patients for Burt to operate on. Russ was a fighter pilot in Europe during World War II.

". . . he told us how he got shot and was the first fighter pilot to bring a damaged plane back to England. He had a big hole in his shoulder. He showed us the bullet they removed—he has it made into a key chain—as well as the scar. He was shot when he was strafing Germany and anti-aircraft fire got him. He believes the Lord alone enabled him to get back."

When Pam was 8 months old, she was sitting on the floor one morning while I was getting breakfast. She ate breakfast as usual, and we went about our business. About noon she started vomiting and had loose stools.

"I saw parts of a bug in her vomitice and stools. I kept giving her milk to make her vomit which she did about three or four times, and by that time most of the bug was out. We realized that evening that it was a blister bug. The bug, if it sits on you, leaves a discharge which raises blisters and is very poisonous. In fact, the Africans cut them up in little pieces and put them in the food of their enemies if they want to kill them off. Very simple. We realized that Pam had eaten one—we recognized it with finality when we saw the red colored wings that she vomited. She was very sick until bed time and very listless and pale." Her crib was next to my bed and all night long I would wake up at intervals and get up to see if she was still breathing. We prayed without ceasing!

"The Africans also say that what kills the person is the blisters that they raise in the intestines. Pam's ability to get rid of it fore and aft was what saved her, they say. Anyway, we praise the Lord."

It wasn't unusual to have dead bugs lying on the floor each morning. They were attracted to our lamps and came in through the cracks in the windows and under the doors. Usually, the ants would have a feast during the night and clean up the floors, but apparently they were smart enough to avoid blister bugs. They are no dummies. Even the Bible commends the wisdom of the ants. It wasn't too long after this incident, that Pam discovered the art of standing up and holding onto the furniture.

"Today Pam is 9 months old. She took her first steps a few days ago, and she's raring to go. We stand her up alone and move away, and then she starts to haltingly walk. She's taken 9 steps at once now. Cherry was our earliest walker, at 10 months, but the way Pam is going, she should beat even Cherry."

The annual doctors' conference was coming up from the 27th to the 29th, and this time I decided to go with Burt and see our kids. I was especially anxious to find out how Johnny was faring at school. I also needed some dental work done. The Kraays were back from furlough, having left their two oldest children at Ben Lippen School.

"Nov. 1, 1959 from Kano. A week ago Sat. we left Galmi, arrived in Kano about 6:30. We were limping in on our flat spare tire. Came all the way without benefit of battery because the starter shorted it out. Had to be pushed every time we stopped. Monday we got passports in order and Burt bought 2 new tires. Tuesday morning we flew to Jos. Burt stayed there for doctors meeting, and I bummed a ride to Miango. It was sure good to be with the kids for a few days. Johnny is making 2nd grade all right. Thursday afternoon Burt came out and we returned to Kano on Friday morning. Tears from 2 members of the family—Lanny (!) and Cherry. John just walked away rather bewildered. Yesterday Burt put the car in the garage to have the starter worked on. VerLees are here studying language and should be on their way to Galmi in February. We're thinking about furlough and have applied for air out of Kano with stopovers in Zurich, Frankfurt, Amsterdam, Brussels, London and Liverpool where we will board the S.S. United States. Don't know how we'll manage the stop-overs with the little kids, but we'll see."

Doctors' meeting and conference over, and back to Galmi and a full work load. A new nurse, Cathy Klein, came from Nigeria to help us out for a few months before she goes on furlough. About this time, Ben Van Lierop's brain tumor returned.

(From Burt's letter of Nov. 17, 1959 "... it is now about 4 1/2 years since he had surgery. There is little else to do for him ... he is taking it pretty hard, although with good faith. He hates to leave the field not knowing how long it will be till his death, and if long, he will not feel at home in America away from his real work. He bears it very well as to pain, head pressure and all. Main worries are the family. They have three kids, one in second grade two in high school in England. These two visited their folks out here this summer, as a gift of their grandmother. I guess they thought the time would be short for Ben. They are going on furlough next month. They have a home of boys in Dogon Doutchie, most of whom are in various government schools, one has graduated from Tsibiri SIM Bible School, one has just graduated from government veterinary school, several are in teacher's college, etc. They have all signified that they will carry on the work at Dogon Doutchie and evangelize the area all around to try to establish offspring churches for the mother church at Dogon Doutchie. So it leaves things in a fair state of preparation which leaves him a great deal of consolation for the work."

The Van Lierops made their furlough home in Holland, Michigan where Ben's family lived. I will skip ahead a little and mention that we arrived home for furlough in June of 1960, rented a house in Chicago on N. W. Circle in Norwood Park, thanks to the efforts of Ruth Reuter. It was late summer or early fall that we got the call from Gwen that Ben had gone home to heaven. Shortly thereafter, she came to stay with us for about a week. Gwen did return to Niger and spent more than 30 years more in Dogon Doutchie and Maradi before her retirement. During those years, she often came to stay with us for a few days or a week and considered us her shoulders and confidants. She is retired in Toronto but has visited us in Sebring twice. Her daughter, Muriel, is married and lives in Toronto, and her two boys, Bernard and John make their homes in England.

Back to 1959. Pam was walking all over now. If she started to lose her balance, she stopped and rested and then started out again. Her eyes turned a piercing brown and her hair became darker red rather than strawberry blonde. About this time one of our missionaries, Bill Strong, had an accident. He had two nurses with him. He was traveling behind a bus, eating his dust, and decided to pass the bus even though he could not see. He ran into a culvert, the car turned over and the gas tank was punctured. The doors were jammed, but the Lord provided a way of escape. The whole windshield separated from its frame like a door, and the girls crawled out and were able to pull Bill out, although his arm was badly burned. Minutes later, the car went up in flames. The bus stopped and took them to Niamey (about 5 miles) where they were treated.

Christmas came and went and so did the kids. Burt drove to Miango to get them. The kids got up at 5:45, had breakfast and they went all the way to Sokoto in one day, 450 miles. Got there by 8 p.m. Made stops most of the way every 25 miles to let the kids out and check the oil, etc. Had one good meal at Gusau about 3 p.m. Then they ate again at Sokoto. The next day, they left Sokoto by eleven. I'll let Burt tell the rest.

"Then, on the road, where I had gone through 6 inches of water going down, I plunged in and sank in 18" of water and conked out. It was a good thing I didn't get in any farther as it was a yard deep a few feet farther on. Same pool. It is spring fed apparently and gets deeper at times. Took a lot of cajoling to get pulled out of there by the Africans. Fortunately there is a village near there. Motor would not start so we pulled and pushed it out and up the hill till the back was downward so the water could drain out of the exhaust pipe and then started it by compression in reverse backing down the hill. So we had to take a wide detour through deep sand and got pushed two more times in it. Then we got to customs during their rest hour and had to wait an hour for them to get up. So we didn't finally get home till about five."

. . . they (the kids) are really excited about being home. Johnny has grown so, it's hard to recognize him as the same boy that went to school three months ago. He's put on weight. Pollens took off after supper with Johnny Van Lierop to go to Dogon Doutchie, pick up the Van Lierops and be off to Niamey with them the next day. About 10:30 p.m. they were back—they had forgotten J.V.L's passport which Burt had brought with him from Jos. So they spent the rest of the night here . . . we had 11 sleeping here that night.

Christmas was a happy time. Christmas morning we were serenaded by the Hausa ladies and Virginia Fridal. She had taught them "Silent Night" in English and French. So they serenaded us in three languages and it was a cold, blustery morning—65 degrees with high winds. After that, everyone was awake so we turned on the Christmas tree lights that we had strung up in the house, and they ran off our wind charger and converter. So after that, we opened up presents but before that we hooked up the tape recorder and got a spontaneous tape of "Christmas morning at the Longs." Soon, vacation was over and we had to say good-bye, but with the prospect of seeing them in February for a few weeks and then wind down for furlough in June.

"Rollie was a little broken up about leaving for school, because he had said good-bye to his black friends for the last time and hated to leave them and his boy-hood home. None of our kids know any other home or country, except for the year in America, and when they say good-bye here for good, it's like leaving a part of their life here. This is their home and Rollie loves it more than the others. (Remember when we first left America and arrived in Paris and then in Africa, Rollie wanted to go home. Home was where Fran and Bill were.) K.A. of course is a vital part of their life, but that also goes when they leave Africa."

The church was having problems. Tanko, a professed believer who worked in the dispensary, impregnated a young girl, Hassana, who was working at the hospital. Hassana complained of pain in her abdomen and when Burt examined her he found her to be 5 months pregnant. She was shocked. Apparently she didn't know how she got that way. She was only 16 years old. Tanko was fired and put under church discipline for a year, which included giving the baby his name and having his name on the birth certificate to make the baby legitimate. Hassana was also put under discipline for 6 months but she kept her job. Hassana gave birth to a boy and he was named "Istiphanus", Hausa for Stephen. Genevieve Kooy mothered both Hassana and "Isti" for years, sent Isti to school at Tsibiri, then to secondary school, and Isti has been "her boy" even though not legally. Hassana married Cisu, and they had several other children, but Cisu died as a young man of an aneurysm and that left Hassana a widow with small children, and Gen continued to support all of them, although Hassana worked in the hospital as well. After secondary school, Isti got a good job in Niamey and has turned out to be a fine young man. He married the daughter of Abdou, who was one of the Van Lierops' boys. Abdou held the Dogon Doutchie station and church together for years, and it was less than a year ago (1996 or '97) that Abdou went to be with the Lord.

On Pam's first birthday Dr. and Mrs. Dion Warren arrived and their two children. They were stationed in Jos caring for the physical needs of missionaries, and this was their holiday. Getting out into bush work was a change for them as well as an eye opener. They were with us for two weeks, and Dr. Warren did surgery with Burt and also separately from Burt. So in those two weeks a lot of surgery got done.

Sometime after that, the Ver Lees arrived from language school in Kano. They moved into the house next to ours. They came with four kids. Alice, Don, Peter and Faith. Finally we had a second doctor, but it would only be for a few months because we would be going on furlough and leave Jim to handle the whole hospital alone. We heard later that at times he was overcome with the responsibility and Wilf Husband was a good encouragement to him.

We did get to Miango in February/March and celebrated Sue's birthday there. We invited all the children of French country and had cake and Kool-aid. She loved the attention. Pam was walking well by now and mimicking sounds beautifully.

"When she wakes up in the morning, usually before anyone else, she just sits up in her crib or lies there until someone gets up, but as soon as someone is up she demands 'out'. Cherry had the lead part in the school play—Pinocchio—and the four Long kids got 12 ribbons on Field Day."

While we were at Miango, word came to us that George Powers had been killed riding his motorcycle in Maradi town. A truck without brakes plowed into him at an intersection and dragged him about 30 feet. George was going to town on business for the B.D. The next day, SIMair brought Iva to Miango where her two children were in school, Lillian in 5th grade and Danny, in 3rd.

On the way home, we had the usual car/road problems: "Just 35 miles from home we ran into an impassable road. They are building an all-weather road from Sokoto to Konni and the deviations (detours) are many and impassable. We got into one dilly that was nothing but sand for 2 miles. We finally couldn't go any further because the ruts made by trucks were about a yard deep, without exaggeration. We waited until 6 p.m. (from 4:30) for a road grader to come and pull us through the 2 miles and get us on to the dirt road again. Then there were a few more sandy spots that we had to be pushed through, and it didn't help matters to have the battery go dead as a result of many stops and starts. So we did the last 35 miles in 4 hours. Home never looked better."

On holiday we got word that my father had died, and I have covered that earlier. Our children never knew my father although Rollie had met him when he was 1 1/2 yrs. old in California on our way back from Alaska. So the only grand parents that our children knew were Lasca and Ritchie, Burt's folks. Apparently when Johnny heard us talking about Dad's death, he said, "Our granddad is dead, isn't he?" We assured him that the granddad that he knew was still alive and well.

Back at Galmi work began on the east wing of the hospital and a house for the nurses, which we called the motel. Carey Lees and his crew of carpenters and masons arrived, and soon there was a big hole in the ground next to the hospital. No bull dozer did the job, but a lot of Africans with pick and shovel. We hoped to see it finished before we went on furlough.

The Husbands stayed with us in our house for six weeks while the houses were being built, so with their two children, Steve and Danny, and our two at home, we were quite a family. We did have a break when we went on holiday for three weeks, after which the Husbands took a short holiday. Wilf and the boys returned, but Esther remained in Jos until Bonnie was born on July 3.

"April 2, 1960 The building work goes on. The Husbands have moved from our house into the nurses' house, and although the two nurses are still there, it is easier from them to be there than here . . . They moved on Wednesday and that was the first day since Burt took the kids back to school in January that our family ate together without guests, not counting our holiday.

"It has been terribly hot since we've been back. It has been 105 in the house, and one afternoon, it registered 107 in the house and 130 out in the afternoon sun . . . We are sleeping outdoors at night. The heat along with her vaccination has made Pam out of sorts and needing a lot of petting. She is covered with prickly heat and has some small boils on her chin and upper lip as well as a big scab from her vaccination. As a result, she is not eating much, but I presume she will be through this phase before you get this letter.

"May 25, 1960 Carey Lees is here, having returned from Madaga to finish up the building work on the hospital and girls' house, and he is eating with us. Wilf Husband is back from holiday and he is eating with us. So having two extra 'farm hands' to feed three times a day, adds to the work. We are sorry we won't be able to move into the hospital wing and actually work in it before we leave.

"If all goes as planned, we will be in Zurich a month from today. There is a mountain of work to do yet"

Somehow we made it. We met the four school kids in Kano, flew BOAC to Rome (a 7 hour trip—2200 ft up at 300 miles/hr cruising.) Landed in Rome about 5 A.M., had a 4 hr. lay-over in the bleakest air terminal in the world. It was like a huge barn. Barely inhabited. Then we flew to Zurich.

"June 25, 1960—Zurich airport—6:30 p.m. Just a note from Zurich. We've had a good trip so far, although it's rained in Zurich since we've been here. Took a bus tour to Lucerne yesterday and a tour of the city today. Everywhere we go we are a spectacle what with six kids in tow. We've had two compliments from strangers on how well behaved they are, so they're making a good impression anyway. Hope it holds out.

"Took an Irish plane to Zurich. Alps were beautiful all around with snow. Rollie and Lanny spent some time up in the cockpit with the pilots. In two hours we'll be in Frankfurt, leave there on Monday morning for Amsterdam, then Tuesday for London and Thursday to the boat. Bye for now."

Chapter 10

SECOND FURLOUGH—1960-1961

Now here we go again, and I have to rely on my memory. That means this chapter will be short. We got to London without any hitch and stayed in a Christian missionary home, not related to SIM. We then boarded the S.S. United States for the next to last leg of our homeward journey. The boat was one of the newest traversing the Atlantic and it was the fastest. All the passengers scrambled for deck chairs, but we traveled so fast and the wind was so strong, after the first hour or so, everybody deserted them. So whenever we wanted a chair on deck (and it wasn't often) we were able to get one. When people saw a family of eight, they either shook their heads in awe or in disdain. What can you do but shrug your shoulders! We may have been traveling on a first class boat but we weren't traveling first class. We could see the upper deck where people were swimming in a fancy pool, but we swam a few times in the tourist class pool, about the size of a 12 x 12 ft. room.

The Queen Mary (or was it Elizabeth?) left before us and I believe it was the 2nd day out that we passed it up. When we arrived in New York, we found that two other boats had just docked and the customs and immigration room (it was a huge barn-like structure) was jam-packed. We collected our luggage in one spot, and with the six kids in tow, Burt took the passports and stood in line. He had a splitting headache. After about two hours, he went around to the head of the line and spoke to those in charge. He told them, "Look,

I have a family of eight, we've been waiting all this time, I have a splitting headache. Can't you do something?" With that, the customs officer very apologetically came over to us and checked the baggage without opening anything and waved us on. I forget how we got to the mission but we got there, spent a few days there debriefing and getting physicals, and then headed to Chicago. I don't remember how we got there. You kids are going to have to help me walk through this year.

I believe we stayed in a house on Wesley Street in Wheaton around the corner from Fran and Bill for a few weeks, and then rented a house on Circle Ave. in Norwood Park, thanks to the efforts of Ruth Reuter. The rent was a fabulous $200.00 a month—an amount we thought was terribly high, but with a family like ours, what could we do? It was a house that met our needs and we were thankful for that. Nowadays (1997), one can't rent a room for $200.00 a month. Lance remembers that he and Rollie and Johnny slept upstairs and the only heat source was through a vent in the downstairs ceiling, and they huddled over the register each morning waiting for a whiff of warm air to rise to their heights. It really wasn't adequate and they remember those COLD mornings. The living room and dining room were large, and the dining room had a raised platform near the side bay window on which was our telephone stand. The kitchen itself was small so that only one person could occupy it at a time, but it did have a dishwasher—a first for us in 1960! The eating area was large enough to have a round table that seated our family of eight beautifully and a small working table. The two bedrooms downstairs (or were there 3 bedrooms?) took care of the sleeping quarters for the girls and us.

Being in Chicago meant that we could get to the Center in about 10 minutes, so the children were able to be a part of the Awana clubs. Hank and Gertie Holmbo lived not too far from us, and Hank usually picked up the boys for club. Hank and Ruth Reuter also lived near us and we had good fellowship with them. Closer than any was Neva Kletzing, Burt's aunt, who lived on Neva Ave. which her father named after her before the road was paved.

Lanny, Cherry, John and Sue went to the Norwood Park Elementary School. Cherry was in fourth grade and had Lois Mutchler for her teacher. Lois was a member of the Center. She had graduated with Burt from Wheaton College. Sue spent half a year in kindergarten and half a year in first grade, so when she went to K.A. on our return to Africa, she started in second grade. John was in third grade, and I guess Lanny was in 6th. Rollie had finished grade 7 at K.A. and Burt took him down to Jones Commercial High where he was tested to see if he might be able to get into high school. He tested very well, so he enrolled at Taft High School as a freshman in the fall of 1960. Pam, of course, was at home with us, not quite 2 years old.

I told you that you kids have to help my memory out. So Sue, then five or six reminded me today of one of the few things she remembers about our furlough there. She said that once I was so frustrated with all of them, I just sat down in the middle of the floor and cried. It so impressed the kids that they decided to behave themselves. You know, I don't even remember that.

I remember going to the Center on Sundays and we sat as a family in one row, closer to the front than the back. Many were the time I was so moved by the choir and the beautiful music that tears just welled up in my eyes. I was so starved for good music!

I remember that we had a trash burner in the basement and once during the end of our furlough when we had a lot of packing residue, Burt had a fire going so hot that it heated the inside walls of the chimney to the point that we thought we would have a chimney fire. But by the grace of God, it didn't happen and he learned a lesson.

Ruth Frame (now Van Reken) was living across the street with her grandparents and aunts while she went to high school and her folks were back in Africa. She would come over and do my ironing. We paid her, of course. It was her way of getting some spending money and my way of getting some help.

Toward the end of furlough, it was packing time again, and the basement was cluttered with drums. Unfortunately, we had to get out of the house after a year and our visas had not come yet. Hank and Gretie Holmbo came to our rescue and gave us their garage to store our drums until we left. More than that, they opened up their home to us. We thought it would be for just two weeks, but the visas were delayed time and time again so our two week stay turned into 4 and then 6 weeks. The Holmbos were most gracious although we know it had to be a very trying time for them.

Most traumatic was leaving Rollie at home. He stayed with Fran and Bill who had moved to Carol Stream and he attended Wheaton

Academy as a day student. The Academy was out at Prince Crossing then. His experiences at the Academy were sweet and sour. Fran and Bill made wonderful surrogate parents, and we are forever indebted to them. Later on when we left more of our children at home for college their home was our children's home away from home. Speaking of homes that impacted our children's lives, I must mention Howard and Lina Duncan who fed our gang and were their transportation to and from the Center many a time. We are forever grateful.

Now I have just about exhausted the highlights of our second furlough and the rest is up to you. If you will write down your memories of things that happened on furlough, I will incorporate them into this autobiography, even if I have to re-write this chapter.

Cherry's additions and recollections:

With reference to our trip home on the S. S. United States, it took 4 days to cross. This is when the fog horn blew and Pam about jumped right out of Dad's arms. It's also where she learned to eat butter patties, I believe. It's where I learned about shuffleboard and tourist class. We weren't allowed on Deck A. We were Deck B people.

(This was the furlough that we lived on Circle Ave., in Chicago.) It was a 2-story house with a living room-dining room combination, a small kitchen with a galley section and just barely room for a table. There was a study, a bathroom, and a bedroom which you shared with "the baby"—Pam—on the first floor. Upstairs were 2 bedrooms off a hallway. The back room housed Sue and me, and the front one at the top of the stairs had a small room off the back of it which Rollie used by himself and Lance and Jack had the big room. There was also a large walk-in closet for all three of them. They had a desk in there—a "secretary" where the front pulled down. Boy! I'd love to have it now! The full basement came in handy for rolling up Rollie's newspapers for his delivery job. We all had to help him prepare the papers, but he got the pay! (He did the delivery.) The front screened porch was a great place for quiet work—even in fourth grade I remember enjoying being there. One day I made a book of some sort with a title page. I was so proud of it, and when I showed it to Dad, you acknowledged it, but then said I should have done the title in all capital letters instead of mixed capital and lower case. You were right, of course, but I remember feeling completely deflated. Many an hour Sue and I worked together on that porch—I was "teaching" her writing in order for her to make a transition into 1st grade from kindergarten.

For Christmas I had received a plug-in child's stove. One day I asked if we could cook the pan of cocoa on my stove. You said yes, and I was so pleased. Something happened then to spill the whole pan all over the floor, and this was on a school morning! You were so patient, Mom! (I believe this was while Dad was gone out west to do speaking in churches, and we were home alone—that is, you were there with all 6 of us kids!) That kitchen was really crowded with all of us in it at the same time!

I also remember how cold it was in the winter and hot in the summer. Rollie, Lance, and I would grab our clothes in the morning and get "dibbs" on the heating vent in the dining room next to the kitchen to get dressed on top of.

When Grandma & Grandpa Long came to visit, Grandpa and I worked together to untangle the string in your string can. It made me feel pretty special to be working alone with him. But I got a very clear impression that he was a disciplinarian, and I'd better be careful. That year you also burned some stuff off Grandma's face and neck. She also took me downtown on the bus one day and we had a ladies' day out. She bought me a dresser dog which I may still have today in my scrap box! I remember going out to Carol Stream to visit Fran & Bill's new house under construction. They said it was costing them $17,000. I loved that house, and to this day I regret not buying it from them when they were ready to sell. They gave us first dibbs, but we didn't know what we were doing and didn't think we could afford it. It would have been our best financial move so far! Within two years the value of that house went up by $20,000!

That year (speaking of Awana) I would often go with Carol (Hawkinson) Sisson to the Center on Saturday mornings on the bus. That was the year we really got to know her. That was the year she and Dick became an item. There was also the time when Dad dropped Sue and me off at Awana and someone from the alley ran into him. Eventually he had to go to court downtown over this. One evening when he wasn't home after supper, we asked you where he was, and you said he was at court. I thought he was going to go to jail! You set me straight on that!

I also remember that was the year we were inundated by Christmas gifts from Elmwood Park! We had never seen so many! It was great!

I was in 4th grade, Jack in 3rd, Lance in 6th. When we got back to Africa, of course we were in the next grades.

Ruth Ellen told me in the past couple of years that ironing was so boring that she was always glad when either you turned on the T.V. or we came home and we turned it on so that she could watch while she ironed! She was too shy to ask you if she could watch T.V. and iron at the same time!

(At the Holmbos) It was 6 weeks. I remember how crowded it was sleeping on mattresses on the floors and never being able to find things. I attended their neighborhood school for a short time before leaving for Africa, and my 5th grade teacher was very intimidating to me. One day I left my watch (my first watch and therefore beautiful and valuable) in the gym after PE. I was afraid to ask the teacher to let me go get it, so a friend did it for me. But the teacher knew she didn't own a watch, and chewed her out in front of everyone for lying. Then I had to approach her anyway to tell her it was my watch and could I go get it? She said o.k. Surprised me! Also, on the first day, Sue and I got lost trying to get "home" for lunch. Finally, Gertie sent her son Don (Jack's class) to find us, which he did, and we were all turned around! We hardly had time to eat. But I was so humiliated by getting lost! Everyone laughed and thought it was so funny. I had my birthday while there, and I got a Barbie doll—the one with the black and white striped swim suit. I wish I had it today—it's worth a fortune! It also had a gorgeous lace wedding dress. Gertie and Hank were cool. Remember picnicking in the back yard? (As I look back on it, I can see how that was logistically the easiest thing to do with all of us!)

Also, I remember going downtown to buy shoes for the next term with Dad. He had bought so many that when they were tied together, they looked like more merchandise. Dad set me guard over them, and a customer came over and began to peruse them I was too shy to say anything to them, but I got Dad's attention, and you told them they were already sold! I vaguely remember the questioning look in the person's eyes—that you were buying so many at a time! I remember that on the way home from that excursion we stopped at a small shop and got ourselves milk shakes!

Saying goodbye to Rollie was very hard for me, too, Mom. I was sitting next to you and crying as we waited to taxi away in the plane. Even to this day when I think of saying goodbye to Rollie, I feel the sadness all over again. We were close enough that he was a brother to me—my big brother no less—and though I'm sure he wasn't thinking about me at the time, I already missed him.

Thanks Cherry, for the memories. There are some things in your essay that I had completely forgotten. That you all survived and turned out so well is a token of God's grace to us as a family. And it continues to this day. Since Lance and Cherry are the only contributors to this section, I'll wrap up this chapter and go on to our 3rd term at Galmi—unless someone else wants to contribute.

Lance's reflections:

"We were in Wheaton for a short time before moving to Chicago. One night, I awoke and saw the lights on downstairs. Knowing Dad wouldn't leave a light on overnight, I was sure the Rapture had happened and I was left behind. I crept downstairs quietly (just in case the Rapture had not happened—I didn't want to be caught out of bed). What a relief to see the two of you reading in the living room! I snuck back upstairs and made sure of my salvation right away. I guess I was 11 yrs. old.

"When (I was) at camp, you moved in to Chicago. The Circle Ave. house: huddled over the grate in winter trying to get warm.

"Rollie was in high school. We were fighting. Mom spanked me but when it was Rollie's turn, he wouldn't let Mom spank him. Unfair!

"I wore shorts to school the first day. I was laughed at and teased. How was I supposed to know? I had a fight with one of the class bullies. It ended up a draw, but Mom scolded me for getting grass stains on my pants.

"I started violin lessons. I would take the Harlem Ave. bus to Diversey and walk to the Ulfengs. I always wished the bus would crash. One time you were to pick me up at Ulfengs. I walked so slowly, you were there before I arrived. You didn't know whether to hug me or spank me. I still have that violin. It's over 50 yrs. old. Made in Germany during W.W. II.

"Too long at Holmbos. One time Gertie scolded me for doing something with Dave. It was okay for him but not for me because I was a missionary kid. In school, I postponed and postponed a major project because I knew we were leaving soon. We left the day before it was due.

"But at K.A., I had to take some make-up classes in Math with Mr. Phillips. But I sure was glad to be back. I remember staying up late with Dad to see the election results.

"Well, I can't think of much more. I didn't start keeping a diary till 7th grade."

Thanks, Lance. That was great! It reminds me that I often wondered if the Rapture had taken place when Fran and Bill got home late. I remember watching from the living room window until they were in sight walking from the street car and then scurrying off to bed.

Chapter 11

FROM OCT. 31, 1961 THROUGH 1962

Too soon furlough was over. The day that we dreaded most arrived. Saying goodbye to sisters and brother, Burt's parents and friends was hard. But it didn't compare to the pain of saying goodbye to Rollie for four years. Fran and Bill would be his surrogate parents and our confidence was in them as well as in the Lord. We enrolled him at Wheaton Academy out in Prince Crossing. Fran and Bill went all out for Rollie. They took him in, loved him and treated him like their son. Relatives—the Hollanders, Cedergrens, Beret, Pat and Ron helped him celebrate his birthday and gave him nice gifts. The Hennixes, Olsons, and Purdues surrounded him with love. The Frizanes, Amundsons and friends were very kind to him and included him in many of their outings. There was just one thing missing. We weren't there for him.

Our last few weeks were spent with Hank and Gertie Holmbo while we waited for our visas. Finally, the visas came through and by this time we were anxious to be on our way because we had imposed upon the Holmbos' kindness too long. In going through letters, I came across some notes that I made concerning our departure and travel. They are on 3 1/2 x 6" note paper and I'll write them down just as I jotted them down on the trip and after the trip. Where I have put parentheses and italics I have added those remarks as I write.

"Oct. 31, 1961 Left O'Hare 9 a.m. after farewell service at airport. Flew Am. Airlines jet to N.Y. 75 min. Nov. 3—Fri. evening left

Idlewild (that's either LaGuardia or Kennedy today, I'm not sure) with the Kings—Cookie and Nolan—KLM to Prestwick, Scotland and Amsterdam at 3 P.M. Sat. To Krasnopolsky Hotel until Sun. aft. 4:30. Sat. went thru a clothing and dept. store. Nov. 5, slept in. Took a walk in aft. along the canals. Supper at airport while plane delayed. Left Amsterdam KLM 8:00 P.M. Arrived Kano airport 6 a.m. Nov. 7, circled for 1/2 hour. A plane had blown 3 tires on runway preventing us from landing so had to fly to Niamey.

So there we were in Niamey, but we couldn't just get off the plane and head east for Galmi. Our ticket read "to Kano." Then, too, the kids had to go on to school, so we waited in Niamey, drank some Fanta, and finally boarded the plane again and went on to Kano.

Meanwhile, back home in Wheaton, Fran started her faithful writing to us. Nov. 5, 1961, was a Sunday and she writes to us: "Yes, you were in New York before I was home. We drove Pat back to her house where we had a cup of tea. By we, I mean Rollie, Beret, Bill, Pat, Agnes and Sam. Then I dropped Beret, Bill and Pat off at the Des Plaines station and took Rollie back to school. Got there at 11:15.

Rollie is working on his leaf collection . . . . Rollie is adjusting very well, and I'm sure he has times of lonesomeness but he seems to be happy . . . .

"Nov. 6 Saw kids off to K.A. in aft. On WAAC. Few tears from Sue. Solemn faces from rest. Cherry fearful of big plane without us. Nov. 7 To airport with Loyd Wickstrom who hit a man on a motor bike on the way. (Not Loyd's fault). Burt went back for Dave Boyes who took us the rest of the way (to the airport). Dave Rutt flew us. Met (in Maradi) by Ockers, Lucases, Gordon Bishop, Edith Durst and Rabi and Mrs. Grafmiller. Flew to Konni, buzzing Galmi. People speculated that it was 'tsofon likita' (old doctor). Met at airport by French gendarme and 3 horsemen. Took us in open jeep to Dr.'s. house. (Degbys) Glad to see us. Had drinks and they sent us to Galmi in their car and chauffeur. Met enthusiastically by Husbands, VerLees, Cathy Klein, Ruth Hunt and Virginia Fridal. Slept in guest house. Started cleaning (our house).

"Nov. 8—Thurs. Many greetings for the next few days.

"Nov. 9—Fri. 3rd, Mr. Daniel Taher, American Vice Consul from American Embassy in Niamey and Frenchman passed through. (Mr. Taher's thank you letter is attached) Nov. 10 Dr. from Madaoua and wife (French) and Dr. and Mrs. Degby (African) from Konni and Margaret (Hayes) came to VerLees for supper with all the gang. Nov. 11—Mrs. Grafmiller and Edith Durst arrived about 1:30. Nov. 12—Tues., Mrs. G. and E.D. left about 3:30. Heard later they ran out of gas and didn't reach Maradi until 10:30 P.M. Nov. 13—Rutens passed through. Nov. 20—Zebs came, brought Cathy's (engagement) ring. Had party here. (Cathy Klein was going home to get married.) Nov. 21—Zebs left.

"Nov. 25 Yahaya and I washed walls in front room. Hung drapes, washed floors. Burt got transistor record player working. Enjoyed Michelson's Touch and Helen Barth and Baylor U. Could see the Center choir singing "It Will Be Worth It All", as Helen sang it. Thank you, Lord, for that song. Thank the Lord for the Center and Doc, etc. standing true to the Word. God, keep it that way always! May this term be worth itself in counting for the Lord! This music tonight takes me back to Center and its music and if heaven has this kind of music it'll be worth it. But heaven's music will be better.

Our K.A. kids were home for Christmas. It was a happy time although "I felt like a mother-hen whose one chicken was not under her wings. Other times when the children have come home from Kent Academy for the holidays, it gave me a certain contentment that we were all together under one roof again."

"Jan. 7, 1962 A month and a half since I've made any entry. The kids went back to school today via SIMAIR Konni after an extended holiday from 15th Dec. Enjoyed the kids very much. Spent the day in bed nursing my nasal congestion and nausea and dizziness. Sue had a hard time leaving, with tears, and I fear she is coming down with measles. Dave Rutt brought up some vegetables from Jos which was a gift from him and his wife (Lyda). It was very kind of him and the Lord, who supplied before I asked. This noon I said to Issou, 'I'm so tired of rice. Are there sweet potatoes in the market?' 'Not until market day,' was his reply. But while I was asking they were being unloaded in Konni—and not sweet potatoes, but white ones. Praise the Lord! And besides the potatoes there were green beans and carrots and cabbages and tomatoes."

This ends my scribbled notes and I'm glad I have them because they are my only points of reference between the time we left Chicago until January.

—

Back to letters again! One of the first things I did when we got back was to start a boys' club based on Awana. This was the end of 1961.

"Jan. 11, 1962 Several weeks ago for the first time we asked for a show of hands on those who wanted to receive Christ. A number raised their hands and eleven boys stayed after the service and Pastor Hassan and I talked with and prayed with each one individually. We're praying that each profession was real. These boys are all Pal-age boys.

"The work in the hospital continues to grow, and with two doctors operating, we are averaging 7 operations a morning. There are over 200 people sleeping in our hospital, half of them patients, the other half, their friends. We have only 70 beds, so when some patients are well on the way to recovery, we have to move them to the floor to make room for immediate post ops."

Yes, Sue did come down with measles. As soon as she got to K.A. she went in to the sick room and stayed there for 2 weeks. Red measles with a temp up to 104 at times. Then when she was well, John got them. Gerry Craig wrote in her note that 9 of the 34 in the infirmary had the red measles, and the rest, the 3 day measles. "She hopes she never sees another measle!" To this day, Gerry reminds us that we sent measles from Galmi to K.A.

We wrote to the kids that on Pam's birthday she was three and "ready to go to K.A." Sue said, "If Pam wants to come to K.A., she can come and take my place." Gerry added a footnote, "Oh, my. We've failed."

Rollie and Lance, do you remember Mai Dabo? One time he took you down to the fadama in the rainy season, and it had just rained, and the water was rushing down the hill but had not reached you yet, and you were on the other side of the gully. Yahaya and Issou were very agitated to hear that you were down there, knowing that the water would gush down the gully and become a swollen stream soon. I sent one of them down to get you, and they got you home before the wadi got filled up. Those were anxious moments for me. We thought that Mai Dabo was a bad influence for you. I wonder what has happened to him. (This is the same fadama where Ishaya, Ibrahim and Lydia's son, was drowned in the rush of water. He was about 10 years old, a promising boy who had made strides in memorizing verses in Awana.

I believe he was really born again. I forget what year it was. I may happen upon that in a later letter.)

Ila was working for the VerLees. "Sha'aybu and Dogari are good helpers in the boys' club. There were 4 more boys saved last week, including Moussa, Dau Duka's son, who is about 7 years old.

Today, 1998, over 35 years later, Sha'aybu and Dogari have gone back into Islam. Moussa became a thief and spent some time in jail. Don't know where he is today. So many of the professions that were made in club amounted to nothing, mostly because of lack of teaching. It would be discouraging except for the few who did turn out okay.

For example, Iliya, the son of Lydia and Ibrahim went to French Bible School, came back to work in the hospital and then went on to some nursing training and is in charge of the nurses in the hospital. Abdou Abou is another of our Awana boys. When we were in Cote d'Ivoire in 1995 or thereabouts we were in the SIM headquarters' office and all of a sudden we heard, "Likita Tsofo!" We turned to see Abdou, who was in anesthesia training in Cote d'Ivoire. Today he is in charge of the anesthesia department at Galmi Hospital and according to Belva Overmiller, who recently returned from a short term at Galmi, he is the best anesthetist that she has ever worked with. He has an outstanding testimony as well.

Then there is Isti, Gen Kooy's charge. Isti was the son of Hassana and Cisu. Isti did all the schooling available in Niger, and today has a responsible job in Niamey. He married the daughter of Pastor Abdou of Dogon Doutchi a few years ago. Pastor Abdou was the protege of the VanLierops and carried on their work when they left there. Abdou died last year.

So there is some fruit that has remained. We wonder where all the other boys and girls that were in our clubs are. Only heaven will tell.

"Feb. 28, 1962 The doctor from Madaoua brought in a patient one evening who had a double twist in his bowel and had a bowel obstruction. Burt and Jim operated . . . the intestine was all blue. They untwisted it, deflated it and put it back in, all the while applying suction from the nose and rectum and giving intravenous fluids. But the patient died at 2:30 a.m. He was too far gone when they brought him to the Madaoua dr. who immediately brought him to us."

At this point, the Africans had their conference in Maradi. Zeb was the speaker and 14 young men and women went from Galmi, including my "boys". Eight of the nine hospital employees went also. So we really had a time of it. I was doing all my own work—cooking, cleaning, dishes. One day my beds didn't even get made. With all the hospital help gone, Burt and Jim had to clean up the body, wrap him in a sheet, dig the grave and bury him.

"Friday night, Dotty Rudolph, Virginia Fridal's replacement, came. She was brought by 3 of the Embassy folk. Since independence (1960) America has an embassy in Niamey. There are 15 Americans there. We gave them supper and beds."

One of the men was with the Dept. of Information and had some films with him. Word went out to the village and about 200 people showed up to see the film, Project Mercury, which told all about the flight of John Glenn and a short history of the space age. The Africans enjoyed them and also the two short films—one on health and the other a take-off on "Chicken Little".

"They just about died with laughter at seeing the barnyard animals dressed in clothes, speaking, smoking and living like human beings .... Sat. nite the VerLees and we went to the Madaoua doctor's house for supper. It was a delicious supper with 7 courses plus white and red wine (which we declined). Shortly before we came home, Pam sat down in a lawn chair, and legs went out under her and her finger got squeezed and pulled her right forefinger nail right out. Well, you can imagine what followed. It is still very sore, but it is healing."

You will remember that Ben Van Lierop died in 1960/61 while we were on furlough. "Monday morning at 6:30 a truck stopped out in front, and Gwen Van Lierop got off. She had arrived in Dogon Doutchie the Tues. before, and came down to Galmi to see us and brought a sick little boy. Gwen had left her 3 children in England. Muriel, who is now 18, is starting med school—a six year course. Bernard is 16 . . . and John is 10 . . . . That same day at noon, Zeb arrived from conference . . . . All of the above happened while our African help was gone (starting with the bowel obstruction from Madaoua). Was I ever glad to see Issou Tues. morning."

That same Monday morning Burt took off for Sokoto to do his leprosy rounds. The next noon, "after I had returned from the hospital, an American male voice called at the front door, 'Is anybody home?' I didn't recognize the voice, but hearing it in English, I said to come on in. I was in the kitchen. It was Ambassador Cook, our

American Ambassador and his wife, who were passing through, and they brought a letter from Maradi. They couldn't stay but said they would return and tour the hospital and extended us an invitation to visit them at the embassy when we go through Niamey . . . . Earlier, the Cooks had made visits to all the dispensaries in Niger. They were appalled at the lack of medicine in the dispensaries. We learned that before we returned, America had sent 2 tons of medicine to Niger to be distributed, but the Minister of Health was from Guinea, then a Communist country, and suspicious rumor had it that he wasn't going to distribute it to the dispensaries but let it become outdated and then dump it so they could say America had not given any medicines. The American Embassy worked at getting it released, and Jim VerLee wrote to the Embassy asking them to augment our sulfa supply. The result was 4 crates of medicines that came through the embassy.

There is quite a bit of meningitis in the area, so we have all taken a prophylactic dose of sulfa. We have two cases isolated outside the hospital, across the road in a makeshift mat house. The first person that came died; he was already in a coma when he arrived."

"March 11, 1962 Tomorrow we leave for Fada N Gourma. We will be gone nine days. The folks in Haute Volta have asked Burt to come and conduct a circumcision class in two or three districts, so that their Christians can learn the delicate art and circumcise their own children. The people in that area are pagans and their circumcision of children is associated with special rites connected with their entering manhood. (Initiation ceremony). Christians therefore need a satisfactory substitute. We will be going through Niamey and hope to spend a little time with Ambassador Cook and his wife."

Pam enjoyed the ferry boat ride across the Niger River and we stayed with Mrs. Bechtel at their mission guest house in Yantala, just outside of Niamey. Mr. Bechtel had died from a snake bite the year before we went home on furlough. The Bechtels were the ones who met us at the Niamey airport when we first arrived in Niger. They were driving along in their truck when Otto spotted a kite (hawk), grabbed his gun and chased it into the bush. He had only thongs on and a snake got him on the back of the foot. His wife raced him to the hospital, but it was too late, and he died.

Mar. 19, 1962 "Today I write from Fad'N Gourma, Pete Strong's station. Besides the Strongs, the Dubizes and Al Swansons are here. Young Pete is in 9th grade at Hillcrest, will be going home with his folks this summer and going to Ben Lippen."

"Since being here (Haute Volta) we have learned more about what goes on at these pagan circumcision camps. The boys go to these camps at puberty, are beaten daily, circumcised, eat and drink contaminated food and water, are made to stay up at night and sing obscene songs, go through mock tribal warfare during the days . . . . All this is to make men of them if they survive. Last year 6 boys died in these camps near Mahadaga."

No wonder our missionaries have set up these Christian circumcision camps. Along with the surgery, done under sanitary conditions, comes about a week of Bible Study and Christian fellowship while they heal.

At Mahadaga and Piela other camps were held and Burt instructed the missionaries in the operation. At Mahadaga, 28 boys were in the camp. From Diapaga to Mahadaga is only 35 miles, but the road was horrendous—bush trails and over a mountain. The Christians from Diapaga and Mahadaga made a "road" over the mountain, meeting in the middle. Three miles across the top—rocks and ruts.

"Next morning we got up at 4 a.m. and went hunting with Telford (Ruten). We traveled about 20 miles over bush trails, up and down dry river bed ruts and saw many herds of hartebeest, dykers, antelope—Burt shot an antelope, and Iver, a bush pig—(wart hog.) So the missionaries and Bible School boys had meat. They seldom buy meat in this country. We didn't see any lions or hippos or buffalos, but they are there and have been seen. Back at Fada again, 22 more boys were circumcised."

"Pam has no one to play with except her imagination. She enjoyed the hunt. We kept talking about seeing game, and she didn't quite understand the game until I made a game out of it and told her that part of the game was getting in and out of the car, walking quietly and not talking and moving on."

"On the way over to Haute Volta we had stopped at Ambassador Cook's house in the American Embassy in Niamey, visited with him in his air conditioned office, met the 15 members of the Embassy and received an invitation from him to have lunch with them on our return."

"March 25, 1962 We kept our dinner date with Ambassador Cook and his wife in their air conditioned home . . . . dinner on fine china stamped with the United States insignia. Glasses, too, had the imprint. Perhaps I mentioned that they are colored, but very white, and when I first saw them, without taking a good look at their features, I thought they were white.

"Had pineapple aperitif, avocado on lettuce with French oil for the appetizer, followed by a fish course, a filet mignon with carrots and potatoes, and cake and coffee. We were there for about two hours, then went back to the mission, changed and headed for the road.

"It never rains but it pours!" In April of 1962, things began to pop!

"April 3, 1962 The Managua doctor came with 8 patients who were victims of a truck accident near Madaoua. The truck turned over. The truck was licensed to carry 42 passengers, but there were over 70 jammed in besides loads, etc. Forty injured, but we got only the 8 worst ones . . . . one remained unconscious, received I.V.'s for 4 days and died. Two had crushed pelvises, one with internal injuries! He was urinating blood. The other Burt thought would get well, since he felt there were no internal injuries but he died Sunday morning. At the same time, the first one, who was only 3 beds away, must have thought he was doomed to die, too, because he went into shock and never came out of it. Burt thinks he just literally scared himself to death. They were all young men, probably in their twenties."

"Rollie, remember NaMari, the canteen owner in town. He bought a car and crashed it up yesterday west of Dogon Doutchie, killing a V.I.P. from D. D. and critically injuring another. He is really in trouble now. Perhaps God is dealing with him. He has heard the Gospel many times."

We learned later that he got off with a slap on the wrist, and it was rumored that he would be given a new car because his car was totaled. Not a bad sentence for having killed a man. We wonder where NaMari is today. We saw him again when we visited Galmi in 1990. He still had his canteen; was still very friendly, but still uninterested in the Gospel. He looked old and worn out, but I doubt he is as old as we are.

Contrast that with what happened to one of our missionaries in Nigeria. Marian Ward made a mistake. She went down a one way street, realized her error, and backed out, and ran over a beggar who was lying in the street, and killed him. She was held for first degree murder, put under arrest and was "held" in the Jos hospital with a policeman outside the window. Finally pressure was brought to remove him. After many anxious weeks, the trial came up. The charge was changed to manslaughter and she was sentenced to 7 years in prison. By this time, Marian was very emotionally ill. It was appealed, and she was "imprisoned" once again in our hospital. Finally the charges of manslaughter were dropped and she was fined $75.00 and her license revoked for three years. She came out of this a nervous wreck and the mission sent her home to recover. "The first court was held by an anti white Pakistani judge who had had it in for the whites and the mission for a long time. The appeal was judged by a white man. So there you are. Draw your own conclusion.

April, 1962 "Two of our hospital workers, Idi and Musa, rebelled at the rule that they have to read four hours a week in order to keep their jobs. Neither of these boys could read or write when they started to work and now they can read a little and feel as if they have arrived! So they walked off the job, took the matter to the labor syndicate in Konni. One of the men came to see us and questioned Burt, and they were very kind and tried to patch it up. However, we did not back down, and since they did not want to read, we would be glad to let them go and pay them their severance pay, and that's the way it was left. They started (the boys) to find ways to come back to work, after they realized their jobs were gone, and after five more days, they decided that if Burt would PLEASE take them back, they would read and make up their last week's reading time. Then they went to Konni and told the syndicate to forget the matter, that everything was all patched up. One good thing that came out of it was the fact that Idi, who is a very strong character, insisted to the union leaders that he was a Christian of his own accord, that no one here was forcing him to believe, and that he would be a Christian until the day he died, whether he worked for us or not. They had a hard time being convinced and laughed at him, telling him he would perish and better return to Islam, but he held his ground. So they are back at work.

"Issou and Yahaya have been accused of having plural wives, and so that thing is hanging fire.

"Another girl who works in the hospital and made a profession about a year ago turns up pregnant.

"This morning, we hear that Labo, our dispenser has been giving shots on the side and making a good profit.

"We wonder what is next. We've been asking the Lord to cleanse the church—maybe this is the beginning of His answer—bringing all these things out into the open at once. Pray with us about this."

Meningitis hit hard this year. We isolated them across the road in grass huts. Many died. Those who came early received sulfa drugs and recovered; those who came in a coma never came out of it. In April we had 30 patients across the road; in a nearby village, 42 died. We ourselves, including all hospital staff, took prophylactic sulfa pills. Since Burt is allergic to sulfa, he took penicillin.

During this time, a Konni doctor and midwife came with a Frenchman and his wife who had been in labor for 3 days. The baby was in a posterior position. About midnight, the mother was given a spinal and the baby was delivered with forceps. A live 8 lb., 8 oz. baby. Madai, Pastor Hassan's wife, also delivered about the same time, without any trouble.

The hot season was in full session and we slept outside. The sky so dark—the stars so numerous! We could see the Southern Cross in front of us near the horizon as we fell asleep.

This thing with Labo came to a head about two weeks later. Wilf Husband and Burt worked out a plan to find out if the accusations against Labo were true.

"At noon each day for four days, Wilf planted himself on the ceiling over a peep-hole watching the dispensary where Labo was working. After all the workers had gone home, Labo was still cleaning up—and I mean 'cleaning up' in more ways than one. He took kerosene, and boxes and pockets full of medicine, which presumably he sold in the market each day. After Wilf and Burt decided the evidence was sufficient, they confronted Labo. Burt asked him what he was going to do with all the pills in his pocket. He said he hadn't been feeling well, and he was going to take them. So Burt said, "All right, I want to see you take them. Take them all right now.' He hedged. Well, Labo was let go, and is now back at Tsibiri where he originally came from. The real tragedy is that he is supposed to be a 'good Christian'. He was an elder in the church and was the S.S. teacher for my boys' class

—

239

on Sunday mornings. He had graduated from Roni Boys' School, was fluent in English. This all came to a head because the fellows started pointing the finger at Issou and Yahaya, so Yahaya said, 'All right, so I have 3 wives, but Labo . . . .' So we started to watch."

The Frenchman and his wife stayed in our guest house for over two weeks. She had a slow recovery because of her ordeal. They ate with us which added to my busyness and ingenuity. How do you vary a diet that consists mostly of rice and onions and goat meat? Fortunately, we had brought a supply of canned and dried foods back with us and we were able to vary the diet a little. Milk was plentiful and I made butter with the cream, and we were able to get a few fresh things from Maradi. They were open to the Gospel. They were Catholic and were concerned about going to church on Easter Sunday—a must for them. They were also concerned about their newborn son, Olivier, and his baptism. Easter Sunday afternoon "I went down to their room and we read together from John, they in French and I in English, of the death and resurrection of the Lord. They were amazed that the New Testament was so interesting. They have received a New Testament in French from us, and we hope they will continue to read it." Burt also had a good opportunity to speak to them about spiritual things. The long term results of their time with us is that we became good friends, and I can't think of their names right now, but he was the "Cotton Man". He introduced a better cotton seed to the farmers which produced larger bolls. The farmers who chose to go along with his plan were given the seed, planted and harvested it and took it to Madaoua to be weighed and sold. From there it was trucked to the big cities for export or sale. Olivier must be 36 years old now. We wonder what has become of the family.

"Dotty Rudolph who is on our station now has a camera (I forget what you call it) that takes and develops pictures right away.

"Lanny is taking violin lessons from Dr. Sandberg. They are stationed in Jos, at the SIM hospital, not Bingham. Here is your next verse—Isa. 30:15 '. . . in quietness and in confidence shall be your strength . . . .'"

The month of May brought a few changes. Gwen Van Lierop came through and returned. Burt went to Maradi with the '54 Chevy motor, came back at midnight on the courier. The Bishops came to replace the Husbands during the latter's furlough. Pollens came back from furlough the end of June. Iva Powers was stationed with us. Gen Kooy returned in July. Cathy Klein left to get married and not return. Fruit basket upset!

We were seconded to the Eye Hospital in Kano for six months. Burt was Doug Hursh's replacement. By June 1, we were settled in, and I was put to work in the B.D. (Business Dept.) The B.D. was quite a hub of activity, and I worked from 10-12 and 3-5. The B.D. is where the action takes place—the comings and goings of missionaries in the Kano district; the fridge filled with cold cokes, lemonade, ginger ale and orange; the mail distribution center, and the food purchasing department. Missionaries in the bush sent in their chop boxes and orders to be filled; then the boxes were trucked out to them. Every six weeks, folks from Maradi came down to get their B.D. orders filled. Most international air flights came and went from here. There were about 20 missionary families stationed there and Kano was like a small oasis in the desert. Every Friday night the compound ate together and had prayer meeting. Our six months there was delightful. Lanny worked in the optical shop at the cash register during summer break and Cherry baby-sat for the Boyes. The Hurshes, Husbands, Hoovers, and Mc Alherans left for furlough. Allister made over Pam, played with her, held her and tossed her into the air. "I was reminded a lot of you, Rollie, when I watched Allister with Pam. Of course, he asked about you."

"Gordon Bishop was down from French Country getting his car fixed. It had broken down on a trip to Maine Soroa . . . a new station out in the Chad area with hundreds of miles of sand between it and Zinder. Carey Lees drove the Learneds' car down from Maradi. The Learneds are going to Galmi to conduct a short term Bible School for 6 weeks, and will be living in our house . . . . Johnny Bishop and Dave Ockers are at Collingwood, and Esther Ockers is going home this summer to join them there."

June 17 was Father's Day in 1962. Just a bit of trivia.

Our family's round robin was in process, and we had received letters from Aunt Ruth, Uncle Harry and cousins Jane and Victor (and wife Dolly) and brother Bob. To Victor, I wrote, "We have a built in swimming pool in our back yard here, too. It's round, about 5' in diameter. Yesterday about 12 kids were in it in two different shifts. It sounded as if they were having a hilarious time. And they were."

To Bob, I wrote, "We are having 'large quantities of weather' too. Right now we are battling temps between 90 and 100 with a rather high humidity.

Kano under the British was a show piece of what an African country could be. Food in the market place and on the shop shelves, colorful gardens and round abouts in town! One could buy almost anything he wanted. We had orange trees in our back yard, and it was Lanny's job each morning to squeeze 14 oranges by hand for us. Delicious! Especially after having lived on the back side of the desert at Galmi for so long. We savored our time in Kano, knowing it would be short-lived.

(1998—Speaking of swimming pools, Victor's swimming pool was a large built in pool located in his back yard. We saw it when we visited Victor and his second wife during our retirement years. Dolly died in Nov. of 1992. Victor married Frances on May 28, 1994, and we had the pleasure of knowing them better since we wintered in FL and they were in Miami. We visited them a few times and they came to our 50th wedding anniversary celebration at SIM Sebring in March 1995. Victor died in Aug. of 1997—almost a year ago. Fran has moved to Gainesville, GA to be with her daughter and family.)

Nineteen sixty two was a historic year in the space age. It was the year that John Glenn orbited the earth. We were all very excited, even in Nigeria. Kano boasted a tracking station for this and other flights. We were invited to see a documentary on the flight of John Glenn.

"We went out to Project Mercury. The film showed Glenn dressing, his entry into the capsule, the various tracking stations with local color all over the world. It showed the blast off and the beginning of the flight, pictures of the world as he was going over. We could see the entire outline of Africa as the capsule orbited. There were many scenes of Glenn himself in the cockpit. We saw his shoulder straps floating during his weightless periods. We noted the various expressions on his face and the 'crushing' facial expression as he reentered the atmosphere. It looked like he was being squeezed together. Most impressive to me was his startled expression when he was informed that plans were changed for the re-entry release of the retro rockets. His signals were registering 'all's well', but you will remember that a false signal was being received at the Cape saying that his heat shield was coming loose. He immediately composed himself and asked, 'What is the reason for this change?' Their response impressed me, too. It told him nothing. "We feel it is the best thing to do.' We saw the capsule in the water, the rescue and transfer by the helicopter, his jubilant reception on board the carrier."

Now, in 1998, all this seems elementary—"been there, done that . . ." sort of thing. In 1962, this was awesome!

Still in Kano and the kids are with us from K.A. for summer break—"July 13, 1962 This morning Pam called from bed, 'Daddy, your sweetie pie is waking up. Come and get her.' Other times, it's 'Your peachirino hurt herself.' There is no humility or reserve with her. She thinks the world revolves around her . . . and in a way, it does.

"We are so glad that Bill is well again. The Lord was good to spare you, Bill. He was good to us is what I mean. The older I get, (41 in '62) the more I realize that we who are left are the losers, and those who go before us, when they enter into the joys of heaven, must realize that they never had it so good and wish that we would hurry up and get there, too. At the same time, the fear of entering into a new experience, the unknown, is always a great deterrent to our desire to hurry up and get there.

"Lanny has changed—he is a bass one minute and a tenor the next. Cherry is a big help, a willing worker, and a cheerful person to have around. One of the missionaries said the other night after church, 'I was watching your oldest daughter, and she is just beautiful!' John and Sue are still little children, most of the time thinking of their own interests, but at other times, very solicitous of the welfare of the rest of us and quite willing to pitch in and help. Sue's hair is very long and looks beautiful in a pony tail. It is almost down to the middle of her back. John's thoughts are on play. He is in charge of watering the garden, so he wishes for rain with mixed feelings. John is my right hand man and "go for". I am giving Sue and John piano lessons this summer. Cherry will be eligible to take lessons at K.A. next year."

During a Friday night missionary get-together, Sue was running around outside and tripped on a barbed wire fence and gashed her arm quite badly. Burt put 16 stitches in it and 2 more in a wound on her chest. It healed up beautifully with only a line like an inverted 'v' scar and she continued to run around. Then, her 'boy friend', Charlie

Brooks, also age 7, fell off a fence post and broke his arm. It was set and cast at City Hospital.

"July 22 The night that Sue hurt her arm, Jess Christensen from Fago, about 60 miles from here, was wiring his house, and he got an electric shock from 220 v. He was on top of his house, and when the electricity went through his body, he was unable to let go of the wire, and the juice went through him for a minute before the electricity was shut off. Mrs. Kretschmer, who lost her husband in an automobile accident last year, got to him immediately but couldn't touch him, so she prayed in German—the last thing Jess heard. Then when the electricity was off, she noticed he wasn't breathing so did mouth to mouth resuscitation. Word got to us about 1 a.m., so Burt and two other men missionaries, went out, arriving at 3:30 a.m., to find Jess in bed, apparently no worse off from the shock, and telling the women they shouldn't have sent for the doc."

The way Jess tells it, "Here, I am, I wake up to find myself being kissed by a beautiful woman! It is also rumored that his wife, Ruth, ran to turn off the electricity and turned off everything except the house electricity, diverting the full force to Jess. Jess had something to say about that, too.

Kano in 1962 was quite different from what it is today. Then the British were still running the city even though Nigeria became independent in 1960, I believe. One of the more modern places was the Central Hotel. On special occasions, the missionaries went there for a meal. One of these was a farewell dinner for Charlotte Bruce, who was going home on furlough. The atmosphere included soft lights and music. You would hardly think you were in Africa. The hotel was run by Europeans. Besides the dining room the hotel ran the "Club" which boasted a swimming pool and tennis courts among other things. It was not only the Europeans who enjoyed this life-style. Well-to-do Africans, mostly associated with the government, had their Mercedes-Benzes parked outside while they enjoyed the good life. Besides the Europeans in Kano, there were about 30 Americans who manned the Project Mercury base and another 25 in the Peace Corps who worked about 25 miles out of Kano. Of these expatriates, a number were Christians, at least in name, and they came to the church services. One of the two morning services and the evening service were in English—keep in mind that English was the official language and used by educated Nigerians. The other morning service was in Hausa. Both morning services were always packed out—about 300 in each service. During each service, in another building, two Jr. Church services for the children were held—one in Hausa and one in English—with approximately 100 children squeezed in for each service. Sandwiched between the two adult services was a large Sunday School. After the evening service, tradition held that the missionaries have a sing song and "coffee and" at the guest house. I like tradition. Kano also boasted a polo field, which hosted many games and tournaments. The stadium, which was the site of many national and international soccer and rugby games was only a block from the SIM compound.

The summer passed quickly. Rollie spent a good part of it at Camp Awana, two weeks as a leader in Pals, and two weeks in Pilots as a camper. He went home with a number of prizes, including the top Bible prize and third prize in All Around Camper prize. Outwardly, Rollie was doing fine. We didn't know the struggle he was having inside. He was happy at Fran and Bill's but had his problems at school with those he called "snobs", kids of well-to-do families who disdained missionary kids. Hindsight is always better than foresight. When we left him at home a year earlier, Hillcrest was not available for SIM kids. It was that year that SIM and Hillcrest came to an agreement that allowed our m.k.'s to attend Hillcrest for high school. Lanny was just finishing up 8th grade at K.A., and he was leaning toward going home for high school, but it didn't work out. One reason for his wanting to go back to the States was the traditional rivalry between K.A. and Hillcrest, and now to become a Hillcrester was almost unthinkable for a K.A.'er. It turned out that he enjoyed two good years at Hillcrest and had we known of Rollie's difficulties at the Academy, we could have had him come out and finish his high school there, too. All of our other kids enjoyed at least one year at Hillcrest—Cherry and Pam graduated from there. Now, 1998, Sue's two boys, Keith and Stephen, love Hillcrest. They both experienced K.A. but K.A. is different today, mostly Nigerians with some Nigerian staff. Hillcrest is integrated but the majority are still m.k.'s.

November 1962 Our time in Kano is over. We are about to return to our desert home, Galmi. But first, we spent 10 days in Jos where

Burt examined missionaries and I took it easy and enjoyed our kids on the week-ends when we got out to Miango.

And now, Galmi, here we come again.—November, 1962

Market day at Galmi was always an adventure. Early every Wednesday morning, we could hear people trekking to the market, heads loaded high with wares and babies on mothers' backs. Donkeys and camels came loaded with wares—mats, spices, cotton, grain, peanuts, cloth, African "medicines" and sometimes limes and eggs. Cows and goats were tethered and driven to the market to await their fate. I stayed away from the market as often as possible. I didn't especially like the attention that I got or the kids following close at my heels. I didn't appreciate their touching Pam or any of our kids. So Burt was the chief purchaser, mostly meat. Our first term, only goat meat was available, but in Nov. of 1962, cows were slaughtered as well. To look at the fly-covered chunks of meat wasn't too appealing, but we brought it home, washed it, and cut it up into roasts, steaks and stew meat. The remainder Issou or Yahaya put through our grist mill and it came out hamburger. Dad always tried to buy the fillet. That was the piece that we cut up into steaks. Even so, all our meat had to be pounded to death or cooked in the pressure cooker. Guess what! We survived and we ate well enough.

"Nov. 28, 1962 There is talk of building an air strip on the plateau across from us—Rollie Mountain. Then our kids can land right in our front yard. This Christmas, however, they will be flying to Konni on Wed., the 19th of Dec. and return about Jan. 8."

That airstrip never became a reality. It wasn't until 1975 that Galmi had its own airstrip behind our compound. Burt negotiated with the farmers to the West and North to buy the land, and finally the deal was consummated, and the land was ours. Then came the leveling with the aid of a road grader that was made available to us from a French company for just the cost of the fuel. Between those two dates, the cement factory opened up in Malbaza, just 13 miles away, and we used their airstrip. It was exciting to hear the mission plane buzz us and know that our kids were aboard. Off to Malbaza to pick them up! A few times, we also used the airstrip at Madaoua. One time, when Rich Schafer was piloting, we noticed a slight lurch as the plane approached the Madaoua strip. When it landed we noticed that the plane was dragging a line that turned out to be the telephone wire. The plane had hit the line which caused the lurch. Our kids, the Harbottle kids, and VerLees bounded out of the plane. We embraced and praised God for bringing them in without mishap. We dared not think of what might have, could have, happened, but God!

"Dec. 18, 1962 . . . the Jos news this a.m. says that the E.T.A. at Konni is 11:30 for 4 Longs, 2 Bishops, 2 Harbottles and 1 Power; 12:00 for 2 Verlees and that plane goes on to Dogon Doutchi with one Pollen, then to Fada with 2 Lochstampfors. So it looks like our kids are riding in the new, 2-engine plane, and I bet they are excited. In fact, this is take-off time in Jos right now—(8:20)" (I was excited, too.)

While we were in Kano, we were able to buy Christmas gifts for the family with money sent from relatives back home, so this Christmas was a little brighter gift-wise than the previous one. Cherry said she wanted nylon hose and a girdle! She was really getting to be a little lady, at age 11, but we didn't think she needed a girdle for her 23" waist. A garter belt to hold up her hose, yes, but not a girdle yet.! That was before panty hose!

The house was decorated with tinsel and ornaments, candles, especially the giant candle Beret gave us which we lit each night, the angel chimes, manger scene and presents. With the money that was sent for Christmas presents and which was spent in Kano and the arrival of our barrels, the children did well. On Christmas morning, they opened their gifts. This is what they got. Lanny: a chemistry set, three books, paint for his models, compass, a model jet and 52 game set. Cherry: a basket weaving set, nylon hose, purse, necklace, shoes, autograph book and a game. John: a pop gun, car run by batteries, target game, archery set, a model and another game. Sue: a necklace, hat and purse, tea set, stick out slip, Willy Whiskers, saxophone and a telephone. Pam: a doll, bathinette, necklace, building beakers, toy motorcycle and purse Pam got a second doll which we put away for her birthday. The family got a target game with three real light balls which stick to pegs. Burt and I spent our money on a new filter which we attached to the water line and eliminated the necessity of boiling the water. Quite a contrast to the previous year when we had very little to give them!

Christmas this year included Sunday evening film strip for the Africans outside the church. Monday, Christmas Eve, compound supper was at our house—23 people, followed by sing-song and performances by the white kids. Pam recited her 4 line piece. The school kids sang and recited some of the things they had learned for their school program. Christmas morning was gift opening and church. No pageant that year. Kids were happy about that! Several African groups sang and recited Scripture. Gordon Bishop spoke. Thurs. we went in to the Harbottles for dinner—29 of us. She killed 15 chickens, half a chicken for each of us. And then, almost as fast as it came, Christmas went.

Remember the candy bar tradition for best grades? Looking back I concede that it wasn't a good idea, and today child psychologists would have labeled it bad for one's self esteem. But we did it as an incentive to getting better grades. We hope it didn't mar them for life! We didn't have all the latest books on how to raise kids and we hadn't traveled that road before. It's amazing that our kids turned out as well as they did.

"Lanny had the best report card last time with all A's. Mr. Phillip's comment on his card was something to the effect that 'Lanny at times entertains the entire class at inappropriate times, which does not affect his own grades but hinders others who need the study time.' Then he went on to say that he enjoys Lanny, etc. Sue's card was almost as good, and she was very confident that she was to get the candy bar. They'll have their cards with them today so perhaps she made it for the 2nd six weeks. Cherry and John are both above average students, but they never get the candy bar."

I don't recall, but I hope the recipients of the candy bar shared with the others. One thing that stands out is the fact that one candy bar was a fantastic prize. There's no doubt about it, missionary kids are a different breed—a wonderful breed. They belong to another world, the world of "third culture kids". No wonder that when they get back to this country, they think that American kids are immature. We are proud of our kids.

About this time, Lanny was warming up to the idea of staying out and going to Hillcrest. The fact that 17 kids from K.A. were staying out for high school and had applied to the Hostel influenced him. Also about this time, Lanny made it known that he was no longer to be addressed as "Lanny", but "Lance".

Just because it was Christmas holiday time didn't mean that the hospital closed down. Quite the contrary.

"Yesterday, I had to stop and go over to the hospital. We did $2000.00 worth of work yesterday morning in surgery—2 hysterectomies, 5 hernias, 1 vesico vaginal fistula and double cataracts. We charged a total of $24.00. Jim (Ver Lee) and Burt were working two tables all morning. Then in the afternoon, two emergencies brought by the Madaoua doctor's car—one, a delivery, arm presentation. Dead baby but mother will live. The other, a girl whose forehead was laid open when a storage house for beans fell on her. This afternoon, Sunday, at 2:45, a woman was brought in with a 5 day labor, so Burt and Cherry and Sue went over. The girls are back and report a dead baby, the woman not out of danger yet—a blood pressure count of 64 which means she is in shock."

Game time was always a part of our life when the kids were home. "Lan, Cherry, John and I just finished a game of Careers. Cherry won." After supper was game time and sometimes "tea time" which did not include tea but a cold drink. It was a time to be together and enjoy each other. Games progressed from Old Maid to Snakes and Ladders to Rack-o to Yahtze, to Careers, to Scrabble, to Rook, to Trivia. What have I forgotten?

Of course, all too soon Christmas holidays were over, the New Year rolled in and the planes came and whisked our kids away—all except Pam. And as Issou said, "The house is too big again," so it was.

Chapter 12

ROLLIE IN WHEATON—1961-1965

You may remember that in Part 2, Chapter 2, we wrote about our time in Paris. We stepped out of the taxi in front of the hotel that was to be our home for a time while we studied French. As we approached the door of the hotel, 3 1/2 year old Rollie made a bee line back to the cab crying, "This is not home! This is not Fran and Bill's house. I want to go home to Aunt Fran and Uncle Bill's home." Eleven years later, his home was indeed that of Fran and Bill's.

When we left in 1961 to begin another term at Galmi, we left part of our hearts in Wheaton. We left a 14 year old boy at home with Fran and Bill. He had a wonderful home with them but there was a void in his life that nothing could fill except his parents and siblings. His days were filled with the usual—school, homework, and his week-ends included a trip to the Dells with the Frizanes, visiting relatives with Fran and Bill and riding his bike.

Except where I mention otherwise, all of these quotes come from letters that Fran wrote to us.

November 5, 1961 "Four o'clock Sunday afternoon . . . . Yes, you were in New York before I was home. We drove Pat back to her house where we had a cup of tea. By we, I mean Rollie, Beret, Bill, Pat, Agnes and Sam. Then I dropped Beret, Bill and Pat off at the Des Plaines station and took Rollie back to school. Got there at 11:15 . . . . I, too, sought strength and comfort from the Lord and he gave me these verses from the 55th of Isaiah. The 8th, 'For my thoughts are not your thoughts, neither are your ways my ways, saith the Lord.' And then, further on in the chapter 'For ye shall go out with joy, and be led forth with peace: the mountains and the hills shall break forth before you with singing, and all the trees of the field shall clap their hands. Instead of the thorn shall come up the myrtle tree; and it shall be to the Lord for a name, for an everlasting sign that shall not be cut off.' I believe the Lord gave that to me to answer the question of 'Why' that I felt. So I fully believe that this term will be one of great blessing.

"Rollie is adjusting very well, and I'm sure he has times of lonesomeness but he seems to be happy. He has really enjoyed riding around the village on his bike. He and Bill went to the football game at the College .... in the evening we went to Pat and Ron's for supper."

From Rollie, same letter ". . . I'm glad you arrived safely in Amsterdam ... what kind of church did you go to on Sunday? How much of Europe did you see? Saturday, I upped and bought a three speed ... works like a charm!"

That first Thanksgiving the family celebrated with Lois and Bill Olson in their trailer. It was a biggee—55 feet long and the living room and one bedroom were about 18 ft. wide so we had plenty of room. Rollie had Friday and Monday off because of the holiday.

November 28, 1961, ". . . he went in to the Frizanes in Chicago again on Sat. morning so that he could go to the Taft-Lane game at Soldiers Field in the afternoon. He stayed overnight and went to Elmwood for Sunday. The Amundsons from Wheaton (Verne and Myrtle) brought him home. On Monday he wanted to stay home and do his homework but he had originally planned on going downtown with Bill and working with him. This week Bill is doing inventory so Rollie did a lot of precounting. He was pretty tired but Bill gave him $5.00 plus his train fare. Then of course, he had to stay up late and do his homework. He is getting along fine and seems to be adjusting.

"We are planning on going to Pat's on Rollie's birthday to celebrate his and ours. Hollanders and Cedergrens will be there .... With the $5.00 you left for him, I bought him a game of Careers (his request) and a light for his bike, and Pat and Ron are getting him a new seat. Has a little left over so will add it to his Christmas money ...."

They had planned to have Christmas at Beret's, but her house caught on fire and she didn't have a roof over her head. About 7:30 a.m. some one rang her bell and she didn't answer it because she was getting dressed, then Mrs.Gurnee pounded on her door and said that the roof was on fire but the firemen were on the way. The roof over her bedroom was demolished and her clothes and some of her paintings suffered water damage. So Christmas was held at Bob and Cora's house. The year ended with Christmas gifts from all the relatives.

Christmas Eve, 1961 ". . . we went to the Carol Stream church and watched Rollie perform in a play called 'Tax Day in Bethlehem'. He was Joseph. Afterwards he went caroling with some of the young people. He has decided to make the Village Church his church rather than the Free Church. He feels more at home there, and they have been very kind to him. They think he is a fine boy as so many people do . . . for the most part he is very happy and tries to please, and we are enjoying him.

"We have a very pretty tree. Rollie put the ornaments on it. He said that it wouldn't be necessary to get a tree for him, but he has enjoyed it even tho' he professed that it wasn't necessary."

Christmas Day ". . . went to Pat's and exchanged gifts; then on to Bob and Cora's where we had supper with the family. We combined our Christmas with a shower for Pat. She was in the hospital the week end before because her hemo count was down to 5 and she had to have two pints of blood."

Christmas vacation for Rollie included a trip to Wayne and Helen's. He went downtown with Bill in the a.m. on the train, then Bill put him on the South Shore train to East Chicago where Helen met him. He stayed for several days, then came back the same way in reverse. Myrtle Amundson invited him to go on a retreat with the young people of Glen Ellyn Bible Church. Aunt Agnes and Uncle Sam were living in the Chicago area about this time but still had their farm in North Dakota. They decided to move back there, which they did, but decided not to spend their winters there. It was about this time that her doctor said her cholesterol was high and said she wouldn't live more than a year. In the same breath, he warned her not to spend her winters (plural) in North Dakota! So each winter they traveled back and forth to John and Sally's house in So. Carolina to escape the cold northern winters, Aunt Agnes made a liar out of her doctor and lived a good number of years after that.

On Jan. 21, 1962 Becky was born, Ron and Pat's first child. That made Fran and Bill grandparents for the first time. Becky was the first of three. Following her were Jimmie and Tom. All three are married, but Becky is the only one with children so far. Today, 1998, Becky has two boys, David and Daniel, getting to be young men already.

"Feb. 6, 1962 The churches in Wheaton got together for a Youth Crusade . . . backed by Dave Mains. Dave Burnham was the speaker, Ed Lyman the music . . . . Rollie went Friday and Sat. and on Friday night he got carried away and put a five dollar bill in the offering that he had been saving for something special. He wasn't sure whether he had a 'glad heart' afterwards or not. He finished his trumpet lessons at the college but Dresselhaus felt that he should go on for another semester, but Rollie said he couldn't afford it, so Dresselhaus is going to give him lessons at his home for $2.00 a lesson and Rollie will use the money he got for Christmas. He is also taking judo lessons from one of the men, John Younglove, at the village church on Thursday nights."

"Feb. 27, 1962 Tomorrow night we are going to hear Rubenstein at the college. Rollie wasn't too keen about going. Rubenstein is the last of the great artists and he isn't long for these parts so we are going to imbibe some culture."

"March 13, 1962 Rollie . . . read *A Connecticut Yankee in King Arthur's Court* and enjoyed it very much. Every once in a while he laughed out loud and he sounded just like you, Burt. He looks more like Ruth but has many of Burt's ways . . . . Rollie begged off going to the Rubenstein concert so we gave the ticket away . . . . Tonight is a farewell for Dr. Bob Cook to which we have been invited. He is leaving to take the presidency of King's College, Percy Crawford's school . . . . I don't think Rollie is actually ever homesick but he did say that he often wishes that he were in Africa. Whether it's because you are there or whether he just likes the country, I don't know."

"April 22, 1962 We went to the Center this morning with the Duncans . . . Rollie wanted to talk to Doc about camp. He is going to work during the first two weeks of boys' camp and be a camper the last two. He said that Bob Hammer was discharged from the service and was bragging to him how he and another kid chase around in cars and try and see how close they can get to hitting the other cars. I asked him about the other Hammer boy and was told that he was a goody-good."

Interesting! It wasn't too many years later that Bob Hammer was killed in an automobile accident.

"June 3, 1962—exams for Rollie. We just bought him a new pair of pants and a summer sort of sport jacket . . . and shoes. He looks real nice in it. He's growing up. Shaved for the first time . . . was elected class treasurer for next year. He missed his letter in track by two points."

The Billy Graham crusade was in progress. McCormick Place was packed out every night. Rollie made friends with a 9 or 10 year old boy who lived down the street. So Rollie invited him to go to the meeting with him. The boy went forward that night. Rollie followed him down to the counseling room so he wouldn't get lost and then they almost got lost themselves trying to find their bus again. Each church supplied their buses. On the final night, Soldiers Field was packed out.

Rollie visited Grandma and Grandpa Long for two weeks that summer. Just before he left for Sulphur Springs, Bill developed pains in his abdomen. He suffered with it for about a week before seeing the doctor. Emergency surgery revealed an abscessed appendix. "The whole mess had imbedded itself in the fatty tissue and attached itself to the bowel down in the pelvic area. He was a pretty sick man for about a week, with tubes in and drains out. People have been so kind and thoughtful during this time and much prayer went up for him. Even our Catholic neighbor said some. He received 108 cards, 7 floral pieces, 6# candy and a pr. of fancy pajamas. The bill was $520.00. Good old Blue Cross. Don't know what the drs. will charge yet. Rollie will be home on Wed." During his time in Sulphur Springs, Rollie worked for friends of his grandparents, the Cains, doing some logging. He enjoyed it immensely but also did some chasing around town at night with his new-found friends. "The popular sport was to see how aggravated they could get the local cop. They would peel off, etc., just staying within the law." It's a good thing he got back home just in time to go to camp.

About this time, "little Bobby" wrote an essay about his father for a school competition for Father's Day. He won in his school and in his district. He was one of 38 finalists out of 600 entrees. "He and Bob and Cora were guests at the Palmer House for a big dinner as a result. A 12 yr. old girl finally won, but we are quite proud of him."

Aug. 15, 1962 We went up to Camp Awana with Bob and Elaine Hall last Sat. Rollie seemed to be enjoying himself . . . It doesn't do too much good to admonish him about driving. He has the days counted until he is 16, confident that he can get a license and drive. He's got the 'bug' and I understand from other folks that if you get it it's fatal.

"Oct. 26, 1962 "Talked to Beret and she is getting to like her new apartment better. Of course, it doesn't have enough space to put things in but that isn't the apartment's fault. She has so much stuff! And she hates to part with it because some day she may use it, such as a winter coat that I'm sure she bought 20 years ago and some day she is going to make it over. I mentioned that the couple below her were Christians and she went to one of the Keswick meetings with them and to Moody's Sunday night. Too bad Redpath is leaving Moody's as she was impressed with him.

Rollie earned his "W" and was initiated into the letter club. He bought a Wheaton Academy jacket, partly with money we sent for his birthday and Christmas. Thanksgiving came and went with 21 relatives at the Buenemans. Gone are the days when families lived close together and enjoyed the holidays together. Well, I guess not all the world is separated by distance, but ours certainly is.

This was the year that Rollie sent us some grapefruit spoons and "salt nuts", but they didn't arrive until after Christmas, mainly because he didn't mail them until after Christmas. But the gifts were appreciated and the spoons lasted a lot longer than the pistachios.

"Dec. 30, 1962 We have had two very bad cold spells and on the first day of the first one Rollie came in from school without his jacket. Someone had taken his and another boy's. We hoped that it was a joke and that it would be returned the next day, but it wasn't, and two more were taken the next day. So Mr. Blanchard started to investigate and found out that 2 boys that had been kicked out of the academy last year had been hanging around school so he went to the home of one of them and while he was there the two boys walked in wearing the jackets. They had removed the name tag that I had sewed in but the needle marks still showed. We were very happy to get it back, needless to say."

Dear Rollie, "We are glad to note that you're quite a poet and painter. Cherry does quite well with art, but I haven't noticed any little poet sprouting here yet.

"Lanny just informed me that he IS a poet. Here is his contribution. 'There was a young lad from the city, Who saw what he thought was a kitty, He gave it a pat and said, 'Nice kitty cat', then buried his clothes out of pity.' He got his inspiration from another poem similar to that.

"The kids are griping about our 'operation beautiful'—making paths with stones and gravel. We're going to put a driveway and a round-about in, too .... The VerLees are gone, Husbands are back."

"July 6, 1963 Dear Rollie, How are things going at Willabay? ... We found an interesting comment in a tablet that you had at K.A. We came upon this notation: 'I love a certain girl called Sherril K. Signed, Rollie Long.' .... Rollie, always remember to destroy the evidence ...."

"Cherry has become quite a good cookie and cake maker. Lanny is busy keeping 3 bikes in running order. Dad let him drive the car and the motorcycle the other day. Sue spends a lot of her time in the operating room with Dad. She likes the medical stuff. John is busy 'doing things' all the time, is usually the last one to say his verse a day—we are learning John 17, have done the first 6 verses so far. 'Little Red enjoys her big kids and is everybody's favorite. She surely is cute.

"1 Tim. 4:12 'Let no man despise thy youth, but be thou an example of the believers, in word, in conversation, in love, in spirit, in faith, in purity. Lots of love—remember that we love you always. Mom"

"July 21, 1963 Dear Rollie, Well, Lanny has gone back to school. It seems funny not to have our two oldest boys around. We are surrounded by little ones again—although they are not so little anymore. Cherry is lovely and in a few more years will send some young heart a fluttering. John is surrounded by the girls, but trying to be a man, although only 10 years old. Sue is fearless and beautiful; Pam is lovely and very quick. I'm sorry you're missing them. And we're missing you."

———————

Back to Wheaton where Fran is writing again.

"June 17, 1963 Did he tell you about the banquet? He looked so nice in his tux . . . . He had a real good time and gained lots of confidence. It was fun watching him get ready. I had a lump in my throat wishing you could have been here. We had to discuss methods and means. 'What do I do when I ring the bell? Should I put the flowers on her? Etc.' Anyway, I guess he came through all right . . . . he fell in love graduation week-end. The tragedy of it is that she graduated and went back to Missouri and he is still in high school, and of course in the fall, she won't be interested in a high school kid when she's in college."

When school was out for the summer, things were pretty dull at home since both Fran and Bill were working. One day, Rollie and a friend decided to ride bikes to O'Hare Field. They got as far as Bensenville and blew a tire. They walked their bikes to O'Hare and left them at a drive in. "When they were ready to come home, Rollie called me to come and get them. Needless to say, I was a little irked, but secretly glad because it was 96 degrees and traffic was terrible. It would have been rough biking back."

About the first of May, Fran had written to Ed Ouland (Ruth Skoglund's relative who manages Camp Willabay) asking if Rollie could get a summer job. They didn't hear from him until June 7 and said to bring Rollie for an interview although it was not their policy to hire high school kids. So Fran and Bill and Rollie drove up for an interview and Rollie was accepted as a worker. He made $15.00 a week and was told that if he worked out well, his pay would go up to $25.00 a week. He worked about 9 hours a day. Camp Awana had spoiled him because they only worked 4-6 hours a day there. But then, they didn't get paid there either.

"July 3, 1963 We drove up to see Rollie on Sunday, the 22nd. He was in swimming when we got there with 2 other workers so we stood and watched him for awhile. The three boys were seeing who could stay under water the longest. He finally saw us and came in. He seems to be having a good time, although he is complaining of having dish water hands.

"Bob, Cora and Bobby are going to the Virgin Islands for a year. The doctor who bought the big house that Bob was building when you were here wants to build a resort down there and asked Bob to do the work . . . . Our family gets smaller all the time—Olsons back in MN; Hennixes in between jobs. The job in Boca Raton didn't last too long.

"I was at the ear doctor's yesterday. Made the decision to have the Stapes Operation on my ear on Sept. 17. I have practically no hearing left in one ear."

The following paragraph is an excerpt from one of Beret's letters to us.

"July 14, 1963 Did Rollie tell you about the two paintings that he made? I guess he was inspired by his visit to the Art Institute. I didn't know that he was doing them and so one night Fran and Bill and Rollie came over and Rollie had two paintings under his arm. I was surprised. They are both very good. One is rather impressionistic and could be or is a landscape. The other is very abstract with a flowing design and a spider. He has a good sense of color and design . . . ."

September 1963 Fran was at home after having had surgery on her ear, Rollie was back at school for his senior year after the summer working at Camp Willabay.

Oct. 14, 1963 "— . . . . Well, Rollie bought a motorcycle! A boy out here in Carol Stream bought a second hand Harley Davidson four months ago for $250.00. Has been trying to get Rollie to buy it. We dismissed it with 'you haven't got $250.00!' Well, the boy finally came down to $50.00 and after much anguish and discussion, etc., we gave in and let him buy it. It's a 3 wheeler (police cycle), has 38,000 miles on it. I worry every time he takes it out . . . . Bob and Cora, in the Virgin Islands, said that the heat and bugs have been bad . . . . Rollie will have Thanksgiving with the Kletzings. He will go home with Dan on Wednesday and come back Thursday night. We won't have much of a gathering this year with Olsons and Hennixes both gone . . . . Aunt Sophia is out of work, Uncle George has been sick. That's all for now. Love, Fran."

Nov. 13, 1963 ". . . I guess I've completely recovered from my ear operation. My hearing is improved although sometimes I hear strange noises and vibration and crackling that bothers me."

"Feb. 9, 1964 You remember that he took the ACT test last Nov., well, two weeks ago he received word that he was high enough on the test to become a semi-finalist. As a result, he has received half a dozen letters from different colleges suggesting that he enroll at their school, two of them offering aid.

". . . Rollie is still wrestling. He won his match yesterday 2-1. He is a borderline case in weight so before every match he goes to the sweat room to lose a few pounds and won't eat anything all day. I feel like shaking him. I'll be glad when the season is over. I don't know which is worse—seeing him eat all the time or seeing him starve.

"Is any of the terrible mess in the Congo affecting you? We've got such a mess here in this country with Cuba. You wonder what our country is doing. Berenice & Ken's boy, Kenny, is being stationed in the Philippines. He's leaving the states this week. Grace Olsen's boy, Floyd, is going to Viet Nam."

(1999—Kenny survived the war, is a pilot with Delta Airlines; Floyd never came back, was listed as 'missing in action'. His plane went down over Vietnam. Much effort went in to trying to locate his body, but it was never recovered. Floyd had met Dr. Larry Ward in Nam and through Ward's efforts, and those of Dennis Stuessi, Floyd's Wheaton college friend, a hospital was erected and dedicated in Hong Hu in 1998 a mile from the crash site. It was named the "Floyd Olsen Memorial Hospital." Among those present at the dedication were his sister, Sandy, and her husband, Rev. George Sturch as well as Dr. Ward and Mr. Stuessi.)

The reason I devote so much space to Floyd is because his mother, Grace, and father, Frank, were good friends of Fran and Bill, and indirectly of mine, and we were all at the North Side Gospel Center together in the early days of the church.

"Six packages have been mailed to you . . . . By this time Bob Swanson has probably come and gone . . . . He was here for supper on the 24th . . . I've asked him to come to Rollie's graduation . . . . Rollie had a wonderful time on the choir tour and hated to have it end . . . . There will be some expenses for graduation. We will invite the Kletzings for graduation and any of the relatives that are on hand at the time . . . .

"Jobs for teen-agers are few and far between . . . . A friend of Ron and Pat's is in charge of a company that cleans out overseas planes between flights. There's a good chance that he can get on there this summer, but it will mean some transportation to O'Hare. He has $343.00 in the bank and he wants to get a motorcycle with it if he can. I maintain a cheap car would be better . . . so we're going round and round. I told him last night that my one ambition was to deliver him back to you safe and sound in body, mind and spirit!"

May 13, 1964 "Rollie left this morning on the Senior Sneak. I don't know why they call it a sneak inasmuch as everyone knows where they are going—Jack and Jill Ranch in Michigan."

June 21, 1964 ". . . Graduation day was lovely. Wayne, Helen, David Kletzing, Beret, Pat and Becky . . . came for it. He received money gifts from Fassolds, Ardith and Ray Hoffmann, Neva Kletzing, J.R. Long, Perdues, Pat and Ron. From Ara Ford, he received a metal file, from Wayne and Helen a Crudens Concordance, from Beret a nice leather travel kit and from us an electric shaver. He started his job on June 13 and he likes it as well as anything." (working at O'Hare, cleaning out planes.)

July 19, 1964 "You will be glad to know that the beauty operator, Bart, was saved a few months ago. I haven't been there but he told Martha Busch that he finally decided to read the book of John that you told him to and now he understands what everyone was talking about . . . . The son-in-law of Russ and Ev. Carlson was drowned up at Eagle River 2 weeks ago. He was married to Marilyn. He left 3 little boys, 4, 2, and 8 months. It certainly was a shock to everyone."

About this time, the Zabriskies paid Fran and Bill and Rollie a visit. Rollie changed jobs and was working for Bill Bueneman. The Lucases arrived for a visit and left Steve with Rollie for a few days. Ethel sold the house in Missouri and went to live with Aunt Sara in Santa Barbara. Helen Gray Zahn had open heart surgery. Marge and Clarence were working for a radio station and were barely making ends meet. The Hennixes were in CA and raving about the weather. Rollie received a check for $50.00 from Norman and Irene Amundson. The Round Robin got sick and was apparently dying.

August 29, 1964 "Thurs. Bill and Rollie and I went shopping for a suit for him. When I said he had to pay for it himself he said he would get the cheapest one he could, but after trying on the cheapest ones, he ended up at Rothschilds and got a $75.00 suit marked down to $64.00. It is brownish and the thing that clinched it for him was the fact that you once had a brown suit, Burt. As he was looking in the mirror, he said, 'My dad had a brown suit.' . . . Don't worry about Rollie now—just keep on praying for him.—

"By this time you probably have heard from Mrs. Boardman. I met her one evening . . . . she says you can have the missionary furlough home.

This job he has taken is a hard one physically. He doesn't have too much pep to do much else. He has been home more than ever for which we are happy. The army won't draft him until he's older and tonight he mentioned going back to school in the fall. After a few months at this job, I'm sure school will look pretty nice.

March 8, 1965 ". . . Rollie is looking forward to your return. You might not think so by his lack of letter writing, but underneath his 'tough' exterior he is tender . . . He goes to S.S. and church with us, which is more than he did when in school . . . . He was using his friend's car to go back and forth to work. Well, it wasn't much good . . . so he felt he had to have a car. That we went along with. He chose an Alpha Romeo; that we didn't go along with . . . .

April 19, 1965 "Rollie quit his job at American Chemical last Friday and started a new one today. Billy Olson is a superintendent at Seco Steel and he has . . . hired Rollie His job is laborer on a dormitory at Northern Ill. College in DeKalb. Today was his first day and you never saw anyone look so tired when he got home! He will make $3.50 an hour, but he'll really earn it . . . . a good thing about the job is that he had to shave off his beard! We were sure glad to see that go!

May 7, 1965 You had better smuggle one of your cooks back with you, if you plan on keeping Rollie filled up. This outside job really makes him hungry. He starts the day with oatmeal and toast, etc., and for lunch I pack him three sandwiches (6 slices of bread), two oranges, a hard boiled egg, cake or cookies and a thermos of milk. When he comes home he's famished.

"In your next letter, tell us your itinerary again!"

At this point, we will leave our story of the years 1961-1965 as seen through the eyes of Rollie and Fran and Bill in the States. In our next chapter we will focus on the same years as seen from Africa through the eyes of Mom and Dad and siblings. At the end of that chapter, we will bring both views into one with our reunion at O'Hare about the end of June, 1965.

Chapter 13

1961-1965

Market day at Galmi was always an adventure. Early every Wednesday morning, we could hear people trekking to the market, heads loaded high with wares and babies on mothers' backs. Donkeys and camels came loaded with wares—mats, spices, cotton, grain, peanuts, cloth, African "medicines" and sometimes limes and eggs. Cows and goats were tethered and driven to the market to await their fate. I stayed away from the market as often as possible I didn't especially like the attention that uwargida (mother of the house) got or the kids following close at my heels. I didn't appreciate their touching Pam or any of our kids. So Burt was the chief purchaser, mostly meat. Our first term, only goat meat was available, but in Nov. of 1962, cows were slaughtered as well. To look at the fly-covered chunks of meat wasn't too appealing, but we brought it home, washed it with soap and water, and cut it up into roasts, steaks and stew meat. The remainder Issou or Yahaya put through our grist mill and it came out hamburger. Dad always tried to buy the fillet. That was the piece that we cut up into steaks. Even so, all our meat had to be pounded to death or cooked in the pressure cooker. Guess what! We survived and we ate well enough.

Early in 1963—a letter to Rollie—"Do you remember Gaji, Rollie? He built the shelter with you one summer near our house . . . . he is a fine looking boy now, tall and pleasant and looking for work, so Dad hired him in the hospital. Pray that he might be saved. There is another friend of yours who often talks about you, and he is working in the hospital. He is Illo. Ila is the VerLees' 'boy'. Attabo we see in town once in a while. He has turned out to be a respectable farmer.

"We will have pigeon stew tonight. Just as we sat down to eat dinner, we heard a thump and the wind charger shudder. We went out to find a beheaded pigeon. Issou has cleaned it and put it in the fridge."

"Mar. 3, 1963 Last week was rather hectic—conference here—68 missionaries. Mr. and Mrs. Stewart from Kano were the guest speakers. Stan and Nyletta Myers came with them We fed 46 adults at our house—the children at the VerLees'. We had them sleeping in our storeroom, the VerLees' garage (couldn't get into ours), 3 tents, nurses' quarters, and four rooms in the hospital. Now the African conference is in progress, and there are about 20 out-of-towners here. Gaji has been attending the meetings . . . pray for him . . . also, for Illo.

"The walls are going up on the new wing and we hope to get the foundation done and the concrete floor laid before the Bishops go on holiday the end of this month. After the Bishops get back from holiday, they will go to Dan Ja for the last year of their term.

"We go on holiday the middle of April to the middle of May. The program is April 17, so we'll get to see it this year. Lanny, Cherry and Sue have parts in the play. Aunt Gerry wrote about taking full advantage of the Longs' talent. (Was this *A Midsummer Night's Dream*?) Did you ever know that Uncle John Herr married Aunt Pauline Grant?" (Beulah Herr had been killed in an automobile accident on the road outside of Jos leading to the Miango road.)

"March 12, 1963 Sue opened her last letter home from school with 'Cherry has to write 'I will not visit in class' 500 times because she was talking in school'." Cherry didn't breathe a word of this in her letter. What would we do without siblings?

"Boys club is tonight. We've been having about 25 kids out, meeting in the dispensary waiting room. A number of kids have made professions of faith."

These were the early days of our Awana clubs at Galmi. It was at one of these early meetings that Paul Bishop was convicted and went home and told his parents he wanted to be saved, and they led him to the Lord that night.

"Pam remembers you (Rollie) and every time she sees your picture, she says, 'That's our Rollie. She remembers your throwing her up in the air and catching her, 'just like Daddy'. Congratulations on winning the bronze medal in wrestling. Dad says he still thinks he can take you on, although he and you weigh the same. (Not anymore—1998) I remember the year you finally beat me in a running race, Rollie. The field is all yours now."

"March 26, 1963 Last Wed. afternoon the gendarme and Konni doc arrived with this man who had cut through his neck—from one side to the other, cutting through jugular vein, pharynx, larynx and other organs and tissues between the two carotids . . . After thirteen hours he was still living. The people didn't bother to bring him right away—first they had to call the police from Konni. They probably figured he would die anyway, and why he didn't we still don't know. Burt sewed him back together again, made him a new tracheotomy, and has been feeding him for the last 6 days with tubes through the nose. There was some dispute over a woman, and apparently he lost, and he took it out on himself—to be a martyr? He is alone and requires 24 hrs. duty for the nurses and workers. Illo and Gaji have been alternating nights with him. He coughs up a lot of pus, and the tubes must stay down for feeding. He has been getting water and soupy liquids down the tube steadily. Pray that he might be saved while he's here. (He recovered.)

"Another blessing is the beginning of the evening Bible school. Two nights a week teaching reading for comprehension, writing, doctrine, personal evangelism and memory work, and marriage and the family. I am teaching the latter; Burt is teaching doctrine. Each of the missionaries has a 45 min. class once a week so it doesn't work too much of a hardship. The amazing thing is the response that we're getting. About 25 local folk are attending and seem to be enjoying it.

"Pam coined a new word the other day:—'twiggle'—She was trying to say twist or wiggle and it turned out to be 'twiggle'. She sure is cute. Has been playing all by herself this a.m., having one tea party after another. She had a radio made out of mud which she 'tuned' in and she immediately started to sing, 'Jesus Loves Me'. Then when she turned the knob, she stopped singing."

Burt had an enlarged node in his neck, so while we were in Jos, Dr. Dion Warren, did surgery to remove it. This is the node that was abscessed and drained when he was a child. It wasn't long after we were back at Galmi that Burt noticed the lump again. Was it a recurrence? He decided that Dr. Warren had missed the node and removed something else! He let it go for a whole year but by this time it had grown so much that Burt had trouble turning his head on that side. On our next holiday Burt told Dr. Warren that he had missed the node. Dion would not admit that he had, but he operated again and this time got the culprit.

This was also the holiday that I fell on the tennis court and bounced my head off the concrete. I had x-rays which revealed no bones broken and a spinal tap which proved no blood in the spinal fluid. But the spinal tap left me with a headache the likes of which I never had experienced before. The last four days at Miango I was flat on my back; the plane ride back to Galmi was torture, and the next week at Galmi was miserable.

"May 24, 1963 Dear Robin Relatives, Springtime and robins! Even here at Galmi Spring is in the air this morning—8:00 a.m. Springtime comes in reverse order here—we have just had our summer—I hope it's over! It is only 86 degrees this morning with a lovely breeze and by noon it shouldn't exceed ten more. If I close my eyes and think HARD (VERY, VERY HARD) I might place myself back in Chicago on Circle Ave. But opening them is reality, this morning here is pleasant, giving a lift (I need them, too), and therefore is a good morning to write to you.

"Pam is a precious red headed jewel. And what would we do without her? You should see her 'swimming' in her pool on the back porch with her neighbor m.k.'s. Or playing with her dolls and doll house, or 'cleaning up' her room."

This reminds me of the time that I finally allowed Pam to wash dishes. She climbed on a chair in the kitchen, and remarked, "This is so much fun I'll be glad to do it the rest of my life."

"May 27, 1963 Monday morning at 11:35. The thought just occurred to me that when I was working at Spiegels (about 25 years) ago, that I was always depressed on Mon. mornings after the good time we had at the Center all day Sunday and the week-end in general, and I would wonder if the next week-end would ever come. It did! And since then, approximately 1300 week-ends have come and gone. Now, as I write, 'Monday morning,' I say, 'Hooray,

266

only Monday, and I have the whole week ahead of me!" (I still do—1999)

"We said good-bye to the kids at Kent Academy on the morning of the 16th about 7 o'clock. The Graham Coxes from Kagoro were driving us to the airport. Such a lot of long faces! Lanny cracked a smile just before we left; Cherry and Sue did their best, but the tears squeezed out of their eyes, and Johnny didn't try to hide his tears. I was having a hard time, too, reminding them that in 3 1/2 weeks they would be home for the summer."

"Several weeks ago one of our missionaries stationed near the border of Tchad (Chuck Forster from Maine Soroa) 500 miles from us, brought us an old Fulani who had a spontaneous fracture of his leg due to osteomylitus. Some time before that Chuck had befriended him, and in appreciation the Fulani had given him a bull. Chuck didn't want to accept it, and the Fulani was quite offended, saying that Chuck shouldn't despise his gift, so he accepted it. There is a gov't. doctor in town but with no operation facilities, and the closest government hospital was 100 miles from them, but the old man preferred to have Chuck drive him 500 miles to our hospital because 'we pray in our hospital'. So the old Fulani produced $60.00 to cover expenses of the round trip and Chuck showed up with him two weeks ago. He is convalescing now, but he is very run down due to absorption of poison from this long standing ulcer and fracture. The road they traveled is nothing but sand the first 100 miles and only a four wheel drive can make it, and only by constantly shifting down, down, down. Pure desert.

"Pam went to the hospital this morning with Burt, and I didn't see her at all until I had to send for her at noon to come home and eat. One thing is sure, our kids take operating room scenes and medical procedures as part of their normal life. Pam sits on a high stool and watches operations, including deliveries, and she's in there cheering with every labor pain as if she's yelling for the football team to 'GO'."

Awana was off to a good start. We marked off a soccer field and an Awana circle behind the chapel. After our games, we gathered under the makeshift shelter for our meetings. Our meetings grew and at one point, we were meeting in the village in the large courtyard of Ibraham and Lydia's house. We were having 50-80 boys at our weekly meetings in town. These were in the evening. Our meetings were not without trouble. Sometimes stones were thrown over the fence and sometimes the kids were unruly and upset the meetings.

"One week as we walked to the village, we were met with a lot of scoffing, jeering kids and older people. We wondered what had happened, although we immediately surmised correctly that the Moslem malams had clamped down, and also the parents. For six weeks we averaged 25-30. But last week, one by one the kids started filtering back in again, some a bit sheepishly, but others acting as if nothing had happened, and we had about 40 out. Either the old ones are letting up again or they think they've got their kids in tow. Little do they know."

"Another time as the hospital kids and Tuni and I were returning from Ibrahim's house, village kids followed us hurling stones at us. The kids (patients or with patients) were scared; they clung to us and everyone wanted to grab my hands or arms. Then out of the blue, Idi Buda, who was sitting alongside the road with the other men of the village, jumped up and shouted at the kids to stop it. They did. And we were grateful that Idi identified with us—all the rest of the men sat there and watched. Idi is our of our believers and hospital workers."

"Each week these kids hear again the Gospel story, and believe it or not, they are the future Christian leaders of Niger. Many of them have made professions of faith, but they must be nurtured, and this takes a life time."

It was during the time that we were meeting at Ibrahim and Lydia's house that Umaru, one of the town boys was saved at our Awana meeting. One evening Burt came home from the hospital and announced that one of "my boys" was brought to the hospital and diagnosed with rabies. He said his name was Umaru. Early the next morning, I went to the village to see him. Sure enough, it was Umaru, who had recently accepted Christ. Umaru had been bitten by a rabid dog a few weeks previous but had ignored it. I found Umaru lying on a corn stalk bed covered with a mat. Indeed, he was a sick boy. His parents hovered over him, but gave place to me. Umaru, said, "Uwargida, sing me the song about the wordless book." I did, and I talked and prayed with him. I assured him that he would be seeing Jesus soon. The next day I visited him again and sang to him and prayed with him. He was near death. I asked his parents to let me know when he died. During the night he died. The parents didn't send me word. They buried him immediately, as is the custom—a Moslem burial. But for Umaru it was an entrance into heaven and a future Christian resurrection.

Later, we built our Awana building. It was a large building with Sunday School/storage/office rooms on either side. The center section was large enough to have an Awana circle in it. Our meetings moved to the Awana building, and we had good meetings with up to one hundred boys one night a week and twenty five girls on a Saturday afternoon. The girls' program included sewing—first project was basting their Awana head scarves.

"For the last two evenings, Isu's brother, Alaha, has brought their horse over for the children to ride. It is a well behaved mare, 9 years old, has had 5 colts, has one now that is 10 months old. They would sell it, and the kids would like it, but it would be quite expensive (especially the upkeep). Anyway, they said they would bring both the horse and the colt this evening, but it's 6 o'clock already and not in sight. Cherry was fearful and would not ride alone. But Suzanne, after her first ride with someone, wanted to go it alone, and had it trotting in just a few minutes. That's the difference between Cherry and Sue in everything."

It wasn't too long after this that Alaha went to Lagos to do some trading. While there he was run over and killed by a truck. We were very sad to hear that, especially because we knew he wasn't a Christian. He was a Moslem and a very upright man. He was the oldest son in the family, and thus responsible for all his children and the children of all of his siblings. Now the responsibility fell to Isu, the next oldest son, and he wasn't more than in his twenties. When we visited Galmi again in 1990, we had a nice talk with Isu and Kwalkwali. They are both old men now by African standards—probably in their sixties. Isu has good farm land which is irrigated by water that is dammed up during the rainy season—a government project.

This was the summer that we met Ron R. He was a 20 year old Peace Corps volunteer, stationed at Kawara. He planted a number of citrus and mango trees there and babied them along. Unfortunately, he was only to be there a year or two. Ron visited us once or twice a week. He was lonely. We made him feel welcome and he had many meals with us. At one point, he was sick and we cared for him in our home. Ron was from California. He said he was "baptized a Southern Baptist, raised a Methodist, and prefers the Lutheran church." We corresponded with him for a while after he returned home and heard that he was attending a Bible believing church. His grove at Kawara died because no one watered the trees. The Africans that he left in charge didn't see the value of caring for the trees if they were not going to yield fruit for a couple of years.

"Ron came down in his jeep and took off with Lanny on Sat. Ron's canvas is off the jeep so they were wrapped in turbans and dark glasses and looked like real Bouzous.

"Continue to pray for Ron. Last week he unburdened himself a little, said when he was young he 'accepted Christ', but knew nothing about the Bible except the stories he remembers from Sunday School. He showed a keen interest in learning more. We invited him to join us for our Wed. Eve. Bible classes among us missionaries, and he stayed that night which was Wed. and said he would continue to come. We are studying Daniel. We also gave him Newell's Romans to study at home and an old copy of DeHahn's Daily Bread."

Lanny went back to Hillcrest the 11th of July, and Cherry, John and Sue went back to K.A. in Sept. Also going to K.A. were three Harbottle girls and Steve Husband, Steve for the first time. Two Comanches came to Konni for the kids. Pam sobbed to see "her kids" go. The summer went too fast. Two weeks before they left, we replaced the ceiling board with plywood. We did each room separately, removed as much of the furniture as possible and covered the rest while they took down the ceiling board. As they removed the slats that held the board, the boards fell and the dust seemed like an atomic explosion aftermath. What a mess! We had six explosions—six rooms. Ten years of dust exploded into the rooms. But the plywood made an attractive difference. About the same time, we replaced all of our pan windows with glass. No more need for window sticks. What to do for discipline??

"July 23, 1963 . . . one of my boys came to me Sunday and wanted to find Christ, so I prayed with him and showed him the Scriptures, and he received Christ and testified in church that morning. Tonight is boys' club again. We had about 50 out last week and they behaved themselves during the meeting. Keep praying."

We received a letter via Wayne and Helen from Mrs. Katharine Engel and a letter from Mrs. Dorothy Rickert who attended the Center, all pertaining to the same thing.

"August 2, 1963 I shall give you some background material on the situation and bring you up to date as far as I am able. You may remember that when we were home on furlough, I made a trip over to the old Luna Ave. neighborhood, and on an impulse, decided to inquire about where my old girl friend, Eleanor Boutz, might be. I rang the bell where she used to live—one of the 3 apartment buildings close to the corner of Catalpa Ave. They did not know but directed me to an old couple, Mr. and Mrs. Engel, who lived a few doors down who had been in the neighborhood for years, thinking they might be able to help me find Eleanor. It was a little white frame house about 3 or 4 doors south of where we had lived. I immediately recognized them, although I had forgotten their names. We had a nice visit. They remembered mother and her goings and comings every day to and from Farnsworth School where she taught. They remembered my brother Bob especially—I suppose he knows why. I told them about us and our family and promised another visit, which I made shortly before we returned to Niger. This time we read the Scripture and prayed together and I left her a few tracts. We put them on our prayer letter mailing list. About 3 weeks ago I heard from Mrs. Richert, that 'a dear old friend of mine', Mrs. Engel, had been in the hospital. Mrs. Rickert had given her a tract, 'Which Church Saves', and this was the thing that brought her to the realization that it was Christ and not the church (R. C.) that saved. Next we heard from Mrs. Engel herself, who had addressed a letter to Wayne and Helen and had enclosed a gift of $2.00. Wayne and Helen decided to send it to Rollie . . . In her letter, Mrs. Engel mentioned that she had been in the hospital with 'stomach trouble', was writing even now although very weak. She is home now. She didn't mention her conversion, although she was happy to send this gift for the Lord's work. Then in the same mail was Beret's letter, which said she met Dorothy Christopher on a walk, who introduced her to a lady who was instrumental in leading Mrs. Engel to the Lord. So there you have it. You can imagine how happy this has made me, realizing that I had a small part in it. I have just written to her. She mentioned in her letter that she had met Mabel Barron at the hospital. From three sources now I have heard about it. It is a real encouragement to me."

"Sept. 7, 1963 We have just come through a violent storm, with wind sweeping the rain across the hills in front of us to give the impression that it is raining upward instead of downward . . . . It is the middle of the afternoon, and I have lit a lamp . . . Our generator arrived last week, and it is in the garage waiting for the wiring to be purchased and then set up. It is an 8 1/2 kw. generator, weighs about 3000 pounds, and it was quite a feat for Carey Lees to unload it with the help of his winch and Wilf Husband and Dave Knowlton, the latter having come along for the trip.

"John has finally stopped sucking his thumb, and two days before going back to school was awarded his football. The next day it landed on a thorn tree and punctured; it was the kind that does not have a bladder in it. He was really disappointed, but he assured us that he was still not going to suck his thumb again."

It was Sept. 20 and I was writing from Kano. We had our usual bad time going from Galmi to Kano.

"We left Galmi at 5 p.m., on Monday, and between Madaoua and Maradi we suffered a broken main leaf on left rear spring, a punctured gas tank, and a broken muffler. At Gidan Rumji we bought some soap and plugged the gas tank, and tied up our muffler so it wouldn't drag, and limped into Maradi at 11 p.m. We went out to the leprosarium in the morning and Gordon Bishop and Burt worked on the spring, putting a Ford leaf on a Chev as a makeshift job and then we headed for Kano about 4:30 p.m. Arrived here at 10:30 same night."

Burt flew down from Kano to Jos for the doctors' meetings while Pam and I waited in Kano. The car was in the garage in town getting the gas tank welded, and we got the spring changed and the muffler repaired before we returned to Galmi. That shows you the kind of roads we bounced along on.

"It is 5:15 p.m., it's clouding up and it looks as if we might have a storm before supper. This is Friday night at Kano, when the whole compound eats together at the big house and then has prayer meeting. I just walked over to the big house and brought back two buckets of warm water for bathing. Pam is in the tub now. She surely is a sweetheart of a four year old. I took her to town yesterday and bought her a pair of white Sunday shoes, a pr. of tennis shoes and some black patent leathers for later. She is thrilled with them, and shows them off to everyone. Well, I have had my bath, and it is now pouring. It's good to be high and dry when it's wet outside.

Back at Galmi again. "We held our DVBS at Galmi last week with an average attendance of 45. Our combination boys' and girls' club is running from 75-100 each Tues. night in town at Ibrahim's new compound.

"Our 30 week evening Bible School classes are nearing an end, and about 10 have been faithful throughout. The medical work is keeping Burt busy even in this 'slack' season, with Burt the only doctor. We have four nurses now, plus Mary Louise Schneider who spends most of her mornings in the wards doing personal work."

Hillcrest's school terms ran on a different schedule from K.A.'s. So Lanny got home on Nov. 22. He was flown to Maradi and then took the bus from there to Galmi. He arrived at 11:45 p.m. While we were waiting for him, we were listening to a concert on BBC and a news bulletin came over saying that President Kennedy had been shot, but that he was still alive. Burt immediately switched to Voice of America, and for the rest of the evening we were glued to the radio. A half hour after the first announcement came the news that he was dead. When Lance arrived he said, "Have you heard the news?" How he heard it while he was riding on the bus I don't know. Probably at some of the many stops along the way, the village people heard it over their battery operated radios. Of course, we were stunned along with the whole world.

"Nov. 24, 1963 It is nice to have him home. He's grown, is now 5'8 1/2 inches, weighs 125 lbs., is like a string bean. Pam tried to stay up and wait for him to get home, but finally decided to go to bed about 11:30 . . . . He was elected president of his Freshman class."

Christmas came and went and the kids were back in school. The plane came to Madaoua this time to pick them up. Pam took their leaving hard. As I put her to bed that night, she started to cry and said, "When we prayed for the kids, I started thinking about them and now I'm sad." She had her birthday party with the two Husband kids. We gave her Fran's old china dishes and my old china dishes which she had been eyeing for some time.

Lanny left on Jan. 7. When the two-motor plane arrived at Konni, Rich Schaffer said he couldn't cut off one of the engines because it wasn't working properly. Our first letter from Lanny after he returned to school said, "We left so fast because we had engine trouble with the left engine. He didn't even bother going to the other end of the runway. He just took off. We flew all the way to Kano at about 100 to 150 ft. off the ground . . . ."

Nineteen hundred and sixty two and sixty three were the years of the round robin. It was fun hearing from the cousins, sisters, brother, aunts and uncles. Then after that, poor robin died, and in recent years we have tried to get it going again, but the robin just won't fly anymore. You would think that in the computer age, it would be easy to get it going again, but it seems to stop as soon as it gets started. Too bad!

And now, 1998, all the aunts and uncles are gone, and five of our cousins are gone. Cousins: Beret, Victor, Jimmy, Billy, Jane. Ten cousins are still hanging on: Fran, Bob, Ruth, Fred, Lillian, Carol, George, John, Bonnie, and Marge.

"Jan. 23, 1964 The Niger Government has decorated Burt with a Knighthood in the National Order of Niger—'Ordre National du Niger—au grade de Chevalier.' This is in recognition of the work of the hospital. At least they appreciate the medical end of the work, if not the spiritual. The American ambassador wrote Burt a congratulatory letter, it was in the *Niger Times*, published in Niamey, but so far we have received no official acknowledgment. We are wondering when they are going to come and pin a medal on him."

"Feb. 2, 1964 Rollie, Your picture shocked me . . . not in a negative or positive way, but just because you've changed so. 'Is that our boy?' We tend to remember you as we last saw you, even though pictures have been coming right along. Isu, Sha'aybu, Idi, Ibrahim, and other Africans all recognized you right away. Your poetry also is something that I never expected from you or from anybody in our family. I confess I have read it twice and still don't understand it all. Congratulations on your wrestling, especially on pinning your 165# man. Somehow or other, writing poetry and wrestling don't seem to go together!!!!

"Lanny and Sue T. have broken up. He's going to stay a bachelor!!

"Mar. 2, 1964 We wish you could enjoy Pam with us. All of a sudden she had grown up, is no longer a baby. Yesterday, Dad brought home four baby pigeons from a village as a gift, and Pam was delighted. Finally she had some pets! She insisted her cats weren't pets, we could get rid of them, but we must keep the pigeons. Dad and I were thinking pigeon stew, but that immediately brought tears. We put them in a cardboard box for the afternoon, Sunday—one of the cats got hold of one during rest hour and had a feast. Pam's heart was broken again, and by this time, our pigeon stew had evaporated, so we put them in the storeroom for the night. This morning we rigged up some chicken wire on a box, and she is happy with her three pets.

"Sat. afternoon, we were brought 3 accident cases from Madaoua. A water tanker carrying prisoners and soldiers turned over in an attempt to avoid hitting a blind man. One soldier and one prisoner were killed immediately, under the truck. Three were brought here with dislocated shoulder and flesh tears. The blind man was also hit, but not hurt seriously.

"The Husbands got back from Kano with a load of supplies. Next is to build 2 more buildings behind the hospital for contagious diseases, especially T.B. Then the building for the generator, followed by some out-patients houses, then a new nurses' quarters. We hear the VerLees are coming back in Sept .... We will be glad to see them. Burt is very much over-worked .... On the 16th we go to Sokoto for a 3 day visit at the leprosarium. The Brabands and Flo. Jackson, who are stationed there, paid us a visit a week ago."

"March 23, 1964 We gave the kids photo albums for Christmas, and we divided up all the duplicates of our pictures since you were born and gave them to the kids. Yours, Rollie, I have kept separately since Christmas and yesterday I spent a little time putting some of them in an album for you .... Pam broke out with chicken pox this morning .... Dad rode to Madaoua with Pam (age 5) on the motorcycle and on the way some goats started to cross the road, then turned back. Pam said, 'They're females.' Surprised, Dad said, 'How do you know?' 'They changed their minds.' Dad said, 'You're a female, do you know that?' 'Yes, and so is Mommy, and Cherry and Sue. You're just a male.' .... We go on holiday May 7 and will bring the kids back from school with us."

"April 5, 1964 We heard first reports of the Alaskan earthquake early Sat. morning, which was shortly after it happened, since we are about 10 hours ahead of Alaskan time. We wonder about our friends, the Laubes, and others with whom we have kept in touch these past years. (They all survived, but Laubes' house was severely damaged. We are still in contact with Laubes today—1999)

"April 9, 1964 About this time the wing of the hospital was finished. Now we have a hospital that looks like a backward E. The new wing consists of semi-private rooms and 5 bed wards which will accommodate another 40 people. We have begun the foundations on some new out-patient buildings as well. We have many patients who come from a distance who do not need hospitalization but daily treatment. These have had to find a place to stay in the village, and it has meant many lost opportunities for reaching them with the Gospel. If they can be on the compound, we can better get the message to them during the day as well as during the dispensary services.

"Lanny is enjoying his Freshman year at Hillcrest. He is president of the Freshman class and has been named 'most witty' in the school for their year book. Cherry is becoming quite a little lady; John keeps plodding along, managing to pass into the next grade each year. Sue has no trouble staying at the top of her fourth grade class. Pam has just recovered from chicken pox, and these hot days she is enjoying her little swimming pool on the back porch.

"During the week we have four children's meetings, thus reaching over 150 kids altogether. We trust that in a few years these kids will be the leaders in the Niger Church.

"About this time we heard that Pastor Bob Swanson was planning to visit us in April—the hottest time of the year. It was also the time of year when the Buzus and Tuaregs came south to find fodder for their camels. A number of these came to the hospital for treatment and heard the Gospel for the first time.

Pastor Bob arrived in Kano via Lagos at noon on April 16, a little ahead of schedule, so when we arrived that afternoon, he was waiting for us.

"Next day we chartered an SIM plane to Jos and had a good week-end at Miango. Bob was certainly impressed with the Rest Home and K.A. We, including our kids, went down to the swinging bridge Sat. aft., after having toured K.A. with Jack Phillips in the a.m. Friday night after supper, Dr. Hicklin came up and threw his arms around Bob. Lo and behold, he's an old Tabernacle man, and he is the brother of Connie Hallworth! Were we ever surprised! Jerry

Hicklin is Lanny's roommate at Hillcrest. After supper Sat. night, we spent the evening visiting with Dr. and Mrs. Hicklin. They are the dentist and wife who are replacing Kraays for their furlough. Sun. morning we went to an African church, and it was full. Bob spoke at the Rest Home chapel that night. Then we said good-bye to the kids and went into Jos, where we picked up Lanny who had been away on a week-end retreat, spent the night at Jos guest house, drove Lanny to Hillcrest next morning, toured Jos. After dinner, we headed back to Kano by SIMair. Next morning we showed Bob some of Kano, then headed toward Maradi. We toured Maza Tsaye, the farm school and Soura, the girls' school, then headed back to Galmi. He picked the hottest time of the year to come—115 degrees. He saw a lot here—operations, two births, villages, even had a short ride on a camel. He attended an Awana meeting with me at Ibrahim's house. He held up better than we expected. The plane picked him up at Madaoua on April 28, and he was on his way again. The same plane delivered Dr. and Mrs. Bob Schofstalhl who will hold the fort while we go on holiday. You remember Mrs. Dreidiger died last year. Well, on May 2, Jack married Joyce Coke. She is an instant mother of five."

July 13, 1964 The kids were home from school again, and it was wonderful to have them all under one roof. We wished Rollie were among them. The Zebs' adopted boy, 10 year old Jacques, half French and half Fulani, stayed with us for about a month while the Zebs were on holiday. I remember one Frenchman who stopped by and came to the conclusion that one little dark boy was Burt's. Well, that was his mind-set because the French have a lot of mulatto children left in countries where they have been on tour without their wives. When the men go back to France, they usually forget about them although some of them do provide for their children. Their wives are very "understanding". Also that summer, a young medical student, Bill Weathers, came to us to work and learn in the hospital. He was in between his 3rd and 4th year of medical school. That meant that I was feeding 8-10 people every day, three times a day, for most of the summer. There were times when I wondered what the next meal would be, but we always managed to eat something. Before our kids went back to school on Sept. 11, the VerLees returned from furlough, so we had six more mouths to feed for a few days until they settled in.

"August 9, 1964. I wonder if you received our letter of July 19 concerning Rollie's coming out for this year if he wishes . . . . The kids . . . latched on to your last paragraph and with one voice voted that you should come . . . . These last weeks have been hectic . . . we have been sewing, getting things ready for school. The trunks will be sent off this Wed., the kids will follow them in about a month.

"This is one of our greenest rainy seasons. In some places, we have had too much rain. Three people were carried away by flood waters in a recent rain. Last Mon. was Niger's Independence Day, and we had planned to spend the day in Madaoua at the Harbottles and have one of her famous chicken dinners. (Either half a chicken apiece or one squab per person.) It started to rain about 8 a.m. and quit around 11, so we couldn't go until 2:30. We piled into both our car and the Husbands' jeep, got as far as six miles out of Madaoua and were met by a quarter mile of water on the road, and the water rushing over it in the middle. It was over our knees deep so we abandoned our car and all piled into the jeep and started across. Half way there the motor cut out, and we were in the middle of the water. Carburetor was soaked. After a 10 min. wait, Wilf started the car again and away we went, this time, much slower. On our return at 7 p.m., the water was only half as deep and half as long on the road."

"Sept. 26, 1964 . . . Pam announced today that she is going to marry you, Rollie, so don't promise anyone else! A bird must have fallen into our fireplace chimney today. At any rate, it flew into the front room during our rest hour, zoomed into our bedroom past us and hit the screen. In a flash, our cat was after it, jumped over Dad, landed partly on me, jumped up on the screen and got it. Then he commenced to crunch it under the bed. That was enough for me! Rest hour was over!

Rollie decided not to come out to Africa which was a disappointment for us, especially me. We were beginning to inquire about housing for our furlough coming up in the summer of 1965. We applied to the missionary furlough homes but Doug Hursh said that there wasn't much hope. However, later we heard that we would be offered the big white house on President. We would have 4 rooms downstairs and 3 bedrooms upstairs. This house was known as the "Dresser house" and was part of the underground railroad during the Civil War days.

"Oct. 23, 1964 For the past 3 weeks Niger has been invaded by communist-led rebel guerrillas who want to overthrow the government. First news we had was when Idi came on Thurs. morning saying the rebels were over the hill in Woro, just across the border. All the men of the town were called out with their bows and arrows and spears and swords to head for the border. The women and children were left alone and were thoroughly frightened. It was both humorous and pathetic to see the men going out with their primitive weapons to face guns. All they found that day at the border were some smugglers running the border with kola nuts. Bands of men are still roaming the border and are being rounded up one by one or two by two. Four were executed openly in Niamey, and that news made the BBC. One of the rebels openly killed the school teacher in Konni, after coming in the night and begging a glass of water. He immediately was killed in return. His body was taken to Niamey and left in the street for people to see. The sarkin tashas at Galmi and Dogorawa were of the opposition and taken away. Rumor has it that they are to be executed today. We got one case in the hospital when a farmer got in the way when government troops and villagers chased a group of rebels near Konni. He had four shot gun wounds. Dad removed two, and two are still in. He is well now. The fear is that Djibbo, leader of the rebel army, will eventually win. They come into villages and offer money and clothes and promises that in the new government they will have good jobs. Labo, the sarkin tasha from Galmi, was promised that he would be chief over the Galmi area. A man rounded up in Dogorawa was commissioned to kill the chief and his son and the commandant, and he would be chief of that area under the new regime."

On the 23rd of November we left for Sokoto to do the leprosy rounds. We picked up Lance at the Sokoto airport since his school was just out and did rounds at the Sokoto Leprosarium and then the various clinics in the outlying villages. Galmi had another war scare and everyone was chased from the market to get their "weapons" and rush for the border. The men came back that night, tired and having seen nothing. The one casualty was a man who stumbled with his sword hanging by his side. He sliced his leg about 5 inches long and 1 inch deep. He came to the house very sheepishly about 4 in the afternoon, so Burt took him over to the hospital and sewed him up.

———

279

"December 13, 1964 Concerning next summer, all the plans that we are making and will make include you, and we don't expect you to be working if we can't be together. We are looking forward to next summer immensely as a time to get re-acquainted and share our thoughts and ideas, joys and sorrows, frustrations and inhibitions and anything else"

Last week was the kind that doesn't happen every week. To begin with, we met Pres. Diori of Niger, who was at Malbaza, inspecting the new cement factory that is going up. We even shook his hand. Then Wed. of this week, the U.S. Ambassador, Mr. Robert Ryan, the Officers of A.I.D., Forestry, and U.S. Information Service in Niger had supper here and spent the night with us. Everybody came over for dessert. All of course were Americans, and it was like a breath of home to have them in our midst. In the morning they drove off with their flags flying . . . the American flag on the right, the Ambassador's on the left. Made me a little homesick. Before they left, they gave us 48 bottles of orange pop, Pam a present of crayons and 2 coloring books, and Dad and me a brand new pack of playing cards! Ryan's photographer took pictures of him and Pam and me by Polaroid and gave them to Pam. She has them in her photograph book."

"April 10, 1965 Our new nurse arrived two weeks ago—Marguerite Upshall. But Virginia Fridal has gone to replace Jo Rogers at the Maradi Leprosarium while Jo is on holiday . . . VerLees are expecting their fifth—the other four are in school . . . . Sue has been in Bingham Hospital with jaundice but is reported to be better now . . . . Remember your sleepy head doll? You got it when you were in Alaska, and slept with it. Pam found it in the drums the other day and latched on to it, and has been sleeping with it lately. She said to tell Rollie she's sleeping with his doll. Last week Pam spelled R U T H. I asked her what it said, and she answered, 'Mother'."

Disappointment came in the form of opposition to our Awana clubs. The school teacher threatened the boys if they attended Awana. They were really afraid of him. So attendance dropped off in our last weeks of that term. We were disappointed in Musa and Gaji, both of whom had paid lip service to becoming Christians, but both kept the fast, indicating that they were back into Islam. Also, Yahaya was dismissed for stealing some roofing pan and Sha'aybu was caught in adultery in one of the hospital rooms and summarily dismissed.

"April 25, 1965 We have a letter from our pastor, Lance and Virginia Latham, inviting us to live in their house during July, including Rollie, and then spending August at Camp as a family . . . .

"May 29, 1965 As I sit here in front of the bedroom window, there is a coolish breeze wafting through the drawn venetian blinds. It is an indication that the back of the hot season has been broken. The temperature in the living room is only 98 (ninety eight) degrees . . . we have seen lightning to the south of us, to the north of us, to the east of us and west of us and rain streaks in the sky to the west of us, but nothing in the way of rain here yet. The Boardmans wrote saying the house will be ready for us by July 12 and we can occupy then and until Sept. 1966, so we are quite pleased about that."

The rains in fact did come! The night of June 13 there was a terrific downpour! We were leaving the next morning for Konni, the first leg of our furlough. We had arranged for the chief's son from Dogarawa to come and pick us up. Between Galmi and Dogarawa a dry gulch had become a stream across the road, and cars could not pass through. The chief's men had parked on one side of the water and had a car waiting on the other. One of the chief's men piggy backed Pam, another carried me through, others carried our baggage, and I don't remember how Burt got through. Maybe he took off his shoes and socks and rolled up his pant legs. Somehow he made it, "if not triumphantly". Then off we were to catch our SIMAIR plane at Konni.

Dave Rutt was our pilot. We headed for Kano where we would meet up with our family. Fifteen minutes out of Konni we ran into a black sky, smack into a terrible storm. Pam was riding with me in the second row. The plane jostled and groaned, and Dave had a nervous look on his face with his ear phones clutching his head. We were all scared. It was 6 yr. old Pam who put her head on my lap and said, "Don't worry, Mom, the Lord will take care of us." We flew out of the storm over Kano. We had been flying so high, we had to circle several times before we could come in for the landing. At noon on June 17, we left Kano. Four and a half hours later we were in Rome, where we spent two days. From Rome we flew to London to spend a week in England as guests of Gwen Van Lierop. Our time in England included visits to the north of England to visit Florence Jackson, formerly a nurse at Sokoto Leprosarium. The town she lived in was famous for their weaving mills, and we visited them. The clacking of the looms was deafening, but we enjoyed seeing the yarn become beautiful colored cloth. We also visited in Gwen's home in Birmingham and enjoyed her children, Muriel, Ben and John. On June 26 we left London for New York, for medical check-ups by John Frame, and finally a couple of days later, for Chicago and home! How good it was to touch down at O'Hare! How excited we were! Waiting at the airport when we arrived were Fran and Bill, Beret. and a tall young man that I did not recognize. In a flash I knew! "Is it you, Rollie?" And then we were in each other's arms. We had left a boy, we came home to a young man! Hugs and tears of joy all around! We were together as a family again!

Chapter 14

FURLOUGH—JUNE '65—END OF 1966

How good it was to see our family again. We were whisked away to Fran and Bill's house. Before we could get into the missionary furlough home at 107 President St., we lived for some weeks in a house on Wesley. That was nice and just a block or two from Fran and Bill. We knew it was temporary so we didn't settle in. I'm not sure how long we stayed there, but it seemed as if we got into the the big white house at 107 President St. sometime in July. The house had been bought by a group of concerned Christians who wanted to make a comfortable home at a reasonable price for missionaries on furlough. We paid $100.00 a month. The house had originally been owned by a well known Wheaton family, the Dressers. There was also some connection between the Blanchards and the house. During the Civil War days it had been a part of the "underground railroad" which helped to get runaway slaves across the border into Canada. We didn't often have occasion to go downstairs into the basement, but when we did, we saw the old coal shed and rooms that were occupied by the slaves, who stayed maybe a night or two before being shuttled to the next stop on the "railroad". It was dank, dark and kind of spooky.

The house was situated in the midst of huge trees and bushes that hid the house from the street. It was a beautiful setting. The house was two storied. It had a large living room, dining room, kitchen and one bedroom and bath on the first floor. Pam shared the first floor bedroom with us while the other children slept in three bedrooms upstairs. There was also a small apartment upstairs that was occupied by a married couple. Sue went to 3rd grade at Lowell grammar school, John went to Edison Jr. High, Cherry and Lanny went to Central High School. Pam was still at home. Cherry had a hard time adjusting to high school as a Freshman. It was hard for her to break into cliques that had been formed by girls in Jr. High. To begin with, her wardrobe didn't measure up to the time, so it was a few weeks before we were smart enough to get her some more modern clothes. To this day, Cherry says that was her worst high school year and she could hardly wait to get back to Nigeria. Sue met some girls in her grammar school that became life long friends, and to this day, they are there for her when she and her family return for furlough. One was Brenda Price, another, Sue Shepherd. And there are others. John and Lance survived in their respective schools, but for both it was a matter of enduring to the end. Rollie was working and preferred to live with his friends rather than be under the authority of his parents. So much for being all together as a family again!

That didn't last long, and soon he was at home with us.

Summer passed and we were involved in missionary conferences locally and otherwise. The North Side Gospel Center, Elmwood Park Bible Church, Grace Church of Elmhurst, Bethany Bible church in Phoenix, The Chapel in Akron, Ohio, Highland Hills Baptist in MI were some that we participated in. Other churches had one time meetings. Of course the family was involved. The children went with us to Port Huron, Michigan where we became acquainted with the Wilson family. We kept in contact for years. We were on another furlough when Mrs. Wilson died, and Roger called Burt and asked if he would officiate at the service, which he did. On one of our return trips from Highland Hills Baptist Church in Grand Rapids, Michigan with the family, we stopped at a restaurant for a meal. It was around Christmas time. Five children! Half way through our meal, a lady came up to our table with 5 candy canes and complimented us on how well behaved our family was. She and her husband had been watching us. We were pleasantly surprised and thanked her for the candy canes. For the most part, those meetings that were not local Burt took by himself.

Behind our big white house was a brand new duplex. Our back doors faced each other with a large yard between. In one side lived the Glassman family and in the other, the Wick family. It was at that time, that Rollie met Margaret Wick, who was still in high school, and a friendship developed that resulted in their marriage a few years later. The Wicks were missionaries with the Presbyterian board in Guatemala.

We were invited to participate in the missionary conference of the Bethany Bible Church in Phoenix. Helen and Don Zahn were instrumental in getting us on their missionary roster in 1960, and that connection was beneficial to us for many years and still is today. It is also beneficial to Sue and Terry who are their missionaries as well and Lance who attends the church today. So we packed the five kids and their school books into the car, a station wagon, and took off. What about Rollie? Lee and Irene Temples were looking for a place to live for their furlough so we said they could stay in our house while we were gone—a month or six weeks. Rollie was to stay there, too. Rollie was to have his meals either with the Temples or on his own in the house, however was best for both parties. He was working for cousin, Billy Olson, in construction.

It was toward the end of our furlough that we got to talking with Rollie about joining the Peace Corps and going to Nigeria under their auspices. He needed to get back to his roots, and this was a way that appealed to him and to us. So he applied and was accepted and went to basic training in La Jolla, CA. He left for Nigeria before our furlough was up. He ended up in Gusau, Nigeria. He worked with the Young Farmers' League and concluded that the African farmers that he worked with were immature and not dependable when it came to meeting a deadline or keeping an appointment. He spent a lot of time with Roy Hirons and his wife and Harvey Stromme, SIM missionaries in Gusau. They were a great help to him. After two years there, he returned home and went to school in earnest and made excellent grades. He started out at College of Dupage in Glen Ellyn, then transferred to Southern Illinois.

In anticipation of having to vacate the missionary furlough home, we went in search of a house to buy. Years before, Burt had talked to Carl Tanis and said if he ever sold his house, we would like to buy it. But while we were in Africa, the Tanises sold the house to some friends of ours, Russ and Evelyn Carlson. While they were living there, their daughter's husband drowned, leaving her with three small children, so she and the children moved in with her parents. Later, she met a widower who had lost his wife to cancer. He had three small children as well. They married and moved out of state. Then the Carlsons were all alone again and thinking of moving to Florida. Burt convinced them that the move to Florida was a wonderful idea, and would they consider selling the house to us? After some thought, they agreed, and we (and Bell Federal Savings Company) became the new owners of 428 Howard St. in Wheaton.

In June Lance graduated from Central High school and we urged him to enroll at Moody Bible Institute for at least a year. About that time, Lance was having a physical problem. He didn't say anything about it so we were unaware of it. But inside, he was troubled—emotionally and physically. Whether it was precipitated by the thought of our soon leaving him home alone or whether he was going to Moody only to please us and really wanted to go somewhere else, we don't know. At any rate, we left him at Moody unaware that he was having diarrhea constantly.

During our 15 months in America, the work at Galmi continued. Word came from our co-workers that "Halilu, one of the boys who is hoping to go to Bible School soon, had a real spiritual problem. It was a real thrill to see the way the Lord answered our prayers and brought him back into real fellowship. It was a real blessing to us too, to see how the native elders took their responsibility in the matter and were a real help to him."

Also an answer to prayer was the fact that the village Moslem school teacher who had made it difficult for the Christian boys and girls in school had been transferred. The new teacher seemed to be interested in spiritual things. And now there was also a good attendance at both the boys' and girls' clubs.

Virginia Fridal wrote: "The three elders of Galmi church had just come out of the church building. They had met to decide the discipline of one of our Christians. The three were walking along conversing. One of the three turned to the one in the middle, asked him a question which was unanswered. Suddenly the soul of the one in the middle departed from the body and went home to be with the Lord and Saviour. The two looking on saw the house of clay fall and screamed for Dr. VerLee and Mr. Husband who were not too far away, having also just come from the meeting in the church. The doctor massaged the heart and did artificial respiration but to no avail. Yes, Chisu, the tall Fulani who worked so faithfully washing surgical instruments and linens in the hospital and who was on his way to work, had heard the call that he had finished his task and was taken serenely into the presence of Christ."

Chisu had high blood pressure and heart trouble, so it was no surprise that he died at an early age. The people in the village and hospital did not hear the screams and wails of a widow. There was just the quiet sobbing of a bereaved widow with four small children to raise, the youngest, just a few months old. Chisu was a witness in the hospital and just that morning he had preached twice to the patients in the dispensary. Someone went to get the pastor from Konni. It was night when he arrived so it was by the light of the pressure lamps that the procession made its way to the graveside, separate from the Moslem graves. They sang Chisu's favorite song, "The King of Love My Shepherd Is". Perhaps that was because he belonged to the shepherd tribe—the Fulanis—keepers and herders of the cattle. One day he found the Great Shepherd as his own Savior. The pastor read from I Thess. 4:13-18 and gave a short message on the uncertainty of life, and everyone sang, "When We All Get to Heaven." In burying Chisu, they took great pains not to bury him facing east toward Mecca, as is the Moslem custom. Hassana and her four children, Istiphanus, Hannatu, Yusufu, and Fibi continued to live on the mission compound.

This happened in 1966, thirty three years ago and the children are adults now. Isti has a responsible position with a company in Niamey, has made at least one visit to the States. He married a daughter of Malam Abdou of Dogon Doutchi. The other three are also a credit to their mother, their godly short-lived father, and the concerned missionaries who helped with school fees for the children and took a special interest in them.

During this furlough, both Wheaton College and Scripture Press did articles on Burt and his ministry. Jim Adair wrote the script for both papers,

Our furlough ended in the Fall of 1966. We rented our house to Bill and Diana Lindberg. After the usual packing of drums and suitcases, we were on our way back to Africa. Instead of heading for Galmi, we were going to spend six months in Kano working at the eye hospital while the regular doctor was on furlough. We left Lance at Moody Bible Institute. Rollie was in Gusau, Nigeria in the Peace Corps, Cherry and John were going to high school at Hillcrest in Jos, and Sue and Pam to Kent Academy We were beginning to feel the empty nest syndrome. We didn't like it too well. I wished, as a mother hen, I could have them all at home under my wings. But it was not to be, and it is not likely it ever will be here. My prayer is that we will all be together in heaven, with spouses, grandchildren, great grandchildren and the great, great grandchildren that we will never know on this earth.

Chapter 15

BERET—THE SUMMER OF 1998

And now for a parenthesis and a chapter devoted to my oldest sister, Beret. I will start with her last days, then proceed to her earlier life. It happened on this wise—

Memorial Day, 1998—Sue and Terry moved in with us for about a week, having sold their house back to the Hoflands and were scheduled to return to Nigeria on June 6. Fran and Bill came from Rockford to help us celebrate the day, and Beret rode the train out to Wheaton. Rudy Levey came too, so we had a houseful and enjoyed our time together.

On June 6, Sue and Terry and Keith and Stephen got away as planned. On June 19, Beret saw her doctor with a sore toe which the doctor diagnosed as gout. Before Beret left, the doctor took a blood sample and was shocked at what she found. She immediately ordered Beret to the Northwestern Memorial Hospital for further testing. After bone marrow testing was done, she was diagnosed with acute myelogenous leukemia. Unbelievable! Beret was a healthy 86 year old, full of hope for what she was still going to do with her life on this earth. All of a sudden the bottom dropped out. I had planned to go to Camp for two weeks. I did go on the 21st while Beret was still in the hospital. On Wed., the 24th Burt picked up Beret from the hospital and brought her to our house. I returned from camp on Thursday, the 25th to become Beret's chief care giver for eight weeks.

—

At first, it was as if Beret were just visiting us. She participated in our activities, helped prepare meals and even went to church two Sunday evenings with me. Once though we walked out early because Beret wasn't feeling well. Beret's medical records were transferred out here and she was under the care of Dr. Isaac Cohen. Hospice stepped in. Chief nurse on her case was Karen Bonkowski; chief social worker was Mary Brooks. They urged us to have me on her bank accounts and be her power of attorney, both for health and general. These things we cared for.

Last winter Beret had a visit from Margaret Wick and her friends, Ann Kennedy and Jo Jordan. Margaret had some of Beret's paintings on her walls at home and Ann visited there and remarked about them and wanted some. They came to Beret's apartment, bought some paintings. Then during the early summer, they came again and went back with about 100 paintings. They invited Beret to visit them. She was not bed ridden. Here is a letter I wrote to the family.

"July 20—Dear Family, Beret spent last week in Ohio with Margaret. She enjoyed herself immensely. What occasioned the trip was a friend of Margaret's, Ann Kennedy, has an interest in Beret's paintings and several months ago, bought a few. Then a week ago, she and Margaret returned, took Beret and some more of her paintings with them to Ohio. During the course of Beret's visit, this friend had a showing in her beautiful home, and her arty friends came and bought $5000.00 worth of them. Well, if that doesn't lift one's spirits, I don't know what would. Margaret brought Beret back to her apartment on Friday and we picked Beret up on Sunday after church and she is back with us. We saw the doctor today, and Beret weighed in at 103, three pounds more than three weeks ago. She is feeling better than she did at first and plans to make a liar out of the doctor who says she has weeks, perhaps two months, to live. She is in a fighting mood. That's good. Attitude helps a lot. She wants to go back to her apartment this week for a few days—says she can handle it by herself—so I'll probably take her in on Thursday and pick her up again next Sunday. We'll see. A lot of people have been praying and maybe that's why she is feeling better."

One week later.

"July 27—Beret wanted to go to her apartment and sort through some of her things last week end, so I took her there Thursday, left her about 4:30 p.m. She had Friday and Saturday to do her project Fri. Bonnie and Bob visited her. I was on the phone with her often. Sun. after church when I picked her up, I found her very sick, slight fever, weak, short of breath, face and legs and feet swollen. I hurried her home to Wheaton, put her to bed. Early this morning, Mon., I called the hospice nurse who immediately ordered oxygen which was delivered about noon. The nurse visited also. Beret has been on and off oxygen since then. When she is on, she feels better, but when she is off of it, she is very weak again. The slightest exertion, such as going to the bathroom, weakens her, and she is back in bed. The week-end finally convinced her that she could not live alone. She had to find that out the hard way. She is still in denial but I think she is beginning to realize that eternal life is not here, but in heaven. Burt is at camp, but if I need him, he is only 3 hours away. So far, I'm doing fine and enjoying my time with Beret and she with me. I am getting an education—learned how to administer the oxygen today. Incidentally, she didn't get anything done at the apartment that she went to do. That's all for now. I'll keep you posted."

As I was e-mailing updates on Beret to friends and relatives, cousin Fred and Marge realized that if they were going to see Beret again, they had better come soon, even though Beret still insisted that she was going to get better. So they, with Fran and Bill and Bonnie came out for lunch on Sat., August 8. By this time, Beret was weak, and they were shocked at her appearance, although I had gradually gotten accustomed to the changes in her. Most of the time was spent sitting around in the living room and talking. Beret was hooked up to oxygen most of the time. The next afternoon Carolyn (Hollander) and Bob Schuldt came to visit Beret. Carolyn mentioned that she was director of nurses at Hearthstone Manor in Woodstock. By now, Hospice was active in our lives—oxygen, bathtub chair, bedside commode, visits by Mary and Karen. It was getting harder to lift her onto the commode and give her a shower. The nights were hard on her. She woke up often, and to her credit, she did not call out for me but struggled to use the commode by herself. She lay there with her thoughts and prayed without disturbing me. It was becoming obvious that she needed more professional care than we could give her here. Likewise, she felt that with more professional care she would get better quicker. She was quite willing to go into a nursing home.

The previous week I had been investigating nursing homes in the area but found none of them satisfactory. Carolyn's visit gave us another avenue to follow. After a few phone calls, arrangements were made and on Tuesday, Aug. 18, 1998 we drove Beret to Hearthstone Manor in Woodstock. She had her own room right across from the nurses' station. For ten days, she received tender, loving care from Carolyn and her staff. The staff and even the patients were very solicitous of Carolyn's Aunt Beret. After the first few days there, she became semi-comatose, and in her last week her response to those of us who talked to her was just a grunt or flutter of the eyes. Obviously she heard. On Aug. 27 at 11:55 p.m., she breathed her last. She elicited no sign of pain She just went to sleep in Jesus. It was just two months and one week from the time of her initial diagnosis until her death. Her funeral was on Monday, Aug. 31, at Olson funeral home in Rockford at 1:00 p.m. Her body was laid to rest in Arlington Cemetery—She was not there. It was a simple service. Burt shared the service with Paul Craig as pastor and cousin Fred Blix who wrote and read his eulogy to Beret. Paul had been pastor to the Seniors at Moody Church and on occasion Beret would attend. Paul also visited her in her apartment and here, so it was fitting that he have a part in her service. Scripture was taken from John 14:1-6. Let not your heart be troubled . . . . Fellowship followed at Fran and Bill's place.

A major task has been to clear out her apartment, and all of her paintings are here with us now except the ones that Ann and Margaret have. Beret's things are occupying two bedrooms downstairs, and will winter here, and when we get back from Florida in the spring, we will try to do something with them.

Now back to the beginning: The beginning for Beret was Jan. 14, 1912. But was that really the beginning? What about conception nine months earlier? And what about Psalm 139 where it says that God knew all about her even before she was thought of. At any rate, Beret Harriet Hollander was born on Jan. 14, 1912 at home on 707 Alles Rd., Winnetka, IL. She was born to Bert and Amelia Henrietta Blix Hollander, both age 26. I have a suspicion that the Harriet was in honor of mother's younger brother, Harry. The birth certificate lists Dad as a mechanic, although I believe he was working for the railroad even at that time. It also lists Dad as being born in New York

City although I believe he was actually born in Budapest, Hungary. Mother was born in Norway.

Almost two years later, Frances Virginia was born on Dec. 19, 1913. Fourteen months later the family moved to North Dakota. Dad had been transferred to Tagus, N.D. Mother travelled alone by train with the two girls because Dad was already there. Below are excerpts from a letter she wrote when they arrived in Tagus.

"Mar. 24, 1915 Dear Folks, The train I came on yesterday, due here at 5:10, has just pulled in and it is now 9:10 P.M. I am glad it wasn't four hours late yesterday . . . . Beret didn't know what to think or say when she saw 'Papa' at last. She sat like a person who had been stunned, and just stared at him for some time. When we came into the house, one of the first things she said was, 'Where is the sink?' There isn't any,' I told her. A few minutes later she asked, 'Why don't you light the gas, Mamma? Ain't there no gas?' Today she asked, 'Is this my house, Mamma?' and another time she said, "Where is the upstairs and the downstairs?'

"I guess everything went as well as could be expected all the way. The children were good. All the way from Savanna, Ill., almost to St. Paul, we followed the Mississippi River. The river was on the left of us and on the right were high cliffs, so high that I could scarcely see the tops of some of them, from the car window. Wherever there was an opening, one could see nothing but hills, that looked like huge mounds of dirt that had been dumped there. Tiny villages would lie in between the hills, and sometimes a tiny shack would be stuck on a cliff side."

"Beret asked, 'What is the name of that water?' meaning the Mississippi. We did not cross the River until after dark, so I was unaware of the episode, but Bert says it happened at Minneapolis at about 11:30 P.M.

"We arrived in St. Paul 15 minutes early. The usher on the C.B. & O., a small black darkey, with a big wide grin, had made himself very pleasant and accommodating and he got me a porter for which I gave him a dime. The porter didn't even take me to the depot, but crossed over trains right to the other train, so I can say that I've been in St. Paul, but I have seen nothing of it. I had him mail your letter and send a telegram to Bert. Beret was very good about being waked up to make the change. She went back to sleep soon after we got on the second train but she knew what had happened, because she looked around and pointed to something on the train and said, 'See, Mamma, that's broke. It wasn't broke on the other train.' You see, the C.B. & O. train was a much nicer train.

"Well, Bert is waiting for me to go to bed, as I won't let him go before I get ready, for it is lonesome, so I'll close here, and write more in my next, which will be soon. I hope you won't forget to write me. I sent Bert to the P.O. today to look for those diapers. Have you sent them? I will send Mabel's waist as soon as possible. We are all well. How is Pa? With love, Amelia."

You may wonder where the above letter came from. I have found out more about Beret and our past in her death than I knew in her life. Beret was a saver. Apparently she never threw anything away. Not just clothes that she never wore anymore, but every little trinket that she owned! Everything was wrapped carefully and individually with crepe paper, or folded neatly and boxed. We shake our heads and wonder why she couldn't get rid of anything. But here is the good news! And it is very good! Among her treasures are letters—hundreds of them. Many are from friends, and I am finding that she had a number of friends from her days at Park House and from her art connections that I knew nothing about. Most of these friends are now gone, but some are alive and I have written to a number of them and have had notes of sympathy from some. Remember, these friends of Beret's are also in their eighties. The best of her collection came in a small cardboard box called "Mother's things." Before Beret died, she called my attention to the box, but I didn't examine the contents until after she died. In the box were Mother's grammar school diploma (1900) and her New Trier High School diploma (1904) plus letters written by Mother to her mother and sisters. I can only surmise that these letters came from Aunt Mabel who passed them on to Beret when Mabel and George moved to Mississippi. These letters, written over 83 years ago, were very fragile, and Beret has each letter preserved in its pieces between transparent folders in a notebook. The above letter was just one of them. My question is, "Shall I type them all out for posterity?" I found a notebook in Beret's things and she started to hand write them out. She got as far as the first two letters, the first one being the one above. Among Beret's treasures, and now mine, are old photographs, most of which bear no name. Yes, I will save some of them, and when I am gone, my kids will rise up and wonder why I saved so many things, but when they find these letters, they may be glad. They read like *Little House on the Prairie* (Ingalls)

Mother's second letter was written the next day, dated March 25, 1915 and contained more detail about their train ride. The conductor told her that her pass was no good and that she would have to get off at the next stop. Mother then asked them to furnish someone to help her with the children and luggage as she could not manage alone.

"Of course, I didn't get off. The conductor gave me a note to give to each succeeding conductor, so that I would have no more trouble with the pass." At one station a couple got on and claimed one of the double seats that I had turned around so that the two girls could sleep on them. The conductor, however, intervened and said he would find the couple a different seat. "At first, when we stopped at stations, Beret would say, 'Everybody is going out, Mamma. We must go, too.' But I guess she soon began to think that we were there to stay. Beret's boil broke the second morning of the trip . . . she wanted to go on the toilet. When she saw the toilet, however, she would not sit on it. She was afraid, because it was open to the ground, and the train was moving over that small piece of track which she saw there. The one on the other train was not open . . . . I have been homesick, but am not saying much about that just now."

"March 28, 1915—Sunday afternoon. Dear Mother and Mabel,

Will try to write a few lines while waiting for my dish water to get hot. The dish water consists of a pan of snow shoveled out of the yard." Water was scarce. They could buy rain, soft, water for 25 cents a barrel. Well water had to be carried a quarter of a mile and it was very hard (alkali). "I baked pie and cake today. We had some beef for dinner with lots of fat and bone on it. Bert got it for 25 cents and we will have about four meals on it."

She fried out all the suet and got about a pound of fat. "It is a good thing, too, for we have to pay 50 cents for a 3 lb. can of Crisco. Flour—$4.25/100 lbs.; sugar, 8 cents a lb.; fresh eggs, 15 cents a dozen; potatoes, 40 cents a bushel; milk, 5 cents a quart."

The house was small but well-built with storm doors and storm windows. The wind blew! In March, they were vacillating between

zero weather and more pleasant weather. They had no clothes
closets, so they used one of the two smaller rooms for closet and
storeroom. There was a cupboard of shelves in one corner of the
kitchen, "and that is my pantry . . . . We are going to have coffee and
cake now."

The last letter I have from Mother from North Dakota is dated
June 10, 1915. In it, she wrote,

"The man we get milk from now filed a suit of bankruptcy last
year, and he has a big ranch full of cattle not far away. That's the way
they do out here. They're a bunch of scoundrels. There are lots of
Norwegians here—Johnson, Charleston, Christiansen, Larson, aren't
those Norwegian names? And they can talk Norsk, too. The town
was named after Tagison. He was Norsk, too . . . . I am expecting
to go back to Chicago in the fall. I don't see any sense in wasting
my days in this place. You needn't be sorry that you can't come out
here, Ma, altho I sure would like to have you. You would probably be
disappointed if you came."

The Hollander saga in N. Dakota, lasted less than a full year.
Mother's letters are so good and give a vivid picture of life on the
North Dakota prairie in 1915. I just looked up Tagus and see that
it is located about 30 miles west of Minot and 50 miles south of the
border of Saskatchewan, Canada. Apparently they left North Dakota
that fall because the next letters were written from Granite City, IL.
Here is an excerpt from a letter written shortly before they left.

"We have just heard that our old friend (?) from N. Dakota, J.
W. Hickey, is working for the Railroad where Bert was working. I
wonder if that has anything to do with Bert's being laid off? This is a
funny world."

In Granite City, they lived in a building with four apartments
on the second floor. There was a hall down the middle of the four
apartments containing the bathroom. Apparently all four families used
the same bathroom and they took turns at cleaning the bathroom, a
week at a time.

"Oct. 19, 1915 We have it as nice and comfortable as we can
expect here. We have nearly every convenience. I telephone my order
to the store, and they bring the things right over. I believe I told you

we had electric lights, with wall switches. Just have to press the button as we enter the door, and we have light.

"Agnes, as a poet reminds me of Walt Whitman. You know he was a great poet, but nobody can understand his poetry. Those who admire him, pretend to understand it, and those who don't, think he is crazy. Take the above any way you like, Agnes, but for goodness sake, don't feel hurt. W. W. was a great man."

How long they stayed in Granite City, I do not know, but the letters that I have stopped in 1915. And now I think I will get back to Beret and finish up this chapter. Winnetka was the Blix home town, and Grandpa Blix had a hand in building their large home there. Beret was born in that home. It was a large house, very impressive and it must have been hard for Mother to adjust to life in North Dakota. At some point the Blix family moved to the north side of Chicago at 2245 Kenilworth Ave., in Rogers Park. Most of the letters were sent to the latter address.

Our real grandmother died somewhere along the way and Grandpa married a Swedish lady, Anna, this time, and that was the only grandmother I knew. The first home that I recall was at 1771 Greenleaf Ave. and our family included Dad and Mother and Beret and Frances and Bob and me, our housekeeper, Margaret Jensen, and at least one cat. I am told that Bobbie tried to put the cat through the washing machine wringer, and Mother rescued it. Mother was teaching at the Eugene Field school. Mother recognized early that Beret had a talent for drawing and she encouraged her. On Mother's death bed, she held Beret's hand and said, "Beret, they don't know you are an artist but I do." Mother had a few more sayings: "Sponge Bath: Wash down as far as possible, Wash up as far as possible, Then wash possible," and the other one, "For every evil under the sun, there is a remedy, or there is none. If there is one, try and find it, If there is none, never mind it."

I uncovered a letter written to Beret, postmarked Mar. 16, 1925. Beret was then 13 years old. This was from one of her grammar school teachers.

"Dear Little Beret, I thot I'd write you and enclose mother's rules on diet, which you so kindly got from home and mother brought it to me on Friday. I certainly appreciate all your kindness and tell mother I shall follow it as closely as I can. I know Dr. Oschner's (?) diets because several friends of my family and my family have taken the same. You see, the Dr. is a personal friend of mine. Have known him ever since I was a little girl like you . . . (Apparently, she was at home convalescing.) I hope I can be back with you on Monday. Then we'll go on with our play, our club and our paper. Aren't you planning another cover? Do! One with birds as couriers—how would that be? We'll keep it a secret between us. Of course, mother may know. Well, I hope you are as nice a little girl when I am away as when I am your teacher . . . . Take good care of yourself. Tell those whom you want to, that I send my love, as I am sending it to you and your dear mother now. Thank mother for her kindness, and remain my dear little Beret. Yours sincerely, Henriette Kleinfell."

Beret started out at Senn High School and loved it. Then we moved to 5530 Luna Ave. in Jefferson Park. Beret had had two years at Senn by the time of our move. She was very unhappy at Schurz and became depressed. She missed her friends at Senn, she missed her art studies and drama, so Mother and Dad allowed her to drop out of school for a semester. Then with special permission, Beret transferred back to Senn to fill out her high school years. That meant she had to ride the street cars from Milwaukee to Lawrence, Lawrence to Clark St., and Clark St. to the school—about an hour's ride each way every day.

One winter day Chicago had a terrible blizzard. Schools were closed, probably early. Street cars were not running. Transportation came to a standstill. Beret was late getting home. We were all worried about her. Where was she? It was dark when she finally arrived. She had walked all the way from Senn High School to our home. We were so glad to see her. And she was so glad to be home.

Beret graduated from Senn high in June of 1930. The Great Depression was in full bloom. It was in the fall of 1929 that the bottom fell out. Beret took some courses at the Art Institute in Chicago. Her interest in art and the aesthetic were very evident, even as a small child. It made her different from the rest of us common people. She was beautiful as evidenced by the many photos we have of her.

During her high school days, she went to Girl Scout camp and also to the camp run by Paul Rader's Chicago Gospel Tabernacle at

Tower Lake first, then later at Chi-go-tab at Lake Harbor, MI. The camp site today is known as Maranatha Conference grounds.

During these camp sessions, Beret trusted Christ as her Savior. At some point in her teen years, she taught Sunday School. She went to the Tabernacle regularly for a while, but when she got into the working world, her focus seemed to be more on art than on Christian things. Although she attended Moody Church from time to time, she never joined or attended regularly.

Beret worked at a number of places: I believe her first job was at Curt-Teich on Irving Park Ave. starting in 1936. She worked at Gartner and Bender, Vogue Wright Studios, Inc., United Printers and Publishers, Scripture Press Foundation, Emmet J. Newman Studio, Plasto Manufacturing Co., Meyercord Co., Silvestri Art Mfg. Co., Stensgaard and finally Marshall Field and Co. At Silvestri she designed a large nativity scene for Carson Pirie Scott where she was able to show her talents in the huge atrium, especially at Christmas. At Marshall Field she worked in the interior design department where she created displays for the various departments. At Scripture Press, she drew pictures for *Power and My Counselor* papers. She did illustrations for some children's books.

She went to the Evening School of the Art Institute of Chicago for four years and took figure painting classes and her report cards (which she saved) are all A's. At Northwestern University—the University College, in 1947 and '48 she took sculpture—again, all A's. Also, the American Academy of Art, night school. During the summer of 1970 she did Graphic Design in Commercial Art at the Central YMCA Community College. In 1984 and '85, she took Advanced Figure drawing at City Colleges of Chicago. Still all A's.

She found time to ski and ride horses, even participating in polo and play some golf. Smitty's stable was about 6 blocks from our house, and she spent as much time over there as she could. One day, her horse ran away with her on it. They sped through the woods, and Beret held on for dear life. She didn't fall off, but she was badly shaken by the experience. I remember winter days when she would be in the kitchen waxing her skis in preparation for going over to the Forest Glen ski jump. Of course, she went down the jump. She spent some months at Steamboat Spring where she worked part time and skied the rest of the time. She had exhibits at New Trier High School, Northwestern

University, Chicago Campus, Navy Pier, Union League, Chicago Art Club and the Chicago Public Library and the Palette and Chisel Academy of Fine Arts. The latter occupied a lot of her time during the last twenty plus years of her life. She did portraits and in 1948-49 did a portrait of the founder of Bethany Biblical Seminary, Dr. Emanuel Beuchley Hoff, which was hung in the library. At that time, the seminary was located at 3435 Van Buren St., in Chicago. During World War II, she worked for the Red Cross doing portraits of men who were in the hospital. They were most appreciative of the attention that they got and there is a letter from Kenneth Garland from Great Lakes expressing his appreciation:

"Dear Beret, You probably have forgotten who I am but I have often thought of you with a sense of deep appreciation and gratitude for the wonderful gift which you gave me while I was in the Naval Hospital. I have often thought of the time and patience you must have to do the type of work you do. I appreciated it a lot also my wife who I now have with me since I have been attached to this station. We shall keep on remembering you all the days of our lives. Ken and Corina Garland"

Another letter came from Katherine Austin, dated May 5, 1944.

"My husband writes you wanted my opinion of the portrait you painted of him . . . . Again I say, the painting was real good and I wish you a lot of success in that line since you're so interested."

Beret never married, but she had many boy friends. The ones I remember that came to the house on Luna were Jimmy S. and Orville H. Orville was an artist, too. I found a landscape that he did in Beret's cache. I have uncovered many letters written by her boy friends. There were Howard D. and John M. and Fred M. But most of all there was Scott B. But Scott was in the (Marine) U.S. Army Corps of Engineers and was sent away to work on the "Third Locks Project" in Diablo, Canal Zone. There must be 100 letters from him that she saved over a period of four years. (We have destroyed them because I think that's what Beret would want.) They first met at Park House.

Park House was a home that belonged to Dr. Robert E. Park, who at one time was an assistant to William James at Harvard. He lived in the east and from time to time, he visited Park House. Jim and Ruth Nobel were the occupants of the large house They opened their doors to young people on the north side of Chicago who enjoyed discussing the arts. "Its essence was communication, not the communication of formal study but the communication that came from questioning, probing, experiencing, and the discussions that followed. It was a place where young people could come and discuss their ideas about life It was also a residence for some, and Beret lived there for several months in 1941. Park House was located at 1508 N. State Parkway in Chicago. Park House existed only 10 years, (1934-44). In 1982, they had a reunion in Solon, Ohio which drew former attendees from all over the country.

In the Canal Zone, Scott was a victim of an explosion that injured his left arm. The arm never really healed well and he was in pain most of the time. Back in the States, Scott and Beret continued to correspond and they saw each other from time to time when Scott got leaves. For some reason or other correspondence slacked off and their relationship cooled. He was discharged from the Marine Corps, did some studying at the university and became a soil conservationist.

Scott went to Iran as a civilian working for the government in soil conservation. This was probably in the late 50's. While there he got sick and was hospitalized in Teheran. "A kidney infection made him weak." Then he went to Geneva, Switzerland for a check-up. Diabetes was found. Had treatments in Geneva. "Pneumonia set in, he became paralyzed in his limbs—was in a helpless and serious condition." This news was from Scott's mother, Mrs. Ada Cronkite. To continue, "A friend of his notified us, and Scott's step brother flew over to bring him home. He was brought back to America in a Navy Hospital plane and put in Oakland Navy Hospital in Oakland, CA. The best specialists were called in. He was operated upon—a malignant tumor was found between lung and heart. Spinal meningitis finally took him after being in a coma for five days." He died on March 31, 1959. Beret didn't hear about his death until October, 1960. Beret didn't write to Mrs. Cronkite until June 25, 1961. Why she waited so long, who knows? She was afraid to open up to anyone. She was not aggressive. In fact, she was just the opposite. But she wrote,

"I only wish that I had been more understanding. I thought his arm was healing for he never mentioned having any pain or discomfort. I'm sure now that he was thinking of me when he said that he was doing the right thing and that it was for the best. (Ceasing to write) But how I wish that I had asked him why and to explain what he meant. If only we had talked about it. One Christmas I gave him a little New Testament. I hope that he might have read it and found in it a source of comfort in his time of need."

A letter Beret wrote to Sally and Anton on Oct. 10, 1960:

"Thank you for writing and letting me know about Scott . . . I loved him very much and hoped that some day I would see him again . . . I wrote to him back in 1949 (I had heard that he was skiing in France) but he did not answer so I never tried to contact him again. I thought of him often and wondered what had become of him."

An interesting letter came to Beret from Mrs. Cronkite written April 4, 1961::

"I recall receiving your letters to Scott years ago requesting that they be forwarded to him, which I did wherever he was located. He talked little of his personal affairs to me or of his new friend after he left home. His cousin, Dorothy Burkhardt, told me she had met you when she was teaching in the Mts. at Aspen, CO. You and Scott were there at the time . . . . Years ago some artist drew a charcoal likeness of Scott. He showed it to me and stated a friend who was a commercial artist had done the likeness. It was very good, and I still have it. Could you have been that artist? I have a photograph or snapshot of a young lady sitting by the ocean or lake. It was among Scott's snapshots. It was unnamed and a very attractive and pleasing pose. I have always wondered again which one of Scott's friends she might have been. Could it have been you?"

Beret answered her but I don't know what she said. Mrs. Cronkite wrote again on May 18, 1961:

"Thank you for your letter and answering my question. I have given one part of your letter much thought where you stated you did not know why Scott broke off with you. His war injury changed his whole life . . . his arm never got well . . . . I found many x-rays taken in many countries where he travelled, also doctors' reports. From these I gathered he was never free from pain, and suspected complications. After a year's treatment he was discharged from the Navy & Marine Hospitals. Was told no more could be done for him . . . . This was the beginning of his foreign travels to S.A. and to Europe which lasted about 10 years. I think he felt he never could get well . . . . To our surprise, he took on a job in Iran."

So there you have the saga of Beret's relationship with Scott. We have heard bits and pieces of someone by the name of Scott from time to time. But Beret was a very private person. And if she mentioned him, she didn't tell the whole story. Now you have the rest of the story, and the remaining letters are heading for the fireplace.

In 1968 she travelled to Galmi, Niger to visit us. She was uncomfortable with the heat but was a good sport and enjoyed her visit with us. Lance was there, too, with a friend of his. With our family of ten and a couple extra visitors, patients, I was feeding about a dozen people 3 times a day. My resources were getting low and the fare was monotonous. One afternoon, a truck stopped out in front and someone came to the door with a stalk of bananas. I couldn't believe it; this had never happened before. I jumped at the chance and bought the whole stalk so we had bananas in the desert for a few days and a change of menu. The Lord knew I needed them and He sent them for that time. To my knowledge that has never happened again.

There's much more about Beret, but you can't put 86 years of living in one chapter, so this will suffice for this time.

Chapter 16

Sami, Ibrahim, LaSani, Nikodimu

I'm going to start this chapter by copying some papers that I wrote when amusing or pathetic things happened at Galmi. The first one is about Sami. You remember him? He was our carpenter at Galmi for many years. This dialogue is between him and me.

"Sami, it doesn't fit!"

"Hmnnn-n-n"

"You can't possibly get that into this space. what have you done? Where are the plans?"

I knew Sami had come back to the kitchen several times during the week and pulled out his tape to measure the space again. At the time, I said, "Sami, are you measuring again?"

"Yes, madam, I'm just making sure."

"Well, just so you know what you're doing."

And so the day came to put my new cabinet in place, and it was one inch too wide.

"Now, whose mistake is this? Let me see my plans. Did I not measure right? Or did you?"

"Well, it's not my fault, mam."

"Well, whose fault is it?"

"I guess it's the wall's fault! You know, the one who built the walls (18 years ago) didn't make them straight. You see?" And he measured the distance on the floor again to show me that it was 24 1/2 inches, exactly the width he had made the cabinet.

—

"But, Sami, you have to accommodate for that. I had already measured at the narrowest width to be sure that it would fit that space."

"Yes, it's the wall's fault. That's what. But don't worry, uwargida. We'll get it in there."

I was afraid he was right. Sami has a way of doing the impossible. I wasn't sure whether he meant to take an inch off the wall or whether he had some other plan, but he started to shove."

I said, "Wait, Sami. I had casters put on the cabinet so that I could roll it in and out easily in order to clean behind it. If you force it in there, I'll never get it out again."

We were able to move the kitchen sink over a half inch. And then he started to plane and plane the sides of the cabinet, until I wondered if there would be any legs left. Finally, after many attempts, the cabinet slid into place and Sami triumphantly beamed. "I guess I fixed that all right. It's too bad about those fellows who can't build a straight wall!"

When I asked Sami to make this cabinet, I had determined I was going to be understanding, kind and considerate in my dealings with him. And I remained that way to the bitter end! I remembered last year's episode and I didn't want a repeat performance.

Sami was commissioned to screen in our side porch. Burt would get him started each morning, but then he would have to leave for the hospital, so it was up to me to see that he did his work right. This Sami resented very much. In the first place, I was a woman, and he didn't like taking suggestions from a woman. In the second place, he was a carpenter, and I didn't know anything about it—or so he thought. So every so often, I would step out on the porch and say, "How is it coming, Sami?"

"All is well, uwargida."

Pause. "Oh, Sami,—I know I'm not a carpenter, but—this frame doesn't look square."

"It's all right."

"Sami, did you use your square? Just by looking at it I can tell it's not square."

Sami had to dig down deep in his tool box to find his square.

"It's off a whole inch, Sami. It won't do. You'll have to take it apart and do it again."

"I'll make it work."

"No you won't, Sami. You take it apart and do it again. We want a good job, not a sloppy job."

"It's only a porch."

"We want it to be a good porch."

"Oh, you want a good porch, do you? Well, I'll give you a good porch, if that's what you want."

Rip, rip. Bang, bang.

One hour later. "How is it going, Sami?"

"All is well, uwargida."

Pause. "Uh, Sami, you have cut this screen on the diagonal. It should be cut on the straight. Now you've ruined a big piece of screen, and we have only enough to do this job."

"Well, I knew we didn't have much screen, so I was making it fit into the space that had already been cut into."

"Do you want us to have nightmares, Sami, when we sleep out here, with every piece of screen cut in a different direction? Take it off and cut another piece, and cut every piece on the straight."

"You're just giving me trouble, uwargida."

"If I'm giving you trouble, it's because we expect you to do a proper job."

"If you, a woman, know so much about it, I'll just walk off and let you do the job."

"I'm telling you right now, Sami, that you're going to finish this job, and you're going to do it the way we want it done. We're paying you to do this job, and already it's cost us half again as much as it should, because you've had to do so many things twice."

I went back into the house. Five minutes later, Sami called, "Uwargida, come." He asked me a simple question. Five minutes later, "Uwargida, come." Another simple question. Five minutes later, "Uwargida, come." By this time I knew he had decided not to pound a nail or saw a board or cut a piece of screen without consultation. Now he had the upper hand. I moved my chair out to the porch and decided I might as well write this week off so far as getting any of my own work done.

It wasn't long before Sami was singing, and we were talking about men and mice and cabbages and kings. The porch was coming along. He was following orders relayed through a woman, and we were friends again. Now Sami points with pride to "his" porch, and we dream pleasant dreams when we sleep out there because the frames are squared and the screens are straight.

Sami Igbayennu started working for us about 8 years ago. He came from Yorubaland in Nigeria where he had learned the carpenter's trade. He is a Christian, and he has had a good influence on Christians and non-Christians here for the most part. It was he who gave Ibrahim Abdou the Bible. Ibrahim (Iyo for short) used to come to the carpenter's shop and Sami witnessed to him. But that's another story.

Ibrahim Abdou

Scene 1: Time: December 1968; Place: Our kitchen; Cast: Yahaya, our gardener; Ibrahim, a local late-teen ager: Ruth: uwargida, mother of the house.

Yahaya: A most amazing thing has happened! Ibrahim, Idi's younger brother, has learned to read in just a few weeks' time. Sami (our carpenter) gave him a Bible, and he's been reading it, and he's never had anyone teach him. You won't believe it. I'm going to bring him over, and you can see for yourself.

Scene 2: Time: a few days later; Place: Our back porch

Yahaya: Here he is, uwargida. Here's Ibrahim. Listen to him read the Bible.
Ruth: Sit down, Ibrahim. where have you been reading?

He opens his Bible to the middle of Exodus and says he started with Genesis. Ruth opens to John 3.

Ruth: Can you read this, Ibrahim? (Ibrahim reads with only slight hesitation.) Who taught you to read?
Ibrahim: No one.
Ruth: Have you never been to school?
Ibrahim: I was in the Koranic School when I was younger. There I learned to read Aljemi. (Hausa written in Arabic script.)

—

307

Ruth: That is no doubt why you learned to read Roman script so easily. What do you think of the Bible, the book that you are now reading?

Ibrahim: It is wonderful. It tells us all about God's love and what we're supposed to do.

Ruth: Keep on reading, Ibrahim. Along with the Old Testament that you are reading, read from the New Testament. Ask God to help you to understand.

Scene 3: Time: Jan. 10, 1969: Place: Open area in center of village. Setting: Ibrahim is surrounded by Moslem malams, crowds increase as word spreads that Ibrahim is "preaching." The malams are asking him questions. He answers from the Bible. They are speechless. They do not understand. This is one of their sons, and he is rebuking them.

Ibrahim: You, malams! You taught me, but you did not teach me the Truth. I have found the Truth. It is in the Bible. If you would teach this Book, then you would not sin; you would not teach a lie. If the world would do what this Book says, the world would not be so wicked.

Malam: You must be mad! He must be a follower of Christ. (To Ibrahim.) Why don't you stand up and say you're a Christian? You just want work with the white man.

Ibrahim: I think I will. I do not want work. This Book has convinced me.

Scene 4: Time: Jan. 12, 1969; Place: Galmi Church. Today Ibrahim stood up during the morning service and openly professed Christ as his Savior.

Abin mamaki—(A Thing of Wonder)

Feb. 16, 1969 Yahaya had just left after washing dishes and I started to bolt the kitchen door and noticed a screw missing from the bolt fastener. We were just preparing to lie down for our after-dinner siesta (a wonderful institution). I said, "Burt, a screw is missing from the lock on the back screen door."

After our nap, Burt set out to fix it. He said, "How long has this been this way?"

"I don't know. I just noticed it!"

"It looks as if the wood has been split, as if it's been broken into. Where's the screw?"

"Don't know."

We looked on the floor but couldn't find it. Burt put another screw in the fastener, and we forgot about it.

That evening, we needed the hospital cash box.

"Ruth, where's the cash box?"

"I haven't taken it. It's probably in its usual place."

Oh, but it wasn't. Then the light began to dawn. Someone had broken into the door while we were at church, and the hospital cash box was missing. Fortunately, the safe had been locked. But we had left the daily cash box out, with the key in it! Only yesterday we had had a more affluent patient who had given us 25,000 francs to keep for him "lest it be stolen", and that was in it plus another estimated 25,000 francs. (about $200.00)

Immediately I suspected four boys who had walked past the house with head loads of hay and stopped for a drink just as we were leaving for church that morning. They knew the house was empty. The next day when they walked by, we called them over, and together with three of our workers, I accused them of taking the money and suggested that if they would return it today we wouldn't prefer charges. I took their names and said that we would ask the commandant in Dogarawa to call them and question them. I figured I instilled the fear of God in them—in fact, one young boy was so scared he couldn't give his name without the help of his friend. They flatly denied having broken into the house, but that's routine. But neither the cash box nor the money was returned by that night.

Burt didn't have time to go to Dogarawa the next day (5 miles away) and on Tues., our annual Niger Conference began, and we were inundated with 67 missionaries, and the matter was forgotten for five days. We had mentioned the theft to our Christians the night that it happened at a gathering in honor of the birth of one of their children.

We were well into the second week after the theft, and I asked Burt if he were going to the Commandant, or should I just throw out those names and forget the whole thing. Each day these kids walked past the house with the loads of hay. They cast furtive looks our way but didn't stop for a drink. What further proof? My soul was vexed as I watched them go by, and we hadn't done a thing about it!

Enter Haruna! And Shama! Haruna was the younger brother of one of the malams in town. He had had a poor farm crop as had the majority of the people last rainy season. He had three small children; he and his wife were separated. He was penniless and everybody knew it. So when he spent 6000 francs on grain and bought himself a new riga (gown) for 1500 francs, that was news. News to the townspeople but we knew nothing about it.

Shama, in better days, worked for us. He worked as a laborer, ironed clothes for me at times and even darned socks for me when the kids were younger. But he came down with t.b. of the spine. We treated him and he wore a cast for a year and recovered. But he was poor. He had become involved in a court case which left him both penniless and wifeless and he had several children to feed. A conversation between the two went something like this.

"Here we are without a franc. Everybody else has money." (Not so!)

"Let's get some money, either from the doctor's house or from the custom's agency."

Shama says, "You'll never get into the doctor's 'box'. He's got it stuck in a wall, and you have to turn a little wheel this way and that until it opens. It's in the bedroom behind the door, but you'll never get into it."

"I'll break into it with a hammer."

Midnight, twelve days after the theft, a voice at the window called, "Maigida (master of the house), the thief has been exposed, the whole village is awake. Come and get him. It's Haruna and Shama."

By the time Burt arrived at the village, Haruna was gone, but Shama was there. He had let the cat out of the bag, had told how they had plotted together, blamed the actual deed on Haruna. He hadn't been sleeping nights, so he had to get it off his chest.

Next morning, Burt went to the Commandant in Dogarawa with the report—not on four young boys—but on two grown men.

—

Sunday evening, the word came that Haruna was back. Three young men hurried to call Burt. By the time they got there, Haruna was gone again. But now the chase was on. The whole village was alerted, and it was a game of "Cat and Mouse". They chased him up and down the little lanes, some villagers bent on hiding him; some bent on catching him.

In and out, up and down. "Here he is!" "No, there he is!" "He was just here. He went that way." Finally, in desperation and breathless, Haruna stopped and shouted, "All right, I'll give it all back. I know where it all is! Just let me alone! I can't run away from your God anymore. I went to Yarbalutu (15 miles away) Thurs. night, took a truck to Sokoto, paid my fare to Ibadan, but I couldn't get on the truck. Your God wouldn't let me. He made me come back. Your God is too strong for me. You Christians have been praying and your God has sent me back here."

"Get the money for us, Haruna."

He produced 29,000 francs.

"Where is the rest? And where is the cash box? And the key?"

"I'll get it all for you. There's the grain in my house, and you can have my riga. That's another 7,500."

Later that night, he dug up the cash box which he had buried in the hill and returned it together with the key!

Burt said, "Haruna, you are a local boy. If you try to get away, you will always be a fugitive. You will never have a home. This is your town. These are your people. Do you want to run away from that all? Get the money for us, and we will tell the commandant to drop the case."

His older brother who has a job in town promised the rest on his next pay day.

The whole village is talking! They are saying, "Those Christians pray and their God answers. We have never seen anything like it. It is an abin mamaki!"

Post script: 1999 I learned a lesson, too. Never to accuse someone if you have no solid proof. I don't remember what happened between me and the boys. I can only hope they forgave me. Perhaps they did and became some of my Awana boys. I hope so.

LaSani and Nikodimu

March, 1969 LaSani and Nikodimu arrived Saturday just as we were eating breakfast, so over coffee and toast we became acquainted. LaSani is an old man with gray hair, bent with years of hard work and with a few front teeth missing.

What is your work, LaSani? What work have you left this month in order to come to our country and preach the Gospel?"

"I'm just an evangelist. All I've done all my life in the way of work is preach. But I'm not a real one."

"What do you mean?"

"Well, I can't marry anybody or baptize anybody."

"Oh, you mean you're not licensed."

"Yes, that's right."

"Well, that doesn't matter. The big thing is to preach the Word."

"Well, that's why we've come!"

LaSani and Nikodimu are two in a group of thirty men who were willing to leave Nigeria and come to Niger for the month of March. They have spread out two by two over a distance of more than 500 miles between our missions. They have left their wives and families alone, separated from them by 700 miles.

"What is your work, Nikodimu?" we asked.

"I have been trained as a school teacher."

We rose from the table. "Let us introduce you to some of our Christians." Idi, our lab technician and one of our elders were at the door looking for the doctor.

Nikodimu was a young man. He with one of our local Christians, went one way and LaSani and Idi went another way. Nikodimu had a good voice. He would start singing a gospel song to attract the crowds and then begin to preach. They went on Sunday afternoons and came back on Saturday afternoons, and Sundays were days of praise and reports of their weeks in the villages.

Sunday afternoon LaSani and Idi were dropped off at Gidan Idir, a large village about 25 miles from Galmi. Sunday was market day, and the town was jammed with people from surrounding villages. The first thing that LaSani said to Idi was,

"Well, here we are. Call the Christians together."

Idi answered, "There are no Christians."

"What? In all this great crowd there are no Christians?"

"Yes, that's right."

And all these people are on their way to hell?"

LaSani wept.

Sequel

May, 1969 Last Sunday, five young men from Luhudu walked 15 miles to fellowship with us in Sunday School and church. These men are babes in Christ, results of an evangelistic effort sparked by 30 Nigerian men who left home and family to spend a month in Niger going out to surrounding villages together with local Christians. Luhudu was one of a number of villages that responded to the preaching of the cross.

DauDuka, who himself came back to the Lord this year, together with LaSani, one of the two visitors who were our church's guests, found great interest in Luhudu, and besides these young men, another handful of young women came to know the Lord. One of the men and one of the woman can read. DauDuka gave them a Bible, and they are reading it together each day.

Pray for DauDuka, who is trying to visit them or have them visit him once a week and strengthen them in the things of the Lord. DauDuka himself is a token of God's grace and reminds us of the Lord's words to Peter in Luke 22:31, 32. "Satan hath desired to have you, that he may sift you as wheat, but I have prayed for thee that thy faith fail not; and when thou are converted, strengthen thy brethren." DauDuka also desires to go to Bible School this coming January to pick up where he left off ten years ago.

Update on DauDuka—1999 Once more DauDuka could not take the pressure from the village and went back into Islam. For some years he worked at the hospital, but he no longer works there. He is an old man by their standards now. He must be in his sixties. He is now a malam in the village. It would seem that Satan has won the battle for him, but the story is not over yet, and we still trust the Lord to do a work in his life and bring him back to Himself.

Update on DauDuka—April 2003 We received an e-mail from Joshua Bogunjoko who was director of Galmi Hospital at that time.

The African conference was going on at Galmi. Joshua said that a man had come forward to say that he wanted to come back to Christ. It raised my curiosity, so I wrote to him to ask him if this could possibly be Dau Duka, our first convert at Galmi, who had gone to Bible School, become our pastor, married a second wife and returned to Islam. Yes, it was Dau Duka.

A Day to be Remembered

I will start my story tonight. It is a story about a boy—his name is Mousa, son of Dau Duka and he is only 15 years old. This is a day to be remembered!

The day itself was beautiful, with the rainy season blue sky, mixed with white cumulus iceberg clouds made of whipped cream. The day itself made you smile, happy to be alive. The tall guinea corn and millet bent slightly with the trees as if to reassure their owners, who had just seen a hungry year, that this year all would be well. Today was Aug. 24, 1969, for Mousa, in addition to the beauties of the day, this was his special day—he was baptized.

The "baptismal font" was along side the road; in the dry season it is nothing but a ditch. A good group gathered this Sunday afternoon—about forty—some, members of the church, some curiosity seekers, some scoffers. Some were boys that Moussa had grown up with—some of these were the scoffers.

Moussa stood there waist deep in the water, flanked on one side by missionary Ray Pollen and the other by Malam Ibrahim, one of the church elders. Moussa began with his testimony. "All of you know my past—my character, my reputation." Indeed we did! Moussa had become a young vagabond, a thief. He had been convicted and sentenced to a reform school, but because of his youth, was let off. "But since I have believed on the Lord Jesus Christ, He has changed my life and the things that I did before, I don't do anymore. Jesus has cleansed me from all my sin and He has forgiven me. I thank Him for saving me." This was something I had never expected to hear from Moussa, and to watch him immersed in the name of the Father, Son and Holy Ghost, was something I had never expected to see. This was only the hand of God at work.

A year earlier Moussa showed up at one of our Awana meetings. His clothes were rags and tatters. I was shocked to see him and said, "Moussa! It is you!" I thought he was in the reform school in a town many miles away. His last episode had been a theft of 50,000 Niger francs plus some American dollars from one of our nurses. For this, he had been tried and sent away. We passed the word along to all the missionaries on the compound. "Moussa is back, keep your doors locked."

Moussa kept coming to Awana every week and spent most of his time in his home. His father, DauDuka, who only a few months before had been re-instated in the church fellowship after many years of back-sliding, noticed a change in him. Moussa visited in the home of the hospital evangelist, Malam Garba, often reading the Bible with him. Gradually an awakening in his soul came, and at one time during the following months, Malam Garba had the joy of praying with him and leading him to Christ. He cautioned us, "Of course, we can't tell if it's real. We'll just have to observe him."

Moussa's entire outlook on life took on new meaning. He continued in the Awana club meetings, he came to S.S. and church every Sunday, he read his Bible at home and didn't roam the village with his buddies. His life was radically different. The chance came for him to go to our mission farm school in Maradi. He applied but was rejected because of his past history. He was almost in tears. I told him to pray and write them a letter. He wrote with great emphasis, "I promise I will obey and do my best, and if I don't you can kick me out—I promise!." On the basis of this letter, they said he might enroll on probation. Joy lit his face as I passed the word along to him and he prayed, thanking the Lord for the opportunity of going. He gathered his clothes in a bundle, and next day got a truck for Maradi—school had started two days earlier.

During the school year, we were pleased with reports that he was doing well in his studies and his character was good. "He has requested baptism and has been examined by the church elders here in Maradi. Shall we baptize him with the others that are to be baptized from the school?" We sent word back. "No. He should be baptized here at home where it means something special. Everyone here knows Moussa for what he was."

And so it came about that this was a day to be remembered.

Sequel

Thirty years later, and I don't know where Moussa is today. Whether he is following the Lord or whether he has gone back to his old ways and is in jail, I do not know. But if he really was saved in 1969, he still belongs to Jesus wherever he is.

Fire!

March 12, 1969 A fire in the hospital doesn't happen every day so that was the farthest thought from my mind when I heard a bicycle speeding up the path and screeching to a stop. It was rest hour. Burt had finished his morning's work at the hospital—the usual run of operations, the examining of patients that the nurse had held for him. He arrived home about 1:30, ate his dinner and was now enjoying a deep sleep, if I could judge by his breathing. I had chosen to read during rest hour, so as the bicycle approached, I wondered what kind of emergency it would be. Should I wake Burt or let him sleep. I waited.

Clap, Clap, clap—the usual Hausa greeting. I ignored it! Let him clap again or say what he wants. If I call to him, I might wake up Burt. Heavy breathing from whoever was standing at the front screen door! Clap, clap, clap, clap, clap. Heavy, rapid breathing, as if he had run for his life. Why doesn't he say what he wants. Then it came out! Gobara! (Fire!)

By this time, Burt was awake. "Mmmmmm?"

"Gobara!" I was on my feet. "Where?"

"Gidan fashi!" (operating room).

I shook Burt. "Burt. Fire! The operating room is on fire!'

Fully awake by then, he was up and gone in a flash. He rode the bike. Mamman, the youngest member of our hospital staff, the one who had come to give the alarm but was speechless with fright, followed him. I hurriedly locked the house. (We were still being careful—it was only a few weeks after "the great theft"). I realized my legs were weak, my knees buckling.

"Slow down," I said to myself. "No sense in running."

It was a good 500 yards to the hospital. Half walking, half running my thoughts were mingled with fears and prayers.

"Oh Lord, don't let anyone be trapped in the operating room.

"Don't run. What good will I be when I get there? It's probably all out now. The men are there.

"I wonder if the sterilizer exploded!

"Please, Lord, may no one be hurt.

"I wonder who was on duty."

I turned into the main entrance and saw men and women with their loads on their heads coming toward me. I saw men sliding along on the floor toward the exit with their legs in casts. There was a general exodus from the men's ward, adjacent to the surgical wing. Smoke was pouring out of the surgical wing doors, but as I had hoped, the fire was out. There were Burt and Ray and Dari and Boube and Mamman and Issa standing in water an inch deep, surrounded by buckets, some empty, some still full of water. It wasn't the operating room, but the scrub room right next to it—the room where they wash for surgery, wash the instruments and sterilize small amounts of instruments. A 20 quart pressure cooker was standing on the two burner kerosene stove, filled with wrapped instruments, but still standing. Two tables were charred—only a few minutes before they had been ablaze, set on fire by the kerosene tank that fell from the stove after the soldering job had melted because of the intense heat. Boube had been sterilizing the instruments, had a good hot fire under the pressure cooker, so hot in fact, that the soldered repair job wasn't adquate. When the tank fell and spilled, fire raced across the tables, aided by the spilled kerosene. Boube grabbed for a bucket, filled it with water, threw it on, but it did no good. He ran for the nurse, Gen Kooy, who was out in the wards and ran to Ray Pollen's house. He must have roused him from his nap, too, because when I saw him, he was shirtless and in his slippers. Ray got there first—his house was closest. Gen ran to the fire, but it was already beyond her. The African workers appeared out of the blue and the bucket brigade commenced.

No one was hurt. Praise the Lord! Word spread that the fire was out. The patients made their way back to their beds. Those who slid out on their bottoms slid back the same way. As I made my way back, the people were joyous—they greeted and shook fists—a most friendly greeting—and said "Gaisheku!" That meant, "You (all) did a great thing getting that fire out so quickly." I greeted them back, knowing that I hadn't done a thing. Then I saw the man in the first bed who had a cast on his leg from the hip down. I feigned surprise. I said, "Are you back in bed? How did you get out of here? I thought you couldn't move." He said, "You'd be surprised what a person can do if he has to." I laughed and went on my way. My legs weren't shaky anymore.

Another Fire

I was reminded of another fire we had a number of years ago. That was before our days of electricity. Then we always had plenty of light because we used our pressure lamps in the big rooms and had kerosene lamps in the other rooms. Now we have a 7 1/2 kilowatt diesel Lister plant, an emergency 2 1/2 kilowatt gasoline plant and the Pollens '1500 watt second emergency plant. Besides that, we have an army field x-ray unit with its own generator in the hospital. But tonight and the last three nights, we have been using the lamps. Only the small ones! The pressure lamps are in the store room—we don't use them anymore—we have all these light plants! So the pressure lamps need a few washers and a little going over! But nobody has time to do that. We don't need them anymore—we have all these light plants! But no light! So we carry the little hurricane lamps from one room to another, and we go to bed early.

The big plant is spread out all over the power house floor. I hope Ray knows where all those pieces go. The Pollens' small plant was in use last week, but "it seized". Ray says he filled it with oil the very night "it seized" so why "it seized" he doesn't know, much less me. The "emergency plant" back-fired the other night so much that it reminded me of the fourth of July back home. The next night it wouldn't even start.

But about this other fire. This took place before we had electricity.

This was when our John was about 5 years old. He was the big boy in the house because Rollie, Lance and Cherry were away at Kent Academy for school. Everywhere his father went, John was sure to go.

A truck stopped. We were eating supper, and it was dark already. You might know it! The truck ran out of gas right in front of our place. It never ceases to amaze us how many trucks run out of gas just at the moment they reach our driveway. If we insist that we have none for sale, they somehow manage to move those trucks to the next stop. Just how, without any gas, I'm not sure. But this night, Burt agreed to sell them some gas. They went out to the garage with a small hurricane lantern, opened the big doors to where the drums of gas stood. As usual, John was right with Burt. Burt set the lantern up high on another drum nearby. John went deeper into the garage. Burt started to turn the bung on the 50 gallon drum of gasoline. While it still stuck to the threads of the bung hole, gas fumes rushed out and up to where the lantern was sitting, and in a flash, the drum was ablaze at the bung hole. Immediately Burt called to John who was trapped inside the garage.

"John, run, run this way! Fast!"

He did. Instant obedience! Right past the blazing gas drum! Both he and Burt ran away from the garage.

"Run, run." Burt expected the drum to explode any minute. The crowd that had been on the truck started to yell, "Fire." They pushed the truck behind the garage!

Jadi was washing supper dishes in our kitchen, and he heard the commotion. He grabbed the big white pan of dish water and ran to the garage.

"All right, Jadi, throw it, but I don't think it will work." shouted Burt. Everyone knows that you don't put out gasoline fires with water.

But THIS dish water did! Jadi heaved from the garage doors, and the water fell in such a manner that it landed right on top of the burning drum and smothered the fire . . . The fire was out. Burt went back into the garage and quickly tightened the bung again. Burt suffered first degree burns on his chest. John was unscathed. The truck driver didn't get his gas that night. Amazing how he drove away without gas!

Burt doesn't sell gas after dark anymore.

Yet another fire!

One other fire of consequence happened in our living room. It happened to Sue. I wrote about it in a previous chapter. Sue knew she wasn't supposed to play with matches, so she carefully hid herself behind the couch so no one would see her. She struck the match, her dress went up in flames. Shayabu pounced on her and the fire was smothered. She was not burned. Praise the Lord! I took her in my arms and cried a little.

Later John asked me why I didn't spank her. "I don't know. Maybe you can tell me."

That was "The year that Sue set herself on fire."

Mai Shanu

I am walking in Gidan Dutse to visit with some of my women friends. I pass the hut where the malams usually hang out together. The following conversation takes place between me and Mai Shanu, who is the chief malam of the village. Other men of the village were there also.

What do you have?

A flannelgraph story.

Show it to me.

No, I won't show it to you. You just want to mock.

No, I won't mock you.

Gaskiya? (Honestly?)

Gaskiya.

Well, then bring me a mat and I will sit down here and you will sit down there, and you will not get up and go away until I am all through.

Mai Shanu himself brought me the mat, and once again he listened to the Gospel story and went away apparently unaffected. I say "once again", for he has heard the story before many times, but since he is the chief of the Moslem malams (teachers) he says he cannot give up his beliefs or his income or his prestige even though the Christ way may be true.

Rumor had it that Mai Shanu was a secret believer. Dan Truax had visited with him many times. The day of his death came while we were still there, and some say that he died a believer. Only eternity will tell.

Another Side of Me

This morning I lit my two kerosene burners, lifted my portable oven onto them and put in six slices of bread for toasting. Then I noticed a baby cockroach on top of the oven. He was running across the top of the oven and came to the ridge at the edge. Then he turned around and crossed the length of the oven only to be met by a similar ridge. His pace accelerated in proportion to the increase of the heat. Faster and faster he raced from ridge to ridge, then, three desperate hops and a final dash and he lay motionless.

During the sixty seconds of this drama, I felt alternate pangs of sympathy, glee, guilt, squeamishness. I felt like an aggressor, oppressor, a big bully. I rationalized and said if he were on the floor, I'd step on him and think nothing of it. Then it was all over and I turned away.

My toast burned!

Yahaya

Yahaya was one of our faithful workers for many years. As for his Christianity, it was an on-again off-again situation. From time to time he was our laborer, our house-boy, our cook. His most enduring job was as our cook and he was affectionately know as "babban kuku", which means "big cook". "Kuku" pronounced "coocoo" had an in-house meaning to the missionaries. He was a good man, faithful. He grew old with us. When we left in 1975, he was in his "off-again" phase. In Jos, a couple of years later, we heard that Yahaya had come back to the Lord and was preaching and having a remarkable testimony in the village. About a year after that, he died, and the Christians had nothing but praise for him. He was buried in the "Christian graveyard."

Years earlier, in one of his on-again Christian phases, he was convicted of having two wives. He decided to build another hut in his compound, put one of his wives in it and care for her but not have married relations with her. He did just that. The only puzzle that we had about it was that he put away his first, older wife and kept his second, younger wife as his legitimate wife. What can you say?

We look forward to seeing Yahaya again in heaven.

Issou

We first knew Issou when he was a teen ager and he carried water on the donkey to our house and to the hospital. As he matured, he

—

321

became our houseboy, and finally our cook. He was a good worker. When we went to Camerouns, he went with us. When we went to Miango, he went along, and when we went to Haute Volta and Dahomey (now Benin) he was our helper and child care giver. We liked Issou very much. He never made an out and out profession of faith, but he agreed with what we were preaching. One day, his world fell apart and we were devastated. Issou stole a large sum of money from our safe and we had to let him go. His big brother, Alaha, pled with us to take him back, but we couldn't do it. I was heart sick because he was such a likable person and such a good worker. Alaha was also a very fine person, and when Alaha was killed in an accident in Lagos, Issou became the responsible one for all of Alaha's family as well as his own. Issou went into farming big time.

When we visited Galmi in 1990, we had a nice visit with Issou and Kwalkwali. Issou showed us his large farm which was irrigated by a dam just north of Galmi. He was doing well financially just from working his farm. And we were happy for him.

Friends

There were many others, I can't mention them all: Ibrahim and Lydia, Chisu and Hassana, Idi and Ashibi, Ila, Sha'aybu, Mai Daji, Amu, A'i and Mamman, Mamman, the nurses' boy/cook, Aminatu, A'i mai Frere, Iyo, Musa and Abdou. And then there were their children who had been a part of Awana and today are adults. Iliya, son of Ibrahim and Lydia, is working at the hospital; Isti, Chisu's son, has a responsible job in Niamey. Aminatu was Gen's adopted daughter. When she was five years old, she accompanied her mother to the hospital—just the two of them. The mother was sick and died and left Aminatu. Gen made arrangements with the family and the authorities and adopted her. She later married; her husband was a police man in Niamey and was killed in a motorcycle accident. She is married to another Christian policeman and lives in Sokoto area. She has a family and they love the Lord.

Amu was a young girl who came to our girls' club and also came to me to learn to read. During one of our classes, she accepted the Lord. When she was about 15, she was married to a Moslem. The wedding was arranged by her parents, and she had nothing to say about it. She was taken to a village north of us and integrated into his family—the only Christian in the whole town. Over the years, she has suffered for her faith. Her Bible has been taken from her and destroyed. She has suffered both physically and emotionally. She manages to get away from her home about once a week to visit the nurses at Galmi, at which time, they study the Word together and pray together and her faith has increased over the years. She has several children—two of them died. She must be 40 years old now. Her life is not easy, but she remains faithful.

A'i Mamman came from Maradi area; Mamman, from Galmi. When Mamman met A'i, he was a professing Christian and working for Jo Rogers. They married and returned to Galmi. Mamman could not stand the pressures of his people in the village and went back to Islam. A'i remained a true Christian and did her best to raise her children as Christians. It was difficult. Finally, Mamman took a second wife and A'i went back to her people in Maradi. In keeping with African custom, their children became the property of the husband only. The new wife did not like the idea of raising someone else's children, and they were neglected. After a couple of years, Mamman woke up to the fact that he had made a mistake. He got rid of his second wife, begged A'i to return. But it was on the condition that Mamman give up Islam and allow her to go to church and take the children with her. Which he did, and I believe they are still together.

A'i mai Frere was one of the young girls who was faithful in Awana, learned many Bible verses, attended church regularly. She was strong enough to resist the family pressure and to this day maintains a testimony. She married a Christian young man whom I don't know but whose last name is Frere—meaning brother.

Garba was our houseboy at one time. So was Sha'aybu. Garba died a number of years ago. I don't think he ever made a profession of faith. Sha'aybu pushed our babies in our buggy. He was just a young boy himself when he worked for us. As he grew older, he became our houseboy. Later, Sha'aybu worked in the hospital. He was a good worker. One day he was found after hours in a hospital room making out with a girl. He was fired. He became our enemy. He renounced Christianity.

Mai Daji worked for the Emmets back in 1951 or so. He was fired for taking what was not his own. I think his concept of being a houseboy included being a part of the family in every way. "What's yours is mine, you know." He was let go. He took up sewing and became a tailor. When we left Galmi for the last time, he bought our treadle Singer sewing machine. When we visited Galmi in 1990, he said, "Uwargida, bring me some cloth and I will make you a riga." And he did.

Iyo, the painter, has been a laborer for as long as I can remember. A fine man, but strong Moslem. There's Kwalkwali and Dari who went out preaching for a season, then quit when they didn't get paid for it. Ila worked in the hospital with Gaji, and together they made a great combination, Ila as a surgical assistant and Gaji as a circulating nurse. Both of them were taught to read and write and taught their work on the job. Both of them quit after we left Galmi in 1975. Neither made professions of faith. Musa was our cook/houseboy our last years and a very fine one, indeed. He still associates with the Christians although I don't know if he really is born again. Only God knows what's in the hearts of these people. They are without excuse, but fear keeps many of them secret believers. You can't build a church on secret believers.

The list goes on, but I must stop reminiscing and bring this chapter to a close.

Chapter 17

1967 and Lance's illness

In January, 1966 an army coup ousted the Nigerian civilian government. Six months later, a counter coup took place. In October, Kano was torn apart by riots. Southerners fled, but not all were able to escape, and the Hausas slaughtered any whom they identified as Ibo or Yoruba. Heroic efforts were made by our missionaries in Kano to hide and aid those who were attacked, but they were not always successful. Some Hausas raided the hospital and killed any patients whom they suspected were not Hausa. Those southerners who tried to flee by car were stopped at road blocks and shot on the spot. The eye hospital closed down. Civil war erupted in 1967 when the Eastern Region attempted to secede under the name Biafra This left hundreds/ thousands of Ibos, Yorubas and Hausas dead. Oil fields were located in the Eastern Region. Had Biafra become independent, the rest of Nigeria would have been cut out of the oil industry. The Ibos and Yorubas were more educated and Christianized than the Hausas who were primarily Moslem. We were back in the States while all this was going on. (In 1970 the nation was reunited.)

For you to best understand the enormity of the situation in Kano, I am quoting from Gwen Hummel's letter dated Oct. 6, 1966

"Have you ever heard the sound of chopping kindling? Doesn't sound bad, does it? But when you know that that 'kindling' is a door or a window, and behind it are not pigs and goats, but human beings for

325

whom there is possibly no escape, for they will be the next kindling, then that is a different thing.

"In our out-patient Clinic we are enlarging our drug storage room. The builders were breaking down the wall today—it gave me chills, for it sounded just like what we listened to helplessly all night on Oct. 1. It will be a long time before such sounds don't bother me.

"Not only was there the pounding and yelling of glee over finding, chasing, beating, and killing humans, but there was also the shooting of the guns. We could distinguish 3 different kinds being used. When we heard the shots bang, bang, bang, bang, bang (just that close, too), I thought they were all aimed at one fleeing soul, but learned later that when they found people in rooms, if it was soldiers who found them, they took them out to a field and lined them up, and each shot sent someone into eternity. The soldiers seemed intent only on demanding money and killing. Our Grace said that when they shot someone they would quickly go over the body looking for money and then leave. Then the civilians would come and carry away other loot. If the soldiers missed anyone, and the civilians found such, they would finish the person off with terribly cruel beating. Sometimes such would faint and be left for dead. These are the wounded we see about us. There are not many of them.

"In Agnes' compound they found a young boy with a Bible (prob. a N.T.) in his back pocket. They made him sit down and open it—I wonder where it was open to, and if it was light enough for him to see the Word—then they shot him from the rear, and it must have been a heavy shot for she said the body flew up into the air."

That's enough of Gwen's letter although there was more. The violence was aimed at the Ibos. But if a Yoruba or Hausa tried to hide anyone, they would also be shot, so when fleeing Ibos begged for entrance into homes, they were pushed out. Sabon Gari was hard hit. St. Stephen's vicarage was in shambles and so was the church. Some Christians, including some of our missionaries, managed to hide some Ibos in the roofs of their homes for days.

The Nigerian war continued. "August 24, 1967 The Kano airport was bombed one day last week, damaging one Czech jet plane that had been sent in. The airport is closed to all traffic, because the Hausas are being 'taught' how to fly the jets that Russia is sending in. K.A.

opening has been postponed until Sept. 14, and we have to take them to Sokoto since there is no air traffic across the border."

While this was going on during our furlough, what was happening at Galmi? Letters written by Gen Kooy tell part of the story.

"January 31, 1967 We were saddened when in November one of the Galmi Christians, Chiso, suddenly went to be with the Lord, after a heart attack. He left his wife, Hassana, and four small children: Stevie, Hannah, Joseph and Phoebe."

Usually when a husband dies, his family claims the children. Chisu's brother, Samuel, also a Christian, came to visit and said that Hassana could keep the children as long as they were receiving Christian training, contrary to the desires of the two younger brothers who wanted to take the children. At this time, the oldest, Stevie, (Isti, for Istaphanus) was 6 1/2 and attending the new Christian school in Tsibiri. Gen Kooy financed not only his education but also that of the other three children as they grew. She also took responsibility for Hassana who lived on the compound and worked in the hospital. Kudos go to Gen for all her help with the children. Isti is a computer expert working in Cotonou at present, is married to the daughter of Abdou from Dogon Doutchie, and they have several children, all loving the Lord. Hassana and Chisu's other three children are also married and following the Lord.

Just a footnote here to keep the record straight. Isti was fathered by Tanko, a hospital worker. Although it was not called "rape", it was determined that Hassana was an innocent victim. Tanko was let go, but Hassana kept her job, bore Isti, and Gen nurtured and discipled her. Later Hassana married Chisu who became a father to Isti and he and Hassana had three more children.

Gen to the rescue again! A mother came to the hospital for help. Her husband abandoned her when she became ill. With her was her three year old daughter, Aminatu. The mother died in the hospital, after professing faith in Christ. And what was to become of little Aminatu? Gen cared for her in her house, then went to Dogarawa to talk to her people, and they agreed that Gen could adopt her. So with all the papers in hand, Aminatu became Gen's daughter legally in 1954. Aminatu went to the Tsibiri school and at age 18. she married Job, a Christian policeman and they lived in Niamey. A few short years later, her husband was killed in a motorcycle accident, so Aminatu became a widow with small children. Several years after that, Aminatu married a Nigerian policeman and they moved to Sokoto where they continue to this day. They maintain a Christian testimony in that city that is predominantly Moslem.

The previous term whenever I visited in Gidan Douche, I made it a point to ask the young boys, who vied to hold my hands or my things, if they would like to play soccer. I had a ball and said that if they would like to come over, we could play soccer and follow it up with a Bible story. They were excited about it. So they came, and I was out there one afternoon a week with a whistle in my mouth and a hat on my head, refereeing a game in 100 degree weather. After the games, I would invite (strongly suggest) them into the chapel for the Bible story. Some skipped out but most came. Later on, we had club in the waiting room of the hospital in the evenings. We would play games and have a meeting. We also had a turn at Lydia and Ibrahim's compound in the village. This went on until furlough. The seeds were planted for an Awana club. Gen was burdened for the girls, so she started a club for girls on Saturday afternoons

During our furlough, we visited Awana headquarters. Art Rorheim fixed us up with flags, T-shirts, neckerchiefs, rope for tug-o-war, belts, badges, bean bags, and markers, club books and more. We were armed for bear when we returned in 1967. But before we could get back to Galmi, when our furlough was over, we were asked to go to Kano for four months to re-open the eye hospital and fill the gap until an eye doctor returned Our scheduled time of departure was the end of January, 1967. But January 26 brought the worst snow storm in many years. All airports were closed, flights canceled, and we were snow bound. We finally got away on Feb. 6.

Dick and Pat Brooks kindly met us at the airport in N.Y., took us to the mission and then returned to their home in New Jersey, a two hour trip. When we woke up the next morning, New York was blanketed with the snow storm that had hit Chicago earlier. Our flight was scheduled to take off that evening, and we wondered if we would make it. We did, but our flight was delayed for four hours, and Swissair gave us a French style dinner in the dining room at the airport. We were met in Geneva by Ted and Addy Emmett, who took us to their home in Lausanne. They showed us the Emmaus Bible Institute and Geneva Bible Institute and got us back to Geneva by 6 p.m. in time to make our flight to Rome. This was on a French Caravelle.—very nice. One hour in the air and then six hours in Rome's barren, barn like, almost deserted airport! At 2 a.m. we connected with KLM from Amsterdam, and then had a very pleasant 4 hr. trip across the Mediterranean and Sahara Desert. I wonder why we took such a circuitous route. Perhaps it was because of canceled flights due to the Chicago and New York blizzards. We were glad to see Jack Driediger waiting for us at Kano on Feb.10. We were happy to exchange winter conditions in Wheaton for 100 degree weather in Kano. It was good to be back in the heat, away from snow and cold weather.

We settled into the Kietzmans' house, and the next day, our kids were whisked away to Hillcrest and K.A and the house was too big again! John, Sue and Pam settled in quickly at K.A., and Cherry at Hillcrest. They were behind in French. John and Sue were put in the same special French class. Actually, Sue had never had French, so she was starting from scratch. They all caught up in time.

The whole Hostel was out to meet Cherry when the plane arrived in Jos. Sue had a similar triumphant arrival at K.A., with all the girls pouncing on her and screaming! She tried out for the Spring program and was chosen to be narrator for *Anne of Green Gables*. After 8 year old Pam had carefully carried Baby Magic all the way from the States, it didn't take long for it to get broken at K.A.

A few days after our arrival in Kano, Rollie and two of his Peace Corps friends surprised us by dropping in for breakfast. Remember, Rollie had joined the Peace Corps and had preceded us to Nigeria. They were enroute to Potiskum, Maiduguri, Jos and back to Minna. He was due in Gusau the end of the month. That made our day. In Jos, he stopped in to see Cherry at the SIM hostel. I'll let Cherry tell you about it in a letter that she wrote back to us from Hillcrest, March 4, 1967.

"We were eating in back. One of the kids said they saw someone from the Peace Corps hanging around—'it must be Peace Corps—the guy has a beard'. So I told all the kids about Rollie's beard, and they were all wondering what he looked like. The visitor all of a sudden said to me, 'Your brother is out there.' Well, I didn't even know this guy, so I said, 'He can't be.' So I sat around. Then he said, 'If you're the daughter of a Dr. Burt Long, he's your brother.' So the kids and I all got excited, and I ran-walked through the house, 'cause I knew he wasn't there, but he had to be. I looked out the window and I tore!!! I leaped 3 ft., I'm sure. Oh man, he was there! They (he and his friends) had had two flats 25 miles away and had hitch hiked. He said he didn't know if I lived here, but where else in Jos would I be? They stayed through Sunday, said good-bye Monday morning. When I got home from school, they were just packing, so it was a glorious week-end."

The folks at Kano had the welcome mat out for us. Burt began work at the Eye Hospital right away. The Eye Hospital had been shut down since the October riots. Dr. Oleari had preceded us by a week, so the hospital was open when we arrived, but Dr. Oleari left a week later, and the work was all in Burt's hands with the help of well trained nurses. Each day 300 patients were treated in the outpatient clinic and each week about 60 eyes were operated. The hospital evangelist visited personally with and preached to the patients over a loud speaker several times a day.

I had a week to settle in before I went to work in the Optical Shop half days, doing correspondence for Dave Boyes.

"You can't imagine what this past week has done for me. I have finally wound down and am more relaxed than I have been in many months. It didn't take any time at all to get used to the afternoon rest hour, and I slept a good part of the first two days."

The biggest and most enjoyable challenge I had was to teach a Bible class at 7:30 a.m. three mornings a week to 5th, 6th, and 7th grade boys and girls who lived at the army barracks four miles out of town. When some of the students asked me to teach this "religious knowledge" class for them, I hesitated because I knew I had only 5 weeks left. But they insisted that I take the class and that someone else would continue it. We finished the study of "Salvation from the Penalty of Sin," and I turned over to my successor. A week after I left, the class came to an abrupt halt, because the fathers of these children were called to war, and the mothers and children were sent home. Only eternity will reveal the effect of this short Bible study.

While this was going on in Kano, drama was unfolding back in Chicago. We had left Lance at home studying at Moody Bible Institute. He had completed the Fall semester while we were still at home and was into the second semester.

February 14, 1967—From Lance

"It's exactly one week since you left . . . . I went down to see about my job at the pie factory and got it. My sore throat cleared up for a couple of days but came back accompanied by a lulu of a cold. I guess I'm cold-prone. I do my best to stay dry and so on but I still get 'em. I'm putting those pills you gave me to good use."

The diarrhea that he had had before we returned to Africa never did let up. He didn't tell us about it, so we were not aware of it. One day we received a letter from Dr. Hursh who said something to the effect that Lance was better now, "out of the woods and would probably make it." What was going on? That was the first we knew that Lance was sick. That scanty news drove me to my knees and I struggled in prayer until I was able to say, "Not my will, but yours, Lord."

Letters began to come. And here the narrative continues with excerpts from those letters.

March 22, 1967—From Fran

"Lance has had diarrhea for about three weeks and the school infirmary has given him kaopectate which hasn't helped too much. Seems to me they should so something more than that. Maybe he's better now."

April 22, 1967—From Lance

"I'm on a bland food diet because of my diarrhea. I don't know what the cause is. I'm down to 135 pounds. The doctor I am with is Aunt Mabel's doctor here in the city. It's quite discouraging to be sick like this. But it'll clear up OK."

April 24—From Fran

"I talked to Mabel Saturday. She had talked to the Dr., and he said that Lance had not told him how long he had had this dysentery nor anything of his African background, so he wanted Lance to contact him again.

"Talked to Dr. Westland tonight and he said that he contacted Moody to have them arrange for a series of tests to be made on Lance."

When his roommate at Moody saw that Lance was crawling to classes and returning to bed, he saw that Lance got to the nurse.

April ?, 1967—From Fran

"Just a short note to keep you informed about Lance. He went to the infirmary Monday and when they realized how sick he was they kept him there. In fact, the head of health service wanted him to be in a hospital. Dr. Hemwall is over the health service, and he has been taking care of him, so I am real encouraged. I talked to the health service this afternoon and they said he was much better today. They are running tests on him, and the first one came back negative, and his hemoglobin was good. They are amazed that he is as well as he is, all things considered. I felt so much better about it tonight so thought I should send the good news along to you. Dr. Hemwall knows that Lance is your son, so I'm sure he'll get the best treatment. Will keep you informed."

From Moody's health service, he was taken to the hospital.

May 4, 1967—From Lance

"Well, it's about 9:00 in the evening. I've got a chocolate malt in front of me, there are four other fellows in the room, 3 watching TV. There's also a pretty girl in here . . . My diarrhea finally knocked me down. It was getting worse and worse, full with nausea and so weak that every minute out of class I was in bed . . . . Friday night I was brought in. I've been here almost a week now. They still can't figure what's causing it. I'm down to 124 lbs. They think it's something I picked up in Africa. Just around the corner is Bud Hey, the guy who got paralyzed some time ago. He had surgery today. His mother, Noma Hey, visits me every day. Pastor Bob comes too. I get visitors from church and school."

From Noma Hey—May 1967

"I was so surprised to see Lance in the hospital. I nearly fell over, didn't even recognize him, heard someone call me and lo and behold! Lance! Bud is in West Sub also, he's been very, very sick. Staff infection in bed sores, anemic, one kidney to be removed because it is nearly all stone and Dr. Michaels says he thinks he can save the other one. Stones in bladder and skin graft to be done on bedsores . . . He's going to surgery in a day or two to remove kidney. So I was thinking about Bud when Lance called me and it really shook me up. I had to leave him cause I was ready to cry any minute, came right home and called Pastor Bob and he said you must be kidding me, and I said, eeh, no!', then he went right over. So I have been stopping in every day to visit with him. Such a sweet boy, today he looked a lot better, he went over and talked with Bud before Bud went to surgery . . . . when Bud came to, he said he wants Lance to come to his room, cause he really likes him."

By way of explanation, Noma Hey was a member of Elmwood Park Bible Church. She was a great seamstress and did a lot of sewing for us. In fact, she had several sewing machines and gave me one of hers—a Husquavarna—which we took to Africa. Noma's son, Bud, (a young man, probably in his 20's) jumped over a fence, stumbled and was impaled in his back and became paralyzed. He fought the complications for a few years, but died not too long after he was in the hospital at the same time as Lance. We've lost track of her; can't even ask Bob Swanson.

May 8, 1967—From Dr. Doug Hursh

"Your sister was in tears on the phone because Lance was in West Sub, and according to her, on his last legs. Hemwall who began seeing him two weeks ago is on his way to Korea and turned the case over to Van Reken. I had him and Dr. Adolph both on the phone after a dozen calls and found that the dysentery has been going on for 10 weeks but he didn't ask for help until 2 weeks ago. He is afebrile and no pathogens have been found as yet—all cultures not yet reported.

He is having a barium enema tomorrow . . . . Your sis was for having me phone you. I said I'll send a cable if necessary, but don't feel it is. I'm feeling almost as bad as she right now."

May 8—From Beret

"I was with Lanny last evening—he was very sick. When I got home. I called Fran; Fran called Dr. Hursh, and you know the story. He is on cortisone.

"I just talked to Bob. He says Lanny is feeling a little better and that he helped him on the commode and there wasn't any blood but he is very weak. He said Mr. Latham stopped in for a few minutes. (He had been away.) I had planned to go out after work tonite but Bob said it was better for Lanny to rest this evening. I will go tomorrow. Bob has been wonderful! He stops to see Lanny in the morning, afternoon, and again in the evening. His sister-in-law washes and irons his pajamas and Bob brings them back. I bought him a pretty pair today. I have been so worried but feel relieved now. I'll do all I can for Lanny—I love him so much! I love you, too! Wish you were here."

May 8—from Fran (4:30 p.m.)

"Yesterday was a bad day for Lance. He was very sick, vomiting and dysentery, so I pushed the panic button and called Dr. Hursh this morning to find out under what conditions a cable or call should be sent to you. So he called the Drs. and talked with me again and said that he would be writing to you . . . . The present diagnosis is that all the stools have been negative for tropical bugs. They feel that he has acute ulcerative colitis brought on by tensions, pressure, inadequate sleep, and it seems that there were a couple of times during the severe weather that he got a terrible chill as a result of being out in the cold. He is being fed right now intravenously with a cortisone solution. There are three Drs. on the case right now. Dr. Nicholas, Dr. Neal and Dr. Van Reken. Nicholas and Van Reken know you, Burt. Dr. Hemwall has gone to Korea and Adolph is only on the case if there was a tropical bug."

For some time the doctors thought that his problem was some African parasite. As they were trying to diagnose him, Lance continued to lose weight. They filled him with i.v. fluids and finally came up with the diagnosis of colitis

May 9—From Fran

"Was in to see Lance this afternoon and talked to the doctor also. He had a proctoscopy and an x-ray this morning. Bob Swanson called me after it was over. He had prayed with Lance before he went up for the tests. When Lance came back he said that he couldn't have stood it if he had not had the Lord with him. Bob Swanson has been terrific, visiting him 2, 3 and sometimes 4 times a day. Since Sunday he has not been allowed visitors except family. Lance told me this afternoon that he hoped that he would never again have to go through a day like Sunday and Monday. Van Reken said that it was definitely ulcerative colitis.

"Now that treatment has been started Lance's morale is better, too, so that is part of the battle. Lance will not get any credit for what he has been taking at Moody's as they will not allow him to make up his work if he does not come back next fall.

"The word has gotten around about Lance's sickness and many people are praying for him, among them, the Catholic nurse at (Fran's school where she works) school, an Episcopalian teacher and a Methodist secretary.

"Bob Swanson just called. He had returned to the church after visiting Lance again. He said that Lance was too exhausted to eat so Bob left orders that he should be given something later after he had slept a little. Bob also called the Dr., and the Dr. said that it would be 2 or 3 weeks more before he would be dismissed from the hospital and that he would have this all his life, but could keep it under control with medicine, diet, but that it would return every time the tension or pressure would mount up."

May 9—From Dr. Doug Hursh

"Van Reken called me last night to say that no pathological organisms had been found and there was nothing to indicate the trouble as tropical. He considers it an ulcerative colitis and has decided against any barium enema for the present . . . . So guess he is out of the woods. I certainly suspected nothing when I saw him at the SIM banquet on April 14, but apparently he had been going for 6 weeks then."

May 11—From Pastor Bob Swanson

"First, may I say that the Lord has undertaken for Lance in a wonderful way. He has been a mighty sick fella—but he is doing very well now. Each day is showing improvement. He is still very weak but happy—his spiritual life has become right and beautiful. He will relate this to you himself.—this I have suggested that he do. So all of this illness has had spiritual value. Pray much for him. He needs to hear of your joy and honesty before the Lord as you personally experience victories. Tell him carefully of your deep love and care for him.

"Some ten weeks before all this happened, he was at Elmwood for Eve. Service. I then said to him, "You are not well, Lance. What is wrong? You have lost weight.' But he replied that all was well. Then Mrs. Hey phoned me Saturday, April 29 at 8 p.m. to tell me of Lance. I had been there all afternoon and just outside his door. I saw Lance that evening—since then have visited him several times a day. He became increasingly weaker. May 5, 6 and 7 were rough days. Finally May 8 the doctors started moving. Dr Neal, the best doctor in internal medicine took over. Some 9 bottles of I.V. While at the Institute he had 72 hours of I.V. Only yesterday did they take him off of them. Lance will continue in the hospital for two more weeks and then he will stay with Fran and Bill. Lance appreciates this arrangement . . . . Lance is a wonderful patient—he is radiant as he sees what the Lord has done for him. He has received many cards, couple of plants, several money gifts. The saints have prayed much for him."

Mothers' Day Sunday from Pastor Bob

"I just returned from West Sub.—had my breakfast there at 7 a.m. Then visited Lance and the other two—Wally Johnson and Bud Hey . . . . Lance was still asleep, but his breakfast arrived at 7:20 a.m., so I left him enjoying his food—he eats a full breakfast—tea,

cereal, milk, soft boiled egg, bacon, toast and jelly—not bad? He is
steadily improving. His bowel movements are still very loose—had
to get up once last night—some 3 or 4 times during the day. Dr.
Neal was in yesterday—he, according to Lance, is satisfied with the
progress. Lance is relaxed and content—has many praying for him.
Beret was up last night—so were three students from Moody. Fran
and Bill come today . . . He spoke so beautifully of your medical work
this morning—he knows and appreciates your faith and dedicated
ministry in caring for the folk in Africa. Heb. 13:20, 21; Phil 1:3.

May 12, 1967—From Beret

"Last night I brought three Mothers' Day cards to Lannie for
choosing and this is the one he chose. I go to see him as often as I
can right after work. The Lake St. "L" is fast and I am out there by
6:00 o'clock . . . . Last night his roommate and another fellow from
Moody's came while I was there. The Forsbergs were there in the
afternoon. He is getting better but it will be a while before he gets his
strength back. The Dr. said he would probably be in the hospital for
two more weeks. We all feel so bad that this has happened to him."

May 15—from Lance and his doctor

"Well, I'm into my third week here in West Suburban Hospital.
About three days before you left, I got this case of diarrhea. I thought
nothing of it, but it persisted and I began losing weight . . . . every
moment out of class I was in bed . . . . I turned myself into the
infirmary . . . . 96 hours of I.V . . . . then to the hospital. Last Sunday
I was sick as a dog . . . throwing up, chills, fever . . . . More I.V. for 72
hours . . . . Things are getting better. Also here in the hospital I've had
a real experience with the Lord and feel so much pressure has been
released. I had been drifting some, but I feel that He has used this to
bring me back to a real relation with Him . . . . The Dr. wants to write
some"
"The ACTH has not affected his sugar—in blood and urine—nor
did he have this at any time. All told, he had 10 I.V. bottles. He has 4
stools per day—practically no RBC. He had low grade fever 10 days,
now no fever 7 days. Hb=11.9=79% with 15,500 WBC recently. He

looks very good compared to when I first saw him. Dx is ulc. colitis. All stools were negative for tropical diseases. He is up and around and should do well. We changed from ACTH to Prednisone 20 mgm Bid as of today. God bless you.

Everett Van Reken."

May 16—from Fran

"We were up to see Lance Sunday, early evening, and he seemed a little weary as he had had quite a bit of company. His latest girl was there holding his hand so that was nice. She seems to be very nice. I talked to him on the phone yesterday and he is encouraged although he still has the loose bowels. At least he can eat and he can sit up for awhile at a time He weighed 122# last Sat . . . . Beret has been going up to see Lance quite a bit and the Moody students have rallied around . . . . Got a letter from Aunt Ruth and she said Charlie was out of the hospital but didn't seem to be much improved."

May 21—from Beret

"I just talked to Lannie on the phone. He is still in the hospital and is getting better gradually. Bob was there when I called. He is taking good care of Lannie. He might be out in a week so the doctor said.

"Friday evening I visited him after work. I brought my camera and some flash bulbs and took several pictures of him . . . . Then Lance showed us Bob's slides of his African trip. He enjoyed all this . . . . I will visit Lannie on Monday evening and on Friday evening of next week. Fran and Bill will go on Wednesday and Saturday. Then I will go again on Sunday if he is still in the hospital."

May 22—from Fran

"I talked to Lance on the phone about an hour ago and he is progressing very well. He has started to put on a little weight at last. He was down to 118#s. Stools are beginning to have a little form. He had a complete g.i. series of x-rays last Thursday and the results were ulceration in the colon, descending and transverse bowel. Lance said this morning that the Dr. thinks he should be operated on this summer and the affected parts removed. This is a decision that only you can make. The idea of recuperating with you in Galmi appeals to him very much . . . . We were up to see him Sat. night and he is looking so much better. If you could have seen him before he started to improve it would have shocked you. Now he looks human again . . . . He is counting on coming home the coming week-end."

May 28, 1967—From Fran

"I just awakened Lance because it is 'pill time'. He has an assortment of pills that he takes every 4 hours . . . . He was dismissed from the hospital yesterday. He had hoped that he could go back to school this week and even if he didn't go to classes, just to be with the kids, etc. as this is the last week, but the school had already listed him as a departure so he could not do so, which was better as he really could not have managed. He is still pretty weak and on a strict diet. I put some peas and some peaches through a sieve this noon but by the time I got through, the peas were cold and the peaches were watery, so we decided to use baby food for fruits and vegetables. Meat and potatoes, etc. are all right as is. We are so thankful that he is getting along. The doctors will not decide about an operation for another month. One is for it, the other against it, and Dr. Van Reken undecided. If he should have an operation my feeling is that one of you should be here.

"Blue Cross covered his hospital bill. Now that he is out of school, this is not covered by them anymore. It wouldn't surprise me it the bill were close to $2000.00.

"I don't know what we would have done without Bob Swanson. He came to the hospital morning and night and sometimes during the day. He talked to the Drs., made calls for Lanny, took care of his laundry and did the countless things that needed doing that were impossible for us to do as we were so far away. Beret was faithful in visiting him and his friends from school, too. Wednesday night we arrived and two student nurses were playing Rook with him. (One was the Frame girl) and three girls from Elmwood were there. We had just walked up without stopping at the desk. After a while the desk called and said that someone should bring cards down as there were two more visitors. Two more girls! So in all, not counting us, he had 7 visitors, all girls . . . . We're all rejoicing at Lance's improvement and now we're working on getting some weight back on him and his blood count up."

May 31—from Lance

"Well, it's been a while since you heard from me. I suppose you've heard all about me from practically everyone else though, haven't you. I got out of the hospital last Saturday about noon. Bob Swanson came for me and took me down to school where I picked up some clothes. Then we met Fran at the Oak Park YMCA and came out here. Sunday we went to the Free Church both times. Monday, I slept all morning, then went in to Moody where I packed all my stuff, said good-bye to a few people . . . Tuesday was Memorial Day. The Leveys took me out to the Center picnic . . . . Then I went with Fran and Bill to the Skoglunds where there were several people. We had a real good time. Today I slept all morning, read a book and started to unpack some of my stuff. It's been a lazy day . . . . I weigh about 125 lbs. now. My lowest was 118 3/4. I feel real good today in comparison with the other days since I was released."

This chapter of Lance's life and our lives comes to an end at this point. I have dwelt at length about it since it so affected so many lives, and I want to pay tribute to those who so faithfully cared for Lance. Besides the doctors, Bob Swanson was his mainstay. Fran and Bill made the trip in to the hospital often, and Beret visited him many times after work. Doug Hursh was faithful in checking with the doctors and corresponding with us. Noma Hey looked in on him often. We might also mention all the girls and a few fellows from Moody who visited him and kept up his morale. Most of those who cared for him are in heaven now—Pastor Bob, Beret, Doug Hursh and Noma Hey. Fran and Bill remain. We will ever be grateful to them; we are so indebted to them. Fran and Bill took him into their home while he recuperated, and he stayed with them until he went to school in Champaign/Urbana that Fall. Some years later, a different diagnosis was made—Krohn's Disease. Today, 1999, Lance is off all medications and is doing fine.

—

If it had been 1999 instead of 1967, one of us would have been home in a flash. Back in those days, it just wasn't done. Mission policy was sacred; transportation was not readily available, so our hands were more or less tied. It wasn't until the 80's that the mission began to relax and allow us to return to the States in an emergency (at our own expense, of course).

Now we return to Galmi and the rest of 1967.

"June 1967 I returned to Galmi from Kano by plane on June 6 and Burt followed by car three weeks later. I was on hand to open up the house for Cherry, John, Sue and Pam, who came home for the summer a week later. The afternoon of my arrival marked the first rain storm of the season. I was alone in the house, and I watched the dust rise and settle in the empty house, while at the same time heard and saw the pan roof rise and settle again and again, up and down, praying while wondering when the roof would lift off. The aftermath of the storm revealed that indeed a part of the hospital roof had been torn away and the walls of the out-patient building under construction had crumbled. As for our roof, Sami, the carpenter, pounded a few more nails into it the next day for good measure."

Summer came and it was good to have the four youngest back home again. We missed Rollie and Lance. The children spent their time in the operating room, at times scrubbing with their Dad, reading, cooking, visiting the nurses and other families on the compound. They helped with DVBS and Sunday School and Awana. The girls took turns at the sewing machine and typewriter. Cherry did a lot of Burt's correspondence. John was surrounded by three sisters but survived. He played soccer with the village boys. We celebrated birthdays—Burt's and mine—and before they went back to school, we celebrated Cherry and John's birthdays. Evenings were always game times. We always celebrated Sue's and Pam's birthdays during Christmas break. This was the summer that Beret went to Camp Awana on her own and taught art lessons. She wrote to us from camp and instigated a letter from the leaders to be sent to me. The summer passed too quickly and too soon the children were back in school. Sept. 23 of this year, Chancellor, ex-president of Wheaton College, D. Raymond Edman, died of a heart attack on the chapel platform. He was speaking on being ushered into His Kingdom, and he just keeled over.

"July 1967 Friday morning a convoy of three land rovers went speeding past the house on the way to Maradi. Those who saw them go by said they were going too fast for safety. A few minutes later they were back. The middle one blew a tire just this side of Galmi town and turned over twice. It was a wedding party, consisting of President Diori's son and his friends. The son was okay as were those riding in the cab with him, but those in the back were pretty hard hit. One was unconscious for 24 hours. Another has a lung injury, and the third has a crushed hand. The fourth, the bridegroom, had face lacerations and apparently either head or internal injuries, because he died yesterday noon. A plane flew in from Niamey with a French Colonel M.D. who was satisfied with their care. Diori's son, and those who were able to go, flew back to Niamey from Malbaza."

Awana got under way that summer. We had the books and the equipment. The boys prepared a proper soccer field, built an Awana circle with rocks and a typical African shelter—tree limbs holding up a grass roof—where we had our meetings after the games. The shelter was just at the edge of the soccer field and Awana circle so we didn't lose any of the boys enroute to the meeting place. We and they sat down in typical African fashion, on mats on the ground. Over a dozen boys made professions of faith that year. It was about that time that I began adapting and translating the Awana books into Hausa and into a culture familiar to farm boys.

Hashi and Dawi in that first year earned their neckerchiefs, T-shirts, hats and belts for memorizing over 85 verses of Scripture plus questions and answers pertaining to the Faith. In other words, they completed their first book. Hashi made a profession of faith, but Dawi held back, due mainly to the threat of his father, who was one of the Moslem malams in the village.

The girls were progressing, too. Gen writes July 27, 1967

"Twenty six girls came this afternoon for Girls' Club; you should have heard them sing, 'Be careful, little Eyes, What You See', plus other songs! These girls are from 6 to 14 years old; we sew for one hour, then have our meeting."

Gen was helped with the girls' Awana by Katie Klein, a new nurse from Germany and Martha Simms. As they progressed with memorization, the girls earned the right to hem their Awana head scarves. One of the objects of the girls' club was to teach them to sew, so this fit in nicely with the program. Their attendance gradually increased to about 40 or 50 a week. Each week they heard the Word.

Sunday School was progressing nicely too, and during the summer we had our DVBS. We averaged 109 children from 4-15 years of age, plus 23 missionaries and national workers.

"One could sense the conviction of sin and realization of need of a Savior in our midst, but fear kept most of them from making a public profession, although we believe many of them are convinced of the Truth."

Oct. 2, 1967 "Awana is sporting a new shelter. White ants, mats, high winds and general wear and tear reduced the original to a skeleton, but it served its purpose in inaugurating Awana here at Galmi. The posts of our new one are cemented into the ground and painted with a white-ant repellent. The roof is made of tin pan, and one side is also covered with pan to keep the late afternoon sun from shining into our shelter. As the number of boys increases, the Satanic opposition increases. Satan is reluctant to give any ground."

I prepared Awana, book 2. Over the next years, boys started with book 1 and progressed as they were able. A number of boys finished the first book and some, the second book. The 3rd book was a Bible correspondence course that only a couple of the boys worked on. Awana grew and many weeks there were from 80 to 100 in attendance. Of course, I could not handle this alone, and several of our missionaries and some of the nationals helped out

"There were about 40 boys at our last meeting, perhaps ten of them Christians. But the other thirty tried every trick in the bag to cause a disturbance during the meeting and then look quite innocent when accused of doing so. Their attitude was, 'Who, me? I wouldn't think of doing that!' Very much like the American teen-ager. We believe the boys are under conviction, and that accounts for their actions."

That same term we built our Awana building, painted an Awana circle on the cement floor, and from that time on our meetings were held there. We went to an evening format. Some evenings we had a hundred boys and after the game time, they heard the Gospel yet another time. The Awana building was also used for Sunday School, for daily reading classes, for a struggling book shop and storage space.

It's 33 years later, and I wonder where all these boys and girls are today. Certainly the Word of God will not return void. We know that some of them are still following the Lord, and wherever the other girls and boys are, God is able to bring back to their memories His Word and remind them of the Gospel message that they heard back during Awana days.

I wish I could say that Awana in Galmi is flourishing today (1999), but I can't. The Awana building has been turned into a well-baby clinic. The present nurses and hospital workers seem to be too busy with hospital work to take on additional work. Furthermore, much of the missionary staff is short term, they don't know Hausa and they don't know the village people. At any rate, Awana flourished until we left in 1975, and the nurses, notably Ruth Hunt and Gen Kooy with nationals continued on with the program for about ten years.

"Nov. 18, 1967 The Schultzes brought Jo Rogers to Galmi to recuperate. She had been ill and found the work at Maradi Leprosarium too demanding. We had to send Marguerite Upshall (Davies) to replace Jo in Maradi, so we got half a nurse for a whole one. It turned out that most of her physical problem was caused by an uncertain relationship with Lofty Grimshaw who couldn't make up his mind whether to marry Jo or not. He was a dedicated missionary who was afraid that marriage would interfere with his ministry. Yet he loved Jo. This left Jo hanging. Lofty was stationed in Jos, and when the v.i.p.'s in Jos realized what was going on, they gave Lofty the ultimatum—either marry Jo or cut off all relationships with her. He came to visit at Christmas time and went back engaged to Jo. They were married shortly after that."

Halilu was baptized the next Sunday in the fadama (stream) a half mile north of us. The water was almost gone, but we found a puddle that was deep enough. In 1964 as a young boy of about 16, Halilu came as a patient with osteomyelitis in his leg. After surgery and during his healing process, he came to our reading classes. His leg smelled to high heaven, but I tried to teach him to read. He didn't seem to understand. He began attending some of our club meetings and Sunday School and made a profession of faith in Christ. I continue to be amazed when I think of how after he accepted Christ, it was as if the light turned on in his head, and he began to understand the phonic system, which we used, and in a few weeks he was reading anything and everything, especially the Bible. He stayed on the mission station and when he was well, found work in the hospital. In 1968, after Halilu was baptized, he went to Maradi Bible School. He later married Kwawa, who also came to the hospital with a medical problem and became a Christian. So far as I know, they are living for the Lord.

"When we got back from the baptismal service, a Peace Corps volunteer, Ron R. arrived from about 20 miles north of us with a bad diarrhea. We kept him in the back bedroom for two days. He had amoebic dysentery and was generally run down. We treated him and he recovered. He became a regular visitor, and we were able to help his loneliness and witness to him for the rest of his two year term.

"The Peace Corp doctor and his wife from Maine Soroa went through enroute to Niamey, Dakar, Ghana, etc. for their holiday. (This was Bill and Barbara Kirker) and we are still in touch with them today (2000 A.D.) On their return they stopped and visited for awhile along with his mother who had come out to Niger to visit them. We invited them for supper and the night which they gladly accepted. Just as we were about to sit down for supper, Gordon and Bill Bishop arrived, so we added two more plates and I threw two more hamburgers into the pan. They have been here all day today and will be here tomorrow and return to Maradi on Mon. So I have been busy with extra meal preparations. Bill will be going to Hillcrest in Feb. for the rest of 12th grade. The doctor and party left last night for Maradi."

Lance was in school at U. of Illinois in Champaign/Urbana. He was living in a rooming house dorm with the Wilkensons as house parents and chefs.

"It was nice of the Browns to give Lance $500.00. We heard from Lance a few days ago. We heard from Rollie this week. He plans to come on Dec. 24, spend 3 days with us."

Christmas 1967 – Christmas vacation came and the kids were home again. An added treat was to have Rollie come from Gusau to join us for Christmas. We had the usual Christmas program, and our girls were angels and John was a shepherd although they were beginning to protest. We had our own family gift opening on Christmas morning. We were able to buy a few things in Kano when we were there and got some things locally in the market. We had the usual compound Christmas dinner and gift exchange and had the Christian Christmas party. The women woke us up by caroling early Christmas morning. All too soon, Christmas vacation was over, the kids were back in school, Rollie was back in Gusau, and 1967 slipped into 1968 without much fanfare.

Chapter 18

1968

In a mission hospital, staff changes often due to holidays and furloughs. In 1968 we got several new nurses: one from Germany, one from Italy and one from England. Katie came from Germany. Everything was new and different for her including the American culture. It was hard for her to adjust at Galmi with no other Germans on the station. Her English was not that good, either. She hated night duty but accepted her turn. Sometimes she would go into her room and weep, but she would never let on. She told me, "I never saw so many bad cases before I came, with organs hanging out, and infections, and even one night a little boy lying in his bed in a whole pool of pus all around him." Katie, twenty plus years after World War II was of the generation that denied the holocaust. Katie was very likable, and we grew to love her and she finally accepted us and the hardships of the work and she lasted out her term but didn't return.

Laura Emmanueli came from Italy. She was saved under the influence of Plymouth Brethren missionaries in Italy. She drinks Italian Espresso, a half cup of which keeps me shaking for two hours. She prefers speaking Italian, French, Hausa and English in that order.

Margaret Hayes is from England, a nurse midwife. Before coming to Galmi, she served with UFM in then Belgian Congo. During the uprising, she was taken captive by the Simbas. She escaped once but when she heard that the Simbas were killing the nationals for not revealing her whereabouts, she decided to give herself up. She was with the Simbas for six months before she was rescued by French/Belgian mercenaries. Her story is told in *Missing, Believed Dead*. She spent a year with us and when the Congo settled down, she returned. Her letters told of the triumphant welcome she received mingled with emotion as she visited the place where her fellow workers were murdered; as she was carried along in the chief's chair on shoulders; as she fellowshipped in the Bopepe church with thousands of believers, among them Bo Martin who had sheltered her in the jungle at the risk of his own life. Tears flowed freely among the Congolese as they saw their "own Margarita" returned to them.

Two years ago, she made a trip from her home in England to Sebring and we had a delightful lunch together with other Nigerien retirees. (1998)

Conference at Galmi was becoming a regular thing. Much of my time was spent organizing the feeding of 54 missionaries including children. All the ladies helped in the preparation and clean-up of course, and we also had our African help so we survived.

Things went on pretty much as usual—Burt at work in the hospital and I doing whatever else had to be done. The VerLees were back from Kaltungo so both operating rooms were going full steam ahead, and 10 surgeries were performed daily. The hospital was a bee hive.

"March, 1968 I finished writing Book I. I don't know how many books will follow but that is the beginning. Another little boy was saved last week. His father was a patient in the hospital, and at last Thursday's meeting, he announced that they were leaving the next day, after having been here for about 6 weeks. I asked him what he thought of what he had been hearing, and he said it was good. I asked him if he would like to receive Christ for himself, and he said he would. I asked him, 'When?' He said, 'Tomorrow'. So he said he would come early in the morning. I forgot about it until at 9 o'clock the next morning, there he was standing on the front porch calling, 'Uwargida, ho!'. So I had a talk with him, and he prayed and asked the Lord to come in, and I followed with prayer. So the Lord seems to be working and kids are coming one by one. Pray for him. His name is Ali."

It was time for our holiday. Along the way, the battery cable slipped off the main block three times and Dad put it back on each time. That is what I call an uneventful, excellent trip considering the "wahala" (trouble) we had had on other trips.

April 1968 Holiday at Miango

It was a great holiday. It was great being with the kids again, and Cherry came out from Hillcrest every week-end. We went swimming in Jos twice. I enjoyed playing the organ with Sue at the piano a few Sunday nights. Sue made the top of the honor roll with a 10.3 average that marking period. Right behind her were four others with a 10.2 average. Sue's closest competitor all through K.A. and Hillcrest was Karen Seger, and they switched places back and forth constantly. Over the Easter week-end, the Jr. High choir augmented by some Rest home volunteers sang two numbers—"We Adore Thee, Oh Savior" and "Since By Man Came Death . . .". These were conducted by Mr. and Mrs. Merle Guy, also known as Mr. and Mrs. Music. They made a wonderful addition to the music and drama at K.A., but their furlough and final exit was due at the end of the school year. There were tennis, horseshoe and volleyball tournaments, all of which we both entered in to.

"The tennis finals were played yesterday afternoon. It was a handicap tournament. The best match was the first match played earlier in the week. It was between Bud Lavely and Enoch Hansen and Dad and Jerry Fawley. Lavely and Hansen beat Dad and Jerry in three bitterly fought matches. But in the match Mr. Hansen fell and broke his wrist. However, he kept on playing, not knowing it was fractured. Then I was asked to take his place for the rest of the match and Bud and I got to the finals. The finals were played and the handicap for us was minus thirty to their plus fifteen. We played against Mr. Bergman and Mr. Warkentine. So every game score started with 15 for them and minus 30 for us, so we were three points down to begin with. However, we beat them 6-4 and 6-3, and that was the end of the match."

On the way back to Galmi we stopped at Gusau and saw the Hirons and Rollie. Rollie went with us to Moriki where Dave and Sue John cared for the leprosarium. After examining the patients, we returned to Gusau, spent the night with Rollie and headed to Sokoto. After some shopping, we headed toward Galmi and it was good to be home again and we were filled with anticipation at the soon arrival of Beret and Lance. But there was life to live before they arrived, and Dad plunged back into the hospital work and I, into mine.

May, 1968

The Awana Girls' Club was doing well with between 30 and 40 girls a week. Much of my time was taken up with the Awana boys program which was coming along nicely. Besides the regular weekly meetings, I spent two afternoons a week listening to the boys saying their verses. One at a time, they would come to the house. For the most part, they could not read, so I had to repeat the verses one by one and have them repeat them after me until they could say them by themselves. This was a long and tedious task. I finally put all the verses on an audio cassette. I spoke the verses onto the tape phrase by phrase, leaving space for them to repeat the phrase until they were able to repeat the whole verse. As they came to the house, I sat them down at the dining room table and turned on the tape recorder. I showed them how to stop the tape and reverse it so they could repeat the verses. When they were able to repeat the verse as a whole, I would listen to them.

"Last week one little fellow of about 10 accepted the Lord. His name is Tandi. He had been coming to the Awana meetings and Sunday School for over a year, and finally the truth of the message has gotten home, and he came to me after one of our classes the other evening and said he wanted to be saved."

"Mamman, about 10 years old, was with his mother, a patient in the hospital. He said he believes. Before he went home, he asked for prayer, that he would have courage to profess Christ in his village."

It was time for the VerLees' furlough. In his place came Dr. and Mrs. Dan Klopfenstein and their little twin daughters. They were from France. "He is serving two years with us instead of doing French military service. Dan speaks no English, Mary Lou speaks a 'leetle'." We were becoming quite an international body.

While this was going on, exciting things were beginning to take shape. Beret and Lance were coming for a visit during the summer. How excited we all were. Even Rollie was planning to visit from Gusau when Lance was here.

The kids came home from school—Cherry from Hillcrest, John, Sue and Pam from K.A.

We eagerly anticipated Beret's and Lance's arrival.

"June 24, 1968 About 11:15 this a.m., the little 4 place Baptist mission plane circled us twice and then went back to Malbaza to land. We arrived there about a half hour later, and they were waiting for us. It was good to see them, to say the least. Dave Keppel was the pilot. He is a friend of Wayne and Helen Kletzing . . . ."

What a happy reunion it was at the airport! Hugs all around! Tears of joy! Back to Galmi then, and for Beret this was the beginning of a most memorable experience. For Lance, it was coming back home!

"Beret is complaining of the heat. She's wondering how she will last out three weeks. She and Pam just went outside to find out how hot it is. It is 106. I have assured her it will cool off tonight—at least to 90. Beret has said that of the four planes she has ridden on each time she is less nervous.

"Yesterday, Sunday, Elvin Harbottle from Madoua rode over on his motor bike, requesting someone to go after his wife and family. The four daughters were sick, so they were brought back and are staying in the hospital and will move into the VerLees' house when they leave, which should be today."

In going through Beret's things, I came across her journal describing her trip, so I am going to excerpt from it and describe their visit from Beret's eyes.

From Beret's journal:

"June 17, 1968 Paul took me to airport. Left for New York at 4:40. Fast flight . . . Left for Paris at 10:00 p.m . . . . 6 hrs. 20 min. at 35,000 ft."

Beret then describes the few days in Paris. They stayed at Hotel Angleterre. June 18—They did a lot of walking. Went to Luxembourg Gardens. Lunched at Wimpy's. Went to Beaux Arts. "At 6:30 Lance and I walked to drug store. Had a good dinner. Walked to Eiffel Tower." On the 20th, they went to the Louvre. Beret met up with a friend, fellow artist, Mr. Bender Kinland, in Paris and they all dined together. On the 21st, Lance went to Versailles while Beret spent time with her friend. "Mended Lance's pocket." June 22 they went to a flea market with Bender. "I bought 6 wine glasses. Feet sore. Soaked my feet. Napped until 7:30. Then Lance and I went to a little restaurant near the hotel and ate some spaghetti." After dinner they took the metro to "the big arch"—Arc d'Triomphe and walked along the Champs Elysee, then took the metro back to the hotel. "June 23, Lance took me to the Palm Museum on metro, then he went to the Bastille. We will meet tonight at the hotel. Left Palm Museum at 2 and walked through Tuilleries Gardens to the Louvre again. Left for airport that evening, boarded plane, then had to get off as something had to be fixed. We didn't get away until 12:45, got to Niamey at 5:30 a.m.

June 24 First impressions

"Very warm when we got off the plane in Niamey, West Africa. Miss Odor, missionary from Evangel Baptist Mission was waiting for us. She took us to her place and we rested and had tea and French bread and jelly. She drove us around Niamey and then to the airport again. Stopped at a mission school . . . saw the Niger River. Saw some fine homes for the elect rulers of Niger. Women wear beautiful wrap-arounds. Boarded a small mission plane—room for four. It took 2 1/2 hrs. to get to Galmi. He buzzed the station, circled it twice . . . John rushed over to the hospital to tell Burt we had arrived. Ruthie and the girls waved frantically to us. So we landed at small airport, Malbaza. Ruth and Mr. Pollen, Johnnie and Pam drove out to get us in a pick up truck. Hard to believe I am here. Very warm. It was wonderful to see everyone.

"Went over to hospital with Pam and Burt to look it over. When we got in, Burt had to go to the emergency room. A man had dislocated his hip bone . . . . he wasn't able to get the bone back into the socket. I got upset and decided to leave. Saw all the misery and felt faint. Sat on the hospital step. Native woman tried to offer help. I decided to go back and felt dizzy. Couldn't see too well. It was hot. Dr. VerLee came along. I told him I felt faint. Could he help me? He walked me to the church step. Then I said he should go on, he was needed at the hospital. Another lady helped me back. I can't eat too well. I have some pain on right side again. Washed out a few things and hung them out. There is a breeze, but it is still hot. Cherry is sewing a dress, so is Sue. I may cut my hair.

"This morning Burt got man's hip in place. A man came over and we bought some material from him. The head Moslem malam came over and greeted me. I took several pictures of natives. We are all resting now—after lunch rest hour. Then Ruth had boys' Awana group . . . . Sewed up holes in the mosquito netting. So thirsty for Chicago water. The temperature today was 102, yesterday, 106. It stormed the night before—wind and lightning. Cherry and Sue have been sewing dresses. Lance reads, so many activities here. The Harbottles are here . . . . Uma is in kitchen washing dishes. I saw two yellow birds. They look like canaries and sing a sweet song. Lizards are all over the place. Camels, goats and sheep pass all the time; horses, too. Bugs and spiders and huge grasshoppers, ants, etc. are aplenty . . . . The native boys have given me a name which means peace, 'Salamatu'. The house of the Longs is large—a living room with a fire place. Books and magazines all over the place. A large bedroom off living room (Ruth and Burt's), high ceilings, a dining room, another bedroom, bathroom, 2 kitchens, another bedroom (study). A porch where Lance, John and Pam are sleeping. No mosquitoes yet. The natives smell bad. The hospital wards really smell. The operating room is all right though. Desert date is one of the pretty trees. They have a garden started. Corn is growing—too soon for any yield.

"June 26 Ruth and Sue went to hospital with me. Took pictures of a camel on the way. Took pictures of Burt giving a spinal. Went thru wards. The hospital smells bad and it is hot here!. After dinner and siesta, went to market . . . . It sure was an experience. It was hot! It smelled bad! The children crowded around me. The meat area looked pretty awful. Burt bought meat. Sue bought material and sandals. I bought a pineapple, oranges and limes, too. Helped with dinner. At 8:30 the nurses came over and we listened to a tape by a Mr. Hunter. Talked to a pretty Italian nurse (Laura Emmanueli). I am reading an interesting book, Missing, Believed Dead by Margaret Hayes. I met her. She is helping here at the hospital. Will go back to the Congo in December.

"June 27 Took pictures of Pam in barrel of water. Also pictures of back of house with Ruth, Cherry and Pam, also natives and landscape in back . . . . Walked to hospital with Cherry to see baby born.

Nothing yet. This afternoon a woman brought her child to Burt. He took something out of child's eye. Lance and Sue held child down so he wouldn't move. I prepared some tapioca pudding and some baked beans for supper. It was hot, and it isn't like at home. Everything is harder here. Ruthie went to Awana, Pam played in water barrel all day. The heat bothers me. Writing letter to Camp Awana. Ruth and Burt went to prayer meeting tonite. Girl next door came over (Judy Pollen). Kids played records.

"June 28, 1968—Friday. Burt helped me fix a board so I could paint. Took pictures of Sue and John on motorcycle. Went up to hospital. Saw four new born babies. Took picture of Margaret Hayes and black baby. Burt examined a leprosy patient and had me come up close to see. As a result, I am reading <u>Alone No Longer</u> by Stanley Stein. Missionary prayer meeting this afternoon. Burt is reading Luke 17. I am writing this on the enclosed sleeping porch and can hear them. Sheets are flapping in the wind. Sue is sleeping on the other bed (rest hour). It is hot! Tonight another prayer meeting. I am reading <u>Run While the Sun is Hot</u> by Harold Fuller—all about the Sudan. Felt so hot tonight. Back hurts. Feel miserable, felt like crying. Asked Ruth if she would feel hurt if I went home. Oh, for a good glass of Chicago water and ice! I could never be a missionary in this climate!

"June 29 Feel better this morning. A little breeze this morning. Would like to paint but it is so hot, I get out of the mood. Went up to the hospital this morning and took pictures of Burt doing a hysterectomy. First time I have ever seen an operation . . . . It is still very hot. I took off my slip and now only wear dress, pants and bra . . . I am perspiring so!

"June 30, Sunday. Last night slept out on porch under net in Lance's bed. Lance and John are sleeping in VerLees' house . . . . Bed too soft. Will go back to other bed. Went to church and S.S. this morning . . . . Burt was our teacher in S.S. Washed my hair. Ruth took pics of my long hair. Then Sue cut it and curled it. Sewed up more holes in mosquito net. Three men were struck by lightning—one killed.

"July 1, Ruthie gave me a permanent wave. Heard on radio that Rollie would be coming either today or tomorrow. Last night I woke up about midnight. I thought I heard foot steps outside and then the door open. I called out 'Ruth'. Told her someone was in the house. She got up and looked and said no one was here, but door was unlocked. My hair looks nice, but it seems strange not to have the knot in back. It's good for a change. Everyone at home will be surprised. Composed letter to Mr. TerMeer. We had a big rain storm last evening, early before supper. It was beautiful. Took a few pics. Prepared water color paper for paintings. In bed by 10:30. Another wind storm. Slept well.

"July 2, 1968 Tried a watercolor this morning—so did Ruth. It was cooler today. I didn't do too well as there was a wind. Kind of a grey day, walked down to hospital and took a few pics . . . . Rollie came about 4 p.m. on his motorcycle . . . . A little native boy was kicked in head by a horse. I feel rather nervous today, especially at table. Too much coffee?

"July 3—Did an oil landscape this morning looking out back porch. After rest hour went to market. Went to Doris and Ray Pollen's for supper. It was pleasant weather today. Rollie looks good. After supper we listened to a tape. Then the family all talked into a tape. It was fun to hear the voices. I talked, too. Heard from Olga.

"Rollie left this morning. Made an abstract water color landscape. Hot again today. Helped with dinner. Lance went to Malbaza. I walked over to village and took a few pics . . . . then into hospital. Cherry and Ruth are trying water colors, too.

"July 5—made a small oil painting this afternoon looking out back. Can't seem to do too well. Before supper tonite we rode over to a blacksmith in the village and saw the way a primitive blacksmith works with charcoal and bellows worked by his assistant.

"Went over to village with Marguerite this morning. I enjoyed seeing the natives in their homes . . . . The kids followed me around as they do at the market. Kevin Ahearn (Lance's friend from school) came in a plane while we were there so we hurried back so Lance could go and get him in the car. A quiet day. Wrote to Fran.

"July 7—Sunday. Went to S.S. and church . . . After rest hour, Ruth, Burt and I rode over to the lake on motorcycles. Took pic of child with face eaten away. Tonite we had a sing song here. There are 23 white people on the station. Nurse invited me to dinner tomorrow night.

"July 8—Just came back from witnessing the Cesarean birth of a child. It was thrilling. Also watched Burt operate for cataract on a man. He prays over each patient before he does the operation. I am getting used to watching now and didn't even feel faint . . . . This evening we had a big storm. First you could see a big cloud of dust coming from the north. I was invited to Genevieve's for dinner, so I decided to go over before the rains came. It was a terrific storm. Typical for this time of year. We couldn't hear ourselves talk. We had pizza and mango sauce and blueberry cake and coffee. Laura, Marguerite, Gen, Martha and Tuni were there. After we ate we all went our ways—Laura to the hospital. I borrowed a rain coat and flashlight and came home. Am writing a letter to Dorothy Mackin. Cherry is typing. Ruth and Lance are playing chess. The piece 'Sound of Music' is on the record player. Burt is reading. John and Sue are reading. Kevin? Must get pictures of nurses and staff at hospital.

"July 9—Started a portrait of Pam today. It looks good. It is 19" wide and about 34" tall. Hope I can finish it by Friday, so I can take it with me. Had supper at Martha's house tonight. It was good. There was a beautiful sky tonite (clouds in sky.) Owls kept me awake all nite. Finally fell asleep about 4:30 in the morning.

"July 10—Uma has hepatitis. Hope we don't all get it. Marguerite left early this morning. Lance drove her. Painted arms and dress on Pam's portrait. Hope I can finish by Friday. Very hot today. Went to market. Bought another riga and had tailor start dress . . . . Burt picked me up on way home. I was glad as I was getting over-heated . . . . I went to bed early. Owls started to act up. Burt went out and took a shot at one. They started again and I shined a flash lite outside. Later it began to blow but it didn't rain. Slept well.

"July 11—Wrote letter to Virginia Latham in morning. After dinner I started painting Pam again. Burt said a lady was going to give birth to a baby so we walked over. He put the cord back in (it had come out). Burt explained the situation to me . . . . I painted until 4 o'clock. Pam was a little wiggly today, so it was harder. It is hard. Ruth and I walked over to the area back of house where some African Christians from Nigeria live. Poverty and inconvenience are their way of life. They are used to it and take it for granted. Prayer meeting for Ruth and Burt. Wind storm tonite. Beautiful sky again tonite. To bed early—10 p.m.

"July 12—Must finish portrait today so it will dry be Mon. night. Ruth and I went to the village. I took several pictures. Saw Uma, too. Went over to the hospital and watched Burt do a hernia and also a large tumor from down near prostate. He explained as he went along. I'd like to try scrubbing on Sat. or on Monday. After dinner, I painted Pam again . . . Walked up the hill with Pam before supper. Man brought blouse today. It was too small. He let it out and then brought it back. He is going to make another. Then I'll buy more material.

"July 13—Sat. Before breakfast we all had a camel ride. Took pictures. I must finish portrait today; Tues. I leave. Will miss everything here. Hope I'm not too homesick for Ruth and Burt and the children. Finished portrait today. The eye on left still doesn't look right. Burt says it should be rounder on left edge. He might be right.

"July 14—Sunday. I'm going to pack tomorrow. Went to church this morning. Burt spoke on Romans 2 . . . After dinner, two men came over. Ruth showed my portrait to them . . . . Over a cup of tea, Ruth, Cherry, Sue and I and Lance discussed short skirts and rules at Kent Academy. After dinner, a boy came over with rings. I ordered one and so did Kevin. Tonite we had a sing song at the nurse's house.

"July 15—Am getting ready to leave here. Packing things, washing clothes, etc. Ruth and Burt took me to the canteen to buy more material. Rode on motorcycle with Burt. Then started packing . . . All kinds of flying ants in house tonite.

"July 16—Before breakfast word came from hospital that a woman was in labor and that I should hurry up there so I did . . . . Baby wouldn't come. Finally Margaret took forceps and pulled the baby out. It started crying right away . . . . Then back to house for breakfast and packing. Glad I was able to see the birth of a child. Ruth, Burt, Lance, Judy, Sue and Pam drove me to Malbaza airstrip where I boarded a plane (mission). We prayed before taking off. Waved to all of them as we circled the strip. Flew above clouds. It was beautiful. Got to Kano 2 hours later. (Left at 12:30.) I asked Mr. Andrews (pilot) if I could take a picture of the airport. He said sure so I did. It was a mistake. Several guards with their rifles at their sides stopped me and I had to see the sergeant. They were going to take my film away from me but I pleaded with them and was about to cry. I said, 'No, you can't have my film—I've got pictures of the birth of a baby on my film.' I promised to destroy the picture of the airport if they'd let me keep it . . . . Finally they said okay, and I thanked them. Nigeria was at war (Biafra). We drove to the guest house after seeing some other missionaries land by plane. Lots of people ride bicycles in Kano. Went uptown with LeRoy Andrews (pilot) and looked in a few stores. Had dinner at the guest house. Met several people—Mr. Bishop, director of the work in Niger. Also Janet (Schneiderman?) went to the church with me and we saw a film about a Liberian—Samuel Morris. Then we toured the eye hospital. I can't believe that I am in Kano, Nigeria.

"July 17 In Kano, Mr. D. (Driediger?) drove me, Mark and Mr. Andrews around Kano this morning. Went into the old section. Then he took us to airport and we boarded a Comanche plane and headed for Jos. One hour at 7,500 ft. Beautiful clouds all the way. Landed at Jos. Mr. Andrews drove me to the guest house. Had lunch there. Mr. ? drove me around Jos. It was raining. Saw the new hospital and the school, Hillcrest, and the dorm where Cherry and John will stay . . . Met Dr. Cummins at the hospital. Saw the market, saw the pharmacy, the other hospital where Cherry was born. Mr. Kastner and his wife drove me to Miango where Kent Academy is. We had a good dinner and toured the school. Later, tea at the Kastners.

"July 19 Flew from Jos to Lagos. Had Mr. Andrews for a pilot again—a 3 hr. flight. A man and his wife in back seat of plane. At 10,000 feet had an embarrassing moment. Drove to guest house in Lagos. Had supper there. Met Doretta (Dail?) Taking off from Lagos at 6:40 p.m."

And that's Beret's three week sojourn at Galmi. Notice the transitions from excitement to surprise, to unbelief, to despair, to near fainting, to wishing she could go home. That was the bottom. Then notice how she began to feel better, even though it was still hot and the hospital still smelled, and the little kids still followed her around in the market place. And when it came time to leave, she was a bit sad to leave us, although I don't think she was sad to leave the heat and the smell and the inconveniences.

Just one thing I want to include about her visit. Our food didn't have a lot of variety to it We didn't get much in the way of fresh fruits and vegetables. And I was a bit pushed to feed our family of 7 (8 when Rollie was there) plus Kevin and Beret three meals a day. We had plenty of rice and onions and wheat and meat, although after Beret saw all the flies on the meat in the market, she lost her appetite for a time. In despair I cried out to the Lord, "I don't know what to feed this mob." That same afternoon there was a knock at the door, and a truck parked out on the road. A man stood at the door with a stalk of bananas in his hand. He asked if I wanted to buy them. You know what my answer was. So we had bananas for dessert and enjoyed them for a few days. We had never had a truck stop before and offer to sell us some fruit or any kind of food, and it never happened again. Coincidence? Or God's loving kindness and tender mercies! No question about it.

Beret flew from Lagos, Nigeria to Liberia where she met her long time friend, Olga Hodel, who was working for the American Embassy there. Olga showed her the town and the Embassy and its grounds which were very beautiful. You enter the embassy gates and you forget you are in a foreign land. It is a touch of America. Next day they visited ELWA

"July 20, 1968—Toured the station, then stopped at a friend's house where we had coffee. It is very beautiful on the ocean with palms all along the beach. Met Dr. Schindler and toured the hospital. We talked of Burt and Galmi Hospital. He wants to visit there sometime and told me to tell Burt to visit him at ELWA"

The next day Olga took Beret to the hotel where she picked up the airport bus. She was the only passenger on the bus. The other bus had already taken the crew.

"It was raining. We were stopped on road; a truck was standing sideways. We all got out. Took pictures. Men finally pushed truck to side and we continued to airport. Took off KLM at 11:00 a.m. We stopped at Freetown, then Las Palmas in the Canary Islands, then on to Madrid."

Beret visited the Prado Museum. The next day she took a bus trip to Toledo. Saw El Greco's home and his paintings. She took pictures of Toledo and bought pictures and when she got home, she drew a beautiful oil painting of Toledo. She sold that for $1000.00. She visited the Palace the next morning, and the afternoon of July 25, flew to London. The next morning she visited Trafalgar Square and the National Gallery. It was cloudy and crowded and she didn't enjoy her stop in London. Took boat train from Waterloo Station to South Hampton, where she boarded the boat. She had a small state room—no shower, no window. From July 26-31, she was on the boat.

She spent her time between the deck in her rented chair, the dining room, the lounge, and her stateroom and it began to get a little boring, but she met some interesting people.

"After breakfast, we docked. Went thru customs and got to hotel at noon. Paul called from Chicago . . . I feel depressed here. Wish I were home. Called Mildred Gunderson (Bissell) and she came and got me, and I spent a day or two with her. Also stopped to visit Sally and Anton as they lived near the Bissells. They drove me to airport and I arrived at O'Hare and was met by Paul, Jeanne and Fran and Bill. Good to be back home."

What an exciting summer! Hard to top that one. And then all of a sudden, it's over!

"July 30, 1968 It hardly seems possible that tomorrow the kids will be leaving—i.e., Lance, John and Cherry. It has been good to have Lance here this summer. He hasn't changed much, and we will miss him when he's gone. Kevin was a very nice boy, although his being here took Lance away from us a good deal of the time, and so I was disappointed in that respect. But that's a purely selfish reaction. As far as Cherry and Judy Pollen were concerned, they were delighted to have Lance and Kevin here because it gave them something to do and someone to do it with. Mothers have to be weaned sometime, I guess.

"Kevin left this morning by truck. His flight out of Niamey is scheduled for Thurs. afternoon.

"After tomorrow, Sue and Pam will be here alone for the month of Aug. Then during Christmas holidays, those two will go back after 3 weeks and Cherry and John will be here another 3 weeks. It's going to be very quiet tomorrow.

"Monday, Burt and Lance and Kevin went cross country into Nigeria, which is 12 miles south of here. There is a wide path, sometimes called a road, between Galmi and the border town of Yar Balutu, which is where all our local merchants get their supplies for resale. Kevin rode on the back of Burt's motorcycle, and Lance drove the smaller B.S.A. It took an hour and a half each way.

"Your letter dated July 8 came a couple of weeks ago, but the pressures of people, work and departures followed by an acute attack of depression have not been conducive to letter writing."

Other things happened in the world that summer and in the year 1968. Our friend and founder/president of Scripture Press, Victor

Cory, died of a heart attack. The story is that he had cut his hand the day before, had to have stitches. He was up walking the floor during the night when he died.

That was the year that Martin Luther King was shot and killed. It was also the year of riots in Chicago during the Democratic convention. The Viet Nam war was going on and Floyd Olson, son of Grace and Frank Olson, old Centerites, was missing in action.

Bob and Cora returned from their work in the Virgin Islands. They felt that tensions were too great between the blacks and whites to expose their son, Bobbie, to possible harm.

In Sept. we had our annual Vacation Bible School.

"A daily average of 109 children from 4 to 15 years of age plus 15 African workers and 8 missionaries were packed into our small church in the 100 degree heat of the afternoon for studies in the Word. About a dozen boys and girls publicly witnessed to their faith in Christ. One lad of 13 accepted Christ and testified to it two days later. Already he is being taunted by the other fellows. This morning I asked one of the boys why he didn't accept Christ, having heard the Gospel now for several years. He admitted that he and the others were afraid of being persecuted by the other kids and their parents. I asked if he thought what we were telling them was the Truth, and he readily admitted that they all thought it was. So I suggested that all the boys accept Christ at the same time—then they could poke fun at the others. He didn't answer. Maybe that's the only solution.

"Haleru was converted last year in our Vacation Bible School just before he went off to the big city to attend high school. He came back for the summer and said that he no longer believed. He attended this year's Bible School, learned the extra Bible verses that entitled him to a Hausa Bible and hymnbook, said he didn't want them, then later said he wanted them to study. He came two mornings to read with Ruth, then the next we heard, he had sold the Bible to a patient in the hospital. He is a mixed up boy, returns to school in a few days. I asked him if he really and truly accepted Christ last year, and he said he had. We feel he is under conviction and at the same time he is trying to put on a front with the other local boys whose greatest sport is to taunt the Christians. Will you pray with us for him?"

———

Nov., 1968 Gen Kooy writes:

"This patient is dying; will you come and pray with her?" called Margaret Hayes one morning. The woman had just been brought in, after five days in labor! She had never heard the gospel before, but as I told her about Jesus, our Saviour, she said she believed in Him. About an hour later she passed into eternity. Leaving her, I went into the ward, where another young woman, a post-operative patient, was also dying, and the Spirit led me to talk to her, too. She had heard the gospel before, as we had visited her village, and an evangelist lives there. Only fifteen minutes after she expressed faith in the Lord, she also was gone. Several others recently professed Christ before departing this life—only God knows if they understood enough to be saved."

Do you remember Aminatu, Gen's adopted daughter? She was married to Job in December. Gen writes:

"December 9, 1968 Well, the wedding is over; the bride and groom are gone, and my house is empty and lonely! Job arrived on Friday morning, and said he was due back at work in three days and wanted the wedding on Sunday . . . . He brought a suitcase full of beautiful clothes for her: 4 blouses, 7 wrap-around skirts, 6 headscarfs, 4 pr. sandals, cloth for two or more dresses, soap, perfume, talc, and 6 pr. earrings. Her wedding dress was made of white nylon, with an over-blouse, and she pinned a square of the same material over her head . . . . The groom wore a yellow robe and the best man a red and white T-shirt . . . . she gave her maid of honor, Kwawa, one of her outfits; it was dark blue with light blue and white design, African print . . . . Aminatu took along a little girl, a niece of hers, about 6 years old. She said she couldn't stay home alone all day while Job works! Quite often new brides do that . . . we were surprised, though, that Aminatu's relatives let her have the child . . . . Job was happy when they left. She looked kind of sad, and a good many of the rest of us were crying. Last night Dije said her house was like someone had died, that no one would eat supper. Aminatu had been eating there—she, Dije, Kwawa, and Dije's brother and sister cooked their meals together. I believe one reason for the sadness is because she is going so far away, N'Guigmi, and we don't know when we will see her again. John Ockers came from Maradi to marry them, and they rode back as far as Maradi with him. It will take 3 or 4 days to get to N'Guigmi."

Tani and Elisha were married at Galmi just a week before Aminatu and Job. Mary Louise Schneider had been supporting Tani in school. Elisha was a lab technician at Maradi Leprosarium, a widow with four children. A year or so later, Tani died in child birth, and later, Elisha married A'i who had come from Sokoto with her children after her Christian husband had taken a second wife.

Christmas, 1968

Cherry, John, Sue and Pam were home for the holidays. We had the usual Christmas program—Christmas Eve for the hospital patients and Christmas morning for the villagers. The place was packed out both times, with kids sitting in the windows.

"The Husbands arrived from furlough on Monday, the 21st, and ate with us until supper, the 26th. That made 12 at our table each meal, and on Christmas day, the entire compound ate here along with Jacques (Zabriskie), who came from Niamey where he is in school, so we numbered 25. Thursday I had one of my headaches. I wonder why. I recovered in time to greet Jack and Grace Frizen on Sat., and they stayed with us over the week-end. That was a very happy time without pressure, so we enjoyed that."

"Last Sunday Halilu and Kwawa were married and have gone back to Bible School. The Tsibiri and Farm School African kids returned to school. Ruthie Bishop came on Sunday and stayed until Friday, and John escorted her back to Maradi on the bus . . . . This week we are expecting three visitors . . . from an architectural and contracting company in Ohio . . . doing some work in Niamey. They met Edith Durst at home, and these men want to meet the parents of the three Africans whom Edith is mothering in the States. And now 1969 is here."

This is a fitting time to pay tribute to our nurses, especially those that were with us in the early years of Galmi Hospital. Martha Wall and Addie Raidt (Emmett) were the first two, but they didn't stay longer than a year. Gen Kooy, Ruth Hunt, Virginia Fridal, Martha Simms, Jeanne Marie Berney were the back-bone of the nurses. Of them all, Gen was the one who persevered the longest—she spent forty years at Galmi, and she was the most reliable of them all. Gen came in November of 1952. She had just arrived when our John was born. Burt was sick, but he delivered John and returned to home and to bed while Gen finished up the job. What an introduction to what was to be her life style for almost a half century. But it wasn't only the hospital work that our nurses entered into—it was also the spiritual ministry. Their concern for the patients led them to do personal work at their bed sides. Beyond that, there were the kids' clubs, the village visitation and the special reading classes. From day one our desire was to use medicine as a means to reaching these people with the Gospel, and our nurses fulfilled that desire to the honor of the Lord.

Today, 2000 A.D., Gen is in a nursing home in Sebring, battling with Parkinson's. Ruth Hunt is in Ohio retired but still working with correspondence courses with children. Martha Wall is in a nursing home in CA about to celebrate her 90th birthday. It is doubtful that she will reach 91. Addie is with the Lord. Virginia Fridal has just retired after about 40 years at the Maradi Leprosarium where she went after a term at Galmi and she plans to live here. Martha Simms is working in the office here in S.I.M., Sebring. Jeanne Marie is retired back in her home country, Switzerland.

And here we are! And the VerLees are in Michigan, retired. And the work at Galmi goes on. Other doctors including Jim and Mary Lou Ceton and Harold and Bonnie Jo Adolph have come and gone as have other nurses. Things are different at Galmi these days. Plenty of water, new and better equipped operating rooms, more construction. We pray that the spiritual ministry will progress hand in hand with the medical.

Chapter 19

Leprosy Rounds/A Funeral/Tea Time

Come along on our quarterly trip to Sokoto in November of 1968

"Estimated time of departure is 10 a.m. Monday. Nine forty-five, and I'm not ready—I need at least another hour. A quick look out the window shows me that Burt is still working on the car, so I relax a little. At 11 a.m., Burt and Ray Pollen have the carburetor spread out on the dining room table, so we plan on lunch at home. By 2 p.m., the carburetor is working, so the Africans push the car to get it started, and Burt takes it up on the ramp for a look at it bottom side up. A broken shock absorber and a faulty electrical connection!

"By 4 o'clock we're away. Thirty miles to Konni and a police check-out. Five miles to the Nigerian border and a customs check-out and another police check. Now we're in Nigeria and must remember to drive on the left side of the road. Here's the Nigerian police check-in, (hope we didn't forget our passports). Nigerian customs check, followed by another police inspection 45 miles later. By 7:30 we're in Sokoto at our mission station. There's nothing like a good meal and bath and sleep after a day of traveling. In the morning we must see the Immigration Officer, and then we drive the final 12 miles to the leprosarium, and by 10 a.m., we're ready to see the first of 400 patients. All day we check patients and discharge 32 as symptom free.

"Wednesday morning we do surgery, and in the afternoon, we're on our way back to Sokoto town. Thursday we have to shop. Not

365

only for our needs, but also for the needs of our fellow missionaries at Galmi. We start out in the canteens. No, not in a super market. A canteen is not a water bottle. It's a small, private store with perhaps a couple dozen shelves with canned goods, toilet articles or hardware supplies. There's a 'cold store', too, and we get some bacon to keep in our refrigerator until the kids come home for Christmas. Burt succumbs to buying a tiny piece of blue cheese. At a 'goods store', we buy 100 blankets for the hospital and look over all the bolts of material on sale. There is some bright red cloth which would make good neckerchiefs for Awana, which I buy. All the bolts of material are a great temptation to me, but I manage to resist them this time.

"Now to the market. Stall after stall for almost a square mile, each displaying its own wares—bicycle parts, plastic shoes, enamel ware, flashlight batteries, lanterns, trinkets, soaps, perfumes, 'jewelry', glassware, shirts, hats, fruits, vegetables, meat, patent medicines that cure everything, grain, native food, peanuts, cloth, notions, you name it. We go up and down the rows, kicking up the dust and coughing as we go along, the hot sun beating down, followed by beggars and kids who want to carry our purchases for a penny.

"Friday morning, a few more purchases, and a final attempt to buy a starter for the car with no luck. We pack the car—a station wagon—from behind the front seat to the top and all the way back, knowing that our spare tire is in the tire well but hoping that we won't need it. After dinner, the final push, and we're on our way home. Ten miles out, and yes, the tire's flat. So with a heave and a ho, out comes some of the stuff, the tire gets changed, and we re-pack. And another push and the car starts. Same police and custom checks, a forty five minute wait at the border because the customs official went into town and nobody can do his work, and we're finally home, and home looks good. Only disappointment—we didn't get a new starter. So we're still pushing the car to start it, and you know who does the pushing while Burt sits behind the wheel and starts the car by compression! The good news is that when it starts, he stops and waits for me to get in the car before he takes off!"

An eerie light!

"Quite by accident Burt saw a native burial in the middle of the night. A wind storm woke us up and we saw a light beyond a distant hill increasing in volume and brilliance, then gradually fading away and finally disappearing only to reappear in a few minutes. This went on for awhile. It was a bit eerie but we were sure it was of this world and not of another. Africans might have said it was evil spirits. Burt got on his motorcycle and at 2 a.m. traced the light to its source, which turned out to be the funeral of our cook's mother who had taken ill and passed into eternity without Christ. The light was a bonfire which was kept going with dry grass, and when we saw the light increasing from our window, more grass had been thrown on it. Our curiosity was satisfied.

"The next day our cook, who is a Christian acknowledged that his mother wasn't a believer, and I pointed out to him that since she wasn't saved, she was lost, and that her eternity without Christ had just begun. I don't know whether it made any impression on him or not. I'm sure that even we don't see the enormity of such a thing. We say we believe that those who are not saved are lost, but if we really and truly believed it with all our hearts, our prayer lives and our witness would be different.

"It was less than 10 years ago that the hill across the road from the hospital had its last annual 'tsafi'. The entire village gathers, a feast is prepared, and a black ram is sacrificed, the drums beat and the dancing goes on into trances and spirit possession. Each person in attendance is given a small piece of the sacrificed ram and when it is eaten it keeps away the evil spirits for the coming year. We weren't here at the time so we don't know why the practice was discontinued, but we do know that many of these dances are held in private compounds and they usually end up with someone who has given himself over to Satan, becoming possessed of demons. We have never seen them, but we are told that that's what goes on, and even as I write tonight, the drums are beating, and we wonder what is going on behind the drum beat.

"As I tucked Cherry into bed recently, she said she didn't like to think about dying. I told her not to worry, because dying was just going right on living with Jesus in heaven. Before we said good-night, Cherry asked Jesus to come into her heart."

The Forsters—1967/68/69?

"Chuck and Lois rumbled in from Tahoua today. We could see their new, white Ford 1/2 ton truck round the bend a half mile away.

There's not too much foliage here on the back side of the desert to obstruct a good, long view! Distinctive about their truck is the huge box sitting on the bed of the truck! Painted white, too! This is their home on wheels. Not bad! Three beds (one for little Paul), adequate storage space, a 50 gal. drum of water, supplies of one sort and another all contribute to make their trekking ministry as comfortable as possible. Tahoua is not their home. Tahoua is a sort of jumping off place into the desert. A few miles out of town, and unless you stay on the 'road', you're in deep sand and deep trouble. The Forsters' home base is Maine Soroa—at the other end of Niger, and that's real desert! The house is built right on the sand. However, their faith is built on the rock.

"The Forsters have a unique ministry. They spent two weeks at Tahoua and the environs showing film strips to crowds anywhere from 500 to 1000 people. Intense interest! They have their own generator, loud speaker system, tape recorded scripts, film strips and screen. Their screen is a large sheet draped across the back of the 'box' and tied to the top of the truck. Another pipe at the bottom of the sheet keeps it taut and prevents it from sailing away on windy nights. They're here with us now for 10 days and enjoying good reception everywhere they go."

Around the dinner table, Lois said,

"I suppose you remember the Arab woman that was here at the hospital a few years ago."

"No, we don't know her, but we heard a little about her. We were on furlough when she came."

"We had a tremendous time with her in Tahoua last week. Esther kept pressing Wilf to find out where they lived. (Esther and Wilf Husband were working at Tahoua for awhile, in the absence of a furloughing couple.) Finally, Wilf found out where they lived and found out the 'Open Sesame' formula for his wife to go and visit her.

"Well, Esther went one afternoon last week, knocked on the door, announced herself and said she was from Galmi Hospital and was immediately ushered into a dark passage way, through one room and then another and finally was brought to her Arab friend. (I don't know her name—we'll call her Aishatu.) There they sat and talked for a long while.

"Aishatu said, in a hushed voice, 'They've taken away my Bible and my record player, but they can't take Jesus out of my heart.' She went on to say, quietly, 'I have a little radio, and I can't get much on it, it's so small, but sometimes I can pick out Kaduna on it, and I hear the preaching of Jesus Christ. That gives me joy.'"

Lois went on with her story.

"While Aishatu was thus talking, one of her little maids must have swept the room next to them three times and no doubt heard what her mistress said. At the close of their visit, Esther asked if she could come back in a few days with two of her friends and the visit was allowed.

"This time, Esther and Ann and I were ushered through the preliminary passageways, were met by Aishatu, and then we went up some narrow, circular steps to a sort of penthouse. Aishatu followed with her tea preparations. The furnishings were luxurious—beautiful rugs and draperies, and we sat on pillows on the floor. There was a balcony around us, and we felt as if we had been transported out of Niger and into Arabia (on a magic carpet)—the kind of Arabia we read about in story books.

"She fixed her tea on a little brazier on the floor. Then she poured it over the tea leaves into another pot. Then she threw out the first water, repeated the process, and finally on the third time, offered us Arabian tea. This time our conversation was very guarded, and she was cautious and we wondered if something were wrong. Esther asked if she could come again and take her picture. Aishatu is a very attractive woman. Her skin is as white as mine. Her clothes were made of the finest materials. She told us that when she was allowed out, she had to cover all of her face except her eyes.

"On the day appointed, just before Esther was to go back for her third visit, a messenger came with a big platter of dates and a note saying that Aishatu was out of town. When we inquired further, we found that she had gone nowhere. Apparently her husband has forbidden further 'contamination'."

"Is that the end of the story? We don't know. We do know that her husband can take everything away from her, but in her own words, 'He can't take Jesus out of my heart.'"

The story began three years ago right here at Galmi. Jim VerLee was the doctor in charge. We were at home. She and her entourage came for medicine. Esther ministered to her and became her friend. When Aishatu heard the Gospel, she gladly received it and returned to her home rejoicing in the Lord.

Margaret Hayes returns to Congo

In Chapter 18 I mentioned that Margaret was with us for a year. In February of 1969 she returned to the Congo. "We wish you could share her exciting letters about the triumphal welcome she received, mingled with emotion as she visited the cross that marks the place where her fellow workers were murdered, as she was carried along in the chief's chair on shoulders, as she fellowshipped in the Bopepe church with a thousand believers, among them Bo Martin, who had sheltered her in the jungle at the risk of his own life. Tears flowed freely among the Congolese as they saw their 'own Margarita' returned to them."

Sai Galmi

". . . a hospital located in the town of Galmi has acquired a reputation for taking seemingly hopeless cases and restoring them to health. If some illness or accident seems nearly incurable, the people say, 'Sai Galmi' (only Galmi Hospital can help). The expression has become a part of popular speech, and now if a car is badly wrecked, its extreme condition is, 'Sai Galmi'."

So said Hamani Diori, the President of the Republic of Niger, during his recent State visit to Canada. He was addressing a gathering of Toronto officials and S.I.M. missionaries at the S.I.M., Toronto headquarters. The *Toronto Daily Star* on Oct. 4, 1969 had this to say:

"Christian missionary work, often assailed by African states as expression of Western colonialism, has been praised by the Moslem head of one of them . . . In Canada for a 10 day state visit, Hamani Diori, President of the Republic of Niger, requested that a visit to the mission be included on the itinerary. He invested mission director, Dr. Raymond J. Davis, as an officer of the National Order of the Republic of Niger. In conferring the order, Diori said he was expressing his country's gratitude for the contributions of missionaries to Niger."

—

Mr. Diori went on to say,

"We have known your missionaries in many capacities long before we knew your government. We would like to express our gratitude for the hospital you operate, for the leprosarium, for the agricultural school and the school for boys and girls . . . . The seeds of kindness sown by these missionaries long before we became independent have been a factor in the friendly relations we now enjoy with your government . . . I have only one regret. The government of Canada has not understood the magnitude of what you are doing. During this visit I want to tell them more about you."

Prior to his visit to Canada, President Diori visited Galmi. The hospital was the gathering place, and thousands of people from surrounding villages were on hand to welcome him and his party. Niger, Nigerian, and Canadian Press and TV were out in full force. Mr. Diori had nothing but praise for the work of the hospital and the mission in general.

Did I mention in an earlier chapter that Burt had been honored by the Nigerien government in 1964? He was not in Niamey for the presentation—his nose was to the grindstone at Galmi, so the certificate was mailed to him. This is what it says:

ORDRE NATIONAL DU NIGER
Fraternite Travail Progress
LE PRESIDENT DE LA REPUBLIQUE DU NIGER
Grand Maitre de l'Ordre
delivre a Monsieur LONG BURT E
Medecin-Chirurgien—Konni
le present brevet de CHEVALIER de l'Ordre
en reconnaissance des services rendus a la Republique du Niger
Fait a Niamey, le 19 Oct. 1964

Le Grand Chancelier de l'Ordre Le President de la Republique

Grand Maitre de l'Ordre

Both the Chancellor and the President signed this.

Christmas 1969 Two young Awana boys who were converted about this time were Mamman Hassen, age 16, a boy with seven years of grammar school education and who was interested in going to Bible School and Dan Ladi, a young patient at the hospital. When Dan Ladi was dismissed from the hospital, he returned to his village, some 200 miles away. We all know what he faced—a complete Moslem environment with no Christian encouragement. Did he remain true to his profession? We don't know. Heaven will tell. As for Mamman Hassen, we have lost track of him. We continue to pray that he is following the Lord.

Christmas 1969 found Rollie at the University of Southern Illinois, Lance in Chicago, Cherry in Wheaton and John, Sue and Pam home from school for the holidays. We looked forward to Christmas 1970 when we would celebrate Jesus' birthday together. And on this happy, forward looking note, I will close this chapter.

Chapter 20

1969

A quiet Sunday afternoon at Galmi.

"Jan. 5, 1969 Dad is reading and listening to a play on BBC, sitting in his favorite overstuffed green chair. Sue is sewing. Cherry and Pam are having rest hour in the motel—the nurses' long house, which they have taken over this holiday, and I have just finished my afternoon siesta. John is spending the afternoon with Bill Bishop in Maradi."

Rollie returned home from the Peace Corps and went back to live with Fran and Bill. Their open arm policy with Rollie, in fact with all our kids, is appreciated to this day. We can never repay them for their kindness. On his trip home, he injured his arm while doing some weight lifting—"pressing", I guess it's called. From home, Dr. Doug Mains wrote to us, "My impression is that he has torn the insertion of the pectoralis major which is now healing back." There was some thought of doing surgery but was not done, and it has healed by itself over the years. Rollie enrolled in College of DuPage for the second semester. It was sort of a test semester for him, to see if he was really motivated to go on to a four year college. At the same time, he had to check in with the draft board. He went downtown for his physical. Fran wrote, "The draft board seems to delight in taking fellows who have dropped out of school and then gone back. They feel that they are doing so to escape the draft."

March 16, 1969 Doc Latham turned 75! The Center had a birthday party for him, and Fran and Bill and Rollie went. Then Fran and Bill drove to Florida on spring break, and Lance came home to Fran and Bill's from school. So Rollie and Lance were left to fend for themselves for awhile.

Cherry was applying to Wheaton at that time but hadn't heard anything yet. Fran writes, "Tuition there has gone up again. It is now $800.00 a semester. That does not include board and room, books and incidentals." Thirty years later, it costs $20,000.00 a year to go to Wheaton.

In Feb., 1969 we had conference at Galmi. That involved three meals a day, cooked in three different kitchens for 70 people. The food was brought over to our house where we had tables set up in the front room, study/bedroom, and screened in porch. Everybody pitched in and had their jobs to do, so the actual conference week wasn't such a burden on me, but the planning and preparation that went ahead of it was considerable. Our speaker was a Mr. Tony Wilmot, a Scot businessman from Lagos.

"Burt goes to Drs. meeting this coming week. He will drive to Sokoto. I have decided to go with him, and if there is room on the plane I will go to Jos with him. It so happens that Sue is playing in a K.A. piano recital on Friday night, and I would like to be able to hear her, since we get to enjoy so few of our children's performances. I'll be glad to get away, since I've been on the station since last May except for a few days in Sokoto."

We flew from Sokoto to Jos, rented an SIM car and drove out to Miango to see Sue and Pam. We returned to Jos, where Burt was busy with the meetings. Friday we went out to Miango and spent the day and evening. The piano recital was excellent and Sue's grand finale was "Crescendo" by Par Lasson, and it was the best performance in our eyes. "She has talent and real possibilities."

March 25, 1969 Lance wrote expressing his desire to come out "next year" and work at the hostel. He really wanted to do this. When we got to Jos, we talked with those in the office who felt that Lance was too young to be responsible for high school kids and there was no apparent opening at K.A. This was a real disappointment for Lance and also for us. However, he did get out after he graduated from Wheaton and helped out in the hostel. We suggested that he come out and spend a year in Niger, either with us or at the farm school where he was invited, but that didn't materialize either.

March 29, 1969 To Rollie and Lance: "This morning Yahaya killed an African Beauty snake in our garden. It's the same kind that you killed last summer, Lance, that was in the motor scooter, only this one measured 3' 8" and was twice as fat. It's a back fanged snake, and consequently not so poisonous.

"Monday night we had an Awana party in the dispensary waiting room. We limited the number of kids by writing out tickets for those who had been to at least one Awana meeting during the past year. There were 93 tickets, and 64 of them got their tickets from me or at the Awana meeting the previous week. Many more came to the door for tickets but their names weren't on the list. They knew we were going to have refreshments, so we could have had all the kids in town if we hadn't restricted it. We had a good time. Dad did some of his 'magic' which fascinated the kids. We played some games, but the game the kids liked best was blindfolding two fellows, holding each other's left hands, and swatting the other fellow with a paper wad. Boy, that was great!! On the last try, Dad blindfolded Dawi and left the other one open. Did Dawi ever get it! Finally, we asked for the 'smartest boy to reveal himself'. Dan Ladi, the TB boy with whom you wrestled last summer, Lance, immediately responded. He had to balance a penny on his forehead and toss it into the funnel at his belt. You know the rest of the story. He got a pint of water down his trouser legs. He took it with good grace. He has come a long way in his Christian growth."

Now that I have copied from the letter, I am asking myself how pouring water down a boy's leg relates to his coming a long way in his Christian growth.

Letter from Fran May 26, 1969 in which she includes a sonnet which Rollie wrote for school:

AGAIN, RETURNED AGAIN

I had unto the soil at last returned
From which the heritage to me was given
of pride and strength, And yet inside there burned
The lust to travel and from there be riven.
So great the force that surged within my breast
That I grew restless and began to hate

The givers of the heritage. And lest
The rage too much become I changed my fate.
I fled the land my fathers gave to me
Unto a barren wilderness of sun
Where wild winds blow the sands erratically
And bronzed Tuaregs on their camels run.
But as the tumult of my rage died low
I heard the call of home and had to go.

Meanwhile, what's going on back home? Letter from Rollie—April 8, 1969. SIM banquet in Wheaton; job offer for the summer at a tree nursery—$2.75/hr.; Four piano concert with Doc, Merrill Dunlap, Ed and Eleanor Sherry; "saw Grandma last Sunday—is in great shape for a grandma; Ken and Grace Frizane invited Lance and I (sic) and Pastor Bob out to dinner. Good times. Lance left for U.of I. Sunday afternoon; Fran and Bill on vacation in FL. Sure am enjoying myself. Never as happy as when I'm being worked both mentally and physically to full capacity . . . ."

Both Lance and Rollie do well in school—Lance at U. of Ill. in Champaign and Rollie at College of DuPage in Glen Ellyn. In the summer they move in to a house near Sunny Ridge home together with five other young men. It is an old mansion that a developer has bought. Both boys with the help of Margaret Wick cleaned up their rooms. "Theirs are, I think, the cooks and the cook's helpers rooms as they are right off the kitchen . . . . I wish you could see Lance when he gets off the garbage truck, especially when the temperature has been 90 and over, which it has been around here when it isn't raining."

Tense times for Cherry and us, all of whom had our sights set on Wheaton for Cherry. She was rejected because of lack of space, but put on the waiting list. What joy when she heard there was room for her!

June 17, 1969 Letter from Beret—"Just a year ago today I boarded a plane at O'Hare airport and was on my way to Africa . . . . I went to the Awana banquet and heard your tape. It was good to hear your voice. I gave Art Rorheim 5 slides to show that evening . . . . I showed my slides to the Ed Rei group. They enjoyed seeing them . . . . I'm trying to do a little landscape painting this summer at the park."

June 22, 1969 Letter from Fran—"We are happy for Cherry and will be glad to help her in any way we can. As for shopping, we'd better take Margaret Wick along as I'm a little out of it when it comes to what the well dressed college girl wears."

June 29, 1969 Cherry, John, Sue and Pam home for the summer. "The kids have their jobs to do daily, plus other tasks that they do willingly (Pam, grudgingly at times.) Included in their jobs is 'baking day'. John and Sue have each had their days at baking bread, and John has made cookies his two other days so far . . . . we're all enjoying John's initiation into the club. That's what happens when he's outnumbered by girls, three to one.

"Last night we had one of the worst dust and sand storms in my recollection. Just as we finished supper, we noticed the billows rise from the north east, so we shut everything up tight, but still the dust billowed in, and when it was over about 20 minutes later, and followed by an average to heavy rain, we began the clean-up job . . . . we swept mounds of dust out of the house. Pam had bought Perito's baby goat from Yahaya and had built him his house out of empty drums, putting a roof of plywood on top, held down by rocks. But Perito's son was being neglected by his mistress, so we threatened to sell him back to Yahaya if she didn't keep him out of our garden, and yesterday the ax fell and we sent him home with Yahaya. Pam was upset, but after the storm, she was glad that her baby goat had been taken away, because the drums were all scattered, the rocks and plywood fallen down, and the yard this morning was a general mess. Yahaya found one of our drums on the hill across the road; the wind had lifted it over the fence and rolled it up there. So if the goat had been here, he would doubtless have been killed or wounded so that he would have had to be slaughtered.

"Lance, we are still waiting to hear what your plans are. We received a letter from John Ockers, 'Lance could be useful to Wilf Husband for a year. My answer is 'very definitely'. There are numerous things he could do within his capabilities. There is a place for him in an apartment; he would be welcome. Wilf added his invitation. 'He can eat with us and be like our oldest son.' . . . We hope you come."

"Cherry leaves Kano Aug. 7. Travelling with Belva Overmiller, Martha Neufeld and one other single woman. They will spend 2 days in Vienna, 4 days in Switzerland, and 4 days in Scotland and arrive in N.Y. on the 17th."

She was met in New York by Jack and Grace Frizen. They took her in for a few days during which time they bought her some new clothes, in style for a Freshman coed. Then on to Chicago and Wheaton. Fran and Bill met her at the plane and saw that she had a room in our house at 428. Bill and Diane Lindberg were living in our house at the time. When school started, Cherry moved into Williston Hall for her first year. She was in a triple room with two class mates who were as different from Cherry as could be. They were worldly wise and in their estimation, Cherry was a neophyte. It was a miserable first semester for her, but she was able to change roommates for second semester and met and roomed with Cindy Brewer who became her life long friend.

July 1, 1969 "Beret, we enjoyed your pistachio nuts very much. They are just about gone! They don't last long with 6 of us going at them. I rationed them out 5 at a time which means 30 at a throw. Thanks so much for sending them. When I get home, I think I'll buy a can of pistachio nuts and sit down and eat them until I feel like stopping. Happiness is eating pistachio nuts until you don't want any more."

July 19, 1969 Letter from Fran—"We're all excited about the possibility of astronauts on the moon. President Nixon has declared Monday a National Holiday so that people can stay up Sunday night to watch what happens on t.v . . . It will be an exciting moment to watch it live."

Burt to his mother—"Do you realize that the astronauts will be landing on the moon on my 51st birthday?"

The actual landing took place on Sunday, and it was evening in Niger, and we were all at the nurses' house for sing-song, but were connected by radio to BBC and got the news. Of course, the Africans wouldn't believe that there was a man walking on the moon, and we couldn't convince them.

July, 1969—"These past weeks have been hectic . . . I can't say that I haven't enjoyed them, but they have worn me out. Two weeks ago Tues. the Zebs and Jacques stopped in enroute to Maradi where they are stationed this term, and just as we were sitting down to supper, Dr. and Mrs. Kirker from Maine Soroa, a former Peace

Corps doctor, now working for the Niger Gov't came with an educated African, married to a Frenchman in Maine Soroa for an operation. Dr. Kirker didn't want to do the operation since she was such a good friend. She is a Fulani woman, Marianne, so we had 12 for supper, and from that time until 16 days later, we fluctuated at meals between 10 and 13. During that same time, Dr. and Mrs. Ray Davis, general director of our mission, paid us a 3 day visit—he is touring the fields, and during those three days the Godbolds came down from Tahaoua (plus 3 kids), and Elvin Harbottle came from Madaoua, and Chuck Forster, our new district superintendent (replacing Gordon Bishop who has gone on furlough) came and went twice. The Pollens shared in feeding the mob, but it was sort of difficult to think up meals for the mob 3 times a day. Rick Armstrong is with us for the summer, a student from Westmont, is 21 years old, which adds to the interest of the Pollen girls as well as ours. One Sunday night for supper and Mon. for breakfast we had an Am. Negro Peace Corps doctor (Naylor Fitshugh) and a French Catholic priest added to the crowd. Now we are down to seven, including Rick. He is eating with us this week. He alternates weeks with us and the Pollens. Thursday morning, our patient, Marianne, was operated. Her nurse, Vickey Ike, arrived the following day, to nurse her, freeing Dr. Kirker and his wife to go back to Maine (600 miles east, almost to Lake Chad.) Fortunately, I had canned green beans during the bean season and tomatoes and tomato juice, and all my jars were filled, but now I have only one jar of beans left and 1 jar of tomatoes, but have just touched the juice, since we had oranges and grape fruit that we brought back from Zobolo on our return from holiday. Twice Marianne made us an African dinner with chicken and gravy and African spices (reduced in quantity for our palates) and couscous. It was delicious."

July 2000—Whew! Just re-reading the above paragraph exhausts me. I don't think I could handle that now. Especially when food was so hard to get, situated as we were on the edge of the desert.

Same letter—"Dropping out of school for awhile may be the best thing you can do, Lance, and we're all for it. We'd still like to see you come out here if you would like to and spend your time either with us or elsewhere in Niger.

"Rollie, congratulations on making the Dean's list.

379

"Cherry is due to land in New York on Aug. 19, KLM 621 from Glasgow at 17:05 o'clock. We have heard from Jack and Grace Frizen and they would like Cherry to stay with them over the week-end, which means that if she leaves them on Mon., Aug. 25, she will be home on that date. She can call you when she gets her plane reservation and let you know when she will arrive at O'Hare.

"Fran, you asked how the kids were able to get visas back into Nigeria for school. The way it's done is to get a return visa before leaving Nigeria. How was the family picnic? We heard from Charlie and Ruth this past week. How are Bob and Cora? Seldom hear from them. How is Carolyn's boy—the one who had colitis? Sue has been doing some sewing. She shortened two of the dresses Pat made and grew out of, and they fit nicely. Then the third one, she made an Empire dress out of it. She is quite a good sewer. Cherry gave me a permanent today."

Aug. 17, 1969 from Fran "We are anticipating Cherry's arrival. I wrote to Frizens last week and asked if they could arrange a flight for her here on Sunday the 24th or in the evening on Monday. Both the boys will be wanting to meet her and it would make it easier all around.

"We spent the week of Aug. 4th at Maranatha . . . had a wonderful time. The weather was perfect and we really enjoyed the lake. Mr. and Mrs. Ray De La Haye were the missionary speakers and we enjoyed them very much. Maranatha has changed considerably with all the homes encroaching on the grounds and at first I resented it; to see a house where the dorm was, using the old tennis courts for their patio, to have a house on the promitory overlooking the lake where not too many years ago we had camp fires made me feel bad, but the things that I like the best, the water and wind and the sun and sand and the spiritual emphasis were still the same.

"Rollie has had a meeting with the draft board and it looks like, unless a miracle happens, they are going to win."

It was Sept. 7, 1969. It had rained during the night. Godbolds had been with us overnight enroute to Maradi. We thought they should delay their departure a few hours, knowing that there would be delays at rain barriers. But no, they insisted on leaving at 8 a.m. They arrived at Maradi at 3:30 p.m.—7 1/2 hours later—a trip that ordinarily takes 3 to 4 hours. Our concern was for Pam who was traveling with them to

Maradi enroute to school. Otherwise we wouldn't have cared. Besides that, Pam had her sore leg. She and the Pollen girls and the Godbold kids were all in the back of the truck, open to the elements.

Regarding Pam's sore leg. "On market day ten days ago, Dad took Pam on the BMW, rode past the market about 4 miles, then turned around. Two and a half miles out of Galmi, in order to avoid a man on the path at the edge of the road—the smoothest part of the road—he turned out, only to hit a hole and fall. The BMW wouldn't start again, so he parked it in the bushes, and he and Pam started walking home. Burt had severe arm abrasions, and Pam had severe leg abrasions. Burt had 3 stitches in his elbow and Pam, 5, above her ankle. The man carried Pam piggy back for awhile, then Pam walked, then back on his back. Finally, about a mile from the market a young fellow came along on his motorbike, and Dad put Pam on it and sent her to the hospital. Then the fellow came back for Dad by the time he reached the market. Pam suffered some shock and all night long she vomited, probably as a result of the morphine that was given her. The lesion being where it was, she was confined to her bed for most of the next week, and was only getting around on crutches when she left. But with an ace bandage, she was able to limp around, so she left the crutches here.

"Tues. of this week, I must have gotten stung by an insect—perhaps a blister bug—but I don't see any blister. As a result, I have a draining, purulent sore on my calf about the size of a 50 cent piece. It hurts."

July 2000—Thirty years later, and the scar remains. It took a long time to heal. Still don't know what caused it.

Still Sept. 7, 1969 The coming of President Diori of Niger was at hand. "Last Saturday he was due at 3:30, but because of the storm he was two hours late. The whole village was lined up orderly in front of the hospital, all the way toward the top of the hill and almost to the Chapel. The circle was filled. Everyone was single file. I've never seen such an orderly crowd—5000 people at least. His avant garde arrived, set up a microphone in front of the entrance, took pictures of the flag strewn road and flag draped hospital. Two French Canadian t.v. men were shooting pix of the Pres. for a preview to be shown in Canada. Mr. Diori is planning a visit to Canada soon. Another journalist from the New Nigerian was in the party. A Chinese (Communist??), several French and a lot of Niger dignitaries completed the party, not to mention his bodyguards. The Pres. and his wife were met at the road by Burt and Ray Pollen, then they came to the hospital entrance where we shook hands with them, then toured the men's wing and surgery, came out for the speeches. The first speech was made by the Minister of Agriculture (Cabinet level), who was Rabi's father. She is the girl in the States with Edith Durst. Then the Pres. made a speech, praising the work of the hospital. We got several slides of him and his wife. His wife is very pretty."

July, 2000—It was after this visit that President Diori visited Canada and SIM headquarters in Toronto. It was there that he made his famous "Sai Galmi" speech about which I have written in Chapter 20. I think it was within the next year or two that Niger had a coup that ousted the President. His wife resisted arrest and was shot and killed. President Diori was put under house arrest in Zinder, and after many years, I believe he was released. Since then, word is that he has died.

Still Sept. 7, 1969 "A week ago in Konni a truck turned over, killing one laborer and injuring several others. We didn't get the patients; apparently they were taken to the Konni dispensary.

"Fran, you asked if folks help with the food bill when they come. We don't charge people, but many of them bring some food along to help out. The patient (Marianne) and the wife of the doctor from Maine Soroa (Mrs. Kirker) passed through the other day enroute to Niamey. They brought us 20 lbs. of potatoes and some French bread. So we do get some remuneration. Now that the Husbands and Zebs are stationed in Maradi, we always have a place to stay as guests when we pass through. Otherwise, we would pay in the guest rooms.

"Next week, the 15th, we start our annual DVBS here for 5 afternoons. We're going to teach The Three Aspects of Salvation. There will be 10 lessons, plus hand work, plus memory work. This coming week, I will be very busy with preparations."

Letter to Pam at KA and John and Sue at Hillcrest, July 7, 1969 "We miss you, but we know that you are having a happy and profitable time. Pam, we are glad that you are growing up. We know you are growing up because you said that you were going to be friends to those whom you wanted to be friends with and not listen to your roommates. Even if they didn't want to be friends with somebody else, you would still be friends to them. That is good, and it is the way Jesus would want it. How is your foot?

"Sue, I was glad to hear that you decided not to go steady with David. I think David is a very nice boy . . . but it's better not to be tied down to one fellow or one girl. And John, if a girl doesn't want to go steady with you, it doesn't mean she doesn't like you. She usually wants to have fun with all the boys, and if she becomes someone's 'steady', the other boys usually keep hands off. So date several girls, not just one."

A letter from Fran written Sept. 22, 1969 "Cherry arrived, is settled in. She shares her room with two others. She was disappointed with her room mates but has adjusted. They are border line hippies. Up to now there is only one bed in the room and 2 mattresses on the floor. So you can imagine the disorder, inasmuch as it is a room big enough for two people. That's the negative side. The positive is good. She likes school, she's met lots of people, she is working in the P.E. Dept and is really keeping busy. Before school started, she, Margaret and I went shopping at Yorktown. She probably told you Frizens gave her $100.00, fifty of which was spent in New York and some of it here. She has gotten some nice things.

"All three went to Awana over Labor Day. Margaret went with Rollie and a friend of Lance's, named Margarita, went with Lance. They reported a good time. Now about Rollie. The draft got him, and he is leaving for the army on Oct. 8. He was upset at first inasmuch as he had everything arranged at S.I.U. including schedule, etc., but he is adjusting to the idea and is willing to go. He doesn't say much about it except agree with me when I said that he must have been born under an unlucky star!

"Lance moved into Chicago. He is renting a house, sharing it with Frank Woyke and Jerry VanDer Molen. He quit his garbage job the end of August. I'm back at school doing the usual chores. My new principal is nice, very considerate and careful not to give me too much to do. I guess he was warned that I was pretty fed up with my job last year and did quit one day."

Lance wrote a super long letter on Sept. 8 mostly describing his life on the garbage truck and his close calls while driving a fully loaded truck. Empty, they average about 9 tons. "Last Wed. we ate at the Buenemans, and he had a letter there which was just one sentence. His orders to report for induction had been canceled. This was because Nixon canceled the Nov. and Dec. draft calls, so October's call is being spread over those three months. He may still have to go, but on the other hand, he may get a student deferment. Thursday, I drove him down to Carbondale and brought the car back."

Sept. 24, 1969 "Three weeks after my 'blister bug' episode, my leg is finally healing. The infection reached the size of a doughnut and was very painful. Was on penicillin for about a week. Now it has stopped draining, is scabbing and showing new skin underneath, but there will be some scarring, I expect. Now dad is hobbling around. He and Ray were fixing the car, and a piece of a jack hit him in the shin, and he's got an infected shin. Ray and Burt took the car to Malbaza for some welding. After our letter about pushing the car to start it, some people, the Scholtens of Grand Rapids decided to send us a starter, so they wrote asking for particulars. Burt mistakenly said it was for a '67 Chev. He realized his mistake and sent them a letter saying it was for a '57 Chev. They had already shipped the first one, so now we have two starters on the way. In the meantime, I'm still pushing. Some questions: Where do the Bishops live? What is their address? Who is Charlie Brown?

"We had a good DVBS last week with an average of 114 kids, plus 19 leaders. Jammed church! Hope the youth building will be ready by next year."

A letter from Fran written Sunday, Sept. 28, 1969 "Wednesday a letter came from the selective service and it so happened that Rollie, Lance, Cherry and Margaret were coming for supper that night. When the kids got here around 6, Rollie opened it and you can't imagine the excitement! It was just a brief statement that his induction into the armed service had been canceled—no explanation. Well, he gulped his supper, went to his house and packed, and Lance drove him down to SIU the next day. School was to have started on Thursday and the previous Sunday he had written to the school to tell them that he wasn't coming, but he got there before they had finished processing. Cherry is on a retreat this week end for P.E. majors—an obligatory one."

October 19, 1969 "Burt left for Bimbereke, Dahomey, 400 miles from here, to relieve our Dr. Elliott for two weeks. He plans to be back the day Dr. and Mrs. Klopfenstein leave. They have finished their military tour of 15 months.

"My leg is healed after 6 weeks. But I have a round red area about 3" in diameter, which should fade eventually.

"Sue was top of the whole high school for the first six weeks, with a 10.7 average out of a possible 11 points. She uprooted a boy who has been on top for 3 years. He got a 10.4 average. I wonder how he feels to be taking 2nd place. She has a very full schedule—French, Biology, English, Bible, Geometry, Phys Ed. She is taking piano lessons—she's very good—in school choir, in G.R.A. and in the school play. She and 3 other girls are practicing an 8 hand, two piano, arrangement of Hungarian Rhapsody, which will be given on their Spring Program. Biggest surprise, however, was that John got a B—average.

"On the way home from Jos, we stopped at Moriki where we saw 590 leprosy patients and dismissed 115. (David and Sue John's station.) Then, back to Gusau and on to Amanawa where we saw 400 leprosy patients and did surgery, then in to Sokoto for some shopping, and got home on Wed., Oct. 15 after almost 3 weeks away."

Letter to Cherry at Wheaton Oct. 19, 1969 "You've got some 'real' roommates! Don't be discouraged. Maybe the Lord put you with them for a purpose. You can probably make a change the end of the first semester if it gets too difficult. We appreciate the fact that you believe in showing respect to God in the way you dress, etc . . . . We're praying for you every day and praising the Lord for you, too. You make our hearts happy knowing that you are seeking the Lord in your daily walk. Never turn from that wonderful path. See you in 9 months."

Letter from Fran Oct. 20, 1969 Rollie got another induction notice, this time for Nov. 5. He had the school write and ask for a deferment which he got until the school year ended. "Margaret went down to visit him over the week-end. We shopped for a winter coat for Cherry. It is brown and has a wide belt, and a fur collar. She is happy with it and we had fun shopping for it. I don't know whether Bill did or not but he was very patient and I'm sure he enjoyed people-watching while he waited."

"Sam and Agnes are on their way to So. Carolina and are stopping in this area for a few weeks so the family is getting together for dinner next Sunday. A tornado hit Sam's place in MN this summer, knocked off the chimney on their house and ripped off the roof of the addition that they put on a few years ago, ripped up about a dozen of the big trees and destroyed 2/3 of the tenant-farmer's crop. It took about 30 seconds to destroy what it took years to build and grow.

"Cherry called and was on cloud 9. She got a B on a Bible test. She really studied for it, app. 5 hours."

Letter from Fran Nov. 4, 1969 "This morning a special delivery letter arrived telling him (Rollie) that his induction had been canceled. I forwarded it to him right away . . . . So he has been spared again . . . . It seems that his 'girl interest' has narrowed down to Margaret. Which is all right. She seems to be a fine girl.

"Lance started to work at the American National Bank last week and is liking it. He's working in stocks and bonds . . . . Frank isn't living with them anymore so they are looking for another room mate.

"Yes, Cherry has her winter coat as you know from my last letter . . . . she is working every afternoon, except one. At first she called me every day, then it tapered down to twice a week and now, once a week. She called tonight. She had just written to you and I think was feeling a little homesick. She said she still missed Africa. I guess we were the next thing to Africa. I'm picking her up tomorrow night to go to church and hear Brother Andrew. He is speaking here tomorrow night. She read his book while in Africa. It is about his smuggling Bibles into Russia.

"Pat is going to have another baby. As usual she is sick . . . . Jamie will be two this month. He sure is a honey. Becky is getting to be quite a lady, and a very sweet young thing."

Nov. 20, 1969 to Cherry "Dad and I keep listening for Abarshi's truck as we eat our Sunday morning breakfast from trays in the front room on Sundays and listen to Stephen Olford . . . . We have three nurses here who speak French—Jeanne Marie Berney, Janine Lanier, and Esther Egli . . . 2 from Switzerland and Janine from France. The Klops. have gone.

"We changed Awana to Wed. night and last night was our first nightly meeting. We had a treasure hunt. The prize was "moon dust" that Armstrong brought back with him on his first journey. He dropped some off here—candies. We started a contest to the moon, and have a large contest board with the moon capsules—one red and one yellow—racing from earth to the moon. It's quite an impressive looking board with the earth on the bottom of an 8' piece of plywood and the moon on top. We had 22 kids out last night, which was a good beginning to the night-time meetings. We had it at the church.

"We're looking for our kids on the 19th or 20th. Planes are still not flying, so they will have a long, hard trip. The Haute Volta kids will have even longer."

Nov. 20, 1969 to Fran and Bill "Now that Intrepid and Yankee Clipper are 'hard docked' and our supper is over . . . It was 4 months ago (Burt's birthday) that the first two men stepped on the moon . . . . Your sentence about Frank not living with them anymore is intriguing, because just a few days before, we heard from the Forsbergs that Lance's roommate was in trouble and what a hard time Lance had over it and that they were praying that the Lord would work it all out now. Would you mind enlarging upon this?

"It's getting quite cold here these days, except in the middle of the day. We're under a sheet every night now and will add a blanket soon, I think . . . . We would like Cherry and Rollie to live in our house over the Christmas holidays . . . . Sue and John will be home for six weeks, but Pam will have only 3 or 4 weeks—we don't know for sure yet."

Nov. 30, 1969 to Rollie, Lance, Cherry and Fran and Bill "Rollie's letter came last Sun. a.m. and gave us the first news of what happened to Frank. We are terribly sorry for him and for his family and for his friends, including you who know him well.

"We have experienced a shock this week, too. At the end of my last letter, I mentioned a VC-10 going down just outside of Lagos killing all 87 on board. A few days ago, word came that our missionaries, Ross and Mavis Carson and their four children had boarded it at Kano enroute home to New Zealand. They first came out 13 years ago and were stationed their first term at Talata Mafara in Sokoto Province, their second term at Lagos, and the last year at Maradi B.D. This was the first VC—10 air crash in its history, and it was Nigeria's one and only VC-10. It had European pilots, although it was Nigerian owned and operated. It had come from London, stopping at Rome and Kano. The Carsons were going as far as Lagos to connect with a plane to New Zealand. For them they are with the Lord, but for the family waiting to meet them at home, it comes as a tremendous blow. Pray for them.

"We received a nice letter from Margaret. SIMAIR is flying again but only to limited places and no international flights. Dad has gone to the hospital to do a Caeserean section. Time for African sing song in the chapel."

Letter from Fran Dec. 12, 1969 "Cherry spent the Thanksgiving holidays with the Kletzings, going home with Brian on Wednesday night before Thanksgiving. and coming back on Sat. Lance went up to Wisc. near Milwaukee, visiting the family and friends of an ex-girlfriend from Moody's. He drove up with some students from Trinity. Rollie and Margaret came here along with Beret and a friend of hers, Jeanne Young, and Pat and family . . . . We are happy to hear that Margaret and Rollie are planning on getting married next December. If I had had to pick out a wife for Rollie I don't think I could have chosen a better one.

"Lance said he wrote to you about the tragedy of Frank . . . . we have much to be thankful for that he did not attack Lance or Jerry as they would have been able to defend themselves and in so doing could have killed him and then how could they have proven it was in self-defense without trials, etc."

(I, Ruth, don't have that letter so I will add here what I remember about it. Frank was having strange visions and apparently his folks came from somewhere out east to try to help him. They registered at a hotel in Chicago and brought Frank with them. Frank was in a room next door to his parents, and during the night, he slipped into their room and killed them. His father, by the way, was a pastor with the North American Baptists (I believe) and Woyke house was named after him. Correct me, kids, if my memory has become distorted after 30 years.)

From Fran: "Don't see too much of Cherry but she calls 2 or 3 times a week. She needs to talk over her problems and decisions.

"Alec Minor, Dr. Jack Minor's son was married on Oct. 4 and they went to Canada to live and operate a Marina. It was a family project I understand. Anyway, last week he was goat hunting in the mountains and fell from a 1000 ft. cliff and was killed. I cut the clipping out of the Journal and am going to mail it to Rollie as he spent a little time with him, and I think attended Elmhurst at the same time he did."

Dec. 21, 1969 "The kids are home for Christmas. Pam came home sick, and she spent the first night and next day in bed with fever, ear-ache and vomiting, but she is perking up now. Yesterday Sue put up the decorations for Christmas . . . . Christmas day we will have a service, then all of the compound will eat together. We are 19 this year . . . All the single workers' houses are occupied, which makes 10 single girls—8 nurses and 1 lab. tech and 1 personal worker. Nigeria seems to be getting sicker and we are getting more personnel from Nigeria. Nigeria has a lot of Russians walking around the streets, we understand. We know the Kano airport is loaded with Migs."

Fran has the last word in 1969—December 29, 1969 ". . . we are all glad that Rollie has been spared from the draft . . . . from now on there will be a lottery. Rollie's # is 56, I believe, if I remember correctly so if he is called up while still in school he has a good chance of getting deferred again.

"Frank is still in the county jail awaiting trial. Rollie visited him. He talks and acts very rationally but refers to the killing as 'that thing I did.' His lawyer is trying to get a speedy trial so that he can be hospitalized for treatment. Since then Jerry has moved out. Lance has two new room mates now, the third one is a friend of Don's (the first new roommate). Both of them were financially low at the time of their moving in so Lance has had to carry the main burden of rent, etc. until they get on their feet. Poor Lance, he's always the good guy.

"Pat is beginning to feel better. At lease she has more good days than bad ones.

"You mention the cold. We had 11-14 inches of snow this past week. Rollie, Lance and Cherry were here for Christmas along with Beret and the Von Busch's. We had a nice day. Cherry stayed at Lindbergs and has been keeping busy with her social life, coming here on days when she has nothing on the agenda. She spent yesterday with us. Rollie stayed at Lance's. Today Beret is starting a new job. She finally left Field's and is going to work for the Chicago Academy of Science and History in Lincoln Park. She will be painting scenery, etc.

"It is 4:30 now and beginning to get quite dark. I don't have to light the kerosene lamps though. Something to be thankful for!"

Good night!

Chapter 21

January-June 1970

Nineteen seventy started on the happy note that Christmas activities were over and we could relax and enjoy the younger half of our children for a few more days before they had to return to school, Pam to K.A. and John and Sue to Hillcrest.

Jan. 25, 1970 "Our Christmas time was fun, mostly because we all enjoy being home together at that season. Lots of family games get played to make up for lost time and to have something to do together. Rollie has announced his engagement to Margaret Wick, M.K. raised in Guatemala, and hopes for a next Christmas wedding, but he is student deferred for the draft still—always an unsettling feature."

With the Biafran war over, the planes were running internationally again and they arrived in Malbaza three weeks apart to pick up our kids along with the Pollen girls. No sooner had they left than preparations for our annual Niger conference began and it was to be held at Galmi again. Much of the planning for the mechanics of the conference fell to me and Doris Pollen.

Jan. 25, 1970 "Our conference starts on Feb. 5. Buying and arranging for all the food for 17 meals for 63 people is quite a headache, especially since we can't go to the nearby shops and pick it up. Most of the canned and packaged things have already arrived from Maradi, and Maradi will be sending fresh vegetables on the plane that comes on Feb. 4 . . . . That should include cauliflowers, cabbages, carrots, radishes, beets. We bought 37 lbs. of beef last market day and have it freezing in the refrigerators of the missionaries. Next market day we must buy another 50 lbs. and the following market day another 50 lbs. Storing it is a major task. We need 25 lbs. of meat for each dinner (five dinners) plus ground meat for spaghetti and meat loaf. This is all ground by hand. We have arranged for potatoes to be purchased here locally and tomatoes and lettuce and paw-paws. Talk about detail work. Then there is the task of bedding down the mob. Most of this is in the province of Doris Pollen, while my task in concerned mainly with feeding the inner man. This is missionary life—the kind that never entered my head when I said, "I'll go."

Conference came and went.

Feb. 15, 1970 "The final count was 57 noses. They arrived Thurs. aft. My biggest responsibility was in the food department. Everyone had assigned jobs, so when the actual time came, each did his own thing, and the food appeared on the tables at the right time. Vegetables were done at the nurses' house, salads at another house, cakes, pies and cookies were brought by all who came. Morning coffee, afternoon and evening teas were held at Pollens'. We were responsible here for morning cereal, cooking the meat for dinner—23 lbs each day, coordinating it all and putting it on the tables here. We had serving tables in our dining room and eating tables in the back bedroom, living room, study-bedroom and screened in porch. Actually the planning and preparation were harder than the conference itself. The conference was good, but when they all left on Wed., I couldn't say that I was sorry to see them go. We are gradually getting our house back in order, moving our furniture back from our bedroom and other corners. Speaker for the conference was Rev. Walter Angst, president of Institute Biblique Bethel in Lennoxville, Quebec."

Good news! Dr. Jim Ceton and his wife, Mary Lou, arrived at Galmi right after conference—"a young couple, enthusiastic, dedicated, but overwhelmed! He is capable but lacks experience. He is also humble—a rare trait among guys just out of internship. Our French doctor thought he had nothing else to learn."

With the Cetons' arrival, we were able to go to Miango for a short 2 week holiday. On our return from holiday, a surprise met us. We learned that Rollie and Margaret were married on March 21. We were disappointed that they did not wait until our arrival in June, but Rollie's relationship to the draft was a factor.

February also marked the death of Dr. Jeanette Troup. Jeanette was in Wheaton with me, a year or two behind me. She was working in Jos and cut her finger while doing an autopsy on an African patient. Prior to that, Lily (Pinneo) had contracted Lassa fever, had been air-lifted out of Nigeria and treated in the States. She almost died and a lab technician who attended her did die. Penny recovered and tells her story in the book called *Lassa Fever*. Penny had built up anti-bodies for the disease and was rushed back to Nigeria in order to donate her blood to Jeanette but arrived just a few days after Jeanette died. Jeanette did get blood from an African who had recovered from the disease, but it was too late.

After our holiday the wheels were set in motion for our upcoming furlough beginning in June. This trip was to include stop overs in Sweden and Norway.

Genevieve Kooy kept us informed while we were on furlough so I will be giving some space to her letters to us below. But first I want to tell you a little bit about Gen. She arrived at Galmi on the eve of the birth of our John Richard on Nov. 13, 1952. Burt was sick when he delivered me, and as soon as John was born, Burt took off for the house and was in bed for a day while Gen finished the job. That reminded me of the tribes where the father goes to bed after his wife gives birth and the mother goes about her regular duties. The idea is that when the evil spirits come to haunt the weak mother, they will find the father there in bed who is strong enough to fight them off. What an introduction to Gen's 40 years at Galmi.

Gen was from DeMotte, IN, had graduated cum laude from Lutheran Deaconess Hospital school of nursing in Chicago and was valedictorian of her class. Besides being brilliant, she was the most capable nurse we ever had at Galmi. Along with that went a heart for the people of Africa so her ministry didn't end at the hospital. She, along with Ruth Hunt, were regular visitors in the villages and often entertained the village women in their homes. When five year old Aminatu was left at the hospital after her mother died, it was Gen who formally adopted her, put her through school, arranged for her wedding as any mother would. Then there was Isti, Hassana's son by Chisu, whom Gen supported at school and through his marriage. Gen still keeps in touch with both of them. Aminatu lives in Sokoto with her husband and children (her first husband was killed in a motorcycle accident), and Isti has a good job in Cotonou and is married to the daughter of Abdou, who cared for the ministry at DogonDoutchie during and after the Van Lierops left there.

Today, August of 2000, Gen is with us at Sebring, FL, but not exactly with us. Instead of being in the SIM village, she is in a nursing home in town with Parkinson's. Having been such an active person, her confinement to a wheel chair is frustrating to her.

From Gen's letters:—1970 and 1971

March 10, 1970 Dr. Jim and Mary Lou Ceton arrived in Feb. 1970 together with Linda Kasper. Longs immediately went on holiday. Linda began helping Bernice Thompson with hospital evangelism.

Dr. Jeanette Troup, missionary doctor in Jos, died in Feb. of Lassa fever. "This newly discovered disease last year took the lives of two missionaries (one, an SIM nurse); a third (Lily Pinneo) was flown home to N.Y. and recovered, but her doctor contracted the disease, also a laboratory technician (the latter died). This is described in TIME magazine, Feb. 23, 1970. A number of Africans have died recently in Jos of this virulent disease; pray that its spread will be checked."

March 20, 1971

A'i, from Sokoto, who ran away from her husband in Sokoto after he, a Christian, took a second wife and went back into Islam, has worked for us for two years. She also witnessed faithfully in the women's ward. She was married Jan. 31 to Elisha, lab. tech. at Maradi Leprosarium. Elisha's first wife died in child birth as did his second wife, who was Tani about whose wedding we wrote in a previous chapter.

April 14, 1970 Mai Zama, our dispensary worker, has a good testimony for Christ. Plans to be married next Saturday to a Christian girl from Madaoua.

Andrew, a prince from Nigeria, surgical technician is with us.

DauDuka and Mai-Dubu (Ma'u) in Bible School. D. D. not doing well, failing in his studies.

Dorothy Kallock, who left us in Feb. for Maradi, to do the Bible correspondence, is also teaching first and second grades (in French) at the Tsibiri School!

April—Abraham and Idi have returned to fellowship, having left it in December because of a disagreement with Dr. Long over discipline.

April 14, 1971—"Precious in the sight of the Lord is the death of His saints." Ps. 116:15. We praised the Lord God, through our tears, for the hope we have in Jesus, our living Savior, as a few days ago we laid to rest the body of Dije, one of our hospital workers. As we stood on the barren, rock-strewn hill, with the sun beating down on us at about 120 degrees, we praised that she was free from her pain and troubles, with Him in Paradise. Though only about 30 years old, she had not been well most of the time since we first met her about 13 years ago. Her 'son', little Johnny, who will be six in July, was an unwanted baby, left by his unmarried mother. How we struggled to keep him alive, sitting up many nights. Now he is a bright little boy. Pray for him and his new parents, Halilu and Kwawa, at Bible school; yesterday he left to join them—had been with me since Dije's home-going."

That's all I have from Gen.

April 5, 1970 "Back at Galmi! And it is HOT! It is now 110 outside under the bagaruwa tree at 4 p.m. It was 116 when we came home from church. We have just risen from our afternoon sauna (bed of sweat). We arrived here on Mon., March 30. On March 31, the compound had a dinner in our honor—our 25th anniversary."

The only thing bad about our holiday was that it was too short. We stayed in the Eye Hospital cottage which had two complete bathrooms with hot and cold running water. The weather was wonderful—cool enough for tennis, hot enough for swimming at the pools in Jos, which we enjoyed twice. After two weeks in Miango, we went to Jos for the doctors' meetings. Rendels were in charge of the guest house. The Monday night we arrived in Jos for the Drs. mtgs, we had supper at the hostel with Sue and John; Tues. night at the Brian Walls, and Wednesday, at the Hicklins, Herb and Yola. Herb was an old Chicago Gospel Tabernacle man. Herb was a dentist. His wife died when their two children were very small. He took the children to his dentist's office and they stayed with him all day. In between patients he fed and diapered them. Later, he married Yola and they had several more children. Herb is a brother of Connie Hallworth King.

Royce Van Gerpen, a Sr. medical student from U. of Iowa and brother of Emory Van Gerpen, came for four months to help and to learn. He stayed in our small study/bedroom for awhile. When the Pollens went on holiday, he moved over to their house. Bill and Candy Lyons came for a week's visit from Miango to test the waters. After their furlough, their plans were to return to Galmi and set up a dental clinic there, which they did.

April, 1970 "The operating room is buzzing these days, with fifteen operations a morning. Three operating tables are going at the same time—Jim and Mary Lou at one; Martha Simms, one of our nurses and Andy, our Nigerian scrub assistant, at another; and Burt and Royce Van Gerpen at the third. This keeps our staff hopping and the 180 beds filled, plus the floor space between the beds. The outpatient department is seeing 400 patients a day as well. There are at least three preaching services for the out-patients a morning. We thank the Lord for Linda Kasper and Berenice Thompson, who spend their mornings doing personal work in the wards."

Letter from Fran dated April 6, 1970

". . . you know that Rollie and Margaret are married, Lance is back in the hospital and Cherry is in Detroit for spring vacation visiting with her roommate's family.

"To start with Lance: he had a recurrence of the colitis and tried doctoring it himself. He was supposed to be Rollie's best man at the wedding but just wasn't able to. He did manage to come to the wedding for a part of it but went into the hospital on Sunday. When I talked to Van Reken on Monday he seemed to think that an operation would be necessary. He suggested that it might be a good idea to cable you folks. But I talked to Mr. Forsberg and we decided to wait a few days and Lance did start to improve so Mr. Forsberg wrote you instead. He is still there but on the mend. He has some hospitalization through his job but it won't begin to cover all of the bill.

"Next, Rollie: It was really a lovely wedding even though we had a limited time to plan it. It was a beautiful day, the one and only real nice one we've had so far this spring. Margaret's sister and Cherry stood up for her and Jay had to step into Lance's place at the last minute and Jerry helped out, too. Rev. Wick and Bob Swanson shared the ceremony. The wedding was at the Village Church here in Carol Stream, but we had to bring all of the dishes, coffee pot, etc., as the church doesn't have its own. But everything worked out and it went off beautifully. I mentioned Mr. Wick taking part in the ceremony. They flew home a week before the wedding and that took some of the responsibility off of me. It was to be a very small wedding but after they got here they began to invite a number of their friends so it grew until almost 100 were present. The only folks from the Center that Rollie had were the Duncans and the Lathams and I've heard that some of the Center folks were disappointed that they weren't invited.

"Pat's family and Beret were here for Easter and then Becky stayed overnight. Bill took Monday off and we went into Chicago for the day. We visited the Conservatory (Easter flowers), the zoo, the Historical Society and the Field Museum.

"Berenice Kott and I have been asked to serve on a committee to plan a Guard reunion for this fall . . . . John Busch died on March 12 . . . had been on a kidney machine . . . his heart gave out. Pastor Seume had the funeral. It was an inspiring message, especially so since Seume is suffering from the same thing."

April 19, 1970 "Did I tell you that Sue made the top of the honor roll for the second time? This time with a 10.9 out of 11.0 average? When we tell her she's a brain, she insists that it's just hard work. That may be so. She also works hard at her piano, enjoys the organ—played at one of the church services recently, is on the Student Council, is in G.R.A."

June 17, 1970 "This will be a short one, for we are in the midst of our packing. In six days we will be saying goodbye to Galmi for a while and heading home. Simair is picking us up at Malbaza and taking us to Kano on Monday, the 22nd. We will fly out of Kano on the 24th on Sabena. Between the 24th and July 2nd, we will be in

Madrid, Copenhagen, Stockholm, Oslo, Bergen, so we are not having too much time in each place. We arrive in New York on July 2nd at 3:50 P.M., Flight SAS #913 out of Oslo at 11:40 A.M. on July 2nd. Our physicals are on July 3, and we will head toward Wheaton as soon as possible after that.

"Last Sat. night, the Christians and workers in the hospital had a farewell supper for us at Idi's new compound. We had tuwo da miya and barbecued ram. It was very nice.

"Must close now. It is now the 19th, and work is piled high, with just a few days left in which to do it. Will call you when we arrive in N.Y."

As I write in August of 2000, I am acutely aware that in a few short months, 428 Howard St. will no longer be our home, our destination every furlough, our home that we always head back to from wherever we travel, the place our kids have always called home and the only place our grandchildren have known as their grandparents' home, for we have sold it to the college and our SIM retirement village will be our final earthly home. Burt calls Sebring "our SIM launching pad."

But there is more to come. We still have 30 years to cover and I'll keep working at it next year and the years to come.

PART IV

Chapter 1

GEMS FROM THE '50's

In looking over the material I have from 1970 on, I have run across some "gems"—original letters, essays and thoughts from back in the 50's. I know I have put the 50's to bed, but these are too good to omit, so I will copy them for you or at least a part of them because I think you'll enjoy them.

You may remember our April, 1958 prayer letter in which we describe Maman and A'i's wedding. You will remember how her folks were against the wedding because the kids were Christians. I'll recap it below because I want to give you the "rest of the story."

1958—Mammadu was married last week. A'i made a lovely bride in her borrowed clothes. But why borrowed clothes? Hadn't Mammadu given her the proper gifts which consisted of blouses, wrap-around skirts, jewelry, brilliant head gear? And hadn't he paid his bride price to the family? The bride price in itself was outrageous—30,000 francs ($143.00) A more proper price is 10-15,000 francs.

Bur A'i's parents are not Christians nor does she have a single Christian relative. When A'i was younger, she ran away from her people and voluntarily entered our girls' school at Maradi where in the past years she has developed into a lovely Christian girl. The day of the wedding, the family refused to give her her clothes—all the lovely ones that Mammadu had bought for her—not even one outfit to get married in. But all of this is overlooked, for after the wedding, Mammadu will take her to his home, and all this business will be over with. But that's where we are wrong. A'i doesn't go home with Mammadu. Oh no, the family steps in and says she must stay with them for another week. So off they go with the unwilling bride and Mammadu stands helplessly by. During that week she will be given various medicinal drinks which are supposed to break up the marriage and bring her back to them. Will she stand the test? We haven't heard yet. But the rumors are that Mammadu will have to pay an additional sum of money to redeem her after the week is up. Have you prayed for our Christians lately?

The year 2001. Feb. 2. Forty three years later. Over the years we watched A'i and Mammadu and all has not been clear sailing for them. They were living in Galmi, Mammadu's home. There was a time when pressure from his Islamic family was too great for Mammadu and he went back into Islam and took another wife. A'i had already given him several children. A'i couldn't tolerate the situation so she went back to her family in Maradi even though it meant leaving her children with Mammadu. Whenever there is a divorce, the children belong to the father—automatically. Mammadu's new wife got tired of taking care of A'i's children and therefore neglected them. Mammadu woke up and decided he'd better get A'i back. She came back to him at Galmi on several conditions—he get rid of his other wife, and allow her to go to church and take the children with her. He agreed.

Over the years, A'i and the children came to church; she even worked for some of the missionaries. The children grew and each of them attended Sunday School and Awana. Jonathan was the oldest. A'i stood her ground even while Mammadu persisted in Islam.

The day came when Mammadu could no longer resist the Holy Spirit and he came back to the Lord. He has had a good testimony for the last 20 years, is or has been an elder in the church. In the meantime, his children have grown up, have been educated and are living for the Lord.

Now here's the rest of the story, but not the end. For the last year or two Galmi hospital has undergone worker unrest and strikes. There are over 100 employees—not all are Christians. That is not to say that if they were all Christians, there would be no problems. And who has been the mediator this past year? Jonathan, son of A'i and Mammadu. He has a responsible job in Niamey but was able to come to Galmi and arbitrate with the leaders of both missionaries and workers. At this writing, negotiations are still underway for a settlement. Perhaps before next Christmas I'll be able to conclude this chapter in the lives of Mammadu, A'i and Jonathan.

Now here's another gem

This one is from March, 1956

Few people thank us for our help—about one out of ten. Dan M . . . was numbered among the ten percent, and he wanted his gift to be extra special. He knew that the white man eats eggs—a thing that a black man does not do lest he become sterile and unable to bear children. Two months after we amputated his finger, Dan M . . . brought us a gift of 75 eggs. We thanked him profusely, and after he was gone, we put them in water to test them. Anybody but city folk knows that a bad egg or an old one floats. Those that are good lie flat on their sides at the bottom of the water, while those that are questionable turn on their ends in various degrees. Fifty seven of these eggs rose like Mexican jumping beans; eighteen were questionable. Dan M . . .'s heart was in the right place—he must have started saving his eggs from the day he returned to his village.

And yet another one from the same date

To be childless in Africa is a thing of great shame and grounds for divorce. Nana, an old woman who brings our milk and has borne 13 children in her day, has a daughter who has been married six years and is childless. Last week Nana and her daughter took a truck the 35 miles to Konni to visit the "crying tree." They made their petition before the tree, and if the daughter bears a child within the year, they have promised to take a cow or a goat to the tree in thanksgiving. When she told us, our cook scolded her saying, "Here you are, you have heard the gospel in this very kitchen, and you go and worship this tree that your daughter might have a child. Why doesn't she go to the hospital and get medicine from the doctor?" (Sometimes it works!) We then suggested that she wait a year lest the doctor's "strong" medicine help her and she take the cow to the wrong place.

Whatever happened to Dau Duka?

Dau Duka was our first convert at Galmi. That is to say, Martha Wall led him to Christ while she was teaching this young lad of about 16 to read. He learned to read very rapidly, went on to Maradi Bible School, then returned to Galmi as our pastor—a very eloquent Bible teacher. Eventually, the Islamic pressure from his home village became too much for him—his marriage went down the tubes, he married a second and third wife, denounced Christianity and returned to Islam. He got a job at the hospital. His second wife had a dream one night—a bright light swept over her and a voice said, "Christianity is the true way." This happened several times. In the morning, she sought out one of our nurses who led her to faith in Christ. Ma'u has followed the Lord ever since. Dau Duka continued to work at the hospital, still holding on to Islam. She is divorced from Dau Duka, who is married to another wife. Dau Duka has retired now from the hospital. We wonder how the final chapter will read.

Chapter 2

FURLOUGH – 1970-1972

June 1970—SIMAir picked us up in Malbaza. We met John, Sue and Pam in Kano. We flew out of Kano on Sabena on Wednesday, the 24th of June. We flew to Madrid, spent a few days there enjoying the city, then flew on to Copenhagen. We visited Stockholm as well, then flew on to Oslo, visited a number of sites, then rode the train to Bergen. After a day or two there, we flew back to Oslo from which we began our return flight back to good old U.S.A. We arrived in New York on July 2, had our physicals on July 3, and then flew to Chicago and Wheaton.

The down side of being at home is that I didn't write letters home because we were there. So I don't have any proof of what I am about to write from memory. You kids will have to fill in on these. So what I am going to do is write what I think I remember, and I would like you to correct me or add to it and then I will revise this chapter.

It was so good to see Rollie and Mar, Lance and Cherry again as well as Fran and Bill and Beret and other relatives and friends. Being back at the Center again was a joy; enjoying the music, the message and friends. Living in our home at 428 Howard St., in Wheaton was contentment. Having our family except Rollie and Lance under one roof made me feel like a mother hen again with all of her chicks under her wings, even though our chicks were quite grown up.

John and Sue enrolled at Wheaton North High School and Pam was in 5th or 6th grade at Holmes School across the street from us. Cherry had finished her Freshman year at Wheaton College and now moved back in with us and enjoyed her second and third years under our roof. Cherry's first semester at Wheaton was quite traumatic since she was rooming with two girls who were opposites in their life style and upbringing. But she met Cindy (now Buher) and roomed with her the second semester and Cindy has remained a good friend ever since. Cherry arranged her schedule so she could come home mornings for "tea time." During John's time at Wheaton North, he enrolled in a work/school program and spent a few hours a day at a bank in Wheaton. It was there that he met Mary and they started going together. John graduated from Wheaton North in June of 1971 and Sue became a Senior. John started at College of DuPage. We stayed home for two years in order to see Sue graduate and get into Wheaton College. Lance was working at a bank in downtown Chicago and living in Oak Park with friends.

Rollie was married to Margaret Wick and they were both in college at Southern Ill. Un. in Carbondale. The army loomed over Rollie's head, and he was drafted before Diana was born in Sept. of 1971. Diana was born in Elmhurst Hospital and Rollie was able to be home from the Army for her birth. They stayed with us for about a week and then I went back to Carbondale with Margaret while Rollie returned to N.Y. I stayed with her for about a week and then took the train back to Chicago and Wheaton. Rollie was making a name for himself in the Army, being Soldier of the Month a couple of times and excelling in racquet ball. As a result of his good record, he was given the choice of where he wanted to serve and what he wanted to do. He chose Chaplain's Assistant and Fort Sheridan, north of Chicago. That meant that Rollie and Mar and Diana moved to Deerfield, IL, and we enjoyed being close to them during the rest of his army time.

In June of 1972 Sue graduated from North High School and in that Fall, she started Wheaton College and Cherry started her Junior year there. Cherry was a resident assistant in one of the dorms that year. It was during this time that John's girl friend, Mary, became a Christian and was baptized at Wheaton Bible Church. She invited her parents and big brother to witness the baptism. They had never been in a Protestant Church before, so this was a real step of courage.

We invited the family back to the house for some food and fellowship, and it was there that Cherry met Mary's big brother, Chip. He had recently been discharged from the air force after a four year stint. Chip began calling Cherry after that and wanted to take her out. She was afraid to go out with a non-Christian guy, but agreed if he would go to the Bible study at Lois Peterson's house in Chicago. After three weeks, Chip became a believer. That friendship blossomed and two years later, they were married.

John and Mary's relationship became quite serious and they wanted to get married. We opposed the marriage on the grounds that they were too young. John was 19, and Mary was 18. The upshot of it was that we persuaded John to return to Africa with us for a year and Mary to get a year at Moody Bible Institute, and then if they were still of a mind to get married, we would give our consent. So Mary started at Moody and John returned with us to Galmi in the Fall. We hadn't been back too long before John got a "Dear John" letter from Mary saying that she had dropped out of MBI and was marrying someone else. John was broken up about it for a time, but later he realized that it was the best thing that could have happened to him. After a year with us at Galmi, John returned to the States again. He worked at Four Seasons Hotel on Roosevelt Rd. where Howard Duncan was the manager.

Sept. 1972—The time came for us to return to Galmi. We had been away a little over two years. Rollie was married; Lance was working, probably for Sonny Burnier as a garbage man, Cherry and Sue were in Wheaton College, so we returned to Africa with Pam and John and a special friend, Kathy Duncan. It never got any easier to say goodbye to family. And we knew that when we got back to Nigeria, Pam would go one way to school, and we would go north to Galmi. Always a separation! Although we didn't like it, we trusted the Lord to walk through these experiences with us and with each member of the family. We counted on the Lord's promises that in the long haul, "all things would work together for good," and we can say that they have. Even today, (2001 A.D.) it's not a smooth ride for any of us, but the Lord is with us, He does not change, and His promises are sure.

Kids, read this chapter for your comments, corrections and additions. I will not finalize it until I hear from you.

April 15, 2001 Here's what Sue has written:

"Mom, here are my memories about our time in Wheaton from 70-72: It was a nice hot summer, but despite that I gained 15 pounds in three months as soon as we got home!!! I distinctly remember being amazed at that since I'd never had to watch my weight before! Interestingly, I never totally lost those 15 pounds until my first year back in Nigeria. :-)

The first two girls I met at Wheaton North were MKs—I introduced myself to Sarah Brooke waiting for the bus, and she was new from Cameroun. Then, as we were chatting in our seat, Kathi McFall, from Congo, who was sitting behind us, said, "Hey, I'm an MK too!" I don't know where either of them is now. My best friend those two years was Janet Swackhamer (Hoekenga) who was another transfer student. Janet and I took the same bus and were in choir and drama together. Of course, choir overshadowed those two years and was the highlight for me. Mr. Daebellhien (I'm not sure of the spelling—pronounced Dublin) was excellent and we gave concerts all over the city, and even did a dinner theater once. We had a choir Christmas party at at our house my senior year, remember? I played the piano for choir along with Barb Bates, who attended Wheaton Bible Church. I also played the piano for "Fiddler on the Roof," the musical my senior year, which was another fantastic memory for me. I got a dozen roses for graduation.

Camp was a highlight those summers. I was up there the full eight weeks after both my junior and senior years, and those summers cemented friendships I still enjoy today.

I remember that we had to go to the Center or Elmwood for both Sunday services AND Wednesday prayer meeting, and we went without murmuring and complaining, even though it was a drag to go on Wednesday. We kids (Jack and I) preferred Elmwood and got quite involved with the youth group there on Sunday evenings, particularly because of the Benshoof (Max and Betty) and Harbeck kids. I had a crush on Tom, and Max had a huge crush on me. It was a dilemma! Max used to drive all the way to Wheaton and back on Sunday nights just so we could stay and participate in the youth activities.

I went to Michigan with Dad one weekend when he spoke at a church. On the way home, it was late at night and he was tired, so he pulled over on a lonesome, desolate road and slept for awhile. I was very alert and quite nervous!

Those were two fantastic years of my life! At graduation from Wheaton North, I wondered how I could ever be any happier, and then I found out that college was even better! I'm not sure, but I think I moved into the dorm at Wheaton the day or the day after you left to return to Niger. Brenda Price was my roommate and we became fast friends with Mark Lutz and John Abisamra right away. Gordie Pullen and Alice VerLee were also at Wheaton (classmates from KA). Cherry and Chip were my mainstay. No email in those days, and letters came by snail mail. Cherry and I visited you the summer of 73, you came home the summer of 74, I went to Israel, Greece, and Rome the summer of 75 and then visited you in Jos, and you came home in 76, so I saw you each summer I was in college.

Anyway, these are my memories, and it's YOUR memoires, so you can choose what you want from my ramblings.

Love you,
Sue

Chapter 3

1972-1973

"Back to Galmi we must go, we must go, we must go . . ." and with a fair lady in hand. Kathy Duncan returned with us for about six weeks. With Pam away at school, she was company for John as they were the only young people on the compound. Kathy got a taste of surgery and medicine. She became acquainted with 15 year old Sahiya, in fact, became quite attached to her. Sahiya was from a Muslim family in town but she made a profession of faith. Her family didn't openly oppose her faith, but they didn't encourage her either. At the same time, Dr. Bill (dentist) and Candy Lyons took an interest in her. Between the Lyons and Kathy, they paid for Sahiya to go on to school. Over the next few years, Sahiya got a good education, went on to work in Niamey, went to the EERN church in town. There she met a young man and became engaged to him. Before they were married, however, he was killed in a motorcycle accident. Sahiya thought of us as her mom and dad and when we visited Galmi in 1990, she rode the bus from Niamey to Galmi to greet us. We were quite moved that she would do this. We wrote occasionally and about a year ago, we learned that during an operation in Niamey, something went wrong and she died on the table.

But I must back-track a little bit.

Sunday, Sept. 17, 1972 "It doesn't seem possible that it is only one week since we were with you. It also seems unbelievable that from the time that I walked out of the house at 428 at 3 P.M. and entered our

—
410

front door here it was only 39 hours. We are six hours ahead of you here and when you go back to Central time, we will be seven hours ahead of you.

"We had good flights and were well fed. We arrived in Kano at 7:50 P.M. Tues. night (21 hours after take-off from O'Hare.) We French Country people were sent right up to Maradi without going through customs in Nigeria. Our planes were waiting for us. It was quite a shock for me and Pam to be separated so abruptly. We thought we would have a day or two in Kano. Instead, we had two hours together at the airport while waiting for our luggage, and then Pam went home to some missionaries' house in Kano for the night and was to go to K.A. the next day.

"We left Kano that night in three mission planes and arrived in Maradi at midnight. We slept there and next morning we flew to Galmi.

"It is very hot and humid. The temperature is running in the 90's. The rains have been sparse this year, like they were the summer you were here, Beret, and the crops are poor. It will be a year of hunger for many. We have been welcomed by the Africans who have been coming to the door all day long to greet us. They are very happy that we are back. The kids are anxious to get Awana going again.

Oct. 19 "This morning Kathy and John and Jeanne Marie went for a camel ride over to Milela. They came back very sun-burned and tired, and have been relaxing all afternoon. The camel caravan leader walked, so they could go only as fast as he walked, so they were disappointed that the camels didn't trot."

From Burt: "Well, we're back at it and I sort of feel that we're right where we belong for now. We're filling a need. Ruth is having a terrific success with Awana, and I'm elbow deep in blood a lot of the time. We have an SIM plane stationed in Niger now and this is the busiest station in the country (18 missionaries when we're all here.)"

Nov. 4 "John and Kathy Duncan left a week ago, intending to spend a couple of days at Maradi, a week at Zinder, and fly to Kano on the 8th. From there, John hopes to go to Jos to spend a few days, while Kathy plans to fly out of Kano to Brussels on the 10th. We are very sorry that Kathy is not getting to Jos, because that would have been the most pleasant spot in her whole visit in Africa. In Brussels, she will step into winter, after coming from 116 degree weather. Both she and John insisted on riding in the back of a truck to Maradi and Zinder. It was 'more exciting'. The bus was 'too sophisticated' for them. Well, to each his own.

Nov. 19 "John is helping Dad scrub on surgery now, and is enjoying it. Gen Kooy is in Jos with hepatitis, but is due home this week. Martha Simms in on holiday. Pam is having quite a struggle with French because she is 2 years behind, and that's quite some gap. Also, she's doing poorly in Math and Science .... There is a wonderful spirit of unity at K.A. this year, coupled with a revival at both K.A. and Hillcrest. Kids at Hillcrest are gathering together for prayer and Bible Study for their lunch hours. Pam rededicated her life to the Lord. We rejoice in evidences of God's working in all your lives.

"I'm pretty excited about Awana. Last week we had 70 boys there. The youth building is super, and it has made a tremendous difference in our meetings over last term. Best of all, DauDuka, Halilu, and Mamman (he's new) are faithful in helping. As a result of Awana, we have been having about 20 new boys in S.S. Last Sunday I had 12 teen age boys in my class. Do you remember Hashi? He's grown up, has lost his pot belly and hangs around and does odd jobs. He is a Jr. leader in Awana, along with Jonathan Mamadu, Iliiya Ibrahim, and Idi Yahaya. Remember Dawi? He's back from Sokoto, all grown up. I didn't know him when I saw him. Do you remember Mamman Dille? He was Mamman, the girls' cook's nephew. He was the boy who always used to come around trailing his pet ram with him—just like a dog. He was in Lagos working, and was shot and killed one night when he was an innocent bystander in a fight over a woman. He must have been about 20 yrs. old."

(As of the year 2002, here is a post-script relating to the above mentioned young men. DauDuka went back into Islam. Halilu continues in the faith, is an operating assistant in surgery, Hashi has gone back into Islam, Jonathan is an outstanding Christian and holds a responsible job in Niamey. Iliya Ibrahim continues in the faith and is in charge of a ward in the hospital. Idi and Dawi have gone back into Islam.)

Rich French, Candy Lyons' brother, visited about this time. He was familiar with a variety of machines. He was a super welder, a builder, photographer.

"In fact, there's nothing that he can't do, if you ask him. And he's only 24. He is a nice guy, but he only eats potatoes. No meat or vegetables—says he gags on them and has since he was a baby. Oh, yes, he also eats bread. He's been a Christian just one year—from California and quite a surfer."

Nov. 27 8:15 P.M. "It's Monday night and I am all alone. Dad went to Cotonou to pick up the truck. We got word at midnight Fri. night that our truck had arrived. (Bill Lyons returned from Maradi with the news.) And the plane was coming through on Sat. and would stop for Burt to go to Niamey if he wanted to catch it. So he caught it, week-ended in Niamey, and is scheduled to fly from Niamey to Cotonou via 'Air Kepple' (formerly with the Baptist Mission, but now on his own, supplying air service to any who can afford it). Ray Pollen is with him as his car came on the same boat. He will probably be home this week-end sometime. It's a good 3 day trip from Cotonou.

"John is out this evening. He is usually out in the evenings—visiting the nurses—especially Jeanne Marie. (Insert—June 19, 2002 Yesterday we learned that Jeanne Marie Berney went to heaven on Sunday, June 16, 2002. She had an inoperable brain tumor.) When Kathy was here, the three of them did a lot of things together, and now that she's gone, the two of them do. Yesterday, they went in to Madaoua to the cotton plant, courtesy of M. et Mme. LaFitte, who sent their chauffeur to pick them up and returned them later that night. They spent the afternoon swimming in their private pool. They also had a French style, many-course supper. Mrs. LaFitte is not well and spends much of her time coming and going to the hospital. Both Jeanne Marie and John have had upset stomachs today, and I wonder if it was something they ate or drank yesterday."

Dec. 10 "You won't believe it, but my fingers are so cold, it is hard for me to type, and this is Africa! I will say that I prefer this weather to the extreme heat, so I shouldn't complain. It is 60 these mornings, but the winds are so strong, that outside the wind chill must be about 40. Inside, it is 73 and you must think I am crazy to be complaining about the cold.

"I have put a number of Awana verses on cassettes, and the boys listen to them and learn their verses. Just a few minutes ago, a boy of about 11 years old, came to the door so I invited him in and he is listening to 2 Tim. 2:15 while I type. He is using the ear phone, so all

I hear is his repeating the verse phrase by phrase, over and over again, as I have recorded it on the tape.

"Cherry, we received a real nice letter from Chip, which we will be answering soon . . . . John has entered into the chess foray and is winning as many as he is losing. You had better brush up on your chess, Lance, for when John comes home, he will be good competition for you."

Burt returned with the truck and the motorcycle and the news that our loads had all arrived in Cotonou. But he had to go to Maradi with the truck and motorcycle to go through customs. He had to leave the motorcycle there to go through customs when our loads got there. So the truck with our loads on them went by Galmi going to Maradi and then had to make the return trip to Galmi. What a bummer.

"I do miss all of you lots (Rollie, Lance, Cherry, Sue), but nevertheless, I see the Lord working here, mostly through Awana. Last week, three boys came forward after the message by Halilu and stood and acknowleddge their desire to become Christians. I prayed with them later. Already they are having trouble in the village with ridicule. So pray for them if you think of it.

"We celebrated Thanksgiving here on Fri. night with the whole compound eating here, each person bringing part of the meal . . . . I am writing a Christmas play for the Africans . . . . This week while Dad is gone, John is helping Rick French build the new generator house. The two 25 kw. generators are here, the wiring is finished on the houses, and all that waits is the generator house. Today they finished pouring the cement for the floor. For the generators they have a sub-floor and a floor . . . . The painters finished our house Fri., and it is nice and clean and fresh . . . . Green is the predominant color—in dining room, kitchens and John's bedroom, cream in bathroom and bedroom leading out to the porch."

Sunday, 5:45 P.M., Dec. 31, 1972 "If I were to say this is the last time I'll be writing 1972, I would probably be wrong, because if I follow my usual pattern, I'll be writing '72 well into '73. This afternoon Pam and I worked on her long dress, the one she is going to wear to the Spring banquet, while we also made pop-corn balls. At the moment, she has a boy friend at school, Steve Brown. I don't know the family, but it's not the family of Harold Brown who was a friend of Rollie's and Lance. So now Pam is one of the "couples that stand under the tree!"

"Christmas Eve we had the S.S. program in the church. I worked with the S.S. kids about 5 weeks, and they did a real good job presenting the Christmas story, memorizing their parts very well, so I was quite proud of them. We had it in the Youth building, and there were at least 250 people there, many of them standing along the walls. On Christmas day all the missionaries met at the Lyons' for dinner, and we had a gift exchange as well. We played games for awhile, then went over to Israel's (the carpenter) house and had rice and miya and spit-cooked ram. Later that night, we went back to the Lyons' for some slides and more games. So Christmas day was a day of relaxation from 1 P.M. on. In the morning I made 4 pies, boiled 4 litres of milk, spilled 2 litres on the kitchen floor so had to wash the whole thing because my boy wasn't there, so Christmas morning was busy in the kitchen for me.

"Lance, we're glad that you joined the Circle Church. As you say, 'It's good to belong.' How are the Sunday School lessons coming? Writing lessons is a talent, but it also involves asking the Lord for ideas and direction. It's amazing how and when ideas pop into one's head—sometimes during the middle of the night, (have a pen and paper handy, write them down immediately because they'll be gone by morning) sometimes right when you are praying. It's an exciting assignment!

"The Saturday the Cetons were due to fly to Jos for their baby and holiday, MaryLou went into labor, so they had their baby here, at 4:30 that afternoon. David John.

"Hospital patients have built up and there are 90 on the waiting list for surgery.

"John and Mary have become 'dis-engaged' for the time being and plan to remain so until a year after he returns in order to examine their relationship more closely."

1973

The first letter I have is dated Feb. 5, 1973. I don't know where January went, but even today, or I should say, especially today (in 2002), the days, weeks, months, and years disappear before my eyes, so in January, 1973, the month probably just disappeared. Maybe I'll find it down the road!

"It is Monday morning. I have just made butter from cream from a three days' supply of milk. I got about a half pound, which will sustain us until Thurs., at which time I will make another three days' supply. Reason for doing it on Mon. and Thurs. is that we have the electricity on in the mornings, and I can beat the milk with the electric mixer. It's interesting to watch the stages the milk goes through. First it's cream, then it's whipped cream, then it goes into a sort of gunky stage, then finally you see the liquid separating from the solid and you stop beating. Then with a wooden spoon you press the solids together, squeezing out all of the liquid, then you wash it three times to get all the traces of milk out, add a little salt, and presto—butter! I taught Pam how to do it this holiday, so she can do it all summer long, too. I've often thought about making my own butter at home, but where can you get non-homogenized milk these days? I'm also having fantastic success with yogurt—it just melts in one's mouth and is thick and creamy—almost like ice-cream.

"Dad is over at Big Boys' Awana. We split off the group and have taken the 14 year olds and up and made them the older group, and Dad is in charge of that. They have only about 10 boys, but it reduces our younger group by 10, and that helps a lot. Also, these older boys are helping us with the younger boys, and it all turns out to be a kind of leadership program . . . After conference, we're going to get together and do something for the girls."

March 4, 1973 "This week, the remainder of our loads came—those two huge crates, a smaller crate, and two huge cartons of stuff from World Vision . . . We did not come through unscathed. We paid $5000.00 in duty, not counting the truck, which is still being processed . . . . John leaves in early May . . . . He expects to visit Jeanne Marie in Switzerland, who will be going home from here in April for a four month furlough. He and she have formed an unusual friendship, and she has been a great help to him, especially in his bewilderment about Mary. She is 9 years older than he, but they seem to be on the same wave length . . . ."

March 18, 1973—Sunday aft. "It's a hot, still, sunny day, and as I look out the study window to the west, I see scrub trees, sand, rocks, wood pile, cardboard box taken with the wind, empty drums that act as a barrier to the wind when we have a fire to heat water. Directly in front of me is the drain pipe that leads off the roof, bends its way into the cistern through the broken cover. The cistern is empty and was so even in Sept. when we arrived, grim reminder of the drought of last rainy season. The door to the enclosed porch is open, two beds are made up for the moment we need them and are now covered over with plastic. The slat window shades are standing there, ready to be put up—perhaps tomorrow. To the uninvolved, you might call this a scene out of Dullsville, but to us, it's a welcome reprieve from a busy weekly schedule. It is 95 degrees in the house today, probably ten degrees hotter outside . . . . so far we are not dripping with sweat, and the nights are still cool enough for sleep.

"Cherry, and now you are in your last quarter! . . . . I think your 21 years of growing up, the lessons you have learned in and out of class, have been as fulfilling as anyone could possibly want—your early life, your back-ground, your religious training, the stability of your home life, even though there have been separations, have all combined to make you what you are today, and so with confidence we can see you graduate and take up the next chapter in your life. Knowing that the Lord is leading you adds to our confidence in you, because it is in a very real sense, in Him. We wish that we could see you graduate, but we are excited about the prospect of seeing you and Sue shortly thereafter.

"We started Awana for girls 3 weeks ago, and last week we had 52 girls out. So pray for them as well as the boys. Dad and John drove to Maradi on Thurs. and brought back the motorcycle, which was just released from Customs. Then they emptied the two big crates that arrived, so we are sleeping on new mattresses—firm!"

April 8, 1973 It was harmattan season which brought the temperature down to 90 from 100 degrees.

"For the past three days it has been blowing sand and dirt, and our house is literally covered again. The sun looks like a light ball up there, its rays cannot get through to make us miserable."

On the 28th we drove to Kano for eye exams and then went on to Miango on the 30th.

"Cherry and Sue, your report cards came this week, and we are proud of you. Lance, congratulations on being accepted at Wheaton. John went to Niamey last week and spent a few days there while waiting with Jeanne Marie for her plane to Switzerland. He came back with Zebs who were on a return trip from Haute Volta. He has been working with Don Williams, who is the new maintenance man. John is learning a lot about maintenance which will be of value to him in later years."

May 3 from Miango "It is so different here—cool and humid and comfortable after months of dust and heat! Everything is green and beautiful. We are enjoying some tennis as well as fellowship with other missionaries and K.A. staff.... John leaves on May 11 and will spend about a month in Switzerland visiting with Jeanne Marie and her folks. If Mary thought there was anything 'going' between John and Jeanne Marie, she should have known that J.M. is 35 years old and was a 'sounding board' for his problems only. She has definitely helped him, and John realizes now that he is 'lucky', and is 'off' girls indefinitely. Pam is doing well, growing taller.

The old swinging bridge is out of use, and many of the wooden planks have been removed to discourage crossing. It has been replaced by a new cement bridge that handles automobiles and trucks, so traffic has increased on the Miango road to Vom and other parts.

"Fran, it was nice of you to have the kids up and have a birthday cake for Lance and Bobby" (Hollander).

On our way home from Miango, we stopped at Zobolo where Harry and Cora Cox live. They had some cousins visiting them, the VanderMolens who live on Geneva Ave. in Wheaton. They were going to take the Coxes to East Africa on a safari and pay all their expenses. Not bad, eh?

From Kano we returned to Galmi via Gusau/Sokoto. Harvey Stromme fixed us up a beautiful meal as only Harvey can do. He was living in the Hirons' house, so we slept in his old house. The Hirons were back home. Gertrude Hirons was dying of lung cancer.

Back at Galmi, June 3, 1973 More dust storms, waking up and bringing the beds in off the porch, sealing up the house as best we could, and then sweltering in bed the rest of the night and sweeping up the next day. People were suffering from hunger since the previous year's harvest was meager.

"Believe it or not, my melon harvest has been beyond all expectations. While we were gone, Idi did the watering and he said he picked 7 melons, but since our return, we've had at least a dozen, and we counted about 17 on the vines in various stages or ripeness. The largest one weighed 13 1/2 lbs. and resembled a small watermelon in size. They are averaging between 5 and 10 lbs. And delicious, too. I hope that we will still be having them when the girls get here. We have planted some corn, beans, carrots, tomatoes and swiss chard.

"Believe it or not again, as I type this, the fan is blowing on me. A blessing of having 24 hr. electricity."

Cherry was about to graduate from Wheaton College, and we were sorry we weren't there to rejoice with her. I wrote to Fran, "A week before graduation, we would like you to send to Cherry a bouquet of flowers from us and an appropriate graduation card with our love and congratulations. We would like these to be sent to her room a week before graduation so she will have them to enjoy during the excitement of last days of school. These will have to take the place of our being there."

Pam was due to come home from Hillcrest on Sat., the 9th, and Cherry and Sue were due to arrive on the 14th. Cherry had graduated from Wheaton and Sue had finished her Freshman year. They flew into Kano and then SIMAIR flew them to Malbaza. And that was the beginning of a wonderful summer with our three daughters!

June 18, 1973, Mon. nite "On the one hand, it doesn't seem real—on the other, it seems quite natural—to have Cherry, Sue and Pam here. We have spent the last five days catching up on the year's news and enjoying it thoroughly.

"Pam arrived on Saturday, June 9. She was due at Malbaza at noon, and we waited for 3 1/2 hours! It was 100 plus degrees and no shade, for awhile . . . . as the hours wore on we got more shade. After taking off from Kano, the plane started to sputter (3 minutes out), so Rich Shaeffer turned around and landed again at Kano. Then he changed the sparkplugs, but that didn't help, so he telephoned to Jos, and Bill Tuck brought another plane to Kano and gave it to Rich and worked on the first plane. Hence, the delay. Just a week prior to that Rich took off from Jos, and the engine died about 100 yards up. He got it turned around, fooled with all the dials and it still didn't start, then he nose dived 50 yards and the engine caught again and he was able to bring it back into the airport—to the very edge, and it died again. Rich was pretty well shaken up after the first one, but he took off an hour later in another plane and made his daily run. Then to have this second experience was somewhat disconcerting.

"Cherry and Sue arrived in Kano at about 11:00 A.M. on Wed. morning, over-nighted there and got here at 12:30 on Thurs. Then from the airport, we went over to the Malbaza restaurant and had steak and rice with tomato sauce for dinner, together with Al and Eva TerMeer, Ann Beacham and Dotty Rudolph.

"Fran, I'm so sorry that you have been sick . . . . Thanks for all the shopping and chasing you did for us in connection with the girls' coming and also for your seeing to the needs of our kids—and this goes for Bill, too."

The July 1 letter mentioned Rollie and Mar's proposed trip to Guatemala with Diana to visit Mar's folks, Stan and Betty Wick. It contained admonitions on housing for John and Lance in Wheaton, Fran's improvement health-wise, Lance's room and board options when Lance enters Wheaton in the Fall. Work was going ahead on paving the road. They were working toward Galmi from the East and expected to be at Galmi by the end of July. Both MaiDaji's and MaiDawaki's and the other shops on the hill were ordered to move because they planned to reduce the size of the hill and straighten out the road. Also, "we just had a dust storm alert . . . someone yelled 'Dust!' and we all jumped up and I think we shut all the doors and windows in 20 seconds. Now, dust is swirling around and the wind is howling, and we are hoping that it will result in rain."

Sunday July 15 "Uma dusted yesterday, and I am at the dining room table, staring at the big oil painting—a mountain stream, trees on either side and the mountain in the background—'strictly amateur' according to Beret. At the side of it is the green clock. In the living room are several other evidences of Uma's dusting yesterday. All I am trying to say is that the pictures are all crooked, because he never can put them back straight after dusting, so if you will excuse me for a moment, I will adjust the pictures in front of me before I get a crick in my neck. There, that's done, and I am greatly relieved.

"A storm is brewing in the East—dark clouds and thunderings. The grain that is 6" up is sleeping (suna kwana) and the Africans say that it will die if we don't get rain soon. Our compound is overrun by women and kids who are pulling weeds to take home and eat themselves and feed to their animals. Animals are walking skeletons and so are many of the people.

"The Husbands were here for 4 1/2 days, and we made eleven around the table. We had a great time. Both Danny and Steve are almost 6 ft. and good looking, and it was refreshing to have these high schoolers with us. Bonnie and Pauline have grown up too and we always enjoy Wilf and Esther. Last Sunday aft. we drove over to Milela to the dam, and there is quite a bit of water in it now, although it's only up to 1/10th of its capacity. We had a picnic supper there, too, after we played some 'Bounce or Fly out' (That's played with a bat and ball, you know.) They stayed in their old house which is now being used as a Guest House.

"Last Sat. night Burt was called to the hospital. Some Fulanis had let their cattle into a field of newly sprouted grain. As might be expected, the Hausas, whose field it was, arose in righteous (?) indignation, and there was a flashing of swords and bashing of heads with clubs. Five were brought in here. One died. Dad was gone from 10:30 p.m. to 3 a.m. He left the front door unlocked, and while he was gone, we had visitors (or one visitor). They (he) must have blown some sleeping powder in my direction, for there I was, sleeping away while he went through my dresser drawers, emptying my top dresser of some 140 francs, rifling through the others and finding my Norelco tape recorder (the one the Center gave us) and making off with them. He took my African bag off the hook and emptied it in the kitchen. He went into Pam's room (back bedroom) and she slept through it while he took a piece of cloth that she had just bought to make a dress with and her African bag, which he likewise dumped out in the kitchen. There was nothing of value to him in them, so he left the contents on the kitchen floor. I'm just sick about losing the tape recorder. I'm thankful though that he didn't take my camera, which was more or less camouflaged in my camera bag. It was right next to the tape recorder. It seems to me like an inside job, because he knew right where to go for both petty cash and recorder and bags and cloth. However, there is no way of telling. We collected a foot print in the dust on the living room floor the next morning. It is wide enough to be Idi's but too short. It is short enough to be Uma's but too wide. Here comes sand! To the windows! (Two hours later Yes, it was a good rain. Thank you, Lord.)"

August 5, 1973 "Niger celebrates two Independence Days. Thirteen years since Niger became completely independent! The first, Dec. 18 was independence from France. The second, Aug. 3, independence from the other French countries. That means two paid holidays .... They keep all the Christian (Catholic) holidays and all the Moslem holidays. All paid holidays, too. Some deal.

"The Godbolds from Tahaoua have been after us for some time to visit them, so we decided to go on Independence Day because Tahaoua usually puts on a big parade, with speeches and colorful displays, including dances, horse shows and races and camel races and even a beauty contest. So we started at 5 a.m. to get there for 7:30 breakfast. At Bada Gishari, which is the first of four valleys, we encountered a flood of water. It had rained in the hills the night before and just shortly before we got there, the water started to cross the road, like an avalanche. People were wading through it thigh high going to their farms. They said if we didn't go through now, it would get worse in a few minutes and we wouldn't get through. They said they would push us, so about 20 men and boys started pushing and we started through. After the first 25 yards, in the middle, the motor died, but the men kept pushing and in another 10 yards, the motor caught again. Water covered the cab floor in the deepest part. After that, there was no more trouble, and we arrived 15 minutes late for breakfast. The eggs and muffins and coffee really tasted good. Sue and Pam rode in the bed of the truck. Coming home, we took the back road from Tahaoua through Keita and Buza and Madaoua. Beautiful hills and scenery. Some lush forests along the river bed, while a few yards away, desert sand. Typical oases-in-desert scenery. The trip home took 4 hours for 150 miles against 2 1/2 hrs. for 90 miles. Buza is a village set among the hills with many houses built right into the cliffs.

"To get back to our day at Tahaoua! We went to the ceremonies. There were a couple of speeches, then the human parade of different groups—army, widows of soldiers, girls; then the announcement that due to the famine, there would be none of the games or spectaculars, and even the evening celebrations would be canceled. So that was that!

"We visited around the town, saw the hospital—there are five German doctors there and they all speak English. Most of the hospital buildings were built by the German gov't. which continues to staff it.

Had a nice visit. Returned to the house where Ann Godbold had fixed dinner, and we got into their Land Rover and rode out of town to a big sand dune like the ones of Lake Michigan, and ate there and played around for awhile. Then we left for home about 5 p.m.

"We have been hit hard by famine, and people get skinnier, but they are still able to get to their farms and cultivate them. We are praising the Lord for 13 good rains to date, and it is amazing to see the valley below us turning into a velvet green. Keep on praying. But in Tahaoua the Buzus, Tuaregs and Fulanis have really been hit hard. Many people have been brought to the hospital and treated for starvation, and we saw one man with I.V. tubes in his arms who was a mere skeleton. They have lost all their cattle, and anywhere along the road you might see dead cows. We met a German journalist who had just come from Mauritania where he saw within an 80 kilometer area dead cattle every 10 feet. We are glad to hear that Tahaoua is also getting good rains this year. The Harbottles tell us that Madaoua is not getting them, although they have had a few."

My Sept. 23 letter told of the departure of all three girls—Pam to Hillcrest and Sue and Cherry back to the States. During the summer, Don and Sherilyn had a son, Andrew Donald Douglas Williams. He was premature. Sherilyn was in a serious situation during her 9th month—toxemia. Her body swelled up and her mind didn't function properly. One night she was found wandering around the compound in her night gown. She came to our door and Burt led her back home. He decided to induce labor which he did the next day. We also needed a certain medicine which we did not have, so one of our missionaries drove first to Konni,—no luck—and then to Tahaoua where she was able to find some. Sherilyn delivered Andrew who weighed 4 lbs. 4 oz. He survived and grew up and Sherilyn gradually regained her strength and mind.

We were empty-nested again, so Dad and I took our supper over to the dam at Milela. The lake was large—about the size of the lake at Camp Awana. The Van Vertigans (cotton man) dropped in enroute to Niamey to take their two children to the plane for France. Their kids had been out for the summer. They asked about all of you kids.

"Rains have stopped prematurely. and it looks bad for the dawa crop but not too bad for the hatsi crop. Some farmers are wiped out again, but others have good farm land and will realize good crops.

Probably there will be about a 50% harvest on the average, so 1974 looks rather grim, too, but perhaps not as bad overall as 1973. Talk about locusts! They are as good as a piece of candy, and I had a hard time making the kids leave their grasshoppers outside the door as they entered for Sunday School this morning. 'That's meat,' they say."

October 7, 1973 The rains were over, the crops, what there was of them, were in. Many people were talking about leaving the area and moving south into Nigeria. A few weeks earlier a Peace Corps girl died at Tahaoua.

"She and her co-worker had traveled from Niamey by truck, had been on the road 2-3 days. They arrived at Tahaoua at 3:00 a.m. exhausted, with no advance notice of their arrival, and looked for a place to sleep. Some Africans gave them a hut, which they swept out. This one girl came down with an asthma attack, and while the other tried to find help, died alone in the hut. At 8 a.m. the Godbolds were alerted because they were the only Americans there, and Cash took the body, after getting it released from the medical officer at the hospital where it had been taken. He contacted Niamey asking for an American plane. He prepared the body, but the plane took more than 24 hrs. to come and already the body was beginning to deteriorate. The girl's co-worker was sure that her parents would have the body sent home, so the body was sent to Niamey, and from there no word has been received. It's too bad the plane couldn't have been used to bring the girls in the first place. And where was the communication between Niamey and Tahaoua including preparations for their arrival?

"We had a visit on Friday from the new Candidate Secretary and his wife, Gary and Glenda Johnson. They will be taking over the Forsbergs' job, but will be living in Cedar Grove. Along with them was Charlie Guth, former missionary to the Sudan and now in the Toronto office doing S.I.M. publications and art work. Charlie was in Wheaton with me—class of '47, and it was good to see him again."

(As I write this in Nov. of 2002 Charlie and Betty live in the village with us. Betty is in the nursing home in town and is not expected to live much longer.)

Nov. 20 "We received the tape the other night. It was so good to hear from you and Beret and the kids. We're glad that you can get together once in awhile, and it was good of the kids to have you. No reason why they shouldn't, after all the times they've been at your place. Sometimes young people don't think about those things, but I'm glad ours did."

Days were filled with two Awanas a week, teaching school two hours a day, visiting in the village, Sunday School and keeping books, and it was very wearying at times. Hospital work picked up after the Fast, and Burt was kept hopping there. We had dinner with the French Dr. and his wife in Madaoua one Sunday. She had delivered at Galmi two weeks previously. We rode in on the motorcycle.

The Africans were in the midst of a severe famine which means a deterioration of health as well. "We get the liver and kidney deficiencies of poor nutrition and less resistance to the ever present parasites. These last for many years after the famine, over which period many more of them die. Immediate starvation deaths are the exception, although many have starved to death in areas hit worse than ours. This year's harvest has also been very poor. Mary Haakenson was due next week. She finished language school in Kano. The Africans were talking of building a church in town—the first step—talking and praying.

Dec. 2 "We just got back from Malbaza (Sun. aft.), and after a bite to eat and a shower, I feel pretty good for not having had a rest hour. The Senegalese fellow who is in charge of building the bridges for the new road invited us to come for a visit, and we spent two hours with him talking and drinking Cokes. He also wants us to come for the Big Salla, which is in a couple of weeks, and he's going to kill the biggest ram that I have ever seen—stands chest high and fat with vicious horns. It was a very interesting afternoon—conversation all in French—with him and his wife and a Dahomean cook, who is hoping some day to go to America and be a cuisinier in a hotel there and make lots of money. This man in charge of making the bridges, Gorgy, makes 180,000 francs a month—$900.00 This cook says he is a Christian. He has one wife here and one in Dahomey. Gorgy likewise has one wife here and one in Senegal. He is a staunch Moslem. The cook probably is a Christian as opposed to being a Moslem. The road is paved all the way to Galmi now, and work is being done west of us."

Dec. 16 "You won't believe this, but Fran, two packages arrived from you dated Feb 23. One was nuts and candy; the other, a puzzle. I wrapped up the puzzle for Pam for Christmas. I hope it will occupy some of her alone moments this holiday. Last year there was John, too, but this year, she will be the only one.

"I just got back from a flying trip to Niamey. The 'flying' part of the trip was only one way. The return trip was anything but 'flying'. I started out Sat. aft. at 2 p.m. in a 404 Peugeot pick-up, riding in the cab with the driver and one other male passenger. Of course, I had the middle seat, right over the hump, and underneath my cushion a part of the car jack was poking itself in my bottom. I thought it was probably a broken spring so didn't say anything about it until we stopped at Dogon Doutchie. Then the driver said it was probably the jack, so I asked him to remove it. I took this 404 to Konni, about 275 miles, and we got there this morning at six—sixteen hours after we left Niamey. Five of those hours we spent sleeping. The driver and other cabin passenger slept outside wrapped in a blanket, and I slept on the seat, with just a plaid shirt over my dress. So when the shirt was on my top, my below-the-waist parts were cold. When I switched, the top was cold. The driver was in no hurry to leave, so at 8:30 I arranged with a truck to take me the rest of the way. I got into the front seat, and got home at 9:40—an 18 1/2 hour trip. What an experience! I hope I never have another one like it. I could have waited until next Thursday to come home by plane, but I didn't want to spend that much time there, since what I went to do was accomplished and Pam was coming on Wednesday.

"My primary reason for going was to see if we could get some grain for the hospital patients and village people who were hungry. I had a nice talk with the U.S. AID man who is in charge, and he thinks we might get some. I also made arrangements for purchasing electric fridges for the people on our station, including one for us. The chief in Dogoraoua has already bought our 20 year old kerosene fridge which still works like a Trojan, and he is anxious to get it."

(A sequel to that is that the chief didn't keep the wick clean. Burt showed him how to clean it every week, so the fridge didn't last very long. When we were in Niger this year (2001) we visited the chief—he had played with Rollie as a boy. He was on his bed, dying, unable to speak, but when Burt spoke to him and told him who he was, there was a sign of comprehension on his face. No one said what he was dying of, but we have an idea—he was very promiscuous and also had many wives.)

"Incidentally, as we were waiting in Konni this morning, we saw a bright light in the West going from North to South. It looked like a bright airplane light, and it traveled just near the horizon. I'm sure it was Kahoutek, but there was no tail. The Africans there were all bewildered and I told them it was a 'new star', and they had had no prior knowledge of it. This was about 6 a.m."

Just so you know that the weather at Galmi is not always unbearable, this is what I wrote on December 23. "These past few weeks we have enjoyed cool nights and pleasant days. Actually at this season of the year, it's really beautiful, our garden is pretty with green leaves and flowers and we forget the unpleasantness of the dusty season and the hot season.

"This aft. I made a batch of peanut brittle and penuche. The other day Pam made a batch of cookies, but they are all gone already. I made a fruit cake about 3 weeks ago, and we'll start to peck away at that on Christmas day."

December 28, 1973 It was the cold season, and we enjoyed our fireplace in the living room. We moved our dining room table into the living room to have breakfast around it. This land that could be so blisteringly hot in the hot season was now uncomfortably cold, and we bundled up during the day and during the night we slept under several blankets. We used our old wood stove for cooking meals so that would provide us with some heat in that area. This particular Christmas, we didn't have a compound dinner. Rather each household had some African Christians over for a meal, thus sharing with them Christmas in a more intimate way.

"We had 15 over, 6 adults and 9 kids, and two babies on backs. We all sat at 2 tables put together in our dining room. We had rice, African type gravy with meat and vegetables but not so much spice in it as they use, lettuce salad and coffee, tea and cup cakes. Other families had other Christians, so all were invited out some place either Christmas Eve or Christmas day."

Three days later 1973 was put to bed, and 1974 was ushered in. Cold season abated and harmattan increased. Routine set in, hospital work increased, clubs, reading lessons continued, hot season began to creep back in, and things continued as before.

Chapter 4

1974-June, 1975

January 1974 "What do you do when you get a toothache?" That was a question that came often to our minds as we contemplated missionary work twenty five years ago. Some of the old-timers took drastic action—getting their teeth pulled out and false ones made, even when it was not indicated. That seemed too traumatic for us—we wanted to hang in there until it was necessary. So we came to Niger hoping for the best.

"First term—third year—yes, a nagging toothache. We heard there was a French dentist in Zinder—300 miles east of us. Our builder, Don Darling, was here and going to Zinder in his truck in a few days, so with two small babies—one and two years old—John and Cherry—I made the trip in two days, saw the dentist and lost a molar. A week later I was back home, wearied by the truck rides but free of pain.

"A few years later, our first missionary dentist (Wes Kraay with his wife, Char, who became the new K.A. nurse) was installed at Miango Rest Home in Nigeria, and we rejoiced with this new development, which meant that each year as we had our vacation, we would be able to combine it with a visit to the dentist, and in case of an emergency, we could make our way to Miango either by car, or by plane, and be assured of adequate care.

"Now, in 1974, here at Galmi, we have a new dental clinic, a young dentist and his wife and child. Dr. Lyons is busy treating both

—
428

Africans and foreigners (that's us). His wife, Candy, is his assistant. Missionaries from Timbucktu, Mali; from Dahomey; from Nigeria; from Haute Volta as well as from Niger have visited the dentist here. Peace Corps volunteers and other Europeans working in Niger have been patients. Africans that we have known for years and who had lost some of the front teeth show up smiling with a full set of front teeth. Others who have suffered for years with toothaches are finding relief for the first time in their lives."

A lesson in fruit bearing: "Last June I transplanted some cuttings from a Cape Gooseberry bush that we brought back from Nigeria with us. We envisioned bowls of gooseberries topped with sugar and milk. In October, the cuttings had become large, lush bushes, nourished by fertilizer and abundant water. But no fruit. I gave instructions to my helper to cut them down, but he suggested that we leave them to act as windbreakers for the rest of the garden. His suggestion prevailed. Last week I noticed that the bush was loaded with pods, and inside each pod is a little berry, almost ready for the milk and sugar. How surprised I was! I thought, 'There must be a 'just right time' for these to bear fruit. I would never had known if I had had them cut down. Some fruit takes longer to bear than others."

"Sunday was another 'just-right' time. This, too, has taken a long time, but 'in the fullness of time', the Galmi church commissioned Halilu and his wife, Kwawa, to be our first missionaries to a village about 20 miles north of Galmi."

Background: In 1963, Halilu, about sixteen, came to us as a patient with osteomyelitis of the leg. He came from a village about 25 miles away. While he was being treated he came to reading classes. He seemed to be quite dull at first, and his cast smelled "to high heaven," and I hated to sit too near to him. He came to some of our club meetings and Sunday School. After a short time of hearing the Gospel, he accepted the Lord as his Saviour. At the same time, it seemed that his intellectual lights turned on, and he immediately made great progress with his reading. When the rainy season came around in 1964, he went home to help his family farm. He went with his Bible and literature. At Christmas time he came back from his farm to continue with his reading. He expressed a desire to go to Bible School. He helped us with the Awana club, and became a worker in the hospital. He ended up in the Surgery Dept.

In 1966 he had a real spiritual problem and it was a real thrill to see the way the Lord answered our prayers and brought him back into fellowship. Two years later, Halilu was baptized and then went to Bible School in Tsibiri, about 125 miles from us. In 1972 Halilu did some hospital follow-up evangelism by bicycle in some villages a little ways away. Halilu and Kwawa were married in our church on the hospital station.

When we returned to Galmi in 2001, Halilu was working as a scrub assistant in the operating room. Not formally trained, he had learned his skills from Burt, Jim VerLee, Jim Ceton and the variety of doctors who came and went. He is very good and does minor operations on his own. He is still the only Christian in his town and has a good testimony in Galmi.

January/February 1974

"It's really been cold here, and we have been eating in front of the fireplace for several weeks and doing other work at the table there, too. This cold season seems longer and colder than in many a year. This has been the year of the 'mostest'—coldest, hungriest, what else? Another break-in. Ruby Day's home. Got a tapestry, 8000 francs and her tape recorder. Had visits from the Al Swansons and Alberta Dubisz. Alberta's purse was stolen out of Lyons' house when she was there! Found empty two days later behind the fence."

March/April, 1974

"We have just come through a particularly windy and cool cold season with a lot of dust; most of this is a mile high cloud which is constantly stirred up and which sits upon us day after day. We sweep it around and out, we wash it off and it gets blown back in; we breathe it all the time and it gets into our respiratory tract and supplies us with many, many patients in distress and plagued even unto death.

"We are getting into the warm season and it is very warm. The Africans love it because there is no prospect of being cold and they need no clothes for warmth. They can dress for show if they can afford it, but they just wear rags if that is all they have, and no shivering.

"The famine is really showing its teeth now as most of the stored food, and all that was reaped from last fall's poor harvest are gone. As always when there is poverty there are some who are wealthy; many of these have speculated with the food grains and supplies, and are now reaping financial rewards, as the price has hit a very high level, running about $20 to $25 a bag of about 160#. But who can afford it?"

Meat available! Have you ever eaten camel meat? One day a truck killed a camel on the road a few hundred yards from us. The Africans dressed out the meat, and we ate camel meat for the first and only time in our lives. We may have eaten horse meat unknowingly during our travels in France. In Paris, there were shops devoted only to the sale of horse meat. Their identification was a marquee with a horse's head in front of the shop. But we had never eaten donkey meat or heard of anyone doing so until . . .

"last week! A herd of donkeys was being driven down the road to a market some 20 miles from here. Our houseboy said, 'See those donkeys? People have sold them so with the 1500 francs that they are worth ($7.00), they can buy grain to last them a few weeks. The donkey herder will take them to market across the border where they will be slaughtered and sold. People who buy the meat won't know it's donkey meat, and they will have something to eat.' We asked, 'Do Moslems eat donkeys?' Issou answered, 'No, it's just this year, because they are hungry.' They pretend that it is beef."

Famine really hit Niger hard—all of it, not just Galmi. Many people went without food for a few days at a time. Many of the men left town to look for work in the big cities, with the intention of sending money back home to feed their families, but usually they made only enough money to sustain themselves in their work. We were able to help a few of them.

When the U.S. or any other country sent relief grain to Niger, as soon as it went through customs it came under the jurisdiction of the recipient country. Much of it was kept in Niamey, the capital, stored in their warehouses to be sold later at high prices. So much for gifts to the people of Niger! It was at this time I made my trip to Niamey (see chapter 3) to see the U.S. Embassy people. They introduced me to some French dignitaries and with my broken French and the help of the U.S. Embassy people, we pleaded for some grain. Not too much later, a big truck load of bags of grain arrived.

Over a period of six months, the hospital with the combined efforts of the local church, distributed over 100 tons of grain. This distribution covered an area of 100 square miles. Without this help, many would have died. Along with the grain went a witness to the Gospel, and both were received gladly. This left an open door for the preaching of the Word in many villages. The Awana youth building was used as the distribution center.

The Tuaregs, Buzus and Fulanis, these once fierce desert warriors and their slaves, were reduced to nothing but their lives. Camels, cattle, wealth, land, all gone, and those who survived huddled in refugee camps on the outskirts of Niamey, Maradi, Tahaoua, Zinder where they found shelter and food provided by foreign gifts. Dead animals spotted the country side from north to south, east to west.

April 15, 1974 "At the moment the Niamey airport is shut down since yesterday the army overthrew the government and is in charge. President Diori is a prisoner in his own home and all the cabinet members are in jail. This includes Rabi's father, (Edith Durst's little ward), who was Minister of Something or Other. Today we hear that Mrs. Diori was shot dead when she tried to defend her husband and shot at the intruders, wounding them, and they in turn shot her.

"We think the 'last straw' is this relief grain which nations have been pouring in to the nation, but the people haven't been getting the grain . . . . Even what gets out to the villages is exploited at the lower level. We have an evangelist friend out of a town called Galma, who said that 8 bags of grain were brought in for the whole village. But that wasn't all! The village-head kept 6 bags and distributed the other two. Each person got one handful . . . . Everyone agrees that the president himself is not a bad guy, but the people under him are out of his control."

An airstrip at Galmi? For months we had been negotiating with the farmers whose land was adjacent to ours just north and west of us so that we could build an airstrip. About 5 or 6 landowners were involved and bits and pieces had to be negotiated separately. "Saturday, we were able to complete the purchase of a 35 meter wide strip just behind the compound, from west of our house to the edge of the hospital on the east. This will be sufficiently wide and long to care for our planes, so perhaps they will be landing here soon."

Cherry and Chip: John was going with Mary Sabathne while he was doing a work/school project through Wheaton North High School during our two year furlough in '71-'72. Mary had recently become a Christian, and she was baptized at the Wheaton Bible Church one Sunday night. We attended, and so did her family, staunch Catholics, who had never before been in a Protestant Church. We invited them over for "coffee and". Accompanying Charles "Bud" and Dorothy Sabathne was their son, "Chip", for Charles. They all met our family, and Chip was immediately attracted to Cherry. He phoned her several times for a date, and Cherry said she would let him take her to a weekly Bible study at the home of Don and Lois Peterson in Chicago. He agreed. After studying the Bible and hearing the Gospel for the first time, this Catholic boy who had gone all through school in Catholic schools, accepted the Lord. We wondered at first whether it was for real, or was he making a profession of faith in order to date Cherry. It proved to be for real!

Cherry finished her year at Wheaton College and worked for a year. During that time they became engaged. Letters went back and forth to Galmi between us and Chip and Cherry, and the date was set for June of 1974. Then we had to set the wheels in motion for us to get home for the occasion. I left on May 20 in order to help Cherry with the details of her wedding.

Burt writes: "Pam couldn't get out of school early to go home with Ruth, so she arrived in Galmi two weeks after Ruth left. She and I had a very interesting 10 days together at Galmi. We tried to wash clothes once using bleach instead of detergent and wondered why the clothes didn't get clean. In between frying hamburgers and steaks that Ruth had prepared for us before she left, the nurses took pity on us and had us out for meals at their houses. Many special relationships develop when one is isolated with one of the children, and Pam and I had a good time at Galmi and also traveling home together. She is not too good an airplane traveler, and so her last flight was rather miserable with being sick, but we were stuffed from our hotel and airplane supplied meals."

Chip and Cherry were married at our home church, the North Side Gospel Center, in Chicago, and Pastor Dick Sisson and Burt officiated. Sue made Cherry's dress and did a beautiful job. Pam and Sue were bridesmaids. It was a 10:30 a.m. wedding followed by the reception in our church basement, catered by Fran Minarik and her family. Although it was a rainy day, 200 guests braved the weather and honored us with their presence. This was our first experience with a morning wedding, and we found it a delightful way to enjoy the whole day. Chip and Cherry were able to be with the guests until they all left, then we had a few hours together at home with the family before they took off for their honeymoon in the Wisconsin Dells.

Our six-weeks at home sped by, and before we knew it, we were on our way back to Galmi.

August 10, 1974 "I would like to erase the past two weeks from the record. After suffering the crushing blow of having our new tape recorder, Pam's tape player (the red and white one), our camera and Pam's instamatic camera stolen in Niamey while we were sleeping, plus a few clothes of Dad's and two pair of his shoes, and some of Pam's school clothes and the battery charger for the calculator, it has taken me two weeks to come out of it. In the tape recorder was the tape of the 4 piano concert, which I was listening to on the plane, and in the camera was an almost finished roll of 36 colored prints. That included shots I had taken of the family, the wedding day and after, so that's gone, too. I know that they are just 'things', and I keep wondering what the Lord has to teach me through this experience. Maybe it's that I shouldn't set my affections on things of this world, but on things above. I also keep reminding myself that they are not vital to my existence here, and when I consider that Pastor DauDuka's house collapsed during one rain and he is living in a borrowed house until he can build a new one, and that Aminatu lost her husband in the motorcycle accident, I feel angry with myself for being so upset over our losses.

"The first two nights we were back Pam was very fearful sleeping in the back bedroom by herself. First night, during the night she woke up and begged to sleep with us, which she did. (Just like old times!) Second night she woke up but managed to spend the whole night in her bed, and after that she was all right."

"We said good-bye to Pam on Wed., the 7th, and presumably she got to Hillcrest okay. Between days and hours of house-cleaning (you can't imagine how dirty this house was what with the sand and dust storms over a period of two months), we managed to get Pam ready for school. She did most of the name tapes, and I did a little bit of mending for her, and she left here with a foot locker chock full, plus two cartons."

"The rain! We were amazed at how much rain has fallen so far. Last Monday we had a downpour from about 3 a.m. until noon. So much rain fell that between here and Dogorawa (5 miles) in that low stretch, the road was covered for a couple hundred yards. It washed away much of the shoulders and part of the pavement on the new road. It was a fast flowing current which in places came up to the thighs. Next day it was off the road but still rushing under the bridges and through the culverts. The road to Tahaoua is also out—a big bridge has collapsed. Many houses in town, Dogerawa, Konni and elsewhere have collapsed.

Dau Duka's daughter, Chimma, woke up during the night having heard a strange sound and awakened the rest of the family, and they all got out before the one side fell down.

"Dad and some of the missionaries decided to go to Sokoto on Thursday. They got as far as Konni, went south through Konni, and before reaching the Customs House, there was a road wash-out. There was no way to get through. The water was chest high, all the huts this side of the main Customs House were gone, and the Customs House itself was threatened. So they came back!

"A week ago Friday night there was a road wash-out four miles east of Magariya, and a big tanker loaded with fuel oil ran into it. The cab fell down into the hole and the trailer kept right on going over him until it spanned the gap, resting on the cab. So far as we know, it is still there, 8 days later, and one body is under it yet, and the smell of death is all around. Another body was removed and buried, and the driver is in the hospital recuperating with a fractured femur. He either was thrown out or jumped out of the cab.

"Just yesterday we heard that the dam at Milela (behind our house and over the hill) had broken, and water gushed through, ripping up the farm land in its path, taking away the crops with it. Now no water is left in the lake for the coming dry season.

"Now it hasn't rained since Monday, and we are hoping that all the rain wasn't dropped in July. The crops are looking good, but the rain must continue or everything will die as it did last year. So keep on praying."

435

Sunday. Sept. 9, 1974 "The atmosphere is right. At my right is a dish of pop-corn, to the right and slightly behind me is a drink of lime-ade, Mary Haakenson's stereo tape recorder is hooked up in the bathroom while the stereo boxes are one on the desk and one in the hall, and you might guess that I have moved my desk into the back bedroom. Bev Shea is singing, 'Thou blest rock of ages, I'm hiding in thee.' (Contentment in a hostile setting.) Now I have written 7 lines and told you nothing, but perhaps I have set the scene.

"It just started to rain—6 p.m. Dad is out on his motorcycle, so he might get wet. We had two good rains the day before yesterday night and the day before the day before yesterday night, and the people are terribly excited about the prospects of eating some of their own grain in about ten days. Before those two rains, there had been a lapse of twelve days without rain, and the people were really worried as they saw their crops droop. But these latter rains have just about assured a crop. Praise the Lord! Lord, please keep the locusts and grasshoppers away."

"Rain is seeping through dining room and back bedroom windows. This may be disastrous. Wind from the north. Rain is sweeping past in a horizontal position. Just knocked down the drain pipe to our cistern. Cistern leaks anyway. Starting to rain again and sky is getting darker. Hope Dad gets home soon. Here he is!"

Burt speaking now. "Well, the front of me got soaked on the trip home. It rained with hail in Magaria, so I waited it out there. Then I started home and a guy wanted a ride. I was at the front edge of the storm all the way. Had to go fast to beat the storm, but the rain was so sharp in the face, 40 mph was the limit. Scared the passenger. Storm really broke after I got here and so many trees were broken it was that terrific. Some crop damage, too. Along with the rains have come mosquitoes, caterpillars, pests of all kinds. This desert is absolutely beautiful here now because the rains have been so good.

"Mom had a great week-end: beat me in a game of horseshoes Sat. and Scrabble last nite."

August 24, 1974 "The other night a child arrived at the hospital having traveled two days by donkey. Their house had fallen in and she suffered a huge gash in her cheek, which was already infected, and a broken jaw. The trip left her completely exhausted and exposed to the elements and she had pneumonia by the time she arrived. Burt was called, and by the time he got to the hospital, she had died."

Mary Haakenson's folks visited for about three months. They were in their sixties, and very helpful. He did a lot of handy-man work around the place and she did nursing a couple days a week in the hospital. Margaret Gwilliam came for dental work and wanted to be remembered to those of you who were at K.A. when she was teaching there.

"We have heard from Pam several times, and she seems to be enjoying herself at Hillcrest. Her letters are short and to the point because she's 'terribly busy'. Her roommates are Joy Beacham and Patty Warkentine. Her last letter was 13 lines, and the last line, 'Bell rang—must go—razor broken.'

"Mr. Ottermiller, houseparent at Elm House (Lutheran) in Jos, passed through on way to Niamey, returning today. Spent the night. Mrs. Iver Ruten and Liz Chisholm were here last night, slept in the guest house (Husbands' old house). A thief stole 30,000 francs ($120.00) from Mrs. Ruten's purse. The thief went through Mr. Ottermiller's Land Rover but apparently didn't take anything. Left a camera that was on the front seat. Just wanted money."

October 13, 1974 On Saturday night, Oct. 5, Roland Pickering's life was snatched from him in a terrible automobile accident. Roland was the acting Francophone general director. The African chauffeur, a friend of Roland's from early Dahomean days, was driving. It was night. He started to pass a truck. At the same time, the truck started to pass a parked truck and edged Roland's car off the road into a ditch. The driver recovered control, came out of the ditch back onto the road but ran into an abutment on a bridge. Apparently, Roland was killed immediately. The driver sustained a broken leg. The other two passengers, Pat Burns and Jo Ann Franz, were injured. Pat had a compound fracture of her arm and facial injuries, and Jo Ann, liver damage and 3 broken ribs. Pat was airlifted to Jos. Roland's death came as a terrific shock to all of us. He was well liked by all and a relief to 99% of the missionaries in Francophone, who were tired of the officious ways of the general director, who was on furlough.

"The Beachams arrived a week ago. Mae is working in the hospital, a nurse, and George is taking over Al TerMeer's job, business manager. I am in the process of turning over all the books to him, thus releasing me from that frustrating burden which has occupied so much of my time for the last 6 years. Mr. and Mrs. Robert Shell and Mr. Bud Accord visited us for half a day ten days ago."

November 3, 1974 We were getting lots of visitors, which was nice, but it made extra work for us, too. Most of the visitors came for dental work. Formerly we all had to go to Miango in Nigeria, but now folks were coming to see Dr. Lyons, at the "bush" station of Galmi for dental work. Candy, his wife, was the guest house keeper, and it was a full time job, feeding guests and preparing their rooms. But she enjoyed it, since she was tied down with their new baby, four months old, and Ronnie, 3 years, and it was something she could do in the house. Among the guests were Ed and Alberta Dubisz from Upper Volta, Elaine Berdan Carpenter from Dahomey, Joyce Beacham, (Gordon's wife) from Dahomey, Helen Watkins, Ruth Warfield, and Kay Buck from Kano and 2 Peace Corps girls. George Learned came to teach his monthly Theological Extension Course to our African Christians and Bev Botheras and an African friend to get some tips from George on how to do T.E.E. work.

"Awana got off to a good start on Wed., with 75 boys in the first meeting, and 45 girls in their meeting. The weather has turned colder during the nights, and we are having refreshing nights for sleeping. Days are still warm. Winds are increasing, and in another month the harmattan will be settling in on us.

"The harvest was terrific this year. People were hilarious as they brought it in. Harvested it one stalk at a time as each one became ripe. Gloated over the delicious new grain, and the full feeling as there became enough to fill the tummy. Then enough to start filling the granaries. The granaries had been unused for so long most of them had to be rebuilt. Nobody is selling grain unless they have to. They will keep it in case next year is another bad one. The memory of hunger is too acute."

What a joy it was to see the villagers go by with bundles of grain on their heads or strapped to their donkeys' sides. Those who had carts loaded them with bundles of grain and put their donkeys to good use pulling them. All were praising God (and Allah) for an abundance of grain this year. "Our Christians have set aside in a corner of one African believer's compound over 500 bundles of grain which is their tithe and there is more to come."

—

On November 12, 1974, Douglas Heck, American Ambassador with the Embassy of the United States of America, located in Niamey, Niger, sent an invitation by land mail to us and the American missionaries on the compound inviting us to Thanksgiving dinner at the Embassy.

The invitation reached us on November 30, eighteen days after it was sent, and after Thanksgiving. Niamey and Galmi are separated only by 300 miles, but that was an example of mail service in Niger and to and from Niger. We hastened to write back and express our regrets at not having been able to attend. (See attached.)

November 16, 1974 "We are really disappointed and perplexed about Bob Swanson's failure to come today. He had written saying that he would be arriving in Niamey at 4:45 this morning. Dave Knowlton got up to meet the plane, but he wasn't on it. So when our SIM plane came to pick up some passengers from here, no Bob. We wrote to him twice—once to a French address, once to England. We wonder if he got the letters since there was a French postal strike. If he didn't get our letters, he probably decided that we weren't going to be here.

"We have had another missionary loss. On Nov. 5, Alan Gibbs was killed in a train accident between Parakou and Cotonnu, Dahomey. His passenger train hit head-on with a freight train. Alan was riding in the first coach, which was completely crumpled and burned. The story goes that the passenger train was supposed to wait on a siding while the freight train went through, but the engineer either didn't get the message or didn't heed the message. Alan was the brother of Alberta Dubisz. He leaves 5 children and his wife, Ruth. Two children are in K.A., three are pre-schoolers."

Shortly thereafter, Ruth was stationed at Kent Academy as a dorm parent and music teacher.

"Last week Jim Grant of Wheaton and his photographer, Heinz? showed up. They were making two films for SIM, one of Francophone countries. They took pictures of the hospital and Dad and then some of Awana in action and me. They are shooting all three Francophone countries—Niger, Haute Volta and Dahomey, and the total film will be 30 minutes, so you can guess how much time we'll have.

"For three boys' Awana nights, we have had 75, 80, and 80 kids out. It's really too many to play the games well, so we won't mind if it drops away. We expected it to drop down the second week, but it didn't. We started out with 45 girls the first time, and have been running about 20 since on Sat. afternoons.

"Pam seems to be enjoying Hillcrest. She has had several dates with Doug Bergan. Hillcrest is out Dec. 11, so we expect her the next day or so."

December 8, 1974 "The cold season has come in with a bang, and early! Three days now we have been having a fire in our living room fireplace, and for a week now, we have put the old wood stove back into service. Each hot season I say to myself we should get this stove out of here, but each cold season, I am very glad to have it. When the Awana boys drink their "coffee" (chocolate), they drink it in front of the kitchen stove; when they say their verses, they say them in front of the living room fireplace."

Work on the airstrip was commencing. SATOM, the road building crew, agreed to build our airstrip. They left a bulldozer with us for a week, and since their man to run it was in the hospital with an infected hand, Don Williams was permitted to level the ground with it. The final result will be a laterite top with a 10" base. Cost estimated to be $7,500.00.

Mr. Brian Nelson, SIM missionary in Lagos, was with us for a week. He had put up with a toothache for two years, tried a number of dentists in Nigeria (French, Egyptian, etc.) with no relief. Finally, two teeth were abscessed, so he flew over a thousand miles to Galmi. He left free of pain for the first time in two years.

December 29, 1974 We finally got word concerning Bob Swanson's failure to come to Niger. He had written a letter from Yugoslavia on Oct. 22, which arrived two months later, saying he had broken his ankle and wouldn't be making this leg of the trip. He went directly back to the States.

"Christmas celebration started last Sunday with the Sunday School program in the morning. That Sunday night we had sing-song at our house and I served Hungarian coffee cake and an ice cream/water melon ice combination plus hot chocolate. The cake and hot chocolate were a success, but the ice cream/water melon ice was rather weird. Monday night we had our compound Christmas dinner at Lyons' followed by games at Chappels'. Tuesday nite, Christmas eve, we had the nurses over for supper. Christmas morning we opened gifts, had church service and then the Women's Fellowship had dinner together in the youth building, the national women bringing tuwo da miya and goat bar-b-qued. We brought rice—Candy, Sherilyn Wms. and I."

There were four paid holidays during the Christmas season. The Moslems celebrated their "big Salla", the Feast of Sacrifice about the same time and Dec. 18 was a holiday remembering Independence Day within the French Commonwealth, and New Year's Day was a holiday. Four paid holidays—the only rub was that we were doing the paying.

At this same time, Tchad was having great persecution. The principal of our school in Tsibiri (Maradi) was Tchadian and he reported that his father-in-law had been martyred. Also, Dahomey was declared a socialist state and "will follow the principles outlined in the teachings of Marx and Lenin. So far, Niger and Nigeria, while under military governments, still have freedom, but we wonder how long it will last." At this same time, Ethiopia was expelling all the missionaries. Usually they give you 24 hours to leave and you leave all your possessions behind. It is a kind of robbery. Sudan is in trouble, too.

January, 1975 was filled with an unusual amount of out-of-the-ordinary happenings. Monday, the 20th of the month, an Aztec, 6 passenger, 2 motor plane circled the station and finally settled down on the end of the airstrip, coming to a halt 3/4 of the way down the strip. Accompanied by SIM pilot, Bob Forward, three French aeronautical inspectors came to inspect our finished airstrip. After months of negotiations with the farmers from whom we wanted to buy some land and the road paving company who agreed to do the work, finally the all-weather laterite topped airstrip was completed. And now here were the inspectors! And who else was there? The whole town, of course. It was like market-day. At least a thousand people came running from every direction to see this "big bird come down out of the sky" and land in our backyard. And who else was there? We missionaries, of course. We were just as excited about it as the Africans were. No more running back and forth to the airstrip in Malbaza, 14 miles away. No more waiting for planes scheduled to come but delayed along the way. No more wasting the pilot's time after he buzzed our station, giving us the signal to meet the plane. From now on, we could be in our houses when the plane landed and be out on the airstrip by the time the plane taxied to a halt. No more transporting ill or wounded patients for evacuation to the other airstrip subjecting them to further hardship.

Would the inspectors approve? After parking the plane, they rode down to the end of the strip west in the V.W. Bug, then back up to the east end behind the hospital, and after a cup of coffee at the Lyons' house, they gave their approval. Permission was granted just in time, for within a half hour we were expecting a plane of our own to buzz us with two passengers, and ordinarily we would have had a 25 mile round trip to the Malbaza airstrip. So when the plane buzzed us, the pilot saw the other plane and hordes of people, and we gave him the signal to come on it. Thus, on Jan. 20, 1975, our little airstrip was inaugurated.

On Tuesday, Dr. and Mrs. Ray Davis, SIM director and wife, arrived with a tour group of 13 others from Grand Rapids. Among them were Paul and "Dotty" Gordon, who were in Wheaton College with me; in fact, Dotty and I played on the women's tennis team together. What fun it was to see them again after 30 years. The group spent 24 hours with us.

Pam was back at school. We had hoped that she would be the first passenger from our airstrip, but the strip wasn't ready before she had to leave.

Steve Godbold was with us for two weeks. He was not in school. He started out with a correspondence course but threw it "to the winds" and was bumming around that year. We arranged for him to spend some time with us. His parents were really concerned about him. He behaved himself while he was with us. Cash and Ann really appreciated our opening up our home to him. (Today, years later, he is married and has a family and is a life-time missionary in Tchad!)

"We heard that Dave VanGerpen is in prison back home and Grant Cail is in prison for 'life' after being involved in the killing of a policeman. Every day I praise the Lord for you kids. My heart would break if one of you got into that kind of trouble. I praise the Lord for His faithfulness to us and to you. You kids have been covered with prayer all your lives, not only by us, but also those who pray for us and support us."

March 1975 "Four French youths stopped off at the hospital to greet us enroute to the Chad Republic with a 20 ton truck loaded with hospital supplies for a Christian French doctor and his hospital. (This turned out to be the hospital where we did a short term in 1991—Bebelem.)

Two of the boys were in the truck. The other two were driving a Peugeot. Fifty miles later, the Peugeot turned over, the boys were thrown out of the car. A few minutes later some Peace Corps girls were passing in their car, found them, administered first aid, then took off to find help. The truck which was following about 5 minutes behind them, came upon them lying alongside the road. The boys picked up the wounded, laid one of them on the floor of the cab widthwise, the other on the seat with his head on the driver's lap. While the fourth boy stayed with the Peugeot, the truck made the return trip, arriving at the hospital about 3 in the afternoon with the wounded. Three of the four are Christians, the one that is not was the one most seriously wounded—fractured pelvis and concussion. The other wounded boy had large leg and head lacerations.

Trips to retrieve what was salvable from an otherwise "totaled" car, trips to Madaoua to see police and make phone calls to Niamey, arrangements made in Niamey for a plane pick-up here and an evacuation out of Niamey all followed successively, while here the wounded were hospitalized. Next morning our SIM plane arrived, the boys were removed, one on a stretcher, the other, able to sit up. As we watched the plane speed down the airstrip, get airborne, fold its wheels into the body of the plane, circle and head west, how thankful we were that the airstrip was available.

March 1975 The hot season suddenly descended upon us and along with it came meningitis. By the end of the season, we had treated more than 250 cases. Many died. Those who came early were treatable, the rest had no chance. All of us, including workers at the hospital and those who came from town, took prophylactic sulfa drugs. Towns all around us were severely hit this year. The first rain usually ends the epidemic.

"Dad and Dr. Lyons went to the doctors' meeting in Jos this week. Dad saw Pam two nights. The first night she wasn't feeling good—boils on her legs which caused her to vomit. The next night they went to the Hillcrest play—The King and I—and Dad said it was excellent.

"Last week-end, Candy Lyons and her baby and I attended the Zumuntar Mata (Women's Fellowship) conference in Maradi. In previous years, our women have gone down to Nigeria to participate in their conference, but this year Niger decided to go it alone. There were over 200 women from Niger present (plus 200 babies on backs and another 50-100 toddlers). It was quite a noisy time and consequently hard to hear the speakers, who were also Niger women, but the fellowship was good. I drove our truck and we took 10 women from here. Twenty seven villages were represented."

The story of Awana at Galmi. As I walked through the paths in the village, little kids would follow after me, vying for position to hold my books or hold my hands. One day I asked them if they would like to come to our compound and play soccer, and afterward, I would tell them a story. They came. We set up some goal posts and I brought out our soccer ball, and they had a good time. We built a little shelter nearby and after the game, they sat down on the ground and listened while I told them a Bible story. This was the beginning of the Awana program. I translated into Hausa portions of the Awana books, adapting them to an agricultural theme rather than to an Indian or pioneer theme. There were 80 Bible memory verses in the first book. We built a youth building, brought out supplies from the States, painted a proper Awana circle on the floor and had an authentic Awana program going. Each week, we reached out to from 20 to 100 boys and girls, separate clubs, and many of them made professions of faith. There was a great deal of opposition from the Moslem parents of these kids, but the kids somehow managed to slip away from their homes long enough to come to the meetings.

Local boys had a hobby of making toys out of corn stalks after the harvest. We capitalized on that, and a tradition was born. Each year we challenged the boys to make a model of a truck, car or bus out of cornstalks. Then we had a panel of judges (missionaries) choose the winners, based on originality, design and workmanship. The contest in 1975 occurred just about the time the airstrip was opened, so it was logical that the project would be to make an airplane out of cornstalks and the prize was to be something related to it. We asked the pilot, Bob Forward, if it would be all right if the winners could sit in the plane while he showed them some mechanics of it. Bob agreed, the contest was held, and next time the plane came to Galmi, two boys had the privilege of sitting in the plane while all the other fellows wished they could. They also had their pictures taken with Bob.

These same kids became the nucleus of Vacation Bible School during the summers and the establishment of Sunday School. In one of the VBS's we had a contest, "Going to the Moon". It was the year of the first landing on the moon.

It was time for a contest to stimulate attendance in Sunday School as well as punctuality. How should we go about it? What was the prize to be? For a long while, I had had in the back of my mind what I thought would be a super prize for the winners—a real, honest-to-goodness airplane ride. I talked it over with the Sunday School teachers, both missionaries and Africans alike, and they liked the idea if it could be arranged. Next time Bob Forward put down at Galmi, I approached him on the subject, and he agreed, so the prize was promised. Next, the contest.

(Following are excerpts taken from a letter I wrote to Christine Ferrier, from Canada, SIM, who wrote asking about our Sunday School contest for inclusion in one of SIM's publications.)

We made a large contest board with pictures of our SIM planes and four different towns—Galmi, Tahaoua, Maradi, and Zinder. We decided to "take a trip". We started at Galmi, "flew" to Tahaoua, then to Maradi, then Zinder, and then finally, non-stop back to Galmi. Every pupil would get 5 points each Sunday for attendance, and 5 points for being on time, which meant before the first song was finished, a possible ten points a Sunday. It would take 30 points to get to Tahaoua, 30 to Maradi, 30 to Zinder and 30 to return to Galmi. It was possible, with perfect attendance and punctuality, to accumulate 120 points before the contest was over and those would be the winners. In order to keep interest alive, if a person missed one Sunday or was late one Sunday, we gave prizes when the child reached each place, regardless of how long it took him. Tahaoua is known for its dates, so the Bob Smiths from Tahaoua co-operated by contributing about 50 lbs. of dates. When the pupil accumulated 30 points, he was given two handfuls of dates. When the kids reached Maradi we "sent them to the market", while "the plane was refueling." (Use your imagination.) They "bought" two small packets of biscuits (cookies).

Then off to Zinder. Zinder is know for its leather, so we purchased small leather purses, which were the prizes for reaching Zinder and having 90 points. Whereas 51 kids got the dates, the field was down to 19 who "reached" Zinder in 9 weeks and were still eligible to be grand prize winners. Three weeks to go and we faced a dilemma. There were only four prizes—four seats in the plane, and 19 kids still eligible. We "left" Zinder for the return non-stop flight back to Galmi. On the 11th week, there were still 7 who had a perfect score. The final Sunday came, and three of the seven were either absent or late, disqualifying them, and there were just four winners. They were Amu Hamadin, Ibrahim Alhassen, Ian Hamidin (not related to Amu) and Azizi Haruna.

In the meantime, Bob Forward had come down with hepatitis and was sent home, so we wondered whether the whole contest and all the build-up was for naught. But Jim Rendell was more than willing to give the winners their ride. So amidst the crowd of people that always gathers when the plane arrives, these four winners were ushered into the plane, their seat belts fastened, and were whisked away for a 5 minute ride over the area. They returned to the cheers and envy of all the rest of the kids and towns people. They were a little dazed, bewildered, and happy to be back on terra firma after being somewhat apprehensive about the flight but happy to have had the ride.

Don't get the idea that the whole Sunday School period was taken up with the contest. At the most, it took 10 minutes out of each Sunday morning's opening session to award the lesser prizes. A total of 102 children and teen-agers were registered which meant they had come at least once during the twelve weeks. Fifty one reached Tahaoua; 33 reached Maradi and 19 reached Zinder.

April, 1975 Whatever happened to these four winners?

AMU, aka AMUKA. Amu was about 12. She started coming to Awana, then did odd jobs for Gen Kooy. Gen encouraged her to come to our reading and writing classes in the afternoon, and she caught on quickly. During one of these sessions, I asked her if she were a Christian. She said, "No." Then I said, "Would you like to receive Christ now?" She said, "No, not yet." She continued faithfully in her work, in Awana and Sunday School, learning more verses and earning more parts to her Awana uniform. She was the first girl to learn the required number of verses together with questions and answers relating to various Bible truths. Several months later, during a reading lesson, the time seemed right to ask her if she were ready to accept the

Lord, and this time she said, "Yes", without any hesitation. We prayed together. Like all little girls who come from Moslem homes, she was promised in marriage at a very early age. Two weeks after her airplane ride, she was taken away to a village about 5 miles from Galmi for her wedding to a Moslem man about 10 years her senior. She went with a good knowledge of reading, a Hausa Bible and song book and other literature. Periodically she made her way back to Galmi for a visit. She said she was not hindered from reading her Bible, and whereas she would rather be back at Galmi, she is not unhappy. The marriage seems to be more a convenience for her mother-in-law who has more help with the household chores. The husband has gone off hundreds of miles to look for work until next rainy season. This is customary for the young men who would be doing nothing for 8 months of the year during the dry season. (The rest of the story of Amuka is found in Part V—Chapter 2—Back to Niger)

Ibrahim Alhassen—Ibrahim's father (Alhassen) was a long term out-patient asthma case. When he first arrived for treatment several years ago, he realized being near the hospital was his only hope for life, so between asthma attacks, he built his hut across the road and moved his family there. When Don and Phyllis Chapple were with us, they sort of "adopted" Ibrahim, who did work for them. Phyllis taught him to read and write, and he caught on rapidly and made great progress. The Chappels wanted to sponsor him at Tsibiri school, but his parents, strong Moslems, refused to let him go. Ibrahim became active in Awana and attended Sunday School and reading classes regularly. For the first six months, he would never say that he "believed." Family and peer pressure were too great. I don't know when the turning point came in his life, but sometime during the last 6 months of Chappels' year at Galmi, his attitude changed, he identified himself with the Christian kids, and if we asked him if he were saved, he answered in the affirmative. (There's more about him in Part V—Chapter 2—Back to Niger.)

Ian Hamidin—he was a boy from town who attended Awana but was not outstanding in his efforts until the S. S. contest began. Then he had a perfect record. He says he is a believer, but I do not know when he received Christ. I am aware that sometimes the kids will give me an affirmative answer to please me, but if challenged in the village, they will deny it.

Azizi Haruna—aka "little Azizi Haruna", about 8 or 9 years of age. His older sister was a tuberculosis of the spine case. She came to the hospital unable to walk and after six months' treatment was well and walking, although stiffly. The mother came along to nurse her and brought Azizi and his other sister, just older than he. During the course of their stay at the hospital, both the patient and mother came to know the Lord. The younger sister and Azizi became active in Awana and S.S. and both accepted the Lord. Azizi was ready and jumped at the opportunity the day I asked him if he wanted to pray and ask the Lord to come into his heart. Azizi did not take to reading and writing. I think he spent 6 months on the first reading lesson, and we finally gave up on him. But he is a charmer and a winsome fellow, and maybe when he gets a little older, he will be more inclined toward books.

You will notice that two of the four kids involved are results of the hospital's presence. Two are originally town kids. Coupled with the hospital ministry has been the evangelistic thrust that has made the work at Galmi unique through the years.

Word from home was that Sue was going to Israel for a summer course, and that she was hoping to extend the trip to visit us. She was also chosen to be the Director's Assistant in the girls' dorm for her Senior year. John was back in school—and doing well, getting an A in Physics, of all things, and B's in the rest of his subjects. Congratulations to both.

"We just heard over the radio that Chad has had a coup. The President is dead, and the military has taken over."

Holiday was beckoning and about mid-April, 1975, we were off to Miango. Since Pam was at Hillcrest, twenty some miles from us, we saw her only on week-ends. What a relief it was to get away from the heat and the pressures of the work and replace them with fellowship of other missionaries, cool weather, colorful flowers, trees and shrubs, tennis, plenty of mangoes and citrus and good food, and not having to prepare it and no after-meal clean-up. A different world. "It sure is different not having any kids at K.A."

From Burt—"We took a weekend trip to Yankari Game Reserve and (on an early morning safari) saw most of the animals on the animal stamps. Most interesting sight: a 6 inch thick python swallowing a half grown crocodile. The crocodile was dead as it probably had been previously crushed by the python. When the wardens saw it, they started beating the python (very unorthodox for game wardens), but most Africans go berserk to kill any wild meat they see. I insisted they stop, but when the python spit out the crocodile, we all took off at top speed (to the truck). Nobody wanted to be hugged by that one! That would be too much affection displayed in public. We saw monkeys, eagles, water buffalo, bush buck, hartebeest, water buck, crowned hornbills, warthogs and baboons. The morning trek before us had been charged by the bull elephants, but we never saw them—too spooked by the experience.

"The game reserve is a big valley with rivers and dense forest, rising uplands with grass, and a well developed chalet system for guests. We had a bungalow with all facilities, including kitchen, and used the restaurant. Many go to relax and play, not to see game, and most of the guests now are the upper class Africans."

May 17, 1975—A bolt out of the blue! Transferred to Jos! Our holiday at Miango was coming to an end and we were beginning to think about getting back to Galmi. We had one year to go before our furlough. The Mission had been undergoing some changes in management, and instead of each of our Francophone countries being a law unto itself, the Mission decided that all of Francophone was to be under one head, and Howard Dowdell was appointed Director of Francophone. We weren't too happy with the "hierarchy" and their remote control of the hospital from Niamey. Burt objected to this, and told Howard that the hospital couldn't possibly be run from behind a desk in Niamey some 300 miles away and furthermore, apparently Niamey was unconcerned about trying to find another doctor to relieve the work load and pressure. Howard didn't take kindly to that so he called for a Francophone Council meeting in our absence and without our knowledge. Thus, it came as a shock during our last week at Miango when Charlie Frame visited us from Jos headquarters with the news that the Francophone Council had met, and we had been transferred to Jos. The Council stripped Burt of his authority and decision making prerogatives in the hospital, and we were told to go home and pack up. At first they said we should go back to the States and return to Jos after our year's furlough, but we chose to spend the year in Jos and go home for our regularly scheduled furlough.

A year before we had toyed with the idea of working in Jos, so that we could be with Pam. Since nothing was done about it the previous year, we figured that we would coast along for our last year and then ask for a reassignment before considering a return to Africa. However, the Council decided that the time was now, so we received this news with mixed emotions. We were hurt; yet we looked forward to the move. We hated the thought of leaving the Africans in whom we had invested so much time and love. It is comforting to know that the Galmi staff was up in arms and down in tears at the change and writing letters of protest, but that apparently didn't alter the "law of the Medes and Persians." The Nigerian Council grabbed us up immediately and gladly, and assigned Burt to Evangel Hospital and me to teaching Bible Knowledge classes in town.

"Now that the initial shock is over, we are looking forward to leaving the desert and enjoying "Paradise." We will be living on the Evangel compound in Dr. White's house. It has 3 bedrooms, combined living and dining room, kitchen, utility room and garage, and the gardens around the house are beautiful, and grapefruit and orange trees are laden with fruit. Dad will be working with three other doctors, and according to E.J. Cummins, Medical Director, they aim at a 40 hour week for their medics, and I will be teaching 15 hours a week. It will be like a holiday all year long. Now we are going to go back and start packing up."

Back at Galmi, life went on. There was another doctor there, a Canadian, retired from the Indian army, older than we, who was there during our holiday. He was scheduled for six months; after that, who knows. He was sort of caught in the middle—so many people wanted to see "the old doctor" who was "relieved of his duties" in the hospital. So our days were full with packing what we were to take and getting rid of things we didn't want to take.

During those weeks, Haruna, the 8 year old son of Ibrahim and Lydia drowned in the "gebe" (stream) down below our compound. In the dry season, it was a dry wadi, but in the rainy season, it was a fast flowing stream. Haruna was a sweet little boy, in my Sunday School class, and a fine little Christian. It was a shock to parents and friends, and after the initial grief, the family accepted it quite well.

"In Sunday School this morning Ibrahim said that very Friday morning when the family was having their devotions together,

Haruna's voice could be heard over the rest, and he was always the first one up in the morning and got the others up for devotions. Then Ibrahim added that they didn't realize that morning that it would be "ban kwana"—(good-bye), but that heaven was much closer now. He added that God had given them 8 children and had decided to take back one, whereas God had only one Son and had given Him freely, so how could he begrudge this one's going home."

Also during those final weeks, Ralph Faulkingham stopped by on a return visit to Magariya to follow up on the anthropological work that he and his wife had done years earlier and also to attend a conference in Niamey with USAID on just what Niger's aid needs were. We are not talking about AIDS as we know it. In 1975 AIDS was not an issue, not to say that it didn't exist, but it was still "in the closet."

Sue was going to Israel for a study program that summer and after it was over, she hoped to visit us in Galmi but since our place of residence was changed, hers had to change, too. So Jos, Nigeria was her destination.

Chapter 5

Sue's summer trip to Israel – 1975

As told by Sue

Our summer school trip to Israel started with a strenuous three-week cram session at Wheaton. It was during the excitement and pressure of books to read, atlases to study, reports to write, tests to take, and last minute shopping that I found out the price of a round-trip ticket Rome-Kano-Rome was $807. The news was a shock. I had anticipated $500 to make the extra jaunt, which was all that I had on hand. Coupled with this I sent my passport to New York to get a Nigerian visa, and it was late in returning. Three days before our departure, I shared these two concerns with 51 others in my group. They prayed continuously and seemed to be more concerned than I was. I had committed both to the Lord knowing that if it were His will, He could drop $300 in my mailbox without any problems and also bring that passport back.

Miracles started happening and they kept up all through the summer. The day before I left, I cashed a check of $125 which I had recently received. Lance lent me $100, and a friend gave me $75 to use for my trip home—exactly $300. Three hours before we left campus, my passport with visa arrived by special delivery.

452

So, 52 of us arrived in Tel Aviv airport, eagerly anticipating 4 weeks in Israel, one week in Greece and 4 days in Rome. Those were fascinating, exciting, busy, learning, growing weeks. We studied at the American Institute of Holy Land Studies on Mt. Zion, located just outside the Old City walls. Unless we had field trips, we had classes all morning and were then free to roam around Jerusalem. The city is comprised of several distinct groups, each trying to establish its culture to its fullest in its particular segment of the city.

We had five guest lecturers, each with a different viewpoint—a Palestinian, a Moslem, a traditional Jew, a Zionist, and an Arab. I began to understand how complicated the political scene in Israel really is.

We visited the holy sites in Jerusalem but quickly lost interest in the huge, richly decorated churches or monuments built over them. Far more important than visiting holy sites was traveling over and experiencing the land. Our 5 field trips took us from Jerusalem all across Israel—east to Jericho, Ai, Bethel, southeast to the Dead Sea, Qumran, Ein Gedi, Masada, south to Bethlehem, Hebron, Beersheva, west to the Mediterranean and the Philistine Plain, northwest to Tel Aviv, Caesarea, Haifa and Mt. Carmel, north to Shiloh, Shechem, Samaria, Nazareth, the Jezreel and Armageddon Valleys, northwest to Mt. Hermon, Mt. Tabor, the Golan Heights, the sea of Galilee with Capernaum and Tiberius. Each place made an impression on us; after spending a day in the Judean Wilderness, for example, I appreciated the months of conquest there by the children of Israel and Jesus' 40 days of solitude, thirst, heat, dust, agony. The Galilee area is beautiful. I can see why most of Jesus' ministry was there. One day we had a worship service overlooking the valley called Armageddon (named after the Old Testament fortress of Megiddo) where many, many battles have been fought. The city of Nazareth borders the lush, green valley, and I thought of how many times' Jesus must have stood where we were sitting and ached over future strife in the valley, even though He would shortly die for all men's sins. The whole land held impressions such as these. We came away different from what we were at the start of the summer.

—

In Greece and Rome, we visited the cities of Paul's ministry and the latter early church. Of course, our group became very close as a result of nine weeks together. Through them I realized more than ever before what Christian love in the body of Christ really is.

My ticket troubles started again in Rome. When I heard about the coup in Nigeria, I called Nigeria Airways and found out that flights had been cancelled. (From Rome, only two flights go to Nigeria per week, both by Nigeria Airways.) Because of the coup; I wondered if Mom and Dad had even gotten to Nigeria. Also, we had had no communication, due to the faulty mail service. I didn't know for sure if I should go ahead despite the cost of $800, and I knew I couldn't wait in Rome another whole week. Another phone call assured me that the Kano airport was open again, but that flights were full already. I was thoroughly confused about what to do and prayed that God would give me wisdom. Also, I considered that He might want me back in Wheaton, not Nigeria, for some reason. This was hard to accept. I knew there was a purpose in all of this, though; too many crazy things were happening just at the right minute about that ticket. (I mean, of all the weeks. of all the years, why did Nigeria have a coup the week I needed to get there?) The next time I called, I said I was coming down to the office to buy a ticket and I would stand all night if need be for a stand-by seat. I needed that seat! I've never been so bold before, especially with something as awesome as an airline, but I prayed for courage and walked in.

"I'd like a ticket on tonight's flight, please."
"I'm sorry, there are no seats left."
"Yes, I know, but I called earlier and said . . . ."
"Oh, are you Miss Long? Yes, we have a seat for you!"

I couldn't believe it, but I didn't argue. And, I think he was amused at my gratitude.

I arrived at Kano at 5: 30 am. Because nobody knew I was coming, nobody met me. However, a European man, who had come to meet someone else, offered to drive me to the S.I.M. headquarters. "Mom

—
454

would have a fit, but yes, please," I said. I got a ride to Jos the same day.

So, I'm here, finally, and it's great! It's been fantastic to see how the Lord allowed me to go through so much confusion but was leading me all the way. This summer, for the first time in my life, I faced problems that I had to rely completely on the Lord for—passport, money, ticket. In all three, I did as much as I could and then watched the Lord work miracles. This summer has been beautiful. I am thankful to many friends, my parents and family, and especially the Lord, for making, it so.

SUE LONG

PART V

Chapter 1

July 20, 1975

Dad's birthday, his 57th. Well, here we are in Jos . . . . We finally got away from Galmi on Tuesday morning. Reached Sokoto about 2 p.m., left there at 3, and Ken Platts from Sokoto telephoned to Harvey Stromme that we were on our way. We arrived at Gusau for supper and the night, and Harvey had received the phone call at 5 o'clock, and when we arrived an hour later, he had a beautiful supper spread . . . two meats, two vegetables, salad, mashed potatoes and gravy, pie alamode and cream puffs and coffee! What more could you ask for than that? Well, a bed, and he provided us with those, too. All around us it rained, but we thank the Lord, for He held it off for us. We had our fridge, our stereo and other sensitive things on board and no protection other than tarps. The 5 ton truck had come on Sat. and loaded our stuff and it was here in Jos waiting for us on arrival. So we are settling in.

"Oh, what a contrast! Instead of sand and dirt, there are flowers, trees, grass, fruit trees—it's just beautiful here, and we have a beautiful big lawn. Lots of rain these days, while Galmi is (or was when we left) still waiting for the big planting rain. We are in the home that used to be Dr. E.J. and Marge Cummins. Lots of built in cabinets and cupboards and even an automatic hot water heater that gives us hot and cold running water all the time. It's just like home in America.

"We damaged the drive shaft coming down when a part of the tarp slipped through between the cab and the back and got tangled in it. However, we were able to run on it, and now that the damage is assessed, we need to get a new rubber ring, for it was ruined. We bought a 1970 Cortina yesterday, so we are planning to sell the truck . . . . It's really nice. Bucket seats, four gears, a deluxe model. It cost about $2000.00 but we should get at least that much for the truck.

"We have dined well. Wed. night at the Verbrugges', Thurs. noon at the dentist's, (Pinningers), Thurs. evening at Marilyn Morgan's, Friday evening at Don TerMeers', this noon at Truxtons', tomorrow night at the Charlie Frames'.

"Well, there was a bit of excitement at Galmi before we left. Jim Rendell came in for a landing one afternoon, and when he put on the brakes, he found there were none, so he coasted off the end of the runway and nose-dived into the ditch at about 15 mph. No one was hurt, but one wing and the prop and the nose were damaged. Jim was with a summer worker/pilot/mechanic and Betty Longman. They were all shaken up but we were all thankful that they were not hurt. When Betty got off the plane, her knees buckled under her and she went to the ground. When Jim saw the inevitable, he tried to spin it around at the end of the runway . . . . this evening the men phoned Jos from Malbaza, and the next day another plane came in with Bill Tuck, master-mechanic and they made arrangements to take the plane apart and send it back in the K.A. truck. Sat. morning before they could start to take it apart, the Niger Aeronautics plane flew in from Niamey to inspect the damage—the same plane that inspected our strip originally, so finally about 10 a.m., they were able to take it apart. The K.A. truck arrived on the scene Sunday morning, and Mon. a.m., they loaded the dismantled plane—just the wings, so they had the body and the wings packed into the truck and took off that Monday night."

Yes, we had moved to Jos, Nigeria so it is fitting to mention a few things about that city and country. It is a place we had visited but where we never expected to live.

"August 20, 1975 It is a plateau at 4000' elevation and is considered to be the health resort area of Nigeria. Most of the missions maintain or occupy holiday and rest areas, and many also have hospital facilities here. Way back in 1893 when the SIM pioneers (Kent, Bingham, and Gowans) dedicated themselves to the interior work in West Africa, starting with Nigeria, their health problems prevented them from getting very far. Two died and Bingham went home and directed the work from there. The first SIM doctor and others immediately recognized the value of the plateau as a place to regain health for those who did not need to go home to do so, or who did not die before they got to Jos.

"Evangel Hospital is the present facility of the SIM, both for Africans of all economic levels and for the missionaries of all the missions who wish to use it. Therefore, this hospital has a better level of most facilities and equipment than our other hospitals, and it becomes an important element in treatment of missionaries whenever possible on the field in order to avoid the very high costs of medicine in the home countries . . . ."

It was a month to the day since we arrived in Jos, and we were well settled in. I was enjoying the modern kitchen with lots of cabinets. We still didn't have our work permits so Burt spent his time touring the various SIM dispensaries in the Nigerian "bush". I hope they come soon so that I can begin teaching Bible Knowledge in the schools this Sept.

Sue was with us by this time after having harrowing experiences first in Wheaton, then in Israel and Europe and even in Kano when no one was there to meet her.

Aug. 16, 1975

No one knew when she was coming and she arrived at 5:30 a.m. A kind European gentlemen took pity on her and deposited her at the mission in Kano. She waited on Driedigers' door step until Mrs. got up—about 6:15, and was she ever surprised to see Sue sitting there in a drizzle. Well, from then on, she got a ride down with the Van Gerpens who were leaving for Jos that day. And now she is here, and we are happy to be together. She and Pam are at a party tonight at the Hostel.

"Last night I was very sick during the night with vomiting that lasted about 6 hrs. At 1 a.m., (Dad is away, you know), I asked both girls to fetch Marilyn Morgan. She saw me and gave me some injectible dramamine, then she called Dr. Lonnie Grant, and he gave me a shot of thoroxene (sp.) about 2 a.m. and after that I went to sleep and the bowel relaxed and I didn't vomit after that. I have been weak all day and have slept most of it, but have eaten today and am gaining back my strength. I don't know what I'd have done without the girls, who ventured out into the night twice and who attended to my every need. Dad and I really have some wonderful kids—all of you!

"Sue is disappointed that it is cold and rainy. She had anticipated days at the pool, but when you're sleeping with 3 blankets at night plus sometimes a hot water bottle at the feet, it's not conducive to swimming the next day.

"Pam is enjoying Hillcrest and especially having Sue here to help her with the homework and encourage her along the way. She is riding to school on the Rock Haven school bus, which goes past our house on the way to school."

August and September passed quickly without our receiving our work permits, so Dad made some more trips, one to Kwoi/Kagoro area and one to Keffi. He also flew to Egbe and chaired a seminar for dispensary attendants. I spent my days preparing for the classes, and although I could not teach, I prepared and sent questions for them and graded their papers at home, so I was pretty much tied to the typewriter and mimeograph machine. That was before computers and printers were a way of life. I don't know for sure, but perhaps they didn't even exist—at least the P.C.'s.

Wed., Oct. 1 was Independence Day, so Pam spent the day at the swimming pool with the rest of the hostel kids, came home looking like a red lobster. The long week-end followed and Friday night was hostel night out for the kids who didn't go home for the long weekend. We had 5 kids over for supper and the evening—Debby Forster, Annagret Schalm, Joy Beacham, Norman Hodges and Michael Schalm.

Oct. 5, 1975

We met the house parents of Woyke Hostel a couple of Sunday nights ago and asked them if the house was named after any relation of Frank Woyke, Rollie and Lance's friend. He said it was named after the father, Frank Sr., who has married again.

"It is fantastic the way things grow here. We have been eating lettuce, sweet potatoes, strawberries, oranges, grapefruit, tangerines, papayas and guavas all from the garden and trees on our property. The lettuce is the only thing I planted—the rest we inherited. But we have planted corn, tomatoes and beans, and the beans are now coming ripe and the corn is beginning to tassel. The tomato plants are small but look healthy."

My letter of Oct. 27, 1975 was written from Galmi. Yes, we were back there again. We knew we had to make another trip to take care of final affairs, and since our permanent visas had not come, this was the time to make the trip. Burt cleared out the garage and found things he had "lost" years before. We had a buyer for the '57 Chev who said he would bring the money that day. Don Williams got Burt's BMW fixed up so he could drive it to Jos while I drove the truck. I didn't relish the thought of driving alone even though we would go tandem.

"We arrived here (Galmi) on Wed. night, coming via Sokoto. We had spent the night in Gusau with Harvey Stromme. What a super cook! He put on his usual 6 course meal for us. Harvey teaches Bible Knowledge classes in Gusau and keeps about a dozen school boys on his compound who have been rejected or orphaned by their families. He provides well for them—housing, food, Christian fellowship, and after they have finished school and are on their own, they often come back to visit Harvey who is their "father". He has a very fulfilling life, even though he has never married.

"The Friday after our arrival back at Galmi, the plane came from Jos going to Niamey, and since there was an empty seat on the plane, I took it and got additional 3 month visitors' visas for us. So now we are good for another 3 months in Nigeria—through January, and surely by that time our regular visas will come. If not, we will leave the country again and go back in. I guess this can be done indefinitely.

"Lance, I talked again with Dick Fuller just before we left Jos, and he is looking forward to your coming to K.A to help out.

"Last Thursday one of our missionaries out of Kano (at Gani), Florence Geiger, was changing gas bottles for her stove, and the valve had been turned to open, and when she took off the cap, the tank exploded. Her clothes caught fire. Her cook got the fire out, then commissioned someone to ride 80 miles to Kano on motorcycle (in 2 hrs. over bush roads). Thad Jackson came out with a nurse, they got her to Kano, flew her to Jos. She has burns over 70% of her body, 30% of them 3rd degree. Daily reports over the radio have been encouraging. Today's report said, 'Dr. Verbrugge says that her condition has deteriorated witin the last 24 hours.' Five days later she died. She was just a few months away from retirement. She was alone on the station. Her colleague, Carol Edgar, was on holiday.

"When we get back to Jos, Dad has two big trips ahead of him—one to Egbe area and one to Kano area to visit dispensaries. I will continue to write my lessons and send them even though that is only second best.

"We are taking Alhassen back with us to be our 'boy'. He will do both outside work and inside. All the Africans were happy to see us back at Galmi. Many of them jumped for joy and thought we were back to stay, but their joy was short-lived when we told them it was for about 2 weeks. Gaji's wife (his 3rd one—he divorced two others because he didn't have any children by them) got pregnant and carried the baby to within 3 weeks of full term, then delivered a still-born last week. He was really disappointed. Dad has always felt that the fault was not necessarily his wives' but Gaji's, and the fact that something may have gone wrong with the development of the fetus might add to that theory. However, we hope that is not the case, and that someday Gaji will have an heir. God bless you. We love you and hope there will be mail from you when we get back to Jos."

Our trip back to Jos was a spectacle—a white woman driving a loaded truck and a white man on a motorcycle with a black young man on the back following the truck. No wonder people stared as we passed by. At times Alhassen rode with me; at other times, he rode on the back of the BMW with Burt. For the most part, the roads were passable and mostly paved. But potholes abounded and between Zaria and Pambeguwa they were so bad that Burt decided to ride ahead with me following behind. It was a horrible pot holed, high crown, one lane road with very rough shoulders—shook the whole load and truck to get off and on. So Burt kept his three motorcycle lights on and grandly waved all opposing traffic off the road while I followed down the middle. Only one large truck and one small bus failed to leave the road so we went bush. It was like a v.i.p. motorcade, but I didn't feel very important and was very glad to get off that road and onto the final pavement that took us back to our new home in Jos. The question was, "How long? When would our permanent visas arrive so we could go to work?"

Our two weeks back at Galmi was a painful reminder of the past 25 years of dry, dusty, hot, desert weather. We had seen years of famine and years of plenty. This year's crop was poor, and the people were facing another year of crop failure and starvation. Our hearts went out to them. Saying goodbye again to missionaries and African friends was difficult. We would have stayed with them for our whole missionary career, but our move was not our choice. But having been compelled to move, we accepted the challenge of a new kind of ministry. Along with that came the joys of fresh fruits and vegetables, canteens loaded with merchandise, cooler weather and new friends.

December 6, 1975—Christmas in Jos was quite different from Christmas in Galmi. Celebrations went on with SIM people and with those of other missions, ECWA churches and Hillcrest School. Downtown Jos was alive with Christmas shopping—just like home, but on a smaller scale. On this particular night I was home alone.

"Saturday night—an unusual night for me. I am all alone. Dad went to Kano on Tues. to attend and help conduct a seminar for dispensary assistants for three days. This morning he was planning to leave and to visit some of the dispensaries in the Kano district. I expect he will be back about Wed. or Thurs. of this week. Pam is also out tonight. The Hostel is having its annual Christmas supper and party and the SIM kids who live in town are also invited. That leaves me here by myself, so I have the stereo on and am enjoying the Reader's Digest album of Christmas records.

"I have attempted to get a fire going 3 times now, but it's gone out each time. However, it is still smoking, so I'll give it another blow. The trees in this yard have been shedding their leaves, and as they dry we are burning them in our fire place. Also, about two months ago, one of the big eucalyptus trees in the yard was responsible for a break in the water line. A root had split it. At the time, the laborers dug down to the pipe and the root and chopped out the root and fixed the pipe. We laid claim to the root which was 12" in diameter and 8 ft. long, and Dad and Alhassen have sawed it into 12" pieces and so with the root, the dry leaves, and sticks on the lawn that keep dropping down, we have a good supply of wood. The supply will increase on Mon, since we are buying a cord of wood from the tree that was taken down last week.

"A crew of Africans came to take it down. All they had were axes and machete like knives (addas) and heavy rope to work with. They started by chopping down some of the limbs, and when they were satisfied with that, they started to chop away at the base of the tree. They had the heavy ropes tied from it to other trees. The trunk of the tree is about 3 ft. in diameter. I began to wonder if they knew what they were doing or whether the tree was going to fall on our house, but they made their cuts—one slightly above the other. Then about six men started to pull on one of the ropes. They keep pulling and pulling, swinging on it like monkeys, shouting and laughing as they were doing it. Then it started to crack and fall and the men scattered like scared rabbits. The tree fell with a mighty thud, and it missed every bush, every tree, every flower. In fact, it landed in the open space just where they planned for it to land, and to say the least, I was surprised. So, with that supply, we will be well supplied for this cold season. (The fire is going nicely now.)"

A tradition at Christmas is singing parts of the Messiah with the Jos Community Choir directed by the Hillcrest School faculty and held at the school's auditorium. This year I was part of the 70 voice choir. We sang the first half of the Messiah—the part about Christ's birth—plus the Hallelujah Chorus. It was thrilling and until you sing in it yourself, you can't fully appreciate it. This was the first of a number of years that I was able to be a part of that chorus. Handel wrote the Messiah in 24 consecutive days "never leaving his room, often forgetting to eat, and at times mingling his tears with the ink on the page." Handel said, "I did think I did see all Heaven before me, and the Great God Himself."

Our first Christmas day in Jos we were invited to Dave and Lyda Rutts' for dinner. Also invited were the Swingles and Lee Buchanan. Lee was taking over the Guest House temporarily until the Thad Jacksons arrived from Kano to take over.

"Last night we went caroling at Evangel Hosp. and the General Hospital in town. We had an Evangel Compound supper and gift exchange last week. Last Friday we had Debby and Paul Haken, Mary Marbaugh, Dianne Cunningham, and Shiela Pritchard in for a meal and evening. We have been busy.

"The high school put on its Christmas concert, the church meetings were oriented to Christmas, the Sunday School had its Christmas program, and there were other mission/church get-togethers of which we were a part.

"First school term is over, and today I finished marking exams for the Bible Classes. We still have no regular visas, so keep on praying that they will come before the end of January. I have certainly found plenty to keep me busy. What with writing the notes for the classes and stenciling and mimeographing them, plus writing Sunday School lessons for the manual, plus serving on the Editing Committee for said S.S. lessons, I don't have any spare time. I also attended a board meeting for the Elfon (Evangelical Literature Fellowship of Nigeria) which puts out the S.S. manuals, plus other literature, yesterday morning. I will also be attending a 3 day conference in Jos from the 12th to the 15th for Bible Knowledge teachers.

"I have been having neck aches for some time, so I saw Dr. Cummins last week. X-rays show a lordosis of the neck spine plus some calcification and deterioration. He has given me some pills to take if it bothers me too much and has me doing a few exercises of the neck each morning. The X-rays also pointed out a node below my goiter, in front of my larynx, which he thought might be a tumor, so he referred me to Dr. Verbrugge, and I saw him yesterday, He thinks it is a node on my already existing goiter, so he put me on two thyroid pills a day for 5 weeks. Then if it hasn't decreased, 'he wants to take a look at it'. He assures me that 'it is a low-risk' operation, and I will only be hospitalized 3 days. He doesn't intend to take out the goiter, just the node—i.e., if the thyroid doesn't shrink."

December 26, 1975 Bad news! Byang Kato drowned last Friday. He was a Kwoi boy who was dedicated by his parents to be a juju priest when he was born. However, he got saved when he was a boy. He went through all the local schools, Bible Schools and Seminary, then went to a Bible school in Canada and finished off his Th.D. at Dallas Theo. Seminary, and finally came back to Nigeria about two years ago. He has held many important positions in world wide Christian organizations, and his latest job was General Sec'y. of the African Evangelical Association of Churches of Africa. (AEAM) This is the evangelical voice against the liberal voice in Africa. He was in Mombasa, Kenya, where he was working. He took a walk down to the river by himself and he apparently slipped off the edge and his foot wedged between the rocks and held him there so he couldn't ascend out of the water. He was alone and his absence wasn't noticed until several hours later and it was the next day that he was found. His death is a tremendous loss to the evangelical arm in Africa. He was 39 years old." Boxing Day is an old British Tradition. Its original intent was to give gifts (boxes) to tradesmen, servants, postmen and public servants. It has become a legal holiday. Pam says it's to give away the gifts you got for Christmas that you don't want. And so it is that the day after Christmas is Boxing Day and a day of vacation for all workers. Of course, Nigeria, as part of the Commonwealth, observes the national holiday. And so did the Jos Christian community.

"We joined them at Hillcrest High School campus for a hamburger fry and picnic supper. We had a soft-ball game, and the side that Dad and I and Pam were on won by one run, 19-18. After supper we had a camp-fire on the tennis court and sang Christmas songs. After we got home, we three were having a game of Rook, when Berenice VerBrugge came over and asked if we wanted to see Dicken's Christmas Carol on T.V. They just bought a T.V. for Christmas. So we went over in time to see the last part of Beverly Hill-Billies and all of Dicken's Christmas Carol. What an experience! Here in Africa, to watch television, coming right out of Jos studios, and believe it or not, no commercials! This living in Jos is fantastic. The Africans love to watch American movies and programs, and their favorite one is 'I Love Lucy.' They only have T.V. from 6 p.m. to midnight or whenever it's done before midnight.

"The pastor of Bishara #1 Church here in Jos, his wife and 6 kids started out on their Christmas vacation to Biliri in their V.W. Bug last Monday when he crashed into a tree on the Bauchi Road just 2 ½ miles out of Jos. His wife was killed, and the pastor and 4 kids were hospitalized. One little one is still in a coma, but two have been discharged. The pastor, Dan Juma, is in much pain with broken hip and other injuries but is expected to make it. The youngest child is a 3 month old baby. Pray for the family.

"Cherry, There is a girl whose first name is MarJo, who is out here with her husband as house-parents for the Hillcrest grammar school, and she said to greet you. I forget what her maiden name was and don't know her married name."

Good news! Just after Christmas we learned that our visas had been approved. So another trip to Galmi was in the works. When

Burt was on his last trip, on the way to Gani (40 miles from Kano), he hit a buried stump in the road and crumpled the frame and tie rod. So the car had been in Kano since then (about 3 weeks) getting repaired. "Hopefully we can pick it up when we go through. At the same time, learned that Lance would be arriving in Kano on Jan.8. We had known that he was coming but didn't know exactly when. We arrived at Galmi on New Year's Eve and sent our passports on to Niamey. It took a week before our passports came back. Then we hurried on to Kano and arrived at the S.I.M. Guest House at 7:30 p.m., just ½ hour before Lance arrived. The next day we returned to Jos. Lance went on to Kent Academy where he was going to lend a hand in doing something for his grammar School Alma Matre.

Pam was back at school. Since we lived next door to the Polo Club and Pam loved horses so much, often she went over there and watched and talked with the owners. As a result they asked Pam to ride their horses whenever she could, because the horses needed exercise and many of the owners didn't have time to exercise them. So Pam spent much of her free time over there riding horses as a "favor to the owners" and was in seventh heaven doing just what she wanted to do. "She turned seventeen this week."

Now that we had our visas, Dad was working full time at the hospital and I was teaching 12 classes of Bible Knowledge a week at a commercial college in town. The first week was a challenge and a joy. It was a mixed bunch—some interested and eager to learn, others, not so. Instead of the students moving from class to class, they stayed in the same room and the teachers moved from classroom to classroom. The Moslems had to stay in the room and some were indifferent to the material and showed their contempt by reading a newspaper or something else. However, though they appeared to be indifferent, a certain amount of Bible knowledge filtered through to them. In my six classes, I had a total of 201 students who met twice a week and twelve of them were Moslems.

So 1975 is wrapped up—an interesting year! And 1976 loomed on the horizon. Only six months would we be in Jos, because in June we were scheduled to fly home on the charter for our furlough.

Chapter 2

JANUARY THROUGH JUNE, 1976

January 28, 1976 We were pretty well settled into our new missionary life in Jos. We continued to marvel at the comfortable weather, and when we heard complaints from others about the heat, we could only shake our heads, and say, "If you only knew." We enjoyed the proximity of Miango where we could take a quick run out on our days off, and we enjoyed the fellowship of the Hillcrest people with missionaries from other missions. Yes, the Southern Baptists, the North American Baptists, the Brethren, the Lutherans, the Christian Reformed, Assemblies of God, as well as SIM'ers joined together with one voice in reaching out to Nigerians with the Gospel and coming together for Hillcrest services. It is a well known fact that the missions programs of the denominations are much more conservative than at home. I don't think we'll all have our own separate corners in heaven. One of my biggest thrills was practicing and singing in the Messiah each Christmas with the Jos town's people sponsored by Hillcrest.

Lance brought out a number of gifts from Fran including some tapes. "Pam was especially appreciative of the 'Happy Birthday' song sung by the ensemble! I woke her up with it the morning of her birthday. She enjoyed that, although it is doubtful if she ever enjoys waking up in the morning, either by song or by word of mouth."

"Dad took a spill on the motorcycle last Sunday. There is a new road in the making on the way to Miango, and he was just about 2 miles out from here on it with Pam on the back, and he plowed into some sand. The cycle did a 'u-turn', but Dad and Pam kept going forward. They slid about 6 ft., Pam landing on top of Dad. She was unhurt except for a bruise on her knee. Dad has a bruised shoulder which is painful and some black and blue marks on his trunk and legs. The motorcycle needs some repairs, too, before it will be road-worthy again.

"I am enjoying my classes at Gwosh College, ('College' meaning 'Secondary School' meaning High School). I have 12 hours of teaching a week—six different classes. Each class meets twice a week, and there are two sections for each grade. So I have to prepare three different lessons twice a week which takes about six hours. So approximately 18 hours are tied up in Bible Knowledge. Repeat—I enjoy it very much.

"We understand Lance is doing very well at K.A. and 'the kids love him!' For two days, he taught Miss Wiebe's (later Edna Robfogle) Math classes until she returned from Canada. I hear he taught some Science classes with Jim Crouch, pertaining to Astronomy. He has done well in leading the Alpha Teen Sunday School group on Sundays, so he is making a good impression."

February 24, 1976 Nigeria had another coup. The Head of State was killed and several other influential people, so a curfew was set and the airports were shut down for ten days. As usual, America and the CIA were blamed for the coup. There was a demonstration in front of the American Embassy in Lagos and they burned the Embassy. There were more demonstrations in Kaduna, Zaria and Ibadan by university students.

My weekly piano teaching classes started at K.A. and I had nine pupils. For the most part, I flew out, leaving Jos by the airport bus at 7:30 a.m. The flight itself from Jos to Miango was five minutes, but the whole process took about an hour. It was a pleasant day; my classes were in the K.A. lounge. We returned to Jos the same way about 2:30.

"Pam and I went swimming at beautiful Hill Station on Saturday. She went in the morning with Bonnie Husband, Velma Neef, Lydia Grant, and I went in the afternoon. The pool is beautiful, water clear, and the pool is set in the hills, and surrounding it are chairs, tables, mats for lying on. It is a lovely country club setting. The all day price—come and go as you wish, is 50 kobo, about 85 cents. By the time we got there, Pam was 'well done', and she is trying to be brave and tell us it doesn't hurt.

"Dad was in Egbe taking Dr. Jackson's place for a week when the coup took place. He was delayed for five days and finally had to drive up with some other folks who were coming to Jos since the airports were closed.

"Lance came in yesterday for two days, and he and Dad just went out the back door to play some tennis. I'll join them as soon as I get supper under control. Pam should be home from school pretty soon."

How different our missionary life here in Jos is compared to Galmi!

March 11, 1976 "Last week-end the Hostel kids went to YanKare. Lance was invited to go along, but Pam was not, since the town kids were not invited. That hit Pam pretty hard, but she has survived. The kids got to know Lance a little bit and found out that he wasn't such an ogre even though he was classified as staff.

"In April he will be taking a trip to Niger, then get another visa into Nigeria and return. The hostel staff has asked him to live there for a month when he comes back. He worked out beautifully at K.A. He got a hair cut two weeks ago, and he looks great. He also has trimmed his beard back.

"The mothers and women staff at Hillcrest have got a soft ball team and are entered in the competition with the high school girls and Jr. highs. Of course, I had to join. We beat the Jr. highers 24-7 and the first of the high school teams 27-9. Our team is red hot. We have five more teams to play.

"Jim Grant, the film maker from Wheaton, is here. He filmed last year in Franco-phone. He titled the film 'What it Takes', and we were supposed to be in it. It is being shown here now. Our voices are in the script but not our faces. The other night Jim explained to us the reason: one speck of sand got into the magazine and ran a streak down the center of 400' of film that he shot at Galmi. Well, I guess that was our last chance to be movie stars, but it's nice to know why."

March 28, 1976 Shortly after Nigerian borders were opened, Niger had another coup, so the borders were shut down again for two weeks. I learned what the African peace dove says—"Coup, coup, coup!"

The term in the African school system closed and exams were held. All Bible Knowledge students from Forms (grades) 1—5 sat together for the exams, but they were all separated to insure no cheating. All questions were essay questions, so it took a long time to grade the papers.

It was about this time that Nigerian Provinces were chopped up into about 50 states. So Benue/Plateau Province became Plateau State, and Benue was divided into two different states.

Furlough was looming on the horizon. Three more months, and we would join others on the June 4 charter and be back at 428 on the 5th. We were counting the days—96 to be exact.

Chapter 3

Furlough
June 1976 through summer of 1977

Well, we made it home all right and furlough was ahead. We were met at the airport by family, brought to our home in Wheaton, and I can't express the feelings that I had as I walked in the front door of 428 Howard St. This was home! This was home to our kids. My heart was filled with gratitude to God and family, and I relished every minute of our homecoming. At the same time, I knew that the days would fly by and in a year we would be saying good bye again. Will it always be this way?

Was this what was meant by "letting go of our kids?" Or was it that the kids were letting go of us so that we could do what we felt was the Lord's will for us? They sacrificed for us as much as we sacrificed for them.

Our furlough year was a time of getting re-acquainted with family and friends, our two home churches, our alma mater, Wheaton College, of speaking at many missionary conferences in the area and beyond. Of special delight was to be home for Sue's graduation with honors from Wheaton College.

The Bethany Bible Church of Phoenix, AZ had its annual missionary conference and we were invited to be there. It was bad timing, though, because Jessica was born on Jan. 15, just days before our departure. I regretted that I didn't let Dad go alone and stay

---

to support Cherry. Hind sight is always 20/20. But he needed my support, too. So we took off for AZ and the West coast with Pam, who was able to take her school assignments with her.

Furloughs have a way of coming to an end—too soon. I never accepted the fact that Galmi or Jos was "my home." Home was where family was, and that meant, for the most part, in Wheaton. Well wishers at home would often say, "I'm sure you can't wait to get back home, meaning Africa." NOT! I remember sitting in church at the North Side Gospel Center with the family, with tears running down my cheeks. The choir music was so beautiful, the piano, the organ, the message, the friends, the family! This was indeed home! So reluctantly, we said goodbye again! This time, to all of our six children.

Rollie—very happy in the medical school program in Springfield, IL
Lance—at Trinity Evangelical Divinity School in Deerfield, IL
Cherry and Chip and Jessica—in the Wheaton area.
John—in his six month internship in biomedical electronics in Springfield, IL.
Sue—Employment coordinator for Scripture Press in Wheaton.
Pam—a Senior at Wheaton North High and will be heading for John Brown University in Arkansas in the Fall.

Chapter 4

September, 1977

Saying good-bye again! Our return to Nigeria on the September charter was uneventful, which is what we like. Delays along the way were frustrating but that was to be expected. Having said our good-byes and boarded the plane at O'Hare we waited and waited and waited. At 2:40 they announced that our plane had tire trouble and off-loaded all the passengers. We hoped that the family would still be there, but only George and Grace Gouzoulous remained. Rollie and Mar were apparently flying somewhere on another plane, so we rushed over to where they were supposed to take off but heard that the plane had already left. We returned to Grace and George and visited with them over a cup of coffee. Rather than fix the tire, they put us on another plane and told us that the departure time would be 3:20. Probably it was just as well that we didn't have to say goodbye again, but at the time, we would have enjoyed seeing you all again."

We flew to New York to meet up with the rest of the SIM'ers who were on the charter. Our trip across the ocean took 8 ½ hours. Our first stop was in Monrovia, Liberia where our ELWA missionaries deplaned. Then another 3½ hours later, we landed in Kano, 6 p.m, Kano time. Imagine the confusion at the Kano airport with a plane full of missionaries with tons of luggage. Besides that, a British Caladonean plane landed at the same time, so there were two plane loads of passengers going through the lines. Well, eventually, we made it and then made our way to the Kano guest house where we spent the night. Then the next afternoon we arrived in Jos, where we spent a few days in the Jos guest house until we could move into the Truxtons' house while they were away for five months. Along with the house came Heidi, their beautiful German Shepherd dog. She makes a beautiful watch dog. Over the months we fell in love with her.

I began teaching Religious Knowledge (Bible) at Narraguta Secondary School, 2 ½ miles north on the Zaria road. I taught Form 1 to five different classes twice a week, a total of ten hours. That left three days free, and one of those days I went out to K.A. to teach piano. There were about 40 students in each class. I continued teaching at Narraguta until we retired in 1984 and kept up with several students after our retirement. Unfortunately, I've lost track of all but one, Jonathan Nwafor. Jonathan and his wife and children live in West Germany and he is in business related to his family's business in Nigeria.

Oct October, 1977

"Today Dad flew to Egbe for a seminar which he is helping to conduct and will be back Friday for the week end, then fly to Mkar again. These flights to Mkar are being done in the C.R.C. plane. My week there was pleasant and I'll probably have another week down there before the month is over.

"Yesterday was the annual Jos S.I.M. picnic. It was over at Hillcrest, and we had a mixed doubles tennis tournament. Dad and I beat our first opponents but then bowed to Verbrugges who went on to win the tournament. Last Sunday we went out to Miango, spent the afternoon with the Husbands. Fawleys are in charge of the rest home. Fullers are in charge of K.A.

"I miss you all very much and wish that all of you could be transported over here, out of the rat-race of America for awhile. Things are a lot less hectic out here. We keep busy, but it's not a frantic busyness.

"We bought a 1974 Opel-Rekord, 1974, 4 door sedan with 30,000 miles on it, so we have wheels now.

"Dr. and Mrs. Hicklin are back, and he is setting up his dental practice at Miango again. Their daughter Sue, got married in August and she and her husband are taking care of the vineyard.

"I have made arrangements with Darlene Reiner, the organist at Hillcrest, to give me lessons on the organ, and I have permission to practice on the organ, so I'm looking forward to that. I will be attending a Management seminar for six days. I have memorized 2 Tim. 2 and 3. I started at Camp and decided to keep on going.

"Mary Haakenson is staying with me (Burt is in Mkar). She is on holiday at Miango, and I brought her back with me on Thursday, and she will go back tomorrow if she can get a ride, otherwise, on Tues. in the Miango car. She says I learned my management course well—I have managed to get her to make two batches of cookies and a pan of brownies so far!"

November, 1977

"Last night we presented The Messiah. It was beautiful, and it was thrilling to me to be one of the 93 chorus members. Mr. Korhorn was the director, Glenn Verbrugge and Darlene Reiner shared the organ while Jim McDowell and Miss Braun (new at Hillcrest) shared the piano. I'm sorry it's over. Even the practices were thrilling. After Christmas we are planning to begin practicing Brahm's *Requiem* for Easter."

When Burt got back from Mkar, he signed a contract with the government but stayed in S.I.M. After 18 months, we would be eligible for a 3 month leave since we get five days for every month served. That will bring us to the summer of 1979.

Living and working in Jos was almost like having a holiday all year long. Fun things went on all the time. Next was a men's doubles tennis tournament at Hillcrest. Dad played with a Hungarian radiologist, who was working at Evangel; Don Ter Meer and Glen Verbrugge played together; Ken Kastner and Wally Braband played together. Jim Crouch and Art Redekop played, but not together. (That was 27 years ago, and they have all aged along with us.)

Following that, we enjoyed the play, "The Mad Woman of Chaillot." It was the Sr. class play. It turned out that the woman was not as mad as she was thought to be; rather, she was the cleverest one of all. Debby Tuck was the "mad woman."

We had a compound Thanksgiving dinner with the TerMeers, Penny Pinneo, Jean Bacon and Dad and me. Verbrugges were with their C.R.C. people.

"I gave a Bible exam last week. I thought I had 275 students, but a total of 352 took the test. The marks ranged from 0-97. About a third of the students made from 70-100; another third made from 40-70; and a third failed. A grade of forty is passing. Some of them are Moslem and don't give a hang. Others have problems with English, having had just Primary School education in English.

December 11, 1977

"Two weeks before Christmas! This afternoon we will be going out to Miango to hear K.A.'s Christmas program. Linda Glerum is in charge. She is doing a good job in the music dept. at K.A. We have picked 150 tangerines to take out to K.A. today, so that each kid can have a tangerine in his stocking for 'stocking night.'

"On Christmas day, we plan to go to Miango and have dinner with the Husbands. Hillcrest had their grammar and middle school program on Thursday night, and it was very good. Friday night we went to the high school choir and band concert, which was also very good. It was conducted by Miss Janet Flory. The Couleys have left Nigeria for good, I think. Mr. Korhorn, incidentally, led the Messiah this year and last. The McDowells are leaving for a year's furlough, and the Coks are due back after Christmas.

"Since we are only temporarily in the Truxtons' house, we haven't opened all our drums, so I don't have any Christmas decorations up yet. Hopefully I will be able to find some in the next few days. It will be lonesome without you kids. My school is out now for 5 weeks, so I have a little breather. Two mornings next week I promised the Christian Ed. Dept. to help edit some Sunday School lessons. I am also on the committee to write some Jr. lessons for S.S. books."

December 15, 1977

"This a.m. I've been busy in the kitchen; have bread rising; peeled half a squash, (Dad had cut it up into little pieces last night), cooked it, put it through a sieve and have almost 15 cups of squash ready for pies. I have put 12 cups into the freezer in 4 cup containers, so have them divided into enough for two pies at a baking.

"This is the cold season and I live with cold hands and feet. Temperature gets down to 50 degrees at night, warms up outside during the day, but doesn't seem to penetrate into this house at all. Too many trees around it. Remind Pat that she said she was going to write us a letter some day. She said that years ago. You all have a Merry Christmas and blessed New Year."

December 30, 1977

"I feel a little sad writing the date. 1977 will be over and gone in a few hours and never be around anymore. It seems as if it just arrived, and now it is leaving. It is like saying goodbye to a friend.

"We have had an enjoyable Christmas season, but I am glad it is almost over. It will be good to get back into the rut. I think man was made to live in a rut, with an occasional break from the routine to appreciate how secure a rut is.

"We have been enjoying Christmas music on tape and records all through the holidays. On Christmas Eve, a group of missionaries gathered in the Teachouts' back yard. We sang carols around a bonfire and had a snack later. On Sunday we left for the Husbands. Got to Miango in time for church, then spent the day with Wilf and Esther and Bonnie and Pauline. Olwyn Kyte and Jim Crouch were also there. Linda Glerum was spending the week with the Winston Adams in Roni.

"On Boxing Day, we went to the Greers for another Christmas dinner at 4 p.m. They are now in Bukuru. Victor Musa and his wife and 3 children were there along with Naomi Sawa and 2 of her children. (Naomi is Col. Sawa's wife, who gave up his army career to be active in the Nigerian Bible Society.)

"Tomorrow, New Year's Eve, the Husbands are coming here in the afternoon for some tennis and supper. Then we go over to the conference center for games, fellowship, a film, and communion service. Sunday, Jan. 1, we will be going back to Miango, this time to have dinner with the Brabands.

"The weather has been terribly cold. It is one of the coldest cold seasons in years. Down to 50's, and with no heat it makes for an uncomfortable situation. The polo games are going in full swing over at the field, Pam."

Today, 2004, as I write this, our co-workers have become our co-retirees. The Husbands live in Canada, the Brabands are here with us in Sebring, as are Mary Ellen Adams, TerMeers and Kastners. Jim Crouch married Linda Glerum and they are working at Kent Academy.

In 2011, as I edit this, Wally and Vi Braband, Ken Kastner, and Jim Crouch are with the Lord.

Truxtons are still in Jos. Verbrugges are still at work in Cadillac, MI.

Chapter 5

1978

January 16, 1978

Pam's birthday! It was good to get back into the routine of teaching and medicine. I taught two days a week—five classes with a total of 352 kids. Thursday I went out to K.A. to teach piano. Dad was at the hospital every day!

Dr. and Mrs. John Elsen from Evanston visited the Cummins. He is the doctor who took out Rollie's tonsils. They attend Moody Church as do the Cummins, and they are good friends. They have a big house and a big reputation of taking in anyone who needs a place to stay. This is in addition to their own nine kids. They had spent a few weeks in Kenya, and stopped off to see the Cummins. We got in on a supper with them on Thurs. night at the Cummins' house.

We entertained Harvey Stromme, our long term friend who was stationed at Gusau and was a gourmet cook and always had a good meal waiting for us when we traveled south from Sokoto, usually topped off with lemon cream pie. When we were back at Jos two years ago SIM had an official retirement get-together for him, but we hear he is back at Miango cooking for the rest home. (2004).

Organ lessons are progressing, and I am learning to coordinate feet and hands at the same time. I sometimes wonder if my brain will be able to sort it all out so that I can read the music, play the hands, play the feet all independently of each other, yet together. My teacher assures me that it will come.

Dad is going to begin to teach a course in English in the Evening Extension Theological School here in the conference center. That course begins tonight."

You may remember Lee Baas who had gone home with a suspected brain tumor. He came back with the diagnosis of "inflammation of the nerve linings due to an unknown virus." He returned to Africa in spite of the severe pain. We don't know what happened to him, whether he is alive or not. He was with CRC mission.

Tony Wilmot, preacher at last night's service said, 'There is no victory without the battle, no courage without the danger, no relief without the pain.' Remember, the battle is not yours, but the Lord's. We pray for you always.

January 25, 1978

"It's 2:30 p.m., and I've been washing and drying and putting away dishes for the last hour and I'm still not done, but I'm tired of looking at the sink, especially now that the pots and pans are staring me in the face . . . . Our company last night was the Quarrels (Aunt Frieda and Uncle Don to some of you), Lee and Norma Greer and Jean Ter Meer. Don T. is at Kaltungo for a day or two. We had scalloped potatoes with ham baked in them, peas and carrots, tossed salad, sliced bananas with mayonnaise and chopped nuts on top, and coffee and Baked Alaska, plus brown bread and date and nut bread. I have never made a Baked Alaska before, but I have seen them and heard about them, so I decided to try, and it was a smashing success. Well, company didn't leave until 10 p.m., so I left the dishes until today. Since I had classes this morning, the dishes were still waiting for me when I got home.

Letters from the kids—John: "We praise the Lord that you were not hurt when wrestling with the would-be robbers." Rollie: "Sorry about your busted water pump. Graduation is almost here. Cherry: "We are so thankful that Jessica didn't smother in her blanket." Reminds me of the time that Rollie (6 months old) got lost in the bottom of the sleeping bag when we were at Victory Camp in Alaska. I just decided to come up from the meeting to check on him (a God nudge) and heard these muffled cries coming from the bag. You can imagine my haste in opening it up and my trembling that followed.

February 19, 1978

"Sunday. A lazy day. Had dinner with Henry and Margaret Martin, houseparents at Girls' Baptist hostel today. Pam probably knows them and their triplets—2 girls and a boy. Also there for dinner—Larry Davis and his wife and two little girls. He continues to teach at the Baptist School. After dinner another Baptist couple came down from Kano and brought Margaret Hayes with them. She is going back to Galmi as a regular SIM missionary this time for two years. Last time she was at Galmi she was on loan from U.F.M. Margaret was the one who was captured by the Simbas during the Congo uprising and held captive for six months until she was rescued by the Belgian mercenaries. Tonight after church, we are invited to have coffee with the Langs over on Woyke compound.

"Another accident week! Two motorcycles down on our road; one 20 ton trailer truck scraped a tree on the road between the Bank and Hill Station on Wed. evening, and turned over. On our way to prayer meeting we saw it (no lights were posted of course) and went bush around it; the Wilmot boy saw it, but hit an oil slick made by the truck and skidded into it; another truck going in the opposite direction saw it, and in trying to avoid it, lost control and went bush and turned over. Thursday a.m., a truck going toward Zaria on the Zaria road just beyond the bridge by the hospital corner, lost control, went off the road and pinned a school boy walking to school, killing him. And so it goes. Those are just the ones we see or hear about. Nigeria, the country with the highest accident rate in the world!

"This week we move into the house that Dr. and Mrs. Grant lived in. The Truxtons are back and are staying in the TerMeers' house for a few days until our house is ready. Africans were in it and the house will be "smoked" out with Gammexene Monday night, and ECWA is to start painting on Tuesday. Hopefully we will begin to move our things out on Tues. evening so the Truxtons can get back into their own house. It is a good feeling to get into our own place again and be able to open up our drums and get back to using our own stuff. Even though the place is a mess now with our things scattered all around, the ceiling, walls and floor are shiny. In a couple of weeks I should be straightened around and get curtains up, etc.

"The weather here is absolutely beautiful. Warm Spring days with gentle breeze. Flowers blooming, trees budding."

March 19, 1978

"Charlie and Betty Frame went home two weeks ago. Charlie had developed a loss of peripheral vision, and brain scans have revealed two masses in the brain. They are doing further tests. Apparently they think the masses are metastases from a primary cancer elsewhere. (Charlie died within the year.)

"Another earth-shaking event this past week was the arrest of Mr. Kutse, father of Ann and Yacoubou and husband of Lillian. His crime is that he is South African, and they are unwelcome in this country. He and his wife were visiting in Jos last week and the Jos police picked him up and have whisked him somewhere, no one knows where, so his wife and two children are in the dark about his whereabouts and naturally very upset. Pray for them as well as for the Frames. (He was subsequently released and expelled from the country.)

"This is exam time and tomorrow I give my Bible exam for end of second term to almost 400 kids. Then I will have 400 papers to mark. If each paper takes me 2 minutes to grade, that will be 13½ hours.

"The women of Jos and Miango had a bridal shower on Linda Glerum who is marrying Jim Crouch, and the wedding comes up on April 2. The Sr. Glerums are arriving this coming week. Friday night was a musical night at Hillcrest featuring classical music. The best number in my judgment was by Mrs. Ruth Gibbs on her violin. She played two numbers plus two encores. Other numbers included a cello, harpsichord, a Bach number on the organ, some flute numbers, the Madrigal singers. Some of the flute numbers were amusing in that two of the flute players began at the beginning and the other two began at the end of the musical score and played the piece, coming together for a brief instant in the middle. The evening was very educational and entertaining. Wilf Shore was in charge of putting it all together.

"This noon we had smorgasbord at the Plateau Hotel with the TerMeers and the new radio-airplane engineer and wife and baby. It was a delicious dinner, and we stuffed ourselves with ham, beef, chicken, rice, salad greens, deviled eggs, jello, desserts and coffee. It is almost two years ago that Lance and Pam took us to Hilltop for a supper in honor of our anniversary. It will be 33 years for us soon. (It's now 66—2011)

"I guess you know that Lasca has moved into the retirement home on Foster Ave. that used to be the Admiral Hotel. She likes it very much, and has nice accommodations."

(It was at this same hotel that years ago—when I was an early teen-ager, that our extended family—aunts and uncles, cousins—gathered here for Thanksgiving dinner, when it was a hotel. It was very exclusive and fancy.)

April 23, 1978—Sunday. Raining

"We are excited about Sue's coming out soon on the charter—in just a few short weeks now. Jim Kastner arrived a week ago with a report of his trip to the East Coast with Sue and her friend . . . . Harold Fuller has been out for the month of April—he is still Director for West Africa, although he spends most of his time at home now. Anyway, he was here for dinner along with the Porters. We had chicken, mashed potatoes, scalloped green beans, cole slaw, mango sauce, pickles, carrot sticks, mango upside down cake and coffee and rolls. It took me an hour and a half to do the dishes.

"The Center sent us a tape, and Sue, we were glad to hear your voice on it. Besides the greetings, Joe Hertel adds music, anecdotes, poetry, etc. Here is a little verse which I picked off that tape, because I thought it was so profound, apropos, yet simple. I like it. Here it is.

'Is it raining, little flower? Be glad of rain.
Too much sun would wither thee, T'will shine again.
The clouds are very black 'tis true,
But just behind them shines the blue.

'Art thou weary, tender heart? Be glad of pain.
In sorrow sweetest virtues grow, As flowers in the rain.
God watches and thou wilt have sun
When clouds their perfect work have done.'"

Fredrick W. Faber

Dad finished up this letter telling about the vegetables we were trying to raise in our own little garden. Then, too, there were also grapefruit, tangerines and oranges for the picking. Being the hot season in Niger brought some of our former colleagues down on holiday which was nice. At this time, Evangel Hospital had been taken over by the government, for a price, so in essence, Dad was working for the government and getting paid by the government. The name of the hospital was changed to Jan Kwano, i.e., Red Roof.

May 14, 1978

Mr. and Mrs. Eickenberry of CBM were honored at the church for their role in the Northern Education Advisory Council of Nigeria. They came to Nigeria in 1946 and over the next 20 years, over 50 Protestant primary schools and numerous secondary, teacher training, Bible and Seminary schools were created. The Eickenberrys were moving to a station near the Cameroun border. They were given 2 sacalas (blankets) and 3 leather foot stools.

We had our week-end at the hostel, and it was more or less just a baby sit since the house-parents had prepared everything before hand. I decided though that I wasn't really cut out for that kind of job and my hat's off to house-parents who had such an influence on our children.

K.A. had a recital Friday night which was excellent and we were invited to the tea afterward. It turned out to be in honor of the music teachers, especially those who came out from Jos each week, which included Ruth Jacobson, Marge Cummins, Jean Teachout and myself. We were given corsages.

Changes in staff for the coming year were: Fullers going on furlough; Brabands taking their place as principal and manager; Jean Campbell, principal, Art and Alice Warkentin moving into the boys' dorm; Husbands stay on as house parents for the girls. Brabands and Hicklins were over for supper. Bonnie Husband goes home and will be going to Briarcrest in Canada. Days have left. Jean has been depressed since her hysterectomy. All Jean Hodges' kids will be coming out this summer for 3 weeks. Sharon Rutt and Becky Tuck were visiting.

—

May 30, 1978

"A week ago Sunday night we did Brahms' *Requiem*. We had practiced so long for it, and the last three weeks we were practicing two evenings a week, that it was a relief to have it finished. But it was GOOD. BEAUTIFUL! Thrilling to give! When we first heard that we were going to do it, we wondered why a requiem. Didn't that have to do with a Roman Catholic Mass for the dead? Well, Brahms' Requiem is, in reality, a sacred cantata, originally in German instead of Latin. In place of the liturgical text, which is used in the mass for the dead, and is in Latin, Brahms used passages from the Scripture in illustration of the joys of the blessed and the glories of the life to come. 'In the liturgical text of the works of other composers, the primary subject is the day of wrath, the last judgment, which threatens the departed with purgatory and the agony of hell, and is only transformed to a day of blessing and happiness through the intercession of the saints and the earnest and humble prayers of those who are left behind. Johannes Brahms, a devout Christian, professes a gentler faith in a joyful resurrection and reunion through the atoning death of Christ.'

"I made mango sauce yesterday. The trees behind our house are loaded. It's a mixed blessing. Every day there is a mob of people trying to get the mangoes down. They pick them before they are ripe, take one bite out of them and throw them on the ground. We must have a couple hundred rotting mangoes in our backyard, and the smell gets pretty 'high' once in awhile. Rotting mangoes! Of course, there is no fence and no way of keeping the people out.

"Sat. late afternoon and evening, SIM had a picnic out at the rock pile across from the airport, then went to the SIM hangar for supper, games and a movie, 'What's Up, Doc?' It was hilarious. The picnic was in honor of the departing souls (those leaving for furlough).

"Thurs. night the Medical Dept. and their spouses had dinner at the Bight of Benin restaurant in honor of the Spadys, who are leaving for good. We were 19 in all.

"The Pollens have arrived to see Carol graduate. They will go home on the charter and return in Sept. to take up their work at the hostel. We had them and Bill and Esther Rogers and Jim Kastner and Hattie Miller over for snacks after church Sunday night. Tues. night we had Roy and Doreen Hodges over for supper. They are going home for a year.

June, 1978

The charter came and went. Sue was one of the passengers, and arrived in Kano with the plane load. We had planned to go to Kano to pick her up and overnight there, but guest house facilities were overtaxed and every available private house was filled, so we had to sit tight and wait for her to arrive on the SIM bus that was due to arrive in Jos at midnight. It was so good to have her with us again! Dr. and Mrs. Verbrugge and family went on the return charter for a two month furlough, so Burt had to assume the responsibilities of being the only surgeon and the "medical officer in charge".

Winston Adams

Several weeks earlier, Mr Coleman brought Winston into the hospital with ulcer-like pains for which he was treated. He had a tender abdomen, obviously peritonitis, and a 24,000 white blood count. So Dad and Dr. Cummins opened him up at 11:00 p.m. (Verbrugges are on furlough). They found a perforated stomach, so they attached a piece of omentum over the hole and closed him up and sent a biopsy of half of the nodes to Zaria and half to the States. They were almost positive it was cancer and were preparing to send him home. His wife and three children were sent for, and then they returned to Kano to pack up everything. He seemed to be recuperating enough to travel. On Thurs., Dr. Carter was called up from Egbe to be clued in on the case and when he assessed the symptoms and heard what was done, he agreed with everything that Dad had done. Dr. Carter is a board certified surgeon and probably the highest trained mission medic. Wed. night at prayer meeting a call for O positive blood was made to the missionaries and there was a great response and about 8 units were taken. This was because Winston seemed to be failing. When Dr. Carter arrived on Thurs. aft., they were considering opening him up again, but were waiting for the biopsy report, wondering why it was taking so long to get back. About supper time the report came from Zaria. It was not cancer, but rather a very rare disease, pasteurella pseudo tuberculosis, which attacked the stomach. This was a great relief to everyone, so they decided not to operate again, and he was already being treated with the prescribed medicine, tetracyclene, etc. Friday night about 10:30 Jean Bacon came running over saying Winston was bleeding rapidly, his blood pressure was already down to zero over zero. They started pouring those extra units of blood into him. Sue went to the Guest House to get Dr. Carter, while Dad went to the hospital, and Don TerMeer went out recruiting more blood donors. About midnight everything was set for the operation, this time to remove the stomach. They found another hole in the stomach, about the size of an orange. They worked until 6 a.m., removing all but a small portion of the stomach and connecting him up again. By this time he was more dead than alive and nobody expected him to live. About 9 a.m. Dr. Carter told MaryEllen, Winston's wife, that there was not much hope—that he also had pneumonia besides the insult to his body. But they continued to work on him, breathing for him and giving him i.v.'s and blood. By about 10:30 a.m., he was still living and they removed the respirator and he began breathing on his own, very shallow breaths. By 11 a.m., they were able to return him to his room and were beginning to hope again. In the meantime, everyone was praying. The message to the mission family went out at 7 a.m. over SIM radio to pray. Jos had a 9 a.m. prayer meeting, Kano was to have a 1 p.m. prayer meeting. Those involved with the operation said that only a miracle could save him. Apparently the Lord is working that miracle, because this is Tues. evening, and he is still alive with tubes going into him through the nose and arms and coming out of him elsewhere. His blood pressure is up, the pneumonia is not cleared up but is no worse. He is still in critical condition but there is now hope for him. He is conscious but sleeps much of the time, is alert when he is awake. While we continue to pray, we are rejoicing over his progress. Dr. Carter is still here and is exclusively on Winston's case because Dad has his continuing responsibilities at the hospital, not only as the only surgeon but also as administrator in Verbrugges' absence." For the rest of the mission family, life went on as usual, except for prayer times for Winston. Sue had been with us for about a month and was now booking her flight back to the States, flying KLM—Kano-Amsterdam-Chicago, arriving in Chicago at 3:40 p.m. on flight #611 on Friday, In the meantime she kept busy, visiting friends, speaking at the women's prayer meeting for the day of prayer, working with the young people along with Jim Kastner, and helping me grade papers. With about 365 papers to grade at 3 minutes a paper, we spent a good 20 hours at the task. She also managed a trip to Yan Kari with friends and a trip to Kagoro to attend the Bible School graduation. (One of the teachers at the school was a young man named Terry Hammack.)

We planned to go home for 50 days, beginning Nov. 16, a new experience for us, being home for Thanksgiving and Christmas. Working for the Nigerian government gave us an annual holiday, tickets paid for by the government. That's probably one reason why the arrangement didn't last long. The government asked the SIM/ECWA church to take it back after one or two years.

Here is a paragraph from Dad dated July 1, 1978.

"I'm really feeling tired tonight with another emergency this afternoon. An older case done a week ago went into shock suddenly after falling down while he was walking. We were out for supper tonite—hamburgers at the guest house. The visiting health officials from Benue and Gongola states were here Thurs., so the Hospitals Management\Board threw a supper for them at Hill Station Hotel Restaurant, and I took Ruth (She was the only woman there, but it's very African to leave wives at home; it wasn't really a stag as such.) We had two suppers that evening because we went to Porters first by a previous invite. Had roast beef one place, chicken, the other."

July, 1978

"A sequel to the Winston Adams case, but not the final sequel, is that his kidneys began to fail, and yesterday, he and his wife and one of our nurses flew to London for him to be put on a dialysis machine. Dr. Carter says that this is a reversible thing and several weeks on the machine to get rid of the accumulative wastes that he has not been able to discard since his operation, should enable his kidneys to function on their own again. So he was transported by stretcher in our small plane to Kano, where an ambulance was waiting to put him on the British Caledonia flight and within a half hour he was transferred to the big plane. Contact had been made with one of our SIM doctors in London to meet the plane, and we hear that the ambulance was to be waiting for him and that a place in a hospital was already secured."

July 23, 1978

Cast: Sue Long, Donna Reed, Joan Pipher, Cora Zobrist, Ken Hoffman, Floyd French, Jim Kastner, Terry Hammack, Diane Cunningham
Time: Summer of 1978
Place: Jos, Nigeria

This was the group of young people, some short termers, others, full time missionaries, that hung together during the summer. Jim and Sue worked together on a young people's meeting every Sunday evening and other group activities such as volley-ball and a trip to Kagoro and a day at Miango. All of a sudden the Longs and Kastners were having meals together. On July 20, Thursday, Jim and his mother, Elsie, were over for supper and the party that followed for Dad's 60th birthday. (Ken was out of town.) At 8 p.m. the Cummins, the Jacobsons, Redekops, Porters, TerMeers, Penny, Jean Bacon, Cora Zobrist, and a visitor friend of the Porters, Dr. Bragg, came for the birthday party. E.J. Cummins and Jim Jacobson were also 60 that year, so we celebrated their birthdays as well. Both E.J. and Jim are with the Lord as I write this. (2004)

Enter Terry Hammack: He was stationed at Kagoro, just finishing up his first term and leaving for a year's furlough soon. Also stationed at Kagoro were the O'Donovans, Bill and Esther. Bill was Sue's Bible teacher when she was a student at K.A. He told Terry about Sue before Terry even met her. Terry managed to break away from Kagoro the week-end that Sue arrived. His home in Jos was with the Redekops. As I waited in line at the gas station, Terry was parked several cars behind. He came up, introduced himself and asked about Sue. I said, "How do you know Sue?" He replied, "I don't, but I'd like to meet her." "Well then, a group of her friends is coming over after church tomorrow night and you're welcome."

He came and saw what he liked. However, he noticed that Jim and Sue were together quite a bit, so he hung back until he realized it was sort of a "brother-sister" relationship. When they were both at K.A. as Jr. Highers, they were a couple that "stood under the mango tree."

"Terry is out at Miango this week-end. He will be staying with Jim and Linda Crouch, while Cora and Sue are in the Husbands' house for the night. The rest of the gang is returning to Jos tonight. Dad and I and Sue and Cora are invited to eat at the Brabands' tomorrow noon (at Miango), so I wonder whether Terry will be there. (He was!)

We were invited to the Redekops for supper and yes, Terry was there.

The DVBS program went well. The summer short termers helped. There were about 140 kids and 16 staff, both black and white. Next night we ate at the Kastners' house. Mrs. K. invited us and said, 'After supper, Jim wants to take Sue out.' "So maybe Jim is waking up. Maybe he is seeing Terry move in on what he thought was his domain. This is all very interesting, and of course, we like all these dinner invitations. Things will be quite dull after Sue leaves. The Kastners are from Solveg, MN and go to the same church that the Sam Olsons do when they are home."

(When I mentioned this to Elsie Kastner, she said she knew the Olsons quite well. In fact, I believe that a relative of hers had dated Johnny Olson at one time.)

WINSTON ADAMS cont.

"He has been on the kidney machine every other day from 4-6 hours. His heart stopped twice a week ago Monday and he was revived. He has been either in a coma or semi-coma since he arrived in England. His kids have been sent for. X-rays showed that his operation and repair have healed nicely, and they have taken brain scans to see if there is brain damage, but the reports are not in yet. There is still a ray of hope. But God! That was Florence Almen's favorite phrase.

"Today I went to a committee meeting on our Sunday School manuals and the committee was well pleased with the work that Sue

—

and I have done to date on the curriculums and outlines. I am to keep at it for the month of August while I don't have school."

August 7, 1978

We drove Sue to Kano, leaving Jos at 2:30 and arriving at 10 p.m. The delay was caused by two flat tires and one spare, so Burt had to repair 5 patches in the inner tube. It was very nerve-wracking knowing that we had a deadline to meet. It held up very well, and we got there before the midnight take-off. The return trip only took 3 ½ hours.

"Life is a little different now without Sue. The young people that she attracted do not come around—except Terry. He dropped in on Thursday night after supper, having come in from Kagoro that day, and visited. We invited him for supper on Friday since the Verbrugges, who had returned the previous day, were eating with us. He knew it was my birthday the next day, so he brought me a large picture of Sue, framed, and a smaller picture of himself inserted in the corner of the larger one. It's a beautiful picture, Sue, and I presume you will see it and perhaps get one, too."

It was at this time that Terry asked for our blessing in pursuing Sue's hand. We said it was all right with us if it were all right with her. Terry soon left for furlough in the States and transferred to Wheaton College from Columbia Bible College so that he "could get to know Sue better." He accomplished that goal and they were married that December!

Sept. 5, 1978

Last report about Winston Adams is that his kidneys have regained 70% of normal function, but he is still in a semi-coma state. To me this sounds ominous, but no one dares to mention out loud that he may spend the rest of his days in a vegetative state, We all hold on to the hope that the Lord is able to restore him to health and strength."

The charter came in on the next Friday, and it included Cora Zobrist's parents, enroute to Cotonou after a week with Cora. Our entertainment schedule was full—meals for the Hays, TerMeers, Lu

Dyck and her children, the Elliots, Lois Brown, Ruth Shustrum and the Larry Dick family. The Dicks were on their way to Kano to take over the Adams' ministry in the Book Shop.

"We just learned that Winston Adams died last night. He put up a good fight. It was a three month ordeal, and since the report says that there was brain damage, it is better this way. Pray for his wife and three kids."

(That's been 25 years now (in 2004), and the Lord has cared for Mary Ellen and Cynthia and Doug and Brenda all these years. The children are married with families of their own. Mary Ellen lives here in our SIM retirement village with our 135 retirrees and is still active.

October 8, 1978

Sunday noon, and Dad went over to the Bishara church #3 to teach his Men's Fellowship class. There were about 70-100 men in the class which met after the morning service. "Bishara" means "good news."

"Even in Kano with its strong Moslem influence they have about 2000 in 3 morning services in our own ECWA (Evangelical Churches of West Africa) church. ECWA also has a Yoruba church in Kano, and then there are all the other denominational churches which flourish. In Jos alone, there are 13 ECWA churches, plus Baptist, C.R.C., C.M.S., Presby., Pentecostal, not to mention R.C. At the same time, there are villages a few miles outside of the central areas where there is no Gospel witness and some remote villages where the people have never heard of Jesus."

Nov. 3, 1978

Sue's letter of this date contained mostly information on the preparation of their wedding.

"Terry and I have been wondering when we'd hear from you and were surprised that you made no mention of our wedding in your last letter. I am quite concerned that we haven't gotten a response, but then, I know it does take awhile."

"We are looking forward to seeing you in just two weeks.

"Plans are falling into place pretty well, though it's difficult to plan a wedding on my own. Cherry has helped when possible."

Sue and Cherry and Beth Funk did a marvelous job of contacting the principals involved. They contacted Fran Minarik for the reception, Beth Funk and an artist friend from work designed the invitations and Wayne and Helen printed them, no charge. They made arrangements to hold the ceremony in the beautiful Evangel Baptist Church of Wheaton, and contacted Pastors Dick Sisson and Robert Swanson to officiate. The date of the wedding was set for December 23.

A member of the church who worked for the Hinsdale Flower Shop was decorating the church for Christmas so it was not necessary to add to the church decorations. Flowers for the main participants were all that were necessary. A local lady was doing the cake.

The ceremony itself was taking shape. Sharon Minarik was to play the organ. Besides the wedding music, Christmas music was included. Dave Gauger, from the Gauger Family Brass, agreed to play the trumpet for both the processional and recessional. Tuxes for the men were ordered. Sue bought her dress—a beautiful winter white with hood, fitting for a Christmas wedding. Material for the bridesmaids' dresses was purchased—dark green quiara with velvet jackets. Beth was maid-of-honor. Her dress was cranberry red. All were hand-made.

I wish we could have been there to help plan the wedding, but Sue did a wonderful job "on her own", and with the help of others, she and Terry had everything under control when we got there.

The wedding itself was beautiful. Everything came to pass as planned. The music was beautiful, the message was challenging, their vows were spoken from memory, the reception was done in the flawless Minarik fashion. Away they went on their honeymoon to begin a life together that has taken them back to Nigeria and produced two great boys and on that happy note, I will wind up 1978.

Chapter 6

January 29, 1979

We were back in Nigeria. We left Winter in Wheaton the first week in January and had a good trip back. It was good to be back in warmer weather—in fact, gorgeous weather. Our time at home was fantastic! Imagine! Thanksgiving, a wedding, Christmas, family, friends all wrapped up in seven weeks!

We were welcomed back by friends. Just think—friends in the states, different friends in Nigeria, friends all over the world. Those poor missionaries! How deprived they are! And their kids—what a pity! Not!

It was hard to leave Lasca; it was harder for her to say good-bye to us, alone in a sea of people and no family at hand save you kids. We appreciate every visit you make to her home and for taking her in from time to time.

February 11, 1979

"We are busier than ever. I keep seeing reminders of you—the gifts you gave us we are putting to good use. The weather is so nice, many are going swimming, both at Elm House and Hill Station

---

497

pools. Pam, have you got your passport yet? When Dad signed the contract for the following year we noted that it was signed from Nov. 15, 1978 to Nov. 15, 1979, so we may be home for Christmas again

February 25,1979

"Rumors abound that the gov't. wants to hand back the hospital to the mission. Simon Ibrahim has been in consultation with the State Govt. officials. The government hasn't the million and a half naira compensation, so it looks like ECWA will be taking it back, which means we won't be home for Christmas next year.

"I was very much interested in the killing of the U.S. Ambassador to Afghanistan. When they announced his name as Adolph Dubs, I pricked up my ears. I went through Schurz High and graduated with an Adolph Dubs, who was a real nice fellow and v.i.p. on campus. Class of 1938." (It was the same.)

March 17,1979

"Congratulations to Fran and Bill on your 45th anniversary. Is it possible? I thought about you today and your wedding at the Blixs' house and my role as the 'weeping mother.'"

Activities in and around Jos kept us busy in our off-work hours. The Driesbacks spent a a week at Miango. They are no longer with SIM. They are independently working in Niger, north of Niamey. End of term is coming up, after which I have 250 papers to correct. All exams in Nigeria were subjective, not objective, so there is a lot of reading to do. But after that, I have a break until after Easter.

"This Fri. night at K.A is the spring recital. I have six out of my nine pupils playing, so we will be going out. When I think of all the recitals and plays, etc. that we missed when you were kids! ! ! !. And now they are all available to us."

—

April 7, 1979

"Twenty hours a week are spent in dealing with food!! Help! Sue, I had to smile when I read about your meal planning, etc.—at least it's different now that you are married . . . . Enjoy everyone of those hours spent in food preparation and house keeping. The Lord is just as pleased to have you do a good job in the home as He is in your doing a good job in the office, or Terry in the classroom or in the pulpit. This pearl of wisdom goes to all my daughters—the home and home keeping can be a real challenge if done with the proper attitude. It is a time for creativity and expression in shaping your family and home. I didn't always feel this way. I often felt apologetic because people might think I wasn't pulling my weight. Now, people's criticisms don't bother me. It took me quite a few years to work this out, so if you can remember that whatever you do, if you do it to the glory of God, you will have the right attitude about it and be happy in it.

"I played tennis this week with the wife of the U.S. Ambassador to Nigeria and wife of Cultural Affairs minister, both visiting from Lagos. My partner was the wife of a dr. from Ogbomosho. We took the Embassy 3 straight sets. The three ladies were staying at Girls' Bapt. Hostel, and early Tues. morning Henry Martin came over and said they were looking for a fourth. I didn't know who I was playing with until after the 2nd set when we stopped to rest."

April 8, 1979

Last week, the Catholic goats got into my two ft. tall corn crop and ate about half of it. (We are next door to the Catholic school compound.) After two trips over to their place, I think they have tethered their goats. At least, the goats haven't been back."

May 6, 1979

We went to an Indian cultural program. There is quite a large Indian community in Jos, most of whom send their children to Hillcrest. They put on dances, explained their meanings, and showed pictures depicting their culture, and had a travelogue on Kashmir. Very interesting.

We went to the Easter Sunrise Service at the Dam site, then had breakfast at the Steve Gibbs'. Doing some entertaining — Redekops, Pollens, Arabelle Enyart, Barbara Forster, Bernice Balzer, Harvey Ratzlaffs. Lots of rain; less tennis.

June 3, 1979

Pam arrived safely May 17. "It is nice having Pam with us. It adds a third dimension to the family." The last weeks were full with end of term (Hillcrest and K.A.) recitals, plays, graduation. We did the *Requiem* by Brahms — a tremendous experience. An African soloist received word that he had been awarded a scholarship to the Rochester School of Music in Rochester, N.Y. He had had no formal training, but he had a rich and powerful voice, and we were all happy for him.

With the coming of t.v. in Jos and the purchase of one for ourselves, we were able to watch some of the old films. Fortunately, the modern day type of film had not reached Jos. We saw some historical films and classics. We watched *Roots*. We saw the life of Lou Gehrig who died at age 39. "He had a spinal cord disease and progressive paralysis of his muscles." We know it today as "Lou Gehrig's disease."

June 24, 1979

"Well, morning church is over, and we have had coffee with Carol and Lee Baas and family and now Dad is at his Sunday noon Bible class. Last summer Lee went home for tests because of an anesthetic and paralysis condition. Doctors were puzzled. At home, he gradually got better and it was finally discovered that his anti-malaria pills were to blame, so now he is recovered and back at his job with New Life For All.

"School is out, papers graded. During one of our Christian Ed. Sunday School Editing meetings, Carol Plueddemann was looking at Sue and Terry's wedding pictures. It turns out that she and Jim were married in the same church 12 years ago. She recognized the red beams and the interior of the church.

"July 1 is the return of Jan Kwano to ECWA, so we are all wondering what will happen.

"The TerMeers have moved over to Rutts' house on Niger Creek compound and in August they are going on a 9 month furlough. We expect to move into the TerMeer house. Rutts left for a year's furlo, and they say that when they come back, they will not be working in Jos.

"Pam was sick for a couple of days last week with diarrhea and vomiting but is back to normal again. She has done some horseback riding and swimming, and yesterday a bunch of them went to the Game Reserve in Jos for the morning and lunch and a hike on Gog and Magog. Tomorrow night, the Bob Campbells, who are visiting in Nigeria this summer, are coming for supper, along with the Kastners. The Campbells have a son by the name of Bruce whom Rollie and Lance should know.

July 2, 1979

"We have been enjoying Pam's company. She is a big help, especially in the kitchen. She had her first bread baking experience last week, and it was so good that she's been elected to do it again this week."

July 24, 1979

"I don't know whether you heard about the drowning of little 4 year old Paul Shephard. They were back in the States, visiting with friends, missed Paul, and found him at the bottom of the back yard pool. What a shock to all! They went home because of the eldest, Scott, who tried to do away with himself by taking an overdose of drugs. Little Paul was a sweetheart, loved by all—a beautiful child. About the same time, we heard that Stan Dowdell was killed in an oil rig accident in northern Canada.

"We are in the midst of our D.VB.S. I am in charge of the 5th and 6th grade girls. We have had a total attendance of about 200 kids.

"Pam took a trip to Niger with Jim Kastner. She got back Friday night and says she really enjoyed her visit to Niger. She says that Galmi has changed a lot, with more new buildings. She was welcomed enthusiastically by both missionaries and nationals alike.

"Tomorrow night they start a week-end at Miango, "babysitting" for the Hillcrest retreat. Jim is taking the high-schoolers and Carol Pollen and Pam are to work with the younger kids. Pam has had a full summer, and I think she has enjoyed herself very much. She has been a pleasure to have around.

"Everybody anticipates Sue and Terry's coming, and it seems to be general knowledge that they will be house parents at K.A. Wally Braband was in the other day and said, 'I wish they could get here by Sept.' They are really strapped for house parents this year. I told Wally it wasn't possible.

Sept. 2, 1979

The Nigerian elections took place, but not without some "rikaci". In some places there were more ballots than registered voters. (Where have we Chicagoans heard that tale before?) The president elect is AIhaji Shehu Shagari from Sokoto State. Just by looking at his name, you know he is a Moslem. "AIhaji" is not a name, but a title—it refers to a person who has made his hadj (trip) to Mecca. "Shehu" means "wise man" as in the Three Wise Men (shehuna—plural for shehu). "Shagari" means to "drink cereal." "Sha" means to drink and "gari" is cereal. The Congress is pretty much balanced between so-called Christians (some born again) and Moslems.

The Ratzlaffs left the field for good for now. Their son, Murray had been pretty wild but recently came back to the Lord. Harvey went home first, then determined that they should stay home for a couple of years to help Murray, so Rose sold out all their possessions and left.

"At the moment, a Dr. Wilson, who teaches anthropology at Calvin College is visiting in Jos and giving a series of lectures on man's origin and the first chapters of Genesis. He is a Wheaton graduate, class of '49. We missed his first two lectures but plan to hear his third lecture tonight after church. Howard and Wanda Jones are also in town this week, holding special meetings, and he will be speaking tonight at the Conference Center, so we will be going there first and after that to Hillcrest to hear Dr. Wilson.

"Because Cherry is expecting, we are planning to come home mid-March through April, being back here for May. This trip will be on us, not on SIM or the government."

September 24, 1979

"As I wrote the date, I was reminded that 94 years ago today, my mother, your grandmother, whom you never met, was born. She died April 2, 1933 at the age of 48. I thought that was old because I was only 11 at the time, but as some of you kids are already into your 30's, you will begin to realize that 48 is quite young to die. Mother had suffered from gall bladder trouble for some time and decided to have it removed. She was operated on a Monday, never fully regained consciousness and died on the next Sunday. She apparently did not have the strength to cope with the operation. Those were the days before anti-biotics. Patients who have gall bladders removed today don't die. She was operated on at Lutheran Deaconess hospital in Chicago, which later moved out to Park Ridge and is now the hospital you work at, John, Lutheran General. Her doctor was a Dr. Schaeffer.

"A couple of weeks ago a picture of the Hillcrest retreat was posted on the Hillcrest High School bulletin board. Dad saw it and said that he saw Lance in the picture. I said it was impossible, it was John that went, not Lance. He proved me wrong, and yesterday, Sunday, after church, I walked over myself. Just before this, Mrs. Ottermiller had said that she had seen both boys at the retreat and that John had knocked himself out getting the pictures printed before the morning that the retreat closed.

"Jim Kastner nearly got himself electrocuted last week. Jim was holding a power tool and his African assistant plugged it in for him into a defective socket and 220 volts shot through his arm, up his head, (his hat was suspended in air) down through his right side and into the ground. He was frozen, but he managed to yell, and in a brief second or two that seemed like forever, the African removed the cord when he realized what was happening. So Wed. night in prayer meeting he gave praise to the Lord for his being here. His right leg was pretty swollen and his face bruised where he hit it when he fell afterwards.

"Yesterday we spent the afternoon at Miango. It is nice to have the Husbands back again. School is in session. The staff is shorthanded, and are very anxious for Sue and Terry to get there. Mary Ellen Adams is a dorm parent; Mrs. Klomparens is a dorm parent, in the boys' dorm She is a young widow with a 2 year old boy, Joel. She and her husband were accepted by SIM for Rural Development work, and he came down with cancer while they were candidating and died within six months.

"Oct. 1 is a holiday, celebrating the day of Nigeria's independence from England (since 1960, I believe).. It is also when Shehu Shagari, the new president, takes office, inaugurating civilian rule."

October 7, 1979

"We have heard from Mom (Lasca) this week. She says that Lance and Laura are very kind to her and visit her often. 'Laura helps me get into the bathtub for my bath, etc.' We certainly appreciate all that you kids do for her in the way of visits, phone calls, etc. She said she had heard from Cherry recently, too. She thinks (and we agree) that she has the best grandchildren in the whole world.

"Biggest news this past week has been the turn-over from military to civilian rule. It all went very smoothly with much celebrating. Each state inaugurated its new governor at the same time, so besides the Lagos celebrations there were local ones and state ones. Jos is the capital of Plateau State so there were ceremonies at the polo club which included marching by the school kids, giving of some awards, inspection of army and police bands and marching units.

The new governor is Solomon Lar, a Christian. We hadn't planned to attend, but in the morning of the big day, we were delivered engraved invitations to the Polo Ground, so we decided to go and were seated with other 'dignitaries' under the canopy with several hundred others. (Truxtons and Verbrugges were also invited.) We also received invitations to a reception at the Governor's Lodge at Rayfied for that evening. These invitations were gold engraved. So we went and drank our coke and Fanta under the stars which were hidden by a light drizzle. The governor and his wife circulated among the guests. The whites that were there could be counted on two hands and feet. The handing over from military to civilian rule came on the 19th anniversary of Britain's granting independence to Nigeria, and theoretically, this is what they were celebrating. Well, it was all very interesting and a break in the routine.

"We hear through Grandma that Neva is going into a home in Rockford, (*Fairhaven)* and that the house at 6010 Neva Ave. is up for sale."

November 25, 1979

"Everyone is excited about Sue and Terry's coming, and I have to pinch myself to believe that it is true. I pray that Cherry might accept her departure well. Sue has been Cherry's right arm in many ways, especially with Chip gone so much of the time. We are planning a week at Miango over Christmas, so we will be with them for that week, at the rest home, but on the same compound.

"I am teaching an additional 3 hours of Bible at Hillcrest school to fourteen 9th graders who are following the British School system. After 9th grade, they have to take 'qualifying' tests to see where they should go on in their studies—to trade school, universities, etc. My job for this year is to teach them everything about Matthew, Acts 1—15 and O. T. from Abraham to Judges. All of their exam questions are subjective—essay and context questions. Here is a sample. 'In those days came John the Baptist preaching . . . repent, for the Kingdom of heaven is at hand.' Matt. 3: 1-2. Relate this passage to its context and discuss its significance in the life and work of Jesus.' How would you do on that one?"

December 9, 1979

This year's presentation of the Messiah was as beautiful as ever. On the dress rehearsal night it was taped and will be cut to an hour and put on Plateau State T. V. as part of five hours that have been given to SIM/ECWA for this season. Governor Lar is pushing hard to upgrade Plateau State T. V. programs. His wife is active in ECWA/SIM circles. Concerning the Messiah, Rusty Verbrugge, age 10, said, "They could sure do it a lot faster if they didn't keep singing the same words over and over again." It would probably take about 15 minutes but it wouldn't be so beautiful. When Handel composed the Halleluiah Chorus, he exclaimed to a servant, "I did think I did see all Heaven before me, and the great God Himself."

"Our schedule for this month includes an SIM/ECWA Christmas party, Dec. 15; Bible Knowledge teachers' conference Dec. 19-21 in Jos; holiday at Miango Dec. 21-28; New Year's party and watch night service Dec. 31 in Jos. Of course, the 13th brings Sue and Teny, and we will probably all go out to KA. for the tea on the 14th, and if their house is ready for them, they will stay; if not, they will return with us for a few more days . . . . Christmas morning we will be breakfasting with the Husbands, and Sunday noon, we will all eat at the guest house.

"Tonight, we are going out to KA. to witness the Christmas program. Linda Crouch and Ruth Gibbs have put together a great program, and Linda, who is used to the fantastic plays that they had in the days of Paul and Jerry Craig., is bringing back more of that type of thing into the programs at KA. Linda is 'great with child'. Cora Zobrist and her boy friend, Ken Clay, will be having supper with us on the 13th, and they leave for Cotonou on the 14th to be with her folks for Christmas. Jim Kastner leaves on the same plane that brings Sue and Terry, so he will get to see them in Kano."

MERRY CHRISTMAS 1979

Chapter 7

1980

Jan. 6, 1980

This was the era of the hostages taken by Iran. Although we got BBC and VOA and Armed Forces Radio, not too much was said about it in Nigeria, although even the Nigerians thought the Iranians had done a bad thing.

Jan. 27, 1980

Things were going on as usual – Dad at the hospital and I in my teaching role both at Hillcrest and Narraguta. Cora Zobrist and Ken Klay announced their engagement and so did Janet Flory and Dale Flatten, teachers at Hillcrest but not with SIM. Terry and Sue were busy at Miango and fitting in well. Jim Crouch had a black-out and was sent to England for tests. He returned with a clean bill of health – heart okay and no brain disease, so they think it was a virus that sent him into a convulsion.

At this point we were making arrangements for our trip home. Plans called for my flying alone from Kano by Sabena on March

14, while Burt would be going to his continuing education course in Kenya and following later.

Feb. 17, 1980

"I spent most of yesterday (Sat.) in the kitchen. Baked bread, cookies, pies, sticky bottoms, made yogurt, and with the mixing, cooking and baking, I had a pile of dishes because I usually dirty every spoon, pan and mixing bowl that I own. Just as I got to the point of 'no return' on the bread – with the yeast and liquid all mixed together, the electricity went off, so I had to beat the bread by hand! I am getting spoiled with my bread beating (kneading) attachments to my mixer. The electricity came back on by noon, so I was able to bake it okay. Last night we went to the guest house for hamburgers and lemon cream pie, so I didn't have to make supper."

"The speaker for the annual conference mission conference this year was Dr. Donald Hubbard, pastor of Calvary Baptist Church in New York at that time.

"He was excellent. He really fed us with the Word, and his messages were the best I have heard for many a year. He was one of few men that I could listen to for an hour and not notice the time go by. Paul Rader was another. Dr. Hubbard replaced Dr. Stephen Olford at Calvary Bapt. Church in New York."

March 27, 1980

C.R. Sabathne arrived! A big boy! His pending arrival was the occasion of our returning home at that time. All went well. Twenty five years later (2005), C.R. is back from Iraq, still in the Army Reserve but going to college in Washington state. Still a big boy – 6' 4", 200 lbs. He recently announced his engagement to Rachel, who is also in the service, stationed in Washington. (Most recent news – C.R. is scheduled to go back to Iraq the first of the year. 2006)

May 24, 1980

"Two weeks have passed since our return to Nigeria, and it seems as if we had never left here. We arrived in Kano on schedule, Thurs. eve., about 6 p.m., then left for Jos about 10 a.m. the next day. We arrived in Jos about 2:30, unpacked, had supper with Verbrugges, and then took up where we left off 8 weeks earlier."

June 16, 1980

The wedding of Ken and Cora at Miango interrupted the routine of hospital work and teaching. Sue and Joanne Parish and Heidi Zobrist were in the wedding party. Burt and I together with the Porters and Fehls cut cake and dipped ice cream at three different tables at the reception.

Two medical students came out that summer. One was Phil Fischer who was related to the Fischer family that lived on Union St. in Wheaton. Rollie had played with Chuck Fischer when he was in 2nd grade when we lived on the corner of Seminary and College Ave. Chuck and Phil are cousins and Phil's father was in Burt's class at Wheaton.

Government schools were out for the summer, but the last week end of school, Narraguta had "revival" meetings at the school. This was sponsored by the Fellowship of Christian Students – (FCS) At the first meeting which was the only one I attended because of the wedding, about 40 kids responded to the invitation and I was able to deal with 5 of the girls who made first-time decisions for the Lord.

Sue and Terry were studying Hausa during the summer and Pam was in Southern France, working with Greater European Mission in a camp for young people.

July 8, 1980

"Sue and Terry were hurt in a motorcycle accident. They are both recovering nicely, so now you can read on. They came in (to Jos) on Sat. morning. After church on Sunday, we came home, then they went up to the main compound to invite Cora and Ken Klay down for Sunday dinner. They had just returned from their honeymoon. On the way back, they had made the right turn at the Hill Station corner (Policeman corner) and were coming down. At the intersection where the Standard Publishing Company is, a van entered the intersection without stopping and made a right turn. Sue and Terry were in the left lane, next to the median (a four lane road). The van crossed over in front of them while making his right turn, so Terry swung into the right lane to avoid him. Then the van swung back into the right lane, pushing Terry off onto the shoulder after hitting them slightly with his right side. Terry still had control of the bike, but there was a car parked on the shoulder ahead, so he had to go down into the ditch. He figured he could coast to a stop in the ditch which would have been okay except there was a rock in the bottom of the ditch which they hit almost immediately. This catapulted them over the rock, bike and all. Sue got hit in the back of the head, apparently by the luggage carrier as the bike flipped over, too. Her helmet had been pushed down over her face which saved her face. Terry got himself up, but Sue was lying in the ditch. After he removed her helmet and found out that she responded to his questions, he told the crowd that had gathered not to touch her, that he would go for her father. The crowd wanted to pick her up and take her to the hospital. So he got a ride to our house (1/2 mile), got Dad and they went and got Sue. Then Dad went back and got Terry. Sue suffered a mild concussion and had 6 stitches taken in the back of her head. She was incoherent for about 6 hours when she came back into reality. She would ask, 'What happened?' 'Is Terry all right?' 'Where am I?' After we answered her, she would ask the same questions. She vomited a little blood the first of three times. By evening she was sitting up and drinking tea and broth. She had about 13 abrasions on her body – arms, legs, back. Terry had a wrenched back and also many abrasions. X-rays of his back showed no fractures.

———

"Monday afternoon I took them back to Miango. They are really sore all over. Besides what you can see, they have muscle aches as well. They wanted to get back so they could go to Hausa class and not miss anymore schooling. The motorcycle is not too badly damaged, and the fellow who hit them and his boss want to settle out of court. They set the price at N300.00 (about $500.00). They brought N100 the first day. Hopefully they will bring the rest today. This van is used for a taxi service, and if we take it to court, they know the van will be impounded until the case is brought to trial and that could be 6 months."

About this same time, Pam was in France at Bourg D'Oisans helping out with the camp work. She wrote that on Mondays she does laundry with a wringer washing machine and helps in the kitchen; Tuesdays she does cleaning, mostly the floors and bathrooms. Most of the water comes directly from a mountain stream and it is cold. Wed. was her day off. When the campers came she also did canteen. "They chose me because I supposedly have the best French." She and staff each day of the week were complimented by the cook, "I looked for work and got a lot done."

"The place is beautiful. It's cold. I've been wearing the ski jacket you gave me just about all day every day. The buildings we are in are at least a hundred years old with no heat . . . . Parts of the building are underground or built into the mountain so they look and feel like caves. Everything is stone and wood, too, so it stays cool – cold all the time inside."

July 30, 1980

Ken and Elsie Kastner left for the U.S. for Jim's wedding to Kathy Hansen, a beautiful blonde. She was out in Nigeria on a short term assignment with a group from Canada. Mostly they worked in the south but on occasion they came in to Jos. The upshot of it was a wedding for Kathy and Jim.

"The Bible School was a great success. We had a fine bunch of staff and an average of 200 kids. The Bible School was able to give the E.M.S. (Evangelical Missy. Society) a bicycle for one of its missionaries. Together with some money we had left over from the previous year and the Sunday night offering, we were able to give them a second bicycle and some money for their latest missionary family who is going to Cross River State. Our theme was Growing, Giving, Living for God, and I believe there were many decisions made for Christ. Next year we have decided to have a two week program, but in all likelihood, I won't be here. .

"On Sunday, Sue and Terry are planning to come in and take us to Plateau Hotel for dinner to celebrate my birthday."

The following paragraph is taken from Burt's part of this letter:

"Boy, we are getting tons of rain. Enough for Galmi for 5 years. I don't mind when I am in, but when I'm out on the cycle, that is just too much of a good thing. Sure nice to get home when soaked and change to dry clothes and get a fire going in the fireplace.

"Did a typhoid perforation in a 9 yr. old Yoruba girl yesterday: four perforations of the ileum and a necrotic spot not quite perforated yet, and sticking its ugly head up out of the largest perforation, a 9 inch ascaris round worm, a beauty, white and transparent. Made one of the white anesthetists sick to see it coming out."

August 10, 1980

Fran wrote that Aunt Sophia died. She and Uncle Fred meant a lot to our family, especially after Mother died. She was a source of help and strength and comfort. Fran and Bill were married in their home. They lived only six blocks from us, and we cousins, Freddie and Lillian Blix and Bob and I, went to the same school. Uncle Fred was my mother's brother. After Mother died, each of us kids stayed with them for periods of time. When brother Bob and I had diphtheria,

Fran and Beret lived with them. I lived with them for some time while I was working after high school. They were mother and father to all four of us from time to time.

Sue and Terry took us out to the Plateau Hotel for my birthday dinner on Sunday after having come in to Jos from Miango, and then on my actual birth date, Dad took me out to the Chinese restaurant at Hill Station Hotel for dinner. Just like home! And so different from Galmi!

Wilf and Esther Husband went home for the weddings of Steve and Dan but were back. Bonnie was still in Briercrest Bible School and Pauline came back with them.

Hillcrest started again. Ramadan was over for the year. Verbrugges were back from their furlough which lightened the load for Dad.

August 31, 1980

"Did any of you go to Camp Awana over Labor Day?

Pam was still in France. She wrote us a postcard. We responded:

"My, your writing is small! I guess you're doing that to save on postage, which is very honorable. It reminds me of Dad when he used to write 'penny' post cards and get a whole letter on them. That's right, when we were young, post cards were one cent, and regular mail, 3 cents.. We're glad you're getting in some touring. Don't omit a trip to L'abri if you can manage it."

Oct. 1, 1980

Independence Day! Twenty years ago (1960) Nigeria and Great Britain broke the ties that bound them, and Nigeria has been doing its own thing since then. (It is now 45 years as I write in 2005.) The Nigeria that we knew is much different today. For the ten years between our first footsteps in Nigeria in 1950, we considered Nigeria the next best thing to the United States. Beautiful flower gardens, stores with goods in them, fruit in abundance, peace!! All that has changed. Isn't there a law of thermodynamics that says that things deteriorate, not improve? It did its work in Nigeria.

But back to that day in 1980. I heard the strains of a band playing from the Polo Field, right next door to us. School kids from all over were there to celebrate by having a "march past" the grandstand where all the dignitaries were seated. It makes sense to call it that since they were all marching past. "Hillcrest is represented there and so is Narraguta, and it stands to follow that I am having a day off, which is a breather for me.

"Sue and Terry are coming in this afternoon so they will be here for the pot luck supper and film this evening at headquarter's tennis courts in celebration of the holiday."

We had a good time at the Hillcrest Retreat. Don Reece, was the speaker (Baptist). Missionaries were dwindling as nationals took over more and more, which meant that the number of kids at the hostels was decreasing. Boy's Baptist and Girls' Baptist combined and were at Crescent Hill. The big, beautiful hostel of Assembly of God had no kids in it anymore, and the McCulleys lived in it all by themselves and it was used as a guest house for their missionaries.

At Narraguta I taught Form IV, which is next to the last year of high school.

"I've had these same kids since Form I when I had 5 sections of them. Now they are cut down to two sections with about 60 kids each. The two rooms are next to each other and at the back of one and the beginning of the other room, which are separated by plywood, some sections of ceiling board are missing, so my voice carries clearly to the next room and the other instructor's voice carries clearly to my class room. Yesterday, the first period, the other section did not have an instructor, and the kids were noisy and carrying on and it sounded like they were in my room. It was terribly difficult. I spoke to the principal about it, and he just shrugged his shoulders and said it was the proprietor's business."

Oct. 8, 1980

"Sunday, 11: 15 a.m., and we have returned from church. At 12 noon, Dad goes to teach his Men's Fellowship class at Bishara #3 church. There are about 70—100 men in the class which meets after their morning service, which usually numbers about 700 in attendance. Even in Kano with its strong Moslem influence they have about 2000 in 3 morning services in our own ECWA church. ECWA also has a Yoruba church in Kano, and then there are all the other denominational churches which flourish. In Jos alone, there are 13 ECWA churches plus Baptist, C.R.C., C.M.S., Presby., Pentecostal, not to mention RC. At the same time, there are villages a few miles outside of the central areas where there is no Gospel witness and some remote villages where the people have never heard of Jesus. This is Nigeria! Niger, of course, is something else again, but even there, Christianity is given a hearing and there is a greater openness that comes with an increase in educational opportunities for the young people. Benin (Dahomey) is struggling with its Marxist government, and the church still functions, except that there are 'indoctrination classes' called by the local governments who set the time for their classes during church time. In Ethiopia, Christians are put in prison for preaching the Word, but the church is growing in spite of it. Angola, Mozambique, Uganda — Christians persecuted for their faith. Nigeria is returning to civilian rule, and next year will be the elections—and who knows what? Well, I didn't mean to start with this prologue when I wrote the first sentence.

"Speaking of the darkness in various places of Nigeria, the other day a 3 day old infant was brought into the hospital to stop bleeding from their having cut out the uvula. This is practiced in places, and that couldn't have happened too far outside of Jos.

"This aft. We are going out to Miango for tea and supper. We will be taking Ed and Alberta Dubisz with us. Ed is being treated for amoeba. He's getting the "works"—about 3 different drugs all at once."

October 29, 1980

"We have enjoyed Dr. Norton both as a speaker and as a friend since he arrived. He has been conducting the Wed. evening prayer meetings for the past month. He is very good as well as entertaining in his presentation. He has also had Sunday dinner with us once and coffee after prayer meeting last Wed. night. This Sun. nite he is speaking at Hillcrest Church and we plan to entertain him after the service for 'coffee and'. The S.S. superintendent was looking for someone to teach the adult class after Christmas, and I suggested Dr. Norton. So we are going to have the Korhorns (he is the S.S. supt.) and Wil over to meet each other.

The Ratzlaffs packed up and went home for good. Rose left six weeks earlier to try to locate Murray. He was found on a Florida beach, under the influence of heavy drugs. "Murray must also stand trial for auto theft." (Today, 2005 word has it that Murray is clean and a changed man.)

"You remember Dave and Shirley Boyes. Dave was saying that their oldest son, I think his name is also Dave, still has a special place in his heart for our John who befriended him on his first trip to K.A. on the airplane. John was a real help to him in getting him off on the right track at K.A. Well, anyway, Dave and Shirley are working in Lagos. Dave was driving his new van on the freeway in Lagos when the car in front of him stopped. Dave stopped, thinking that the guy was in trouble or perhaps had some kind of a grievance with Dave. Dave is the last one to be suspicious of anyone. Two men got out, brandishing machetes and pulled Dave out of his van, slashed his hand and leg, got into the van and drove off. Dave staggered to his feet and walked home—he was only a couple blocks from home.. Shirley got him to the hospital where they stitched him. The next day, he was flown here to Jos and assessed. The Lagos drs. had missed a nerve in a finger, so after a few days, Dave had to have his finger opened up again and Glen VerBrugge found the two nerve ends and attached them and also put a stitch in a tendon that was severed. Then he closed him up again and put him in a partial cast. After the operation, Dave spent a few days and nights with us rather than in the hospital and finally flew back to Lagos. After the thieves went off with the van, they crossed over the median and went back in the opposite direction and crashed it into another car about a block down the road. Then they abandoned it, leaving the two machetes in Dave's car. Dave got his car back, although damaged.

Sunday, Nov. 23, 1980

We went out to Miango to visit with Mr. Jake Eitzen who came out from the States with his son Jim and daughter Ruth. Unfortunately, Dad had diarrhea so wasn't able to join us for dinner or for tea, but I had a nice visit with them. Mrs. Eitzen didn't come—both are 73—and she didn't feel as if she could make it. Jim was especially interested in getting word about Rollie and Lance. Ruth was in the first K.A. class of five in 1946.

"My course at Hillcrest is finished, and the kids have taken their exams. One and a half hours in Old Testament and the same in N.T. Results won't be known until May or so. That's how fast things move in Nigeria. This was a nation-wide exam, taken on the same day all over the country. All essay and context questions—a total of six questions to be answered for each exam!

"I'm still teaching 6 hours (class periods) a week at Narraguta, writing and editing Sunday School lessons for the Christian Ed manuals, and going out to Miango for piano teaching on Thurs., so I don't have time to spare."

Dec. 20, 1980

"Thanks for the word of Aunt Agnes' death. It's hard to think of her as being absent from us, but the miracle of her life is that she lived as long as she did. We shall miss her." She was very knowledgeable about current events as well as Bible knowledge.

For Sue and Terry's second wedding anniversary, we took them out to dinner at a relatively new restaurant, owned and operated by a Lebanese couple. Called the Cedar Tree, it was very clean and served western-style food, and we were pleased with everything.

Benjamin was born to Rollie and Margaret on Dec. 11 and Wyatt was born to Lance and Laura on Dec. 20.

"This past week I attended the annual Bible Knowledge Teachers' Conference for three days. It was our good fortune to have in town a professor of N.T. Theology and Greek, and he lectured us four times. For me, it was his lectures and insights into teaching that made the conference worthwhile. The rest was a repeat of former years. This man, Dr. Ward Powers, has come to Africa at the invitation of ECWA to lecture in some of our Bible Schools.

"We hear that Jim Rendell had a forced landing in Haute Volta and damaged one of his wings. Don't know details, but the K.A. kids from Francophone had to go home by road instead of air."

Chapter 8

VACATION TRIP TO NIGER
Burt and Ruth Long and Terry and Sue Hammack
Dec. 26, 1980 – Jan. 5, 1981

Dec. 26, 1980

Left Jos 10:30 a.m. arrived Kano 2:30. One road block coming into Kano but we were not stopped. Riots had been going on in Kano for about a week between two Moslem sects. Hence, police blockades into and out of the city! For once our skin was the right color. Those Moslems who belonged to the fanatical sect had tattoo marks on their waists, and the practice at the road stops was to lift shirts, and if there was the tattoo, they were shot or had gasoline poured on them and were set fire to. Wholesale slaughter was going on, but when we arrived, it was quiet. After we left, there was a shoot out in which the leader of the sect was killed and things returned to normal again.

It was day of prayer. We arrived in time to unpack the car and go to prayer meeting at the guest house. Then Stan and Char Myers invited all at the prayer meeting to their home for tea. Myers had only been back a couple of weeks. Had supper at Botherases and also breakfast, since the guest house dining room was closed down for the season. After evening prayer meeting, we were invited and went to the VanGerpens for hot chocolate. They are with the Presbys. but were formerly with SIM. Sue and Terry chose not to go. Sue was especially tired. This morning in Kano, Stan said it registered 42 degrees F.

Dec. 27

Left Kano by a back road to avoid the area of trouble. Got back onto the main road just outside of town. No problems. One check point, but only a slow down for us. Good road to Zinder. Usual lengthy border stops at Magaria (Zinder). Stopped at the Book Shop in Zinder, visited with Dankan Dule and Sanushi a bit, then went on to Goure. Dirt road with 66 dips (tabarmun duwatsu) in 115 miles. Got to Lees late afternoon. Judy and Gordon Evans and their 3 children, Christopher, Jeremy, Douglas, were visiting Judy's parents. It was 45 degrees this morning.

Had a good supper and night. Slept in Jean Playfair's house. Spent Sunday there. Went to church – about 20 people there. Carey took us for a tour of the city. Tried to make it to the top of a sand dune in his pick-up Almost made it but not quite. He was a bit chagrined because he has made it before. Of course, sand is everywhere. Sing-song that night at Lees' with Pastor and wife, Laraba, a former Dogon Dutchi girl.

Dec. 28

To Maine Soroa and back. Paved road all the way through desert, desolate country. Had a nice visit with Phil and Carol Short and Lorna Downes and Cathy Jones. Had lunch with the latter. Visited Dr. Kirker's former hospital which is now only a dispensary. He was declared persona non grata after the military coup because he was closely associated with Pres. Diori in establishing the hospital. Back to Goure by 7 P.M. for a nice supper and fire in the fire place. Really very cold weather these days.

Tues., Dec. 30

Left Goure after breakfast. Stopped again at Zinder. In the Book Shop met a half-Belgium, half Zairen man and his Zairen wife. He is teaching in govt. schools there. Introduced himself as a "Christian" and fellowships with the church there. His wife had a baby at Galmi recently. Knows Margaret Hayes and others well.

On to Maradi. Stopped at Maza Tsaye on the way into Maradi. Met the Frangees, saw Emmanuelis. Gwen Van Lierop had planned a get-together with the "oldies" for supper, and we had it at Vi Swanson's house at Maza Tsaye that night. Besides Vi and Gwen, there were Gwen Kelsall, Virginia Fridal, Jessie McGill and Graham Wickett, the latter in charge of the leather works. Had good fellowship, and all the folks wanted to know when we were returning to Niger to stay. This was the theme song all across Niger.

Dec. 31

Maradi to Galmi. Stopped at Madaoua. Had lunch with Lolita. Went on to Galmi. On the road to Galmi, met Elvin who was retuning from there. Visited a bit. We went slowly through the market. Some people recognized us immediately. Arrived at Galmi staion, had cokes with Knowltons and a royal welcome from those who were around. Went back to the market since this was market day, and we were welcomed and greeted royally by the whole town, all saying how glad they were to see us and when were we coming back to stay. Saw many old friends who started a procession to the house where we were staying.

That night we toured the hospital. The out-patient building was entirely new. It faces the road and is attached to the west wing of the hospital by a walk-way. It is a nice building and an addition that was sorely needed. The operating area was chopped up into a lot of smaller areas, which I suppose is functionally better, but sort of gave me a sense of claustrophobia. Perhaps it would have been different in the daylight. There is a good supply of drugs in the pharmacy, some of which comes from MAP. The government won't let them charge area patients. They say they will reimburse for those people, but they are slow in producing any money. This involves mountains of record keeping, and the nurses work long hours on both nursing and bookkeeping. Dr. Ng is the only dr. at the moment and works long hours.

Had supper with Margaret Lacey, guest house keeper. It was especially good to see Gen Kooy, Margaret Hayes and Jeanne Marie Berney again as well as the new personnel which total about 26 adults at the moment. After the tour of the hospital, we had tea at Jeanne Marie's with Margaret. Gen was on night duty. We left there about 10 p..m., had been invited to Knowltons for some Rook. Sue and Terry had already gone to Philpotts, who had invited them. Knowltons had gone over to Philpotts and had left a note on their door, but when we saw their house dark, we went on home. Terry came over later and told us to go to the Philpotts, and we had pop-corn and some 6 handed Rook there. Then to bed and slept the New Year in.

Jan. 1, 1981 Thursday.

Off to Niamey. Stopped at Dogon Doutche and greeted Abdou and Rahila who invited us back for lunch on Sat. on our return. Arrived at Niamey at the guest house late afternoon. Enoch and Phyllis Hansen are in charge. Guest house is at Bible School. Had supper with Hansens.

Friday, Jan. 2

Went shopping in the market. Went to the Museum and Zoo. Sue bought some cloth. We got some dates and cheese. Visited the mosque which is a-building. Work being done and paid for with Petro Dollars by Morocco. Beautiful workmanship, especially the wood carving in the doors. Went up to the minaret since the mosque is not yet dedicated. Took a quick look around the American Embassy. That evening we ate at the Rec. Center sponsored by the

Am. Embassy. Had steaks with all the trimmings. It is a Friday night thing—you get your meat and take it to the bar-b-que pits and cook it. The Royers and Showalters from C.B.M. were there – the former living there now, and the latter on their way across the desert by car to begin their furlough. They said they knew Lance. Royers were former houseparents at Hillcrest. Also, the Bob Williams from So. Bapt. were there. Jim Rendell and his present girl-friend, Sandi, Dave Harling and his fiancée, and Jim French ate with us.

Sat., Jan. 3

Headed back to Galmi. Stopped at Dogon Doutchi at 12:10. Visited with Abdou and Rahila. They served couscous with chicken and miya, lettuce with vinegar, peas (out of a can) and canned pineapple. We told them how much we appreciated their kindness, but they insisted that it was their privilege. Arrived at Galmi around 5:30. We were to eat with Dr. and Mrs. Andrew Ng, the dr. from Singapore. Supper at 7. About 6:30 I began to get sick – vomiting and diarrhea so I missed out on a delicious Chinese dinner, although Burt and Sue and Terry enjoyed it. Several folks came to greet, and Idi, representing the church elders, asked Burt to preach in the Sunday service. Welcomed profusely by the church members. Had dinner with Knowltons – I was better that morning, but Burt and Terry began having diarrhea that day, but no vomiting. Had tea with Belva Overmiller. Had compound supper in the Awana building, followed by sing-song in one of the new duplexes, then cocoa to top off the day. I felt, we all felt, like stuffed pigs. I visited Ai Mamman, Talawai Mamman, Lydia and Ibrahim, MaiDaji, all the while greeting along the way.

Mon. Jan. 5

Left Galmi. Yahaya, who had been one of the first to greet us was there to see us off. All urged us to hurry back. Our return was via Sokoto. About an hour at the border – four stops – two on each side of the border. No problems. Reached Bodinga, out of Sokoto, where

Chris Oswald had a beautiful chicken dinner waiting for us. Sarah Loewen and Grace Rackley were also there. Chris is teaching at an Advanced Teachers' College there and has quarters on the grounds. Left there at 2:30, arrived at Gusau at Harvey Stromme's place about 10 to six. At 7 sat down to about a 14 plate dinner – two kinds of meat, mashed potatoes, vegetables, curry, spaghetti, salad, 3 desserts, coffee – typical Harvey style. Again we were stuffed. Harvey still keeps his boys, and some were still there, returning to their schools the next day or two. He has been a father and provider to about 50 boys in his career. Many of them are out in service, either teaching or working in government or in ministry. He still has some kids in Primary School, and he does this all by himself. He says the grown up boys help support the new ones.

Tues., Jan. 6

Left Harvey's, arrived at Zaria about 11:30. Caught Harris Poole just as he was leaving for school, but he served us coffee and we visited for about a half hour. Then for the final leg of the journey – Zaria to Jos. Arrived here about 2:30, rejoicing in a good trip, safety, fellowship renewal, new places visited and old places re-visited, and a good feeling to be back home again. After hot showers and hair washes, Burt drove Sue and Terry out to Miango.

Chapter 9

1982

August 11, 1982

Before we get too far removed from our furlough year, I would like to include a letter that Janna wrote to me in May during our furlough year. Janna, an SIM missionary, was teaching Bible Knowledge at a different school. She wrote,

"Dear Mrs. Long, Hi! How are you? We just wanted to give you some news about a former student of yours, Rafiu Shehu. Rafiu is from a Muslim family but took Bible Knowledge because he says there was no Islamics teacher. He was at your school, but his guardian had him transferred to our school because of the Islamics thing. For some reason, Rafiu continued in Bible here instead of Islamics. He was the one to call the Muslim students to prayer and was a Muslim leader, however.

"Last Saturday, May 9, Rafiu got saved! He has been given a very rough time, as you can imagine, by Muslim students and teachers. One other Muslim boy who made a decision with Rafiu has already turned back, but Rafiu wants to stand firm. He knows his family will disown him and gets discouraged, but he really wants to be genuine.

Bob is counseling him and praying with him. We also gave him **Black Nomad** about Adamu Dogon Yaro to read.

"Anyway, we knew you'd like to know a seed you planted has germinated. And please pray for Rafiu. The hardest time is in front of him. In Christ, Janna."

Indeed, that was a bit of encouragement to me, knowing that the seed that was planted at Narraguta had taken root and blossomed. (*I wonder where he is today (2005) and whether he is still walking with the Lord.*)

As usual, we had a wonderful furlough with time with children, siblings and friends galore. In eleven months, we traveled 30,000 miles. Our final days were filled with purchasing, packing and arranging for our loads to be shipped. I am amazed that we got away. We wouldn't have made it without the help of family and friends. But it was hard to say goodbye to loved ones and especially to Burt's mom, Lasca, who was living in the Admiral nursing home on Foster Ave. She was a good sport and always had said that she and Ritchie would be disappointed if their son gave up serving the Lord on the mission field for any reason.

"We had a good flight over the ocean, sitting in Business class with plenty of leg room and comfort. But from Amsterdam, we were in Economy. KLM is giving SIM all Business Class flights across the Atlantic for the Economy price because we do so much business with them. From Europe, there are only two classes – First Class and Economy, and KLM hasn't as yet stretched itself to give us First Class. Well, anyway, we got some slippers, free ear phones, and souvenir plaques again.

"Terry met us at the airport and transported us and the baggage to Kano Guest House. Next morning we left about 8 o'clock and drove straight to Miango. It was good to see Sue and Keith again. We got there about 12 noon, We stayed with them that afternoon and night. Keith is a beautiful baby, and he gets around just famously and gets into everything that a typical 1 yr. old does, plus a few more situations besides. We have been given the usual royal welcome carpet by the missionaries. Wed. night we ate at Kastners; Thurs. at Lois Brown's; Friday at Hodges; Saturday at Ogles (Hostel house parents); Sunday noon at Andrews; Mon. night we ate at home and Tues. night at the Leftwiches' (So. Bapt.) house. Now I guess the honeymoon is over, since we have no more invitations for meals left."

All the houses on Evangel Compound were occupied so we were now living on the Niger Creek Compound. We were happy there with good neighbors – Kastners right next door; then Joe Harding and his wife, Kay; Bill and Esther Rogers. Across the circle lived Roy and Doreen Hodges, and the Hostel was directly across from us with the tennis court in the center of the circle. Besides the missionaries, three black families were living there. Our house was being painted and it had fewer cabinets than we formerly had, but we were quite comfortable and that was our home for our final two years in Nigeria.

Dad got right into the work at the hospital, but I had a month before Narraguta school started up.

"I do not know yet what I will be doing. S.I.M. is obliged to supply a 4th grade teacher and a Bible and English teacher for 7th and 8th grades at Hillcrest. Roy Hodges has asked if I might be willing to do either. I do not have a teacher's certificate so 4th grade is out, and I am not sure that I want to be tied down to 30 hrs. of classes a week. Art Redekop is due back on Sat. and Roy is hoping that he will have some teachers in his hat, and so am I. That will release me to do my Bible Knowledge work and continue to work on the Sunday School lessons and help out at K.A. with piano.

November 20, 1982

Christmas was in the air and I was once again singing in the choir that sang the Messiah. It was conducted by one of Hillcrest's teachers (usually Mr. Korhorn) and held in Hillcrest's chapel. Ninety voices made up the choir. A dozen stringed instruments and organ and piano accompanied us. Either Darlene Reimer or Mr. McDowell was at the organ and the other was at the piano. What a thrill to be part of Handel's great oratorio! We performed it twice, once on Dec. 3 and the other, on Dec. 11.

"The Jos Community choir was composed of mostly expatriates, possibly a dozen Nigerians, who come from all walks of life in town or close to town. I was sitting next to a Nigerian bass last practice who had an excellent voice. It sounded good to listen to his booming bass in one ear while I was holding my own with the alto. I complimented him on his voice, and he said he had sung in several different choirs in London. The orchestra is made up of violins, cello, flutes, trumpet, recorders. This Fri. night there is to be classical concert, performed by artists, some of whom teach at Hillcrest and K.A. and others from the town. It's hard to believe the talent concentrated in this city. On Dec. 4 will be the middle school choir, and Dec. 10, the high school band and choir and on Dec. 12, Nine Lessons and Carols. These are all connected with Hillcrest.

"At the moment the Hillcrest Sr. class play is going on. It is Agatha Christie's The Mousetrap. It was a good plot and the performers did an excellent job. Tonight's is the final performance and will be followed by the usual cast party. That means that Sunday School attendance will be down tomorrow in some classes."

Originally, our Niger Creek Hostel had one building for girls and a second one for boys. Later, they built an addition to the first house and moved the seven boys back into the first one. The second building became a self-catering guest house and was getting a lot of use. The regular guest house had been turned over to E.C.W.A. a few years earlier, and had become very run down, so none of our missionaries wanted to stay there. It was overrun by Nigerians, the food was Nigerian style and there was no preparation to water such as boiling, filtering or chlorinating. Two years ago, it was returned to S.I.M., and Grant and Tilly Robinson had the challenge of restoring it to a more livable situation.

December 29, 1982

"The Messiah was superb. I have never heard it or sung in it better that what we did this year, and I mean even in the States. It was magnifique! All the other programs were excellent."

Schools were over for the Christmas holidays, m.k.'s had scattered to their homes, Narraguta was out, and I was grateful for a time to relax a bit. As planned, we went out to Miango with Claudia Long on Christmas morning, getting there in time for the 10 a.m. service. We all had dinner at the Winsors. In the evening was talent night at the Guest house. Some of the numbers were hilarious, not much talent but a lot of humour. We spent Sat. and Sun. nights there and returned to Jos on Mon., Boxing Day. On Jan. 8, Miango sponsored a mixed doubles tennis tournament. Since not many wives played tennis, it was interesting to see how the couples matched up. Ken Kastner played with Ruth Cox; Art Redekop with Claudia; Don Hunt with Barbara Forster; Lorne Shaw with Sue; and Terry with Linda Tiedge. Besides those, there were Dad and me and the Verbrugges. I don't remember who won, but we didn't.

"Looking back at 1982, in many ways I am not sorry to see it go. It has not been an easy year, and as I think of you kids, I reflect that it has likewise been a very difficult year for most of you in one way or another. But with Chip and Pam out of school, and with Lance feeling better, and with us settled in for another year and a half (D.V.), and with Keith becoming a real nice little boy, I look forward to 1983 with anticipation, even though we don't know what lies ahead. Nevertheless, I can say that the Lord has been faithful and I trust him and love him as much as or more than ever before, and I hope that all of you can say the same. We love you all and trust you all had a happy Christmas and that 1983 will be your best year yet.
    Love to all. Mom"

Chapter 10

1983—1984

January 27, 1983

The Nortons arrived along with Dr. and Mrs. Inch, both couples from Wheaton College. They will be teaching at the JETS Seminary (Jos Evangelical Theological Seminary) this term. We had both couples for dinner on Sunday. (Don't ask how they tasted.) The annual conference took place at Miango, and Mr. Richard Strauss, son of the Lehman Strauses, was the speaker. They came from Niger where they had ministered at the Nigerien conference.

The great tennis tournament was held as scheduled. Dad and I lost our first match to Sue and Lorne. That put us into the losers' ladder. We worked our way back to the top, so we were in the semi-finals against Jim Crouch and Joanne Parrish. We each won a set and we lost in a tie breaker. Sue and Lorne went up the winners' ladder to play against Glen and Bernice Verbrugge in their semi-finals. The Verbrugges then went on to beat Jim and Joanne in the finals. It was a lot of fun. We had our full of tennis that day – 10 sets plus several tie-breaker games.

"Both Dad and I were at Miango today (Thurs.), I, for my 8 piano lessons and Dad to man the clinic there. The docs take turns visiting out there every other Thurs., so this was Dad's day.

"Just before Christmas Yakubu Yako and his wife were killed in an automobile accident coming from Kano. Yakubu had just come back from the States representing New Life For All, and his wife and family picked him up in Kano and were returning to Jos with him at night. The driver of their van got a broken leg, and their son was hospitalized for several weeks for injuries. There are automobile accidents all the time, and they become quite common. The Nigerians travel at high speed and take all kinds of chances. We certainly need your prayers as we travel these roads.

"This week, the communications building in Lagos was burned down, so there is no outside communication with the world.

"The loads that we packed in our carport arrived, and the biggest item was the piano that we ordered from New Jersey. It is beautiful. After all these years, I have a new piano! Unbelievable! It is a Kholer-Campbell. It came through unscathed and has a beautiful tone.

"You wouldn't believe this weather. We have been freezing for the last six weeks. Our house stays in the 60's. I live with cold hands and cold feet. My heating pad warms a spot for my feet just before I hop into bed, and the fireplace has been devouring wood mornings and evenings without exception. If we sit within 2 ft. of the fireplace, we can warm up, but most of my work is far afield from the fire-place.

"We are expecting Art Rorheim and Don Wubs on Feb. 18 for 3 days. He/they are scheduled to speak at Miango Sun. a.m. and Hillcrest that night. They are enroute to India and stopping off for a visit with us. Then Verne VanNatta will be following on their heels for a few days."

Feb. 26, 1983

"Dad met Art Rorheim and Don Wubs on Feb. 18 at the new Jos airport in Barkin Ladi – about a 40 min. drive from here out the Bukuru Road. It is almost unbelievable to have them here. They are staying in the Guest House, i.e., the old boys' hostel and eating with us. Don Wubs has been traveling quite a bit with Art the past 5 years. He is quite good at doing 'magic' tricks, and is quite an asset to Art. Sat. a.m., Burt drove the men around town and Sat. aft., we all went out to Miango. We spent the night. Next a.m., Don spoke in the two Sunday School sessions, and he did some of his 'magic', and he was so funny everybody howled. I laughed so hard I cried. His running commentary made all his tricks much more hilarious. Art spoke in the a.m. service; told a little about Awana and gave a good message. After dinner we returned to Jos. I had to be back by 3:30, because Hillcrest was having a piano recital at that time, and 3 of my students were in it. In the evening, Art spoke at Hillcrest and Don performed for about ten minutes. Then on Mon. afternoon, Don and Art had an assembly for grades 1 – 6. Both at K.A. and at Hillcrest two families had kids who had been in Awana clubs, and the kids wore their shirts, which pleased Art no end. One of the families was McDowell's, who is the principal; the other, the counselor's, Don Bates.

"Mon. a.m., Burt took them to the hospital, and their reaction was one of amazement, incredulity, etc. They said it was the highlight of their trip. Tuesday a.m., I drove them to the airport

"We had been expecting Verne Van Natta, too, but we didn't know exactly when he was coming. Monday noon he appeared at the door, having taken a taxi from the airport. Verne was with us until Thurs. afternoon. Unfortunately, he took sick Tues. night and spent all of Wed. vomiting and with diarrhea. Thurs. a.m., we got him back on his feet so we could go out to Miango, I, to teach piano and Burt to take care of the clinic that morning. Verne has part of Sue and Terry's support. Verne spent the day lying on their bed until 3:30 when we left for the airport via the back road through Vom. He was heading for Lagos, Kenya, Zimbabwe and Zambia and So. Africa. In So. Africa he was going to meet up with Art and Don again.

"During the same days, a doctor friend of the Godbolds and their son came to visit. They had been to Niger, trekked out with Ann and Cash, who are out for their yearly 3 month trek to the Tuaregs, visited Galmi, now were visiting Evangel and us. Since we had met the Shamseys in Sarasota when we visited the Godbolds, Cash asked us to take them over. So they also stayed in the guest house and ate with us. However, Joe and Kay Harding are supported in part by their church, so the Shamsays ate some of their meals with them. They arrived on Mon. also and left on the same plane with Verne, Thurs. night, heading for Lagos and Kenya. We were glad that Verne, in his weakened condition, was able to travel with them. So we had a year's visitors in one week, and although it was a busy week, it was also an enjoyable one.

"This afternoon, a group of us youngsters went out to Gog and Magog and climbed to the top. This was a first for us. The youngsters included Penny (age 63) of Lassa fever fame; Burt, 64; me, 61; Bill and Esther Rogers, ages about 58; Barb Forster, in her 40's; and 2 real youngsters, Ian, a medical student from Canada doing his rotation quarter here and heading home next week and Matthew Carr, who arrived today for a 2 year tour, teaching in one of the Govt. schools in the area. For you who do not know, Gog and Magog is a mountain made of rocks, and to get to the top not only involves climbing, it also involves crawling, sliding, being pulled and pushed, jumping and praying. It took about 45 min. to get to the top; a half hr. to get down. We brought our picnic lunches with us and ate in the 'room rock', a rock formation with another rock lying over it. We also met Tilly and Grant Robinson and son Dan, and they joined us for supper and a little sing.

"Our all SIM Nigerian conference was held 3 week-ends ago, and it was a great time. Mr. and Mrs. Richard Strauss were the guest speakers and his main theme was 'God is in Control'. He is the son of Lehmann Strauss. They have a son and daughter-in-law and grandson in Ethiopia with S.I.M. That week-end the cold weather broke, the harmattan lifted and since then it has been warm and beautiful. End of 2nd term exams are starting March 9, so I'll have a few weeks off for Easter break."

It was about this time that Koma people (5000) in the high Cameroun/Nigerian mountains asked for a permanent missionary. The Evangelical Missionary Society (E.M.S.) of E.C.W.A. had already begun a work among them. They were spirit worshippers. E.M.S. responded.

Then there were the Boko people (30,000) who lived between Benin and western Nigeria. They were visited by a Gospel team. Why haven't we heard this good news before?' they asked. Three E.M.S. families were sent.

October 16, 2005

Now I don't have any more letters, unless I find some buried some place in the files. And since there were 15 months yet until our retirement in June/July, 1984, I will have to resort to my memory, and that could be both difficult and challenging. But I'll try.

I remember:

The principal of Hillcrest, Mr. McDowell, asked me if I would be a substitute teacher. I told him I did not have a teaching certificate so I wasn't qualified. He replied, "But you have other qualifications." I thought that was pretty nice of him to say that! The upshot of it was that I taught 4th grade for about 6 weeks until the scheduled teacher arrived. I enjoyed it very much. Oftentimes I had wished that I had majored in Education at Wheaton rather than Anthropology, and minored in Anthropology, since most of my missionary career was spent teaching in some area or another.

I continued teaching piano, going out to K.A. once a week and teaching piano at Hillcrest a few hours a week.

I think the routine of the previous years was pretty well established. I don't remember how I juggled my teaching at Narraguta with my teaching at Hillcrest, but I do remember teaching Bible Knowledge at Narraguta until we left for retirement. The class, which I had had for four years, had a little retirement party for me and gave me two ebony heads as a parting gift. I still correspond with Jonathan Nwafor, whose father owned a business in Nigeria. Jonathan was sent to Germany on behalf of his father's business and came back to Jos several times, married a Nigerian girl, Nkiru, and they returned to Germany and have lived there for about 20 years and raised several children. Just this past year he became a citizen of Germany.

We had a few "garage sales" and sold a lot of our things. The naira was about $1.50 to the dollar, so we did all right. Was it that year that Jean Bacon taught me how to knit? I knit a little sweater for Jessica. That was my first and last knitting attempt. I preferred tennis.

At the close of our term, in May or June, SIM had a retirement party for those who were retiring. There were several of us, but I don't remember who the others were.

That about wraps up our years in West Africa – 25 years in Niger and 9 in Nigeria. Well, you know what they say about the farmer. "You can take the farmer out of the farm, but you can't take the farm out of the farmer." So it was with us. You could take us out of Africa but you couldn't take Africa out of us." And we have been back 6 times for short terms, up to 3 months – 3 times to Galmi and Jos; twice to ELWA, Liberia; and once to Chad.

There is more to come. PART 6 will deal with our return trips to Africa during our retirement years. The Lord has been faithful. "It is of the Lord's mercies that we have not been consumed, because his compassions fail not. They are new every morning: great is thy faithfulness." Lamentations 3:22, 23.

PART VI

Chapter 1

E.L.W.A.
MONROVIA, LIBERIA
1986

1986

Two years into our retirement, we were asked to go to Liberia for a three month short term. E.L.W.A. – Eternal Love Winning Africa – had not only a radio station but also a hospital, and they had need of a surgeon. When the phone call came, Burt immediately said, "Yes!" We packed our bags and were on our way in January of 1986. We landed at Roberts Air Force base near Monrovia, were met by fellow missionaries and driven to the ELWA compound. What a beautiful compound it was! We were impressed! The paths and roads were lined with majestic palm trees. The only negative — it was hot and humid!

On the compound were the well equipped hospital, the ELWA studio, a school for missionary kids, a chapel, a print shop, offices and work shops as well as comfortable homes for the missionaries.

Camp Lawana (Liberia Awana) was located at the far end of ELWA's compound. Jim and Chris McNally were in charge of the camp together with capable nationals. Jim and Chris were missionaries from the Center. I had the privilege of teaching a series of lessons on the Grace of God to two one week sessions of girls' camp. I also helped the girls in swimming. Not that we did much swimming! Mostly we tried to keep our balance against the sometimes giant waves that tried to knock us down. Swimming in the ocean was a new and fun experience. Yes, the water was salty and inevitably at times I got a mouthful. The water was warm, probably in the 80's.

Burt enjoyed his work at the hospital. He found the schedule much less demanding than what he had had both at Galmi and in Jos, but he didn't mind the slower pace. He operated every day, at least two patients, but there were always emergencies that came in. Besides surgery, he had the daily rounds and daily outpatients to examine. He also had some speaking engagements at the English speaking church on the compound and the hospital chapel.

While Burt spent most of his time in the hospital, I was kept busy with a variety of activities.

I helped Steve Kehr in the office; I did some work in the library, spoke in the m.k. school and at a women's meeting. But the most challenging opportunity I had was to teach an "Introduction to Biblical Christian Education" for four weeks to the Senior class at the Monrovia Bible College, situated across the road from ELWA and run by the Carver Mission. It was exciting and I learned a lot myself. I prepared notes and questions for the class, and when it all over, the principal asked me where I got those questions. When I told him I wrote them myself, he was amazed – "they were excellent!"

The studio was well equipped with its transmitters and buildings. The shelves were loaded with tapes and videos from all over, mostly the States, and familiar speakers were aired on a daily basis. Many of the programs were produced right there in their own studios by their own people. The Gospel went out over the airwaves to a good bit of Africa by short wave and locally by FM. The antennas were away from the compound in an open field.

The beautiful palm trees swayed to a delightful breeze. Flowers and bushes abounded. It was a beautiful scene. One night as Burt was walking over to the hospital for an emergency, he heard a plop a few feet from him. It was a coconut that fell from a tree. After that, he avoided walking under the palm trees.

Awana had been introduced to Liberia and flourished. John Gay, a Liberian, had received training in the States and returned to Monrovia to become the Liberian Awana director. During our time there, Art Rorheim, Arne Abrahamson and John Deck, visited Liberia on behalf of Awana. John Gay and his family lived in Monrovia, a few miles from ELWA.

Art was the executive director of Awana, Arne was his associate director, and John, an Awana missionary in Northern California. They came to Liberia to encourage the clubs and the Liberian director. They held Awana Olympics on the grounds of the Mid Liberian Baptist Mission near Monrovia, and there were about 200 kids from five churches who participated, all in their colorful Awana uniform t-shirts. Just like back home! Sunday afternoon, we attended the dedication of a brand new building to house the director and an Awana office and store-room for supplies for the entire country. The building was called the "Lance Latham Memorial Building" in honor of Lance Latham who developed the program and who had died just the year before at the age of 91. It was an impressive ceremony and Burt had opportunity to give a tribute to Lance, since we had grown up in his church and knew him well. Art, Arne and John and some nationals all gave tributes, and a plaque was nailed to the wall which read:

IN MEMORY OF
LANCE B. LATHAM
AWANA

Monday, the day after the dedication, Burt accompanied the three visitors along with the Liberian director, John Gay, on an overnight trip 100 miles into the "bush" where there was a club, and the following day they visited another club on their way back.

We got our first taste of shark meat one day when some fishermen caught a shark and sold it to the guest house proprietor. They invited us in for a sample.

It was the end of March and our time in Liberia was over. We packed up and said goodbye to ELWA . Our experience at ELWA was delightful.

"We will miss the beautiful Atlantic Ocean, which shore lies just 50 feet away from our front door. We will miss the beach and the warm, tropical water that we have swum in; we will miss the palm trees that line the beach and the road, the fellowship of missionaries and Christian Liberians, and we hope that some day we will be able to come back and thus be blessed again and be a blessing to others in turn."

In 1990 Liberia had a civil war with much devastation. In 1994 we returned to Liberia for another three months.

March, April, May, 1994 — Return to ELWA

When we returned to ELWA, we were astonished at what we saw. The war of 1990 devastated the land and left people in poverty The once beautiful SIM compound was reduced to bare naked trees, the buildings were pock-marked, the radio station reduced to broadcasting just a few hours in the local area whereas it had gone out all over Africa before. The staff, both black and white were greatly reduced.. An uneasy peace prevailed in Monrovia, but there was still fighting up country, and many civilians were caught behind the lines and couldn't get back to their homes. Children were separated from their parents and living with extended families.

March 12, 1994

"Many refugee camps exist and the U.N. is providing food and shelter. It is not a good situation. Hunger prevails unless you are among the fortunate who have scarce jobs. Seldom a day goes by that we don't have women and children at the door asking for food. Inflation is rife. Wages are low, and sometimes a bag of rice for the Liberian household takes a month's salary of those who have work. Many do not have work.

"The ELWA studio was demolished in the war, the transmitters destroyed. The antennas withstood the onslaught. The rebuilding has begun, and a local FM station broadcasts for about 6 hours a day. The long wave radio station is operating and a small 50 kw. short wave reaches out to the neighboring African countries, but ELWA's voice doesn't reach out the way it used to. A lot of damage was done to the homes here, and along with the shelling came the looting. ELWA is recovering slowly.

"It is so sad to see the stumps of former stately palm trees lining the main road on the compound. ELWA station became a haven for refugees. The refugees themselves cut down the trees to eat the pulp. New trees have been planted, are about 4' tall now, but it will take years before they get to their lofty heights of other years. Lois Balzer's house is a shell as is the Dave Schultz house. The one we are in (the Steve Befus house) is one of the best, but many of the windows don't completely close. We have electricity in only part of the house, and the electricity goes off at 10:25 and comes on at 5:30 a.m. All the other buildings are pock-marked with patched shell holes. Destruction of buildings and trees go hand in hand with neglect to a deteriorating environment.

We visited the site of the Awana Building. It was a shambles, just like most of the buildings in town. John Gay had fled the country and was now a refugee in another country. There was a bullet hole in the plaque on the Awana building on the "B" in "Lance B. Latham."

"War still goes on outside of the capital city. In Monrovia, the ECOMOG troops consisting of soldiers from Nigeria, Ghana, Sierra Leone – African countries on a mission comparable to the U.N. troops in other parts of the world – are trying to keep peace between the three contending Civil war armies. (One is funded by Kadafi, Libya, for

Muslim evangelism and encouragement.) Previously, Islam had very little support in the population. Just a few miles beyond Monrovia in all directions the war continues, tribe against tribe, separating families and friends. Many are the refugees that have fled into Ivory Coast and many families have loved ones "behind the lines" and whom they hadn't seen for three years. Despite poverty, war, deaths in most families, split families, and much illness, (most treated by indigenous witches and sorcerers), many are Christians and many are turning to Christ."

"Physical needs abound and Burt keeps busy in the hospital doing surgery. Once people heard there was a surgeon here, they began to come. Now he's booked up to the last day and can't take anymore except emergencies. There is one thing holding some back — money. Most operations cost $10.00 but big ones are $20.00. It takes some of them a long time to save that much. The nurses get $29.00 a month for 40 hr. weeks — all the hospital can afford.

March 14, 1994

Went 'swimming' Sat. afternoon. Actually, it wasn't a swim. I just stood in the water up to my knees. The surf was so high and strong, it come in and swamped me up to my neck. With difficulty I maintained my balance. I managed to keep my mouth shut, remembering from past experience how salty the water is.

March 18, 1994

"The other night we had a terrific wind and rain storm. The wind blew doors shut, mainly our bedroom and bathroom doors. In the morning, when we get up, the first thing I head for is the bathroom. Ashe! The bathroom door had blown shut in the locked position. I was in big trouble. I went through all the keys in our possession but none of them unlocked the door for me. In the meantime, Burt went outside. I think I knew what he was doing, but that didn't help me any. On returning, he worked with the keys and got one of them to work. What a relief!

"I've been trying to do a bit of water coloring. I brought water color paper, paints, and I remember choosing some brushes to bring but apparently I didn't bring them, so all I have for a brush is the one amateurish brush that came with the paints. Have been trying to capture the waves as they break beneath our windows. I find it hard to do with water colors. The foam is white and how do you do white spray on a white background?

"I am back in the business of making yogurt, saving plastic bags, re-using Saran wrap and aluminum foil, saving empty jars and cans! Just when I was getting Americanized to the point of having no guilt feelings about throwing out those things! When I get back to the States, I'll probably have to go through a period of recovery again before I can get back to the American extravagant, wasteful mentality. I'm back to breaking eggs one at a time into a cup. Back to baking from 'scratch'. No 'scratch' for sale here. Every evening there are a half dozen vendors at the door with fruits — pineapple, paw paw, watermelon, citrus, bananas, avocados, and some vegetables. So we don't lack for food.

March 27, 1994

Saturday, a relaxing day for me but a busy one for Burt with a number of emergencies. After I finished washing clothes, resting a bit, doing a little water coloring – this time a landscape view looking away from the ocean and our house up toward the road leading to the hospital, I went to the beach for a 'swim.' The waves were so strong, they knocked us down and we kept coming up for more and had a good, relaxing time in dangerous waters.

April 5, 1994

"We are keeping busy here and the days go by rapidly. Not like when we were in Chad and I had nothing to do all day. I spend my mornings over at the offices here. I helped to organize the files, and I'm doing some work in the library, cataloging books, and at the same

time, I'm writing some letters for our services director. The fellowship
is good and the air conditioning in the offices is great. Because of the
library, we have done more reading in a week than in a month back
home. No T.V.

"Dad is working hard at the hospital, comes home very tired. He
doesn't have the same energy that he had years ago. Lots of C-sections,
hysterectomies, D and C's. Did his first hernia this week. Several
deaths; one placenta previa — patient bled to death; one 12 year old
boy who had part of a wall fall on him. Dad removed a portion of his
ruptured bowel, but he died a few days later.

"Yesterday we got a note from the U.N. office in Monrovia saying,
'Your brother is critical. Your daughter will call again at noon here at
the U.N.' Our first thought was my brother, Bob. It turned out to be
Burt's brother, Paul. (Paul passed away while we were there).

"Have you ever seen a refrigerator bake bread? I hadn't either, and
I hardly believed it possible until I saw it with my own eyes. Here
she was, Esther, baking 8 loaves of bread at a time in the refrigerator
in the shed behind her house. She showed me how it works. Make
a hole about a foot in diameter in the floor of the fridge, build a
charcoal fire in a head pan and set it in the hole, and the heat of the
coals permeates the insulated fridge that ordinarily would keep things
cold. Esther makes delicious bread, and she has quite a clientele,
not only among the missionaries, but also among certain Liberians.
Esther works as a midwife at the hospital and augments her salary
by baking and selling bread, rolls and cinnamon rolls. The cost of a
loaf of bread – 60 cents; rolls – 40 cents. We applaud her enterprise
and expertise.

"I continue to be fascinated by the ocean. Here we are, just a few
yards from the Atlantic, and as we look west and a little bit north, we
watch the sun set on Argentina. The ocean speaks with many voices.
Sometimes it shouts, screams, is in a tantrum, furiously mad. It is
restless, agitated, always in a tither. It sends its waves bouncing off
the rocks, washing them smooth, and the breakers end up in boiling
pools on the beach. The sound is deafening. If I close my eyes, I see

a snow blizzard, 40 degrees below zero. Sometimes it sounds like the rumbling of an earthquake or a distant freight train rumbling toward a neighboring town. Then it accelerates into a 'boom' as an incoming wave meets one going back out. The power is unimaginable, the noise unceasing. They say we will get used to the constant sounds. Not yet!

"Other times, the ocean speaks in gentler tones. It speaks in inviting tones, saying, 'Come in and play with me.' The surf is just right; the waves are moderated. But these tones can be deceitful, too. With abandonment, one can become careless and venture too far out, and the ocean claims you for itself. Treacherous!

When the tide is low, there is comparative calm, but even if it's calm, it is powerful.

"One thing in common about these many voices of the sea is that they never stop speaking. Relentlessly, they carry on day and night, never ceasing, always speaking, never resting. The hymn writer was right when he talked about the 'wild, tempestuous sea'. Sometimes, I wish they would be quiet. I tire of the constant sound. What would happen if the oceans stood still for a minute? Probably a cataclysmic disaster. I am glad God is in control. I am reminded of Psalm 104:9 'Thou hast set a bound that they may not pass over, that they turn not again to cover the earth.' And Job 38:4, 8 – 11 'Where wast thou . . . Or who shut up the seas . . . and said thus far shall thou come, but no farther and here shall thy proud waves be stayed.'

April 6, 1994

"The U.S. Embassy is here in Monrovia and every 2nd Saturday they open their doors to American and European families that are not connected to the Embassy for a buffet lunch. As you enter the premises under heavy security, you pass from poverty into wealth. You see a covered pavilion with patio type tables and chairs set around, some down by the pool and in the gardens. Beyond the pool are two tennis courts, and within the premises are apartments where the embassy personnel live.

"Saturday we went to the Embassy with Martha and Stan Bruning and Helen Inman as a belated anniversary present to ourselves. Their buffet lunch was really a dinner for eight American dollars. There were 3 kinds of meat, potatoes, lasagna, egg plant, other vegetables, rolls. The atmosphere was nice. The food was excellent. You would never know that poverty exists outside the doors. The situation is unreal. Nothing is ever too good for U.S. government workers. Then you remember that you came to Liberia for a different reason, to bring the Good News to a needy people. You feel a little guilty about being here at the Embassy, but enjoy the few hours you are here and rationalize that you don't do this very often. We have gone once, to celebrate our 49th wedding anniversary."

In 1986 Firestone Plantation was a thriving industry with thousands of acres of rubber trees that produced latex to sell overseas. ELWA was privileged to go into the hundreds of camp sites and start Bible classes. The war stopped everything. It was just the year before our return that ELWA was able to travel the 40 miles to Firestone and hold classes once again. Workers were beginning to return to the camps which were also filled with refugees from the war. Firestone was hoping to start up the industry again. The whole project is subsidized by Firestone Co. in Detroit. Donna Welch and John and Marge Campbell spearheaded the weekly visits to the camps with Liberian Bible teachers. On occasion I was able to accompany them

As in 1986, we couldn't pass up the opportunity to visit Sue and Terry and the boys in Nigeria as long as we were on the African continent. From Liberia, we flew to Abidjan where we picked up our flight to Kano on Middle East airlines. The plane ride to Nigeria was fine, but the hassle at the airport was frustrating. When we left Liberia, our luggage weighed 42 kilos. We did not add anything to it or even open it, but at the Abidjan airport, it weighed in at 55 kilos. All the arguing was useless. They charged us for 15 kilos of overweight baggage and we knew they had tampered with their scales. The bottom line was that we got there safely with our baggage.

Our ten days in Nigeria were great. We not only saw the Hammacks, but we saw many of the Africans that we had worked with and grown to love. We also saw a lot of missionary friends of long ago because our time there included graduation week at Hillcrest and many missionary families came to see their kids graduate or else pick up their kids for the summer holidays.

One evening we had supper with our good friend Hauwa Kadima and her son, Daniel. Her pastor husband, Ameche, ran off with another woman in 1983, the year Daniel was born, taking their other children with him, but leaving her to rear newborn Daniel by herself. Tears of joy flowed as we saw each other again; tears of sorrow as we parted, perhaps never to meet again this side of heaven. (Daniel, today, in 2005 has just completed four years at LeTourneau College in Texas.)

Another highlight was spending time with cousin, Claudia Long, who at the time was a physical education teacher at Hillcrest. All too soon it was time to say good-bye. From Jos to Kano, from Kano to Brussels, Brussels to New York, New York to Orlando and back to Sebring. We had come full circle in three and a half months.

Chapter 2

Chad –

Republique du Tchad Jan. – March 1991

I don't remember what the circumstances were that initiated the plan for us to go to Chad for three months to help out in the hospital in Bebalem. Bebalem is located two hours by plane out of N'djamena, the capital of the country. SIM seconded us to TEAM for the duration.

We arrived in Bebalem by M.A.F. air in the midst of a missions conference that included several missions, including TEAM. We moved into our little apartment – kitchen, bathroom, bedroom and all purpose room. It was filthy! It had been empty for some months and prior to that it had been occupied by a bachelor. The drawers and cabinets were filled with rat and cockroach dirt. It took me five days to wash every shelf, cabinet, dish, pot and pan. For those first few days, we ate with other missionaries and had chicken 5 times, which fortunately I liked but Burt didn't. Morning fare was bread and coffee.

"This house had neither gas stove nor bottled gas nor fridge. When I said I was planning to do all my own cooking, one of the missionaries lent me her stove because she never uses it. All the missionaries' homes have outside cook stoves and ovens make of bricks. For the ovens, they are made with 2/3 of a drum (barrel) with the lid serving as the door. Underneath is a place where the wood fire is built. Amazingly, it works. They do all their baking in them, including bread, etc. All the missionaries have cooks who do <u>everything</u> — local Chadians who have been taught by missionaries. I am amazed at their capabilities. For the cooking on top of the stove, there are two "burners". The fires are started with wood and followed up with charcoal. You would have to see this to believe it.

"There is not an extra working fridge on the compound, but by the first of February, a big truck will arrive from France loaded with medicines and supplies. They think there are two new fridges on it. These trucks come periodically, crossing the desert and going right past Galmi enroute here. Until a fridge is found for me, I will be using a shelf in my neighbor's fridge. There are about 18 adult missionaries here – all European and mostly French and Swiss. One Swede!

"Let me tell you about the toilet seat situation. This apartment has none. When I asked abut it, they said there was none available. One Canadian missionary who was here for the conference and stayed a few days extra, was very helpful to me, especially in the area of language. Everything is in French, RAPID French. She told me that the French didn't think it (a toilet seat) was a big deal. Most of the houses do not have toilet seats. So I'm getting used to the feel of the cold, narrow porcelain on my bottom.

"Do you remember the Klopfenstein family who worked in Niger? Daniel and his family were at Galmi for two years in lieu of military service. That same system holds, and his nephew, Philippe and family, are here. He is also a doctor, just out of medical school, doing his military service. Another doctor and his family are here doing the same and one left (a bachelor) yesterday. (*Apparently the French think that the hardship of serving in Africa is equivalent to serving in the military!!*) Others – nurses, maintenance, etc. are also here for two year stints, mostly, and the hospital runs on short termers.

"There is a Chadian doctor who got his training in Russia. What a story he has to tell of his experiences of discrimination there, both as a black and as a Christian. He is a very capable 'chef de medcin' here and keeps the continuity going. He has been back about eight years.

"Then there is a Chadian male nurse who does operations. He learned from missionary doctors along the way and he is very good. He does everything – hydroceles, hernias, hemorrhoids, hysterectomies, etc. Both missionaries and Chadians alike have great confidence in him.

"I think of myself as a 'seasoned missionary', but I have never seen situations like this. I think I am very soft and spoiled compared to what both missionaries and Chadians put up with. I thought Niger was on the bottom of the list in terms of poverty, but Chad surpasses all. It also has the distinction of having the largest mosque in Africa in N'djamena. Moundou is 40 miles and two hours away by road, so you know what condition the roads are in.

"But the Christians here far surpass the Christians that we have known in Niger and Nigeria in terms of spirituality and growth. We went to church on the compound Sunday, and there were about a thousand in attendance. In town, Bebelem, about a kilometer away, there are three more churches.

"This is a 250 bed hospital and there must be about 100 Chadian nurses and aids. Everyone who works at the hospital must have had Bible School. There are no others. There is an exceptionally good relationship between TEAM and the church."

Feb. 1, 1991

"I think I mentioned the outside stoves and ovens that the missionaries use. For a whole week of cooking with gaz, I have disdained them, but I decided yesterday to give mine a try, so I bought some wood. This morning, I tried to make a fire to boil a large pot of drinking water. Boiling drinking water takes a lot of gaz and my one bottle of gaz has to last until we leave. I did all the right things – put paper in, then twigs on top of it, struck a match, and voila, a fire! Then I added the charcoal and voila, it went out. My neighbor's stove is back to back with mine, and she had had hers going since early morning, so she told me to use her stove since she was finished with it. So much for my first attempt.

Then I decided to give the oven a try. It is a 50 gallon drum mounted on a brick base with space for a wood fire underneath. I tried to get a fire going but failed, so my neighbor's "girl" (woman) came to my rescue and got it going. The two houses share the same oven. I decided to make some muffins from a mix. My neighbor had bread in the oven while I had my muffins baking. It was so successful I decided to make a hot milk cake while the oven was hot. So, — one cup of sugar – an estimated cup because all measures are done in liters and their parts — it takes 40 cubes of sugar to make one cup. I borrowed my neighbor's mortar and pestle and pounded the cubes; one cup of flour – sift out all the potential bugs; one cup milk – mix your powdered milk with water, then measure. Crack your eggs first into a cup to ensure their goodness. Finally, put them all together and into the oven – a success!

Feb. 4, 1991

"Saturday I successfully started a fire on my outside stove! When I had finished boiling my water, I had some nice hot charcoal so decided to roast some African sweet potatoes and carrots in them for dinner (lunch). I wrapped them in foil and put them on the charcoal, too. Forty five minutes later, they were charcoal, too. Then Burt suggested putting some small stones on the coals and the food on top, which I did. Then after 10 minutes, I turned them, gave them another 10 minutes, and they were delicious. I can't believe this – that at 69 years of age and 'retired', I am doing all these things.

"Saturday a.m. Dad and I went for a walk in the little village adjacent to this compound. It is a beautiful village with large and small trees and bushes and round brick houses with thatch roofs. Ground cover is dirty sand, trod upon for centuries. But on the whole, the village is pretty clean as African villages go.

"Church in French is at 7:30 a.m. so yesterday we went to the French service. I got about 25% of it. There are about 100 in attendance. The Gambai service is at 10 a.m. with about 1,000 in attendance. After church Dad and I walked over to the market in the town of Bebelem, about a kilometer from here. It's about the size of the Wednesday market at Galmi. We bought what we thought was 'acha', the cereal that Miango serves for breakfast. We brought it home and were informed that it was sesame seed! What do I do with about two cups of sesame seed?

"In connection with the hospital there is a Bible school which is not in session now. There is also a school for kids of African employees. As far as the eye can see, all the buildings and property belong to the hospital.

"On Jan. 5, a 10-wheeler truck, a six wheeler truck and a Toyota passenger car left Southern France for Bebelem. Saturday, Feb. 2, they arrived. They crossed the Mediterranean Sea, traveled through Algeria, Niger – going through Arlit and Tahaoua and Galmi – they spent a Sunday there – then on to Kano, Maidugari, N'djamena and here. The trip took 30 days, and almost half of them were spent at border crossings. The trucks were loaded with medicines and supplies. There were also some goodies for missionaries and last night we all enjoyed figs, dried fruit, pistachios, potato chips and prunes. Six Frenchmen – 5 men and 1 woman – accompanied the trucks. The trucks will be sold here in Chad. The six return to N'djamena today and fly back to France tomorrow. A Christian group in France supplies everything and sends trucks loaded with supplies from time to time. The men said they were given a rough time at the Algerian border because of the Gulf crisis, so there will be no more trips until that is resolved.

"Dad is enjoying his surgery, but I have a lot of time on my hands to miss you all.

—

Feb. 11, 1991

The hot season was beginning to show its teeth. Days reached 100 degrees but at night we appreciated a sheet over us. There was a generator that was on in the mornings and from 5 to 9 p.m. at night. At first I was disappointed that it went off so early, but then it broke down and we were out of electricity altogether and had to resort to borrowed lamps and one pressure lamp. It gave us an opportunity to sit out on the porch and enjoy the stars and God's handiwork that first evening without electricity.

"I came in at 8:30 to take a shower. I got wet and two arms lathered and suddenly, no water. I called for Dad and a bucket and he managed to squeeze a helmet full of water out of a lower pipe line, so I finished my shower but was left with a soapy feeling because the water is so soft. Except for drinking water which is in bottles, that was the last of the water until the morning. We hadn't realized it, nor had other missionaries thought about telling us, but without the electricity to pump the water, we had been draining the water tank of its supply. About 8 a.m., we were supplied with a drum of water for our house and our neighbor's house and told that the generator might be fixed by noon. So I was able to wash my face and "flush" the toilet and wash dishes and was very thankful for the drum of water. Whereas two nights ago I was wishing that the lights would stay on later than 9, now I am thankful for electricity from 5 – 9 p.m. which also runs the pump that brings the water through the pipes to the houses.

"About 1 p.m., the lights went on and shortly after, I turned on the spigot in the kitchen sink and out spurted beautiful brown, rusty water. Even in its filth it was a beautiful sight. After about 10 minutes, it came through clear. The same routine took place in the bathroom sink and shower. Water is the most precious commodity in the world in my viewpoint, and we don't appreciate it until we don't have it.

"No fridges came on the trucks so I am continuing to use a shelf in my neighbor's fridge. But the trucks did bring 15 tons of medicine and supplies, and I have been helping in the pharmacy to unload, sort and stack medicines on shelves. I have also been "popping pills", i.e., pushing them out of their plastic wrappers and putting them in cans, thus saving a lot of space. It helps to fill my mornings, which is good.

I think I'll call it quits since its that magic time between 5 and 9 p.m. when the lights are on, the water runs through the faucet, and it's time to make supper."

Feb. 20

"The biggest news this week is that we got a toilet seat! After four weeks of juggling on the porcelain rim, getting a rim around my bottom, one of the missionary families brought over a seat. It was their own personal property which had come on the truck two weeks ago. Mind you, this is not just an ordinary toilet seat as we know toilet seats. This is a white, hard, thin plastic seat, complete with white, hard, thin plastic cover. We sit on it gingerly, so as not to crack it. There is nothing quite so painful as a cracked toilet seat. So we want to avoid it at all costs. And besides, it was very generous of the Ankers to let us (this house) have it. I am very thankful for it and once I am seated comfortably on it, I can catch up on my reading without discomfort. As I have always said, 'It's the little things in life that matter' — such as toilet seats.

"It came about in this manner. Saturday night we were playing Pictionary with some of the missionaries, in French of course, and Burt drew a picture of a toilet seat on the board. After our initial noise about there not being a toilet seat in the house, everyone forgot about it since there was no way of buying one in these parts. But this one had come on the truck with the Ankers' loads, and obviously they didn't need it at the moment. Burt's drawing reminded them so next day Nicola came over with it.

"As you will notice by my lengthy dissertation on toilet seats, there is not much to write about. The medicines are all stacked on the shelves, and everyone is so busy they don't have time to give me a job. Days become very long and monotonous. Dad is very busy at the hospital doing 4 – 6 surgeries a morning and he is enjoying his time here. I like nights best here, even though the lights go out at 9 p.m. I can go to bed and wake up in the morning and it's the next day, one day closer to going home. Five and a half weeks to go. We have word that a new fridge is on the way from N'Djamena, so we may have a fridge the last five weeks of our stay here.

"Beret will be interested to know that I have been sketching some scenes of Bebelem. It is hot here – well over 100 degrees."

March 4, 1991

"Yes, we got a fridge and what a difference it makes! It's a new one. A missionary's loads had been misplaced for a year and a half, and finally were discovered some place in the country, probably in a government warehouse. In the meantime, he has been working in a town where there is 24 hr. electricity, so he bought an electric fridge and sold this one. So TEAM or the hospital, (I'm not sure which) bought it, and we are back to a kerosene refrigerator again. It is not as big as the Servel we had at Galmi, but it is adequate for the two of us and works well. It is called 'Dometic' and made in Sweden.

"This week-end I am going to a TEAM ladies' retreat which is being held at Bere, a mission station about 40 miles from here. I'll be flying MAF on Thursday. It's a ten minute flight or 1½ hours by road. I'll be coming back on Sunday by road with a missionary who is coming to Bebelem for some reason. So I'll have both experiences

"The next week Dad and I will be spending a few days in Moundou with some missionaries who have invited us." (Paul and Ruth Cochrane)

This letter ended with a discourse on how hot it was. Hotter than Galmi? Yes and no – Ruth, yes; Burt, no. It was about 110 degrees in the shade. A surprising rain tempered the temperature on Feb. 28 but increased the humidity for the next few days. Then a decrease in the humidity made it bearable again.

———

I had never read much of Amy Carmichael, but with time on my hands, I did a lot of reading. She was able to put into writing the feelings that I had each time we were separated from our loved ones. Her *Candles in the Dark* says it well. Here it is:

Candles in the Dark

" . . . . commit them to Him. It is the Wounded Hands that part you. That was said to me when the stabbing pain of the parting was almost too much to bear. It was the thought of their pain that broke me; it may be like that with you. Then take the Word that comforted me, 'It is the Wounded hands that part you, one on them, the other on you', and He will not leave them comfortless. It is hard to say goodbyes, like being torn in pieces without chloroform. But it is for His sake; that carries one through."

Amy Carmichael was able to put into words my heart's desire for all my children, my grandchildren, my great grandchildren and those generations to come whom I haven't met yet. A blessing that came out of being in Chad was getting acquainted with Amy's writings.

Father, Hear Us

Father, hear us, we are praying,
Hear the words our hearts are saying.
We are praying for our children.

Keep them from the powers of evil,
From the secret, hidden peril.
Father, hear us for our children.

From the whirlpool that would suck them,
From the treacherous quicksand, pluck them,
Father, hear us for our children.

From the worldling's hollow gladness,
From the string of faithless sadness,
Father, Father, keep our children.

—

Through life's troubled waters steer them,
Through life's bitter battles cheer them,
Father, Father, be thou near them.

Read the language of our longing,
Read the wordless pleadings thronging,
Holy Father, for our children.

And wherever they may bide,
Lead them Home at eventide.

Amy Carmichael

Chapter 3

Back to Niger
October 14—Dec. 17 , 2001

This morning — it was about 11:30 on Sunday — as we were lifting up our hearts and voices in praise to God in our church in Sebring, my thoughts went back to Galmi, Dogarawa, Malbaza, Magariya, Gidan Arna, Hillcrest, Tudun Wada where six hours earlier, hearts were lifted up in worship to God — all churches that we had visited over the past three months in Niger and Nigeria. At the same time, thousands of other congregations in Niger and Nigeria were worshipping the God, our God, of the Bible. Add to that the thousands of congregations in all of Africa and let your thoughts wander to the whole world, and you would count millions of people who had already gathered together to worship the Lord and those in the West who would be meeting soon. Put all the voices together and what a mighty choir that would be! Imagine what heaven will be like!

Twenty seven years ago, when we left working at Galmi in Niger, there were no churches in Dogarawa, Malbaza or Gidan Arna in Niger. What has been amazing to us this trip is that in village after village, churches have sprung up, pastored by indigens, and although congregations are small, there is a voice in the midst of Islam, and people can hear the Word if they so desire, and thus are without excuse. There is religious freedom, although in some areas local opposition to Christianity is visible. God is at work in the world — we here in America are but a small part of the whole!

In a sense, our visit back to Galmi was a closure to our missionary experience. True, after we left Galmi, we spent nine more years in Nigeria, but having spent the first 25 years of our missionary career in Galmi, our formative years, it was only natural that we would like to go back once again.

That dream became reality when, with passports, visas, and tickets in hand, we left Sebring on Oct. 14, 2001. In Orlando, we boarded a Delta/Air France plane and arrived in Niamey, Niger, via Paris, France, the afternoon of the 15th. We were met there by our good friends, Gordon and Judy Evans and spent two days with them. Judy is the daughter of Carey and Shirley Lees, who worked alongside of us in Niger and for some time, with us at Galmi. She and her siblings were playmates of our children at Galmi and at K.A. and Hillcrest. Gordon has been the director of SIM Niger the past four years . In Niamey we visited with Jim and Sandy Rendell and Jim and Connie Knowlton. Both Jims are m.k.'s. Jim Rendel is the son of Betty and George Rendel who worked in Nigeria, and Jim Knowlton is the son of Dave and Hazel Knowlton who spent their missionary career in Niger, part of it at Galmi. It is amazing how many m.k.'s are back on the fields as missionaries. We had lunch with Pat Irwin who invited Hannatu Cisu to visit. Hannatu is working in the library at Sahel Academy and is the daughter of Cisu and Hassana. Cisu has been with the Lord for many years, having died of an aneurysm. Hassana raised her children alone with the help of some of our nurses, and the children as adults have responsible jobs and are walking with the Lord.

Jim Rendel flew us to Galmi on Thursday, Oct. 18. Another m.k., Ian Rideout and his wife and family, pilot son of missionaries who were contemporaries of ours in Nigeria, has recently joined Jim Rendel in Niamey as a second pilot. He went along to get acquainted with the terrain. A number of old friends greeted us at the Galmi air

—

strip, among them Hassana, Kwawa, A'i, Uma, and more. And since then, we have seen many, many African friends. We were ushered to our little apartment and the first three evening meals were with missionaries, Doug and Quimby Wilson, Alan and Deb Waters and Mathias Kohls — his wife, Iris, was in Niamey for a week.

There are three doctors here regularly now. Everyone is interested in how it was back in the early days and fortunately, at the suggestion of Iris Kohls, I brought pictures taken back in the 50's, 60's and 70's.

The compound has changed. There are about 30 houses around it. The front of the compound is the back and the back is the front, and all the new houses face each other or are situated diagonally. We are in one of the new guest houses. It's right behind the old three-room store room/boys' house facing the air strip, the first building at the station. Nobody is living in our house so it stands empty and deteriorates. But it could be fixed up and made livable again.

It is hot here. Don't know the temp but HOT. And this is not the hot season. We have a swamp cooler and ceiling fan in the bedroom and fan in the living room. It's quite bearable, and the nights are cooling off a bit.

Everyone asks about all our kids, and we go through from top to bottom and give them the news. They remember your names — Lari, Haro, Johnny Jack, Cheri, Suzanne and Pum.

Galmi has become an oasis in the desert. In 1950 when everything was so barren, Mr. Dave Osborne, director of Niger, said to me, "Some day this will be the garden spot of Niger." I thought he must be dreaming, but didn't say so. Fifty two years later, his dream is reality. The difference is water and lots of it. Some time after we left, the government co-operated in digging a deep well on the compound, at least 1000 ft. deep. Warm artesian well water gushed up to within a hundred ft. of the surface, and from there, it was easily pumped out in abundance. Now the station is almost a jungle — trees, bushes, flowers, vegetable gardens.

Early Friday morning, the first of a string of visitors arrived. Number one was Issou — a special visitor. Issou had been our houseboy, then cook, then only worker for many years. As a matter of fact, Issou started out as a water hauler early in our missionary career. On either side of a donkey a 5 gallon tulu (clay water pot) was hung, and Issou made trips back and forth to the well and brought back water and poured it into 50 gallon drums in our kitchen and bathroom. It was fitting that he was the first to greet us. He is about 70 years old now, the patriarch of his family. Before he left, Ila Tanko joined him. Ila had worked in the operating room while we were there, but left after we were gone due to some confrontation. Together we reminisced for awhile. Kwalkwali is dead. Dari is dead. Kourma is dead. Kourma's brother, Idi, is dead. Yahaya is dead. Hashi is in prison! Kwalkwali, Dari and Yahaya all professed to know the Lord and so did Hashi.

A'i Mai Frere and Madubu were among our visitors. A'i was one of our Awana girls, married a non-Christian, divorced after some years, then married Mai Frere, a Christian and hospital worker. Madubu was the former second wife of Dau Duka. One night she had a vision — an extremely bright light shone on her and a voice said, "The Christian way is the right way." This vision came and went several times. The next day, she walked over to the hospital and talked with one of the nurses who led her to the Lord. At the same time, Dau Duka began to deny Christ. They were divorced. Madubu continued in the Way, but Dau Duka drifted farther and farther away.

Another A'i was the wife of Mohammadu. She was a Christian from Maradi. Mohammadu was a local boy who went to Maradi and found work with Lofty and Jo Grimshaw. He professed to know Christ. After he and A'i were married, they moved back to Gidan Dutse. He couldn't stand the pressure of his family and neighbors and went back into Islam. After several children, Mohammadu took another wife and A'i returned to her family in Maradi. As custom dictates, the three children were left with the father. The new wife didn't appreciate caring for the children, and finally in desperation, Mohammadu pleaded with A'i to come back. She returned under the condition that she and the children could go to church. He agreed.

Eventually, Mohammadu came back to the Lord and is active in the local church. Lydia, widow of Ibrahim, and Ashibi, wife of Idi Noma visited, then Uma, former cook and boy, and Hassana, wife of Cisu. Thus ended Friday, our first day back

Saturday was also a busy day getting settled in and entertaining visitors. Our first Sunday back, we visited the UPEEN church in town, a break off from the EERN church of Niger. It meets at 8 a.m., and the other one meets in the same building at 10:45, although the UPEEN church is building its own structure on the same compound as the first one. Seems strange. Each has its own pastor. We think they should get together and be one group instead of presenting to the village of Galmi a division among the believers. Individuals in each group are friendly with each other. It may be that the church leaders of each church do not want to relinquish their positions — for instance, who would be the pastor, the elders, etc.? Politics!

A typical church service includes choirs from every group — the women, the young people, special groups, many of them accompanied by the drums, gourds filled with stones and tambourines. A service lasts at least 2 hours. There are testimonies, announcements, offering, (sometimes two) prayer requests and prayer, then finally a message. All in Hausa, of course, and of course, the women on one side of the church and the men on the other.

On this particular morning, as we walked from the hospital into town and back, we were stopped and greeted along the way so often, that the trip took twice as long. So much so, our missionary friends told us they were going on ahead. Among the church announcements was that the founder of the hospital and his wife were in the congregation that morning. And much to my surprise, the pastor called on me to close in prayer. In Hausa! Why me? A woman! And her husband sitting with the men on their side! Amazingly enough our Hausa came back readily so I managed all right. That same thing happened again in another church — I forget which one — but I was called on to close in prayer. I found out that it was not unusual for pastors to call on the women to pray.

That same afternoon we climbed Rollie Mountain. We took some pictures. Unfortunately the indicator that tells what number is up stopped at number 17. And from that time on, all the pictures that I took did not develop. I wasted 2 1/2 rolls and got nothing. Especially disappointing to me were the pictures that I took of "my kids" who were now adults, and I promised to send them copies. When we got home, I took my camera in to a shop for possible repair. They told me it was a lost cause. The camera is about 20 years old. They said that the average life of a camera is 10 years and that I had already gotten twice the amount of time out of it. They told me to throw it away! I could buy a new one for less than the price of fixing the old one.

That afternoon climb up Mt. Rollie proved to be a disappointment to me. Along the road and reaching up the base of the hills was trash, mostly discarded plastic bags, all the way west from the hospital to our old house. Rain had washed away a lot of dirt, exposing rocks in abundance and creating deep wash-outs. The climb was hazardous. Graves dotted the hills, and it took some doing not to step on them. We had to zigzag in order to avoid the thorn trees that had been planted to prevent more erosion. I decided to stop before I got to the top, but Burt went all the way to the top and then walked east toward the hospital, while I slowly descended at the level of our old house. He ended up in Gidan Dutse and came down through the village. He met Dau Duka, who has three wives and 17 children at the present time. His oldest son, Mousa, is dead. He was a paradox. As a boy, he made a profession of faith. Then he began to steal. Then he repented and was baptized. But we heard that he went back into thievery, roamed the country, did drugs and alcohol. Death claimed him. Was our work with him in vain?

Monday, Oct. 22.

Burt started work at the hospital in O.R. Here are some paragraphs written by Burt:

"I went back into the operating room again for the first time in 17 years. This seemed normal, but a few differences in program, procedure and equipment made it a bit difficult. Most things have been improved and there is no lack of help. Hospital workers have increased to 120 from 19. There seems to be a big crowd in the O.R. area. Now we have African — mostly Niger men — anesthetists, and we step grandly into the scene with the patients already on the table and under anesthesia. Spinals are still the modum for lower body surgery.

"Doug Wilson is here with Matthias Kohls — American and German respectively and both very capable men. A few minutes into a c-section with Doug got me oriented and a bit of guidance kept me up with changes. Doug wades right into most anything, today a wide and apparently scarred and thickened ureter with no stones involved, though a provisional diagnosis."

Mai Muna washed clothes and floors for me. In the afternoon, I went to the office in the old dental building which Bill and Candy Lyons had built and used. I helped Zachari with typing lessons. As I returned I found Minne, Kourma's wife, waiting for me. That same day, Hawa, Issou's wife came to greet, then Dawi and Alhassen, both Awana boys who have gone back into Islam. Alhassen is now known as Langalanga — tall, thin. Souley came to greet.

Souley is working for the Wilsons and had previously worked for the Knowltons and the Evanses. When we re-visited Galmi in 1990, Souley was working for Gordon and Judy Evans, who were living in our old house. The Evanses had made our living room into two bedrooms to accommodate their family of five children. Among other things, Souley baked bread for the Evanses, so I knew he was capable. I engaged him one Saturday morning to come and bake bread for me. It was then that I asked him who had taught him to bake bread and he said it was Nicky Knowlton. I watched him as he threw in some flour, some melted butter and milk in a bowl and tossed in some dry yeast, never measuring it, then an egg or two, more flour and then he kneaded it until it felt right. Then he left it to rise, but not for long — maybe a half hour. He beat it down and made some sticky bottoms, some rolls, and three loaves and let them rise again. I carried on from there and after an appropriate time, struck a match, turned on the propane gas and lit the oven which brought the project to a satisfactory conclusion. All that was left to do was to eat and enjoy. Souley has heard the Way for many years, and he is an honest, trustworthy adult, and he nods in agreement when we speak about the Lord, but I doubt whether he is saved.

In our day, Kwalkwali and Dari visited outlying villages and preached to the people. After a while, they decided that the missionaries or the church, or someone, should pay them for what they were doing. Nobody agreed to their requests, so they quit going out to the villages to preach. Dari's sons are Christians. Sanusi attends the church in Dogarawa. Both he and his brother, Mamman, were Awana kids. Heinz Reulicke worked with Sanusi in recent years, discipling him He came to greet one morning. I had a picture of Dari which I gave to him. He was thrilled to see his father when his father was young, not married. His wife, Saratu, is expecting in four months, so I gave him a baby's undershirt. We read Scripture together and prayed together. Then Mamman visited again.

Then Ibrahim Alhassen came. He reminded me that he had worked for the Chapples — Don and Phyllis — who were at Galmi for a term and are now missionaries in Ecuador. He was one of the boys who earned an airplane ride in a contest we had in Awana. He said he still believes in his heart, but he has trouble saying so publicly. We read John 14:1-6 together and I prayed with him asking the Lord to give him strength to make a stand for Christ.

Kourma means deaf and dumb and that he was. Although he had a name, he was known as Kourma. Meningitis caused his deafness as a child. Yet he was able to make himself understood by sign language, grunts and actions. He was our faithful water boy for years, carrying on for as long as we needed donkeys with tulus to fill our drums and the drums at the hospital. Kourma worked for Galmi station from the beginning; he was Zeb and Irene Zabriskie's boy before we arrived. Kourma's brother, Idi, was the father of Souley.

Tuesday, I helped Quimby Wilson with Hausa for about 45 minutes. She wanted to learn Hausa just by using phrases, said she wasn't all that good or interested in learning the grammar which is the way I wanted to teach her. However, I went along with her, but it wasn't more than a couple of weeks that she said she didn't want lessons anymore. Was too busy.

Mai Daji and Alhassen came during the ten a.m. break. Burt was there for tea and after a good visit, Burt and Mai Daji left but Alhassen lingered. I wondered why but took advantage of his being here by confronting him with what he had learned as a boy. Then I asked him if he could still read and he said yes, so I asked him to read some Scripture for me and opened the Bible to John 14. He read it well. When he got to 14:6, he said it from memory. He said he remembered and still believed, but one wonders, since he is doing Salla. Alhassen was one of my Awana boys who learned all the verses that were required up to that point. He even went to Jos with us when we moved there and worked for us a little while. But after some weeks, he returned. He was homesick.

On Wednesday, Issou visited again. He is old, looks old, acts old. He is probably 70, the maigida of his house. Has many children; says he is poor. We remember that his older brother, Alaha, was killed in Lagos when a truck ran over him, and Issou raised his children, too, since he was next oldest. I read to him from John 14. Had morning tea at Wilsons along with the rest of the missionaries. Wed. is a special morning tea time for the missionaries. The plane came. Jim Rendel was the pilot and he was breaking in Ian Rideout, the new pilot. Ian's wife and several others were on the plane. Ian's wife is expecting and saw the doctor and made arrangements for the baby to be born at Galmi. After tea, I went back to the O.R. with Burt and Doug and watched Burt amputate a toe, and Doug do a C-section. Things are different now in the O.R. I had to don gown and shoes as well as cap and mask before they would let me in the O.R.

After lunch we went to the market. It is huge and filthy and disorganized to our way of thinking. We were greeted by so many we couldn't even shop, so we came home. There is a new, large, beautifully painted mosque with turrets in the center of town. But there is garbage all over the town. We saw Attabo who greets Rollie. Below is another one of Burt's paragraphs:

People in the area have gotten wind of our arrival and are flocking in to greet us. All Ruth's old Awana boys are middle aged men in appearance. Africa is a hard place and these should be young looking men in the U.S. and European climate. Today was Wed. and we walked to the Galmi market. Many recognized us and were totally surprised to see us. Some were so taken aback they had to ask around before they'd believe it really was the old likita, tsoho, gwabro (very humorous and getting lots of laughs"), lokotoro, etc. Several showed old surgical scars and demonstrated healed lesions. Happy to say thanks again but not one gave witness to salvation in all the market. Islam is the majority and few can stem the tide.

Burt met Hassada — "a Buzu (Tuareg?) who remembers us and asked about 'Zabriskie', who with Irene taught him Bible, no doubt in Tahoua. He is a believer."

My first visitor on Thurs., Oct. 25, was Madubu, who works for Iris and Matthias Kohl. She had five children by Dau Duka. Kanduwa had three by him. Kanduwa visited one morning and brought us up to date on her children. Besides Musa, whom we mentioned earlier, there are Haruna and Esta. Haruna is a judge in Maine Soroa. He sent Kanduwa money to build a new house in Tsarnawa, near Konni and supports Dau Duka. Their daughter, Esta, lives with Kanduwa. Kanduwa says that she and Esta go to church in Tsarnawa, are still "following." I gave her a picture of Binta, her sister, I believe.

Then Dawi came and Burt arrived for 10 a.m. break. Mai Muna went to the market for me to buy wheat (alkama) and onions (albassa) for the Evans in Niamey. After Burt returned to the hospital and Dawi left, Madai Hassen from Madaoua came to greet. Hassen, who was at one time our pastor in Galmi, died a few years ago, so Madai lives in Madaoua town with some of her children and grandchildren. Then Fatima, Dari's wife, came. I had another picture of Dari which I gave her and she was delighted. Now she could show her grandchildren a picture of their grandfather! Dari died of liver failure two years ago.

—

I made some yogurt ice cream today. Just like old times!

On Friday, Mamman, the plumber, came to fix a slow drain in our kitchen. I found out later that the plumber was a relative of the Fulani family who lived on the hill — Mousa and Hauwa. As a boy, something frightened Mousa and he jumped right over our fence — not climbed but jumped! One afternoon I visited Hauwa on the hill. Mousa was away for the afternoon but Mamman was there. We learned about the Fulani young man who climbed a telephone pole to get a better look at his herd, reached out with both hands onto the wire. He dropped to the ground. Both hands were cooked, and he may have lost both of them, for sure he lost one. He was treated at the hospital. That's a hard way to learn about the properties of electricity.

Saturday afternoon I did e-mails and in the evening we and the rest of the compound had tacos at Deb and Alan Waters' house..

On Sunday, Oct. 28, we went to church in Dogarawa with Alan and Deb Waters and Matthias and Iris Kohls. Alan is English; Deb is American. They met at Galmi a few years ago when both were here on short term assignments. Alan is in charge of the pharmacy. Matthias is one of the doctors here and Deb works in the office. They are on a two year assignment and this summer they go back to Germany where he finishes up his medical program. They have a 13 month old daughter, Anika and are expecting a son soon after they return to Germany. There is a church in the village of Dogarawa pastored by Nomo, a graduate of Aguie Bible School and his wife, Jimma. The church is really an extension of his house, a cornstalk enclosure with benches and pulpit. Very few attend but at least there is a Christian presence there. He had a good sermon on the second coming of Christ. We returned to the Kohls' house for "coffee and".

In the afternoon Idi Yahaya came. We gave him a photo of himself. His father, Yahaya, was our cook for many years, became known as "babban kuku," (great cook). Early on he made a profession of faith. He had a problem, he had two wives — one old one and one young. The dilemma was "What to do?" On his own, he decided to put away one of them. We thought that was wise. But he chose to put away his first, his older wife, and keep the younger one. We didn't exactly agree with his choice, but putting away multiple wives is always a dilemma. He made a wise decision though in that he built a hut for his first wife in his compound, cared for her there, kept and fed her but did not sleep with her. At least that is what he said! For many years he remained only a nominal Christian. After we left Galmi, he came back to the Lord and became an outspoken Christian, fearlessly standing up to the malams and Muslims of the village. After two years of witnessing, he died. His testimony remains.

Wed., Oct. 31, 2001

The wife of Mai Shanu, Fatsima (?) came to greet in the morning. Mai Shanu was the head malam of Gidan Dutse. He also had at least one cow as his name indicates — possessor of cows. He had sold us milk at one time. Speaking of milk, Fulani Nana and her family supplied us with the bulk of our milk needs — up to 4 litres a day. Mai Shanu was a good friend, even though he was a staunch Moslem. When Dan and Mary Truax worked at Galmi, Dan talked to him about the Lord. Mai Shanu was interested and was very cordial to us, at least to our faces. Some years later, perhaps in the 60's and 70's when I would go to the village, I had to pass by the hut where all the malams convened each day. When they saw me, Mai Shanu would invite me in and ask me to read to them from the Litafi Mai Tsarki. (Bible) At first I said, "No, you just want to mock me." But they assured me that they were sincere, and Mai Shanu brought me a chair, the only chair and with broken slats, and they usually wanted me to read to them about the second coming of the Lord. I would turn to I Thess. 4, and I Cor. 15 and eventually get to John 14. Each time I visited them, they were very gracious and nodded in agreement to what I said. Mai Shanu also encouraged me to visit his wife and read to her, which I did occasionally. From some outward signs, both to me and to Dan Truax, he indicated that he believed. But for the head malam to believe would cost him everything — position, friends, family, his living, so he never made an outward profession. He died while we were still in Galmi. I wonder if he was a secret believer. We shall see!

The next day I started teaching Nick Palmer Hausa. He is a career doctor from New Zealand. His English is incomprehensible the first time around. After "Huh?", "What did you say?", "Say that again.", I finally made out what he was saying. Then I met his wife, and her English was even less comprehensible. But they were a lovely family and as we got used to their English we enjoyed their fellowship.

Hassana Cisu came for a visit. I asked Hassana to tell me exactly how Cisu died because her daughter, Hannatu, had asked me when I saw her in Niamey. I wanted to get it straight for the "horse's mouth," so I could relate it to Hannatu. Hassana said that the church elders had been meeting on a Sunday afternoon at the church concerning a case of discipline for Dije, (mai-ciwon-kafa). When they left the church Cisu was walking between Idi and Ibrahim. Dr. Jim VerLee was walking on the path at the time, possibly in the other direction. Cisu started to fall. Idi and Ibrahim caught him before he touched the ground. They called to Jim, who turned around and went back. He tried artificial respiration by mouth, to no avail. He died on the path of a ruptured aneurysm. Hannatu never knew her father; she was born after he died. I was glad I could send a full report to her.

Later that afternoon, Saidou, Issou's grandson, came to guide me to their house. He is about twelve, is in 5th grade. On the way we saw Ila at the hospital. Took picture of him and also of Saidou. On the road to Issou's we met Mamman, who had worked for the nurses. Musa, his first born, has a responsible job in Niamey, has something to do with the telephone or electric company, working on the lines outside. We also met Musa, the Fulani who lives on the hill with his wife, Hawa, whom I have already mentioned above. Also, Iyo, the former painter and Garba, a former laborer, both of whom are retired. At Issou's we sat and chatted for awhile. Hauwa was holding a new-born grand daughter. Because we were surrounded by noisy, staring little kids and their mothers, I couldn't speak much about the Lord. Took photos of Hawa and Issou together.

On the way back, I met Idi Nomo and Mohammadu, Ai's husband, whom I mentioned earlier. Their son, Jonathan, is in Niamey. Another son is in the States. Also saw and met Dogari. Others on the road coming and going greeted. Stopped to talk. They all knew me and many were once Awana boys or workers. It was a heady experience for me — just walking to town and back! We had supper with Matthias and Iris and Anika's tonight.

More about Mohammadu and A'i. Their daughter, Salome, married Balla. Where he came from, I don't know. He wasn't there when we were there. Balla was Galmi Hospital director for the last few years and was highly acclaimed for his testimony and work. In most recent years, they lived in our house, after the Evans and others. Word from Galmi came that Balla was not well, that he had T.B. Eventually he died, and the final word was that he died of AIDS. To compound the sorrow his wife, Salome, became ill, went to Niamey for diagnosis and treatment, came back with the report that she too was HIV positive. She was given some medicine that has improved her condition, at least temporarily.

Saturday afternoon, Nov. 3, was a busy day. This morning we got up at the usual hour — 6 a.m. and went to the first of two naming ceremonies of Christians in Galmi town. We drove with 12 other missionaries in one of the 5 mission vehicles. Drove to the market, then turned right, going beyond Issou's house. There must have been 100 people there — men sitting on the ground in the outer area and women ushered into the mother's house, unable to hear the message or the pronunciation of the baby's name. Segregation. The baby was named Ayouba (Job). After the usual tuwo da miya, we went to the other naming ceremony. This was in Galmi, not far from the church in the village and close to Gazarawa. This time, the segregation wasn't as severe. The women sat on mats at one end of the compound; the men at the other. The baby's name is Saratu (Sarah). Then home again for an hour and back to the church in town — walking — this time for a double wedding. Do you remember Jimma who lived in the "boys house" on our compound for awhile? She married and has had a number of children, the last ones being twin sons. The twins were married in the church. The church was packed with people standing — perhaps 200 or more there. Singing by many choirs; the brides and grooms were seated in big overstuffed chairs in the center of the room and after the singing was over, the pastor preached a sermon on

———

573

women obeying their husbands — what else? — ah, yes, but he added that the men must love their wives as Christ loved the church. Then both couples repeated their vows, and it was over. We didn't stay for the feast!

Believe it or not, I am wearing a sweater to the 6:30 a.m. prayer meeting. The weather has turned cool and except for the heat of the afternoon, is quite pleasant. Dust is everywhere, but as Souley Idi has said, "It's not like it used to be because we have so many trees, it keeps the dust down. I can say "Amen" to that.

Issou came again during Dad's break from the hospital. We drank tea together and then Dawi came and drank with us. Salamatu, Mai Zama's wife came. Then Friday night, Nyalia came bringing rice and miya (gravy with meat) and dankale (sweet potatoes) deep fat fried. On Sunday, we visited the EERN church in town. Same building, different time. This was at 10:30. Good singing, but hard to hear the message — mike too loud.

On Tues., I visited at Minne's house, widow of Kourma. I already mentioned that Kourma died some years back. A baby grandchild was there who had had scalding water spilled on her twenty days earlier and her front and back were raw flesh. I asked why they hadn't taken her to the hospital, and they said they couldn't afford it. I knew there was a benevolent fund available, so when I left I took her with me to the hospital right into the area where Burt was working. He looked at her and wrote a note to the African in charge of the benevolent fund. She received free treatment—some kind of medicated salve. She came back about 3 weeks later to visit me and we both rejoiced to see that the wounds were healing nicely.

Although we have missionary nurses on the compound, (three of the wives are nurses), they don't do nursing but are involved in other things. The nursing is all done by Africans, and there are 120 employees of the hospital and compound. At first, the missionary nurses tried working with the African nurses but they found it too frustrating to work alongside of nurses with different standards of nursing care. There are four midwives — 2 missionaries and 2 Africans and they are kept busy. It seems that there is an average of one C-section a day, but the doctors do them. One of the doctors is a Nigerien. The dentist is a Singapore Chinese. The dental clinic that the Lyons built is used for the offices and the dental clinic has been set up in the front part of the former Awana youth building.

The Awana building has been taken over by an "Under Five Clinic" which is a great disappointment to me. The building was meant for the youth and children, and we used it to capacity when we were here for Awana, Sunday School, reading and writing classes, small book store, relaxation and consultation, and now there is no youth work going on at all. We cannot fault the present missionary staff because the one who has been here longest says it was that way when she arrived 15 years ago. Missionaries and African helpers kept up the children's work for about five years after we left in 1975 and the Africans who were helping did not keep up the work after the other missionaries went on furlough or left. And now, even if there were some people with a heart for kids, there is no place for them to meet with them.

Friday, Nov. 9, Amu came. She is still a believer. She is so grateful for Esther Egli and Jeanne Marie Berney, who showed her the way of salvation. She learned to read and said she still reads her Bible. She lives in a village near Dogarawa, is married and says her husband who once was very much opposed to her faith, has softened and allows her to read the Bible to their children. She believes he is close to believing and asks us to pray for his salvation. She mentioned that she had been having tooth trouble. Already her two front teeth are missing. She said one of her back teeth — probably her wisdom tooth — had been killing her with pain, but that it was quiet at the moment. She didn't have the 6000 (about $5.00) francs that they say she must pay. I talked to the dentist about her and he said he would do the extraction if she can get past the "screener" and the cashiers. I determined to go with her and pay for her if the benevolent fund wouldn't take care of it, but she didn't come back.

Nov. 11

Our fourth Sunday at Galmi we went to church in Magariya with Linda Hardy who teaches a weekly women's Bible class there. You will recall that Magariya is about half way to Madaoua. Elvin Harbottle started the church there many years ago. The church building is similar to our old chapel with cement benches but a little smaller. There were about 30 in attendance. Pastor had a good message. Incidentally, our old chapel is now the school house for the m.k's. on the station. We had lunch at Linda's with Vee Travers.

Our Sunday evening sing-song tradition with the missionaries has evolved into a more formal meeting in the Convalescent center. About the Convalescent Center, it has been built since we left. It is situated just west and behind where our old house is. It is set up to care for missionaries who need care after surgery or who are sick, and it is also used for guest rooms.

There is a large central room which is used for conferences, special events and for monthly day of prayer services. Each Sunday evening, the missionaries meet for church services — in English — an escape from always listening to sermons in Hausa. It's a very nice all-purpose building. This particular evening, Burt and I gave reports to the missionary family on how it was in "the good old days." They weren't all that good, were they? Now there is 24 hr. electricity, thanks to the government. A footnote about the government electricity — Nigeria sells its electricity to Niger. The dam is in Sokoto Province. Apparently Nigeria wants the money more than electricity, and the people in Nigeria suffer from lack of it while Niger enjoys their electricity.

Do you remember that we had a "Christian cemetery" just west of the station? The compound has grown to the point where houses and the Convalescent building have encroached upon it. We wandered over to the cemetery to find it covered with weeds. Nobody on the compound was even aware that anyone was buried there. When I mentioned it, they were surprised. I suggested we clean it up and identify it. About that time, Mamman, the son of Issaka the hospital sweeper in our time, came to greet us and was also looking for work.

Although his dad was illiterate, Mamman was educated through secondary school. I asked him if he would like just a morning job for one day, and he agreed. So the next day, we walked over to the cemetery and he started to clean it up — dug out the overgrown weeds, re-set the stones marking the area of the graves. The regular compound worker, Usuman, helped him, and the job was completed in the morning. I paid him 1000 francs for the job. Those buried there are Cisu, Soumai's baby son, the wife of Mamman from another town who died, and an unidentified grave. I charged Usuman to keep it up and he agreed.

Nov. 14

Amuka came this afternoon. Amuka was one of the young girls from the village who came to Awana. In girls' Awana, led by Gen Kooy, besides the usual program, Gen taught the girls to sew. They sewed their blouses and scarves which they earned by learning verses. Amuka wanted to learn to read so she came to my afternoon reading class. As we sat around the table in the Awana building, I asked Amuka if she were a Christian. She said, "No." I said, "Would you like to be one?" She said, "Yes." So right there I had the privilege of leading Amuka to the Lord. She was about 12 years old. She was faithful in Awana, learned all of the verses in the books, continued her reading and writing lessons. As a child she had been promised in marriage, and when she was about 15, a camel procession came from a village about 5 miles away to take her to her Muslim husband. Gen Kooy, one of our nurses, who is now in heaven, rode another camel with her. Amuka was properly veiled in the Muslim custom, and the wedding train, led by her husband-to-be rode to his village. She became the youngest of several wives and became their slave. Her husband was very opposed to her faith, he trashed her Bible and hymn book. We left Galmi shortly thereafter. Amuka held fast to her faith and whenever she could get away, she came back to the hospital and read the Scriptures and prayed together with the nurses.

When she came to visit this afternoon, I was delighted. She thanked me over and over again for bringing her the "bishara", the good news of salvation through Jesus Christ over 25 years ago. She reads well; we read the Scripture together; we prayed together; we rejoiced together. Although her husband is still opposed to her faith, she is walking with the Lord. They live in Milela, a town about five miles away and she walks the five miles and back to visit her friends as often as possible. One of her good friends is A'i Mai Frere. A'i works on the compound — she cleans and cares for the guest houses on the compound. Thursday was her day off so she came and we had a delightful 2 hour visit. A'i is Dawi Abubakar's sister. A'i stands firm in her faith, but Dawi no longer identifies himself as a Christian. A'i told me that although she had been a faithful Awana girl and made a profession of faith as a child, she didn't quite understand it all until later in life, when she definitely invited Christ into her life.

The dentist, Hsun Tau Chow, and his wife are from Singapore. She, Yook Wai Chow, is a pharmacist but does not work in the hospital because she has 3 sons that she home schools. They are 6, 5, and 4, Paul, Jabez and Elisha. I taught them for three days while their mother had to do a 3 day stint in the pharmacy. These Singapore people have English but their accent is strong and hard to understand, and their kids speak the same kind of accented English. Hsun Tau and Yook Wai are good tennis players, and we played with them several times.

An unwelcome visitor arrived. Harmattan! Dust everywhere! Chapped hands and stuffed noses! The redeeming factor is that it is cooler.

Although there are 22 adults here, only six are Americans. They are: 1 Frenchman; 3 New Zealanders, 1 Australian; 5 English; 2 Singaporean; 2 Germans and 2 Nigeriens. Altogether there are 9 children. It makes for good international relationships, and all are compatible with each other. We all decided to celebrate American Thanksgiving. We celebrated with a pot-luck supper in the Convalescent Center with turkey and all the fixings. One of the American doctors gave a brief resume of why we celebrate Thanksgiving. . The hardest folk for me to understand are the New Zealanders, next are the Singaporeans. English is a second language of the latter, so they are excused, but New Zealanders — wow! One of the English girls has what sounds like a cockney accent which is also difficult for me to understand. It makes me wonder who has the accent — they or we!

Dau Duka came for a visit this week. He and I had a good talk. He was our first convert, went to Bible School at Tsibiri and then became our first pastor. Then some years later, he went back into Islam. He admits that we cannot know his heart and indicated that he still believes in Jesus Christ. We prayed together. He is keeping the Moslem fast and does his Moslem prayers and refused a drink of water or tea. He has 17 children by three wives. Kanduwa bore Musa, Esther, and Haruna. I asked if he still had a Bible and he said , "No." I said, "If I leave our Hausa Bible with you, will you read it?" He said he would. I said he should come back on such and such a day in about 2 weeks time just before we were to leave, and I would give it to him. I didn't really think he would come back then, but he did. So Burt inscribed it and we left the Bible with him, and he promised again to read it. It is hard to stand in a difficult Moslem area but we did hear this morning that there are 22,000 Christians in Niger. A drop in the bucket, to be sure. And there are over 300 churches in the country. Fifty years ago, there was just a handful of believers and churches.

As I was buying vegetables at the compound stand, Hashimu (Hashi) appeared on the scene. We were overjoyed at seeing each other and spontaneously, we embraced each other, a very unusual thing for an African to do. I had heard Hashi was in jail in Konni for having stolen money from Balla and Salamatu, who lived in our old house. He then returned with me to our house and I offered him something to drink, but he refused — he is keeping the fast, too. Hashi was one of my Awana boys who learned all the verses and earned all the rewards he could. I didn't question him about his past or how come he was in jail and able to visit now, but he said he had to get back to town to go back to the "farm" in Konni, and a car was going to pick him up at noon, so I assume he was on a work assignment sponsored by the "government". I gently reprimanded him for trading his Christian faith for another, and like DauDuka, he gave the same answer — in his heart, he knows the truth. We prayed together before he left. The following day, A'i Mai Frere said that in fact, Hashi was innocent. The man whose house was broken into exonerated Hashi, but his wife wouldn't, so she carried it to court and Hashi was given 2 years in jail in Konni. I believe he gets released the end of this year. To this day, Hashi says he is innocent.

The next Sunday, we went with the Kohls and Chows to church in Malbaza. There is a small church there now and Yamba, who was originally from Guesheme, and his family live in town. His son, Samuila, a young man probably in his twenties, is working with the youth of the church. Yamba's mother, Kaka, was in church, but Yamba himself was not. He comes "once in awhile", they say. On the way back, we stopped at Yamba's and greeted him. He has a grain grinding business. He and Dan Rani had come to Galmi from Guesheme as teen-agers. They worked at Galmi for awhile and then went on to Bible School at Aguie. Dan Rani went on to teach there. Yamba has become a nominal Christian. His son, Samuila, went to Bible School in Nigeria, and now he is working with the youth in the Dogarawa church.

As I was doing some work in the office, Zainabu came in, and we talked for a little while. She works in the Under Five Clinic together with Kwawa, Halilu's wife. Zainabou and Musa arrived from Nigeria while we were still here. He worked in the lab but is now retired. They have nine children. Their oldest daughter is in London working with BBC. She expects to be transferred to Niamey soon. Six children are in Nigeria in universities, all on scholarships of one sort or another. Their son, Daniel, is in charge of maintenance here. An excellent worker and a fine Christian! Their last daughter is still with them, in school here. What a joy to see such a fine Christian family.

On Sunday we returned to Dogarawa for church. We met a man who looks like a Fulani. He came from Tchin Tabaradin. He is a teacher and will be teaching in the CEG college in Dogarawa. From there, we visited Kadiri, the chief, who is bedridden. Kadiri was a teen ager when we first arrived in Galmi. His father, Attawal, was the chief. When his father died, Kadiri became chief. He was always a sort of careless living person, with several wives, but he was a congenial man and a friend. It's always good to have the chief as your friend. During our association with him, he bought our kerosene fridge and our '56

Chevy station wagon. The fridge didn't last too long because he didn't care for it properly, although Burt explained to him how to keep the wick clean. Now he just lies in bed, senile, degenerate, not knowing anyone, dying. When Burt spoke to him, he seemed to acknowledge him but didn't respond. Is he dying of AIDS? It may well be since he had multiple wives and no doubt as many women as he desired. He must be about 60 years old.

Monday, Alhassen came again. He seems to desire the fellowship and he comes during his break or on his day off. We read together John 3:1-17. He did the reading. Is doing azumi. That evening we had dinner with Anna Barton and Jessica Whitworth, two English medical students who were spending six weeks with us. Delightful girls.

Tues., Nov. 27

This morning I visited the CREN. What is the CREN? I'm not sure what the initials stand for, but in the northeast corner of the compound — where the t.b. dorms were located, is the CREN. It is an outgrowth of the post natal department. Women whose babies are not gaining weight or are sick for one reason or another live there with the babies for a month. Theoretically, after a month, the malnourished babies have gained weight, and the mothers have been instructed in how to care for their babies and nurse or bottle feed them. The rooms make up the east wall and the north wall, and other walls are erected on the south and west sides to form a square. This construction becomes their compound where the mothers do their grain pounding and cooking. There may be a dozen women at a time. A'i Yahaya is in charge of the compound, does the instruction classes and teaches Bible lessons. Her husband, Yahaya, works in the Under Five Clinic, and they came from Nigeria some years ago.

On Friday, I visited with Lydia in her home. Ila Tanko was there. Talked about the past. He seems bitter about things that led to his leaving his job after we left. He was a good operating room assistant, even did some small operations. Still a strong Moslem and very vocal

---

about it. Lydia and I walked over to see Hassana, but she wasn't there. Then I bought some onions but Lydia insisted on paying for them. Then we visited A'i's daughter, Salome, whose husband, Balla, died of AIDS. She has since been proven HIV positive. She was lying in bed, weak, but communicative. Bought some Nile perch this morning, which proved to be a nice change in our diet.

On Dec. 4, Amuka and grand baby Samaila came from Millela for a visit. She sang choruses and the Awana song, remembering the words better than I. We prayed together. When I write, I must address it to her c/o A'i Mai Frai or Abdou Abou in the O.R. She wants me to greet Gen. Today was Founder's Day. I led the evening prayer meeting at 6 p.m.

Wed., Dec. 5

Rollie's 55th birthday! Went to the hospital after break with Burt. Watched Doug Wilson and Halilu repair a botched up colon cancer operation. The whole area was herniated. He put a mesh in it. Watched Burt and his assistant do a hernia repair. Watched Andrew Ng do a v.v. fistula. Went to O.B., saw Ashibi, then Lydia and Iliya and others. Met Nana, the only woman chaplain. She took me to the office of the chaplains. Met. Malam Abdou, one of the 3 male chaplains. He is also the pastor of one of the churches in town. One of the other chaplains was on holiday, and it was the day off for the other one. Met Nadelou for the first time. He is in charge of outpatients, including the benevolent fund. In the afternoon, Hawa Ibrahim visited. She and Ibrahim came from Dan Ja originally. Hawa works in the O.B.; Ibrahim in the lab. Nice visit and prayer.

On Thurs., Dec. 6 Madai Hassan stopped in this morning after taking a sick grandchild to the hospital. Then Jim Rendel flew in with Virginia Fridal and Dorothy Kallock, both retirees. Virginia was on her way to Dan Ja, the leprosarium, for a month's visit. Virginia was the mainstay at Dan Ja for twenty plus years. For a few days before going on to Dan Ja, she stayed with Nyalia in town. They invited us to have supper with them Sat. night. Nyaliya lives in a typical African house. The inside is a little bit better than most. She has electricity, which not everyone has, because it costs a monthly fee. Nyaliya works in the pharmacy. We had spaghetti and miya (gravy), spicy but not too much.

Back to Jim Rendel — he had tea with us before he took off again with Dorothy for Maradi, then Aguie, where she will be working with Phyllis Erickson. At the same time that Jim and we were drinking tea together, we had two more visitors — two Tamajak (Tuareg—desert people) men. They were father and son, Mr. Abdoul Moumouni Phiza, Sarkin Zongo a Konni, Dept. de Tahaoua and his son, Ibrahim Abdoul Moumouni. Ibrahim is pastor of the Tamachik Church just outside of Konni with over 50 believers — Evangelise de l'eglise Tamachik de Konni. They live in Konni. The father was led to the Lord through the ministry of Cash and Ann Godbold who included Konni in their itinerary while they were living in Tahaoua. We had a good time of fellowship and prayer. We were delighted to be able to drink tea together — a testimony that they indeed were Christians and not keeping the Fast.

Another visitor that day was Arzika Asuman. He also is a pastor from Konni — pastor to the Hausas. He is a local Galmi boy who was led to the Lord by Iva Powers when she was stationed at Galmi. She nurtured him as a child, sent him to school. He told us of his conversion. He had a dream that a large snake was chasing after him. The snake's body was bigger than the trunk of a tree. Arzika was running as fast as he could but the snake was gaining on him. Then he saw a vision of a bright light and a man in white in front of him. He knew it was Jesus. He called out, "Yesu, Yesu". When he looked back, the snake was gone! Arzika counts his conversion from that moment. He went on to Aguie Bible School. We had a time of prayer together, too.

In the afternoon, Saidou, Issou's grandson, brought a gift of lettuce.

Soumaye's wife also came. Soumaye was one of Zeb and Irene's adopted boys. They cared for him from the time he was a young boy. For many years he worked at the cement factory, then moved on to Niamey where he is now working. Saratou and Soumaye have homes in both Niamey and Malbaza, but they live mostly in Niamey. Another of the Zabriskies' boys was Jacques. One year when he was about five years old, he stayed with us for a month while the Zebs went on holiday. Jacques became a leader in one of the new churches in Niamey, then through some upset, he left the church and didn't attend anywhere. We heard recently that he has come back to the Lord and is worshipping with the brethren again.

Thursday, Dec. 6, is not over yet. It was an evening to remember! The hospital staff and missionaries put on a big "ban kwana" for us. (farewell). We were like a king and queen, seated in plush furniture in front of everyone in the Awana building. Chairs and benches were set up. Microphone was in place as well as canned music. Over 100 Africans were there to wish us well and reminisce. People from town who knew us back then as well as the present staff came and sang our praises. Dad spoke and I spoke. We greeted them all for all of you kids and many want to be remembered to you. Rollie, Ayouba, son of Mai Shanu, and another Mohammadu, all said they played with you when you were boys and said to greet you abundantly. Ayouba is the head malam now. The women worked all day cooking rice and miya, and you know how they pile the plates full, well, everyone had their fill and then some. After eating, and some hadn't eaten all day — the Moslems are keeping the fast — the program continued. Among other things, each hospital dept. came up — O.R., Outpatient, West Wing, X-Ray, etc., etc. — 14 in all, and each dept. was given a question, e.g., "How old is Likita Tsofo?" "How long have they been married?" "When did the hospital open?" etc., The question that stumped them all was "Give the names of their children." Then it was open to the audience and Dau Duka came forward and said "Rolli, Lanny, Cherry, John Jack, Pam da Suzanne!" He was roundly applauded. They were given prizes for the right answers. You know Dau Duka went back into Islam. Then monetary awards were given for those who had retired and those who had completed 25 years at the hospital. Pictures were taken galore, but I only took 3 shots, and I hope they turn out because I have been having trouble with my camera. (They didn't turn out.) We were and have been treated like the patriarchs of old, which I guess we are! Our stay at Galmi was well received by Africans and missionaries alike, almost as if they are in awe of us. Unbelievable! And what a send off! A far cry from our non-send-off of 26 years ago. We were given a brass plated antelope and 12 brass plated shishkabobs from the missionaries and two tee shirts on which the Africans signed their names. An evening to cherish and remember!

On Saturday, the 8th, I talked with Mani Ato who works at the hospital. Mani originally came from Galma (not to be confused with Galmi.) Galma is north of Madaoua. Mani says that Elvin Harbottle brought the good news to Galma as well as Magariya and other areas, and the work has flourished with many believers in both places. Played tennis with the Chows in the afternoon.

On Sunday, the 9th, we went to church in Malbaza again. The visiting pastor did not show. He was away at a conference. So out of the blue, they called on Dad to speak. He had about 25 minutes to collect his thoughts during song time, but he came up with a good message in Hausa based on Mt. 24:16, "Heaven and earth shall pass away but my words shall never pass away."

Another surprise this week was the unexpected departure of one of our doctors and his wife, Doug and Quimby Wilson. Quimby has not been well and is quite depressed, so it was felt that if they went home for Christmas it might help her. They will stay home indefinitely, for as long as necessary. He is a top surgeon and will be sorely missed, not only for his medical expertise, but also for his good relationship with the townspeople. Another surgeon is away this week for an AIDS conference in Ouagadougou, Burkina Faso (Haute Volta), so they will be short handed this week. The dentist and family (Singapore Chinese) leave for furlough this week, and we leave next Sunday.

The work here is enormous — people come from as far away as Lagos. A week ago, the Niamey hospital referred a patient here. The other day the doctors scheduled a facial cancer where they will be taking a flap from the neck to cover the spot. Now that the doc who was scheduled to do it has gone I wonder if it will be done. The dentist has done a number of mandibular operations since we've been here as well.

Maybe you remember Kwawa and Halilou. As a teenager, Halilou came as a patient with an osteomylitus of his leg which Dad treated. He was healed and became a Christian. He is one of the surgical assistants and also does some minor surgery. One of the anesthetists is Nuhu, son of Ibrahim and Lydia.

Had a nice visit with Mamman (the cook for Gen Kooy and Ruth Hunt and others) and his wife, Talawai yesterday. I visited in their home, then I walked up the hill farther to visit with Hawa, the wife of Musa, the Fulani family. When we were here, they were alone on the hill with their goats and sheep, but now the village has surrounded them.

So these examples and many from our own ministry are gems that we are taking back home with us. Even though some of our "converts" have gone back into Islam, there are those who have been faithful, so we are satisfied that what the Lord started with us has accomplished its purpose. We laid the foundation and others have built upon it. Being back at Galmi for two months has been a wonderful experience for us.

This is the Wednesday of our last week here, a holiday. We're not quite sure what holiday it is, but it has something to do with "two days before Salla". We hear that it is supposed to be a day and night of prayers to Allah with visions and dreams from Allah in order to prepare for the big Salla, which occurs either Sat. or Sunday depending on the sighting of the new moon. Salla is the big day of celebration, when a ram or goat is sacrificed and the villages have big celebrations. Some big towns like Kano will be having horse races while those in Niger may be having camel races. At any rate, everything is shut down today, the hospital is operating on Sunday routine, and the office here is closed.

By 8 o'clock on Sunday, December 16, we were on the road to Maradi with Dr. Andrew Ng. In Galmi town, we waved to the few who lined the streets at that early hour. As we passed through town, I looked back and with some nostalgia had a feeling of sadness, knowing that we would never return, and that we would never see some of our friends again, not even in heaven for some of them. We pray that they will turn to the Lord. Others we will know as we and they get to heaven. On our way we stopped at the Madaoua compound, all walled in. The Schmidts were there and in the morning service. We also stopped at Gidan Arna, half way between Magariya and Maradi. They were in the midst of their service, too. Elvin Harbottle was responsible for this church as well.

We arrived in Maradi at noon. Sallah was in full swing, both on Sunday and on Monday. We were given our guest room in a new guest facility, a combination of rooms with a large central area with self catering facilities and lounge. Andrew took charge and fixed us some soup and then we went to visit the leprosarium in Dan Ja. Now hear from Burt.

We toured DanJa that afternoon — "a very well kept institution. Leprosy is so well treated now that the place is used much more for general dispensary work and is a notable medical institution for the whole area in all directions. We returned to Maradi and were happy to know that all personnel from the area were coming for a Sunday evening sing and devotional in the guest house. That way we met them all without having to travel to each home. Andrew had gone right on back to Galmi where he was to be on call the next day (Monday)."

The next day, we left Maradi in a chartered taxi at 7:45 a.m. for the Niger/Nigerian border. Streets were lined with people dressed in their best garb. This was Babban Sallah — the great holiday after the month of Ramadan fast for the Muslims. Early morning group prayers were performed in the open field and in the mosques. A party mood prevailed. Shops were closed, but market stalls were open. The drive to the Niger border took about a half hour. I was sitting in the back seat kitty corner to the driver and Burt was in the front passenger seat. From time to time, I saw the driver bow his head, then lift it up again, then down again and up again, and I realized he was doing his Moslem prayers as he drove. We arrived safely at the border. His prayers or ours?

Burt again: "First time we ever had a Muslim taxi driver do his 2nd morning prayers while he was driving the cab at 60 mph! Ruth was a bit shaken. However it wasn't a bad road — only occasional pot-holes, and we stopped for immigration and customs to get out of Niger and a few miles farther to get into Nigeria. Immigration and customs use two different stops so the process took 45 minutes or more. I am always amazed at the primitive government offices. The officers hardly know where to look to get info in the passports, but they are very attentive in Nigeria to give one day less than you need so you'll have to go through a lot of stress the day of departure to get renewals (and be tapped for bribes.)"

Now we were in Nigeria! What a relief and delight to see Terry and Keith and his girl friend, Lauren, at the border waiting for us. Soon we were on our way again heading for Kano, then Jos and a very special month with our kids!

Chapter 4

Nigeria, Ho!

December 17, 2001 – January 18, 2002

"In our day", i.e., between 1950 and 1975, whenever we traveled to Nigeria from Niger, as soon as we crossed the border, the world seemed to brighten a bit! Grass looked greener, trees were more abundant, and shops were filled with commodities. Also, "English was spoke!"

Nigeria was our supply house. Goods, supplies, food, fresh fruit and vegetables were in abundance, and we loaded up our car on our return trip. Usually there was one annual trip to Kano and perhaps two or three trips across the border through Birn'n Konni into Sokoto each year.

Now, in December of 2001, being with Sue and Terry and the boys for a month was enough to make our days, but Nigeria itself had changed. Houses were walled in; guards were at the gates, shop windows were barred. This particular day, December 17, 2001, the streets were lined with people, all dressed in their finest garments, making merry. The fast was officially over, the prayers had been performed, shops were closed, the rams were slaughtered, and feasting and merry-making were the order of the day.

589

We arrived in Kano about noon, and were welcomed by Istifan and Gazella Patikai, doctor and doctor. Mrs. Patikai worked at the Eye Hospital; Mr. Patikai was a psychiatrist at the university in town. They are friends of Terry and Sue from the days when the Hammacks were living in Kano. And now they are our friends as well. We had dinner with them — a delicious Hungarian dinner, for they are Hungarians working in Kano under the auspices of the Christian Blind Mission. My father's roots are in Hungary, and before we left, the Patikais had wrapped up a Christmas present for us — a beautiful picture book about Budapest. We have an invitation to visit them in Hungary if we ever get back to Europe. Lovely people! They live in the former Myers' house. Their home is enclosed in the walled-in compound.

We met Dr. Kiru and his wife who live in the former Kietzman house. Dr. Kiru gave us a tour of the Eye Hospital, and just before we left Kano at about 3:30 p.m. we had a short visit with our friend, the Russian lady who led one of Terry's attackers to the Lord before his execution. You remember the armed robbers who attacked Terry with his two boys in the car while the Hammacks were living in Kano. We arrived in Jos about 7:30 just as darkness was beginning to envelop us. Terry did an excellent job of maneuvering the car up the Plateau hills and around the curves in the dusk, and then worming his way through the Jos traffic to their home on the Niger Creek compound. Burt again, "An old English law which applied to Nigeria in the colonial days stated that auto lights must be turned on no later than a half hour after sunset. This is interpreted by the Nigerians to mean "at" 30 minutes after sunset, so there are many surprises until about 7 p.m. with cars appearing suddenly out of darkness with no lights. By 7 o'clock, the tension was over when all were finally lighted.

"Sue was waiting with supper when we finally pulled into the Niger Creek Compound — mainly a 13 hr. day riding in a crowded Peugeot 505 wagon, but no unexpected complications made it complete. Lauren is testing the Nigerian culture, for Keith has told her this is where he is going to spend his life! Like a kitchen with two offers — take it or leave it. We finally go over to a guest room, revamped from Nigerian workers quarters on the Apollo Crescent compound. Very nice! The beds were very restful, and the first eight hours of their use was very refreshing. We're here! In Nigeria!"

Christmas was in the air, but Sue and Terry still had to keep working. On Tues. morning, we visited the brand new ECWA headquarters building — a two story large concrete structure. ECWA offices are on the first floor — SIM's are on the second. Sue's office is lovely, with working area separated from visiting/interviewing section with table and chairs. Terry's office is down the hall "a piece", not as handsomely decorated but functional. In the afternoon, Terry took us to Evangel Hospital where we met Dr. Greg Kirschner who gave us a tour of the hospital. Some of the nurses remembered Burt and greeted him joyfully.

Dec. 19, Wed.

In the morning we attended the final Hillcrest assembly which signaled the close of school for Christmas holidays. We met a few old friends, including Larry ?? and his wife and John and Nancy Sawyer. In the evening we all had supper with Peter and Bette Verkaik who are with Word of Life and working in Jos. Their ministry is largely with the Fulani. Their home was decorated with Christmas, American style, and we had a lovely meal and good fellowship.

Lami and Bakari are house parents for missionary kids of the EMS, (Evangel Missionary Society), the ECWA missionary arm. These kids are all Africans whose parents are missionaries mostly to other parts of Nigeria. Some of the parents are in Niger or adjacent countries. Of course their pre-school kids are with them just as ours were before they went away to school, and the school kids join their parents for holidays and vacations. The children were on Christmas break so they weren't there when we visited with Lami and Bakari on their compound for supper on Thurs. the 20th. The teachers were gone too. They are using the ACE method, which will equip them for America style schools if some day they go to America for further study.

Sunday, the 23rd, was Sue and Terry's 23rd anniversary. We went to the ECWA Tudun Wada church in the morning. There were about 1000 in attendance. After the service, we drove out to Miango for dinner and a visit. The Voths are in charge. Lois is the daughter of the Hieberts, who were SIM missionaries, now with the Lord. The exterior of the guest house has not changed; neither has the interior physically. But in the corner where the radio used to be is a large t.v., and we spent a little time watching C.N.N. Can you believe it? The piano is in the same corner, and it's the same piano and hasn't been tuned for who knows how long! You remember "piano corner" — it's the same piano that fell off the truck years and years ago and no one missed it until they got to Miango and the piano wasn't in the truck. They back tracked and finally found it. Hence, the name "piano corner."

Back in Jos — we had a visit from Daniel Nwoso. Daniel is the son of Nwoso who was a friend of Burt's. Daniel lives in Zaria and came to see Burt. He is in the dog breeding business and doing quite well. We also had a visit from my friend, Hawa and her son, Daniel. Hawa was married to Ameche and they traveled to the States with us when we came on furlough. They were on their way to Wheaton College for advanced degrees. I believe it was in 1980. After they returned to Nigeria, he became the pastor at Plateau Chapel, a very good pastor. They had several children, and Daniel was just a baby when Ameche left Hawa, went back to his own home in Yoruba land. He took the older children — except Daniel who was still being nursed by his mother. Hawa raised Daniel alone, saw that he got an education. He graduated from Baptist High School and not too long ago, graduated from LeTourneau University in Texas.

On Christmas eve, Hillcrest had a lovely fireside service. Sue was at the piano. There were a number of special numbers and an appropriate Christmas message. Christmas Day dinner was shared with Claudia Long and George Janvier at the Hammacks. It was a quiet morning with gift opening and dinner preparation.

Christmas week was one of relaxing and visiting. Baba Philip is a guard at Niger Creek compound. When he learned that we were coming, he was overjoyed. He had worked in the lab at Aminawa, Sokoto, when Burt visited leprosy patients there while we were still at Galmi. He visited us at Sue's, then again with his wife and daughter, then gave a very pretty framed scenic picture to Burt with a "Happy Birthday" greeting on it. Of course, it wasn't Burt's birthday, but that didn't matter. He inscribed the back of it, "from Baba Philip and family to Dr. B. Long." How does one respond to such gratitude? Just say, "Thank you" and accept it? That's what we did. We were at all times surrounded with respect and appreciation by the Africans, both in Niger and Nigeria.

Was it Friday, Dec. 29 or Saturday that we drove out to Miango for a pot-luck with Linda and Jim Crouch? It matters not. The de la Hayes, Ray and Marcia, were there with all their kids. The Voths joined us, too. It was a get-together with those who were old K.A.'ers. Ray was a contemporary of Lance; Linda, with Cherry; Lois preceded them all. Our day was relaxing and enjoyable. What made this day one to remember was not our gathering, but the drive out!

We thought it strange to see so many Fulanis with cows on the road coming our way. There was a large group not just of shepherds, but women and children with loads on their heads, babies on backs, little tikes trying to keep up with their parents. All were in a hurry. One group would pass, then another and another and it seemed that the whole road was lined with people in a rush to get somewhere! "What's going on?" we asked ourselves. We found out when we got to Miango. It was rumored that a Fulani had killed a local man. So the locals in revenge had raided, ransacked and burned the Fulani village that morning. Hence, the flight! That night, the Fulanis camped out somewhere between Miango and Jos, and their ultimate destination was purported to be "East." Another episode in the "peaceful area of Jos!"

Amazingly enough, this is May 28, 2002 and just when I am writing about this, this e-mail came from Terry today: " . . . And we got word that some of the Fulani who were chased out of the Miango area at the New Year came back recently. There was not enough water and grazing area in Bauchi State where they'd gone so herders were hungry and cattle were dying. To show their 'gratitude' for being back in the Miango area, some of the Fulani took revenge for the January killings and murdered four Miango people last night . . . . This taking of revenge, even for imagined slights, is all too common among the Fulani. This type of hit and run tactic happens in at least five localities every year around this time just before the rains get strong. The Fulani really do need the Lord."

Welcome to the new year! Jan. 1, 2002. We slept the New Year in! In the evening, the Jos missionaries had a pot-luck supper in Beachams' back yard, (Steve and Beaj) and on Wed., Jan. 2, we rode out to Miango with Chuck and Judy Brod for the annual Nigerian conference. We were housed in Ebenezer left and Sue and Terry were in the right. The porch entry way was locked with a metal gate!! A sign of the times. Paul and Virginia Haney were up from Aba and already settled in. Burt led devotions in the evening, and then we went over to the de la Hays for a visit.

Conference began on Jan. 4. The speaker was Danny McCain who is a lecturer at Unijos. His wife is Mary. Their daughter is Carmen, who is doing post graduate work at the university. Danny's messages were very good and relevant, relating to cross-cultural ministries. He started out with Abraham. "Abraham", he said, "had a definite call. Some have a definite call. Others are led step by step. Joseph did not know what God was going to do through him. He had a cross-cultural ministry. God calls people in different ways." Then he talked about "real" missionaries versus technical missionaries with Nehemiah as his central character. A negative example was Jonah who also had a cross-cultural experience, much to his dismay. What kind of missionaries are we?

Several days we played tennis with Peter Fretheim, Vake Kantyaddas, Jill Tau and by ourselves. Sue played for most of the meetings, and a highlight was Sue and Heidi Gibbs Tolar's piano duet — *Poet and Peasant*. Greg and Carolyn Kirschner were in charge of music. He played the keyboard and she led the music. Most of the missionaries who attended were new to us, but Harvey Stromme was one of the old-timers, and on Sunday afternoon, there was a special program in the living room to honor him in his upcoming retirement, after 36 years in Nigeria. Most of his years, starting in 1966, were at Gusau where he took in boys who needed a home. He clothed them, fed them, saw to their education. Many of the missionaries gave testimony to his hospitality and cooking. I added that he and the Hirons befriended Rollie when he was in the Peace Corps and posted in Gusau. The Haneys were honored as well. They were 1 1/2 years into their two year commitment to Aba. During that time they celebrated their 50th wedding anniversary — not much celebration. As a belated gift, SIM arranged for a SIM driver to drive them back to Aba. Their trip up took 12 hours on an African bus. What a fantastic gift, and were they ever pleased! They will be back in Sebring in June.

On January 9, Barnabas visited. He used to work at Jan Kwano but was let go for some reason. Of his five children, one was deaf. She had just finished Unijos. On Dec. 15, 2001, just a few weeks before, she died of typhoid fever. Barnabas was somewhat discouraged.

On Sunday, we took the Hammacks out to the Cedar Tree restaurant for dinner. Then we visited Aina and Eric, who are independent missionaries in the "bush". They are hoping to start an orphanage and retreat center for indigenous missionaries. A gracious Nigerian couple, living by faith in a pagan village! They have 200 plus chickens, goats, pigs, sheep which they raise and sell to aid in their support. We had a good "tea/visit" with them.

On Monday, Jan. 14, Hawa came by taxi to fetch us to her house for breakfast. Had acha and kosai and tea. Visited with her and Daniel. They have TV with satellite, radio, and the latest in communication equipment. She is a communications major working on her Ph.D., which justifies her owning the latest equipment. She ordered a taxi and returned with us in it, then went home in it.

About 11 a.m., Yeri Bako came. She had worked for us when we were in Jos, both at Jan Kwano and at Niger Creek. It was an effort for her to come, took several taxis, wasn't quite sure where to find us. She finally was directed to Apollo Crescent. She said she just had to come and visit or it would have been an insult not to, knowing we were here. She had only heard a few days before. I think it was Barnabas who told her at church the day before.

That same evening, we had a great family time for supper at Claudia's. We were four Hammacks, two Longs, Lauren and Claudia. Claudia even built a fire in her fireplace, which made it nice and fuzzy. The next night we had supper with Kwang Yun (David) and Young Boon (Joanna) Lee, who are working with the Evangelical Missionary Society, the missions program of ECWA, born out of SIM and are living at Apollo Crescent on a hill behind the house we were living in, so it was just a short walk up the hill. The tension connected to this was that the Lees were offered that house for a dwelling place after it had been promised to Claudia and occupied by Claudia. The mission asked her to move to smaller quarters so that the Lee family could live in her larger quarters. Well, that caused quite a stir between Claudia and headquarters, which also touched on Sue because she was part of headquarters. However, Sue says that the decision was made without her. Well, Claudia did move, but there were hard feelings all around for a long time, and to this day, I doubt whether Claudia has been reconciled to it. Claudia's claim to a larger house is that she has a lot of equipment related to her camping program which has to be stored. When the Camp buildings are finished and there is a full-time director living at Camp, there will be room for the equipment, but in the meantime, Claudia has to store her camping equipment in a garage. I can feel for Claudia, because the house we were having supper with the Lees in was a lovely, large modern house. Nothing was said during the supper meal for which we were grateful. This was the eve of our departure. We left there and about 8 p.m., Terry and Sue and Keith and Lauren came over for about an hour, and then to bed.

Wed. a.m., Jan. 16

(Pam's birthday) Terry picked us up at 8:15 a.m. With him was a friend of Terry's who had drawn a pencil picture of Burt and me from a snapshot that Terry had given him. He presented it to us, and the likeness was excellent. In the background he sketched in a typical

Nigerian village. We were deeply touched by the gift from someone whom we did not even know, but family is family, and we were part of Terry's family.

We loaded the car with our luggage and drove over to the Hammacks. Said our good-byes to Sue, Keith and Lauren. Stephen was already at school. Then Terry drove us to Abuja. It took about three hours. It is a very modern city, the capital of Nigeria. Terry gave us a tour of the city. We got a taste of the elite class of Nigeria by walking through the Hilton Hotel — as fine as any in the States. We ended up at Peniel apartments. That's another story. These are like an apartment hotel, owned and operated by Christians. Florence, who worked for KA at one time, now works there. The owners dedicate some of the apartments to Christians in transit who need an overnight. Florence put in a good word for SIM and as a result, our missionaries are given free lodging and meals. Terry checked us all in, had a nap and then ordered our supper off the menu in the room, and it was delivered to our room. Not "just like back home", but better than back home. All for free.

At 7:30 p.m., we left for the airport. Got checked in by 10:00 p.m. Said good-bye to Terry before going through emigration, boarded the British Airways flight #777 about midnight for the 12:15 a.m. flight. It was a newer plane, not full, so we were about to stretch out and have about a 2 hr. nap. T.V.'s were on the back of each seat. It was a good 6 hour flight to London. After a five hour wait in London, we boarded an older 747 plane, not quite so comfortable or modern for our 9 hour 20 minute flight to Orlando. We flew over water from the time we left London until we touched down in Orlando. A good flight. Any flight that you can walk off safely is a good flight. Lloyd and Marge Wickstrom were there to meet us, and we arrived back in Sebring by 7:15 p.m. on January 18, 2002 after about 36 hours from start to finish. Thank you, Lord. And here we are at Sebring on this day, the second of June, 2002, and it has taken me four and a half months to write up the report of our final hurrah to Niger and Nigeria.

Chapter 5

THE LAST HURRAH!

November 18, 2004

Eighty years ago, Mr. Ed Rice, an SIM missionary in Nigeria, had a burden to enter into Niger with the Gospel. He trekked into southern Niger and established the first SIM mission station at Zinder. From Zinder to Niamey, east to west, many mission stations were opened over the next eighty years. Today, in 2004, there are 120 churches established in that great expanse of land. Through the years hundreds of missionaries have come and gone, and some are there today.

The Nigerien church throughout the land wanted to show their appreciation to the SIM and to the former missionaries for bringing the Gospel to them, so they invited all who were able to come and be a part of the celebration.

We couldn't resist the opportunity, so it was that on November 18 of 2004, we left Sebring and were on our way to Niger to celebrate the 80th anniversary of the church in Niger together with the national believers.

TO NIGER FOR 80th Celebration
NOV. 18 – DEC. 7, 2004

Thurs., Nov. 18

Drove to the airport with John and Anne Ockers. Flight was at 2:05 p.m.. Flew from Orlando to Atlanta, then to Paris on Delta. Arrived at Charles DeGaulle International Airport in Paris at 9 a.m. Friday, the 19th, and our next flight was in four hours to Niamey, Niger.

Friday, Nov. 19

Paris needs to take some lessons from the U.S. First, we debarked on an apron of the runway and had to take a bus to get to the gate – about a 5 minute ride. From there, we were directed to take another bus to a different part of the airport, and after asking many questions, were directed to our gate which involved a good walk. As we headed toward our gate, we heard that there had been a security crisis, and there was a delay. All flights were delayed, and we were among hundreds of passengers all trying to get to their gates. We joined them and stood in line for about an hour. Apparently there had been some kind of a threat; people who were already on board their flights had to get off the planes while the planes were scrutinized and the airport inspected. Finally, the crisis was over and our individual scrutiny began. We even had to take off our shoes. Finally, we made it through, hurried to our gate about an hour late, and the plane was still there waiting. We found John and Anne already seated in the plane because John was escorted by wheel chair in all airports, so they went whizzing through all the check points. Also on our flight were Gillian Reynolds and Maurice and Martha Glover who had come from England and Virginia Fridal who had arrived in Paris on another flight. We were all headed for the 80th celebration reunion of SIM's entry into Niger via Zinder.

We were met at the Niamey airport by our SIM pilots, Ed Chamberlain and Ian Rideout at 5:30 p.m. – a less than 5 hr. trip from

Paris. Because of their connection to the airport, the baggage of all of our missionaries on board passed through customs and immigration without a second look. They drove us to the guest house where we had supper with others and bed.

Sat. Nov. 20

At 9 a.m. Ed Chamberlain picked us and the Glovers up for our flight to Galmi. Other retirees along with Gordon and Judy (Lees) Evans had gone by road two days earlier to Guesheme and Dogon Doutchie. We arrived in Galmi by noon in time for lunch. We were met by missionaries and Africans, some of whom we knew. Sat. night was the big meeting in the old Awana building, now used as an "Under Five Clinic". The place was packed with missionaries, hospital and compound staff and towns people. Each retiree was introduced – Pollens, Husbands, Glovers, Lees, Ockers, Virginia Fridal, Gillian Reynolds and us. Each retiree had a couple of minutes to tell where they had worked, and when, and the retirees on the station they were then visiting had the lion's share, so Burt and I each had about 10 minutes that night. At each station, the process was repeated and a 20 minute power point presentation of pictures of the early days was shown. At Guesheme, the Pollens starred; at Maradi, the Ockers held court; at Goure, the Lees; at Dan Ja, Virginia Fridal, but each of us was put on display at every church and school and told where we had worked and what the Lord had done through us. The idea was to acquaint the new missionaries and new generation of Nigerien Christians to the beginnings of SIM in Niger. The hope is that the history of SIM in Niger will not die.

Sun. Nov. 21

Sunday morning at Galmi, the two churches who meet in town next door to each other, combined their services. It was also the dedication of the UPEEN church. Both choirs sang, both shared in the meeting. The split off from the EERN church all through Niger some 13 years earlier was gradually being healed, and there is a new unity among the different groups throughout the country, and it was evident that morning. The service lasted 3 ½ hours and the church fed us rice and gravy afterward along with bottled pop. Then we returned to the conference/convalescent center to top off our dinner. That evening we had a service in the Conference Center with just the missionaries on the station and charged them to carry on the good work. There are 120 SIM related churches in Niger now; eighty years ago there were none.

Mon. Nov. 22

Still at Galmi, in the morning, we visited the Christian elementary school which was started by the EERN church a few years ago. There are grades 1 and 2 now with about 50 kids in the school. Each year a grade is added. The school is located a ways behind the market and we rode to it over sandy, rocky, rutted paths. This is completely a church function, not SIM, so these kids, some of them Muslim, are being taught their ABC's integrated with Christian teaching. It's a private Christian school and parents pay school fees for their kids. Located to the West of Galmi about a half mile is a new government secondary school, and many of our Christian young people attend. Although it is not a Christian school, our Christians like it because their children do not have to go away to attend secondary school and perhaps get led astray. This way, they can live at home and have their home Christian influence.

From there, we went to Madaoua where the Schmidts are. We had a service there. We were introduced again. The power point pictures were shown. Food was served. From there we went on to Maradi. We were housed in the guest house, were more or less responsible for fixing our own food, but guided by the guest house caretaker, Gail Klippenstein. That evening there was a pot-luck supper provided by the missionaries who live in the area. We then had a short meeting with the usual introductions and power point presentation.

Tues. Nov. 23

In the a.m., we went to Dogon Gao, out of DanJa, where there is the Hausa Bible School, a preliminary school before entrance into the Aguie Bible School, which I believe is in French. Dorothy Kallach is one of three teachers. The other two are nationals. Besides the Bible School students, there is a school for the children of the Bible School students. We visited their school as well, giving testimonies in both places.

On to Dan Ja for a visit in the school for the children of the leprosy patients and staff. We visited the wards. Then we had a meeting with power point and introductions of the missionaries, followed by a lunch of miya, meat and tapioca. We were back at the guest house at 3 p.m. to get ready for the evening meeting.

The service at 7:30 was a combined service of UPEEN and EERN churches. About 500 people were present. Many choral groups and children sang. Showed power point and all of us were introduced and had some words to say about the "old days". Following the meeting, they served us Fanta, biscuits and cake and candy. Ali Dan Buzu and Cherif were there..

Wed. Nov. 24,

We visited Soura. Joel and Alice Mathews are our SIM missionaries there. They have a son and daughter, Shanti, whom they home school and a daughter at Sahel Academy in high school. I took a picture of Dan Nana, his son, Elisha, and 2 grand sons. There were other nationals there. Joel works in agriculture. I took a picture of the well where Gordon Bishop was killed.

On to Tsibiri, where there is an EERN school of 210 students, about 150 of them boarding school students; the rest, day school students. They seem to think that they may not teach religious knowledge classes on school time, but for the boarding students, they have devotions in both the a.m. and p.m.

Then we visited the Chief of the Gobirawa area in his "grand room." The chief belongs to the Marafa family. (Musa Marafa is dead.) Dan Nana and Jadi were there. Jadi is the uncle of the chief. He is also the father of Lydia Ibrahim of Galmi. Introductions were made all around, as we sat around sipping Fanta. Jadi, from his posiiton on the floor, gave a bit of history of Tsibiri concerning his relationship with David Osborne, himself and Dan Nana. He also gave a resounding testimony of Jesus and His love to the chief and all his attendees, although they were Muslim. Why not? Jadi is the chief's uncle and much older than the chief himself, so he is highly respected..

Four p.m., and we are off to the Maza Tsaye farm school. On the way, we stopped at the leather shop that has grown out of Gwen Van Lierop's ministry of teaching former (or present) leprosy patients a trade.

At Maza Tsaye, John Ockers "held court" while former farm school "boys" hurried to greet him. John was honored everywhere in the Maradi/Tsibiri area. SIM leased the farm school to EERN for 15 years. During their 15 year lease, the property was left to itself and became a pile of weeds. EERN took the fence down and made use of the wire. They dismantled the 8 windmills and took the blades off of them, either to sell or use. They removed a barn, brick by brick. In fact, they vandalized the place. In 2003, the 15 years was up and SIM took back the property again. Peter and Sally Cunningham are the SIM missionaries on the property now and are trying to restore it to its original state.

Thurs. Nov. 25

Off we went to Aguie, 50 miles east of Maradi. Phyllis Erickson is holding the fort there, but as of now, she is on her way home both for furlough and medical help. This is the Advanced Bible School station. We had a meeting with the students and some church workers, and went through the usual routine. We saw Dan Rani, who was teaching there. One, Hassan Boratawa, got up in the meeting and criticized SIM for denying them a proper French education in the early days.

It turns out that he was one of John's farm school boys who did well in school. The Ockers paid his way to a Bible school in France. After a year, the proprietor of the school in France said Hassan should not return – he was struggling and not able to keep up with the class work. He has been bitter ever since and running down the missionaries.

We returned to Maradi the same day.

Fri. Nov. 26

In the a.m., we visited the Computer school in Maradi. It is owned and run by EERN, although SIM people have been helping to get it off the ground. They hope to start in Jan. They want to teach people who will be teachers of computer science. Thirty four people are registered.

After lunch, we headed back to Galmi. Wilf Husband was the driver of the Land Cruiser. In Gidan Roumji, we had a flat tire, so Wilf, with Burt's help, changed it, and we were on our way again.

Sat. Nov. 27

We were at Galmi from Friday night to the next Thurs. morning. Sat. a.m. was the day of prayer held at the convalescent center. It went from 9 to 12 a.m. with "tea" half way through. Soule Idi came to visit. Amuka came from Milela with a 15 year old boy who accompanied her. We reminisced about Awana. She knows and recited her Awana verses and sang the Awana song. I commented to her on her memory, and she said "They are in my heart", patting her chest.

Idi Yahaya came and greeted. Walked over to the hospital. Peeked in the door and saw Burt doing a hernia operation. Walked back on the road. Saw Uma and Dau Duka. Salome, the daughter of A'i and Mohammadu, and her sister, came to visit our neighbor, Silke, a Swiss doctor. I met them in the hallway. We talked for awhile. She was married to Balla, who died of T.B., brought about by Aids. He had been hospital director and they lived in our house. She contracted Aids from him, or perhaps she was only HIV. Three years ago she was bed-ridden; today she seemed to be in good health, after being on medicine. Her brother, Jonathan, lives and works in Niamey and he was instrumental in getting her the medicine.

Sun. Nov. 28

Went to the EERN church in Galmi with Bev and Carol Botheras. In the afternoon, Dau Duka and Uma visited for about 2 hours. Minne Kourma also visited. Gave her shirts and 1000 francs. Husbands visited in the evening.

Mon. Nov. 29

Hassana Cisu and Fibi visited. Took picture. Also, Fibi's son, Abdou. Sue and Terry arrived from Jos. Withdrew money at Galmi — $150.00 – 77,135 francs @515 cfa./$1.00. Had previously withdrawn $100 in Niamey – I believe at 535 cfa/dollar. Saidu, Issou's grandson brought lettuce.

Tues. Nov. 30

Mamman Habu, son of Awana, works at the hospital. Says he's a believer. Alhassen works in the ward. Sanusi Dari works with A'i Mai Frere cleaning guest houses. Went with Sue to visit Issou and Hawwa and family. Long walk. Saidu came to lead us. Took photos of Issou's family. Took 4 pics. Took picture of Mai Gari of Issou's section and Malam Mamman MaiWa'azi sitting along the way. Moslems! On the way back, saw Ibo with a long beard. Looks awful. Hashi visited us in the evening. Ila has 18 kids (2 wives). Doesn't work. His kids support him. He just eats. Is heavy. Big tummy. Says he can still beat Rollie wrestling. I told him I didn't think so.

Wed. Dec. 1

Toured the old house with Sue. Termite ridden. Took pix. 87 year old Alhaji from Kawara came to see Burt at Botheras' house. We went over. Wed. 10 a.m. "coffee" and fellowship at Zoolokowski's house – Christ and Helene Warkentine. Christ is a doctor; also interested in Awana.

Thurs. Dec. 2

Mamman Musa – gave him our address. Write to him in care of Botheras or Kendrick Lau (Alisha is his wife). Alhassen Ango visited. About 9 a.m. started our drive to Niamey, with Sue and Terry in their car. Took 6 hrs.

Fri. Dec. 3

Toured National Museum of Niamey with Sue and Terry. That evening we had spaghetti supper at Sahel Academy sponsored by the Sr. class who are raising money for their senior get-away. Gave our testimonies.

Sat. Dec. 4

Visited Foyer. Took pic. of Scott Eberle and a STAer from Quebec, Karen, who has been helping at the foyer. Reading rooms and computer rooms are used by university students.

Sun. Dec. 5

A combined service of at least 8 churches in Niamey at Centre Biblique under tarps! Estimated that between 900 and 1000 were in attendance! We missionaries gave our testimonies again. John Ockers gave a history of Niger beginning with the arrival of Ed Rice coming from Nigeria to Zinder in 1924. Four hr. service. It didn't seem long. Translators went from Hausa to French and French to Hausa.

Traffic in Niamey is unbelievable. On the J.F. Kennedy bridge, you would see cars, vans, camels with heavy loads, donkeys laden, donkey pulled carts, bicycles, motorcycles, trucks piled high with goods and people piled high on the goods.

Mon. Dec. 6

Sue and Terry started their drive back to Maradi at 7 a.m. with a stop at Galmi for lunch with Botherases. Their passenger was Andrew Ng, who was going all the way to Jos with them, and then going on by taxi to Egbe and back to Galmi. About 9:30 we were driven over to the Bible School guest house for a farewell pow-wow with the retirees who were leaving that afternoon. Before the Hammacks left, Terry suggested that there might be two places on the flight leaving the next morning (12:35 a.m.), so we decided to give it a try. We talked to Gordon Evans, who in turn sent Falke to Air France to see if it could be arranged. It was—all the way to Orlando. We had to be ready by 3:30 p.m. to go to the airport to check in our baggage. So when our meeting was over about 11:30 a.m., we hurried back to the guest house and packed in a whirl. And we made it. Because of another flight leaving earlier, we were not able to check in our baggage until 5:30, so we waited in the airport. After all was checked in, Eliane Martinez took us to the Palais Hotel where we had shushkabobs and frites and ice cream. Then we went back to the guest house and changed into our traveling clothes and were picked up at 10 p.m. to go to the airport. The Air France flight to Paris was okay – under 5 hours; we waited in Paris for 6 hours, then flew to Atlanta on Delta and after a 3 hr. wait, on to Orlando on Delta where we were met by Wally and Vi Braband who brought us home to Sebring. We were home by 11:00 p.m. on the 7th of Dec. Glad we went and glad to be back home.

Home again! A wonderful trip! Wonderful to be home again — AMERICA — HOME SWEET HOME!

CPSIA information can be obtained at www.ICGtesting.com
Printed in the USA
243675LV00001B/2/P

9 781462 868322